Fighters in the Shadows

Fighters in the Shadows

*A New History of
the French Resistance*

ROBERT GILDEA

The Belknap Press of
Harvard University Press
Cambridge, Massachusetts   2015

First published in the United Kingdom by Faber & Faber Ltd in 2015
First Harvard University Press edition, 2015
First Printing

Typeset by Reality Premedia Services Pvt. Ltd.

Library of Congress Cataloging-in-Publication Data

Gildea, Robert.
Fighters in the shadows : a new history of the French
resistance / Robert Gildea. — First Harvard University press edition.
pages   cm
Includes bibliographical references and index.
ISBN 978-0-674-28610-8 (cloth : alk. paper)
1. World War, 1939–1945—Underground movements—France.
2. France—History—German occupation, 1940–1945.
I. Title.
D802.F8G465 2015
940.53′44—dc23   2015018188

To my Mother
In memory

Contents

List of Illustrations

Photography was treated by the Germans as spying under the German occupation and resisters did not take pictures of themselves for security reasons, so contemporary photographs are rare. These images were nevertheless all created at the time, with the exception of that of the Paris Liberation Committee.

De Gaulle and Giraud at Casablanca, as Roosevelt and Churchill look on, January 1943 (Imperial War Museum)

Marianne on a Bourg-en-Bresse plinth proclaiming the Fourth Republic, original photo and publicity mock-up, 11 November 1943 (Collection Musée de la Résistance Nationale, Champigny-sur-Marne)

Maquisards about to be executed at Lantilly, in Burgundy, 25 May 1943 (Collection Musée de la Résistance Nationale, Champigny-sur-Marne)

The *Affiche rouge* demonising resisters of the Manouchian group as 'the army of crime', February 1944 (Collection Musée de la Résistance Nationale, Champigny-sur-Marne)

General Leclerc in Normandy, 1 August 1944 (Musée de l'Ordre de la Libération)

Paris Liberation Committee, posed after the Liberation (Collection Musée de la Résistance Nationale, Champigny-sur-Marne)

Henri and Cecile Rol-Tanguy (copyright reserved)

Funeral of Pierre Georges/Col. Fabien (Collection Musée de la Résistance Nationale, Champigny-sur-Marne)

Madeleine Riffaud at the site of her triumph (Collection Musée de la Résistance Nationale, Champigny-sur-Marne)

Gaullist march-past, 18 June 1945 (Collection Musée de la Résistance Nationale, Champigny-sur-Marne)

Unveiling of the bust of Missak Manouchian at Ivry by his widow, 1978 (Collection Musée de la Résistance Nationale, Champigny-sur-Marne)

ENGLAND

English Channel

Dunkirk
Brussels
BELGIUM
GERMANY
Lille
Abbeville
Dieppe
Amiens
Charleville-
Mézières
LUXEMBOURG
Saarbrücken
Metz
Cherbourg
R. Seine
Bayeux
R. Moselle
Nancy
Strasbourg
Brest
Avranches
Drancy
Paris
Pithiviers
Troyes
Quimper
Rennes
Le Mans
Beaune-la-Rolande
Belfort
Vannes
Châteaubriant
Orléans
Angers
F R A N C E
Dijon
Besançon
Zürich
R. Loire
Berne
Nantes
Montceau-
les-Mines
SWITZER-
LAND
Châteauroux
Moulins
Oyonnax
La Rochelle
Bourg-en-Bresse
Vichy
Roanne
Annecy
Plateau of
Glières
Limoges
Lyon
Clermont-
Ferrand
Le Chambon-
sur-Lignon
Grenoble
Château
d'Uriage
Tulle
Le Puy
Vercors
Massif
Bordeaux
Vals-les-Bains
R. Rhône
ITALY
R. Garonne
Montauban
Nîmes
Saint-Jean
-de-Luz
Albi
Montpellier
Cannes
Nice
Antibes
Toulouse
Béziers
Marseille
Gurs
Le Vernet
Rivesaltes
Saint-Cyprien
Argelès
SPAIN
Mediterranean Sea

Bay of Biscay

N

0   100 km

0   100 miles

■ Internment camps

French territory occupied by Germany June 1940

Vichy France (occupied by Germany Nov. 1942)

Territory occupied by Italy until 1943

Occupied France, 1940–44

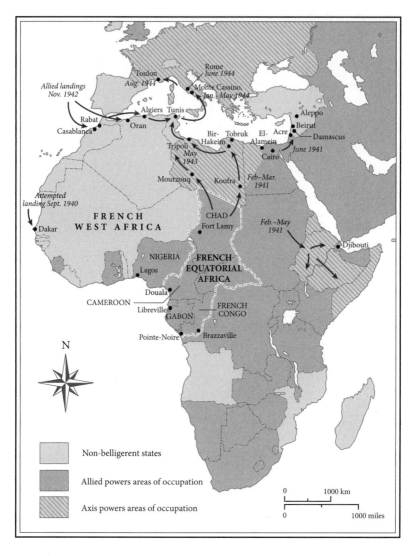

The French Empire in Africa and the Near East, 1940–44

Acknowledgements

My thanks are due first of all to Lucy-Jean and the family, who gave me leave of absence to spend a year in Paris to research this book, accompanied by my daughter Georgia, who pursued her studies there at the same time. This research was generously funded by the Arts and Humanities Research Council. I am also indebted to the Leverhulme Trust, which awarded me a Major Research Fellowship to complete the writing of the book.

Although my work sometimes goes against the grain of French historical writing, I have a trio of French historians to thank for their advice, their encouragement and their critical reading of my work. Laurent Douzou, Guillaume Piketty and Olivier Wieviorka have been trail-blazers and companions along the tortuous road of research and writing. In the UK I am indebted to the assistance of Samantha Blake at the BBC Written Archives Centre in Caversham. Navigating the French archives is never easy but always brings rewards. For their patience and help I would like to thank Patricia Gillet, Olivier Valat and Pascal Rambault at the Archives Nationales, Dominique Parcollet at the Centre d'Histoire of Sciences-Po, Anne-Marie Pathé and Nicholas Schmidt at the Institut d'Histoire du Temps Présent, Cécile Lauvergeon at the Mémorial de la Shoah, André Rakoto at the military archives of Vincennes, Pierre Boichu at the Archives départementales de la Seine-Saint-Denis, Chantal Pagès at the Archives départementales de la Haute-Garonne, and Isabelle Rivé-Doré and Régis Le Mer at the Centre d'Histoire de la Résistance et de la Déportation at Lyon. The welcome afforded me at the Musée de la Résistance Nationale at Champigny-sur-Marne was particularly warm and sustained and my warm thanks go to the team of Guy Krivopissko, Xavier Aumage, Céline Heytens and Charles Riondet.

For their support and inspiration I would like to thank a number of colleagues: Hanna Diamond, Matthew Cobb, Julian Jackson, Nick Stargardt, Lyndal Roper, Daniel Lee and Ludivine Broch. Ruth Harris read and commented on the whole manuscript and offered unfailingly sharp and insightful advice. Neil Belton at Faber and Joyce Selzer at Harvard have been more than just editors: they believed in the project and pressed me to make the text tighter, more readable, and more persuasive. My agent, Catherine Clarke, has been unstinting in her enthusiasm and generosity, coupled as ever with a critical eye. Gabi Maas compiled the bibliography with her usual aplomb and goodwill, while Christopher Summerville impeccably copy-edited the manuscript. The production and marketing of the book was expertly overseen by Julian Loose, Kate Murray-Browne, Anne Owen and Anna Pallai at Faber, and by Silvia Crompton at Whitefox.

I began research on this book shortly after my mother was diagnosed with cancer and she died while I was writing a first draft. I owe everything to her intelligence, her wit, her love and her understanding of humanity. This book is dedicated to her memory.

Introduction:
Remembering the French Resistance

On 16 May 2007, the day of his inauguration as French president, Nicolas Sarkozy made a pilgrimage to the Bois de Boulogne on the outskirts of Paris to pay homage to thirty-five resisters executed by the Germans during the final momentous days of the liberation of Paris in August 1944. 'The resisters were young. They died. But what they embodied was invincible. They said "no". "No" to subjection, "no" to dishonour, "no" to what belittles human beings, and this "no" continues to be heard after their deaths because it is the eternal cry of human freedom against enslavement. It is the cry that we still hear today.'[1]

In his speech, Sarkozy proclaimed that those who died for France were not simply patriots who gave their lives to liberate their country. They were martyrs of humanity who died for the universal and eternal values of freedom and dignity. He was keen, moreover, that this message should be transmitted to all young French people, who were invited in numbers to the commemoration. One high-school student read the last letter to his parents of Guy Môquet, a seventeen-year-old resister executed by the Germans in 1941. Sarkozy pledged that this letter would be read out every year in all French schools. Guy Môquet had been a communist. His father was a communist deputy who had been imprisoned and the twenty-six men with whom Guy was shot were also communists. But the Cold War had been won, the French Communist Party was a shadow of its old self, and the moral that could be drawn from the young man's death was again a universal one that 'the greatness of man is to dedicate himself to a cause that is greater than himself'.

The story of the French Resistance is central to French identity. The country was defeated in 1940, overwhelmed by a German *Blitzkrieg* that lasted a mere six weeks. The northern half of France was occupied immediately, the southern half in November 1942, in response to the Allied landings in North Africa. Power was assumed by Marshal Pétain, the hero of Verdun, who promptly abolished the French Republic and set up an authoritarian regime with its capital in the spa town of Vichy in central France. The French divided between those who collaborated with the Germans, those who resisted them, and those in the middle who resigned themselves to the situation and 'muddled through'. The Vichy regime succumbed to pressure from the Germans to deport 75,000 Jews living in France – 24,000 of them French and 51,000 of them of foreign origin – to the death camps. The French waited four years for the Allies to return to French soil to help them drive out the Germans. Paris was liberated in August 1944 and the Germans were finally pushed out of the country. French troops drove into Germany and set about recovering lost colonial territories in the Near East and Indochina and with that some of their former national greatness.

To deal with the trauma of defeat, occupation and virtual civil war, the French developed a central myth of the French Resistance. This was not a fiction about something that never happened, but rather a story that served the purposes of France as it emerged from the war. It was a founding myth that allowed the French to reinvent themselves and hold their heads high in the post-war period. There were several elements to this narrative. First, that there was a continuous thread of resistance, beginning on 18 June 1940, when an isolated de Gaulle in London issued his order to resist via the BBC airwaves, and reaching its climax on 26 August 1944, when he marched down the Champs-Élysées, acclaimed by the French people. Second, that while a 'handful of wretches' had collaborated with the enemy, a minority of active resisters had been supported in their endeavours by the vast majority of the French people. A third element was that, although the French were indebted to the Allies and some foreign resisters for their military assistance, the French had liberated themselves and restored national honour, confidence and unity.

This myth was orchestrated very effectively right from the very moment of liberation. After Charles de Gaulle was welcomed at the Hôtel de Ville in Paris on 25 August 1944, he addressed the crowd in the streets outside. His words, frequently quoted, may be seen as a first bid to define a myth of resistance and liberation, even before the liberation of France was complete:

Paris liberated! Liberated by its own efforts, liberated by its people with the help of the armies of France, with the help of all of France, that is France in combat. The one France, the true France, eternal France.[2]

The narrative was elaborated in a series of ceremonies after France finished the war and took the surrender of the Germans in Berlin as one of the Allied powers. At a parade held in Paris on 18 June 1945, the fifth anniversary of de Gaulle's appeal, the Free French forces who had continued the armed fight eclipsed the forces of the internal French Resistance both in number and style. Tanks rolled past, representing the arm in which de Gaulle had himself fought, and a flypast drew his symbol, a Cross of Lorraine, in the sky.[3] De Gaulle's resistance myth was military, national and male. It was sanctified by a new chivalric order, the Compagnons de la Libération, founded in November 1940. Numbering only 1,038, they were handpicked for their deeds of valour during the epic of liberation; 81 per cent were serving officers, only 5 per cent were foreigners and a mere 0.6 per cent were women.[4] The national dimension of the Resistance narrative was imposed by marginalising any idea that it might be seen as an international struggle against fascism and Nazism that was fought in part on French soil by resisters who might be Spanish republicans or Polish Jews. On 11 November 1944, in the company of Winston

Churchill, de Gaulle laid a wreath at the statue of First World War premier Clemenceau at the bottom of the Champs-Élysées, and announced the Resistance as only an episode in a Thirty Years War fought with Germany between 1914 and 1944.

Such a myth, powerful though it was, never exercised complete hegemony over the minds of French people. Communists, who played a leading role in resistance combats and emerged as the largest political party after the war, were happy to subscribe to the dominant narrative so long as they enjoyed power, but when the Cold War came in 1947 and they were ejected from the government, they insisted on their own separate story.[5] The Communist Party (PCF) defined itself as the party of the 75,000 *fusillés*, their estimate of the number of communist victims shot by the Germans. This was undoubtedly an overestimate but the Communist Party highlighted one dramatic case of martyrdom: the twenty-seven communist hostages – including Guy Môquet – who were shot at Châteaubriant in October 1941 in reprisal for the assassination of the *Feldkommandant* of Nantes by a communist hit squad. A monument of five muscular men tied to a stake and plainly singing the 'Marseillaise' or 'Internationale' was unveiled in October 1950 in the clearing where they had died. Rivalry for the ownership of this memory was symbolised by the fact that the city of Nantes raised its own monument (in October 1952) to the sixteen non-communist hostages shot in Nantes, as well as to the communists executed at Châteaubriant. The mayor of Nantes praised the role of the Vichy authorities who had intervened with the Germans to prevent a second round of executions threatened by the Germans and the good people of Nantes who had endured the reprisals with dignity. This ceremony was pointedly boycotted by the communists, who held their own separate vigil and demonstrated how sharply divided memories of resistance could be.[6]

What might be called the Gaullist myth of resistance suffered the setback of being divided against itself during the Algerian

War of 1954–62. North Africa had been the military and political platform from which France had been liberated but the war fought to retain Algeria ten years later used brutal methods, including the torture of insurgents. The camp of former resisters split between those who equated liberation with the restoration of national greatness and those who were troubled by the 'Nazi' methods used by the French military against Algerian rebels. In order to restore unity to the Resistance camp, the cult of Jean Moulin – who had briefly united the competing factions of the French Resistance under the direction of de Gaulle in London and who had died a martyr – was duly promoted. In December 1964, in advance of the first presidential elections under universal suffrage since 1848, in which de Gaulle hoped to triumph, the remains of Jean Moulin were solemnly transferred to the France's hall of heroes, the Panthéon. This was the apogee of the unifying Gaullist myth and de Gaulle was duly re-elected to the presidency the following year. However, the legacy of the Algerian War divided Algerian immigrants and French settlers repatriated after Algerian independence in 1962 and nurtured the extreme-right-wing populism of the Front National in post-colonial France.

De Gaulle's fall from power in 1969 and his death soon after weakened the carapace of the central myth of French Resistance and allowed other stories to come to the surface. The commonplace assertion that only a few French people had disgraced themselves by collaborating with the Germans while the overwhelming majority of French people had supported the Resistance was called into question by Marcel Ophüls' 1969 film, *Le Chagrin et la Pitié*, subtitled, 'Chronicle of a French city under the Occupation'. The film suggested that the French had not been heroes but rather time-servers and cowards if not traitors.[7] One of the leading resisters interviewed, Emmanuel d'Astier de la Vigerie, declared, 'I think you could only have joined the resistance if you were maladjusted.'[8] Because it undermined the official resistance story, *Le Chagrin* was banned from TV

5

screens for ten years. Meanwhile President Pompidou, who had succeeded de Gaulle in 1969, held out an olive branch to former collaborators by pardoning Paul Touvier, the head of the Militia in Lyon who had waged war on resisters and Jews and had spent years after the war in hiding. Pompidou had not taken part in resistance himself and had a negative view of its achievements. 'Is it not time,' he asked at a press conference in 1972, 'to throw a veil, to forget that period when French people hated each other, tore each other apart, killed each other?'[9]

Another narrative of resistance under occupation now captured public attention. It claimed a leading role in the French Resistance for foreign anti-fascists and in particular foreign Jews. The French had liberated themselves but not without the help of foreign resisters, whose contribution had initially been glossed over. It was brought back to light by two films that highlighted the tragedy of a group of twenty-three resisters under the Armenian Missak Manouchian, who were executed at Mont Valérien fort on 21 February 1944. Frank Cassenti's *L'Affiche rouge* of 1976, titled after the German poster that seized the opportunity to demonise resisters as foreigners and Jews, was followed by Serge Mosco's 1985 *Terroristes à la Retraite*. Unfortunately, this latter film had to compete with another, Claude Lanzmann's *Shoah*, also released in 1985, which concentrated on Jews as victims of extermination rather than as violent resisters. This shaped a powerful new paradigm that increasingly saw the Second World War not through the lens of resistance but through that of the Holocaust. It was reinforced in 1987 when former Gestapo chief, Klaus Barbie, was brought back from hiding in Bolivia to the Assize Court of Lyon and tried for his part in the deportation of Jews from France to the death camps. In particular he was indicted for the deportation of forty-four Jewish children from a home at Izieu, near Lyon, to Auschwitz on 6 April 1944. Barbie, who was known in resistance circles as the man who had tortured Jean Moulin to death, was not on trial for this crime. Instead, the victims of the Holocaust in France were heard giving testimony against their accusers and prioritising the story of the massacre of innocents. Sabine Zlatin, who had cared for the children of Izieu, exclaimed:

Barbie always said that he was only concerned with resisters and *maquisards*, that is, the enemies of the German Army. I am asking: what were the children, the forty-four children? Resisters? *Maquisards*? What were they? They were innocents. For this terrible crime of Izieu there can be neither forgiveness nor forgetting.[10]

Not only were the resisters upstaged, but they were also put metaphorically in the dock themselves.

Barbie's defence counsel, the enigmatic Jacques Vergès, floated the rumour that Jean Moulin had been betrayed to the Gestapo by none other than Raymond Aubrac, hitherto considered (with his wife Lucie) as a giant of the French Resistance. The honour of the Resistance was impugned and had to be defended. Jacques Chaban-Delmas, who had been one of Jean Moulin's successors linking de Gaulle and the Resistance in France and who became prime minister under Pompidou, stepped up: 'If there were traitors in the resistance,' he asserted, 'these were not *of* the resistance but collaborators who infiltrated it very cleverly, but had nothing to do with us.' Facing down attempts to blacken the Resistance as a whole by tarnishing some of its leaders, Chaban addressed the new generation: 'Young people must know that French people behaved honourably and they do not have to blush about France or about the conduct of their fellow citizens under the Occupation.' The resistance, he continued, capturing the emerging discourse that centred on the rights of man, had begun as a campaign to drive the German invaders out of France but in time became something far more universal, a war against Nazism, which was 'a curse, contempt for the human being'.[11]

Barbie was condemned for crimes against humanity and sentenced to life imprisonment but the deportation of 75,000 Jews from France could not be blamed only on the Germans. The role of the French state that had collaborated with the Third Reich was also questioned. Pressure built up for the state to acknowledge its part in the Holocaust. President Mitterrand refused, claiming that the crime was that of Vichy, not that of the Republic, but in 1995 his successor, Jacques Chirac, solemnly recognised the role of the French state in the round-up of Jews that led to their deportation. He used a discourse of human rights to condemn the actions of the French state and to offer an apology: 'France, country of the Enlightenment and the rights of man, land of welcome and asylum, on that day accomplished the irreparable.' In the same speech, however, he cited the statistic provided by Serge Klarsfeld, who had brought Barbie back for trial and acted as counsel for the prosecution, that three-quarters of Jews in France had not been deported. The conclusion to be drawn was that the same values that had been betrayed by the French state had lived on in the hearts and minds of ordinary French people and inspired compassion and generosity towards persecuted Jews. Chirac therefore praised the 'humanistic values, the values of liberty, justice and tolerance that constitute French identity and bind us for the future'.[12]

The story of a minority of armed resisters, supported by the mass of the population, was now replaced by that of a mass of generous souls, supporting a minority of rescuers, who had found safe hiding places or escape routes for Jews persecuted during the German occupation. These Gentile rescuers had been honoured as the Righteous Among Nations in a limited way by Yad Vashem, the Jerusalem body founded in 1953 to document and commemorate the Holocaust. In Paris, over fifty years later in 2005, a Memorial to the Shoah was opened in the former Jewish quarter of the Marais. Inside the edifice the names of all the Jews who had been deported from France were inscribed on a Wall of Names. Outside, a Wall of the Righteous, with the names of all the French Righteous among Nations, was unveiled in 2006. On 18 January

2007 Jacques Chirac and Auschwitz survivor and stateswoman Simone Veil presided over a brightly lit ceremony in the Panthéon to celebrate the Righteous of France. Chirac rehearsed a language of reason and rights cloaked in moral righteousness. True to 'France, that country of enlightenment and human rights,' he said, 'very many French men and women demonstrated that humanistic values were enshrined in their souls.'[13] This ceremony consecrated a new image of what resistance meant. It was no longer the military and patriotic struggle intended to drive the Germans out of France but the unarmed work of rescue to save a persecuted minority from the clutches of the Nazis that duly allowed France to reclaim its identity as the country of liberty and the rights of man.

Myths are narratives developed to define the identity and aspirations of groups or countries and need no factual basis in the historical record.[14] Historians, however, are bound by the record of written, oral and visual sources from the past, duly scrutinised and tested for veracity. Just as de Gaulle was elaborating a myth of resistance from the moment of liberation, so former resisters and historians mobilised the services of the state both to preserve and to build a historical record of France's experience of the Second World War. As early as October 1944 a Commission on the History of the Occupation and Liberation of France (CHOLF) was set up under the Education Ministry in order to gather wartime documents from a wide range of other ministries. Its general secretaries were the medieval historian Édouard Perroy and Henri Michel, formerly history teacher at the Lycée of Toulon and socialist resister in Provence. Another body, the Committee on the History of War (CHG), was founded in June 1945, immediately after the end of the war in Europe. Chaired by the historian Lucien Febvre, with Henri Michel again as general secretary, it was directly answerable to de Gaulle and designed to have more leverage with ministries to secure the release of documents. It was soon realised, however, that these two bodies had overlapping functions and personnel, and in 1951 they were amalgamated as the Committee for History of the Second World War (CHDGM).[15]

The first target of these committees was documents held by the various government ministries. However, some ministries were reluctant to hand documents over to the National Archives, at least in the short- or medium-term. Once in the Archives, documents were still subject to a fifty-year rule of confidentiality before they could be consulted. The written archives containing official documents relating to the Occupation, Vichy and the Resistance remained virtually closed until a law of 1979 facilitated access, although even then access to many files was only accorded with special permission or *dérogation* from the Ministry of Culture. Other sources therefore had to be exploited. For nearly forty years the history of the Resistance was written from the oral testimony and memoirs of former resisters while the archives remained unexplored.

One of the key functions of the Committee for History of the Second World War was to build up an archive of interviews with former resisters from which later histories might be written.[16] The methodology was far from the oral history practices of today. Interviewers and interviewees belonged to the same milieu, so that the process of 'snowballing' from one resister to another led to interviews with more of the same: educated people, mostly men, who had belonged to the Free French or to the mainstream non-communist metropolitan networks and movements. In the climate of the Cold War virtually no communists were interviewed, and even fewer resisters of foreign origin. The interviews were not recorded and it is not clear whether they were taken down in shorthand. Typescripts of the interviews were not set out verbatim, as question and answer, but as summaries of the conversation. There was little appreciation that witnesses might be telling *their* story, which might be different from *the* story of the Resistance. Henri Michel thought rather that by cross-referencing a mass of partial stories it would be possible to extract from them 'the sap of truth they contain'. Material from these interviews, suitably anonymised, and other documentation, such as the Resistance press, provided the basis of the first histories of the Resistance by former historians turned resisters or former resisters turned historians. Henri Michel published the first textbook account of the Resistance in 1950 and other volumes on the ideas of the Resistance in 1954 and 1962.[17] Marie Granet, one of the lead interviewers of the CHDGM, brought out a series on individual resistance networks.[18] Working at a distance from this 'official history', two former resisters, Henri Noguères (who had belonged to Franc-Tireur in Languedoc) and former communist Marcel Degliame (who had worked with Combat), wrote a ten-volume history of the Resistance between 1967 and 1982. They regretted that the archives were closed for fifty years but could not wait and had relied on 170 written or oral testimonies. Had they not, they said pointedly, 'it would have meant giving up on the option that this history might be not only written and discussed but also controlled by those who lived it'.[19] The assumption was that an élite of resisters themselves would write their own history. Meanwhile in 1975–6 Jean-Louis Crémieux-Brilhac, who had worked with the Free French in London, edited the messages that had gone out to France from the BBC in London, inaugurating a brilliant career as the most authoritative resister-historian of his generation.[20]

The memoirs of former resisters were the other initial source for a valid history. In the early years there were few accounts of ordinary resisters. One was that of Agnès Humbert, who had been involved in the Musée de l'Homme resistance network and had been deported to do forced labour in Germany.[21] More usual were those of high-profile or self-promoting resisters[22] and the great military and political leaders who were anxious to be first on the scene to establish their story for posterity.[23] A second wave of memoirs appeared after 1968 and, particularly after the death of de Gaulle and the decline of the Communist Party, wider space was opened up for a variety of former resisters to tell their own account.[24] For a long time the testimony of former resisters who had been close to the centre of decision-making insiders wielded great authority. Confidence in their gospel, however, was shaken in 1973 by the publication of the memoirs of Henri Frenay, the leader of Combat.[25] Still fighting his wartime battles, he accused his rival Jean Moulin, who had now acquired the aura of a resistance hero and martyr, of being a communist agent. He repeated the accusation with another book in 1977 that provoked a media controversy.[26] To defend Moulin's reputation, Moulin's former radio-operator, Daniel Cordier, decided that the only way to rebuff these accusations was to analyse the whole available archival record. His mission coincided with a professionalisation of the history of the Second World War, symbolised by the passing of the torch from Henri Michel's Committee for History of the Second World War to the Institute for the History of the Present Time (IHTP), founded in 1978 under François Bédarida. Born in 1926, Bédarida was a schoolboy member of the Resistance but above all a scholar who saw it as his mission to historicise studies of the Second World War. Bédarida and Cordier thus joined forces to challenge the trustworthiness of testimony, either written or oral, in the name of the primacy of written archival sources. Cordier's four-volume history of Jean Moulin, published between 1989 and 1999, both made the case for an archival history of the Resistance and made Moulin the centrepiece of that history.[27]

This cult of the archives stimulated research by a new generation of *agrégés* and doctoral students born in the 1950s and 1960s, who now turned to the Resistance as a legitimate historical subject. Those based in the provinces researched histories of the Resistance in their area, in the Franche-Comté, Provence or Brittany.[28] Those based at the Sorbonne and Sciences-Po in Paris wrote and published theses on the main non-communist resistance organisations: Laurent Douzou on Libération-Sud, Alya Aglan on Libération-Nord and Olivier Wieviorka on

Défense de la France.[29] Guillaume Piketty wrote a thesis on Pierre Brossolette, Jean Moulin's intermediary between London and France, and together these publications concentrated on the 'royal road' of metropolitan resistance.[30] A 1996 thesis written on the Front National, through which the Communist Party built bridges between communist and non-communist organisations, was not published.[31] Around the time of the 40th anniversary of the Liberation these historians also used the conference as a scholarly tool to share the most-up-to-date research and research methods.[32] They also embarked on a Dictionary of the French Resistance that was, in 2006, the state of the art of current thinking about the Resistance.[33]

Many of this new generation of researchers interviewed former members of resistance organisations and Piketty used interviews undertaken by Brossolette's widow in the 1970s.[34] Their supervisors nevertheless maintained an undisguised scepticism about the validity of oral testimony and the interview was used primarily to complement the archival record. At an IHTP round table on oral history in 1986 Daniel Cordier admitted that the interview had the 'aesthetic benefit of freshness' and could recreate 'atmosphere' but when it came to detail it was useless. 'Chronology is extremely vague because the witness is naturally unable to situate his past in time. When a witness says to you, "It took place on 21 June in Avignon", it might be the 15 August 1943 or the 10 September 1942.' François Bédarida, director of the IHTP, concluded a round table in 1986 by declaring that 'the Resistance, which hitherto had been seen as the chosen territory of oral history now appears as the site of the triumph of written history.'[35]

Outside the academy there was a greater faith in oral and written testimony and a greater interest in recording the testimony of resisters who had not taken the 'royal road', notably Jews, communists and foreigners. Around 1968 Anny Latour undertook a series of interviews, both in France and Israel, with Jewish resisters for a book she was writing on the Jewish resistance, that were preserved at the Centre de Documentation Juive Contemporaine (CDJC), now part of the Mémorial de la Shoah.[36] The Musée de la Résistance Nationale at Champigny-sur-Marne, which opened in 1985, had a communist and labour affiliation. It collected the written testimonies of resisters from communist backgrounds, often of immigrant origin. It also archived the original returns to a call in 1984 from the communist daily *L'Humanité* for testimonies from 'the unknown of the Resistance', a wide repertoire of resistance gestures and memories sent in by ordinary people.[37] Finally, the Centre d'Histoire de la Résistance et de la Déportation in Lyon, which opened in 1992, began a programme of video-recording interviews with former resisters. These included mainstream resisters but prioritised interviews with foreign resisters, often of Jewish origin, and women.

The vogue for autobiographical accounts enjoyed a new wave with the publication in 2004 of Irène Nemirowsky's posthumous *Suite française*, a fictionalised account of families fleeing Paris in 1940 and living cheek-by-jowl with the Germans in occupied France.[38] Interest was revived in what could be gained from memoirs, journals, diaries, letters, and oral testimony. The memoirs of Agnès Humbert, originally published in 1946, were republished in French in 2004 and English in 2008.[39] The diary and memoir of the American Virginia d'Albert Lake, who was involved in an escape line for downed airmen, came out in 2006.[40] Academic historians returned to subjective accounts with new confidence. Laurent Douzou acclaimed a new genre of writing by the children of resisters, notably their voyage into the hidden past of their parents.[41] Some of these introduced readers to resisters who were not French by birth. After his mother's death in 1994, the scientist Georges Waysand wrote *Estoucha*, an account of her resistance activity. Esther Zilberberg, known as Estoucha, was a Polish-Jewish communist medical student who migrated to Belgium in the 1930s, served as a nurse with the International Brigades in Spain and the communist resistance in northern France, giving birth to Georges in 1941 before her husband was executed by the Germans and she was deported to Ravensbrück.[42] Claude Lévy, also of Polish-Jewish origin, had written his own account of foreigners in the French Resistance in 1970.[43] In 2007 his son Marc assumed his father's voice and role in *Les Enfants de la liberté,* exploring his father's experience with Jewish and Italian resisters in Toulouse and trauma of the 'ghost train' that deported him and his younger brother in July–August 1944.[44] In 2009 Guillaume Piketty published a superb collection of first-person writings by resisters, from the diaries of Free French soldiers to the letters of Claire Girard, a resister shot by the Germans in 1944.[45] Two years later François Marcot co-edited a collection on writing under the Occupation that privileged diaries as a source.[46] Ironically, Daniel Cordier, who had led such a vigorous campaign against the validity of testimony, published his own memoirs, *Alias Caracalla,* in 2009. 'If a diary is by nature limited,' he conceded, 'it is nevertheless incomparable: it is a snapshot of the past that brings to life lost passions.'[47]

This study of the Resistance is squarely based on testimony, both written and oral. It takes the view that only first-person accounts can lay bare individual subjectivity, the experience of resistance activity, and the meaning that resisters later gave to their actions. Testimony is taken from the widest possible range of sources in order to underline the breadth and diversity of those who became involved in resistance inside and outside France, most of them French but many of them foreign. The first six chapters of the book explore why a small minority of individuals opted for resistance under the impact of defeat and armistice in 1940. While most French people were relieved that the war was over, trusted Marshal Pétain to defend their interests and cohabited more or less peacefully with German occupying forces, a few said no. They came from all parts of society, from the extreme left to the extreme right, educated and uneducated, French soldiers who left defeated France for England or were undefeated in the colonies. Were they oddballs and eccentrics or idealists who had undergone a political apprenticeship and were moved by principles? Were they in some way conditioned by their families and background, or did contingency and chance play a part? The story then investigates ways in which resisters came together in small groups, isolated from the conformist mass of the population, to think about what could be done to resist. All resisters were confronted by the challenge of breaking the law and of putting their own lives and those of others at risk. All were bound by intense bonds of comradeship, fraternity and solidarity – even love. Since resistance was originally conceived as refusing defeat and continuing the fight, women were not immediately in the front line, but the failure of men to defend the country in 1940 and the fact that 1.5 million of them were prisoners of war meant that much responsibility devolved onto women. Women navigated between gendered expectations of their roles and the opportunities that appeared for extraordinary achievements. We look at how resisters constructed their underground world and invented new identities and new roles for themselves. This had something theatrical about it but risked discovery, arrest and death. Invention gave resisters the opportunity to pretend what they were not, but also gave the opportunity to informers to pretend that they were resisters. Comradeship and trust among resisters was too often compromised by deceit and betrayal. From time to time resisters emerged from the world of shadow into the light, in order to publicise their message and their activities, and sometimes this moment of transition was the most dangerous of all.

Resisters were always a minority but emerged from a rainbow of different milieux. They had very different views and were fighting for different aims. Some were simply patriots who disagreed with the Vichy regime about what patriotism meant. Their profile might be very like supporters of the Vichy regime, except in their opposition to collaboration with Germany. Some saw themselves as fighting an anti-fascist war that had started with volunteering to resist Franco's crusade against republican Spain that was supported by Fascist Italy and Nazi Germany. After the defeat of the Spanish Republic in 1939 many retreated to continue the struggle on French soil. This was a struggle that was also fought in the Low Countries, Central Europe, the Balkans and behind German lines on the Eastern Front. Men and women of Jewish origin were an important part of the Resistance in France, fighting the war against Germany but also a 'war within the war' against both the Germans and Vichy to prevent their own extermination. They were often young Jews who had lost their parents or other family members in the round-ups and deportations and joined resistance groups as the best way to survive. Some were French Jews for whom the liberation of a tolerant France was the main goal, but others were Polish or Romanian Jews who dreamed of founding socialist republics in the countries from which they were exiled, or else of leaving old Europe to found a new homeland in Palestine, which was then a British mandate.

The Gaullist narrative of a straight line of resistance between 1940 and 1944 and of a France that liberated herself, albeit with some help from the Allies, comes under some scrutiny. The armistice of 1940 left the French Empire intact and the few who joined de Gaulle's Free French battled for control of that Empire in Africa and Syria-Lebanon with the armies of Vichy which, collaborating with the Axis powers, opposed them at every step. De Gaulle in London enjoyed the support of Churchill but was an isolated figure, even among the French in exile. The Americans had an almost visceral dislike of him, and kept an ambassador in Vichy with the main aim of ensuring that Marshal Pétain did not enter the war on the German side. When the Americans landed in North Africa in November 1942 they did a deal with Vichy's Admiral Darlan and then, when he was assassinated, backed de Gaulle's arch-rival, General Giraud. De Gaulle also had great difficulty establishing durable connections with resistance

17

movements that were emerging in metropolitan France. The communist resistance movements escaped him entirely and even the non-communist ones jealously guarded their own autonomy. Eventually, in 1943, de Gaulle's envoy Jean Moulin brought together the threads of the metropolitan resistance movements under the General's authority, and at the same time de Gaulle established himself in North Africa alongside Giraud. Unfortunately, however, Jean Moulin was arrested by the Germans in June 1943 and tortured to death. Links were broken with the internal resistance movements, which at the same time became increasingly popular as the German demand for forced labour for factories in the Reich provoked strike activity and drove many young men into hiding and some into the *maquis* of forest and mountain. Some came under the control of well-organised communists who had a strategy of immediate action and national insurrection; others were provided with weapons by Allied agents (who were parachuted in) but were encouraged to delay any offensive action until after D-Day.

The D-Day landings provoked an explosion of resistance activity as fighters came out of the shadows to attack Germans in the rear. This initially had disastrous consequences as resisters had huge optimism and energy but very little training, strategy or leadership. Conflict broke out between the two models of resistance: the communist desire for national insurrection, in which participated the full rainbow of foreign resisters, and which would usher in popular government and far-reaching reform, and a well-timed seizure of power as German sources retreated, to enable de Gaulle to reassert the authority of the French state and stifle any chance of popular revolution. The Gaullist account reaches its climax here, with the General marching down the Champs-Élysées to the applause of the crowd before France returned to business as usual. But for those who had resisted, life did not simply end here and their testimonies trace their hopes and fears, triumphs and disappointments after the Liberation. Many resisters joined the French armies that continued the advance on Germany, and some of them did not return. A minority went on to take part in founding the Fourth Republic, but this was generally at the expense of the aspirations of resistance movements. Others returned from deportation camps to rebuild their shattered lives, or dedicated themselves to putting back together the shattered lives of those around them.

The book ends with the battle for the soul of the Resistance, which over the following decades set individuals and groups against each other, as they fought to impose their own collective memory as the dominant narrative of the French Resistance as a whole. Immediately after the Liberation the Gaullist gospel, military, patriotic and essentially masculine, became supreme. This was contested by a communist memory under siege during the Cold War and controlled by a Stalinism that purged the memory of dissident communists who had been at the forefront of resistance. The Holocaust memory that became the main lens through which the Second World War was seen from the 1990s ironically marginalised the memory of a Jewish resistance that was beginning to emerge. The dominant narrative of resistance today is a humanitarian and universal myth of the struggle for the rights of man, which allows a greater role for women and rescuers of Jews, and a lesser role for freedom fighters with Sten guns. The memories of resisters of dissident communist, foreign and Jewish origin survived as group memories but not as dominant narratives. One of the aims of this study is to bring these back into the mainstream.

I

Awakenings

The sight of the débâcle revived an old nationalist reflex, deep humiliation and fury at the idea that those people were at home in our homes. And at the same time a very deep anti-fascism, a hatred of all that.

(Jean-Pierre Vernant, 1985)

Madeleine Riffaud was not yet sixteen when the German armies, triumphant after Dunkirk, burst into northern France on 5 June 1940. Her family fled south, *pêle-mêle* with tens of thousands of other terrified civilians and punch-drunk soldiers, their possessions loaded onto cars, carts and horses.[1] Her parents, who were both schoolteachers in the Somme, had the additional burden of a grandfather who was dying of cancer. Some weeks later, with France defeated, they made their way slowly back home to what was now German-occupied France. At the bombed-out station of Amiens, Madeleine went in search of a stretcher from the Red Cross to carry her grandfather on the last leg of the journey. Attractive in her 'little summer frock, and long hair down', she was molested by a group of German soldiers. An officer called them to order but at the same time, she recalls, 'he gave me a huge kick in the bottom which sent me flying. I was so furious, it was humiliation, anger, and in my anger I vowed to myself that I would find the Resistance. I will find those who are resisting. It all started from there.'[2]

The humiliation of defeat was suffered by the whole French nation, from its leaders to ordinary people. It was an unexpected defeat, because the French had gone to war in 1939 with their tails up, confident in the strength of their army, navy and air force. It was an inexplicable defeat because in 1914–18 French forces had kept German armies at bay for four years and in the end climbed victorious from the trenches. This time, however, their armies were overrun in a mere six weeks.[3] It was a critical defeat because it destroyed the Republic that had embodied French democracy and patriotism since 1870, and gave way to an authoritarian regime prepared to do business with Germany.

Events moved extremely quickly. On 17 June the French government, which had retreated from Paris to Bordeaux on the Atlantic coast, sued for an armistice. Paul Reynaud, who had replaced Édouard Daladier as prime minister in March 1940 and had made an agreement with Great Britain not to sign a separate peace, lost his majority in the cabinet. He handed over to Marshal Philippe Pétain, the victor of Verdun in 1916, who with General Maxime Weygand had been brought in to strengthen the government in May 1940, when the Netherlands and Belgium crumbled before the German assault. Unfortunately, Pétain and Weygand's thinking was not only military: defeat for them offered the opportunity of having done away with the Republic that was increasingly attacked by conservatives as opening the door of political power to Jews, communists and Freemasons. The Republic had come within an inch of falling on 6 February 1934 in Paris, when fascist and reactionary paramilitaries stormed the French parliament building. To stand in their way an anti-fascist movement had formed on the streets and within the trade unions, endorsed by the socialist, communist and centre-left radical parties which came to power as the Popular Front in 1936, under Jewish prime minister Léon Blum. Although the Popular Front prevented fascism from coming to power as in Italy and Germany and avoided the civil war that ravaged Spain between 1936 and 1939, fascists and reactionaries lay in wait for their moment to have revenge, which came in 1940.[4]

In his broadcast at midday on 17 June Marshal Pétain announced that, Christ-like, he was offering himself as a sacrifice to end the war with honour and to redeem France:

Sure of the affection of our admirable army which is fighting with a heroism worthy of our long military traditions against an enemy superior in numbers and weapons, sure that by its magnificent resistance it has fulfilled its duties towards our allies [. . .] I am making a gift of my person to France to attenuate its misfortune [. . .] It is with a heavy heart that I tell you today that we must cease the fight. Last night I sent word to the adversary, as between soldiers, after the battle and in honour, to enquire whether he was willing to explore means to end hostilities.[5]

Under the terms of the armistice concluded on 22 June 1940, Alsace and part of Lorraine were annexed by the Third Reich, the northern half of France and the Atlantic coast down to the Spanish border was occupied by the German military, the total French Army was reduced to 100,000 men and a huge war indemnity had to be paid to Germany as punishment for declaring war alongside Great Britain in September 1939. Less than three weeks later, on 10 July, the French parliament was summoned to the spa town of Vichy in unoccupied central France. It was persuaded by Pétain's political *éminence grise*, the veteran politician Pierre Laval, to surrender full powers to Pétain to make a new constitution. Pétain immediately made himself head of what was now called the État français, abolishing the Republic. He proceeded to give himself complete executive, legislative and constitution-making power and adjourned parliament indefinitely.

The reaction of most of the French population was one of relief. The armistice meant that the fighting was over and there would be no carnage on the scale of the First World War when France had lost 1.4 million men. Instead, 1.5 million soldiers were captured by the Germans, but it was imagined that they would soon be released. The passing of the Republic that had so clearly failed both militarily and politically was not unduly regretted. Conservatives felt that France now had a saviour and strong leader who would purge the Jews, communists and

Freemasons who had undermined the country from within and who would restore her unity and strength.

A few people saw things differently and were prepared to act. One of these was Charles de Gaulle, a comparatively unknown general who had spent half the First World War in a German POW camp. He confessed to his mother in November 1918 that 'the immense joy I share with you about events is combined for me with an indescribable regret, more bitter than ever, not to have taken more of a part in them which will stay with me for the rest of my life.'[6] Since then he had proved himself as an authority on tank warfare and commanded the 4th Armoured Division with credit at Abbeville near the mouth of the Somme in late May to early June 1940, attempting to open up an escape route for troops holed up at Dunkirk. He was appointed Under-Secretary of War in Reynaud's government on 5 June and was described by Churchill's envoy as observing the rising panic and defeatism in stony silence, 'ceaselessly smoking cigarettes, lighting one from the other'.[7] De Gaulle was one of the minority in the government who had favoured continuing the struggle; isolated, he now feared that he might be arrested. Early on 17 June he and his aide-de-camp, Lieutenant Geoffroy de Courcel, boarded a small plane at Bordeaux, provided by the British, and flew to England as Pétain was making his broadcast. The next day, 18 June 1940, de Gaulle made his famous riposte on the airwaves of the BBC:

I, General de Gaulle, now in London, invite French officers and soldiers who are on British soil or who find their way there, with or without their weapons; I invite engineers and skilled workers in the munitions industries who are on British soil or who find their way there, to contact me. Whatever happens, the flame of resistance must never go out and will not go out.[8]

Although according to the Gaullist myth his message marks the founding moment of the French Resistance, not many people in fact heard it at the time. Because resistance was at first imagined only in military terms it was addressed in the first instance to the military – to the 30,000 soldiers, sailors and airmen who were in Britain, having been taken off the beaches at Dunkirk or escaped from other Channel or Atlantic ports in ships fleeing the disaster. It was also addressed to the remains of the French Army in retreat across the southern parts of France. However the message was also heard by some of the civilian population, many strewn along the roads leading to southern France or in the towns and villages where they sheltered, weathering the storm. Confused, angry, humiliated, they were not in a position to continue the fight straightaway. They too had to decide whether to return to their former lives and buckle down under the new regime, or whether to begin to seek like-minded people with a view to 'doing something', whatever that might be.

Those who later became involved in resistance activity were keen to demonstrate that they had been resisters 'of the first hour'. Their honour flowed from how promptly they had answered de Gaulle's call to resist. Rallying to de Gaulle was, nevertheless, always a minority activity, and that minority was often frustrated by a majority sceptical about de Gaulle's haste and ambition to create a government-in-exile in opposition to Marshal Pétain.[9] The first potential source of support was the French expatriate community in London and influential French people passing through, but support was in short supply. The director of the French Institute, Denis Saurat, a professor of literature at King's College and an authority on Milton, Blake and Victor Hugo, went to see de Gaulle on 19 June at his lodgings in Seymour Grove (now Curzon Place) to offer his contacts.[10] One of these was the writer André Maurois, who nevertheless refused to work for de Gaulle, fearing reprisals against his family in France, and instead sailed for the United States to lecture at Boston.[11] Jean Monnet, who had been involved in negotiating logistical support from the United States and had designed a forlorn Franco-British union on 16 June 1940 as a last chance for France, found de Gaulle's initiative too personal and too dramatic, and sailed for New York in August.[12] Alexis Léger, a diplomat who also published poetry under the name of Saint-John Perse, refused to join de Gaulle not least because he had been sacked as general-secretary of the Quai d'Orsay for being too much of an appeaser by Reynaud, who then brought in de Gaulle, and Léger also went to the United States.[13] The French ambassador in London, Charles Corbin, opposed de Gaulle's bid to set up a French National Committee to represent the Free French and resigned after the British government recognised it on 23 June, making his way back to retirement in France via Rio de Janiero.[14] Not until 1942 did a significant member of the diplomatic community rally to de Gaulle.

De Gaulle's success was slightly greater with military personnel who found themselves in England, although even here only a minority came over. One early recruit was Georges Boris, whose Jewish family from Lorraine had opted for French nationality when the province was annexed by Germany in 1871. He saw himself as 'born on the left', shaped by the battles of the Dreyfus Affair that set intellectuals and Jews against conservatives and clericals, and was a committed socialist. Suffering from TB, he did not fight in the Great War but worked in Switzerland for the Inter-allied Commission for the blockade of the Central Powers and was later denounced as an *embusqué*, having a cushy job behind the lines. He had experience of government, running the private office of Léon Blum in his second Popular Front ministry in 1938, working with Treasury minister Pierre Mendès France on a Keynesian plan to restimulate the economy. This short-lived ministry came under vicious attack by the right-wing press as a 'Jewish' cabinet.[15] In 1939 he was keen to make up his patriotic deficit and began the war as a common soldier. Promoted to sergeant, he worked as a liaison agent with the British Army and was evacuated with it from Dunkirk on 28 May 1940. On 20 June 1940 he went to de Gaulle's headquarters to offer his services but – in the light of the Popular Front and indeed the Dreyfus Affair – expressed a concern that 'the participation of well-known Jews and socialists might not undermine the work of General de Gaulle, alienating conservatives and military people of whom he had need'.[16] He was taken on in the press department and maintained a liaison with the BBC but always felt uncomfortable in the presence of more right-wing and military elements in de Gaulle's entourage.

The dilemma of whether or not to join de Gaulle was well illustrated by the case of General Anthoine Béthouart, who had graduated from Saint-Cyr military academy in the same cohort as de Gaulle and had commanded the French contingent of the Anglo-French expeditionary force sent to Norway in May 1940 to cut off a German invasion. This included the 13th Half Brigade of the Foreign Legion and units of Alpine Chasseurs. Repatriated to France when the Germans burst through in June he had briefly fought there before escaping to England with his troops. He heard de Gaulle's appeal and had lunch with him on 26 June at the Rubens Hotel in Victoria. Although he understood his fellow officer's action he felt that his duty lay elsewhere. He recalled their conversation:

'Have you seen what I have done?' asked de Gaulle. 'Naturally.' 'So what do you think?' 'I think that you are right. Someone has to stay and fight with the Allies, but personally I have 7,000 men to repatriate and can't in conscience abandon them before they are safely home.'[17]

At this stage it seemed very possible that France's war against Germany, which had ended on the Continent, might continue in France's North African colonies of Morocco, Algeria and Tunisia. Béthouart reflected that to take his forces back to Morocco was 'tempting because hostilities may be resumed from there'. He continued, however, that 'It is not very clear what is happening but it appears that all the top military leaders – Weygand, Darlan, Noguès, Mittelhauser – are following Marshal Pétain.'[18]

De Gaulle was recognised by the British government on 28 June as 'leader of all the Free French, wherever they may be, who join him for the defence of the Allied cause'.[19] Joining him or not was a drama that was played out among all French forces then stationed in England. While the Alpine Chasseurs were an élite force, the 13th Half Brigade included large numbers of Spanish republicans and Jewish refugees from Central and Eastern Europe who were not eligible to fight in the French Army proper and were regarded by the officers as respectively communists and intellectuals.[20] They now joined other French soldiers and sailors who, after France had sued for an armistice, were held in makeshift camps set up on racecourses near Liverpool such as Aintree, Arrowe Park, Haydock Park and Trentham Park, or in London at the White City Stadium dog track.[21] De Gaulle went to Trentham Park on 30 June but was unable to rally many troops. There was a conflict between the military hierarchy that trusted in Pétain and some of the younger soldiers and junior officers who were more rebellious in spirit and persuaded by de Gaulle.[22] There was also a political dimension: within the Foreign Legion the Spanish republicans feared being sent back to Franco while Central Europeans Jews feared Hitler.[23] Thus of 700 Alpine Chasseurs all but thirty decided to go back with Béthouart, while of the 13th Half Brigade of the Foreign Legion 989 out of 1,619 stayed in Britain. Many of the Spanish republicans joined the British forces. Among the 1,600 French serviceman held at the White City Stadium in London a traditional Anglophobia was spiced up by French Catholic chaplains ministering to the servicemen. Only 152 of these joined de Gaulle, while thirty-four joined the British Army and thirty-six the British Royal Navy.[24]

Two officers of the 13th Half Brigade of the Foreign Legion who followed de Gaulle came from traditional military backgrounds. They belonged to provincial noble families in the west of France, but something in their past incited them to dissent. Jacques Pâris de Bollardière was the son of an officer from Brittany who had served with Marshal Lyautey in Morocco. Jacques was ten when his father died in 1917 and felt that he had to continue the family tradition. However, he revolted against the discipline of the military academy of Saint-Cyr and when he graduated in 1930 said, 'I only had a sergeant's stripes instead of those of a sub-lieutenant.'[25] After serving in Morocco like his father he was promoted to captain during the Narvik expedition and later reflected on 1940: 'I was terribly ashamed of the defeat [. . .] Henceforth I wanted to reject that cowardice and to fight as long as I had to so that together we could recover the right to look at each other without shame.'[26] Gabriel Brunet de Sairigné, aged twenty-seven, came from the Vendean nobility, which had fought against the French Revolution, and attended Saint-Cyr. He fought at Narvik and in Brittany as a lieutenant in the 13th Half Brigade: 'Shameful armistice' he wrote in his diary on 23–25 June 1940, 'What will North Africa do? Repatriation is being talked about, perhaps to Morocco. Discipline impossible: the Spaniards are leaving.' On 1 July he witnessed the departure of all but a few Chasseurs and 700 Legionnaires: 'Emotion at the station as the colonel said goodbye. Everyone making excuses. We all know that Morocco will not fight. Almost everyone is motivated by personal questions.'[27]

The decision of whether to stay or return was not easy to make or indeed easy to predict. André Dewavrin came from a solid industrial family in northern France, attended the élite École Polytechnique and served in the Chasseurs Alpins under General Béthouart in Norway and France before sailing to England on 18 June. He missed de Gaulle's visit to Trentham Park and was sensitive to insults levelled at those who decided to stay, such as 'war to the knifers' and 'English traitors'. 'The Pétain virus was starting to work,' he said. Right-wing himself and loyal to Béthouart, he need the latter's approval before he stayed:

I hesitated until the last moment, and accompanied the expeditionary force to Barry Docks, where it shipped. After a final conversation with

Béthouart who supported my plan, I decided to stay in England and to join General de Gaulle.[28]

On 1 July he met de Gaulle in the dilapidated St Stephen's House on the Victoria Embankment, where the Free French were temporarily located before they moved to Carlton Gardens near Pall Mall at the end of the month. He was put in charge of the General's intelligence services and became more commonly known by his pseudonym, Colonel Passy.

Soldiers who were in France at the moment of the armistice were officially demobilised and most returned to home, family and jobs. A small number, however, reacted against the resignation and passivity they found among their fellow officers and struggled to get out of the country to continue the fight from Britain. Claude Bouchinet-Serreulles, aged twenty-eight, described himself as 'born with a silver spoon in his mouth' and continued the diplomatic career his father had had to interrupt because of illness. He served as a liaison officer with the British Army at Arras, then retreated to the French military headquarters at Vichy, where he heard Pétain's appeal on 17 June:

We were in the mess, each with his nose in his plate, stunned. All our hopes of continuing the war alongside the British with a president of the Republic and war cabinet in Algiers fell apart in an instant. An abyss opened up, silence. Except at our table where, after the speech, artillery colonel X of the general staff exclaimed, 'Bravo, we will continue with the Germans and give the English a good licking.' After a pause he added, 'Here's to more stars!' He was only thinking of promotion. I felt sick and had to excuse myself and leave the table. Alone in the corridor the idea came to me for the first time that I would have to desert![29]

Bouchinet went to Bordeaux and managed to board the *Massilia*, which was sailing to Casablanca. There he met up with Jacques Bingen who had been serving as a liaison officer with the 15th Scottish Division. Wounded in Normandy, Bingen had swum to a fishing boat which got him to Cherbourg. As the Germans closed in he jumped from a hospital train heading for Bordeaux, and took a French cargo ship from La Rochelle to Casablanca. There Bingen and Bouchinet managed to board a Polish ship going to Gibraltar and thence to England. Bingen wrote in English:

Here I am, escaped safely from Naziland and ready to join the British Empire and fight Hitler to the end [. . .] I have lost all I had, my money (not a penny left), my job, my family who remained in France and whom I will perhaps never see again, my country and my beloved Paris, but I remain a free man in a free country and that is more than all.[30]

Docking at Liverpool, Bouchinet and Bingen went to London and met de Gaulle at his headquarters at St Stephen's House on 22 July. Bouchinet was reunited with his schoolfriend from the élite Catholic Collège Stanislas in Paris, Geoffroy de Courcel, who had flown to London with de Gaulle, and while de Courcel ran de Gaulle's military cabinet, Bouchinet headed his civil cabinet. He later reflected that 'the clan of military men [around de Gaulle] were uniquely right wing. They were fierce partisans of the war against Germany, which set them against Vichy, but otherwise, like Vichy's men, they were anti-republican and anti-parliamentary.'[31] Bingen, who in his previous career had been the manager of a shipping consortium, was given the task of gathering together what he could of the French merchant fleet for the benefit of the Free French.[32] Like Georges Boris, he sat slightly away from the centre of power but his contribution was no less significant.

Those who joined de Gaulle in London in order to continue the fight were not all prominent figures and not all men. Hélène Terré began the war in September 1939 in a conventional way as a Red Cross nurse, evacuating children from Paris. She campaigned to set up an ambulance service and told a general staff officer at the War Ministry, 'We want to serve in this war. We are not nurses and we want to wear a French uniform.' 'My dear lady,' she was told, 'please understand that in this war no woman will set foot in the war zone.'[33] After the defeat she decided to go to England where women had been recruited since 1938 into the Auxiliary Territorial Service (ATS). She arrived there in September 1940, travelling via Spain and Portugal, but was immediately arrested as a suspected fifth columnist and spent three months in Holloway prison. On her release in December she read in the paper that de Gaulle had set up an auxiliary service for women, the Corps féminin des volontaires françaises, and was put in command of all its 126 women in October 1941.

One of those who joined the Corps féminin was Tereska Szwarc, whose Polish-Jewish parents had come to France and converted to Catholicism without telling the grandparents in Lodz. Tereska attended the Lycée Henri IV and read Proust. In January 1940 she wrote in her diary:

Riddle: Who am I? I am legally French but the French think me Polish because my parents are. I am Jewish but Jews want nothing to do with me because I am also Catholic. I am a Jew of the Catholic religion, something that cannot be, although I am.[34]

Her sense of Polishness and Jewishness was sharpened in September 1939 when, returning from seeing the family in Poland, German armies invaded the country. The synagogue in Lodz was burned and her grandfather died of a heart attack. She feared that what had happened in Poland would happen in France, and as the Germans invaded France the family fled south to Saint-Jean-de-Luz, where boats were taking on British and Polish soldiers:

In the street I met Elisabeth, who told me of the appeal of General de Gaulle. As they tried to board a boat at Saint-Jean-de-Luz a friend said, 'You must all flee, the Germans are coming. You are Jewish and in great danger.' I want to go to England to join de Gaulle's army.[35]

Tereska's decision to join de Gaulle was a way of escaping her Polish-Jewish identity and affirming herself as a patriotic French woman. The family got to Lisbon in October 1940 and a boat took them to Gibraltar and thus to England, where Tereska become one of the first recruits to the women's branch of de Gaulle's Free French Army.

The people who joined de Gaulle in England were a happy few, but only a few. In England too they were completely reliant on the good offices and generosity of the British government, which accorded de Gaulle limited recognition as leader of Free French and provided material support under an agreement of 7 August 1940. The biggest challenge for de Gaulle in terms of military weight and legitimacy was to rally the French Empire. This extended from the French West Indies to North Africa, French West Africa and French Equatorial Africa to the French mandates of Syria and Lebanon and in the Far East to Indochina. The African possessions were supported by the 140,000-strong Army of Africa, composed largely of European regiments such as the Zouaves and Foreign Legion and North African regiments under French officers, the Moroccan, Algerian and Tunisian Tirailleurs.[36] These were backed up by forces in Syria and Lebanon under General Mittelhauser and 40,000 troops in Indochina under General Catroux, the governor-general who was dismissed by Vichy at the end of June 1940 and came over to de Gaulle.[37] The Empire was defended by the second-largest navy in the world after the British under the command of Admiral Darlan. If these ships could be brought over to de Gaulle's Free French, his position would be massively reinforced, but to prise them away from Marshal Pétain, who was head of government and commander-in-chief of the armed forces, would not be easy.

This idea of continuing the war from North Africa had already occurred to twenty-seven French parliamentarians and former ministers, who set sail on the liner *Massilia* from Bordeaux on 21 June and arrived at Casablanca on 24 June. They included former premier Édouard Daladier, former interior minister Georges Mandel, and Pierre Mendès France, who opposed the armistice and wanted to carry on the struggle from North Africa. Unfortunately the Pétain government had facilitated their departure in order to get them out of the way and on their arrival had them arrested and interned on the ship with a view to putting them on trial as traitors.[38] On 19 June de Gaulle sent a telegram to General Charles Noguès, commander-in-chief of all North African forces and resident-general in Morocco (effectively the Sultan's prime minister) saying, 'Am at your disposal either to fight under your orders or for any approach you may think useful.'[39] A further message on 24 June read, 'General, the defence of North Africa is you or nothing. Yes, it is you and it is the essential element and the centre of continued resistance.'[40] The overture was reinforced by a visit from General François d'Astier de la Vigerie, who had been an air ace in the First World War, commanded the air battle in north-east France in May–June 1940, and had plans to continue the air war from North Africa. D'Astier initially found Noguès 'vibrant, dynamic, super-patriotic' but on a second occasion Noguès was in tears. He had contacted Weygand to say that North Africa did not accept capitulation, at which Weygand demanded his resignation. Noguès then concluded, 'On reflexion, I could impose the capitulation' and, said d'Astier, 'he became the collaborator we knew'.[41]

For Great Britain, the most urgent issue after France dropped out of the war was to keep the French Navy out of German hands. Such an eventuality would threaten the naval routes that were crucial to her own survival and destroy her superiority in sea power. The French fleet was divided between Toulon, the Algerian port of Mers el-Kébir outside Oran, and Alexandria. On 2 July the British issued the French commander at Oran with a choice: sail to fight alongside the Royal Navy, or sail with reduced crews to the French West Indies to be disarmed, or be sunk. The French commander refused this ultimatum, claiming that France's word that the fleet would not fall into German hands was enough. In the early evening of 3 July the British commenced a naval artillery barrage and air attack from the aircraft carrier *Ark Royal*; within minutes the bulk of the French fleet was destroyed at its moorings with the loss of 1,300 lives. While Churchill received a standing ovation in the House of Commons the French broke off diplomatic relations with Great Britain, de Gaulle was condemned to death for treason by a military tribunal in Clermont-Ferrand and was widely regarded as a prisoner of perfidious Albion.

North Africa rallied strongly behind Vichy and only a minority thought otherwise. José Aboulker, a twenty-year-old medical student from a prosperous and well-known Jewish family in Algiers, had become a reserve medical pupil-doctor, 'the lowest army rank for medics who joined it'. 'At the armistice,' he remembered, 'almost everyone hoped that the North African territories would continue the war alongside the British' and cheered air squadrons from France that touched down there. But within a short space of time opinion in the army changed. General Weygand arrived as delegate-general of French Africa on 5 September 1940 and undertook a tour of officers' messes in North Africa to bring them into line and nip any signs of Gaullism: 'I saw Weygand when he came to our barracks,' remembers Aboulker. 'The next day you could say that the men had been turned around. The great general told them that they had to follow the Marshal in his policy of collaboration.'[42]

Further south in Africa, the battle for control between the Free French and Vichy was more fiercely fought out. Three thousand miles from Oran, at Pointe Noire on the sea coast of French Congo, Jesuit-educated Captain François Garbit, aged thirty, who had commanded indigenous troops in Sub-Saharan Africa since he graduated from Saint-Cyr in 1932, wrote to his mother on 30 June 1940. He described the draining away of hopes that the Empire would continue the war, as people resigned themselves to the new situation, with only a few, like himself, keen to fight on:

It is done. The armistice is signed. We hoped at least that this armistice, like that of the Netherlands for example, would only concern the metropolis. We have been disappointed. The armistice has surrendered the fleet and been extended to the Empire. We hoped that the Empire would rise up, rebel, refuse to obey a government that surrenders its forces intact and hands over its trump cards to the enemy. However, unity has not been possible [. . .] Those who want to fight are champing at the bit while more and more accept the fait accompli and dream about their little comforts as if they could have them back. Only the voice of General de Gaulle gives a clear, clean, loyal, convincing sound. But here, so far from everything, without information, how do we know which way to go? May the Holy Spirit guide us.[43]

For a short time there was hesitation. Pierre Boisson, governor of French Equatorial Africa (AEF) at Brazzaville, a hundred miles inland from Pointe Noire, appealed for calm and maintained an ambiguous line about the armistice. Blanche Ackerman-Athanassiades, the wife of a colonial businessman at Brazzaville, described how 'everyone looked at each other suspiciously. No one knew who was going to rally [to Vichy] and who wasn't.'[44] On 14 July 1940, however, Boisson flew to Dakar, the capital of French West Africa, and declared it for Vichy. He was followed by soldiers such as Major Raoul Salan, who described himself as a 'a soldier of the Empire, of that Empire that is indispensable for French greatness'.[45] He had fought in the colonial infantry since 1917 and commanded a battalion of Senegalese Tirailleurs in 1940. Horrified by Mers el-Kébir he sided with Vichy and worked for the Colonial ministry there before becoming head of intelligence in Dakar in 1942–3.

Other soldiers, nevertheless, moved in the opposite direction. They gave birth to the Free French, giving de Gaulle a foothold in Africa.[46] Garbit's commanding officer, the Corsican Jean Colonna d'Ornano, flew from Brazzaville to Lagos in Nigeria, to meet de Gaulle's envoy to Africa and Jean Monnet's former assistant, René Pleven. The British colonial administration in Nigeria offered financial and economic support to the components of French Equatorial Africa – Chad, Cameroon, French Congo and Gabon – to join de Gaulle and Pleven was in talks with them.[47] Pleven and d'Ornano then flew east to Fort Lamy, the capital of Chad, whose position was threatened by Italian forces in Libya to the north and where – reported Garbit – 'they were welcomed with flowers by a population which overwhelmingly wanted to continue the fight'.[48] Félix Éboué, the black governor of Chad, declared to the assembled notables, 'You have heard our decision. Those who are not in agreement may simply leave.'[49] The rallying of Chad to the Free French on 26 August 1940 was a key moment in the balance of power between the Free French and Vichy. According to Garbit it 'lit the powder' in French Equatorial Africa.[50] Garbit himself went to Chad to join Colonna and the offensive against the Italians in Eritrea on the Red Sea.

In the plane with René Pleven, as it landed in Lagos and then in Fort Lamy, was Major Philippe de Hautecloque, a Picardian noble who had graduated from Saint-Cyr and served in the Rif war against Morocco rebels in the 1920s. In 1940 he was on the general staff of the 4th Infantry Division. Taken prisoner twice and escaping twice, he hid in his sister's château in Anjou before making his way via Bayonne, Spain and Portugal to join de Gaulle in London. On 4 August 1940 he broadcast on the BBC, praising the patriotism of those French people who refused to accept defeat and telling them that around de Gaulle 'I had the joy of seeing that everyone, soldiers and civilians, are pursuing only one goal: the struggle. I did not find refugees but fighters. Be reassured, France still has its defenders.'[51] Taking the name of Leclerc, by which he would henceforth be known, and kitted out in colonial gear by the British, he flew to Africa with Pleven on 6 August. He orchestrated the rallying of Cameroon to the Free French at Douala on 27 August, although in Gabon soldiers and civilians whipped up by the local bishop remained loyal to Vichy until the Free French took charge on 10 November.[52]

In the meantime de Gaulle had attempted, in a seaborne expedition supported by Britain, to seize control of the port of Dakar and with it the whole of French West Africa. The assault on 23–25 September was a failure, as Governor Boisson held fast and shore batteries and the battleship *Richelieu*, which had escaped from the British attack on the French fleet at Mers el-Kébir, fired back at the assailants.[53] 'I wanted to avoid a pitched battle between Frenchmen, so I pulled out my forces in time,' de Gaulle wrote to his wife in London, adding, 'the ceiling is falling on my head.'[54] Although he went on to be warmly received in French Equatorial Africa on a tour between 8 October and 17 November, the Free French had suffered a massive blow to their confidence and at the British War Cabinet on 30 September there was debate about whether they had backed the right horse or should reopen talks with Vichy.[55]

There was a great distance both geographically and psychologically between what the Free French were doing in far-flung parts of the French Empire and the choices that were open to individuals in metropolitan France, where the military option was not available. In German-occupied northern France there was no French military force, all paramilitary groups including boy scouts were banned and all weapons, including hunting rifles, had to be handed in on pain of death. In the unoccupied or Free Zone, where Vichy held sway, there was an Armistice Army, 100,000-strong, available to keep internal order, but this was entirely loyal to the regime.

In a few isolated minds, even so, thoughts about resistance of one kind or another began to germinate. In which minds were these thoughts entertained? Were these early resisters patriots who instinctively reacted against German occupation? Were they idealists who reacted against Vichy's authoritarianism and policies of discrimination? Were they simply oddballs and mavericks who did not go along with the conformist majority? Were there deep family or social reasons for their resistance or were their choices purely contingent, explained by chance?

All French people claimed to be patriots, although their patriotism meant different things. At the heart of the narrative was France's bravery and endurance in the Great War, next to which the war of 1940 was a humiliating failure. This impacted on individuals in different ways. Some saw themselves in a tradition of fathers who had served heroically in the First World War and who worshipped Pétain in 1940 as they had at Verdun in 1916; they followed their fathers out of filial piety. A second group felt that they had been unable to match up to fathers or siblings who had excelled in the Great War. They had fallen short when their own turn had come in 1940 and their masculinity was impugned. Resistance was their way of recovering lost patriotic ground and a sense of self. A third group had fathers whose roles had been less than heroic in the Great War; they had been unfit to fight or let the country down in some way. It was the task of the younger generation – whether male or female – not only to prove themselves but to redeem family honour.

'Since my father was an officer and I graduated from Saint-Cyr, I was steeped in the military world from my earliest childhood,' said Henri Frenay. 'I belonged to that traditional, poor, patriotic and patriarchal French Right without even being aware of it.'[56] His father had died in the First War when Henri was a boy and he was brought up by his mother. A captain in 1940 he was taken prisoner on the Maginot Line but escaped and went south to Marseille in late July. 'In the southern zone,' he recalled in 1948, 'the immense majority of the population welcomed the armistice with an infinite relief and the Republic disappeared on 10 July to general indifference.' He did not hear of de Gaulle's appeal until the end of July 1940 and 'this did not have a noticeable repercussion at the time; Pétain was the head of government, De Gaulle was nothing and we did not have the means to join him'.[57] The popularity of Marshal Pétain as the saviour of the French people was at its height and for Frenay he was initially a surrogate father or grandfather. He described the Marshal's official visit to Marseille on 3 December 1940, when he reviewed 15,000 men of the Légion Française des Combattants, in which all veterans' associations were now combined, and was acclaimed by the crowd:

The head of state alights from his car, grave and dignified. He is in uniform. Without a smile he surveys the electrified crowd which he salutes with a flourish of his stick. With his hair white as snow and pale blue eyes, his calm has a powerful effect [. . .] People break through the barriers and throw themselves at the Head of State. Dumbfounded, I see an old man kiss the Marshal's hand. A large woman with a wide, pleated dress, probably a fishwife, kneels and piously kisses the hem of his coat. I have never witnessed such religious fervour.[58]

Frenay believed that Pétain was playing a 'double game', keeping lines open to the British while dealing with the Germans. In December 1940 he was appointed to the Deuxième Bureau (Intelligence) of the army general staff at Vichy and saw himself in a position to uncover military intelligence that might be used by the British. It was not until January 1941 that the scales fell from his eyes and he left the army to think seriously about resistance. His mother, as guardian of the family's military honour, threatened never to speak to him again.[59]

Philippe Viannay, aged twenty-two in 1940, was very clear that 'the origins of my resistance owe nothing to my family'. His father had served under Pétain at Verdun and would not have a bad word said against him. His career as a mining engineer took him to Poland, which was very much in France's orbit between the wars, and Philippe enjoyed hunting there. The family was extremely Catholic, one uncle a priest while two sisters became nuns. His elder brother went to cavalry school at Saumur but Philippe was destined for the priesthood and attended the seminary of Issy-les-Moulineau. Two years later he upset his parents by deciding to quit and went to the Sorbonne in 1938. When war came he was mobilised in the colonial infantry and after the armistice returned to the Sorbonne, where friendships led him towards resistance. Fear of his father, who 'was convinced that Pétain was playing a very clever game and wanted to confront the Germans', meant that it was some time before Philippe broke with the cult of Pétain: 'In his eyes I was committing the sin of pride by challenging the established order.'[60]

Jacques Lecompte-Boinet was one of the second group who found it impossible to live up to his heroic father and felt his masculinity challenged. At the outbreak of war in 1939 he wrote in his diary, 'I am obsessed by the memory of my father. I return to that day, 2 August 1914, when my father gave his last pieces of advice to my mother before going off to war on horseback. The only bit of the memory that remains is him telling her to hide the pictures that recall the war of 1870 in a cupboard behind the wardrobe and I think that things were much simpler twenty-five years ago.'[61] His father had been killed at the front in 1916, when Jacques was eleven, and he did not manage to match his father's heroism in 1939. A tax official in the Paris Préfecture, he was not called up because of his poor eyesight and because he had four children. Instead, he was given a job at the Gare Saint-Lazare directing refugees going to Normandy. His sense of military inadequacy was increased by the fact that he had married one of the daughters of the legendary General Mangin, and that the husband of one of Mangin's other daughters, Diego Brosset, had pursued a brilliant military career. On 13 June 1940 Lecompte-Boinet joined the exodus south on a bicycle with two of his colleagues, but was appalled by the reaction to the armistice of people around him, such as 'the schoolmaster who criticised the royalist agitator Maurras for being too left wing and saw only one thing: "the Jews will leave and order will be re-established".' Two years later, deep into his resistance career and after the birth of a fifth child, he reflected, 'I thought constantly of my father. I had not been able to fight normally in the war but I did not want to leave my children with the memory of a father who had spent that time with his feet snugly in his slippers, waiting till it blew over.'[62]

In some cases the heroism of siblings was just as much a challenge as that of the father. Emmanuel d'Astier de la Vigerie was fourteen years younger than his brother General François d'Astier and three years younger than his brother Henri, who had joined up in 1917. 'From August 1914 – I was fourteen years old,' he said, 'I was very miserable. Everyone else went to war but I was *embusqué* because I wasn't old enough to fight [. . .] I was the only one who could not become a hero.'[63] After the First World War Emmanuel went to naval school but disappointed his father because he did not pass out in the top ten out of 150. After seven years in the navy he dropped out and attempted to become a writer but failed at that too. He was encouraged by the darling of the extreme right, Drieu la Rochelle, but suffered the 'traumatism' of having his first offering turned down by the *Nouvelle Revue Française*. While his brothers again became heroes in 1940 he achieved nothing. He was a naval intelligence officer at Saint-Nazaire as the French armies collapsed. With five men under his command he set off to try to get a boat to England or Africa, first from La Rochelle, then from Saint-Jean-de-Luz, but even that did not work out. His involvement in resistance at this point went back to a deep sense of failure. For the first time he heard the words, 'we must do something.'[64]

The third group was composed of those who wished to save family honour from the shame of a father who had not been a wartime hero. Agnès Humbert was the daughter of a former soldier, journalist and senator of the Meuse who had made a reputation before the First War for exposing military incompetence. However, in 1918 he was himself accused of accepting German money and, though he was acquitted, his career was in ruins. Divorced from a painter, politically a left-wing anti-fascist, and a historian at the Musée des Arts et Traditions populaires in Paris, Agnès was on the road fleeing south when news of the armistice came through. It was her moment to be brave and she recalled taking on a different personality. 'All around me men were weeping silent tears. Jumping out of the car, I stamped and yelled, "It's all lies, it's all lies, it's the German radio that's saying that just to demoralize us. It can't be true, it's not possible." I can still hear my voice, as though it were someone else shouting.' Arriving at her mother's house in the Limousin she found it teeming with French and Belgian refugees. De Gaulle's voice came over the radio and she thought, 'It's not over yet.' Again it was the men, even the soldiers, who did not share her sentiments. An old captain to whom she told the news replied, 'Oh yes, he's a right one, that de Gaulle. Oh, we all know about him, don't you worry! It's all a lot of nonsense. Me, I'm a reservist anyway. All I want is to get back to my business in Paris. I've got a family to feed. He's a crackpot, that de Gaulle, you mark my words.'[65] Agnès returned to Paris at the end of July but in her case it was to join one of the first resistance cells.

In other cases the shame of the father was that of omission rather than commission. Jean Cavaillès was a brilliant young philosophy teacher who defended his thesis in 1938 and was appointed junior lecturer at the Arts Faculty of Strasbourg; when war broke out he was recruited to the army's deciphering department. His father, a soldier who had taught at the military school of Saint-Maixent, was invalided out of the First World War and died during the German invasion of 1940. 'Our father lived in close communion with Jean, who always kept a picture of him on his desk,' his sister Gabrielle recalled. 'He was proud of this son who was realising his life's ideal – this philosopher son, this soldier son.'[66] In the military, and then in the Resistance, Jean fulfilled the aspiration to heroism that his father had never quite realised. To help him he fell back on a family legend of resistance as persecuted heretics and Protestants in Provence. Gabrielle wrote, 'Our father was in fact the descendant of the countess Malan de Mérindol, who was buried alive in the twelfth century because she refused to abjure her faith. Jean was thus the heir of men and women who defended their ideal at the risk of their lives,' she continued, 'the heir of Marie Durand who carved the word "resistance" into the stones of her cell.'[67] The story of Marie Durand, who had been imprisoned as a Protestant for nearly forty years in the Tour de

Constance at Aigues-Mortes was a common reference among those who engaged in resistance to the Germans.

Resisters are often seen as idealists as much as patriots, striving after a better world that had been frittered away by the Republic and perverted by the German occupation and Vichy. One of the questions asked of former resisters by the Comité d'Histoire de la Deuxième Guerre Mondiale was how they had reacted to Munich. It was assumed that their prescience in seeing Munich as an appeasement of Nazism that was condemned to fail led them directly to resistance when the Germans occupied France. In this sense they were unlike the crowds of 'cons' berated by Daladier (under his breath as his plane from Munich touched down in Paris), who thought that the agreement had brought peace in their time. Opposition to Munich might provide a clue to the thinking of some resisters but in the case of communists, who vehemently criticised Munich, it was complicated a year later by the Nazi-Soviet Pact.

For some, resistance was a continuation of the anti-fascist movement that had given birth to the Popular Front in 1936. That said, resisters were in fact drawn from all parts of the political spectrum, from the extreme left to the extreme right, and included socialists and Christian democrats who belonged to a long and controversial tradition of prising Catholicism away from the established order and reconciling faith with freedom. Some of the extreme right moved naturally into collaboration with the Germans, but the nationalist thrust of extreme-right politics could also lead them to oppose servility. Resisters were often political idealists who thought a great deal during the Resistance of the world they would build after Liberation. Rarely, however, were they partisan political animals, as the political parties had failed in their mission to defend the Republic: 569 deputies and senators voted full powers to Pétain on 10 July 1940, while only 80 voted against and 17 abstained. They tended to be political nonconformists who opposed the Party line where that line was determined by political expediency rather than principle.

Pierre Brossolette was an exemplar of Third Republic social mobility, a brilliant student at the École Normale Supérieure who was the son of a primary school inspector in Paris and grandson of a peasant.[68] His mother died when he was a child and he was described by his friend Louis Joxe as having 'a rather anxious character, wondering whether he was going to achieve great things; it was something that haunted him'. He carved out a career as a journalist, writing for papers such as *L'Europe Nouvelle*. He was also an activist in the French Socialist Party, but failed to get elected with the Popular Front in 1936, and was not one of the successful young socialists close to the prime minister, Léon Blum. In that sense he was not a party man. Having long been committed to reconciliation with Germany 'he was', continued Joxe, 'the first among us who understood fairly quickly where we were going, that is, towards war, towards a fight to the death, well, between democracy and fascism'.[69] He was resolutely opposed to Munich and came into his own in 1940 when he was promoted to infantry captain, described as 'the officer in the midst of his men, a real warrior'.[70] Forced to retreat, news of the armistice came through to his unit near Limoges. Here Brossolette and his men disagreed, as one of his sub-lieutenants recalls:

The men welcomed the armistice with a joy that was understandable because it put an end to their present sufferings, even if it was out of place. Brossolette was deeply pained. 'They don't understand,' he told me, 'that we are beaten. They don't understand what it means. But I fear that before long they will understand only too well. They don't know the Boches. We are going to be very unhappy.'[71]

At the far right of the political spectrum were resisters who were often First World War heroes and politically no different from Pétainists and maintained contacts with Vichy. In the inter-war period they had gone into industry and associated with right-wing organisations such as the Maurras' royalist Action

Française, George Valois' Faisceau and Colonel de La Rocque's Croix de Feu, which recruited initially only from those who had seen action at the front in 1914–18 and which tried repeatedly to overthrow the Republic.[72] They diverged from Vichy's strategy of collaboration because they believed that the war was not yet over and that military intelligence should be passed to the British, who were still fighting. Among them, Alfred Heurtaux was an air ace who had been wounded in a dog fight above Ypres in 1917, worked for General Motors and Renault between the wars, and was active in the veterans' movement, accepting responsibility in Vichy's Légion Française des Combattants formed in August 1940 to unite all veterans' organisations.[73] Another, Alfred Touny, who finished the Great War as a much-decorated captain and pursued a career in law and industry between the wars, had been involved in the Croix de Feu.[74]

Communists were perhaps the most radically inclined to resistance, although the path from Party to resistance was a complicated one and not all took the same route. Communism was the most dynamic force that had taken on fascism in Italy and Nazism in Germany. Crushed there, it had played a leading role in the Spanish Civil War, and the International Brigades that volunteered to fight there were recruited by its international body, the Comintern. With 328,000 members in 1937, the French Communist Party had been a key factor in the Popular Front, although the Party refused to serve in what it regarded as a 'bourgeois' government. It had campaigned for intervention in Spain and was at the forefront of opposition to Munich. However, this direction of travel was sharply reversed by the Nazi-Soviet Pact of August 1939. Feeling abandoned by France and Britain after Munich, Stalin opted for a non-aggression pact with Hitler as a breathing space and cover for territorial annexations. Communist parties everywhere were thrown into a spin. Was the anti-fascist line of the last decade suddenly finished, and the new enemy the imperialist and warmongering powers of France and Great

Britain? The French government under Daladier immediately banned the Party, expelled its members from local government and began to arrest its activists. Party members were confused and divided: the leadership generally followed the Moscow line: after all the Soviet Union was the home of socialism and must be safeguarded. Many of the rank and file drifted away.[75] A small proportion of activists, particularly those who had fought in the International Brigades, persisted in the anti-fascist line, which meant distancing themselves from the Party until the German invasion of the Soviet Union in June 1941, when resistance behind the German lines became officially sanctioned.[76]

Among communist activists who became involved in resistance three groups were apparent. The first might be called Jewish Bolsheviks of foreign origin, whose attitude to the Nazi-Soviet Pact depended on how closely they identified with the French Communist Party. The second were the students of the Latin Quarter in Paris, who were bloodied by the anti-fascist street fights of the 1930s and did not always follow the Party line. The third were communists of working-class origin, who were influenced both by Moscow and the anti-fascist line and were also divided by the Nazi-Soviet Pact.

Lew Goldenberg was born in Paris in 1908 to Polish-Russian revolutionaries who were close to Rosa Luxemburg, and who fled to France after the failure of the 1905 revolution, his father working as a doctor. He was educated in the French system, including the Sorbonne and Paris Law Faculty, changed his name to Léo Hamon, and became a barrister at the Constitutional Council in 1930. His parents subsequently returned to Soviet Russia and Léo himself joined the French Communist Party after the riots of 6 February 1934, mainly because he saw the Party as 'the heirs of 1793, devoted to liberty and full of salutary hatred for what they called fascism', but partly because privately he imagined that it would help to get his mother out of the Soviet Union. 'Munich outraged and disappointed me,' he recalled. 'I experienced it for what it was: capitulation, abandonment and a mistake.' Equally, though, given his view that fascism must be opposed, he was 'stupefied as much as outraged' by the Nazi-Soviet pact and did not see why French communists should consider themselves bound by it. He joined the army but soon found his unit in retreat. Opposed to the armistice, he took the view that each French person was now free to continue the fight as best they could, in Britain or the French Empire if possible.[77]

Another foreign Jewish Bolshevik, Roger Ginsburger, was a rather more hard-line militant. Born in Alsace in 1901, when it was part of Imperial Germany, he was the son of a rabbi who was also university librarian at the University of Strasbourg. His upbringing and education were thus German up to the *Abitur*, which he took in 1918, although at school he was bullied as a 'dirty Jew' or 'Yid'. In 1919, when Alsace was restored to France, he went to a special class at the Lycée Saint-Louis (in Paris) for bright children from the recovered province, and then studied architecture in Strasbourg, Stuttgart and Munich. He was seduced by the Bolshevik Revolution, abandoned his Jewish faith, and tried to combine art and politics in the Communist-party-inspired Association of Revolutionary Writers and Artists. In 1934 he became a permanent member of the French Communist Party, writing for *L'Humanité* and the *Cahiers du Bolchévisme*, and was promoted to the Central Committee in 1935. Like all French communists he was hostile to Munich but had a very different reaction to the Nazi-Soviet Pact from Léo Hamon. His argument was that communists should show solidarity with those who now faced government persecution as traitors. To criticise the pact, he said, 'at a moment when comrades faithful to the Party are being driven out of town halls and trade union leadership, and some indeed arrested, when the pro-Munich press are calling communists Hitler's agents, would be to justify these repressive measures and to betray one's comrades'.[78] He attempted to keep the communist press going under the German occupation, but was himself arrested by the Vichy police in October 1940, and did the rounds of a number of prisons and camps until he managed to escape in January 1941. The *nom de guerre* he invented for himself in the Resistance was Pierre Villon.

The Latin Quarter students included Jean-Pierre Vernant and his older brother Jacques, who had lost their father at the front in 1915 when they were small children. They nevertheless shared brilliant academic careers, Jacques coming top in the philosophy *agrégation* examination in 1935, Jean-Pierre achieving the same in 1937, aged twenty-three. Jean-Pierre traced his commitment back a long way: 'I was a communist militant from 1931, starting with the Friends of the USSR at the Lycée Carnot. I attended my first political meeting in the Latin Quarter when I was in the philosophy class [of my Lycée] and was still in short trousers.' The years 1932–4 were particularly tough, he remembers, 'because the Latin Quarter was effectively in the hands of extreme-right groups: the Camelots du Roi, who supported the Action Française students, the Jeunesses Patriotes, the youth section of the Croix de Feu, the Francisques. There was an atmosphere of physical violence, we got beaten up and even ejected from the Sorbonne.' The fierceness of the battle nevertheless bonded him with a group of young people who subsequently became key players in the Resistance in the Free Zone, including Lucie Bernard, 'with whom I sold the *Avant Garde* and who had the same qualities of extraordinary nerve that she demonstrated later'.[79]

Lucie Bernard was initially destined to become a primary-school teacher (*institutrice*) but managed by sheer force of will to get into the Sorbonne and pass the *agrégation* in history in order to become a secondary school teacher. In the Latin Quarter, she agreed with Vernant, 'We fought, literally. Activism involved physical confrontation. I punched, I punched.'[80] During her time as a student there she met Raymond Samuel, later known as Raymond Aubrac, who came from a bourgeois Jewish family that had left Lorraine after 1870, and was training to become an engineer at one of the leading *grandes écoles*, the École des

Ponts. Raymond moved in the communist circles of Lucie's group without actually feeling enough of a 'member of the family' to become a communist, and though not himself a practising Jew, he remembered that 'in the Jewish milieus I frequented anti-Semitism was considered a return to medieval barbarism.'[81]

These communist students were fiercely opposed to Munich but were less keen to follow the Party line over the Nazi-Soviet Pact. Jean-Pierre Vernant was already mobilised in the army and recalls that the pact 'hit me between the eyes'. He argued that 'the Russians are doing that, I don't know why, I don't know their thinking. But that does not change our position.' Known in the army as a communist he was not selected for officer training and remained a sergeant, but reasoned, 'When you are faced by Hitlerism, there is no alternative but to fight.' He had retreated to Narbonne and was with his brother when Pétain told the country that he was asking the Germans for an armistice:

I was felled by shame and anger [. . .] I was convinced that for us it was beginning. The sight of the débâcle revived an old nationalist reflex, deep humiliation and fury at the idea that those people were at home in our homes. And at the same time a very deep anti-fascism, a hatred of all that.[82]

Vernant's anti-fascist reflex never really faltered. Neither did that of Lucie and Raymond Aubrac, who had married in December 1939. Raymond was taken prisoner after the defeat but was extracted from a POW camp at Saarbrücken thanks to Lucie's cunning. She tracked down Raymond's brother, a doctor working in a POW hospital in Troyes, and from him obtained a substance which, placed under the skin, produced the symptoms of tropical fever. After he was transferred from prison to hospital, Lucie extracted him once again by flirting with a guard, providing Raymond with workmen's overalls, and hiding him under a train wagon to cross the frontier back to the Free Zone where together they began resistance activity.[83]

The working-class constituency of French communism was extremely important. The labour movement had organised itself from the end of the nineteenth century into trade unions, which came together both nationally as trade federations and locally in Bourses du Travail, the union of unions. Politically it was represented by the Socialist Party and the Communist Party, which split from it in 1920 over the question of loyalty to Moscow. The working class was heir to a powerful political tradition that went back to the Paris Commune of 1871 and to the Revolutions of 1848 and 1789. The communists, however, also saw themselves as part of an international communist movement ranged against capitalism and imperialism, and were loyal to the Soviet Union, which was acclaimed as the first socialist society.

The tension between 'Moscow' communists and veterans of the International Brigades went down the middle of Lise Ricol's family. Her father had come from Spain to France in 1900 to look for work and became a miner at Montceau-les-Mines, moving to Vénissieux, a working-class suburb of Lyon, in the early 1930s. The family was entirely communist and had wide communist connections. Lise's elder sister Fernande, born in 1913, married Raymond Guyot, who became national organiser of the Communist Youth and went to Moscow in 1936 as secretary of the International Communist Youth. Lise, born in 1916, became a secretary at the Communist Party's regional headquarters in Lyon, where she met and married a Party official, Auguste Delarue. When Delarue was sent to train at the Lenin School in Moscow in 1934 Lise followed him, working as a typist at Comintern headquarters. There she met the love of her life, Artur London, a Czech communist who was also working for the International Communist Youth. Lise abandoned Delarue and returned to France with Artur to live together; Lise was involved in setting up the International Brigades while Artur went to fight in Spain with the Brigades.[84] The family divided over the Nazi-Soviet Pact. Guyot, who had been elected a communist deputy for Villejuif in 1937, staunchly followed the Moscow line. Mobilised to his regiment at Tarascon, he continued to enjoy immunity as a deputy until he appeared in the Chamber of Deputies on 10 January 1940 and remained seated while honours were voted to the French Army. Twenty-seven communist deputies were sent for trial in March–April 1940 and were taken to a succession of prisons in France before being moved to the Maison Carré in Algiers. Guyot deserted and was spirited away by the Party via Belgium to Moscow, following on the heels of PCF leader Maurice Thorez. Given the betrayal of the Munich agreement and the invasion of Prague by the German armies in March 1939, however, Artur London stuck to the anti-fascist line of the Czechoslovak Communist Party. This approved the organisation of a Free Czechoslovak Army fighting alongside Britain and France, which Artur joined at Agde in August 1939.[85]

André Tollet was a typical product of the Paris working class and was something of a hybrid in that he had connections with both Spain and Moscow. Brought up in Paris, the son of small tradesmen, he left school at thirteen in 1926 to become an apprentice upholsterer in the Faubourg Saint-Antoine:

The Faubourg had kept its old traditions. The Revolution of 1789 began there. We sang songs of the Commune by Pottier and Clément in the workshops and we commemorated it by processing to 'the Wall', the Mur des Fédérés at Père Lachaise [. . .] I was not yet fifteen when I paraded for the first time.[86]

He became involved in the Woodworkers' Union and the Communist Youth and was invited by Raymond Guyot to represent them at a meeting of the Red Syndicalist International in Moscow in 1936.

Back in Paris he took part in the strikes of May–June 1936 that ushered in the Popular Front and, having had his request to join the International Brigades turned down by the Party, organised collections in support of the Brigades and went to Spain with a convoy of shoes in 1938. Despite his confusion he came down on the side of the Nazi-Soviet Pact, saying, 'We had two ideas: [. . .] either it was totally stupid or else the Soviets probably knew much more than we did. As a result we did not want to condemn the pact.' He was called up to fight but was unmoved by the defeat of France, which seemed more interested in repressing its own people than in winning a war. After demobilisation he returned to Paris and tried to bring traumatised communists back together through neighbourhood committees and clandestine trade unions. However the Vichy government organised a massive clampdown on communists in October 1940, as a result of which he was arrested and sent first to Fresnes prison, then to camps for dangerous internees at Rouillé and Compiègne.[87]

One of the International Brigadists whom Tollet met in Spain was Henri Tanguy, a political commissar of the famous XIV Brigade. Tanguy was a Parisian of Breton origin, who left school at thirteen and was sacked from a succession of car factories for organising strikes until in 1936 he became a permanent official at the Metalworkers' Union. There he met his wife, Cécile Le Bihan, a secretary at the Metalworkers' Union, whose father François was a long-serving communist and active in the Secours Rouge International, so that she often met Czech, Hungarian, Yugoslav, Italian and German political exiles who sheltered with them. Tanguy secured permission from the Party to go to Spain, where he joined the International Brigades and fought there in 1937 and in 1938.[88] 'My anti-fascist determination never failed,' he insisted. 'Perhaps it was because I had been in the Brigades and seen fascism at first hand.'[89] In 1939 he was mobilised, then sent as a skilled worker to an arms factory near the Pyrenean border, and in 1940 drafted into a regiment of colonial infantry. He remembered hearing Pétain's speech at a water fountain in the Limousin but was in a minority as far as his dismissal of the Marshal and thoughts of resistance were concerned:

As I knew the character and his role as French ambassador to Franco, I could not stop myself saying, 'It's not him who will get us out of this mess.' There was a chorus of protests. I had to beat a hasty retreat. I really thought those good people were going to attack me.[90]

His wife Cécile, left in Paris, meanwhile suffered a string of disasters. Her father François Le Bihan was arrested in April 1940, accused of attempting to reconstitute a dissolved organisation, the Communist Party. She had a seven-month-old baby, Françoise, who fell ill as medical staff fled from the Paris hospitals with everyone else. The baby died as German armies marched into the capital. Soon afterwards she agreed to undertake resistance activity for the Metalworkers' Union because, she said, 'I had nothing left. My father had been arrested, I didn't know where my husband was and I had lost my little girl. What was keeping me back? I got involved. It helped me. It gave something back to me.'[91]

Even more a product of the Paris working class was Pierre Georges, who was a born rebel. The son of a Paris *boulanger*, he belonged to a large communist family in the Belleville-La Villette area of Paris. His older siblings, Daniel and Denise, dragged him and his younger brother Jacques into the Communist Youth. He was sacked at the age of fourteen for striking back at his *pâtissier* boss and became a riveter. Overcoming the reluctance of the Party, Pierre Georges went to Spain at the age of seventeen in November 1936 to join the International Brigades, rising to become an officer in the XIV Brigade until, wounded in the stomach, he was evacuated back to France in 1938. In Paris he found work in an aircraft factory and was promoted to the central committee of the Communist Youth, where he met and married Andrée Coudrier.[92] The family was deeply affected by anti-communist repression after the Nazi-Soviet Pact. Pierre Georges, his pregnant wife Andrée and younger brother Jacques were arrested. The men were imprisoned at La Santé, the women sent to La Roquette. Andrée was released in February 1940, while

Pierre caught up on Balzac, Maupassant and Dostoevsky. 'I am reading a wonderful novel at the moment,' he wrote to Andrée, 'It's Stendhal's *Le Rouge et le Noir*. I bet it will make you cry.'[93] As the Germans approached Paris in May 1940, Jacques was transferred to the Pyrenean camp of Gurs and was given an eighteen-month sentence by a military court; Pierre was transferred to another camp but escaped en route, disguised as a soldier. He made contact with the Party again at Marseille and was sent back to Paris to develop communist resistance.[94]

The conflict between the Moscow communists and more freewheeling veterans of previous struggles was sharply highlighted by the case of Charles Tillon. He enjoyed heroic status in 1919, at the age of twenty-two, as one of the mutineers of the Black Sea Fleet who refused to fight the Russian revolutionaries and were sentenced to terms of hard labour. In 1936 he was elected communist deputy for Aubervilliers in the Paris red belt and was sent by the Party leadership in October 1939 to reconstitute the Party in the Bordeaux area. He was troubled by the way the Party, locked into the Nazi-Soviet pact, blamed the war on the rich bourgeoisie and Anglo-French imperialists but did not criticise Nazi Germany. He was hiding in a mill owned by a peasant family when he heard Pétain's call on 17 June to cease the fight and took it upon himself to call for resistance:

A youthful sense of revolt fired me up. I gulped down good Mme Jouques' soup and went upstairs to draft a tract. It was an appeal to ensure that the representatives of the people did not remain voiceless when they saw France invade, subjected, and kept in cowardly ignorance of the true nature of fascism.[95]

He drafted a manifesto, which was duplicated and slid surreptitiously between the pages of newspapers on sale the next day. Preceding even de Gaulle's appeal by a few hours, it beat the official communist appeal of 10 July by nearly a month and later landed him in serious trouble with the Party. It called for:

A government fighting against HITLERIAN FASCISM and the 200 families. To negotiate with the USSR for an equitable peace, fighting for national independence and dealing with fascist organisations. People of the factories and fields, shops and offices, artisans, shopkeepers and intellectuals, soldiers, sailors and airmen still under arms, UNITE in action. [signed] The Communist Party.[96]

Many stories of resistance are easily be traced back to patriotism or political commitment, and commitment to resistance seems to arise from a strong sense of belief. In other cases, resistance seem rather to be an effect of contingency. Like Madeleine Riffaud's experience of a German kick in the backside, they were an immediate response to shock and humiliation. There is, nevertheless, generally a backstory that places the humiliation in context and through which the resister makes greater sense of the decisive moment.

Madeleine Riffaud, for example, was brought up in Picardy, in the battle zone of the Great War. Her father had been wounded in that war and she remembered going with her stepmother, 'veil of mourning blowing in the wind', wandering among the tombs of a military cemetery one 11 November to see if the body of her husband had been identified.[97] However, she also traced her resistance reflex back much further to a family tradition of revolt. She was brought up on the story of her great-great-grandfather who, as a conscript, had refused to fire on the revolutionaries of July 1830, and after leading peasant opposition to Napoleon III's coup d'état in his home village in 1851, was sent to do forced labour in Algeria. He was for her a rebel convict like Victor Hugo's Jean Valjean. Closer to home, her grandfather, whom she was brought back from the exodus on a stretcher, was a former agricultural labourer with the reputation of being a 'red'. Her later trajectory into communist resistance was thus shaped by family history.

Geneviève de Gaulle, a student at the University of Rennes in 1940, was also clear about the precise moment of her conversion to resistance: 'The first thing that made me a resister was to hear

Pétain [on 17 June]; the second was to see the arrival of German motorcyclists.' She had joined the exodus to Brittany but the motorcyclists who fanned out ahead of the main German force soon caught up with them. Naturally there were other stories in the family cupboard. Charles de Gaulle was her uncle but her father, the General's older brother, who had fought in the Great War, took her on a regular basis to visit the battlefields. He had been a mining engineer in the Sarre, which was provisionally attached to France after 1918, and campaigned during the plebiscite in 1935 against its restoration to Germany. He was a conservative and admired German culture and music, but he had read *Mein Kampf* and hated 'the Prussian spirit' and Nazism. A commander at the military camp of Coëtquidan, near Rennes, he led the retreat of his troops into Brittany, where there was briefly a plan to set up a 'redoubt' of military resistance. Geneviève followed with the rest of her family, including her grandmother. When a local *curé* reported hearing the appeal of 18 June her grandmother took him by the arm and said, 'but Monsieur le curé, that is my son!'[98]

Hélène Mordkovitch, who would later meet Geneviève de Gaulle in the same resistance group, followed a very different trajectory. In family terms she was torn between Red and White Russians. Her father was a Russian who had served in the French Army in the First World War, and met her mother while she was working as a medical student in the Franco-Russian hospital. In 1917 her father returned to Russia to take part in the revolution and Hélène, born in Paris that year, never saw him again. Her mother remarried a White Russian and worked in the kitchens of the Russian college at Boulogne-Billancourt, which was attended by White Russian émigrés. In search of her own identity, Hélène opted for being French: 'Are you not ashamed that a little Russian girl is top in French?' her schoolteacher would ask the class. She got to the Sorbonne in 1937 and after her mother died the next year survived by taking a part-time job as librarian of the Sorbonne's physical geography department. In 1940 she joined the exodus south and was horrified by the egoism and passivity of the French people in the face of defeat. She stayed with a family in Rodez, where the grandfather took to his bed and passed away, the parents could only think about the fruit harvest and the children went out to applaud the Germans as they marched in. 'In three generations,' she reflected, 'it was an extraordinary image of what France had become.' Until then she had not felt herself to be Jewish but on a train of refugees returning north to Paris on 6 September 1940 the guard said that Jews were prohibited from crossing the demarcation line into the Occupied Zone. At the crossing point at Vierzon a huge swastika flag was flying and she went one better than Madeleine Riffaud: 'We were arriving in Germany. I was so stressed that I slapped the German soldier who addressed us.'[99]

Awakening to a consciousness that resistance was necessary took place in thousands of minds, in those of the Free French who joined de Gaulle in Britain and the French Empire and in those of the individuals who refused to accept the armistice in metropolitan France. Sometimes this awakening was explained by patriotism, sometimes by idealism, and sometimes by contingency. Often a family story of honour or shame or revolt was drawn upon to make sense of the impulse to resist. In some cases a deep political commitment to communism shaped direction, but it was a nonconformist kind of communism that embraced the International Brigades in Spain and refused the Nazi-Soviet Pact. An awakening to consciousness was nevertheless not enough. The next steps would be communication, organisation and, not least, agreement on the way forward. Few individuals would be willing to embrace that challenge.

2

Faire quelque chose

The only remedy is for us to act together, to form a group of ten like-minded comrades, no more.

(Agnès Humbert, 1940)

During the night of 10–11 November 1940 a sixteen-year-old schoolboy and a student climbed the tower of the cathedral of Nantes, the great Atlantic sea-port, and shimmying up to the highest point fixed a tricolour flag to the lightning conductor. The population awoke to behold the national colours, which were banned in occupied France, floating in the grey morning sky. The Germans were incensed by this commemoration of the date that symbolised their defeat in 1918 and ordered the authorities to remove the flag. It took several hours for firemen to seize hold of the flag and bring it down, during which time news of the exploit had spread across Brittany and the Loire valley 'like a powder trail' and it was acclaimed on the BBC as an act of resistance.[1]

Life in occupied France is often described as being 'under the German jackboot'. It was a military occupation that expressed itself both by spectacle and by instilling fear. German troops paraded regularly on the main streets of cities, most notably daily on the Champs-Élysées, in order to dramatise their superiority. They were billeted in regular French barracks but also in schools and convents. Groups of officers took over hotels and châteaux and individual officers were billeted in bourgeois houses where they expected to be waited upon. German forces, it is true, concentrated in the towns and cities and were rarely seen in the countryside, where they felt less secure, especially as the Occupation wore on. The German military administration was clamped on top of the French civil administration, with a *Feldkommandantur* in each departmental capital where the prefect was based and a *Kreiskommandantur* in each *arrondissement*, run by a sub-prefect. *Feldgendarmes* or military police were highly visible on the roads; the secret police much less so. A demarcation line was established between the Occupied and so-called Free Zone, which closely controlled the movement of people and goods in each direction at checkpoints. A permit or *Ausweis* was required and issued only for good reason. Individuals or groups tried to cross the demarcation line, normally from north to south, with or without the help of guides who demanded payment, and anyone caught was liable to be sent to prison.[2]

Military security was the Germans' obsession. The *Wehrmacht* had to be uncontested and any threat to it, even by cutting its telephone cables, was punishable by death. France was disarmed and rendered incapable of re-entering the war. It was allowed an army of 100,000, which was precisely the number that the Germans had been permitted after the armistice of 1918, but only for the purpose of keeping internal order. The call-up and military training of all young men aged twenty was abolished and replaced, in the Free Zone alone, by six-months' training in the Chantiers de la Jeunesse, which were no more than glorified scout camps. Scouting movements to regenerate French youth flourished in the Free Zone but were banned in the Occupied Zone on the grounds that they were paramilitary. French citizens were required to hand in all firearms at their local town hall under German supervision. Some hid their hunting weapons, since all had been licensed to hunt since the Revolution of 1789, but being found in possession of a gun also risked the death penalty. To attack German personnel was beyond the imagination of any resister until Germany invaded the Soviet Union in June 1941 and communist resistance became serious, but the Germans had instituted a hostage system as an insurance against such eventualities and perfected the practice of collective reprisals to ensure order. The women of a defeated nation were, as always, regarded as legitimate prey by the victorious nation, and though the occupiers did not sanction rape tensions were heightened over approaches to French women by German soldiers. France was also disbanded as a nation. All symbolic manifestations of patriotism were prohibited in the Occupied Zone. There was to be no commemoration of Armistice Day on 11 November, or of Joan of Arc Day in May, or of Bastille Day on 14 July. Even in the Free Zone the Vichy authorities were concerned lest such demonstrations upset the Germans and prevented them with a heavy police presence.[3]

The Vichy regime in theory exercised sovereignty over the whole of France, but in the Occupied Zone its reach was subject to the goodwill of the military authorities. The regime was authoritarian, having disposed of parliament, and remained highly suspicious of former politicians, who were sent back to their fiefs and whom they suspected of plotting to restore the *ancien regime*, as the Third Republic was now known. The Légion Française des Combattants, which brought all veterans' associations together, acted as the transmission belt of Vichy's National Revolution, which promoted the values of Work, Family and Fatherland.[4] Certain categories of people regarded as anti-French were excluded from public life altogether, namely Jews, communists and Freemasons. Jews were also excluded from economic life under the process of Aryanisation. Vichy carried out its own anti-Semitic policies without prompting from the Germans, including the internment of foreign Jews.[5] The regime was against the class war that had defined the Popular Front period and against the activists who were seen to foment it but not against workers as such. The Charter of Labour it introduced in 1941 was supposed to encourage blue- and white-collar workers to collaborate with employers rather than to fight them.

The loyalty of workers (and other elements of the population) was dependent on the economic situation, and this was not good. The Germans took huge resources out of the economy in the shape of reparations, purchases with an artificially strong Reichsmark and shameless plunder. Shortages were increased by the blockade imposed by the British on a power they now regarded as an enemy. Goods and foodstuffs sold at exorbitant prices and the imposition of price controls only drove transactions underground: the black market was rife. The dislocation of the economy by the defeat and the division of France into different zones drove up unemployment. Petrol was in short supply and the use of cars restricted to Germans, the administration and key professionals. One of the most common sights of the Occupation was people on bicycles pulling trailers and heading off to the countryside to buy food direct from farmers. Farmers, together with shopkeepers and other middlemen, generally did very well out of the system: city-dwellers, especially old people, a lot less. People learned to improvise: long-lost country cousins with food supplies were rediscovered, bicycle tyres were stuffed with straw, cars were run on charcoal and rabbits were kept on the balconies of flats. This was the famous Système du Débrouillage or Système D (i.e. 'Getting by').[6] Later in the Occupation, the German war machine created a massive demand for military hardware and other supplies. Aircraft and car factories and shipyards were inundated by German orders and took on more workers. Unemployment disappeared, labour became scarce and the Germans instituted various schemes to recruit forced labour from occupied countries. In France labour was drafted to build an Atlantic Wall to repel any Allied invasion and from 1942 to go to work in war factories in Germany.[7]

What was the response of French people to all this? Most of them muddled through. Their horizons narrowed, they limited their gaze to their family, their neighbourhood and their means of livelihood and kept going until help came. The Germans were prepared to let people live their lives as before so long as they did not challenge the security of the *Wehrmacht*, although increasingly they tightened the screws to ensure a supply of labour. To collaborate with the Germans seemed like a good idea to some people, not least because it exempted them from forced labour, but in the long run exposed them to reprisals from resisters. Resistance was even more dangerous, exposing individuals to arrest, deportation and even execution. And yet, for a small number of individuals and groups, resistance called to them.

A clear definition of resistance has long been sought by historians but in a word, it meant refusing to accept the French bid for armistice and the German Occupation, and a willingness to do something about it that broke rules and courted risk.[8] That 'something' involved different circles of activity. For de Gaulle it meant military resistance, which could only in this early phase be undertaken by the Free French. Resistance for others began in metropolitan France with gestures that were spontaneous, sporadic and symbolic, such as raising a tricolour on a cathedral tower. This has been called 'resistance outside the Resistance' or 'the penumbra of Resistance'.[9] In time some of these activists organised into small groups with sustained activity and a material contribution to the war effort. This was Resistance with a capital 'R', providing intelligence for the Allies, escorting downed airmen to safety, spreading propaganda against the Germans or Vichy, sabotage and, in the last instance, armed struggle.

Since the Germans prohibited all symbolic manifestations of patriotism, such gestures became in themselves acts of resistance. In Nantes on 11 November 1940 school and university students tried to lay a wreath at the war memorial but were prevented by the municipal police and *Feldgendarmerie*. The students also sang the 'Marseillaise' on the steps of the municipal theatre.[10] More spectacularly, in Paris, students gathered at the Tomb of the Unknown Soldier at the Arc de Triomphe and paraded along the Champs-Élysées, carrying sticks known provocatively as *gaules* on their shoulders. This reclaiming of a symbolic space where Germans now daily paraded was too much for the occupying authorities; they arrested dozens of students and closed universities and *grandes écoles* until further notice. Benoîte Groult, a student whose friend was arrested and held for a week, noted how badly he had been treated and what this spelled for the future. He was:

lined up with his comrades against the wall of the Cherche-Midi prison, all night in the rain. They were kicked, hit with rifle butts and spat on by German soldiers. They were told that they would be shot in the morning, which could not have made standing up any easier. One of them fainted in the night and was left lying there. These boys were certainly not the same when they got home [. . .] It was not abstract, like reading *Mein Kampf.* A kick in the face does more than all propaganda.[11]

A safer way of communicating dissent was to write to the French service of the BBC, which broadcast daily to France.[12] The Free French were given five minutes a day, usually the voice of Maurice Schumann, but this was followed by *Les Français parlent aux Français*, featuring a team around Michel Saint-Denis, known by his stage name of Pierre Bourdan. The numbers of French people who listened to the BBC rose from 300,000 in 1941 to 3 million in 1942,[13] This was in itself transgressive, because the BBC was banned in the Occupied Zone in October 1940 and in the Free Zone a year later; those caught listening to it risked a heavy fine or even prison. The post was strictly censored so that letters to the BBC had to be smuggled out via the Free Zone or through consulates in neutral countries. Correspondents were not in general men of military age but veterans, women and a significant proportion of young people. 'A real French woman' from Bourg-en-Bresse told de Gaulle in August 1940 that 'immediately, at 8–15, the whole family falls silent and drinks in the words of the English radio, of our Free French [. . .] an invisible thread ties us to you.'[14] A woman who called herself Yvonne from Le Havre confessed that she knitted socks while listening to the

BBC and rehearsed a prayer she had heard said by an old priest on the eve of the armistice: 'Dear God, smite our enemies and intercede through St George and Joan of Arc to send England victorious and to liberate France.'[15] The attentiveness of French audiences allowed the Free French to organise demonstrations of support for the Allied war effort. In March 1941, for example, the BBC invited patriots to draw 'V' for Victory graffiti in public places.[16] A young man reported two days later that 'From the early morning the walls of Marseille were covered with "V"s and even "Victory" written out. The number increases massively every day. You see them on trams, inside and out, and on lorries and cars.'[17] Not all those who wrote to the BBC were fervent Gaullists and some saw little contradiction between supporting de Gaulle and Pétain. A group of Gascon women signed off in January 1941, 'Long live England! Long live Free France! Long live the great Marshal!'[18]

Protest was also a response to the hardships suffered under the Occupation. Women were at the forefront, as wives of prisoners of war or imprisoned activists, mothers of large families to feed, clothe and keep warm, and often working women in their own right when work was to be had. The street, after the home, was their domain, as it had been since the Revolution of 1789. Rabble-rousers spoke to other women queuing interminably outside the food shops or in the market-place, blaming German plunder and the black market and demanding that something be done to ensure more food at affordable prices. They marched on town halls and on the Ministry of Supply (Ravitaillement) to demand more rations of coal and clothing.[19] They marched on the house of the so-called ambassador for prisoners of war, Georges Scapini, who had lost an eye in 1915, to press him to negotiate improvements in the condition of POWs.[20] They even marched on the German embassy in Paris to demand – without success – the release of hundreds of arrested communists and trade unionists. Women in factories working for the Germans took the risk of going on strike, as in the camouflage-netting factory at Issy-les-Moulineaux, south-west of Paris, in April 1941. The French police arrested seventeen women who were handed over to the Germans.[21]

Much of this protest was spontaneous, but it was also organised by women's committees that were formed in the large cities, notably in the industrial red belt around central Paris. Behind much of this activity were the women of the underground communist movement, such as Lise London and Cécile Tanguy.[22] Flyers were distributed, then duplicated news-sheets, such as *The Women of Choisy* or *The Women of Vitry*. In her first editorial, recalled Lise London, 'I recalled the march of the Paris women to Versailles in October 1789 to bring back to the famished capital «the Baker's wife, the Baker and the Baker's boy». I concluded by urging the women to be worthy of their forebears.'[23] Lise London became best known for the lightning demonstration organised outside the Felix Potin grocery store on the rue Daguerre on 1 August 1942. She harangued the assembled crowd and urged resistance to the Germans. French police and German soldiers threatened to open fire but she was hidden by the crowd and a communist detachment opened fire on the police. As a result she was called 'the Shrew of the rue Daguerre' by Fernand de Brinon, Vichy's ambassador to the Germans in Paris, and news of the exploit was carried by the BBC and Radio Moscow. Arrested a week later, she would have been condemned to death had she not been pregnant.[24]

This sporadic and semi-spontaneous activity formed a wider context in which emerged small, organised groups that planned a more sustained resistance. Rather than put pressure on the authorities to help POWs, they took matters into their own hands and spirited prisoners out of holding camps before they could be sent to Germany. To help the war effort that was continuing outside France they procured military intelligence about German movements by land, sea or air and delivered it to the Allies.

They undertook propaganda to shock public opinion out of its defeatism and resignation. This might start with graffiti or pasting up *papillons* or slogans the size of post-it notes in public places, and with the distribution of flyers, and then go on to the printing of a clandestine newspaper that gave its name to the organisation.

In an early stage many resistance groups were defined by existing constituencies: combatants and veterans, friends and neighbours, academics and students, doctors and nurses, businessmen and labour leaders, Christian democrats or communists. It was difficult to build bridges between these segmented parts of society, although the shattering of French life under the shock of defeat also brought about encounters between people of different milieux who would not otherwise have met. In the Occupied Zone, where everyone was confronted by the brutality of the German presence and Vichy seemed a long way away and powerless, resistance groups ran the entire political spectrum, from extreme-right-wing organisations based on former military men, businessmen and technocrats to the extreme left of communists, wrestling with the consequences of the Nazi-Soviet Pact. In the Free Zone, where there was a groundswell of support for Marshal Pétain in the establishment and mainstream society, resisters who tried to tried to denounce Vichy as authoritarian, reactionary, collaborationist and anti-Semitic tended to be much more marginal and nonconformist than in the North.

In the Occupied Zone, one of the most dramatic early groups was that which later became known as the Musée de l'Homme network. In fact it was a complex organism composed of what one of its leading members, Germaine Tillion, called 'nuclei'.[25] Tillion was an anthropologist who had been on a six-year research mission to the Aurès mountains of French Algeria before the war. Returning to Paris in 1940 her main concern was the fate of the black and North African troops of the Empire who had fought in the French Army and been taken prisoner; the Germans executed scores of these colonial captives and those who were taken to the Reich were sent back for racial reasons to camps in France. Tillion made contact with two retired officers of the National Union of Colonial Combatants (UNCC), who formed the first nucleus of the network. The UNCC openly provided charitable help to the colonial troops in POW camps or hospitals while secretly trying to extract them and provide them with civilian clothes, safe houses and false identities.[26]

The second nucleus in the nebula was the group at the Musée de l'Homme proper, located in the Palais de Chaillot. This ethnographic museum had been set up by the Popular Front in 1937 under Paul Rivet, an ethnologist who was active from 1934 in the influential Vigilance Committee of Antifascist Intellectuals. The key figures in the Musée were the librarian, Yvonne Oddon, a Protestant from the Dauphiné who had trained at the Library of Congress, and Boris Vildé, a young Russian who had fled the Bolshevik seizure of power and headed the Arctic civilisation department of the Museum.[27] The Musée network participated in the work of spiriting escaped POWs, stranded British officers and downed Allied airmen out of the country via Toulouse and Barcelona. They established links with the American embassy for the transmission of intelligence and produced an underground newspaper in the depths of the Museum with a duplicator that had belonged to the Vigilance Committee of Antifascist Intellectuals, supplied by Paul Rivet. The title of the paper, *Résistance,* was proposed by Yvonne Oddon, remembering her Protestant roots and fascinated, like Jean Cavaillès, by the word 'once engraved on the walls of the Tour de Constance by a group [sic] of Huguenot "resisters"'.[28]

A third nucleus was the so-called 'writer's group' around Jean Cassou and Agnès Humbert. Cassou, director of the Musée d'Art Moderne, had an Andalusian mother and had been sent to Spain for the Popular Front at the outbreak of the Civil War in 1936. He remembered embattled republican president Azaña saying to him:

'You know, Cassou, I have loved France, but at present, France. . .' He gestured as if letting something fall to the ground. Then suddenly, 'Come and see the front.' The windows of the drawing room overlooked the vast Castilian plain. On the horizon one could see the firing line. 'That is your front,' he said.[29]

Agnès Humbert, a curator at the Musée des Arts et Traditions populaires, in the opposite wing of the Palais de Chaillot to the Musée de l'Homme, met Cassou again on the road south during the exodus. When they returned to Paris they both thought about the urgency of doing something. Humbert wrote in her diary:

I find Cassou in his office. He too has aged. In six weeks his hair has turned and he appears to have shrunk into himself. But his smile is still the same [. . .] We talk freely, comparing our impressions and discovering that they are much the same [. . .] The only remedy is for us to act together, to form a group of ten like-minded comrades, no more. To meet on agreed days to exchange news, to write pamphlets and tracts, and to share summaries of French radio broadcasts from London. I don't harbour many illusions about the practical effects of our actions, but simply keeping our sanity will be success of a kind [. . .] Cassou is already joking about our 'secret society'. He has been studying the Carbonari for too long.[30]

The group convened around them never exceeded ten people. It met every Tuesday evening at the offices of the publisher Émile-Paul, who published much of the team's work, including that of Claude Aveline, a Russian-Jewish writer in the group.

Through Cassou's museum colleague, Paul Rivet, the group received a visit at the end of September 1940 from Boris Vildé, 'a tall, fair young man', according to Aveline, who asked them to write articles for the *Résistance* paper he was planning.[31] Shortly after, the members were dismissed from their respective posts by Vichy. With little else to do the group now met at the home in Passy of Simone Martin-Chauffier, whose job at the Foreign Policy Study Centre of the Rockefeller Foundation had been closed by the Germans and whose journalist husband Louis had moved to the Free Zone. She modestly evokes the tone and division of labour at their meetings:

An effigy of Pétain stimulated their eloquence and in case of an unexpected intrusion, permitted them to play the good apostles. Agnès acted as secretary and shorthand typist during the meetings and also busied herself with papers and messages that had to be sent. She called herself the 'corridor rabbit'. My role was just to send away callers and I used to prepare the worker's tray: tea and a little plate of sweet things.[32]

The first number of *Résistance* appeared on 15 December 1940 and four more followed. At this point, however, the network was infiltrated by an informer. Germaine Tillion later observed that 'when a traitor managed to penetrate a part of the organism like poison, his ambition was to climb through the arteries to the heart. It was only too easy and when that happened there was one network less and a few more deaths.'[33] The traitor, they later discovered, was Albert Gaveau, who had posed as one of the escorts for escapees but was in fact working for the Gestapo.[34] Oddon was arrested in February 1941 and Vildé in March. Aveline and Rivet escaped to the Free Zone. Desperately short of manpower, Cassou and Humbert went early in March to visit Pierre Brossolette, who had set up a bookshop and stationers in the rue de la Pompe, providing school equipment to the students of the Lycée Jeanson-de-Sailly opposite, and pointedly teaching lessons at the Collège Sévigné on the 1848 Revolutions in Europe and republican opposition to the Second Empire of Napoleon III.[35] Agnès Humbert was herself arrested on 15 April and Jean Cassou headed for the Free Zone. The Musée de l'Homme group were kept in Paris prisons until sent to trial by a German military court in January 1942. Ten members of the group were sentenced to death; seven men, including Vildé, were shot at the Mont Valérien fort on 23 February 1942; the women, including Humbert and Oddon were reprieved and deported to Germany.

Many of those who became involved in resistance activity were young people. 'Four-fifths of the Resistance in France was made up of people who were under thirty,' claimed Jacques Lusseyran, a student at the Lycée Louis-le-Grand. 'The people over thirty who surrounded us were afraid for their wives and children. They also feared for their property and positions, which made us angry.'[36] He became a member of the Volunteers of Liberty, the high-school extension of Défense de la France, which was set up by a group of Sorbonne students in the autumn of 1940.[37] The initiators of Défense de la France were two contrasting young men who had been friends at the Lycée Louis-le-Grand and were now back from their brief war in 1940 and studying for the *agrégation* in philosophy.[38] One was Philippe Viannay, who came from a Catholic and conservative family which supported Marshal Pétain; the other was Robert Salmon, of a bourgeois and Jewish family, who was sometimes discomfited by Viannay's strictures on 'the London Jews' around de Gaulle.[39] 'Philippe was in the tradition of *mystiques*, I in that of the *politiques*,' said Salmon, echoing the writer and activist Charles Péguy, who had died a martyr's death at the Battle of the Marne in 1914.[40]

Also central to the group was Hélène Mordkovitch, of Russian-Jewish extraction, who financed her Sorbonne studies by working as librarian at the physical geography laboratory, where she met Viannay. 'My reaction was one of pride,' said Mordkovitch of the defeat and occupation. 'We need to drive the Germans out [. . .] I started writing flyers, not very well done. I asked people to spread them around.'[41] She asked Viannay why he was not going to England to join de Gaulle's forces. He was stung by her challenge but was unable to flout the authority of his father. He recalled his response: '"What would you say to an underground newspaper?" The extraordinary flame that lit up her eyes was his answer. Our work together began at once.'[42] Viannay made contact with a family friend and businessman, Marcel Lebon. Although Lebon's sympathies were with Action Française and he had personal contacts with Vichy, notably with Pétain's personal physician and secretary, Dr Ménétrel,[43] he acquired one printer for his own business and another for the students, who set up a secret workshop in the bowels of the Sorbonne to produce their newssheet, *Défense de la France*. On her side, Hélène brought in friends such as Genia Deschamps (née Kobozieff), born in France to a Jewish Bolshevik and a mother of Russian Populist origin (who had remarried a Cossack doctor who had fought in the White Army). Genia had qualified as a nurse and in 1940 helped wounded British airmen to get out of the country. 'It seemed to be something to do, something to do in the face of the calamity that engulfed us,' she said. 'I was fed up with having to get off the pavement for [German] guys who thought they were at home.'[44] Able to circulate freely as a nurse, she was the key liaison agent of the group.

The group was divided over loyalty to Pétain, who was seen by Philippe Viannay as a hero who would in time come over to the Resistance and lead a united France to liberation. Hostility to the Germans they agreed on, but there was also much hostility to the Soviets, shared to some extent by Hélène Mordkovitch, whose Bolshevik father had abandoned her and returned to the USSR, and also to the British, who were seen as regularly fighting wars to the last Frenchman. De Gaulle, it was feared, would come back in the foreigners' baggage train, as had Louis XVIII in 1814. The two big themes that held the group together were 'to defend our soul' and 'to defend our independence': 'Neither Germans, nor Russians, nor English'.[45] It was not until November 1942, when, following the American invasion of North Africa, Pétain demonstrated he would not swing into the Allied camp, that Philippe Viannay was eventually persuaded of the merits of Gaullism. This coincided with the group being joined by Geneviève de Gaulle, the niece of the General, who had been studying in Rennes and had then been in touch with the Musée de l'Homme network in Paris. In the Alps in spring 1943 she met Philippe's younger brother Hubert, who was involved in resistance activity there, and was put in touch with Défense de la France. Only she it seems had the name and authority to wean Philippe off his tribal Pétainism.[46]

In the Occupied Zone resistance networks developed in very different constituencies, from labour to business and from the extreme Left to the extreme Right. The world of labour was divided by Vichy, which denounced class war and clamped down on trade-unionist, socialist and of course communist militants who were deemed to foment it, but was not against workers as such. René Belin, an anti-communist trade-union leader, was appointed Minister of Labour by Vichy. He abolished the central trade-union federations[47] but opened a charm offensive to win workers over to a new Charter of Labour, which aimed to group employers, managers, white- and blue-collar workers in a single trade union for each 'occupational family'.[48] A good many trade unionists saw benefits in this reorganisation, but many were hostile. A small group of these met in secret and published a manifesto on 15 November 1940 denouncing Vichy's attack on the trade unions.[49] Their leading light was Christian Pineau, an unlikely trade-union leader in that he came from an old family in the rural west of France. His stepfather was the novelist and playwright Jean Giraudoux, and he attended Sciences Po and the Paris Law Faculty before going into banking. He was, however, awakened by the extreme-right's attack on the Republic on 6 February 1934 and behind the extreme Right he saw the financial and industrial power of the trusts.[50] He decided to become involved in trade-union activity and became secretary-general of the Bank Employees' Union: 'My family and friends considered me a class traitor and Jean Giraudoux used to say, "For heaven's sake, Christian, your place is not there!"'[51] In 1939 he was mobilised in the infantry and then seconded to the Ministry of Information, which was headed rather ineffectually by Jean Giraudoux. In the spring of 1941 he became an inspector in the Ministry of Supply (Ravitaillement), which gave him the cover to travel widely and legally around the country. After issuing the 15 November manifesto he set up an Inter Trade Union Study Committee, which was tolerated by Vichy, and from November

1940 published a paper, *Libération*, which was typed in the early days by Pineau himself and 'which did not provoke sharp reactions from the Germans until early 1942'.[52]

At the other end of the spectrum was a group called the Organisation Civile et Militaire (OCM), which was composed of precisely the kind of people against whom Pineau had mobilised after 1934. Its first cohort, as we have seen, were First World War air aces and other heroes such as Alfred Heurtaux and Alfred Touny, who had later gone into business and, opposing the rise of what it saw as the anti-business Left, joined extreme-right-wing organisations such as the Croix de Feu.[53] Another group within the network were technocrats – high-placed managers of large firms or the state bureaucracy committed to modernising agendas. They included Maxime Blocq-Mascart, a graduate of Sciences Po and economic consultant to a large industrial group who later observed that 'it was the population of the Occupied Zone, who were supposed to be the vehicle of German penetration, who formed the Resistance's front, morally, intellectually and through action.'[54] They also included André Postel-Vinay, another graduate of Sciences-Po, and young official of the élite Inspection des Finances. He worked with his sister Marie-Hélène and her husband, Pierre Lefaucheux, director of a steel-making company at Montrouge in the Paris suburbs, who was mobilised in 1939 as an artillery captain but then seconded to organise armaments production at the Cartoucherie of Le Mans.[55] Finally, they included Marcel Berthelot, who had graduated from the École Normale Supérieure in 1913 with an *agrégation* in German, had served in the Foreign Office and was now head of translations at Vichy's Ministry of Public Works.[56] This group was superficially part of the Vichy system but used its contacts with Colonel Georges Ronin, who headed the Armistice Army's Air Force's intelligence service at Vichy, to send military intelligence to London.

In the Free Zone, resisters did not have to face the German occupying forces and police. They did have to face the Vichy police, which had specialised brigades for dealing with communists, for example, and a court system that could also be ruthless.[57] In the Free Zone as well as in the Occupied Zone, resisters were also liable to be denounced to the authorities for anti-French activities by citizens who regarded it as their patriotic duty to turn them in. That said, the Free Zone was the destination of choice not only for political activists from the Occupied Zone but also for political refugees and exiles from Franco's Spain, from Alsace and the Moselle departments annexed by the Germans, from other parts of Occupied Europe and from the German Reich itself. It thus provided many possibilities for the encounter of like-minded people and slightly greater autonomy for them to organise.

The hub of resistance activity in the Free Zone was Lyon. The city had not been chosen to be the capital of Pétain's regime, partly because it was occupied by the Germans for seventeen days between 19 June and 7 July 1940, and partly because it was the power base of Édouard Herriot, mayor since 1905 and speaker of the Chamber of Deputies until its abolition in July 1940. Instead, the quiet spa town of Vichy became Pétain's capital and Lyon became the 'capital of the Resistance'. It exploited the density of its population, the size of its working class, now more involved in engineering than in the traditional silk industry, and its importance as a Church centre and a university town. Lyon's significance in the Resistance is sometimes traced to its *traboules* – successions of interior courtyards linking several streets – which made it easy to escape for anyone who was being followed. More important, perhaps, was its position at a crossroads leading east to Switzerland, south and east to Marseille and Toulon, and south and west to Montpellier and Toulouse.[58]

When Claude Aveline fled south from the wreck of the Musée de l'Homme in February 1941 he took refuge at the home of Louis and Simone Martin-Chauffier, the latter having rejoined her journalist husband after the Musée de l'Homme group collapsed.

Situated at Collonges-au-Mont-d'Or, overlooking the River Saône, it was a *pied à terre* and meeting point for many resisters coming to Lyon.[59] Equally significant as a turntable were the offices of *Le Progrès de Lyon*, now run by other Paris journalists who had come south. Yves Farge, a long-time socialist with 'thick tortoise-shell spectacles and greying hair', was the foreign policy editor and also well-connected in literary and artistic circles. Sent in July 1940 with a message to Pétain from the prefect of the Rhône, Émile Bollaert, he returned muttering, 'He's a stupid arse.'[60] *Le Progrès* was crucial as a centre because, as Farge reflected, 'the task in 1940 and even during 1941 was to find and make contacts, to rub up against people. In their original form, the groups and movements that pullulated at Lyon and throughout the Southern Zone had an entirely inorganic character,' and *Le Progrès* helped the process of encounter, rapprochement and structuring.[61]

'For me, the first and most important date for our movement,' wrote Auguste Pinton, a schoolmaster at Lyon's Lycée Ampère, 'was Monday 4 November 1940. I met Avinin at the *Moulin Joli* on the place des Terreaux.'[62] Antoine Avinin, born in Lyon to a family of Auvergnat traders, had a clothing business and was committed to the Christian democratic Jeune République movement that had supported the Popular Front. After fighting in the Alpine Army in 1940 he returned to Lyon scandalised by the right-wing propaganda of veterans who joined Vichy's Légion des Combattants. When Pétain visited Lyon in November 1940 Avinin removed the 'or' from a banner on a triumphal arch proclaiming 'with the Legion or against France'.[63] The group that formed to express common opposition to the regime included a salesman for a metal blind business, a furniture remover and Joseph Hours, a history teacher at the prestigious Lycée du Parc.[64] They sent a message to the BBC in London asking for de Gaulle to declare that he was now the French government. They also expressed the concern that 'the forces of active resistance are dispersed, cut off from one another for fear of arrest. Yet we know that there are dozens and dozens of groups like ours at Lyon, which meet regularly to exchange ideas, news and even plans.'[65]

This group of local resisters was joined by a number of refugees from Alsace who came to the city. Pierre Eude was the Protestant general secretary of the Strasbourg Chamber of Commerce, which moved to Lyon, and came with his Jewish wife and daughter Micheline, who recalled that the annexation of Alsace marked 'the end of my childhood'.[66] Jean-Pierre Lévy was another refugee from Alsace. Born in Strasbourg in 1911, when it was still part of the German Empire, he was educated at the Lycée Fustel de Coulanges, which, when the French recovered Alsace, became emphatically a vehicle of French culture. His father, a retired businessman who had made his fortune in Brazil, died when Jean-Pierre was ten, so that he missed out on university education in order to take charge of the family. Qualifying as an industrial engineer he worked in Nancy for a Jewish firm that made jute for sacks. He was mobilised as a lieutenant in the artillery in 1939 and his unit had retreated to the Dordogne when the armistice was signed. His attitude was shaped by the fact that like Alfred Dreyfus he was both Alsatian and Jewish. 'Around me,' he recalled, 'there was general relief when the news was announced. Both soldiers and officers were in favour of an end to hostilities and didn't hide it. I was almost the only one to refuse to approve the armistice [. . .] I was told, "You react like that because you are Alsatian". I should add that no reference was ever made to the fact that my name is Lévy.'[67] He joined the Lyon group and together they published a flyer called *France-Liberté*, which was the predecessor of a more substantial publication, *Franc-Tireur*.[68] As a commercial traveller for his jute firm he had extensive contacts from Clermont-Ferrand to Toulon that provided tentacles for disseminating the groups' propaganda across the Free Zone.

Lyon was also a religious centre, overshadowed by the basilica of Notre Dame de Fourvière, raised by the Lyonnais after they were spared from German invasion in 1870. One of the refugees it attracted from occupied Paris was a Catholic journalist, Stanislas Fumet. One resister recalled that 'his house at Fourvière and his office in the Terreaux quarter were the crossroads of all those who had gone underground, semi-underground, and opponents of Vichy.'[69] His wife Aniouta called the rather Gothic house 'Kamalot', and another resister commented that 'In any whodunit it would have been the scene of the crime.'[70] Fumet was a Christian democrat who challenged the way the Church hierarchy and right-wing Catholics around Maurras and the Action Française had accepted defeat, occupation and the vindictive policies of Vichy, and was extremely well connected. If the soul of France were to be saved from Nazism, he argued, Christians had to become involved in the common life of the City, legally or illegally. He had been political editor of *Temps présent* in Paris until June 1940 and resurrected it in Lyon as *Temps nouveau* in December 1940.[71] It acted as a focus for Christian democrats, Christian trade unionists, Christian academics and students of the Christian Student Youth (JEC) such as Gilbert Dru and Jean-Marie Domenach, who described theirs as 'the generation of the rout'. They had been too young to fight in 1940 but now became involved in circulating flyers and demonstrating, notably against the showing of the anti-Semitic film, the *Jew Süss*, in May 1941.[72] Such defiance of Vichy led to the suspension, then closure, of *Temps nouveau* by the authorities the following September.

The relay was taken up by one of his chief collaborators in the Catholic Church, Pierre Chaillet, who constituted the second root. Chaillet was a Jesuit priest who had been trained in Austria and Rome, and he had been powerfully affected by the rise of Nazism as a new, persecutory paganism in Central Europe, which forced believers to flee. In 1939–40 he worked undercover for the French intelligence services while lecturing in Budapest and got back to France only with difficulty via Istanbul and Beirut. Landing at Marseille in December 1940 he was shocked by the apathy and acceptance of most French people, including Catholic *bien pensants*, the hierarchy and Vichy, which he briefly visited. Resuming his teaching at Fourvière, he made contact with like-minded Catholics and provided articles for a number of resistance papers in Lyon until, in November 1941, he brought out the first number of *Témoignage Chrétien*. Published as a booklet it carried the message, 'France, take care not to lose your soul.'[73]

Meanwhile one of the Christian democrats in Fumet's circle, François de Menthon, initiated another resistance paper. De Menthon had been a lecturer at the Nancy Law Faculty and captained an infantry regiment on the Maginot Line. Wounded and taken prisoner by the Germans, he managed to escape in September 1940.[74] Crossing the demarcation line he returned to the château of his family of Savoyard nobles at Menthon Saint-Bernard near Annecy, where he set in motion what would become the paper *Liberté*. 'At that stage,' he recalls, 'Pétain was very popular in the Southern Zone: his visit to Annecy was triumphant. One therefore had to be prudent and not attack the Marshal directly.'[75] As an escaped POW he was unable to return to Nancy, but had himself appointed to the Law Faculty at Lyon, where he resumed lecturing in November. He linked up with Pierre-Henri Teitgen, a fellow lecturer at the Law Faculty of Nancy who had briefly been taken prisoner on the Maginot Line in 1940. When Teitgen escaped he was 'very shocked by the attitude of people he met [. . .] 95 per cent of the population seemed to follow Pétain'.[76] Unable like de Menthon to return to Nancy he was re-employed at Montpellier University. Léo Hamon, who had been a law student with Teitgen, recalled going to one of his lectures on the police methods of the Second Empire and afterwards 'falling into his arms'.[77] Together they launched the Resistance newspaper *Liberté* in December 1940.

Two other refugees who came to Lyon in August 1940 were Lucie and Raymond Samuel, later known by their code name 'Aubrac'. After his dramatic rescue by Lucie from Saarbrücken, Raymond as an escaped POW could not work in the Occupied

Zone, and Lucie had resigned her post at the Lycée of Vannes in Brittany. Raymond secured a job running a branch of a patent office, for which he had worked in the USA when he spent a year at MIT in 1938–9. Lucie was without work but went to Clermont-Ferrand, to which the University of Strasbourg had been moved lock, stock and barrel after the Germans occupied Alsace again in 1940. There in November 1940 at the *Brasserie de Strasbourg* on the place de Jaude she caught up with Jean Cavaillès, whom she had known in Strasbourg in 1938–9 while she was teaching at the Lycée, he at the University. At the next table was Emmanuel d'Astier, who had tried but failed to get to England in June. D'Astier was trying to set up a resistance network, which at this point included no more than his nephew Jean-Anet and niece Bertrande, the children of his older brother General François d'Astier. He was impressed by this 'Amazon with the *agrégation*' and they began to work together.[78]

'*Libération* was founded in November at Clermont Ferrand, by a chance meeting,' affirmed Lucie Aubrac, although the first incarnation of the network was actually called La Dernière Colonne, as if it were the last column fighting the war.[79] Its first outing was a campaign to paste up anti-collaboration *papillons* such as 'Read *Gringoire*. You will make Hitler happy' in six towns across the Free Zone during the night of 27–28 February 1941.[80] Lucie organised things in Lyon, where she had been appointed to the Lycée Edgar Quinet, while others went into action in Marseille and Toulouse. Unfortunately disaster struck as the arrest of one activist in Nîmes led to the rounding-up of Bertrande and Jean-Anet d'Astier at the family home. Bertrande was sentenced by a Vichy court in Nîmes to thirteen months in prison, while Jean-Anet got six months. These penalties were halved on appeal but the shock was such that Bertrande escaped to Switzerland after her release.[81] After this the team had to regroup and rethink. Cavaillès' sister recalled that 'It was on a bench in the Arts Faculty [at Clermont-Ferrand] in March 1941 that Jean and Emmanuel

d'Astier de la Vigerie drafted the first flyer of *Libération*.[82]
Raymond took the credit for designing the font for the first
number, which appeared in July 1941 and remembered d'Astier
visiting them in Lyon as 'a spindly personage like a Giacometti
sculpture, nose like an eagle's beak and a questioning smile that
had something aristocratic about it. At least he smoked a pipe.'[83]

Gradually the team acquired reinforcements. Lucie made
contact with her old communist comrades from the Latin Quarter,
who had distanced themselves from the Party after the Nazi-
Soviet Pact. Cavaillès was appointed to a post at the Sorbonne
in the spring of 1941 and re-crossed the demarcation line back
to Paris. He was replaced at Strasbourg/Clermont-Ferrand by
Georges Canguilhem, a tailor's son from the Spanish border who
had been the year above him at the École Normale Supérieure and
was teaching at the Lycée of Toulouse.[84] The Toulouse vacancy was
in turn filled by Jean-Pierre Vernant, who was seen at the school
as 'completely scatterbrained, always in sandals' but linking up at
Toulouse with 'former friends, the little group of fighters who had
battled together in the Latin Quarter'.[85] Vernant reflected that 'the
people around me who formed the active nucleus of the liberation
of Toulouse were either communists or had been communists at
one time, even if they no longer had their party card [. . .] Lucie
Aubrac sold the *Avant-garde* with me, she was in the Communist
Youth, politically she was close to me, very close to me.'[86]

Back in the Occupied Zone Jean Cavaillès began to make
contact with trade-union and socialist circles in order to give
Libération a more popular base in the north of France. A meeting
was convened in Christian Pineau's house, rue du Four, where
Cavaillès was introduced to socialist militant Henri Ribière. The
Socialist Party had been shattered by the defeat and the armistice.
Some of its key figures had rallied to Vichy; others, like Léon
Blum, who opposed it, were imprisoned and sent for trial early in
1942. Under the cover of working for the Interior Ministry Ribière
had cycled from Pau to Limoges via Toulouse and Montpellier in

order to resume contact with socialist militants.[87] Daniel Mayer, one of those militants, a former editor on the Socialist Party daily, *Le Populaire,* was setting up a socialist resistance group, the Comité d'Action Socialiste (CAS), that would group all socialists dedicated to the cause. Mayer described Ribière as 'discreet, silent, almost enigmatic yet humane to his finger tips' with 'an impassiveness that was less British than a tiny bit Asiatic and everywhere at the same time'.[88] His discretion and energy were of great importance in remaking socialism as a force of resistance.

One of the bastions of the Socialist Party was in the northeast of France, the heart of the coal, engineering and textile industries. Early in 1942 Cavaillès made contact with Albert van Wolput, a stalwart of the Socialist Party in Lille. The self-taught son of a café-owner in the suburbs of Lille and veteran of 1914–18 (who had worked as a factory foreman and salesman, sacked for political activism in 1936), van Wolput helped to form a Lille branch of the Comité d'Action Socialiste, which brought together 'reliable comrades' in 'cafés that lay disused or closed under the Occupation'. They also brought out an underground paper, *L'Homme libre,* which later became *La Voix du Nord.* 'It was not about propagating Gaullism, of replying to the famous appeal of 18 June which few people had heard,' he said, but to 'attack Vichy and demand the return of republican liberties in order to allow socialism to recover'. His involvement with the CAS took him to Paris and Lyon and widened his perspectives from a resistance brand of socialism to a much wider form of resistance embodied in *Libération Nord.*[89]

Over a period of time, therefore, everyday discontent and sporadic protest took on greater consistency in the form of small organised groups of resistance. These arose in very different milieux – trade unions and businesses, universities and museums, churches and refugee groups. Divided between the Occupied and Free Zones, they had very different profiles. In the Occupied Zone there was practical work to be done, such as sending intelligence to the Allies or helping POWs to escape, while in the Free Zone propaganda against Vichy's policy of collaboration was at the top of the agenda. There was very little communication between these groups, partly because they came from such different worlds and partly because security dictated that secrecy. They may best be imagined as a honeycomb, but one that was highly fragmented. Most significant, there was very little communication between groups of well-educated people and those formed within the working class, traditionally catered for by the Communist Party. The Nazi-Soviet Pact of 1939 had a devastating effect on the Party, both because of the round-up of its militants and the confusion of the rank and file, who could not understand the pact with Hitler. Resistance took root among the industrial working class as a result of protest against material conditions first and ideology second, when the Soviet Union was invaded by Germany in 1941 and communists of all countries rallied to the anti-fascist cause.

3

'Titi has been avenged!'

*I would prefer to die standing up rather than lying down, suffering
the torture of criminals like a medieval saint.*

(Charles Debarge, 1942)

On 1 May 1941 the population of the northern France coal belt
awoke to see an amazing sight: 'Fluttering from electric wires,
from conveyor belts, from buildings, everywhere,' wrote an
eyewitness, 'were tricolour flags and red flags with the hammer
and sickle and slogans such as "Higher wages" and "Long live
Stalin".'[1] May 1 was celebrated as Labour Day in France from
the end of the nineteenth century, with workers taking the day
off and marching to demand higher wages and shorter hours.[2]
In 1941 the Nord and Pas-de-Calais region was not only under
German occupation but was governed by the German military
administration in Brussels as part of an industrial powerhouse that
could rival the Ruhr and Upper Silesia. The mining population,
massively reinforced by Polish immigrants, was tightly geared to
the German war economy, overworked and underprovided with
food and other essentials.

The 1 May demonstration was only the beginning of the
miners' protest. On 26 May a strike broke out at the Dahomey
pit at Dourges and spread to other pits in the basin at Courrières,
Oignies, Ostricourt and Anzin. The miners demanded a return to
previous work norms and for the provision of fats, meat and even
soap. A climax was reached on 2 June when 100,000 workers out
of a total of 143,000 joined the strike.[3] At the outset the miners'
demands were mainly economic. Yet the flags and slogans of 1
May suggested there was also a political dimension. Communist

activists were, in fact, well implanted at the pits and held secret meetings to plan strategy in isolated spots such as the so-called Jerusalem Wood outside Hénin-Liétard.[4] One of the leading activists was Charles Debarge, a miner who had been in the Communist Youth since the age of sixteen in 1935, was called up to fight in 1939, then sent back to the pits for war work in April 1940. Another was Roger Pannequin, a miner's son who escaped the pit by training as a primary-school teacher, and described Debarge as 'silent, athletic, dark, more of the Spanish than Flemish type'.[5] The two got hold of a typewriter and duplicating machine to set out their material demands in a rough paper called *Vérité*. They also collected weapons that had been left at the front after Dunkirk in order, as Debarge said, 'to copy the example of our Russian comrades in 1917'.[6]

The communists worked to sustain the strike over five days. Debarge paid tribute to the miners' wives and companions who mobilised their street-protesting skills to sustain the strike: 'Our French and Polish wives supported us massively on the picket lines,' he wrote. 'A women's demonstration was even organised and 500 women took part. The police had to use force to disperse it and even charged our girls with fixed bayonets.'[7] Initially the Germans held back, hoping that the mining companies and local police could restore order. When it became clear that they could not the Germans stepped in. About 500 miners and their wives were arrested, and 244 were deported to Germany, of whom 130 never returned.[8]

This brutal repression, which included the arrest of fourteen of his comrades, transformed Debarge and his remaining fellow activists into violent opponents of the German occupation. They launched a series of sabotage attacks on electric pylons and minefield equipment harnessed to the German war machine. Debarge was arrested by the *Feldgendarmerie* on 6 August 1941 but managed to escape while three of his comrades were condemned to death and shot. His wife Raymonde was also arrested and sentenced to three years' forced labour. Debarge went underground and wrote in his diary: 'These were brothers to me, in combat as well as in pleasure. The arrest and sentencing of my wife was unutterably painful too. In the very near future we must hope to avenge them.'[9]

Communist resistance remained distinct, almost in a ghetto of its own, for a considerable time. The main reason was the Nazi-Soviet Pact, which fell on communists like the blade of a guillotine. National unity was constructed over and against them, now denounced as traitors and targets of a witch hunt. Whereas for most resisters, repression on the part of the authorities, whether French or German, was not immediate, for communists it began at the outbreak of war and only intensified under Vichy. The long anti-fascist stance of French communists was derailed by the pact that declared Hitler and Stalin were now allies. The official communist line was that the war had been caused by the capitalist and imperialist powers, France and Britain, who were now waging war on their own people. The Communist Party was banned under the decree-law of 26 September 1939. Communist-run municipalities were dismissed and communist militants arrested and interned in prisons and camps.

For most of the war the leadership of the French Communist Party was either in exile, in hiding or in prison. Maurice Thorez deserted his regiment and resurfaced in Moscow. Jacques Duclos, the most senior communist in France, went into hiding in the Paris region. Members of the Central Committee, such as Léon Mauvais, Eugène Hénaff and Ferdinand Grenier, were moved from prison to prison until they got to the internment camp of Châteaubriant in Brittany in May 1941. Also moved there was Guy Môquet, a Young Communist of the 17th *arrondissement* of Paris, whose father Prosper, a railwayman and communist deputy of that *arrondissement*, was already in prison. Guy had been arrested with two friends in October 1940 for throwing communist flyers from their bicycles as they scoured the district and sentenced under the decree-law of 26 September 1939. His mother wrote to him at Clairvaux prison wishing him a happy seventeenth birthday in April 1940: 'What a disappointment,' she complained, 'Still no letter from you.' He gratified her by replying from Châteaubriant on 16 May 1941: 'We arrived yesterday at 12.30 in our new premises which is none other than a concentration camp surrounded by barbed wire, with huts made out of wooden planks.' Then, on a lighter note: 'We have a football pitch so please send my things as we are going to make teams.'[10] On 18 and 19 June 1941, some of the older communist inmates were able to escape. Hénaff and Mauvais got out dressed in civilian clothes that had been smuggled in; Grenier was allowed out to town on an errand, taking another comrade in a cart under sacks and empty beer crates, and then they cycled away.[11]

The rank and file of the Communist Party were thrown into confusion: their sense of party discipline told them they should follow the official line, while their anti-fascism and patriotic instincts told them that Hitler should be resisted. Charles Tillon, who had gone underground in Bordeaux, issued his own call to resistance on 17 June 1940.[12] Relations with the German occupying forces were ambivalent and communists in Paris even made an approach to the German authorities requesting that their paper L'Humanité be allowed to reappear in the newspaper kiosks. After the war, the Communist Party leadership claimed to have issued an appeal to resistance on 10 July 1940 but in fact it continued to rail against British and capitalist warmongers and Vichy dictators and said very little about resisting the Germans.[13]

Since the Party apparatus was destroyed, activists returning from the front or war industries had to improvise. Some of them organised comités populaires in factories and neighbourhoods, which, while ostensibly demanding work, food or improvements in the conditions of POWs or of hard-pressed workers, were also seeking to reconnect with former comrades. Henri Tanguy, back in Paris in August 1940, sought out his metal-working comrades and became involved in the *comités populaires* with his wife Cécile, who typed flyers and acted as his liaison agent.[14] Albert Ouzoulias, one of the leaders of the Communist Youth, escaped from POW camp in Germany in July 1941 by stowing away underneath a train that was carrying back to France POWs released as veterans of the 1914–18 war, and returned to Paris to organise resistance.

Everything changed for communists on 22 June 1941 when the Third Reich hurled its forces at the Soviet Union. The Nazi-Soviet Pact was no more and communists suddenly knew with forceful clarity where their mission lay. It was to open up a 'second front' behind the German lines to help their Soviet comrades. In addition, they were desperate to throw off the shadow of the pact that had hung over them for two years and to recover (if it were possible) their revolutionary anti-fascist virginity. They were determined to avenge the lives of comrades who had fallen victim to the Germans and to Vichy. This helps to explain why a minority of communists took the road to violent resistance in August 1941.

At its origin were two key encounters in Paris, one between Albert Ouzoulias and Danielle Casanova, one of the founders of the women's branch of the Communist Youth (Jeunes Filles Communistes), the other between Ouzoulias and Pierre Georges, who was also involved in the Communist Youth and hardened by his fighting experience with the International Brigades in Spain. Ouzoulias met Danielle Casanova at the Closerie des Lilas café near the Port Royal metro on 2 August 1941

on a magnificently sunny day. I was in flannel trousers, short-sleeved shirt and espadrilles. Scarcely a week before I was still a prisoner. Danielle was thirty-two, I was twenty-six. We had known each other since 1934, working together in positions of responsibility in the Communist Youth [. . .] When I saw her again in 1941 she was using the pseudonym 'Anne'. She was indefatigable, going from one end of Paris to the other, doing a thousand things to develop the illegal activity of the Communist Party [...] An extraordinary flame illuminated her whole being.[15]

Danielle introduced him to another activist who in turn took him to the metro Duroc where, leaning against a balustrade at the entrance to the metro, 'Fredo' was waiting. 'Fredo' was Pierre Georges, who took over the training of commandos of young people known as the Youth Battalions, which would respond in kind to German executions. Later he became known as Colonel Fabien. An anti-German demonstration had taken place in Paris on 13 August, and among those arrested were two young communists, a 21-year-old metalworker, Henri Gautherot, and Samuel Tyszelman, known as 'Titi', an artisan of Polish-Jewish origin aged twenty. On 15–17 August 'Fredo' took a score of young communists to Lardy, in the countryside on the railway line to Étampes, where he passed on his Spanish Civil War expertise in night marching with a compass and simulated grenade throwing with his recruits. On 19 August Gautherot and Tyszelman were executed in a wood at Verrières-le-Boisson south of Paris and an operation to avenge their deaths was set in motion. Ouzoulias reflected that:

it was not easy to progress from underground leafleting, organising strikes and even cutting cables and sabotage to guerrilla actions. You have to imagine what it was like for an 18-year-old – or indeed for anyone – to go into a Paris street one evening and wait alone for a Nazi officer or soldier and execute him.[16]

One of those young men was Gilbert Brustlein, aged twenty-two, a Young Communist of Alsatian origin, who was one of a team of three chosen to go with 'Fabien' to undertake the first execution of a German officer in Paris, an event that would change the dynamics of resistance for good:

On the morning of 23 August, Tondu and I had a rendezvous with Fabien inside the metro Barbès at 8 a.m. Fabien was going to do the deed while I provided protection. We spotted a magnificent naval commandant strutting on the platform. Fabien said, 'That one'. The train arrived, the officer got into the first-class carriage and at that moment Fabien fired two shots, turned round, and sprang up the steps leading to the exit shouting, 'Stop him!' I followed him, revolver still in my hand, so that the crowd coming down the other steps thought that the shots had been fired by me. Two men tried to grab me. More supple than strong, I managed to get away and rejoin Fabien. We ran as far as Sacré-Coeur.[17]

When they got to Montmartre, all that the breathless Pierre Georges could say was, 'Titi has been avenged!'[18]

The killing of naval warrant officer Alfons Moser had a huge impact. The communists had violated the taboo that dictated German occupation forces should not be physically attacked. It was a spectacular gesture that expiated the guilt that had weighed on them under the Nazi-Soviet Pact and propelled them to the forefront of resistance activity. Unfortunately it also triggered the mechanism of collective reprisals against hostages that the Germans had put in place for precisely this eventuality. Initially they made Vichy do the dirty work. The regime was obliged to set up exceptional courts known as 'sections spéciales' to facilitate summary executions. Six communists were executed immediately and fifty-eight by the end of September 1941.

In response, communist commandos decided to strike outside the capital. Brustlein was selected to take the train to Nantes with a communist of Italian-immigrant origin, Spartaco Guisco, aged thirty and a veteran of the International Brigades. At dawn on 20 October, having attempted unsuccessfully to derail a German troop train, they returned to the city centre and in the half-light under the cathedral, where Christian de Mondragon had raised the tricolour nearly a year before, they came across their target:

It was between 8 and 8–30 when Spartaco saw two officers crossing the cathedral square. I should add that it was by pure chance. We followed them quickly and decided who would go for each Boche. When we got to the pavement on the other side we fired. Spartaco's revolver jammed but mine hit a Boche who collapsed howling like a pig having its throat cut. As we beat a retreat Spartaco told me that my German had to be at least a colonel. An hour later the city was commenting more or less favourably on the execution of Lieutenant-Colonel Hotz.[19]

Brustlein's account was accurate except in his assessment of opinion in the city. Far from celebrating this act of resistance they were horrified by the assassination of the *Feldkommandant* who was effectively the military governor of Nantes. They were even more horrified by the order of Otto von Stülpnagel, the German military commander in France, under pressure from Hitler himself, that fifty hostages would be shot at once and fifty more two days later unless the murderers were found. Minister of the Interior Pierre Pucheu tried to negotiate so that communists held in the Châteaubriant camp should be shot in preference, but the Germans wanted a wider sample of victims, who would include respectable citizens of Nantes. On 22 October the Germans executed forty-eight hostages by firing squad. They included sixteen at Nantes: among these were five veterans arrested for organising the escape of POWs from camps in Brittany and Michel Dabat, who had raised the tricolour on Nantes cathedral a year before. Five prisoners at Fort Romainville in Paris who happened to come from Nantes were executed there. Twenty-seven communists held in the Châteaubriant internment camp were taken to a nearby quarry to be shot. A last-minute attempt to secure a reprieve for young Guy Môquet failed and he too died.

The next two days saw a race against time to prevent the execution of a second batch of hostages. The city fathers – the mayor, the prefect and the bishop – called on the new *Feldkommandant* and pleaded for mercy. The families of thirteen of the Nantes victims also petitioned for a reconsideration. Even Marshal Pétain offered to go to the demarcation line and offer himself as a hostage, but was dissuaded by his ministers. The solemn funeral of Hotz on Friday 24 October was used by the Germans as a test of the goodwill of the French people: 5,000 of them followed the coffin and there were no incidents. Otto von Stülpnagel sent a telegram to Hitler warning that 'Polish methods' of repression in France would be counter-productive. All this ensured that a stay of execution was granted at midnight on 24 October and indefinitely postponed on 28 October.[20]

The execution of these forty-eight hostages widened the gulf between Vichy and the Free French. De Gaulle was placed in a difficult position. An act of resistance had been committed and had to be acknowledged, but the price paid in terms of reprisals against innocent French people was simply too high. He tried to regain the initiative and broadcast on the BBC on 25 October saying that 'War should be undertaken by those whose business it is. I am giving the order to those in the occupied territory not to kill Germans.'[21] That said, he also called for five-minutes' silence on 31 October, during which French people would stop work and stand still in the street as a mark of respect for those who had been executed. The Vichy authorities did everything they could to prevent this demonstration. On 11 November, moreover, de Gaulle awarded an honour he had invented, the Croix de la Libération, to the city of Nantes, citing it as a 'heroic city which, since the capitulation, has met all forms of collaboration with the enemy with fierce resistance'.[22] This, however, was not how the city wished to be seen and it turned down the honour. On the contrary, the prefect reported that the tragedy provoked by reckless and violent resistance had served only to strengthen the authority of Marshal Pétain.

The painful events of Nantes and the excesses of the English radio have caused many people to ponder. Not only have a large number of those who had remained hostile to the policy of Marshal Pétain's government felt the need for all French people to rally round the head of state, but even those who were privately champions of the Marshal but did not dare refute pro-English arguments are no longer afraid to speak out and denounce the activities of those who persist in criticising everything the authorities do.[23]

For communists, the blood of their martyrs created a river between their resistance and the occupying forces that could never now be bridged. They also savaged Vichy for negotiating the sacrifice of communist hostages before all others. Interior Minister Pierre Pucheu in particular was now a marked man. That said, even communists were divided over the question of attacks on German personnel. Some were committed to a strategy of terror and an eye for an eye; others feared that this terror isolated the communists from other resistance movements and made it impossible to build support among the wider population.

Charles Tillon was in the first camp. He was given the responsibility of uniting the various commando groups as Francs-Tireurs et Partisans (FTP) to continue attacks on German installations and personnel. He developed the tactic of small groups of three or four who would attack the Germans and then slip away, like 'blobs of mercury'. He rejected de Gaulle's order to leave war to the professionals: the war was continuing on French soil as well as on Russian: 'We could not accept what de Gaulle said,' he stated. 'Since I had refused to obey Pétain, it came fairly easily.'[24] In the Pas-de-Calais, Charles Debarge stepped up his campaign of sabotage and vengeance. At Christmas 1941, when German vigilance faltered, he organised an explosives attack on mining gear at Ostricourt that stopped work for two weeks and lost the Germans 13,000 tons of coal a day. He was gratified that a German inspection concluded that it was the work of experts.[25] At the end of March 1942 his team sabotaged all railway lines around the town of Lens. The Germans riposted by shooting five hostages and threatening to shoot another fifteen on 14 April if the saboteurs were not found. Debarge decided to get in his reprisal first. Debarge and Pannequin found two German soldiers with local prostitutes on the Césarine Bridge in Lens on 11 April 1942. While Pannequin kept a lookout, Debarge shot and killed one and seriously wounded the other.[26] Writing his diary a month before he was himself shot on 23 September 1942, in a gunfight with German police in the suburbs of Lille, and died in Arras prison, Debarge confessed, 'From the first moments of my underground life I decided to sell my life dearly. I would prefer to die standing up rather than lying down, suffering the torture of criminals like a medieval saint.'[27]

Other communists, however, saw the need for the Communist Party to emerge from its isolation, to build bridges and to widen support. Even before the campaign of terror the order was given to set up a Front National that would be run by communists who need not necessarily reveal themselves as such but gather resisters from a broad political spectrum. A manifesto was published on 15 May 1941 that declared, 'French men and women must unite freely and form a national front of struggle against national oppression by the invader and the traitors in its pay.'[28] The prime mover of the Front National was Georges Marrane, who had been elected mayor of Ivry in the south-east of the 'red belt' around Paris in 1925 but sacked after the Nazi-Soviet Pact. Imprisoned in the south of France, he escaped and subsequently travelled the length and breadth of the Free Zone to make contact with other resistance groups. Whereas the fighters around Colonel Fabien were isolated, Marrane was a networker, keen to forge links with the non-communist resistance. Arriving in Lyon, he went straight to the offices of *Le Progrès de Lyon* to make contact with Yves Farge. Through him he met Georges Bidault, a Christian democratic journalist and former POW who was now teaching in Lyon. Bidault said that before Catholic resisters could join communists they would need the benediction of a 'high Catholic figure'.[29] Marrane therefore had a somewhat unlikely interview with Père Chaillet who, having heard about the aims of the Front National, 'gave his backing to joint action between Catholics and communists'. A few days later, on 6 June 1941, in the offices of *Le Progrès de Lyon*, it was agreed to issue an appeal, drafted by Yves Farge, urging French people in the Free Zone to support the Front National.[30]

Both to evade arrest and to win support, Marrane adopted a personality that was entirely different from the mainstream view of the communist as a man with a dagger between his teeth. He would be seen as an ordinary Frenchman, a patriot, even as a historic character. Madeleine Braun, who in the 1930s had been active in the anti-fascist Amsterdam-Pleyel movement and the Aid for Spain Committee, worked closely with Marrane. She recalled that:

Georges preferred the bicycle because of a liking for sport but also to avoid checkpoints in railway stations [. . .] Marrane always carried a loaf of bread on the back of his bike in order to look like a pensioner on his way back from market [. . .] He always went round with a droopy moustache which attracted the name 'Vercingetorix' from other resistance movements.[31]

This Gallic identity, with his hallmark beard and bicycle, made him acceptable, almost a figure of fun, to non-communists he encountered. The children of Louis and Simone Martin-Chauffier called him 'the cyclist', and Simone recalled that on a subsequent visit 'he was wearing sensational knickerbockers and had traded his beard for a Vercingetorix moustache, which gave him his new name.'[32] The aristocratic resister Charles d'Aragon saw him in Albi in late September 1941:

Marrane exuded a strong sense of a vintage and a *terroir*. He had doubtless been a worker but he looked like an artisan. He evoked the workshop rather than the factory, the people rather than the masses [. . .] Marrane was a pilgrim. His respectability contrasted with his speed.[33]

To build a bridge to the Catholic resistance was a great coup for Marrane and the Front National. Catholics were at the opposite end of the Resistance spectrum from communist commandos. Increasingly, the line of these religious resisters was that they were opposed not only to the German occupation but to Nazi ideology. This was a threat to Christianity as well as to France and had to be confronted by spiritual resistance. Père Chaillet was the pivotal figure here, responsible for the publication of the first number of *Témoignage Chrétien* in November 1941.[34] Printed by 'papa Pons' in his workshop on the rue Vieille Monnaie and hidden in the Saint Augustin bookshop in the rue d'Algérie, it was distributed by a network of far-flung agents. André Mandouze, a lecturer at the University of Lyon, organised distribution by students from the Christian Student Youth (JEC) such as Gilbert Dru and Jean-Marie Domenach. Four hundred miles to the south-west, distribution in Montauban was undertaken by social worker Marie-Rose Gineste. She was as opposed to communism as to Nazism and kept copies of Pius XI's encyclicals *Divini Redemptoris* and *Mit Brennender Sorge* (which condemned each of them in turn) on display in the social security office where she worked.[35]

Resistance in Lyon was as much the work of refugees as of locals. Jean-Pierre Lévy, as an increasingly significant resistance figure in the autumn of 1941, was an exile from Strasbourg. He had made links with locally based resisters and had brought out *France-Liberté*. Links to Farge at *Le Progrès de Lyon* enabled him to put his publishing on a more professional footing and in December 1941 the first number of *Franc-Tireur*, named after the sharpshooters of the war of 1870, appeared.[36] Micheline Eude, aged only sixteen, the daughter of a fellow exile, Pierre Eude, the general secretary of the Strasbourg Chamber of Commerce, became Jean-Pierre Lévy's secretary and liaison agent.[37] The group was also involved in the development of symbolic resistance at Lyon as a way of reconstituting the French people around the image of the Republic that had been abolished. Schoolmaster Auguste Pinton, one of the founding members of the group, described the glorious sense of fraternity rediscovered on Lyon's place Carnot in the early evening of 1 May 1942:

The crowd gathered gradually around the statue of the Republic. It moved slowly, without shouting or noise. Women threw lilies of the valley that gradually piled up. A young man brought a bunch of tulips. I saw grown men weep. How many were we? Thousands, no doubt. Workers, although they were not the majority. Well-dressed people, women almost dressed flamboyantly. Plenty of students, some army officers too [. . .] Afterwards many friends retired to the Brasserie de l'Étoile. You could read in their eyes and the way their hands trembled the joy they felt in feeling a real strength and unity for the first time in two years. 'She [the Republic] is not dead, is she?' they said.[38]

This sentiment of solidarity expressed hostility to Germany, which for the moment had not invaded the Free Zone. It expressed a love of the Republic that had been abolished and was therefore critical of the Vichy government. That said, General de Gaulle had not yet replaced Marshal Pétain as the idol of the French. And for those who were critical of Pétain there were other generals in the frame as possible saviours who did not have the disadvantages of de Gaulle, an exile who was seen to be a tool of the British and advised by Jews. There was still a powerful feeling that resistance would come from within France, owing something to the national regeneration agenda of the Vichy regime but prising the regime away from collaboration with Germany and forcing it to re-enter the war with the Allies. Regeneration meant purging from public life 'anti-French' elements such Freemasons, communists and Jews, and envisaged an order in which Catholics and the military had a prominent role to play. The model was the national resurgence that had occurred in Prussia after its defeat by Napoleon in 1806 and created the power that in turn beat Napoleon in 1813–15.

General Gabriel Cochet, who had commanded the air force of the Fifth Army in 1940, had retreated after the defeat to Le Puy in the Massif Central, and ordered his troops to hide their weapons in caves and quarries, awaiting a time when they would again be of use. On 6 September 1940 he issued an appeal from Clermont-Ferrand:

We must see that the French people do not surrender to the conqueror's will and accept subjugation [. . .] We must at least hold on to what is unfailing, if not unattackable, moral force in the absence of material force: THE WILL TO RESIST even if we do not have the means to do it.[39]

Cochet had a small resistance group around him called the Ardents and brought out a bulletin on the progress of the war that was fairly anti-German. He presided over local ceremonies around Le Puy to mark 14 July 1940 and Joan of Arc Day in May 1941. He was visited by Jean-Pierre Lévy whom he regarded as 'one of the first resisters, of admirable courage'.[40] Cochet also came to Lyon to lecture openly to Catholic students and Polytechnicians.[41] One of those Polytechnicians was Serge Asher, the son of a Czech mother who had settled in Paris as an agent for Viennese fashion houses and who took the name of his Swiss stepfather. Schooled at the Lycée Louis-le-Grand and gaining entry to the École Polytechnique in 1939, he was at artillery school in Fontainebleau in 1940, was astonished that the gun-carriages were still drawn by horses, and retreated with the school to Poitiers without firing a shot. He did not hear de Gaulle's appeal of 18 June 1940 and for a long time thought that Pétain was 'a federator' who united the country and was 'clever, crafty and had outwitted Hitler', negotiating a decent armistice. He was sent to a Chantier de la Jeunesse in Savoy, which was run by officers, and he saw it as a way of doubling the numbers of the Armistice Army. 'We gathered under the stars' he recalled, around camp fires, to recover from a collective trauma with 'romantic evocations of war'. Asher resumed his studies at Polytechnique, which had relocated to Lyon, and after Cochet's lecture of May 1941, met him and one of the so-called 'General Cochet movement' in a café near Perrache Station to talk about resistance. He distributed resistance papers such as *Liberté*, *Franc-Tireur* and *Les Petites Ailes* but without making contact with the groups that were producing them. 'I was both a Pétainist and a Gaullist,' he confessed. 'I have never hidden it.'[42] Graduating as a sub-lieutenant in the summer of 1942 and, still looking for inspiration, he went to study in a medieval castle at Uriage in the Alps, where General Dunoyer de Segonzac was training an élite group of students, youth leaders, industrialists and professionals who would lead the new France. Uriage attracted a galaxy of lecturers who kept open the ambiguity of being loyal to the values of the regime while not endorsing collaboration and leading the way to redemption.[43]

The most outstanding example of this resistance, which hoped for more from Pétain than from de Gaulle, was the Combat movement of Henri Frenay. Frenay was a contemporary of Dunoyer de Segonzac at Saint-Cyr and visited Uriage in December 1941 and September 1942. He was unhappy with Pétain's famous handshake with Hitler (on his way to see Franco, at Montoire on 24 October 1940) but nevertheless accepted an appointment to the Intelligence Bureau of the general staff in Vichy the following December. Given his devotion to the memory of his father, who had died fighting in the First World War, and whose ideas lived on in his mother, it is not surprising that he had to be converted to resistance by a significant personal relationship. Frenay had met Berty Albrecht, who was twelve years older than he, when he was twenty, in 1935.[44] Berty Albrecht came from a Swiss Protestant family that had come to Marseille to do business, had worked as a nurse in the First World War, and then married a Dutch banker whose name she took. Wilful and independent, she separated from her husband in 1931 and divided her time between Paris and the Côte d'Azur, becoming a campaigner for anti-fascism and sexual liberation. She supported the Spanish Republic and welcomed German-Jewish exiles from Nazism to her home. In 1935 Frenay had just entered the École Supérieure de Guerre to qualify as a general staff officer; she gave him both a political education from the left and a passionate romance he had never encountered in his own straight-laced milieu. Moved by the courage and suffering of women in the strikes of 1936, Berty decided to become a social worker and trained at the School of

Factory Welfare Officers (*surintendantes d'usine*) in Paris run by the daughter of a Protestant pastor, Jeanne Sivadon. In 1941 Berty came to Lyon, employed by the Ministries of Industrial Production and Labour to deal with female unemployment and resumed her role as Frenay's political mentor. Frenay resigned his position in the Intelligence Bureau and began to build a network around a resistance paper, *Les Petites Ailes*, first published in May 1941 in time for the feast of Joan of Arc.[45]

The team Frenay collected around him was often from an extreme-right-wing background. They had often been associated with the royalist Action Française of Charles Maurras but had broken with him over his wholehearted endorsement of Vichy and collaboration. Prominent among them was Claude Bourdet, who later described most early resisters as nonconformists or mavericks.[46] His own Action Française background was cut across by his education at the École Polytechnique of Zürich after 1928, where he had been exposed to the views of Jewish intellectuals, Italian anti-fascists and German exiles from Nazism. He had served in the private office of a Popular Front Economics minister, and sided with the progressive Catholic thinker Jacques Maritain against the Francoist hijack of mainstream Catholicism.[47] After a brief war he withdrew to the Côte d'Azur at Antibes, where he set up an oil and soap factory. Frenay met Bourdet in May 1941 on a train between Nice and Cannes and described 'a man of forty-five, decorated, energetic in manner, his face shaped as if by a sickle', travelling under the name of Lefèvre.[48] Bourdet for his part remembered 'a young man with bright blue eyes behind his thick tortoiseshell glasses (probably a disguise), a powerful handshake, square chin, the physique generally but mistakenly associated with the man "of action".'[49] Almost at once, Bourdet was appointed head of Frenay's network in the Alpes-Maritimes.

Frenay's ambition did not stop there. His aim was to establish himself as the leader of the metropolitan resistance movement and to this end he set about negotiating with the heads of other movements. The unspoken assumption was that in this wider federation he would be the top dog. In June 1941, accordingly, Frenay met François de Menthon at the latter's house in Lyon: 'The man who welcomed me was tall and thin,' Frenay remembered, 'He was wearing glasses. His handshake was soft and seemed to be reluctant.' There was a good deal to be suspicious about but there were also pointers to possible cooperation between Frenay's movement, grouped around the underground paper *Les Petites Ailes*, and de Menthon's *Liberté*, run by a core of Christian democratic law professors and other intellectuals. Frenay's movement was conservative and militaristic, although dissenting clerics such as Père Chaillet contributed pieces to *Les Petites Ailes* before *Témoignage Chrétien* began to appear in November 1941. *Liberté* circulated mainly in Languedoc and the Massif Central, *Les Petites Ailes* were stronger in Provence and the Côte d'Azur. Diplomacy between these two movements led to a meeting at Grenoble in November 1941 that agreed to merge into a single organisation and paper, *Combat,* with each movement contributing equal numbers to the organising committee.

More tricky was any rapprochement between Henri Frenay and Emmanuel d'Astier de la Vigerie. They met for the first time in Antibes in July 1941, but the differences between their two movements were too pronounced and the clash between their personalities too strong. Frenay discovered that d'Astier's *Libération* 'was deliberately based on the Left. 90% of its clientele, he told me, was made up of trade-unionists and socialists'. This was a much more powerful organisation than *Liberté* and it was not obvious that Frenay would emerge as overall leader. On a personal level, moreover, Frenay did not feel he could trust d'Astier. 'The man has talent, even class,' said Frenay. 'He knows it and plays on it. His secret weapon is probably his smile, and he smiles often and good-naturedly.'[50]

Frenay's strategy also involved recruiting key military figures to the cause. He began as a fervent supporter of Marshal Pétain but it became less and less clear that Pétain would ever bring the French over to the side of the Allies. Admiral Darlan, his first minister throughout 1941, pursued a high-profile policy of collaboration with Germany and in November 1941 engineered the dismissal of Weygand, who wanted a dialogue with the United States. German concessions in response to the strategy of collaboration were minimal, and as a result of German plunder and Allied blockade the population felt the pressure of food shortages and high prices. On 12 August 1941 Pétain had acknowledged that an 'ill wind' of discontent was sweeping France. At the same time, however, little love was lost between Frenay and de Gaulle. This was partly because of the General's overt and divisive conflict with Pétain, partly because he wanted to control the metropolitan resistance from London. Frenay therefore attempted to find a third way between Pétainism and Gaullism by using a military leader in France who had distanced himself from Vichy but had influence over the 100,000-strong Armistice Army. This leader might be used as a bridge to de Gaulle but also as a counterweight to him.

The first general whom Frenay contacted was General Cochet. They met early in 1941 in a little café in a suburb of Lyon and again, after Cochet had spent the summer of 1941 under house arrest at Vals-les-Bains, in September 1941. There was unfortunately a clash of egos: Cochet wanted to retain his independence from Combat and reported that 'Frenay thought that there was only one resistance movement: his own.'[51] Second on Frenay's list was General de La Laurencie, who had been Vichy's delegate in occupied Paris until he fell out with the Germans and was then replaced by the collaborationist Fernand de Brinon. Frenay persuaded Emmanuel d'Astier to accompany him to a meeting with General de La Laurencie in Valence on 15 December 1941. What made rapprochement impossible was that the General already had his own agenda. He turned up to the meeting with an American minder, Colonel Legge, the US military attaché in Switzerland, which signalled that the Americans too were looking for antidotes to both Pétain and de Gaulle. It became clear, moreover, the General would not act as a bridge to de Gaulle because he wanted simply to replace him. Claude Bourdet, who also attended the meeting, noted the 'irremediable stupidity of La Laurencie. He took himself for de Gaulle. He retained an infinite respect for the person of the Marshal who perhaps made mistakes but who must not be attacked under any circumstances.' Asked what he would do about de Gaulle, who had been condemned to death by a Vichy court martial, La Laurentie replied conceitedly, 'Have no fear. We will pardon him.'[52]

Meanwhile Frenay worked to extend the reach of Combat from the Free Zone to the Occupied Zone. Through Berty Albrecht's ties with Jeanne Sivadon he latched on to a group in Paris led by Tony Ricou, a talented painter who had also worked in the private office of Radical premier Camille Chautemps. His group included an Alsatian Protestant brother and sister, Paul and Elisabeth Dussauze. Paul, an architect, was dedicated to building a radio that would be able to transmit and receive messages to and from London. Elisabeth, who worked for the external relations department of the Comité des Forges and reacted sharply against Nazism on her visits to Germany, was involved in disseminating *Les Petites Ailes* and recruiting new members, such as Jacques Lecompte-Boinet, who worked at the Préfecture de Police, and Henri Ingrand, a surgeon at the Hôpital Cochin.[53]

The Paris group was introduced to Henri Frenay on 3 January 1942 under the cover of a bridge party. Lecompte-Boinet recalled the arrival of the *patron*: 'his blue eyes look straight ahead; he is fair, pleasant-looking. Everyone was quiet. He sat at the desk and placed under our eyes the general plan of the movement's organisation before dealing with the question of information.'[54] This appearance of calm and order under a charismatic leader was brutally ruptured by the infiltration of the group by an agent of the *Abwehr*. It precipitated the arrest of one of Combat's liaison agents who was carrying not only a suitcase full of copies

of Combat but a list of contacts' names and addresses that had
not yet been translated into code. A wave of arrests was now
imminent. Frenay had to think fast. His decision was at the
far end of what communist resisters would have done. Vichy
had responded to the communist attacks on German officers
in Paris and Nantes by handing over communists to take the
brunt of German collective reprisals. But Frenay did not feel
out of place in Vichy. It was only a year since he had asked for
leave from his intelligence post with the general staff. Later the
general staff had wanted to do business with his movement
on the intelligence front, but Frenay had refused this because
it would have meant revealing the names of his team. He now
decided to play on his Vichy connections by attempting to do
a deal. This led him to the office of Interior Minister Pierre
Pucheu, whom communists regarded as responsible for sending
their comrades to their deaths.

Frenay duly arrived in Vichy on 28 January 1942. The deal
he hoped for was to propose his movement reduce criticisms of
the Vichy government, on the understanding that Vichy would
modify its strategy of collaboration and allow space for his
organisation to function and not unleash the police on them.
His first meeting was with the deputy head of Sûreté Nationale,
Commandant Rollin, who underlined his patriotic credentials by
revealing that he had been involved in naval intelligence during
the war, based at Le Havre, and had turned down an offer to
serve as secretary-general of the Interior Ministry because of 'the
opposition [his patriotism] would provoke from the Germans'.[55]
The following day, 29 January, Frenay was invited to meet Pierre
Pucheu himself. The conversation began rather stiffly:

Pucheu: You seem very young, Captain.
Frenay: I am thirty-seven.
Pucheu: So, you are the one who calls me a traitor?
Frenay: Minister, if you are not a traitor appearances are against you.
Pucheu: No one in the government is pro-German. Ministers are trying

to make the most of the present situation, without taking public opinion into account but for the greater good of France [. . .] Your position is easy. You play on people's emotions. It's a kind of demagogy.[56]

The meeting was not conclusive and four days later, on 2 February 1942, disaster struck: Jeanne Sivadon, the Dussauzes and many other members of Combat were arrested by the Gestapo. Ingrand escaped to the Free Zone to join Frenay's organisation there while Lecompte-Boinet was left in Paris to pick up the pieces.

Returning to Lyon, Frenay tried to persuade his colleagues to reduce anti-Vichy propaganda for the sake of the arrested comrades. They initially agreed that he could continue talking to Vichy, to gain time and avoid further arrests. Back at Vichy on 6 February, he had a brief meeting with Pucheu and three hours with Rollin. They agreed there was 'a revival of republicanism at the moment' and that 'people will never accept a totalitarian form of government'. A third interview took place at Vichy between Frenay and Rollin on 25 February. Rollin said that Pucheu had spoken to Pétain directly about the case of the arrested members of Combat. The case would be sent to an examining magistrate in Lyon, who would dismiss it. The arrested parties would be administratively interned, and could then be released at any time.

Unfortunately for Frenay this contact with Vichy was seen in a very different light by most of the Resistance. Frenay later wrote that news of the interview 'spread like wildfire in resistance circles, often distorted or presented in a defamatory way. It was said that a deal had been done with Vichy and that I would personally receive police protection.'[57] At a stormy lunch in Lyon, Emmanuel d'Astier 'attacked Frenay, accusing him of "committing a disloyal act under the guise of human charity" and threatened to write a leader in *Libération* – which in fact appeared – warning resisters against the activities of certain people who thought it was their duty to collaborate with Vichy'.[58] Meanwhile, in April 1942,

Frenay's closest conspirator and confidante, Berty Albrecht, was arrested.

Despite – and to some extent because of – Frenay's attempt to federate resistance movements, at the beginning of 1942 they remained deeply divided. The violence practised by the communist resistance and the collective reprisals it provoked alienated the vast majority of the French population and indeed most of the French Resistance. Attempts by communists such as Georges Marrane to reinvent themselves as ordinary patriots and to build bridges by means of the Front National were in their infancy and vulnerable to frequent setbacks provoked by anti-communism. Meanwhile the non-communist resistance was almost broken in two by Frenay's attempt to make a pact with the devil, the Vichy regime. The incident dramatised a conflict between those who still looked to the possibility of a French revival in France under Marshal Pétain (or a military figure rather like him) and those who saw his rival in London as the only possible unifying force. The support Charles de Gaulle received from the Allies was both a huge benefit and a sign of dangerous dependency in the eyes of those who, since the French Revolution, had criticised *émigrés* who ran for cover rather than battling things out on French soil. Increasingly, however, recourse to London seemed the obvious way forward.

4

London calling

When Rex arrived in France, everything, or almost everything, still needed to be done.

(Colonel Passy, 1947)

On 11 May 1941 a secret agent, Pierre de Vomécourt, was parachuted from a British plane over the Limousin in central France. His mission was to make contact with resistance groups and to assess the possibilities of sabotage in the Occupied Zone. Unsurprisingly, he was no ordinary Frenchman. His great-grandfather had died in the Franco-Prussian war of 1870 and his father at the beginning of the Great War. He and his brothers Jean and Philippe were sent to a Jesuit-run British public school, Beaumont College in Windsor; Jean was old enough to finish the 1914–18 war in the Royal Flying Corps.[1] In 1940 Pierre was a liaison officer for the 7th Cameronians in France, was appalled by the armistice, and left with British forces from Cherbourg in the night of 17–18 June. He went to St Stephen's House to see about joining the Free French and later gave two accounts of why he had not joined them. Having just heard of two Frenchmen being shot at Nantes for having cut German telephone lines, he expressed the view that trained agents should be sent to France to undertake propaganda and sabotage of German installations, rather than leaving it to 'the clumsy initiatives of poor incompetent people'. 'I received a brutal put-down,' he said, 'and was told proudly by a French naval officer, "I am here to fight and not to undertake propaganda or sabotage."'[2] He was also troubled to find at the Free French headquarters 'a certain number of officers who were mainly interested in what their salary would be. Disgusted, he went away.'[3] He went off to find British friends he had known at public school and was duly recruited by the Special Operations Executive (SOE), which had been set up to undertake sabotage operations behind enemy lines.[4] In May 1941 he became the second SOE agent to be parachuted into France.

On one level this is a story of the budding heroism of agents sent to work with the French Resistance. On another it draws attention to the fragility of de Gaulle's position and that of the Free French and the ambivalence of their relations with the British. Pressed by Churchill, the British supported the Free French, but their support was not unconditional. Institutionally, moreover, there was a great deal of suspicion and rivalry between the Free French and British secret services.

Charles de Gaulle was an isolated figure in London. He was at the centre of a small Free French community in Carlton Gardens, with extensions at places such as the French Institute in South Kensington. Not all French soldiers and sailors who fetched up in London joined his little band; some, like Pierre de Vomécourt, were put off by the clannishness or opinions of the General's collaborators and preferred to work with the British. De Gaulle had no support in the French diplomatic community, which broke with Britain after Mers el-Kébir, and most of whom boarded the *Orduna* at Liverpool on 19 July 1940 and returned to France.[5] Influential Frenchmen passing through London, such as André Maurois, Jean Monnet and Alexis Léger, were distrustful of de Gaulle's personal ambition and thought his initiative partisan and divisive. They moved on to the United States, where more often than not they briefed against him and found ready ears in the Roosevelt administration.[6]

The British had recognised the French National Committee in London on 23 June and de Gaulle as leader of the Free French on 28 June. Churchill made an extraordinary leap of faith in backing de Gaulle, but sometimes had second thoughts about his decision. The British also provided the Free French with premises and finance for their enterprise. Far from appearing grateful for this support, de Gaulle chafed at his dependency on British goodwill and often affected a pose of disdainful arrogance. However his behaviour also reflected the real complexity of Franco-British relations. Although the two powers had fought together in 1940 the Dunkirk evacuation seemed to confirm the prejudice that the British were prepared to fight to the last Frenchman.[7] On 16 June 1940 the British government, advised by Jean Monnet, had proposed a Franco-British Union, by which the French could continue fighting, but Paul Reynaud was unable to convince his cabinet that this was not a British attempt to gobble up France and was obliged to resign in favour of Marshal Pétain. The image of Britain as the Big Bad Wolf bent on devouring Little Red Ridinghood's Empire was one of the cartoons that appeared at the time of the Fashoda crisis in 1898, when Britain forced France to back off from the headwaters of the Nile.[8] It was coupled with the myth of Perfidious Albion reinforced when Britain sank most of the French fleet at Mers el-Kébir. This made the French Empire vulnerable not only to the German-Italian Axis but also to British ambitions, should they ever want to take advantage of their military and naval superiority. All this sharpened the Anglophobia of the Vichy regime, which regarded Great Britain as just as much an enemy as Germany. It also made de Gaulle's position, dependent on the British as he was, vulnerable to accusations of submission and even of treachery.

De Gaulle's relationship with Great Britain was undermined by British fears that they had backed the wrong horse and a desire not to alienate the French people, most of whom were understood to admire Marshal Pétain. 'I still wonder if we could find a potential Napoleon from among the French armed forces', Churchill's personal assistant wrote to him on 16 July. 'I doubt if de Gaulle is more than a Marshal Murat', whose highest achievement was to become King of Naples.[9] The humiliation suffered by de Gaulle at Dakar in September 1940 did nothing for his reputation as the man who might bring the French Empire over to France.[10] The BBC pulled back from criticising Pétain overtly, hoping that at some point he would turn back to the British. In January 1941 they called him 'the spearhead of the passive resistance' – a wonderful recognition of what was regarded as the foot-dragging of most French people subject to German occupation.[11]

De Gaulle thus urgently needed cards that could strengthen his hand in the Great Power poker game. Militarily, his hand was very poor. The Free French numbered a mere 2,721 men, including 123 officers, on 15 August 1940.[12] The British had been prepared to help de Gaulle at Dakar because West Africa was not central to their global strategic thinking, but elsewhere things were more difficult. The British Empire formed a crescent around the Indian Ocean from South Africa to Singapore. Its gateway was Cairo, which placed a premium on mastery of the Mediterranean. This was imperilled in April and May 1941 by the German-Italian invasion of Yugoslavia, the German invasion of Greece in support of the faltering Italian offensive, the German invasion of Crete, and by Rommel's advance through Tunisia towards Egypt in support of Italian forces from Libya. As if this was not enough, nationalist army officers under Rashid-Ali seized power in the British mandate of Iraq on 1 April 1941 and appealed to the Germans for support. The Germans put pressure on Vichy to make available airfields in Syria, over which France had a mandate, in order to allow the *Luftwaffe* to support the Iraqi coup. This threatened to tip the balance of power in the Middle East and the British had to act fast. German planes began to arrive at Aleppo and Damascus in May and General Wavell, Commander-in-Chief in the Middle East, scraped together an invasion force of British soldiers reinforced by Australians and Indians from its Empire, commanded by Maitland 'Jumbo' Wilson.[13]

De Gaulle and the Free French saw the opportunity to prevent another capitulation by Vichy forces to German pressure and to oust them from the Syrian and Lebanese mandates. General

Catroux, who had been dismissed as governor-general of French Indochina by Vichy and joined the Free French, was sent out with a small force and instructions to win over as many as possible of Vichy's Levant Army commanded by General Dentz. From Brazzaville de Gaulle approved a French march on Damascus in conjunction with a declaration of Syrian independence in order to undercut nationalist opposition.[14] The British nevertheless had the whip hand and invaded Syria and Lebanon on 8 June. Overwhelmed, General Dentz sued for an armistice at Acre on 12 July, but the Free French then suffered a double humiliation. Firstly, the armistice was concluded between the British and Dentz without consulting Catroux. De Gaulle arrived in Cairo on 21 July and had a furious row with the British about being ousted from their mandates. It was agreed that the Free French would take responsibility for internal order and the British guard against foreign invasion.[15] Churchill was not impressed, saying that 'Free French "pretensions" require to be sternly corrected, even use of force not being excluded. It is important to let them realise in good time that they will be made to obey.'[16]

The second humiliation was that under the armistice Vichy forces were allowed to choose freely between rallying to the Free French and being shipped back to France. Brawling broke out in the streets of Beirut with the Free French accusing the Vichy forces of being 'Boches! Traitors! Renegades! Uhlans! Nazis!'[17] In the end only 15 per cent of the Vichy forces rallied to de Gaulle. The vast majority who landed in Marseille in September were welcomed as heroes to shouts of 'Vive Pétain! Vive la France!' and reinforced the numbers of Vichy's Army of Africa, which was still a considerable force.[18] The only consolation for de Gaulle was the fact that the British now recognised that Vichy would never bring over the French Empire to the Allies and was in fact a leaky sieve as far as German penetration was concerned. After June 1941 Vichy was regularly denounced as treacherous and pro-German and de Gaulle's French National Committee was effectively recognised by the British as a government-in-exile alongside other European governments such as the Dutch, Belgians, Norwegians and Czechs.[19]

Head-on demonstrations of military force were clearly not de Gaulle's strong suit at this stage. An alternative strategy was to demonstrate his indispensability by providing military intelligence about German forces and movements from France. The British of course recruited and ran their own agents through either MI6 or SOE. French people coming to England were interviewed at the Royal Victoria Patriotic School in Wandsworth and many creamed off by MI6 or SOE before the Free French could have a look at them.[20] The British were reluctant to share intelligence gathered by their agents with the French, and insisted on decrypting certain categories of code themselves before passing them on.[21] The Free French thus needed to gather their own intelligence both to be 'in the know' and to accumulate a currency to exchange for intelligence gathered by the British. They also sought the legitimacy that would come from demonstrating that they were in charge of a significant number of French agents and of resistance networks and movement in France.

De Gaulle had set up his own Intelligence Bureau to collect and process military intelligence, which subsequently became the Central Bureau of Intelligence and Action (BCRA). The key figure of this service was André Dewavrin, otherwise known as Colonel Passy. Passy and the BCRA thought of resistance in purely military terms. Politically, they were sometimes accused of being *Cagoulards*, the paramilitary wing of Action Française dedicated to preventing a communist coup in the 1930s. Little distinguished them from Vichy reflexes except that they were in London and in favour of continuing the war.[22] Resistance for them meant the organisation of tight *réseaux* or networks dedicated to the collection and transmission of military intelligence. It might involve escape lines for getting key agents out of France. Later it might involve the sabotage of German installations and communications. Passy distinguished between 'réseaux, with agents sent by us, radio-operators trained by us' and 'resistance movements born spontaneously in France, especially in the Southern Zone'.[23] This, however, generated another form of rivalry, between resisters within France. Some of these might share the view that resistance was essentially spying, escape lines and sabotage. Others, particularly in the Free Zone, developed propaganda though flyers and newspapers and needed a larger number of trusted individuals to disseminate their material. They were *movements* rather than *networks*.[24] In addition they had a political agenda, which was to highlight the evils of the German occupation, collaboration by their compatriots and the Vichy regime, and to begin to think about the kind of France they wanted after the liberation, whenever it came.

The British naturally ran their own agents in France who owed no loyalty to the Free French. One of these was the extraordinary Virginia Hall. An American who had worked at a number of US embassies in Europe, she had been denied a full diplomatic career as a result of a hunting accident in Turkey in 1932. Her left leg was amputated below the knee and she wore an artificial limb she called 'Cuthbert'. In the spring of 1941 she resigned her job at the US embassy in London and applied to SOE. That summer she arrived in Vichy as a journalist on Ralph Ingersoll's new paper, *PM*, and cabled back reports on Vichy politics and French Resistance movements. In November 1941 she wrote to a friend:

My dear Nic. I've moved to Lyons, which is a much better idea. I can go and see things from there, and I've made such a lot of friends, doctors, businessmen, a few newspaper people, refugees, professors. One nice doctor has a *chasse* nearby so I'm shooting again – I shall keep Cuthbert well out of the way.[25]

After the USA entered the war things became more risky for her. SOE sent help in the shape of another agent, Denis Rake. Brought up in Belgium and speaking French, and trained as a radio operator, his other advantages were skills in playacting that came from a career in the musical theatre and the need to hide his homosexuality. Rake was landed from a felucca at Juan-les-Pins near Antibes in May 1942 and made his way to Lyon. He was told to look for someone reading a copy of the *Journal de Genève*, and reflected that Hall was 'a very striking woman who once you had seen you would never forget, for she had red hair and an artificial foot'.[26] The following month Rake was told to return home via Spain but was arrested and kept in prison at Castres until he escaped in November. Virginia Hall failed in her attempt to get him out of Castres and herself escaped over the Pyrenees, arriving in London early in 1943.

Given the brief and dangerous careers of British-run agents there were plenty of opportunities for French agents sent by the BCRA, and success could raise de Gaulle's credit as leader of the Free French. One of the first and most dramatic was the case of Count Honoré d'Estienne d'Orves, who set up the Nimrod network in Brittany in December 1940. A Catholic and royalist noble of Provençal and Vendean origins, he graduated from the École Polytechnique and became a career naval officer. At the armistice in 1940 he was stationed with the French fleet in Alexandria, which rallied to Pétain under Admiral Geoffroy. The sinking of much of the French fleet by the British at Mers el-Kébir confirmed most naval men in their Anglophobia, with the exception of d'Estienne d'Orves, who sailed to Britain on a boat from Aden in September 1940. In London he took the pseudonym 'Châteauvieux', worked for the navy's Intelligence Bureau, and lived alongside Passy in their digs at 69 Cromwell Road. 'His candour astonished me,' recalled Passy, who kept his cards close to his chest. His kindness towards everybody could 'not be equalled. Because of his rather old-fashioned conformism we called him "Old Barrack", the name of a little neighbouring street which echoed his pseudonym.'[27]

Like a latter-day knight errant, d'Estienne d'Orves volunteered to go to France himself to set up a military intelligence network.

Contact was made with André Clément, sales director of the Amieux canning factory at Chantenay near Nantes. D'Estienne d'Orves arrived on the *Marie Louise* at Plogoff on 22 December 1940, travelling under the name of Pierre Cornec and bringing with him an Alsatian radio operator, Alfred Gaessler (alias Georges Marty), and an agent of Dutch origin, Jan Doornik. The local priest later recalled that Christmas was spent at the Cléments' house: 'the BBC conveyed de Gaulle's good wishes to the French. They listened to the "Marseillaise" standing to attention. With the help of a transmitter the count signalled to London that he had arrived safely and London arranged to send the first message for him the next day at 13–30.'[28] Within weeks the group was betrayed by the radio operator Gaessler, who had been thrown out of the Cléments' house for making passes at their maid and had made contact with the Germans.[29] The Nimrod group was arrested during the night of 20–21 January 1941 and sent to Paris, where they were held in the Cherche-Midi prison. In the early days of the Occupation it was normal for resisters to be sent before a German military court and the group duly went for trial in May 1941. On 28 May 1941 d'Estienne d'Orves, the Cléments and other associates were condemned to death. Given the sentencing of a naval officer of noble birth, the head of government, Admiral Darlan, lodged a discreet appeal with the German authorities, which went right up to Hitler. The German invasion of the Soviet Union a few weeks later, however, raised the odds and made compromise impossible. The Cléments' sentences were commuted to forced labour but d'Estienne d'Orves was executed by firing squad at the Mont Valérien fort on 12 September 1941. Although d'Estienne d'Orves became one of the first of new Gaulle's new chivalric order, the Compagnons de la Libération, his actions did not go down well with his own tribe. 'His wife's brother,' said Max André, 'was so collaborationist that the night of d'Estienne's execution he celebrated in the night clubs of Saint-Malo, saying that his fate was well deserved.'[30]

Even more colourful and also more successful, at least in the short term, was the career of Gilbert Renault, code name Rémy, who constructed and ran one of the most astonishing intelligence networks. Having been moved by the power of collective prayers in the Paris church of Notre-Dame des Victoires early in 1942, he baptised his group the Confrérie Notre-Dame. This mysticism was curiously at odds with the hard realities that his work threw up. In particular it dramatised the tension between the Free French, who thought that the purpose of resistance was basically to facilitate military activity to liberate France and Europe, and metropolitan resisters, who realised that the old world had been discredited or destroyed and that resistance involved a political rethinking of how France and even Europe would have to be reconstructed after liberation. This clash of visions had profound implications for the conduct of the Resistance: would it be the secret underground conspiracy of a few in collaboration with the Allies, or would it be a more popular movement of French people who wished to take matters into their own hands and remake their futures?

Like so many resisters, Renault seemed at first sight an unlikely candidate for the work he was doing. A Breton from Vannes, he was Jesuit-educated and a supporter of the hopeless royalist cause. His variegated career included banking, insurance and film production; when war broke out he was making a film on Christopher Columbus in Spain. On 18 June 1940 he found himself on a boat from Lorient with his younger brother Claude, leaving behind his wife and children. He refused to believe news of the armistice which he heard on landing at Falmouth but found de Gaulle's voice 'vibrant with a sombre passion'.[31] He reported to the Intelligence Bureau and found Colonel Passy, 'a seemingly very young officer, prematurely bald, beardless, in riding breeches and white leggings, sitting and reading a document while chewing on his handkerchief'.[32] Passy, for his part, remembered 'a man of about 35, solidly built, with a large round head [. . .] He was full of drive and dynamism but could not help revealing an almost mystical sensitivity.'[33]

Renault volunteered for a mission to France, not least, he admitted, because he wanted to see his wife and children again. Because he had visas for Spain he returned to France via Lisbon and Madrid, eventually finding a way to cross the demarcation line back to the Occupied Zone at the château of M. de la Bardonnie, whom he described as a 'gentleman farmer'.[34] There he met three young men from Vannes who were trying to go the other way, via Spain, to join de Gaulle and he recruited them as the first agents of his network. His main preoccupation was spying on German warships based along the Atlantic coast of France from Bordeaux to Nantes and Brest, and was particularly interested in submarine bases and the movements of the battleships *Scharnhorst, Gneisenau* and *Prinz Eugen*. For contacts he relied mainly on military, naval and air force such as corvette captain Courbon (code name Hilarion) in Brest.

Rémy emitted more heat than light. He was an indefatigable collector of intelligence and contacts, but he also neglected questions of security and was politically naïve, so that his effectiveness as an agent was limited. One of his agents recalled that Rémy was:

A conscientious, hard-working and brave man, fearing neither fatigue nor danger. He spent whole nights decoding messages [. . .] But since no-one is perfect he had his weaknesses. His work methods were clumsy and careless. He wanted to meet all his agents personally, which was sometimes unwise and unhelpful. He took no notice of suspicious signs that were pointed out to him. The arrests of certain members of his network might have been avoided. One striking thing about his personality was his extraordinary faith in the protection of Providence. He had lost two young children; these were the two angels he talked about in his books which from heaven, according to him, would keep him safe from all danger.[35]

That said, Renault's great asset was his contact with London at a time when these were rare and short-lived. He acted as an early conduit between the metropolitan resistance seeking help and endorsement for their activity and the Free French with their links, however strained, with the British.

A crucial link in his chain was Pierre Brossolette and his bookshop on the rue de la Pompe, opposite his old school, the Lycée Jeanson-de-Sailly.[36] Brossolette knew Rémy through a colleague at the Collège Sévigné, where Brossolette sometimes gave history lessons. Brossolette described Rémy as wanting to set up a 'Thomas Cook agency' organising trips to and from London for resistance leaders.[37] As a socialist and journalist Brossolette was himself well connected with those leaders and was able not only to put their leaders in touch with London but also to articulate their political views and demands, which differed a great deal from the purely military goals that primarily concerned the Free French.

In January 1942 Brossolette organised a meeting between Rémy and two resistance leaders in his shop. Rémy recalled that:

I was taken to the basement which he had transformed into a library. Wrapped up in their overcoats, warming their feet against a stove, people were waiting for me. The one wearing big bootees with leather soles introduced himself as Christian Pineau, the leader of Libération-Nord. The other was Louis Vallon.[38]

Vallon was a left-wing socialist who had returned from POW camp in Germany in June 1941. Pineau was keen to go to London to communicate his movement's aims to de Gaulle. Rémy was invited to a meeting of the Libération-Nord leadership in Vallon's flat at the top of the Boulevard Saint-Michel. These included André Philip, socialist deputy of Lyon and a key member of the Comité d'Action Socialiste and Jean Cavaillès, the young philosopher of Libération-Sud who had recently been appointed to the Sorbonne. Rémy was taken with Suzanne Vallon – 'a doctor, slight, merry, mischievous, witty' and rather surprised by the political seriousness of the group he had just met. 'This was the first time I had attended a meeting of members of a "resistance movement", he almost joked. 'In the sitting room they were busy rebuilding France socialist style.'[39]

Rémy was taken by plane to England on 12 February 1942 and impressed Passy by the vast amount of documents and maps he had collected, and his colourful impressions of French slang words for Germans, as he held court in the restaurant of the Waldorf Hotel. He claimed that the French did not want to hear about discredited political parties and that de Gaulle would be ill-advised to take a political stance.[40] Moving in the opposite direction both geographically and politically, Pineau took the train to the Free Zone to meet leaders of resistance movements in order to create for de Gaulle a common front of those who saw the Resistance as a democratic political force. He found many Southern resisters, like Henri Frenay, still nursing the illusion they could bring Vichy and the Armistice Army over to the Allied camp but 'rallied many others behind an agenda for political reform'.[41] He got to London in March and was struck by the difference in atmosphere between free London and occupied Paris:

I was keen to get out, to wander the streets. Walking around London, where despite the recent bombings the crowds have never been so dense, gives one an extraordinary impression of life and liberty. Lots of uniforms, not least those of women. English girls are in any case more attractive in their khaki suits than in their traditional red or spinach-green outfits. Lots of traffic on the street: military vehicles, double-decker buses, little Austins for officials. Policemen in their bell-shaped helmets are on duty and newspaper sellers are on every corner, selling papers with huge headlines and real news, that is news that you want to read.[42]

His enthusiasm soon dwindled, however when he was ushered into a meeting with Passy, who was interested only in military intelligence, not in politics, and with de Gaulle. He recalled the General's command:

'Tell me about France.' I stopped after half an hour, unable to continue. Then it was his turn to talk. Curiously, his speech was in no sense a reply to mine. He talked about the Free French forces, the troops in Africa which for him represent the French Resistance, about the war he was waging alongside the Allies. He was full of pride and bitterness at one and the same time, the latter because of the attitude of the Anglo-Saxons, particularly the British, who were not making things easy for him [. . .] I realise that like Passy he knows almost nothing about the Resistance. His conception of 'France' is military.[43]

Pineau's concern was to return to France with a message from de Gaulle that acknowledged the political aims of the French Resistance and its vision of a new democratic order. De Gaulle, who had a traditional right-wing background, wrote an initial draft that condemned not only the Vichy regime but also the Third Republic that had led to disaster in 1940. For Pineau this unnecessarily alienated trade unionists and politicians who had fought against fascism under the Republic. De Gaulle nevertheless added a phrase that endorsed the political priorities of the metropolitan resistance, namely that 'we wish both for a powerful renewal of the resources of the nation and the Empire through technical intervention and for the actualisation of the age-old ideal of liberty, equality and fraternity.'[44] On 18 April 1942, in a phrase that would return to haunt him, de Gaulle even declared on the BBC that 'national liberation cannot be separated from national insurrection.'[45]

Christian Pineau was not the only resister to benefit from Rémy's Thomas Cook travel agency. Jean Cavaillès, who had met Rémy at the Vallon apartment, knew Marcellin Berthelot of the Organisation Civile et Militaire (OCM) through the old-boy network of the École Normale Supérieure. Berthelot was introduced to Rémy at Brossolette's shop in April 1942. The OCM, run by former military men, industrialists and members of the academic establishment, was not particularly enamoured of de Gaulle and was far more to Rémy's taste as a partner than the socialists around Pineau. Through Berthelot, Rémy was introduced to Colonel Alfred Touny who, he said, 'might have been a bishop or a farmer-general in the seventeenth century but in our own chose to be a company director'. Touny's daily routine, walking his small dog on the tree-lined Avenue Henri Martin, was both a violation of basic rules of security and an excellent cover whereby 'no Gestapo agent would ever pay him the least attention'.[46] Rémy gave them each code names, 'Langlois' for Touny, after the street on which he lived, and 'Lavoisier' for Berthelot, in honour of his intellectual brilliance. Neither of them wanted a passage to England but Rémy acted as their mouthpiece to convey the view that while the French had buried the Third Republic and wanted renewal, they were not necessarily ready to rally to de Gaulle.

Rémy, unfortunately, was steadily becoming more of a liability than a help. His Confrérie Notre-Dame, in which security was always weak, was decimated by waves of arrests in the spring of 1942; even his two younger sisters were arrested in Paris. Rémy himself escaped from Paris to England on a fishing boat from Pont Aven, which was met by a British ship, arriving in England on 18 June 1942.[47] Meanwhile Pineau had agreed with Passy that almost as a *quid pro quo* for de Gaulle's political declaration, he would return to France and set up his own intelligence network called Phalanx, handing over the running of Libé-Nord to Louis Vallon. In the Occupied Zone Phalanx had a separate identity as Cohors, later Cohors-Asturies, which was placed under the command of Jean Cavaillès, the 'Huguenot philosopher' who always walked with books in his hand but had now turned man of action.[48] This provoked a row between Pineau and Rémy, who felt that his Confrérie had been thrown onto the scrap heap.[49]

Brossolette himself went to London on 26 April 1942, seeking like Pineau to sell the political dimension of the Resistance to London. Although they were politically opposed, Passy was immediately impressed by Brossolette's intelligence and vision: 'his mind ground and assimilated ideas at such a rate that few people were able to keep up with his stunning pace. Behind stinging comments he hid a great sensitivity, giving the impression of understanding and foreseeing everything.'[50] Soon after his arrival Brossolette drafted a report that – differing from Rémy's line – minimised the support enjoyed by Vichy and its policy of collaboration, especially in the Occupied Zone. He explained that:

In the Occupied Zone the situation is clear: 95% of people are against collaboration with Germany. This 95% are almost unanimous in despising Vichy, because Vichy preaches and practises a policy of collaboration. In the Free Zone things are made less simple by the government's actions, its press, its Legion and a general ignorance about the German occupation. One part of public opinion is behind the Marshal and accepts everything he does, even collaboration.[51]

What most French people agreed on, he argued, was that the old bourgeois political parties had been discredited by demagogy, corruption and subservience to vested interests and that governmental and administrative 'renewal' was the order of the day. This was wished for by the socialist and the communist parties that were beginning to re-emerge underground, but also by right-wing parties behind movements like the OCM. Given the depths to which France had sunk, argued Brossolette, she could not be rebuilt around an idea or a slogan. What was required was a myth, a myth that had to be embodied in a man rather than in an idea: 'France can only reconstruct itself around the "myth of de Gaulle"'[52]

Brossolette's time in London was cut short by a message that his house in Paris had been searched by the Gestapo. He returned prematurely to France early in June under the name of Commandant Bourgat to get his family to safety. He sent his wife Gilberte and two children to London in July, accompanied by Louis Vallon and André Philip, who became a key factor in developing the political message of the Free French. Brossolette was upset by the fact that Rémy had made an extravagant gesture towards his wife, sending her a bouquet worth 2,000 francs after their house was burgled.[53] He was happy to carry out instructions to salvage what he could of Rémy's Confrérie Notre-Dame and attach it to other intelligence networks. After he returned to London in September 1942 Brossolette denounced the machinations of Rémy to Passy. This pointed up the conflict over whether resistance should be primarily spying for military purposes, or articulating an emerging political and social movement. It also highlighted the rivalry of resistance leaders for the ear of London, which was becoming a precondition of their ability to impose themselves in France. Brossolette reported that:

Rémy never obeyed the orders you gave him in June. Fundamentally indisciplined as he was, he considered them invalid [...] In a recent memo Rémy clearly demonstrated that he did not understand or did not agree with the general policy of the Forces Françaises Combattantes. He violently attacked the trade unionists, resistance movements and leaders representing the French masses, political and social, to General de Gaulle. He thought that Gaullist action in France should be the work of a few agents behind which public opinion would reveal itself as if by miracle [. . .] One feels that he verges on lies, bluff and fantasy [. . .] The ill is all the more incurable because it originates in a deep megalomania and a defined will to play the role that Rémy believes to be the role of his life.[54]

The lack of security observed by resistance networks like Rémy's, the struggle for power between resistance leaders, each of whom wanted to become the most important leader in France, and a growing understanding that resistance was a spectrum of political ambitions as well as a military agenda, caused de Gaulle and the BCRA to conclude that what they needed was their own man in France to bring order out of chaos. To date they had relied on the likes of Rémy who, while hyper-active, had no sense of the wider picture, little political acumen and was a loose cannon who made many enemies. Christian Pineau and Pierre Brossolette had a wider vision but were political animals from well-defined trade-union or socialist backgrounds and they would not be able to build bridges between all resistance movements. D'Astier and Frenay were each ambitious to organise the internal resistance around their own movement and hostile to each other; what they had in common was a reluctance to subordinate themselves to London. These were precisely the people that in the view of Passy and the BCRA had to be united in a single resistance movement and brought under the ultimate leadership of de Gaulle in London. Whether they would accept that unity and that leadership, however, was yet to be seen.

The man found by London to unify the Resistance under de Gaulle was Jean Moulin. Moulin was an administrator rather than a politician, and was prefect of Eure-et-Loire at Chartres when the Germans occupied the city on 16 June 1940. Arrested by the Germans for protecting Senegalese troops accused of rape, he tried to commit suicide by cutting his throat with a shard of glass, and henceforth hid the scar under a scarf.[55] He was dedicated to the Republic and had headed the private office of the Radical-Socialist Pierre Cot under the Popular Front, at a time when sending planes to republican Spain was demanded by the Left and opposed by the Right. With too many left-wing skeletons in his bureaucratic cupboard he was dismissed as prefect by the Vichy government on 2 November 1940. He lay low in the south of France and made early contact with Frenay and François de Menthon. He crossed the Spanish frontier in September 1941 and reached London, where he met de Gaulle in Carlton Gardens on 25 October. Daniel Cordier, who was Moulin's secretary and radio operator in 1942–3, and later his biographer, says that there is no written record of the meeting but claimed that 'we know the outcome: a perfect understanding between two men who were otherwise so different, apart from the patriotic faith that inspired both of them.'[56] Discreet, cool-headed, relatively free of political attachments, Jean Moulin was just the man London was looking for to undertake its mission to draw together the various resistance movements under the authority of London. To this end he was parachuted into France during the night of 1–2 January 1942, code name 'Rex'.

'When Rex arrived in France,' asserted Passy, 'everything, or almost everything, still needed to be done [. . .] Everything had to be organised.'[57] This brutal comment said more about the disdain of the London-based secret services for resistance movements in France than about the reality on the ground. The work of unifying the Resistance had in fact begun before Moulin landed in Languedoc, although it had a long way to go and the very process of rapprochement between hitherto isolated movements threw up distrust and disagreement between highly individual leaders. For resistance leaders in France, moreover, unification was designed to increase their own strength and autonomy, and to avoid being dictated to by London. That said, they increasingly realised that leadership in France depended on being anointed by London. Only London in the end would arbitrate between Jean Moulin and one of the home-grown contenders for supremacy.

Emmanuel d'Astier was first off the blocks. With the help of a British Intelligence agent he was slipped away from Antibes on a British submarine on 17 April 1942 and reached London on 12 May. D'Astier found that he had to deal with Passy to gain access to de Gaulle and they took an instant dislike to each other, amounting almost to physical disgust. D'Astier called Passy 'colonel Bourse', no doubt because he held the purse-strings and described him as 'fair in so far as he had any hair left, a look pale and hemmed by pink, something pig-like in the texture of the flesh and hair, a nasal voice; immediate apathy'.[58] On his side Passy could neither understand nor trust the noble who played at being a revolutionary. He saw d'Astier as a 'combination of *condottiere* and Machiavelli. Tall, thin, elegant, with an aristocratic finesse. He immediately reminded me of that hateful type of "anarchists in pumps".'[59] Once he did meet de Gaulle, d'Astier – like Pineau two months before him – did not feel welcomed or understood by the man he called 'the Symbol'. He was struck by de Gaulle's rigidity, a sort of armour-plating that was a defence against his own weakness:

His most frequent gesture was to lift his forearm while keeping his elbows against his body. At the end of his arms, attached to thin wrists, his stiff and very white hands, almost like a woman's, palms upward, seem to lift a world of imagined burdens [. . .] He is tired. He wades through history as at the time of Fashoda. Even though he is at the head of only a handful of men and a few distant lands, his enemies and his pride have enlarged his size so that he talks as if he was bearing a thousand years of history.[60]

Far from being anointed as resister in chief, d'Astier was sent by de Gaulle in June 1942 on a mission to Washington to try to win over the American administration, which, so far, had seen no reason to abandon Vichy. In his absence, Henri Frenay made a bid to establish himself as the unifying figure of the metropolitan resistance. He wanted to strengthen his hand against Jean Moulin, whom he saw as a foreign agent and rival for power, and against London: 'The very idea of a Resistance movement was completely unknown to the French special services,' he later asserted.[61] Frenay had already absorbed François de Menthon's *Liberté* into *Combat* but the Pucheu affair had for the moment frozen relations with d'Astier's *Libération*.[62] In May 1942 he now met Jean-Pierre Lévy, head of Franc-Tireur, the third main resistance movement in the Free Zone. Lévy was not impressed by Frenay: 'strongly influenced by Pétainism, he agreed to meet Pucheu [. . .] Difficulties are increased by Frenay's slandering character and, dynamic as he is, he wants to become the leader of Resistance in France.'[63] To strengthen his case Frenay called a meeting in July of all the regional leaders of Combat in the château of Saliès in the Tarn, the family property of Charles d'Aragon. They came out in favour of the 'fusion' of all resistance movements, including Franc-Tireur and Libération, as a way of repelling the challenge of Jean Moulin.[64]

To strengthen his hand even more, Frenay made contact with yet another general who – he hoped – would act as an ally and counterweight to both Pétain and de Gaulle. At the end of April 1942 news spread of the dramatic escape of General Henri Giraud, who had led an offensive into the Netherlands in 1940 and been captured, from the German fortress of Koenigstein in Saxony. Giraud did not go to England but made his way back to Vichy, where he told Pétain that Germany could not now win the war. He refused Laval's demand that he give himself up again to the Germans but gave his written word as an officer to Pétain that he would not undermine Vichy's relations with the German government.[65] His château became a site of pilgrimage for resistance movements, although those committed to de Gaulle were scarcely impressed by his arrogance and reactionary politics. He told Claude Bourdet that the most important force in France was the Armistice Army: 'Yes, I know, there are the small Free French forces of General de Gaulle; naturally they are also elements in my game.'[66] Later Bourdet compared notes with François de Menthon who had also been to see Giraud and was incredulous to hear the General's views on the 'social question', saying it did not exist: 'When I was governor of Metz there were big labour movements, strikes. I had batteries of machine-guns erected at the four corners of the town and order was restored immediately.'[67] Giraud was a target for all those resistance movements who were sceptical about de Gaulle. Colonel Touny reported in July that one of the figures of the Organisation Civile et Militaire was in contact with Giraud about supporting him if he decided to renew the war against Germany, and this move was supported by Rémy.[68] Henri Frenay's strategy was to bring Giraud on board before he made an approach to de Gaulle, in order to avoid simply being absorbed by London. He wrote to Giraud on 14 August 1942 describing how he had been an enthusiast for Pétain but had seen his star wane after repeated concessions to the Axis. 'It is in the vital interest of France that you make contact with de Gaulle and make an agreement with him. If you want the prestige you enjoy to serve the French cause you may not either serve the Marshal or deny the attractive force of the symbol of de Gaulle.' However, Giraud had no interest in opening lines to de Gaulle: 'The time for decisions has not yet arrived,' he replied. 'When it does, I will take them in total independence.'[69]

In the face of these military rivals it was increasingly important for de Gaulle to be able to demonstrate to the Allies that the Resistance in France had a military potential of its own and that it was fully behind him. He had won over little of the Levant Army, the Army of Africa was beyond his reach and the Armistice Army in France was still under Vichy control. One of Jean Moulin's tasks, therefore, was to build up an Armée Secrète from the paramilitary organisations of the Resistance movements. The emphasis at its conception was on secret rather than army, for little existed in terms of armed groups outside the *groupes francs* that disrupted collaborationist meetings and premises. There was no prospect yet of cooperation with the communist Francs-Tireurs, whose random attacks on the German military were vehemently opposed by de Gaulle. The Armée Secrète was a virtual army of men who for the moment went about their daily lives and jobs but for whom weapons would be parachuted in and stockpiled and leadership provided, and who would be ready on D-Day to support Allied forces landing on French soil.

Not only did the Armée Secrète have to be formed; it also had to be brought under the orders of de Gaulle. Jean Moulin had strict instructions that the military wing of the Resistance formed by the movements' combined paramilitary groups should be entirely separate from the political leadership. Henri Frenay in particular had other ideas: he wanted to unify all the Resistance movements under his own leadership and also to take personal command of the Armée Secrète. It soon became clear that Frenay was unable to prevail over Moulin's insistence on the separation of the Armée Secrète from political leaders like himself or over other resistance movements like Libération, which did not want to endorse him as commander of that army. Frenay decided that the next best option was to offer command of the Armée Secrète to a general of his own choosing and whom he would be able to control. In August 1942 he therefore went to see Charles Delestraint, who had come out of retirement at the age of sixty in 1940 to command a tank division and had since gone back to retirement in Bourg-en-Bresse. Delestraint expressed his willingness to command the Armée Secrète on condition of receiving written orders from de Gaulle.

For Frenay a trip to London was now inescapable. He would see de Gaulle and try to persuade him to appoint himself instead of Jean Moulin or else agree to the appointment of his man Delestraint. As it happened d'Astier was also returning from Washington to London via Gibraltar and France. They were taken off the French coast at Cassis by boat on 17 September 1942. Pierre Brossolette arrived in London about the same time and soon became a power as Passy's deputy at the BCRA. Passy was not impressed by Frenay, saying that 'though he spoke in a very powerful and even doctrinal way, there was a curious incoherence about his ideas'. He and Brossolette now worked together to persuade de Gaulle of Moulin's indispensability.[70] Frenay again made a bid to lead Armée Secrète, arguing that he had 22,500 men ready to fight against d'Astier's 12,000, but d'Astier was adamant that Frenay should not have the position, so Frenay formally proposed Delestraint. Frenay and D'Astier had little in common apart from their desire to throw off the tutelage of Jean Moulin, and this is what finally brought them together. At the beginning of October d'Astier conceded if not the fusion of Libération, Combat and Franc-Tireur then the convening of a Coordination Committee on which each of the three main leaders would be represented. They returned to France by Lysander on 17 November 1942, by which time events had moved rapidly with the Allied invasion of North Africa and, in response, the German invasion of the Free Zone.[71]

By November 1942, then, links between the Free French in London and the Resistance in metropolitan France were far stronger and more consistent than they had been in 1940 and 1941. Many of the disparate resistance movements, excepting those of the communists and the extreme right, had begun to work together, if not to unite in organisational terms. That cooperation was undertaken in the first place to prevent the bid of Jean Moulin to unify and control the French Resistance. It expressed a fundamental opposition between the metropolitan resistance, which envisaged that liberation would lead to significant political reform, and the Free French, for which that resistance was only to provide help for their great military project, in order to make them a serious force in the eyes of the Allies. That, however, posed the question of how much clout de Gaulle actually had vis-à-vis the Allies. The British tended to back him, albeit with frequent bouts of frustration, but the animosity of the Americans was a major obstacle that was only just becoming clear and was a long way from being overcome. Meanwhile, while all these conflicts were continuing among the alpha males of the Resistance, the contribution of women to resistance activity was steadily taking shape.

5

Une affaire de femmes

Women were the essential links in the Resistance.
(Lucie Aubrac, 1997)

On the day of de Gaulle's appeal, 18 June 1940, Jeanne Bohec, a 21-year-old who worked as a chemical assistant at a gunpowder factory in Brest, boarded a ship bound for England with an engineer who was her 'cinema companion'. Since all foreigners were vetted she was interviewed at Anerley school in south London and placed with a host family in Dulwich. On 14 July she took the bus to Trafalgar Square to see the march-past of the small numbers of Free French, but discovered that 'unfortunately the Free French forces were not yet recruiting women'. She went regularly to the Free French headquarters in Carlton Gardens until a Corps féminin des Volontaires françaises was founded in November 1940; she joined the following January and went off to train in Bournemouth.[1]

In Paris, meanwhile, Agnès Humbert, dismissed as curator at the Musée des Arts et Traditions populaires, joined forces with a number of eminent men around Jean Cassou, together with Simone Martin-Chauffier.[2] Since men of military age had either been dispersed by the defeat or were in POW camps, it fell to women and older men to form the first resistance groups in occupied France. Despite this key role, Humbert defined herself as a 'corridor rabbit', which is 'what they called apprentices who ran errands between the workshops of fashion houses'. Since they could not use the telephone for security reasons she took orders and instructions from one location to another. When the group met to draft a new number of their underground journal,

Résistance, she explained that 'the men write and discuss. I type their articles. Naturally, I am the typist.'[3]

These two stories throw up a number of interesting questions. The *débâcle* ended the conventional war fought on French soil by regular armies. One-and-a-half million young men had been captured and other soldiers were formally demobilised and sent home to take no further part in the war. In spite of an opportunity for women to step into men's shoes and continue the fight, social conventions were still stacked up against the involvement of women outside the home. French women did not get the vote until 1945 and were excluded from formal politics. The Women's Army Auxiliary Corps (WAAC) founded in Britain in 1917 had no sister organisation in France, even in 1940. A combination of paternalism and a cult of femininity confined women to sexually differentiated roles. Women who did become involved in resistance activity often seemed to limit themselves to certain feminine roles, highlighted their use of feminine attributes in resistance, or minimised the importance of the Resistance activity they were undertaking. That said, the defeat of 1940 was a political and social as well as a military *débâcle*. Extraordinary circumstances created possibilities for extraordinary deeds. Vichy attempted to shore up the old order with its cult of Work, Family and Fatherland, but for many women resistance meant resistance not only to Germans but also to gender stereotypes. In May 1942, Marguerite Gonnet, head of Libération-Sud in the Isère, arrested and questioned by a German military court in Lyon as to why she had taken up arms, replied, 'Quite simply, colonel, because the men had dropped them.'[4]

Although the Free French were overwhelmingly a body of men, some women, like Jeanne Bohec, did manage to enlist in their ranks, if only in limited numbers and for auxiliary roles. Hélène Terré had begun the war in France in a conventional way as a Red Cross nurse and was not allowed anywhere near the front. Under the pressure of events, women were in time allowed to work in uniform nearer the action, transporting medicines and blood, proving their worth by driving on black ice 'when military vehicles could not get out'. Even when the military did make changes, however, public opinion was not yet ready to see women in uniform. Hélène Terré recalled:

the jibes to which we were subjected on the streets of Paris. We hardly dared go out in public, and when we came back from missions we quickly changed our khaki uniforms for the navy blue that the nurses wore, or else we put on civilian clothes.[5]

Reaching Britain, Terré was put in charge of the Corps des Volontaires françaises (CVF) in December 1941. Their numbers increased to 300 in June 1942 and their pay from two-thirds of what British Army auxiliaries were paid to the equivalent. On 11 November 1942 she was invited to speak on the BBC after de Gaulle and Maurice Schumann, and took the opportunity to address 'ALL French women volunteers, that is ALL French women who want victory and liberation'.[6]

Life in the CVF was still conditioned by an overwhelming sexism. Its rationale was to take pressure off the male Free French volunteers by doing auxiliary jobs so that the men could think about fighting, the prospect of which was still a long way off. The female volunteers were trained as military personnel but then worked as shorthand typists, telephonists, drivers, nurses and social workers. Tereska Szwarc, who had also come to England via Spain and Portugal with her family, joined the Corps féminin when it was set up in November 1940. She nevertheless complained that 'I joined the army with great enthusiasm but am useless because I can't take shorthand or type. Yet the only thing that counts here is being able to type.'[7] Not all the volunteers had come from France to join up; many were in England already, as students, au pairs, waitresses in cafés and restaurants and 'even, it is said, as prostitutes'. Being thrown together with a community of young women away from their families was exciting but also confusing and even distressing. Tereska imagined that their relationships would be based on a sense of solidarity and sisterhood. In the first winter she fell in love with another girl, Bela, but was rejected. She reflected that women in this peculiar world were rivalrous, spiteful and unhappy:

They envy each other, spy on each other, and get depressed [. . .] Generally speaking there are two kinds here, the women who like men and the women who like women [. . .] Some only speak about men and tell rude stories. Some, who Bela calls 'half virgins', flirt or go out with officers, almost always older than them. The 'women's women' group is more refined and vicious. Instead of getting drunk on cheap red wine they get drunk on pernod and whiskey. Instead of stealing men from each other they steal women. They see themselves as more cultivated and artistic.[8]

Things seemed to improve in the summer of 1942. The women of the CVF began to attract recognition and respect. On 18 June 1942 General de Gaulle smiled at Tereska as she brushed past him on the stairs of Carlton Gardens, and she heard him speak at the Albert Hall. On 14 July she took part in a review at Wellington Barracks and marched through the streets of London, 'amid the indescribable enthusiasm of a huge crowd. My knees were shaking with emotion, I had tears in my eyes and I was carried along by a fervour I have never experienced before.'[9] In September an article appeared in a British paper, featuring Tereska and her friend Jacqueline, both former students of the Sorbonne, both twenty-one, visiting the Fighting French exhibition at Lewis's, 'one blonde and one brunette, both wearing the smart khaki uniform of the French ATS'.[10] A year later she met a young Jewish Free French volunteer, Georges Torrès, who had fled to Brazil in 1940 with his father Henry, a celebrated left-wing lawyer detested by fascists, before coming back to fight. Exile and the dangers before them seemed to create a sudden intimacy: 'We spoke all evening about Catholicism, literature and converted Jews like my parents and Maurice Schumann as if we had known each other our whole lives.'[11]

Back in France women who became involved in resistance were more conditioned by relationships with their families than women in exile in Britain. In some cases their resistance worked with the grain of family activity. The family both made resistance seem natural and protected them from danger. Micheline Eude had fled with her family from Strasbourg when it was annexed by the Germans in 1940 and came to Lyon. Her father had been secretary-general of the Strasbourg Chamber of Commerce and became involved in Franc-Tireur with fellow Strasbourgeois Jean-Pierre Lévy. Micheline studied law at the Faculty while earning money as a typist until, in May 1942, Lévy asked Eude whether his daughter, still only eighteen, would act as his secretary for his jute business. In fact this was increasingly a cover for his resistance activity and Micheline was more liaison agent than secretary, linking resisters in Lyon and further afield. In October 1942 she was arrested but the family and resistance milieu at Lyon rallied round. Berty Albrecht told the procurator that 'a young lady from a good family' should not be kept in prison with prostitutes and she was released after three weeks.[12]

In other cases female resistance was in part inspired by the family but also challenged deeply held conventions about the role of women. Denise Domenach, who was sixteen in 1940, belonged to a bourgeois family in Lyon whose father was an enlightened engineer, but whose mother thought a girl's place was in the home, and whose grandfather was a Pétainist. Her elder brother Jean-Marie and his Faculty friend Gilbert Dru were involved with their history lecturer André Mandouze in the production and distribution of *Témoignage Chrétien*.[13] They initiated her into resistance activity delivering underground newspapers. When she finally went to the Faculty herself in October 1943 and met a young man who appeared to her 'a brave knight in pursuit of the Holy Grail', she became more fully committed to resistance activity. This provoked a good deal of tension with the family:

Mother understood that I might have a private life and left me in charge of my time. Father was anxious but tried not to show it. He was upset by a very harsh letter from grandpa which said that if Jean got himself killed it would be his own fault. Grandpa had been a captain under Pétain's orders, respected authority and would not hear the truth about what was happening.[14]

Denise graduated from distributing journals to working as a liaison agent 'before even knowing what one was'. Rather than using feminine wiles she played on her appearance as a tomboy, wearing her brother's shoes. She organised meetings for resistance groups and took supplies to the *maquis* in a rucksack, on her bicycle. In June 1944 she finally went underground with a false identity as Dominique Duplessys, but for all the tension with her family she could always call upon the knowledge and contacts of her milieu. She was tipped off by a Catholic priest that she was at risk of arrest, and her father gave her the addresses of engineer colleagues in the region with whom she could take refuge.[15]

There were of course instances where a young woman's involvement in resistance activity went entirely against family attitudes and choices and provoked a rupture with it. Jeannette Regal's father was an entrepreneur of Jewish origin in Lyon and close to Herriot's Radical-Socialist Party. He always said that he was happy to have three daughters, as they would not have to go to war. Her elder sister was going out with a medical student who belonged to the extreme-right-wing Croix de Feu but Jeannette took a very different path. Working in the offices of the Comité d'Organisation for the metal industry at Lyon, she met Maurice Lubczanski, a young Polish Jew with a 'sad look', who told her about the persecution of Jews. She distributed leaflets with him on behalf of the Front National, seriously upsetting her parents. When she and Maurice were both sacked from the Comité d'Organisation in 1942 they went underground, acquiring a duplicating machine for printing, on which they worked in the suburbs of Lyon, and survived thanks to a stipend offered by the

Communist Party. She also worked as a liaison agent in the region and often travelled to Paris; with her bourgeois dress and flawless French accent she was less conspicuous than a Polish Jew. When her father died in January 1944 Jeannette did not go to the funeral for fear of blowing her cover. 'We could not cry,' she remembered, 'we had to go on.'[16]

Resistance activity by women was not only shaped by their own families but could also bring shattered families back together. These families might be their own, starting with their own partners who had to be rescued from POW camp or prison, but they might also take the form of wider families of fellow resisters, fellow countrymen or Allies. Immediately in 1940, women were confronted by the fact that their husbands, sons or fathers had been captured during the rout of the French armies and were languishing in POW camps. For a minority, however, all was not lost. Before they were taken to Germany, POWs were kept in what were no more than barbed-wire compounds on French soil. If they were wounded and in hospital it was easier to orchestrate escapes. Pierre Hervé, who had been secretary of the communist-dominated Federal Students Union in Paris before the war and a friend of the Aubracs, managed to escape from a château near Brest, where he was being held before the mass transfer of POWs to Germany. He and his wife Annie moved to Paris, and taught in the suburbs, only to be arrested in June 1941 as suspected communists. She was soon released, but he was held awaiting trial in the cells of the Palais de Justice. Annie managed to smuggle a file into the cell and release Pierre and twenty other prisoners during the night of 7–8 July 1941. They made their way quickly to the Free Zone, where they joined up with the Aubracs. Pierre became involved in Libération and Annie worked with Georges Bidault on the *Bulletin de la France Combattante*.[17]

Two years later, when Vichy agreed to German pressure to send young men to work in Germany, many mothers sprang into action to save their sons. As a young woman during the First

World War, Mme Lamouille had wanted to engage in counter-espionage but when she was 'warned what relations she might be obliged to have with the Germans she gave up on the idea'. When her son, who worked for the SNCF at Chambéry, was 'invited' to go to work in Germany in 1942, she hid him and eight of his comrades in farms belonging to friends around Annecy. Early in 1943 she tried to get them to Switzerland but they were refused entry at the frontier, arrested by French gendarmes and sent to a camp. She urged her son to feign illness, so that he was taken to hospital. Then she simply fetched him in a taxi so that he could join the Glières *maquis* in Haute-Savoie. Having saved her son she became involved in a resistance group, spotting young men avoiding labour service as they arrived by train at Annecy or Thonon, vetting them, and sending them up to the Glières *maquis*.[18]

One of women's key roles was to shelter those on the move or on the run and to weave ties between different resistance groups. Marcelle Appleton was a middle-aged woman in poor health living at Bourg-en-Bresse near the Swiss frontier. She was nevertheless one of the prime movers of Libération in the area. Arrested by Vichy police in July 1941, she was carried out of her house on a stretcher and received a three-month suspended prison sentence and 500-franc fine for 'Gaullist propaganda'. Unintimidated, she spied for the Gallia intelligence network, brought Combat and Libé-Sud together in Bourg and worked with Captain Gastaldo, an army officer who was setting up the Resistance's Armée Secrète in the area. In 1943 she hid at various times a Canadian airman, a Polish Jewish woman and Captain Gastaldo: so developed were her networks that the Gestapo ejected her from her house in order to use it as a trap for unsuspecting resisters.[19]

Hiding resisters and servicemen on the run was often only a prelude to escorting them out of the country along 'underground' routes. Allied soldiers stranded after Dunkirk or Allied pilots shot down during bombing raids on Germany were helped by

Andrée de Jonghe, a young nurse from the Brussels suburbs who, in May–June 1940, had looked after these wounded Allied servicemen. When they were fit to leave she determined to get them out of danger in German-occupied territory and back to Britain so that they could rejoin the war effort. From June 1941 she took batches of servicemen to the Pyrenean frontier, sometimes having to swim over the Somme, which divided the so-called Forbidden Zone on the Franco-Belgian border from the main Occupied Zone. In the Pyrenees she found guides to take her charges across the mountains and negotiated with British consulates in Spain about finance and the best way to keep the fugitives out of Spanish jails. Arrested in the Pyrenees in January 1943, she was deported to Ravensbrück and was later described by one of her team as 'a woman of extraordinary physical courage'.[20]

While some resistance by women was covert, other kinds involved public protest of either a traditional or a symbolic nature. Since women took responsibility for food and were less likely than men to attract brutal repression from the authorities, they had been at the forefront of bread riots since the French Revolution.[21] Women were angry that the German army of occupation was maintained at the expense of the French, and commandeered large amounts of food and resources. The Allies imposed a blockade on occupied territories, which made products even harder to come by. Shortages were dealt with by rationing and price control, which served only to stoke a black market in which much-needed goods could be had but at much higher prices. Hardship was greatest in large cities that had no direct access to supplies of food in the countryside. Amongst the worst off were the working-class suburbs of cities such as Paris, where the Communist Party was traditionally strong. Women of a communist persuasion were particularly desperate and particularly active. Even if their partners had survived the war and POW camp, these men were likely to be pursued as traitors following the Nazi-Soviet Pact and arrested either by the Daladier government or by Vichy.

Women set up 'patriotic committees' that offered aid to hard-pressed families and whipped up popular support to pressurise the authorities to negotiate the release of POWs and increase food supplies. The leader of this activity in Paris and its red belt was Danielle Casanova, founder of the Union des Jeunes Filles de France, and one of the leaders of the underground Communist Party, closely linked with leaders of the armed struggle such as Albert Ouzoulias. Her 'general staff' included Claudine Chomat, whose father had been killed in the war before she was born in 1914, and Lise Ricol, the wife of Czechoslovak resister Artur London.[22] The committees were a major constituent of the Front National formed in May 1941 in order to build bridges between communist and non-communist activists.

Even more audacious, from the autumn of 1942, was women's public opposition to the drafting of their husbands or sons to work in Germany. A Relève scheme had been brought in by premier Laval to send workers to Germany in exchange for some POWs being allowed to return home. But the deal imposed by the Germans was for three French workers to go for every POW repatriated. This provoked a wave of strikes but women also demonstrated at railway stations in Caen and Rouen, where their men were being loaded onto trains. Most famously, 5,000 women demonstrated in the station of Montluçon on 6 January 1943. Many of them lay on the railway tracks to prevent the trains from leaving. Stories of this demonstration had a huge impact and stimulated wider opposition to forced labour in other towns and cities.[23]

Although women did not have the vote, the Republic was symbolised by the allegorical figure of Marianne, and women found manifold ways of representing her. They turned out in large numbers to mark significant anniversaries. They decked out in the national colours that caught the eye of the crowd and challenged the Germans to arrest them. A Parisian women wrote to the BBC in 1941 to declare her bravado:

On 14 July I was Marianne in a blue skirt, white trousers and red scarf and hat, and I was draped in the flag. I went from along the Champs Elysées to the Arc de Triomphe. In front of the Hôtel de Crillon a German officer, outraged by my audacity, looked me in the eye. I held his gaze and smiled ironically in spite of myself, which made him look down.[24]

In the Free Zone it was less dangerous to demonstrate, although Vichy, which had abolished the Republic, certainly did not appreciate Bastille Day. Opportunities for symbolic defiance were nevertheless taken up, and gestures by women could achieve mythic status. Aimé Pupin, a café-owner in Grenoble who was involved with Franc-Tireur, asked:

Is there a citizen of Grenoble who cannot remember that beautiful day when the whole city was in the street, either to demonstrate or to cheer on the demonstrators? You will remember the unknown young woman in a dress with tricolour bands and wearing a Phrygian bonnet who seized a tricolour flag that appeared from nowhere on the place Victor Hugo and headed the procession that was going to the prefecture. It was so beautiful. Immediately [Marin] Dantella and his crew appeared beside her to provide protection.[25]

The commemoration of the end of the First World War on 11 November was entirely forbidden in the Occupied Zone and a challenge to the Vichy authorities in the Free Zone. On 11 November 1943 a dozen boys at Béziers, whose group was called Mon-Mond, decided to answer the call of the BBC to lay a wreath at the war memorial, which happened to be in the railway station. Their leader recalled how timid they were and how they were put to shame by a schoolgirl's courage:

Time passed. Suddenly the band of budding heroes was frozen in surprise. A girl, a high-school student, satchel on her shoulder and walking in little wooden clogs, went straight up to the guarded monument and waited a moment, head lowered. The police, dumbfounded, did not move. The lads looked at each other. It was as if they had been slapped in the face. As one they got up and moved forward. The police started to get agitated. Germans surveyed the scene from the windows of the hotels they had requisitioned. Mon-Mond threw its bouquet to the foot of the monument. A few seconds followed during which the young men heard a policeman say, 'Come on, don't play the idiot.'[26]

Ultimately women stepped into men's shoes. As gaps and opportunities opened up they became involved in intelligence, propaganda, sabotage and even armed struggle. Marie-José Chombart de Lauwe was an eighteen-year-old medical student at Rennes when she became involved in intelligence activity with a group called Georges France 31, which was also working for the British. Her father, a Paris paediatrician gassed in the First War, had retired to his mother's house at Bréhat on the north Brittany coast, and Marie-José was able to use this family reason for cycling around this secure area to spy on the building of the Germans' Atlantic Wall. Unfortunately her group was betrayed to the Gestapo and she was arrested in May 1942. Tried and condemned to death she was reprieved and deported to Ravensbrück in July 1943.[27] Somewhat luckier was Marguerite Blot, the daughter of a family from Lorraine that had moved to Normandy after 1870. Living in Paris, she became involved in Rémy's Confrérie Notre-Dame through Roger Dumont, a former fighter pilot who led a famous attack on a German radar installation at Bruneval in February 1942. Through her friends from Alsace-Lorraine, Marguerite made the acquaintance of a German officer at the École militaire who was involved with railway transport, and passed information to Dumont. Since she owned a beauty salon, the Confrérie asked her to work as a beautician in the Hotel Scribe, where many German girlfriends of high-ranking *Wehrmacht* officers stayed. In this way she was able to find out about the movements of German commanders.[28]

One of the earliest forms of propaganda was the pasting of notes known as *papillons* in public places, such as on lampposts or in urinals. In this way Bertrande and Jean-Anet d'Astier, the children of General François d'Astier, mounted attacks on French collaborationists that provoked the ire of the Vichy regime. Bertrande was imprisoned in the women's wing of Nîmes prison in March 1941 and sentenced by a Vichy court in July 1941 to thirteen months in prison, while Jean-Anet got six months. The court decided to make an example and did Bertrande the credit of recognising her political acumen. Unfortunately, life in the women's wing alongside thieves, prostitutes and abortionists did little for her sense of sisterhood: 'I don't like women and until now I have only known the elite,' she wrote in her diary. 'Physically they disgust me apart from three or four who have some self-restraint. The ugliness, or rather the spectacle of ugliness, is obscene.'[29] Her prison term was halved on appeal in January 1942 but the shock of imprisonment for a woman of her class and sensibility was such that she escaped to Switzerland after her release and took no further part in resistance.

Propaganda was often undertaken in response to calls from the BBC, and not least by women, who made up two-thirds of French people who wrote to the BBC in 1940–3.[30] In March 1941, when the BBC urged people to draw 'V' signs for victory in public places, eighteen-year-old Geneviève reported that in Paris 'there are "Vs" everywhere, on trees, on benches, on paving stones. "Vive de Gaulle" remained for a long time on the Hotel Lutétia occupied by the Boches. When I meet them I sing your song under my breath, "We will clear the Boches out of Paris".'[31] The cinema public also expressed its opinion, especially during the official newsreels. In May 1941 Jeanne, a refugee from Alsace living in Toulouse, went to see *The Little Princess*, starring Shirley Temple. She explained:

The film starts with 'God save the King'. Spontaneously the public applauded for at least a quarter of an hour. They did so at the end of the film when the British Army marches past. That clearly proves that the French people regard collaboration from the point of view of honour, that is, that they remain faithful to the Allies.[32]

Resistance activity was structured, above all, through the writing, printing and distribution of underground newspapers. One of the most effective propaganda teams was grouped around the newssheet *Défense de la France*, but its operations were highly gendered. The pair who led it – Philippe Viannay and Robert Salmon – were highly educated and exercised 'a sort of intellectual royalty' in the journal, which discouraged the intellectually less confident women in the team.[33] Jacqueline Pardon, a philosophy student, nevertheless persuaded Viannay to change some passages and also recruited Geneviève de Gaulle, niece of the General, who was the only woman actually to write in the review.[34] Genia Deschamps, who had qualified as a nurse, was generally happy to leave editing the journal as a 'little boys' thing'. However, as a Jewish immigrant, she was unhappy with Viannay's enduring Pétainism, which Geneviève de Gaulle eventually managed to shake, and had a row with Salmon over an article that he wrote when he admitted that he might just as well have written one arguing the opposite position. 'He had no convictions, frankly,' said Genia. That said, men in that period could not type and the printing process was in the hands of Charlotte Nadel, a science student at the Sorbonne. She had only one hour's training from a professional printer but ascribed her compositing skills to her flair as a pianist.[35] The task of the female women of the team was to organise the enterprise behind the paper: supply, contacts, meetings. Genia Deschamps saw the paper as a way of building a resistance team and organised meetings of the steering committee: 'I took a great deal of trouble over security,' never telling people where the rendezvous was in advance, escorting them one by one from the metro. In a word, she confessed, 'I was ferocious.'[36] Défense de la France had fewer losses than many networks, but Geneviève de Gaulle was arrested in July 1943 and deported to Ravensbrück the following February.

Genia Deschamps said that her role was 'filling holes'. By this she meant 'keeping people together, supplying whatever was needed, from printer's ink to food to safe houses, to 'help[ing] victims'. Sometimes she felt that the men regarded women's role as mending socks but, she riposted, 'if I had darned the socks of everyone who was in the *maquis*, we would never have got off the start.'[37] Sewing back together the threads of resistance did not only mean reconstituting the active nuclei. It also involved dealing with the fall-out from resistance of the imprisonment, deportation and even execution of thousands of resisters. This left women and – when women were arrested – children abandoned and at risk. Resistance networks therefore developed a kind of social service that conventionally fell to women – and to the clergy – to organise.

After her release from prison, Micheline Eude's father said that she should leave Lyon and break with the Resistance. She went to Clermont-Ferrand, where she helped Alsatian refugees, but returned to Lyon at the end of 1943 to work with the social service of the Mouvements Unis de la Résistance, which federated the main non-communist resistance organisations. This involved visiting the families of resisters who had been imprisoned in Montluc, deported or executed, bringing parcels, money and encouragement, and placing children with host families. Charity might still mutate into resistance, for instance, managing to spring a pregnant resister being held under guard in hospital while other resisters blocked the switchboard.[38] Resistance organisations that were increasingly working together saw the advantage of integrating their social services, and this was realised early in 1944 in the Resistance Social Services Committee (COSOR). The key players here were Père Chaillet of *Témoignage Chrétien*, and Agnès Bidault, the sister of Georges Bidault, head of the National Council of Resistance (CNR). They also brought in Marie-Hélène Lefaucheux of OCM, who had helped her arrested brother, André Postel-Vinay, to escape in September 1942, and had then set up a charity, the Oeuvre de Sainte-Foi, to provide support for resistance fighters held in the prisons of Paris.[39] Women were key to this social work. Socialist Henri Ribière of Libé-Nord entrusted this work to Mme Alloy, who ran a nursery school in a Lille suburb, and whose husband had been arrested in July 1943. Two of her female colleagues wished to be involved in resistance 'in a more active way', such as transporting weapons, but Ribière refused their demand on religious and paternalistic grounds that 'he had cure of souls and was responsible for the safety of the two women on behalf of their absent husbands'.[40]

In fact women did become very active at the heart of front-line resistance organisations. Their most important role was as liaison agents or couriers. Because resistance networks were widely and thinly drawn, and because telephones and letters were closely monitored, orders had to be transmitted physically by couriers. They might also be called upon to ferry weapons or explosives. At railway stations passengers inevitably had to pass through checkpoints manned by French or German police, so that cycling was often a preferable option if the distances were not too great. But public transport could not be avoided altogether, and this is where young women often had an advantage. In a world where it was assumed that resistance fighters were men, women were less suspect. In the autumn of 1943, 21-year-old Andrée Monier Blachère was asked by a resister to take a suitcase of leaflets and weapons from Valence to Avignon. 'Women,' she was told, 'pass more easily, especially if they smile charmingly.' On the journey she found herself sitting next to a young German officer who smiled at her. At Avignon she saw that there was a German checkpoint: 'I noticed that my young officer was preparing to leave. A chance. I stood next to him, smiling. We got through, avoiding being searched. Phew!'[41] A few months later, in the spring of 1944, FTP fighter Joseph Rossi was on a coach from Grenoble to his home at Vif, with a map of a planned parachute drop on the Vercors in his pocket, and was shocked to find that the vehicle pulled up at a barracks on the outskirts of the city where a German checkpoint was set up: 'Seeing my embarrassment a young woman – Ginette

Martin – said to me, "Are you OK?" Not knowing what to do I could only acquiesce. "Give me the papers." They vanished into her bra and the Germans did not dare look that closely.'[42]

In communist circles, where security was extremely tight, it was not uncommon for women to act as liaison agents for their husbands. Cécile Tanguy had been her husband's 'war godmother' before they were married, writing to him when he went off to Spain with the International Brigades. When he joined the armed struggle in 1941, she acted as his liaison agent, despite the extreme risks: 'I could do no other,' she reflected, given the closeness of their relationship and the fact that in 1940 her father had been arrested and she had lost her baby.[43] When they had two more children, in 1941 and 1943, her mother helped out with the liaison work, pushing the pram with papers or explosives hidden in it while she wheeled her bicycle alongside. In May 1943 Henri was appointed to the FTP leadership in the Paris region with Joseph Epstein, and Cécile liaised between them. Interviewed just after the Liberation of Paris, Henri Tanguy, now Colonel Rol-Tanguy, with his wife next to him, told the reporter, 'Women? You must know that without them half our work would have been impossible. The only liaison agents I have had have been women [. . .] One of them did 75 kilometres in one day on a bike.'[44]

Cécile Tanguy was in her early twenties when she worked as a liaison agent; Nicole Lambert was only seventeen when she decided to follow her father into the Resistance. Originally from the countryside near Orléans, she had come to live in Paris with her father, who worked for the CGT trade union responsible for office workers, entertainment workers and hairdressers: 'I did not have much education as I left school at twelve,' she confessed, but she listened to her father's conversations with comrades about the 'fight against Hitler' and one day announced that she wanted to join it:

He became very angry and said that resistance was not child's play, that the Germans were not choirboys. He added that once I had climbed over the barricade there was no turning back. Could I coolly imagine torture and death? I reassured him (or think I did) that I would be very careful and in any case would be sliced into small pieces rather than betray one of my comrades.[45]

Nicole was introduced to one of André Tollet's assistants at the underground Paris Trade Union Federation, who taught her the security rules for a liaison agent. She had to be punctual, so that a contact would not draw attention by having to wait for her. She had to remember instructions or else write them on cigarette paper that could be swallowed. She had to lose her identity, including her ration card, and to leave home, cutting ties with what remained of her family and friends. Finally, she said, 'at the time I had a magnificent head of hair that attracted a lot of attention,' but since the first rule of resisters was not to attract attention, 'I had to get rid of it.' Having been trained, her task was to carry messages between the various underground trade unions and to maintain links with other resistance organisations. In the event, her father was arrested in September 1943. He did not talk under torture, and was later deported; she changed her role in the Resistance and carried on.[46]

Despite women's roles in dangerous activities alongside men, very often they were reluctant to talk about them in later years or minimised their importance – where men generally talked up their resistance activities, women tended to do the opposite. In 1984 Jeannette, a seventy-year-old widow who had been a liaison agent in the Black Country of the Pas-de-Calais, was interviewed and began by declaring: 'I don't have much to say.' Her husband was a POW in Germany and they had no children, so when she was asked to help by a communist friend of her husband, she said yes. She continued, 'From October 1943 I was in the FTP. I carried weapons and dynamite that miners managed to smuggle out of the pits. I covered them with lettuce and leeks that overflowed my basket.' Only once was she stopped by the Germans:

I was carrying four sticks of dynamite that were going to be used to blow up an electricity pylon. I had hidden them in large, hollowed-out beetroot and carefully put the fat end back on. I told the Germans, "It's for my rabbits". They did not ask any more questions. But I cycled off with great difficulty. My knees were numb with emotion.[47]

Why Jeannette felt that she had done so little for the Resistance is difficult to say. Perhaps she did not want to upstage her husband, who had spent the war in a POW camp, though he was now dead. Perhaps she felt that as she had only carried weapons and explosives rather than using them, her contribution was less important than that of the men who had pulled the triggers, although she risked deportation or death as much as they did. Perhaps she was just one of those resisters whose modesty was as great as their heroism.

A powerful reason for the relatively low profile of female resisters is indeed that they rarely bore arms. The sharp-end of resistance was military activity, and after the war only military activity was properly recognised as resistance. Women, as we have seen, did serve in the armed forces in auxiliary roles, but the long preparation of a second front did not bring them closer to the front line. The exception to this was that auxiliary service might also be a cover for secret activity behind enemy lines, working for SOE or the BCRA. Here the contribution of an élite minority of women was outstanding, although they were often promoted grudgingly at the time and their contribution minimised afterwards.

Preparations for the second front opened up new opportunities for women, but in other ways closed them down. After de Gaulle arrived in Algeria, in the summer of 1943, he was followed by many of the Free French in London, including the Corps des Volontaires françaises. 'A new era is beginning in Algiers,' observed Tereska Szwarc, 'almost a normal era, with a government and a large, well-equipped army on French soil.' However, this regular army was much more gendered than the clandestine army of the shadows. Tereska became engaged to Free French soldier, Georges Torrès, who left for France in 1944 with Leclerc's 2nd Armoured Division. She herself passed out as a sub-lieutenant, 'after four years of military life' but had to stay in London as a liaison officer with the American forces.[48]

In some cases the auxiliary services provided a cover for secret agents behind enemy lines, working for SOE or the BCRA. Women fluent in both French and English, who had received the appropriate paramilitary training in signalling, firearms and silent killing, were in demand to act as liaisons for SOE agents parachuted into France. Reports on their training could, however, be extremely critical of their abilities in ways that today seem quite inappropriate. Jacqueline Nearne had a French mother and English father and had been working in Nice when war broke out. Her training report said that she was:

mentally slow and not very intelligent. Has a certain amount of determination but is inclined to waver in the face of problems. A reserved personality and somewhat shy – in fact she is a very simple person. She is lacking in self-confidence, which might be entirely due to lack of experience. At present she could not be recommended.[49]

In spite of this, Nearne was parachuted into France on 25 January 1943 by SOE to act as a liaison agent to Maurice Southgate. After an initial panic she did an extremely effective job.[50] Anne-Marie Walters, who was just twenty when she signed up for SOE, received a similarly damning report but one which criticised over-confidence rather than lack of it:

She is well-educated, intelligent, quick, practical and cunning. She has a very strong character, is domineering, aggressive and self-confident. She is vain and rather conceited. She has been badly spoilt and is always 'agin the Government'. She is rather an exhibitionist and hates being ignored. She is inclined to get over-excited and is slightly hysterical. She will not hesitate always to make use of her physical attractiveness in gaining influence over men. In this respect she is likely to have a disturbing effect in any group of which she is a member.[51]

The sergeant in charge of her parachute training was even more damning. 'Immediately on landing,' he told the War Office, 'she invariably removed her protective helmet and shook her hair out, thus advertising the fact that she was a woman to everyone in sight.'[52] That did not seem to inhibit her ability, for when the report was written she had already been parachuted into France to work as a liaison agent for George Starr in Gascony.

Pearl Witherington's parents were both English but she had been at school in Paris and then employed at the Air Office of the British embassy in Paris. She failed to get to England with the embassy staff in 1940 but left Paris when British citizens were being rounded up in December 1940 and got to England via Spain and Portugal in July 1941. She worked as a civil servant in the Air Ministry till November 1942, and then joined the Women's Auxiliary Air Force (WAAF), which gave her cover to work as an SOE agent. Her training report was much more favourable. She was described as 'cool and resourceful and extremely determined [. . .] probably the best shot (male or female) we have yet had'. She was parachuted into France in September 1943 but later reflected, 'I would never have been able to use a weapon against someone in cold blood. I think that's a feminine issue. I think women are made to give life, not to take it.'[53] That said, after the arrest of her SOE boss, Pearl Witherington took command of a *maquis* group in a forest in the north of the Berry region, harassing German forces moving north, a group that was 3,500 strong by the end of July 1944.[54]

Jeanne Bohec, who was French through and through and had joined the Corps des Volontaires françaises, wanted to be more than an auxiliary and to use weapons. She did everything she could to avoid the gender stereotyping that other women suffered. As a trained chemist she worked in an explosives laboratory but was desperate to go on a mission to France. She underwent the standard British training course and her final reports noted that she was 'quite an accurate shot with the pistol', better at practical than theoretical chemistry and 'would make an excellent instructor in home-made explosives'. They also observed that 'she has some powers of leadership and could be relied upon to do any job within her powers. Her inconspicuous appearance should be an asset.'[55] With this training Bohec was finally accepted by the BCRA as a sabotage instructor to work with the FFI and parachuted into her native Brittany during the night of 29 February/1 March 1944. Almost immediately she was confronted by sexist attitudes. The agent in charge of receiving parachuted agents and equipment remarked: '"Well, now they are recruiting in the cradle!" I am indeed only 1 metre 49. But he was also surprised to be dealing with a woman. He did not know that the BCRA was sending women.'[56] She made contact with resistance chief Maurice at Questembert (Morbihan) and then visited her parents briefly in Rennes, who, although 'stupefied' to see her again after nearly four years, 'did not try to stop me, only to be of service'.[57] Having retrieved her bicycle she spent April and May instructing young freedom fighters across Brittany in the manufacture of home-made explosives and organising the sabotage of local railways. In June she took part in the *maquis* of Saint-Marcel, which inflicted heavy losses on the Germans before being forced to scatter.[58] At the beginning of August she had a khaki uniform with 'beautiful new stripes' on the sleeve, but when Allied paratroopers arrived near Quimper and she requested a machine-gun or at least a Colt she was told, 'It is not a woman's business'. The regular army turned out to be more conservative and gendered than the *maquis*: 'It prevented me from taking part in the final combats,' reflected Bohec, 'but it could not send me back to so-called "female" tasks and I remained next to the men who were fighting, although unable to fight myself.'[59]

The crisis and chaos of the final months transformed the situation of women in many ways. They reacted passionately to the arrest, deportation or death of fathers, brothers or comrades. The arrival of the Allies on French soil gave a sudden vitality to the battle-cry of 'Aux armes citoyens' and to the demand for women's suffrage, which had been promised by the Provisional Consultative Assembly convened in Algiers. Many of them suddenly felt able to break out of the gendered stereotypes that had criticised, limited or downplayed their involvement in the Resistance. They reinvented themselves as fully-fledged resisters, but with all the dangers that brought in its wake.

The father and sister of Claire Girard were involved in the Gloria intelligence network, to which Germaine Tillion belonged and, like her, were betrayed.[60] Their arrest in August 1942 was a massive blow to Germaine: 'If I explained everything I am discovering in myself,' she wrote to her brother François, 'you would be devastated. It is all there, rebellion, hatred, a terrible desire not to feel anything anymore.'[61] Her mother, who was involved with the Comète escape line, had a nervous breakdown and gave up resistance activity. Claire might have reacted in the same way but told her brother in the spring of 1944 that 'since father and our sister have gone the idea of the *patrie* has never ceased growing for us. I love my country above everything [. . .] I am ready to throw myself into political action.'[62]

The breaking point came with the arrest of François, who was involved with Défense de la France, in May 1944, at the age of eighteen. Now Claire threw caution to the winds. Hearing of the Normandy landings, she wrote, 'What wonderful news about the war. I am ready for any fight. If, dear mother, we come back together to celebrate our victory, it will have been a formidable pleasure to have been part of the effort.'[63] For Claire, resistance was necessary both to free her country and restore its glory, and to reunite her family separated by arrest and deportation. Although as a woman she felt that she had little to offer, the positive image others had of her changed her mind. The final entry in her diary noted that for the second time she had been called upon 'for important matters. Yet who am I? An ordinary young woman, that's all. But other people think you are somebody, and you must not disappoint them.'[64]

Madeleine Riffaud had resolved to join the Resistance ever since she was given a kick in the backside by a German soldier on Arras station, while ferrying her sick grandfather back home from the exodus of June 1940. She had little opportunity for this until, suffering from TB, she was sent to the sanatorium of Saint-Hilaire-du-Touvet near Grenoble, which was populated by young resisters. One of them, Marcel Gagliardi, a medical student, was also a young communist who had been briefly arrested in 1940. Leaving the sanatorium, she decided to go to Paris to study as a midwife, and joined the Communist Party because of what she had heard about heroes like Guy Môquet and Missak Manouchian. She was tested by the Party leadership and became one of three leaders of the medical students' section of the Front National. Initially she had a conventional view of women's role in the Resistance: 'they were the little fingers of the Resistance, retying the broken threads, darning the secret fabric'.[65] All this changed when she saw the *Affiche rouge*, by which the Germans announced the condemnation to death of the Manouchian group and dismissed the Resistance as the work of Jews, foreigners and criminals. She asked to join the armed struggle and was moved to the medical branch of the FTP. She learned how to attach plastic explosives to German vehicles and provided cover for her comrade Paul when he harangued the shoppers in the Librairie Gibert on the Boulevard St Michel and a German soldier drew a gun on him.

What decided her to kill a German soldier is not altogether clear. After the war the Communist Party reprimanded her for acting without authorisation in a way that discredited them, but in a 1946 interview she said that after the massacre of the villagers of Oradour-sur-Glane, carried out by the Waffen SS on 10 June 1944, communist orders were to kill German officers and soldiers.[66] In 1994 she explained that her comrade Picpus, wounded by the Germans, died in hospital at 1 p.m. on 23 July 1944 and she took up what Paul Eluard later called 'the weapons of grief' to avenge him.[67] Interviewed in 2012 she said that her gesture was designed to shake Parisians out of their passivity as the Allies approached and to help trigger a popular rising: 'I had joined the fight. We needed to impress the people of Paris with spectacular gestures [. . .] We were working on the people so that they would revolt.'[68] For reasons both public and private, Madeleine took a revolver and a bicycle on that Sunday afternoon, 23 July, and, by the Pont Solférino, spotted a German NCO gazing at the river. Casting aside all previous reservations she shot him twice in the head. Immediately she was knocked down by a car carrying French militiamen who shouted, "Terrorist! Bitch! Coward! You will pay for this!' And handed her over to the Gestapo.[69] Miraculously, she escaped execution and deportation and took part in the final stages of the liberation of Paris.[70]

Women had come a long way since 1940. They challenged many of the social and institutional obstacles that prevented them from taking part in Free French and resistance activity alongside men. They played a full part in intelligence work, propaganda, and especially as SOE agents, in sabotage. Some roles, like that of liaison agents, they fulfilled better than men because they were less likely to be stopped and searched. Other responsibilities, such as supporting the families of dead resisters, might be seen to match their social aptitudes particularly well. At the Liberation, things moved in two different directions. Women who had joined the auxiliary services of the Free French found themselves left at home as the men went to war, but women resisters on the ground in France were called upon to take the place of men as they fell. Attached to the Allied armies, Jeanne Bohec was refused permission to bear arms, but Pearl Witherington found herself at the head of a huge *maquis* group in central France, while Madeleine Riffaud's exploit was on a par with that of Pierre Georges, who had first shot a German soldier on French soil three years before.

6

In and out of the shadows

When a traitor penetrated part of the organism, like venom, his ambition was to move up the arteries to the heart.

(Germaine Tillion, 2000)

At the end of March 1941 Simone Martin-Chauffier, who had been working for the Centre of Foreign Policy studies of the Rockefeller Foundation, was waiting for Boris Vildé in a café on the place Pigalle. They both belonged to the Musée de l'Homme network. Vildé was going to collect from her a photo to use on a false identity card. He never turned up. He was arrested even before he had the chance to obtain new papers for himself and create a new identity.[1]

Simone Martin-Chauffier explains very well that to resist meant acquiring a new persona to replace the old identity of family, address and occupation, which until then had been the face one showed to the world. This new identity was the basis of a character who would play a role in a drama involving a small but exceptional cast of actors. The little group linked to the Musée de l'Homme, of which she was a member – along with former museum director Jean Cassou, former curator Agnès Humbert and the writer Claude Aveline, had given itself a literary name, 'The Friends of Alain-Fournier'. They chose this name because they met at the offices of Emile-Paul Frères, who had published Alain-Fournier's *Le Grand Meaulnes* in 1913.[2] They also chose it, no doubt, because the novel is the story of lost innocence, hidden paths and fantastic events and may have captured in some way the mysterious plot which was unfolding for them. Simone Martin-Chauffier was acutely aware, at the same time, of the risks attached

155

to what the Germans would see as spying. Her new role reminded her of the dancer, courtesan and double agent who was shot by the French as a German spy in 1917: 'Secret societies, espionage and counter-espionage require superhuman efforts, starting with lying. I asked Claude, "Do you see me as Mata Hari?"'[3]

The idea that they were entering a fictional world was commonplace among resisters. They invariably concealed their real identity behind a *nom de guerre* or pseudonym, by which they were known to their comrades. This minimised the risk of being discovered and arrested. The name taken, often inspired by a favourite fictional character, could suggest the role that they hoped to perform. Its associations said something about their ideals and illusions as they set out on an unbeaten track.

Madeleine Riffaud was still at school, aged sixteen, when she was abused by a German soldier and vowed to become involved in resistance. As a school student she identified with fictional or historical characters who seemed to articulate her ambitions. Having received 18 out of 20 for an essay on Corneille's *Le Cid* she identified with Don Rodrigo, the Cid, who liberates his country from the Moors and wins his true love. 'He seemed to us,' she said, 'a symbol of an ardent, passionate, generous youth, full of courage and heroism.'[4] Later, when she joined the communist resistance, Madeleine took the name Rainer, in homage to the Prague-born poet Rainer Maria Rilke. Rilke had lived in Paris before the First World War and was invalided out of the Austrian Army in 1916. He wrote in French as well as German and inspired the poet in Madeleine Riffaud, perhaps more than the woman of action.

Denise Domenach, the younger sister of Jean-Marie Domenach, was also at school for most of the war. When Lyon was occupied by the Germans in November 1942, she recalled, 'We each had a *nom de guerre*. At the beginning I chose Loreley, the name of the bewitching siren of German literature, taken up by Apollinaire, as a way of getting back at them.'[5] Because the

French poet had reworked the *Loreley* in 1904 the heroine was fair game for a French girl who wished to ensnare German invaders. To escape German eyes her group met in churches rather than cafés, because they were young, Catholic, and, she quipped, 'the Germans took some time to realise that you could do other things there apart from say your prayers.'[6]

Taking a name and a role helped some individuals to find an identity that pleased them and which had hitherto eluded them. Serge Asher had a Czechoslovak mother who worked in the fashion business in Paris. He had a classically élite education at the Lycée Louis-le-Grand and the École Polytechnique. That said, he confessed that between his birth father, who was Catholic, his official father who was Jewish and whose name he bore, and his stepfather, a rich Protestant Swiss, 'I lived with an identity problem.' He was also divided for a long time between loyalty to Pétain and to de Gaulle.[7] When he joined Libération in the autumn of 1942 he used the opportunity to find a Gallic-sounding name and a character that set him in the right direction. As he loved rock-climbing he took the name of a peak above Chamonix, Ravanel, that was also the name of a mountain guide, Ravanel the Red.[8]

To enter into resistance meant not only taking on a new character and new role but entering a world of shadows behind the real world. For some it seemed as though they were taking part in something unreal, a play, a novel, or a crime story. This might be a good deal more exciting than their ordinary lives, and enabled them to compensate for shortcomings and inadequacies with which they had long felt encumbered. On the other hand it was a shadowland fraught with danger and often reality struck back with brutal effect.

Jacques Lecompte-Boinet suffered from the fact that his father had gone off to war in 1914 as an officer and died a hero when Jacques was only eleven. To make matters worse, he had married a daughter of the celebrated First World War general Charles Mangin, and his brother-in-law, Colonel Diego Brosset, had joined the Free French and would become one of their great commanders.[9] How could he match them? He was short-sighted, a father of four (and soon five) children, and a civil servant. He tells the story of his engagement with resistance as an initiation into a magical new world. Invited by François Morin, who had been General Béthouart's liaison officer in 1940, to meet a contact in a café opposite the Gare Saint-Lazare, on 6 October 1941 he recalled that:

I saw a tall blonde woman appear, wearing a fur coat and very elegant under her fashionable three-cornered hat. François introduced me without giving my name. While he acted as look-out, Elisabeth asked me a few questions about my availability and timetable. Then, suddenly, she said, 'Can you ride a motorcycle and are you in good health?' Then she got up and, speaking very loudly about one thing and another, suggested that I accompany her to the Opéra. We walked through the night. Her English accent (later she would tell me that she was born to French parents in England) gave a touch of mystery to the conversation that was not disagreeable. I learned that her boss is an officer in the intelligence service.[10]

The woman was Elisabeth Dussauze, a member of the Combat network in the Occupied Zone, and her boss none other than Henri Frenay, whom he met at an elaborately choreographed encounter on 3 January 1942.[11] Lecompte-Boinet felt that he was being brought into an adventure that he could only describe in fictional terms. He spoke candidly of 'My joy to be living an adventure that was truly colourful, a joy to be involved in incidents in which I risked each moment disappearing into a hole [...] I have never been so happy as when the adventure had twists and turns and the crime story a succession of episodes.'[12]

Unfortunately disaster caught up with them soon afterwards. Lecompte-Boinet was summoned to a meeting on 4 February 1942 at a flat in the Port-Royal district, but when he rang the bell, nobody answered. He learned that almost the whole team had been arrested. Later he reflected on the theatrical elements of an adventure that lasted scarcely four months, and on what was brutally real, and how what had begun as a comedy ended as a tragedy:

When I now reconstitute this interview and the solemnity of the investiture I can see the degree of pretence Elisabeth used with me. In fact she was acting out a comedy that was a parody of an initiation into a secret society, with its rites and sacramental forms. It is also true that since we were all playing with our lives, that less than two months later all the members of the organisation had disappeared and nine-tenths of them would never return, what looked like a game concealed something that was infinitely tragic.[13]

In this game of illusion and dissimulation, newcomers were often idealistic and naïve, while others already had a good deal of experience. This was the case with communists who had been considered traitors since the Nazi-Soviet Pact in 1939. Witch-hunts succeeded each other, conducted by Daladier's Republic, by Vichy and by the Germans. Jews were also increasingly persecuted and had to choose between conforming to discriminatory legislation, registering as Jews, or going underground with a new identity.[14] Some individuals who were communist, Jewish and foreign were liable to be arrested for a host of reasons and the acquisition of a new identity to evade danger was an urgent imperative.

The young communist Albert Ouzoulias escaped from a POW camp in Austria and got home by hiding under a train that was repatriating POWs who were privileged as veterans of 1914–18. In Paris early in August 1941 he met Danielle Casanova, one of the leaders of the underground Communist Party, Pierre Georges, who had fought in the International Brigades, and André Leroy, who was in charge of the Young Communists in the Occupied Zone.[15] Leroy suggested that Ouzoulias take the name of a famous French revolutionary general, Marceau, who was a scourge of the Prussians and Austrians and was killed at the age of thirty. Young generals thrown up by the Revolution (who were not Napoleon) were attractive role models, but Ouzoulias thought Marceau 'too prestigious' for him. Instead he took the name Marc from the work of one of the greatest living French writers: 'It reminded me,' he said, 'of one of the last books I had read and re-read, *The Soul Enchanted* by Romain Rolland. The battle for peace and against fascism had dominated my life since I was seventeen [1932] and had also dominated that of Marc, who was knifed to death by Mussolini's fascist assassins in Florence.'[16]

The way in which resisters had to learn new characters, with all the details of their lives, as in a mysterious staging, was described by Nina Gourfinkel, born to Jewish parents in Odessa who fled the Russia Revolution in 1925. A friend of the Russian-Jewish writer Irène Nemirowsky and herself an authority on contemporary Russian theatre, she became involved in the rescue of persecuted Jews and was well placed to explore the theatrical analogy:

A whole new society in subdued colours was superimposed on the anxious world of the living. But the skill of the costumiers was not enough to ensure the success of this macabre fancy-dress ball. The clients also had to inhabit their new characters, know about the town where they claimed to have been born, and have a good dose of imagination and humour so as not to trip up.[17]

Another foreign Jew, who was deeply involved in the rescue of Jewish children in and around Nice, also had theatrical experience. Moussa Abadi had come to Paris from Syria to study medieval literature, and soon become an actor. The high point of his acting career was playing Jules Romains' Dr Knock for Louis Jouvet in New York. After the performance the actors were invited for a drink by Antoine de Saint-Exupéry, who was about to undertake one of his flying exploits. Abadi recalls that:

Increasingly bold, I said to him, 'Monsieur de Saint-Exupéry, can you tell me how to go about pushing oneself to the limit?' He looked at me and said, 'It is very simple. You must always try to get above the clouds.'[18]

For Abadi, getting above the clouds came to mean having the imagination to provide new identities for Jewish children threatened with arrest and deportation and hiding them with Christian families across the region.[19]

Even at the time, astute observers thought about the logic of *noms de guerre* and new identities. Gerhard Leo was a young German Jew who fled Hitler with his family in 1933 and came to Paris. Later he became involved with the underground campaign of French and German communists to encourage Germans to desert from the *Wehrmacht*.[20] He saw himself as a romantic hero from a novel, either Julien Sorel from *The Scarlet and the Black* or Pavel in Maxim Gorky's *The Mother*, a hero of the Russian Revolution of 1905. Arrested by the Germans, Leo escaped from the train taking him early in June 1944 to Paris for trial and almost certain execution when it was ambushed by *maquisards* in the Corrèze, whom he then joined. In a brief study of *maquisards* he categorised the names as follows:

1. New first names (Michel, Lucien). 2. Diminutives (Bébert, Jo, Lou). 3. An association with their trade, such as Figaro for a barber or 4. with their place of origin, such as Tarbais. 5. Names which recalled a particular event such as 'La Goupille' [the Pin] for a resistance fighter who primed a grenade when their camp was attacked and then had to hold it in his fist for forty-eight hours. 6. Names that recalled the generals of the Great French Revolution, preferably those who came from the bosom of the people, such as Kléber or Joubert.

That said, the nickname that the *maquisards* of the Corrèze gave to Leo was much more pointed: 'le Rescapé' or 'the Survivor'.[21]

In the world of the Resistance, for reasons of security, one comrade frequently did not know the real identity of someone he or she met or worked with. As in Proust's *Remembrance of Things Past*, external signs had to be read in order to fathom an identity and ascertain whether they could be trusted. Often, encountering colleagues and thinking about building alliances with them, they used literary, operatic, historical or mythical analogies in an attempt to capture a personality. One of the most widely described characters in the Resistance was Emmanuel d'Astier de la Vigerie, a founder of Libération. Some resisters thought that d'Astier, with his noble background, came from an imaginary world or a different epoch. Christian Pineau of Libération-Nord, who met d'Astier at the beginning of 1942, said that 'with his romantic aspect he seemed to come straight out of the great conspirators' scene in *The Huguenots*', the nineteenth-century opera by Meyerbeer.[22] Charles d'Aragon, an aristocratic resister like d'Astier, used heraldic and historical metaphors to describe his comrade's multifaceted and contradictory personality:

With his haughty expression he looked like both Fénelon and Teilhard de Chardin. His tall and undulating silhouette reminded one of both a serpent and a unicorn. The man who would embrace proletarian causes irresistibly conjured up heraldic comparisons. His voice suggested the sixteenth. Less the sixteenth century, in which this hero would have cut a fine figure in Florence or Milan, than the 16th *arrondissement* of Paris.[23]

Resistance activity was based on trust and could give rise to close friendship, even love. But resisters were often ambitious too and competitive for power. In the world of mirrors they inhabited this could give rise to a sort of tactical lying or bluffing. The trick was to make others believe that one was stronger and more powerful than was actually the case. D'Astier and Frenay bluffed de Gaulle in September–October 1942 about the number of men they could bring to the Armée Secrète: d'Astier claimed he had 12,000 men ready to fight, Frenay 22,500 men.[24] Since the Armée Secrète was a virtual army and not due to materialise until D-Day, these estimates were purely rhetorical. The power dimension of the rhetoric may likewise be seen in the case of Pierre de Vomécourt, the agent who had snubbed the Free French and was parachuted into France for British intelligence in May 1941. When he returned to Britain in February 1942 he tried to persuade the British they should marginalise de Gaulle and work with Michel Clemenceau, son of the 'Tiger' who had steered

France to victory in 1914–18, who was now sixty-eight years old. A draft British report on de Vomécourt, behind which one can hear his voice, said that:

He has formed his own organisation in the occupied area, and has assured a titular leadership of certain other spontaneous organisations which he is in the process of attempting to fuse. His work has been carried out through his personal contacts in political, military, religious and industrial circles. He now has some ten thousand personnel in all.

On the draft 'ten' was crossed out and 'twenty' thousand written above it, so that when Lord Selborne, Minister for Economic Warfare, wrote to Churchill making the case, he duly wrote that de Vomécourt commanded 20,000 men in the Resistance, a number that was unimaginable under existing conditions.[25]

Even by comparison with these wild claims, the most notorious bluffer was 'Carte'. The code name in itself was straight out of a thriller. His real name was André Girard, a painter who lived on the Côte d'Azur and who, as a father of four, had been excused from active service in 1939. He had, however, done his military service in 1923 when the Germans were organising underground resistance to the French occupation of the Ruhr, something he said 'gave him a head start of twenty years'.[26] More significant than his limited intelligence work, however, was his imagination. Through the film-maker Henri-Georges Clouzot he was introduced to Maurice Diamant-Berger, a novelist, script-writer and producer for theatre and radio who had gone to Cannes during the exodus. Girard asked Diamant-Berger to join him in resistance and 'this secret and derisory life', remembered the latter, 'seemed to me like a new comedy'.[27] In practical terms Girard had a link to the Armistice Army through Colonel Vautrin, who complained that de Gaulle had accorded him only the briefest of interviews when he had been in London and who was now the head of Vichy's Intelligence Bureau at nearby Grasse. Girard had been contacted by both d'Astier and Jean-Pierre Lévy and tried without success to persuade them to deal directly with the British, cutting out the middleman de Gaulle. He persuaded London to send out SOE chief Nicholas Boddington, who arrived in Cannes in August 1942, to meet him. Boddington was entertained in the Cannes Casino at a performance of *Une grande fille toute simple*, starring Madeleine Robinson, while being taken in by a more serious plot. He was completely seduced by the possibilities that Girard seemed to offer as a figure opposed to de Gaulle who had direct leverage on the Armistice Army: 'This was the most important meeting to have taken place since the Armistice,' Boddington told Diamant-Berger. 'While big disagreements were going on with de Gaulle in London, the English were convinced that they had acquired a direct and serious contact with the Armistice Army. They said to themselves, "We are going to have 100,000 men on the spot who are committed to our cause."'[28] Boddington indeed reported back to London that support for de Gaulle in France was not as great as some resistance leaders claimed and that 'the hitching of our wagon to the unique star of de Gaulle would lose us the cooperation of most of the active and virtually all the secure organisations now in existence in France'.[29] The British were in fact richly taken in. Links with the Armistice Army never materialised and that army was disbanded after the Germans occupied the Free Zone in November 1942. By then one of Carte's agents had left a list of contacts on a train and blown the whole network. The British took Carte off by plane, against his will, and after they terminated relations with him he went to New York. Diamant-Berger, ever the artist, went to London and under the name of André Gillois became a voice on the BBC's French service. He later asked himself, 'How did I not think twice about such a huge mystification?'[30]

The discovery of papers on a train points to a sharp dilemma at the heart of resistance activity. On the one hand, contacts had to be multiplied to get things done, whether collecting and sending information, escorting downed airmen or persecuted Jews, or distributing leaflets and underground newspapers. At the same time it was imperative to be wary of new contacts. Some might simply be careless and make a mistake that exposed the network. Others might be more than efficient but behind a plausible identity and story turn out to be double agents or traitors: 'We recruited too much to live long,' reflected Germaine Tillion of the Musée de l'Homme network. 'When a traitor penetrated part of the organism, like venom, his ambition was to move up the arteries to the heart. This was only too easy to do and when it happened there was one network less and a few more deaths.'[31]

The traitor who did for Germaine Tillion herself was a priest of Luxemburg origin called Robert Alesch. After the collapse of the Musée de l'Homme network, she started to work for a British intelligence network called Gallia. One of its agents, Philippe de Vomécourt, the older brother of Pierre, had been arrested and imprisoned in Fresnes. She made contact with Robert Alesch, who knew a German captain on duty at Fresnes who might be worked on, since he was engaged to a French woman. Gallia offered a large sum to get de Vomécourt out. Unfortunately, Alesch dreamed of climbing the Luxemburg ecclesiastical hierarchy, which answered to the Archbishop of Cologne, and was already working for the Germans. On 13 August 1942 Tillion had a rendezvous with Alesch at the Gare de Lyon, from which he was catching a train. As he passed through the barrier she heard a voice at her shoulder: 'German police. Please follow us.' A year later she was deported to Ravensbrück with her aged mother, who was also arrested.

Meanwhile Pierre de Vomécourt was also in trouble with a double agent, this time a woman. In May 1941 he had landed on his brother's estate in the Limousin with a radio operator who would send messages back to Britain.[32] Late in 1941, however, the radio operator was arrested and contact with London was lost. De Vomécourt was then put in touch with a Franco-Polish intelligence network, Interallié, whose French agent, Mme Carré, went under the name of Micheline or 'La Chatte'. To test her lines of communication, de Vomécourt gave her a telegram to transmit to the War Office, which was acknowledged by the BBC two days later. What he did not know was that both the Polish agent, Armand, and Mme Carré, had been arrested by the Germans in November 1941 and that Mme Carré had been interrogated by Hugo Bleicher of the *Abwehr*, the German Army's intelligence service. He had said to her:

You and I will work together and if you play no tricks you can be assured that you will be at liberty this evening. If you double-cross me you will be shot immediately without trial. Save your own skin, Madame, and get it into your head that England is doomed. Work for 6,000 francs a month.[33]

When de Vomécourt became suspicious of Carré he considered killing her, but instead persuaded her to return to England with him. Bleicher let her go, on the understanding that when de Vomécourt returned to France he would convene a meeting of resisters who would all be arrested, while de Vomécourt trusted that the British Intelligence Service would be able to discover all Mme Carré's contacts. De Vomécourt and Mme Carré got off the French coast to England on 26–27 February 1942, and Carré was promptly arrested. She spent the rest of the war in prison in Aylesbury and Holloway before being returned to France for trial. De Vomécourt returned to France in April 1942 but was regarded by the British as a marked man who could compromise the whole of his organisation. He complained to London of a litany of cancelled drops, missed targets and agents with defective ID, before he was himself arrested in April 1942.[34]

A third story of treachery is that of Roland Farjon, who illustrates the narrow divide between heroism and villainy. Farjon belonged to a leading industrial family of Boulogne-sur-Mer, which built its wealth on making pencils, rubber and other equipment for schoolchildren. His father, Roger Farjon, was deputy and later senator of the Pas-de-Calais and had voted full powers to Marshal Pétain on 10 July 1940. Roland himself had wanted to enrol in the army but was obliged to join the family business. Politically he was shaped by the right-wing riots of 6 February 1934 when, aged twenty-four, he had battled with the youth wing of the Croix de Feu. Fighting on the Maginot Line in 1940 he was captured by the Germans and spent a year in an officers' POW camp before string-pulling in high places got him out and into a job in Vichy's Education Ministry.[35] At the same time he joined the Organisation Civile et Militaire, which recruited in military and industrial circles, and to his superiors he was an active and successful agent. He was, however, arrested by the Germans in October 1943. Realising that they knew everything about his organisation, he decided to avoid the pain of torture and to work with them. When other resisters were arrested he spoke to them in prison, learned their secrets and tried to persuade them to cooperate with the Germans. Many of them confessed, were deported or executed. During the night of 9–10 June 1944, with a file that was passed to him by a German, he escaped from Senlis prison. It is not clear whether this was a reward for good service. In any case he tried to cover his tracks by reinventing himself as a resister at the high point of the liberation of France.

The fact that Farjon had 'talked' broke the golden rule that resisters who were arrested should never talk, even under torture. If it was impossible not to say anything, the advice was to deny everything, to make up stories, to lie. At the very least it was crucial to 'hold on' for forty-eight hours to give comrades time to warn others, to burn papers, to evacuate hiding places and to escape. After Pierre de Vomécourt was arrested he was interrogated, like Mathilde Carré, by Hugo Bleicher. He was told that he and a comrade, who was arrested with him, would be treated as POWs rather than spies if they revealed everything about his organisation. In other words they would be sent to a

POW camp, not shot. De Vomécourt decided to blame everything on himself and his comrade, on the grounds that they were already captured, on another man who he knew had just died in hospital, and on a fourth man he knew the Germans would never reach. After two weeks' questioning he was duly handed over to the *Wehrmacht* and court-martialled in December 1942. Proceedings were suspended while Berlin was asked whether he was indeed to be treated as a POW and he was deported not to a concentration camp but to *Stalag* V-A near Stuttgart.[36]

A similar tactic was adopted by the communist resister Pierre Georges, who was commanding an armed FTP group, twenty-five or thirty strong, undertaking sabotage in the Besançon-Belfort area of eastern France. He was arrested in Paris on 2 November 1942, wounding a police officer while trying to escape. Interrogated and tortured by Vichy's anti-terrorist Brigade Spécial, he only gave up the names of comrades who were dead, or who he knew to be out of reach of the Germans in England or the Free Zone. 'He gave away no names,' said his daughter, 'only pseudonyms, that were often made up. When he mentioned "true" pseudonyms these had no relation to the people who actually used them.'[37] His wife Andrée was nevertheless arrested after him and in March 1943 they were both imprisoned in Fort Romainville, east of Paris, from which his elder sister and Danielle Casanova had been deported to Auschwitz the previous January.

Arrest was often the beginning of the end for resisters, but not always. Theatrical abilities might come into play even at this point. One ruse was to fake illness, be transferred to a hospital, which was less secure than prison, so that escape could be organised from there. Another ruse with the same effect was to fake madness. André Postel-Vinay, Inspecteur des Finances and a member of the Organisation Civile et Militaire, was arrested in December 1941. He had a good deal of intelligence about *Luftwaffe* airfields and German battleship movements and was worried that he would not be able to resist torture. Imprisoned in La Santé, he tried to commit suicide by throwing himself off a second-floor walkway but succeeded only in injuring his back. His sister-in-law, Marie-Hélène Lefaucheux, sent a friend with a message about feigning madness. This he did by jerking and gesticulating during exercises, and he was taken to the Saint-Anne asylum in September 1942. The psychiatrist told him, 'Monsieur, I will now tell you what I think. You have played your role very well, but you are not mad.'[38] He then left him by the lift, saying that he was going to call an ambulance, leaving Postel-Vinay to escape and beg a metro ticket at Glacière station. Berty Albrecht tried a similar trick following her arrest by the Vichy police in April 1942. Sentenced to six months in prison in October 1942 she was taken to the Saint-Joseph women's prison in Lyon. There she feigned madness, screaming, tearing her clothes and calling for her daughter. She was duly transferred to the lunatic asylum at Bron outside Lyon, from where she was rescued by a *groupe franc* of resisters during the night of 23 December. Unfortunately for her she was re-arrested by the Gestapo the following May and transferred to Fresnes prison in Paris. There, fearing the worst, she hanged herself on the night of 30 May 1942.[39]

It was not impossible to spring detained resisters from prison itself, but this required a good deal of cunning and invention. Lucie Aubrac managed to free her husband from prison not once but twice in 1943. He was arrested in March 1943 and pretended initially that he was a black marketeer named Vallet. Lucie went to see the Vichy procurator general in charge of his case and told him: 'This Vallet is in fact an envoy of General de Gaulle. If you do not free him tomorrow you will not see sunset.'[40] The Vichy lawyer duly complied. Raymond was arrested a second time on 21 June 1943, confined in Montluc prison and sentenced to death. Lucie went to see the SS colonel in charge of the affair with brandy and cigars. She was pregnant and pleaded that she be allowed to avoid the shame of unmarried motherhood and illegitimacy by a 'marriage *in extremis*' with the condemned man. To make herself more stately and influential she took the name of Guillaine de Barbentane, the daughter of the château-owner where her father, suffering amnesia after the 1914 war, had worked as a gardener. Guillaine had bullied her when she was a child but now she overcame the intimidation she had once felt and persuaded the SS colonel to permit a meeting with Raymond. This allowed her to give him a message warning him that an attempt would be made to release Montluc prisoners who were transported daily in a police wagon from the prison to Gestapo headquarters for interrogation. The police wagon was duly attacked by a *groupe franc* masterminded by Lucie Aubrac on 21 October 1943 and Raymond was freed.[41]

After major setbacks it was necessary to reorganise the network and move on. Lessons had to be learned about tightening rules of security. Jacques Lecompte-Boinet learned fast about questions of security after the arrests of February 1942. First each leader found a double who would automatically replace him or her if they were arrested. Next, they established a rendezvous, which might be a café or railway station hall, a password and a sign, such as wearing a red tie and carrying a copy of Charles Péguy's *Joan of Arc*. In case of emergency a private letter box was designated, in which a message would give only the date and time of the meeting, the place being known already. Lecompte-Boinet himself kept a list of names, addresses and meeting-places which, having just fathered his fifth child, were kept in a baby's bottle buried in his back garden. The only other person who knew the cache was his own double, Henri Ingrand.[42] The communist Pierre Georges managed to escape from Fort Romainville with a comrade on 1 June 1943. He found his way back to the east of France, where he continued to build up FTP activity in Lorraine and Franche-Comté. His *nom de guerre* was Captain Camille and he was sometimes sheltered by Abbé Maley, *curé* of the village of Magny-Vernois (Haute-Saône). The good *curé* lent Pierre a cassock, a prayerbook, a rosary and an unlikely new identity as a priest, Paul-Louis Grandjean, which allowed him to go about his business unmolested.[43]

This kind of disappearing trick – to abandon their former life and vanish into the shadows – is what resisters called 'embracing *clandestinité*'. Until July 1943 Genia Deschamps had continued work under her own name as a nurse at the Beaujon prison and Port-Royal hospital. She was the only one in her family to have a salary because the Statuts des Juifs prevented her parents from working. Then came a number of arrests and she escaped from a police trap. She left her job and changed her appearance, dyeing her hair, wearing earrings and a flowery dress that she had never worn before. Later she wore clothes that were more sporty. She also acquired false papers and a new identity. At the very least, if she were arrested, her parents would not be in danger.[44] Lucie Aubrac herself worked as a *lycée* teacher in Lyon under her real name, Lucie Bernard, until the academic year 1942–3. Frequently absent on resistance activity she was recorded as on sick leave in January–May, May–June and October–November 1943. She was formally suspended from her post on 18 November 1943 but the paperwork was not completed until 24 February 1944. Her cover therefore lasted until she flew out of the country with Raymond on 8–9 February and gave birth to her daughter Catherine in London on 12 February. Even the baby was given a *nom de guerre* as a second name: Mitraillette.[45]

For some resisters, in the early phase, an assumed name was enough. But to be fully operable, a new name had to be supported by proper documentation: an identity card, a ration book, or demobilisation papers that all told the same story right from date and place of birth. This paperwork was developed to a high degree for agents parachuted into France by SOE to work with French resisters. They tended to have a hybrid Franco-British background, with at least one French parent or a French upbringing, to ensure British loyalty but French identity. They were given a 'cover story' that detailed their whole CV, which they had to learn by heart in case they were interrogated. The best parents to have were dead, especially a father who had been killed in the First World War, since they could not be questioned. The best place to have been born was a location where the archives had been destroyed by bombing or was out of German or Vichy reach, such as North Africa after November 1942. The best occupation to claim was one that justified travelling around, from one zone to another, by day or night, preferably with an official function of some kind.

Philippe de Vomécourt, the elder brother of Pierre, was genuinely French but educated in Britain. He adopted a number of false identities. Through a cousin he secured the papers of a railway inspector with the task of inspecting goods trains, checking they were not overloaded or running behind schedule. He also pretended to be a commercial representative of a firm in Limoges that was well known to him, and he used an aristocratic name, de Courcelles, because it was likely to impress the French police. His last disguise was that of a gamekeeper. In London he visited a makeup artist and was kitted out with steel-rimmed glasses and a false moustache, which he kept in a secret pocket of his wallet. Once, tipped off by a boy that the police were looking for a man answering his description, he 'immediately changed into his gamekeeper's disguise and walked through the cordon surrounding the town'.[46]

Less convincing at first sight was SOE agent Harry Rée. He had no French background but was born in Manchester to a Danish-Jewish father whose business had been in Hamburg. Educated at Shrewsbury School and Cambridge, he was a modern language teacher at Beckenham County School when war broke out. His trainers at SOE described him as 'highly strung and nervy', worried about his 'school standard' French, and this indeed gave cause for concern when he was dropped into France in April 1943.[47] His cover was initially as a seminarist in Paris, but he realised this gave little reason for travelling far from the capital. Active on the Swiss border, where watchmaking was a key industry, he reinvented himself as a watchmaker, first as an Alsatian named Keller and then – after discovering that the police were looking for someone of that name – as André Blied, after a 'well-known watch-making family in Besançon'.[48] Another SOE agent, Richard Heslop, pretended to be a jeweller's representative and was trained by a precious stones merchant in the City of London: 'I was taught to handle tongs, a magnifying glass or "loupe", a weighing balance, in the correct way, how to open and fold a parcel of gems. I had to learn some of the jargon too, like the meaning of "Silver cape" when referring to the colour of a diamond. And in my head were the latest prices of diamonds and pearls in various continental countries.' The severest test he was put to was when an old woman asked him to offer a better price for a brooch than a certain jeweller had offered. Without knowing the original price, he suggested 8,000 francs, 500 francs more than what she had been told, and she was delighted to have been proved right.[49]

Similar inventions were perfected by female as well as male agents. Pearl Witherington's parents were both English but she went to school in France and in 1940 was working at the British embassy in Paris. Parachuted into France in 1943, she was given the name Geneviève Touzalin and posed as a cosmetics representative. She chose this profession because her fiancé's father owned a beauty salon in the rue du Faubourg Saint-Honoré in Paris. She was once pressed on why she never herself wore makeup, but her second string was that she 'looked German, especially as I did my hair in the German style, in a plait round my head'.[50] Anne-Marie Walters, who had a French mother and English father who lived in Oxford, was parachuted into Gascony for SOE with the story that she was a student in Paris who had been unable to continue her studies there and had sought refuge with a farmer who was a friend of her father's from the last war: 'That story took very well,' she later said. 'It was very simple and

FIGHTERS IN THE SHADOWS

normal and everyone around the farm believed it. I should think they still do till this day.' She added:

One had to be careful to be always in harmony with one's surroundings. Sometimes I was in a farm, sometimes a small shop, and sometimes at the home of smart people. My family might not have recognised me had they seen me sitting in a third-class carriage with a beret tipped low over my forehead, wearing an old raincoat and generally looking half-witted while eating a chunk of bread and sausages. Or trying to look like a Toulousaine with my hair piled high on top of my head, long earrings and short skirts. My favourite clothes however were the sabots and the large blue apron I wore on the farm, while I helped to feed the chickens or lead cows to the fields, in the five months before D-Day.[51]

Anne-Marie Walters was the liaison agent of SOE agent George Reginald Starr. With experience as a mining engineer in Belgium but now living in a small Gascon village he passed himself off initially as a Lille engineer who, unwilling to work for the Germans, had come as a refugee. Then the local mayor found him a job as an inspector for the Ravitaillement department, in charge of food supply and the war on the black market. Not only did this give him a car and a reason to travel round the region at any time of the day or night, but he had instructions signed by the minister himself, requesting that all French and German authorities give him every assistance.[52]

When the cover story was not adhered to things could go disastrously wrong. Colonel Pierre Marchal was parachuted into France in September 1943 as a military delegate who was supposed to bring armed resistance groups under the control of London. His cover story was that his father had been killed in the 1914 war and his mother had died in 1930. He had worked for oil companies in Poland and North Africa, for which he was now on business in Paris. He had been issued in London with '1 moustache, 1 pair of spectacles, 1 stick of grease paint, 1 brush, 1 bottle of spirit gum and 1 bottle of methylated spirits' to make up his disguise.[53] Unfortunately, arriving in Paris, he decided to use a code name of his own choosing, 'Moreau'. This was the manager of a real firm and the name was known to the Gestapo. Marchal's arrest on 22 September 1943 led to the round-up of many others in what was called the rue de la Pompe affair.[54]

Most of the work undertaken by resisters was in the shadows. On some occasions, however, they chose to dramatise their activity, to demonstrate to the French public (as well as people abroad) that the Resistance existed and was active. This was designed to raise morale among those smarting under the German occupation, to send a message to the Free French about their resistance credentials, and to warn the Germans that they could not rule France with impunity. Some of these spectacular gestures were violent; these were favoured by the communists. The assassination of German officers in Paris, Nantes or Lille was intended by communists to avenge comrades captured and executed by the Germans, and to demonstrate that after the invasion of the Soviet Union a second front had now opened up behind German lines. Unfortunately, these coups resulted in the Germans exacting collective reprisals, not only against communists but against victims drawn from the wider population.

The deaths of communists gave rise very quickly to a cult of martyrs, which served the growing legend of communist heroism and self-sacrifice. Wreaths were laid in the Châteaubriant quarry where twenty-seven communists had been shot, every October from the first anniversary in 1942. Communist Francs-Tireurs arrested in Paris were summarily shot by the Germans either at Mont Valérien, to the west of the city, or at the Fortress of Vincennes to the east. Many of the bodies were buried in the cemetery of Ivry, in the red belt to the south of the city where, early one February morning in 1942, Renée Quatremaire noticed German lorries arriving, 'full of bodies freshly killed, blood dripping into the street' as they waited for the cemetery gates to open. She described how local women began spontaneously but cautiously to instigate a cult of resistance martyrs:

From that day we began to put flowers on the martyrs' graves [. . .] Women came into the cemetery with little bunches of flowers in their shopping bags and placed them on the bare earth. The Nazis noticed this and began to come unannounced to try to find out who was putting flowers on the graves of so-called 'terrorist bandits'. But among the caretakers we had friends in the Resistance and when the Germans arrived they rang the bell as if for a funeral. At that signal we scattered.[55]

The spectacular coups undertaken by communists served their own cause but rarely won over a wider public. The cost in German repression and reprisals, often against innocent civilians, was simply too great. Different means were found by other resistance organisations to dramatise their presence and carry a message that carried less risk for the population. These aimed to link up with or stimulate forms of resistance activity that were spontaneous, sporadic and symbolic, and might win over at least some of the general population to their cause.

In Lyon, Franc-Tireur was a force behind powerful demonstrations of opinion around traditional moments of commemoration, whether 1 May, Joan of Arc Day, 14 July or 11 November. These demonstrations were mainly spontaneous, as the crowds came out almost by force of habit, but the situation was now more risky, although some leafleting and organisation had taken place. The 1 May 1942 demonstration was silent and passed off without incident, not least because the Vichy police held back. On 14 July things were rather different. Two days earlier there had been an investiture parade of the Service d'Ordre Légionnaire, the tough men of the Légion, who were selected to form an élite paramilitary body that foreshadowed the brutal, counter-insurgent *Milice*. The Vichy police were won over to the new mood and officers on horseback drove back crowds trying to gain access to the place Carnot, where the statue of the Republic stood. This time too, the public was more lively and vocal. Antoine Pinton of Franc-Tireur recalled:

The crowd was densest south of the place Bellecour and the rue Victor Hugo. People sang the 'Marseillaise' and booed Laval. There was in fact a family atmosphere. Lots of children, women (who were more animated than the men) and old people. I came across two little girls with their mother wearing tricolour ribbons in their hair. In the evening the more sedate people went home, but many groups of young people coursed through the streets, singing the 'Marseillaise'.[56]

To demonstrate in the Occupied Zone was of course more dangerous and resistance groups had to be more inventive in how they reached out to the population. On 14 July 1943, the Paris-based group Défense de la France organised a big stunt to assert its strength and galvanise opinion. Its 'Operation Métro' mobilised fifty leafleters in groups of four, protected by two security personnel. They scattered leaflets in metro carriages, alighting at the next metro station and disappearing into the crowd. At street level they took advantage of the holiday crowds relaxing and drinking in the sun: 'There were various operations,' boasted their leader Philippe Viannay, 'of which the most spectacular was a front-wheel drive cabriolet moving slowly up the Champs-Élysées delivering fistfuls of the paper from the running-board to café terraces.'[57]

One of the most striking spectacular incidents took place in the small town of Bourg-en-Bresse in the foothills of the Alps. During the war, on German orders, bronze statues were dismantled and melted down for military needs. Nothing remained but empty plinths. Similarly, busts of Marianne, symbol of the Republic, that graced the council room of every town hall, were removed by order of Vichy. The most famous son of Bourg-en-Bresse was Edgar Quinet, professor at the Collège de France and a great republican who was persecuted under the Second Empire. To mark 11 November 1943, the local leader of a *groupe franc* had the idea of placing a bust of Marianne on Quinet's empty plinth, together with a flag bearing the cross of Lorraine and a painted slogan: 'Vive la IVe [Republique]', and taking a photograph to be reproduced as propaganda, and sold to raise money for the Resistance. At first light on 11 November the bust, flag and slogan were in place and a picture taken by Roger Lefèvre, a member of a *corps franc* who was also a local primary school teacher. The light was poor and the pictures were grey, so a more dramatic mock-up was created by a local photographer. Unfortunately the good citizens of Bourg did not wish to draw attention to themselves by buying the photo, so the stunt passed into legend as a tale of daring, rather than as a material success.[58]

The dramatic, theatrical dimension of resistance was a way of dealing with intractably difficult reality. Fictional accounts of the Resistance emerged even as they were happening. The most famous was the work of a journalist turned novelist. Joseph Kessel was a Russian Jew, born in Argentina in 1898 on one of the Jewish settlements financed by the German-Jewish speculator and philanthropist Baron Maurice Hirsch. He grew up in France from the age of ten, became a reporter in 1915, and joined the army in 1916. After the First World War he became a successful journalist working in the Middle East, Far East and East Africa, and was a war correspondent in 1940. In January 1943 he got to England, and after interrogation at the Patriotic School joined the Free French. He was asked by de Gaulle personally to write a book about the Resistance. *L'Armée des Ombres* was published in Algiers in November 1943 and in New York in March 1944. It followed the movements of a group of resisters around Philippe Gerbier, who had escaped from an internment camp, arguing that 'the national hero is the man underground, the outlaw'. Curiously but understandably, Kessel claimed that the book was not fiction at all: 'No detail has been forced or invented. You will only find authentic, checked, tested facts. Everyday facts of French life.'[59] Some details were based on conversations Kessel had in London with resisters who were passing through, and the book brilliantly captures the secret world of intelligence gathering, escape lines, underground presses and ambushes in the 'prison' that was

France. The main truth, however, is the verisimilitude of the moral drama of the Resistance, the tension between appearance and reality, trust and treachery, and the absence of laws apart from those dictated by circumstance. It begins with the execution of a male informer by resisters disguised as French police, and ends with the execution of a female resister who appears as a tireless propagandist, liaison agent, and mastermind of escapes, and was based in part at least on Lucie Aubrac.[60] Kessel invents a weak spot, which of course many resisters had, for she is a mother of six and carries a photograph of one of her children. When she is finally arrested by the Gestapo and the photo discovered, she talks rather than see her daughter placed in a Polish brothel for the use of soldiers returning from the Eastern Front. On her release, her execution by the Resistance is portrayed as inevitable and banal. The fiction was only a thin veil over a brutal reality. As Philippe Gerbier reflects, 'Today it is almost always death, death, death. And on our side we kill, kill, kill.'[61]

7

God's Underground

The CIMADE had organised what was called an 'underground railway' at the time of American Slavery, to get Jews over the Swiss frontier.

(André Trocmé, 1966)

In May 1940 Madeleine Barot was working as librarian and archivist in the French School of Rome. She had graduated from the Sorbonne and the prestigious École des Chartes, and had been appointed by the School's director, Jérôme Carcopino, eminent ancient historian and author of *Daily Life in Ancient Rome*. Barot, however, was not only shaped by the Ancient World. Her family, on her mother's side, had left Alsace in 1870 when it was occupied by Germany. Her great-grandfather, who had been mayor and deputy of Strasbourg, had walked out of the French National Assembly in 1871 when it voted to surrender Alsace to the German Reich. This was a decisive act of patriotism by one who refused to live under German rule. On her father's side she was a Protestant and identified strongly with the persecution of Protestants in the Ancien Regime. Her Sorbonne dissertation was on the 1787 edict of tolerance for Protestants which heralded their full emancipation in the French Revolution. Her Protestant faith was real and she was deeply involved in the Student Christian Union and Young Women's Christian Association (YWCA).

All this was put to the test when Italy declared war on France on 10 June 1940. Barot and Carcopino returned to France but whereas he became Vichy's Education Minister, she became general secretary of the Inter-movement Committee for Evacuees (CIMADE). Her first task was to look after refugees from Alsace and Moselle (again annexed by Germany) who now fled to the Free Zone. She then became concerned by the fate of German anti-Nazi refugees, interned by the French as enemy aliens but required, under the terms of the armistice, to be handed back to the Nazis. She went to the French internment camp at Gurs on the Franco-Spanish border, where she found 15,000 Germans, Poles, Jews, the stateless, communists, anarchists and prostitutes all piled together. Until this point her horizon had been largely limited to fellow Alsatians and fellow Protestants. This was suddenly widened by the arrival at Gurs on 23 October 1940 of twenty cattle trucks crammed full of 7,000 German Jews, who were surplus to requirement in Nazi Germany, mainly from the Palatinate and Baden. She watched, horrified, as pregnant women, children, old people and the mentally ill were disgorged from the trucks into the camps. From now on the question of saving persecuted Jews became part of her mission.[1]

Madeleine Barot had returned from Rome to a France reeling under the impact of defeat, occupation and amputation. But war was not only a national experience: it was a European war that visited the exile and suffering of peoples from elsewhere on the French. When war broke out in September 1939 much of the population of Alsace and Lorraine – Catholics, Protestants and Jews – was evacuated in a relatively organised way ahead of an expected German invasion to makeshift camps in the Limousin and Dordogne.[2] Invasion did not in fact happen during what became known as the *drôle de guerre*, the Phoney War, and gradually the evacuees were sent home. The German offensive in the West finally came in May–June 1940, pushing ahead of it a wave of hundreds of thousands of refugees, including German and Austrian Jews who had taken refuge in the Netherlands and Belgium, together with Dutch, Belgians and French, Jews and non-Jews. All flooded south across the Loire and away from the advancing Germans, enduring attacks from the air and fearing the worst atrocities.[3] Gradually, after the armistice, many of those people returned home but the

Germans filtered them at the demarcation line between the Free and Occupied Zones and refused to let through Jews and other undesirable elements. Nazi policy during this period was to build a strong, healthy and homogenous racial state. National and racial minorities that did not conform to the model were ruthlessly expelled from the Reich.[4] Those in annexed Alsace and Moselle who refused to Germanise and Nazify, or were regarded unfit to do so, were driven into France. This eviction included the substantial Jewish population of cities such as Strasbourg, Nancy and Metz. In October 1940 they were joined by trainloads of unwanted Jews from the Palatinate and Baden, gathered from maternity wards, old people's homes and asylums, and loaded into cattle trucks bound for France. These Jewish expellees were interned by the French in camps both in the Occupied Zone and in the Free Zone, along the Spanish border, at Gurs, Agde, Argelès and Rivesaltes. Safe for the moment, they were immediately at risk when, in 1941, Nazi policy towards Jews switched from one of expulsion to one of round-up, deportation and extermination.[5]

While a large part of the French population was caught up in the evacuation of 1939 and the exodus of 1940, internment was for foreign refugees and in particular foreign Jews. Most French people were happy to see allegedly insidious elements removed from circulation and interned so that the work of national recovery and regeneration could begin. Foreign Jews were too often variously seen as cosmopolitans and decadents, warmongers and defeatists, capitalists and Bolsheviks. While many activists and agencies, both official and voluntary, were involved in dealing with civilian populations affected by evacuation and exodus, only a small number of activists were motivated to find out what was going on in the internment camps, to seek to improve conditions and to remove to safety vulnerable individuals, such as children and the sick.

Some of those who took a stand and went into action did so for religious reasons: they were Jewish themselves, often from Alsace, or were Christians, both Catholic and Protestant, motivated by a humanitarian desire to help their fellow men. The challenges they faced induced a degree of ecumenism, of working together across faiths. This did not mean that all Catholics, Protestants or even Jews became involved. The Christian Churches had an ambivalent attitude to the Vichy regime, and were prepared to support it in so far as it upheld morality and social order and opposed communism and atheism. Cardinal Gerlier, Archbishop of Lyon, famously said in 1940 that 'France is Pétain and Pétain is France.'[6] Even French Jews agreed to set up a Union Générale des Israélites de France (UGIF), which would negotiate with the German occupation regime in order to protect Jewry as much as they could.[7] The Secours National, which had been set up in 1914 to help civilian populations impacted by the war, was resurrected in 1939 and perpetuated by Vichy. It was, however, more concerned with POWs and their families, evacuation and the wellbeing of the French under occupation than by the refugees.[8] More significant was the Oeuvre de Secours aux Enfants (OSE), which had been founded in 1912 to deal with child victims of the pogroms in the Russian Pale of Settlement. It moved its headquarters to Berlin in 1923 and thence to Paris, and was internationally focussed on the tribulations of Jewish children. Women were very often at the forefront of the work of relief and rescue. They were deeply committed in terms of their faith, whether Catholic, Protestant or Jewish. They often worked for charities on a voluntary basis, which – especially for married, middle-class women – was less controversial in social and family terms than paid work outside the home. Relief work drew on their skills and compassion as surrogate mothers, caring for those who were less able to look after themselves: children, other women, the poor and the sick.

The work of relief and rescue undertaken by these activists was not always illegal. Indeed they operated on two levels. Openly, they acted as legitimate charities to relieve suffering, using contacts, influence and even bribery where necessary. They also tried to persuade church leaderships to intervene with the authorities or even protest in public. As the threats to the camp populations increased and the Vichy authorities became complicit with Nazi policies of deportation, they were forced to go underground. They devised ways of spiriting the interned away to safe houses and along escape lines to the frontier. At this point they themselves ran the risk of arrest, torture and deportation, so that at this point rescue became a very real and effective form of resistance.

French Jewish activists were obviously sensitive from an early date to the persecution of their co-religionists. Andrée Salomon, the daughter of a Jewish village butcher in Alsace and herself trained as a lawyer, was involved in the 1930s in defying British restrictions on allowing Jewish refugees into the Palestine Mandate.[9] After *Kristallnacht* in 1938 she became involved in looking after Jewish children who were refugees from Nazi Germany. She set up an orphanage for German-Jewish girls in Strasbourg, which she moved to Clermont-Ferrand when the Germans invaded in 1940. Another string to her bow was helping Jewish children more generally who had fled to the Free Zone. In Alsace she had set up a branch of the Éclaireurs Israélites de France (EIF) or Jewish scouts, with its national leader, Robert Gamzon, and herself became a national scout commissioner. Jewish scouts became a key organisation in the work of managing refugees, notably in 1939 when many from Alsace and Lorraine were evacuated to the Limousin and the Dordogne. After the defeat, in Clermont-Ferrand, she met up again with Gamzon in order to deal with the scouts who were now stranded in the Free Zone. A fellow scout leader recalled that Gamzon was:

still in the uniform of a lieutenant in the engineers with a military medal on his chest that he had earned for blowing up the telephone centre at Reims under the Germans' noses. We sat round a table in Andrée Salomon's flat and wrote down in bold what the Jewish scouts were going to do in the coming year.[10]

They decided to accommodate the scouts in rural centres around old châteaux where they undertook manual work on the land and in workshops. One of these centres, run by Gamzon and his wife Denise, was at Lautrec, near Albi, while another was at Taluyers, near Lyon. Because the scouts were French, they were entirely legal under Vichy, which encouraged Chantiers de la Jeunesse and youth movements to 'regenerate' young people and until 1942 tolerated the EIF. The centres took the opportunity to teach young urban Jews the farming skills they lacked and to intensify their Jewish learning in preparation for their becoming pioneers in Palestine, which was their ultimate destination.[11]

Having helped launch this scouting activity Andrée Salomon turned to the more troubling question of foreign Jewish families interned in the camps of south-west France. She went to Gurs and Rivesaltes, where OSE work was already being undertaken by Charles Lederman, a Jewish lawyer of communist persuasion. He was trying to persuade the prefecture that healthy males would be better off working outside in the Foreign Worker Detachments[12] set up by the regime, and from which they could more easily escape. He soon became suspect to the Rivesaltes authorities and OSE moved him to Lyon, replacing him with Salomon. She concentrated on getting children out of Gurs and Rivesaltes – legally where she could but sometimes bribing the guards. In this work she was helped by Sabine Chwast, who had been imprisoned in Poland aged sixteen as an activist of the socialist Bund and went into exile to become an art history student at Nancy. There she met a Russian-Jewish agriculture student, Miron Zlatin, and together they set up a poultry farm in the north of France. Now known as Sabine Zlatin, she served during the war as a military nurse with the Red Cross but was promptly dismissed in 1941 as a Jew. Rebuilding her poultry business near Montpellier after the armistice she discovered the atrocious conditions of refugees and volunteered as a social worker with OSE. She saw the need to extract Jewish children from the camps where they were increasingly at risk. With the help of a Catholic priest she managed to get a good number of them from Rivesaltes to a sanatorium at Palavas-les-Flots, near Montpellier. Later, with more help from the Catholic priest and a French official, she moved them for safekeeping to what appeared to be a normal children's home at Izieu, near Lyon.[13]

Andrée Salomon, Sabine Zlatin and OSE were not the only social workers active at Gurs and Rivesaltes. There were also young Protestants – and mainly young women – of the Inter-movement Committee for Evacuees (CIMADE).[14] This organisation had been founded in Paris in October 1939, bringing together a range of Protestant youth movements in order to assist the evacuation from Alsace-Lorraine – which had a substantial Lutheran population – to host areas in the Limousin and Dordogne. The prime mover was Suzanne de Dietrich, secretary of two of the movements – the Student Christian Union and the YWCA – which mobilised a team of scout and guide leaders, Christian Union activists and deaconesses to help the evacuees.[15] After that crisis, and as the country was finally invaded in May 1940, Suzanne de Dietrich wrote to her friends, quoting from the book of Revelation and calling them to resist Nazi evil:

As a truly Satanic power is sweeping over the world, reducing to slavery people after people [. . .] we must ask God with all the strength of our faith to shatter this power. This is not the time for intellectual shilly-shallying, but to give ourselves simply and completely to the service of God and our country. 'Fear none of those things that thou shalt suffer.'[16]

One of the young Protestants who heard her message was Madeleine Barot, who now became a leading light in the CIMADE. The challenge had moved on from refugees to internees and she visited Gurs where she was shocked by the arrival in horrendous condition of 7,000 Jews from Germany on 23 October 1940. Her concern was still primarily for the 600 Protestants interned in the camp, and together with Red Cross nurse Jeanne Merle d'Aubigné, she gained access to the camp and set up a base in one of the huts that served as social centre, library, lecture room and a chapel for the Protestants.[17] In April 1941 she invited sixty-year-old Pastor Marc Boegner, head of the Protestant Federation and National Council of the Reformed Church in France, who was effectively the head of the Protestant Church in France. He was shown round the camp by its director and Madeleine Barot to observe their work and was pleased to attend 'a religious service with our liturgy. Liturgical chant in French but also two hymns in German.'[18] This highlighted the fact that, at this stage, Madeleine Barot and her associates offered the camp inmates rather limited help: 'As French youth movements we did not have a great deal to give,' she reflected in December 1941. 'We asked to live inside the camps, to be with the internees to show our Christian love, our faith in a better future.'[19]

That said, from the beginning of 1942 those interned in the camps were liable to deportation to unknown destinations. The work of Barot and her team, like that of Andrée Salomon and hers, progressed from relief to rescue. The task was to extract people from the camps wherever possible. From the beginning of 1942 places were found where individuals, couples and sometimes families could be removed to, usually on grounds of ill health, and kept safe in case matters worsened. One of the places found was Le Chambon-sur-Lignon, up in the Cévennes, which was a tourist venue for families from Lyon and Saint-Étienne and also a Protestant centre, with a private college run for Protestant families. The local pastor and head of this college since 1934 was André Trocmé, who had a French father and German mother, and who had registered himself in 1939 as a conscientious objector and volunteered to serve with the Red Cross.[20] He was in contact with Madeleine Barot and undertook a tour of camps that might need to send some of their inmates to Le Chambon. By late 1941 seven houses were ready to receive refugees and Trocmé brought in his cousin, Daniel Trocmé, to help out.[21] At this stage the emphasis was on saving Protestants, who were often of German origin, rather than on saving Jews. Pastor André Dumas wrote to Madeleine Barot from Rivesaltes in March 1942: 'Without knowing how many places you are reserving for Rivesaltes, we have chosen only those in whom we have full confidence, who have technical and social skills, and we have given priority to Protestants.'[22] One exception he made was for the Russian Orthodox Boriaff family, whose father had lost his job as an economics lecturer at Moscow University for being a 'non-Marxist', and worked as an accountant for a film company in Paris before scraping a living as a modern languages teacher in Menton and being interned.[23]

The third piece of the activist combination were Catholic activists, who had a somewhat ambivalent relationship with the uniformly Pétainist hierarchy. Most original in this respect was the Abbé Alexandre Glasberg, who in 1940 was curate of the poor parish of Notre-Dame Saint-Alban in the suburbs of Lyon. The parish was itself inhabited by marginals and refugees and in 1940 Glasberg persuaded both his curé and Archbishop Gerlier to set up a Refugee Assistance Committee, which he would run. Jewish by birth, the son of a miller and forester, Glasberg had been brought up in Western Ukraine in a town divided between Jews and Uniates – Orthodox Christians who recognised the authority of Rome – and in a frontier area bled by pogroms and contested after 1917 between the Red Army, Polish Army and Ukrainian nationalists. His family left in 1920 and he journeyed through Austria, Poland, Germany and Yugoslavia, eventually arriving in France in 1932. Converting to Catholicism en route he trained for the priesthood in Paris and Lyon and was ordained in 1938.[24] Nina Gourfinkel, also Russian-born and one of his aides in his work, described him as:

tall, robust, greying. You would think him fifty although he is only thirty-seven. His features would seem heavy if it were not for the extraordinary animation that lights them up, overcoming the thick hair of his ill-shaved cheeks and the short-sighted gaze behind his thick, deforming spectacles. His ancient cassock bears the traces of hasty mending.'[25]

On the wall of his simple room, she said, hung a charcoal drawing of a Spanish Madonna, given to him by a German artist who had fought in the International Brigades. For her it represented both his compassion and his anger, his impulse to fight back in the face of oppression and injustice. The Madonna was 'holding a baby close to her in a gesture both defensive and ready to give battle to the whole world [. . .] I think that he loved Christ very directly, fraternally, socially', continued Gourfinkel, 'It was the Judaeo-Slav dimension of his soul.'[26]

Perhaps it was the mixture of Russian, Jewish, and Catholic origins (and the gratitude of a refugee who had found a home) that made Glasberg so resourceful, so active and so effective in his work for refugees. Nina Gourfinkel called him 'the juggler of Notre-Dame' because he used all his inside knowledge, his contacts with the police and bureaucracy, his ability to exploit loopholes in the law and the hesitancy of officials, in order to extract individuals from camps and get them to safety in five safe houses scattered over the south of France.[27] He had the ear of Cardinal Gerlier, who was not the most outspoken of prelates, and persuaded him to protest to Vichy about conditions in the camps.[28] To fund his work he extracted money from a range of Jewish associations that received funds from the American Joint Distribution Committee, founded in 1914 to help suffering Jews in the Middle East and Europe.[29] He also operated a Robin Hood system, persuading 'paying guests' to pay for themselves and for two individuals who had no resources, which Protestant leaders later thought might also work for Le Chambon.[30] An interviewer in 1946 summed up Glasberg's contribution as 'a war on concentration camps and later against deportation'.[31]

Although Protestants, Catholics and Jews worked separately early in the Occupation, increasing danger encouraged them to work together ecumenically. In 1941 Catholics and Protestants came together in Lyon in the Amitié Chrétienne. It met in the offices in the rue Constantine previously occupied by the *Temps nouveau*, now closed. Its secretary, Jean-Marie Soutou, who was also the editorial secretary of Emmanuel Mounier's review *Esprit*, said that 'Abbé Glasberg was the centre, the pivot of Amitié Chrétienne. He infused the necessary élan and courage into its activists'.[32] The honorary presidents of the Amitié, giving it respectability and clout, were Cardinal Gerlier and Pastor Marc Boegner. More active on a day-to-day basis was Père Chaillet, editor of *Témoignage Chrétien*, who brought out issues of the journal in 1942 on racism and anti-Semitism in order to counter the powerful propaganda of both Nazis and Vichy.[33] After the Liberation Chaillet recalled that Amitié Chrétienne was created by 'the various spiritual families to alleviate the distress of the most abandoned and compromised people who had been thrown up blindly by the defeat and the Nazi occupation'.[34] It was a building block of what he called 'a Christian front to protect persecuted Jews'.[35] The Amitié brought together Protestants such as Lyon pastor Roland de Pury, whose sermons attacked the evils of Nazism, and Catholics such as Germaine Ribière. Germaine Ribière was a student at the Sorbonne who had taken part in the famous demonstration on the Champs-Élysées on 11 November 1940. She was alerted to a round-up of Jewish children in the Marais in May 1941 by a friend whose mother was a headteacher in the neighbourhood. Returning from a camp with the Jeunesse Étudiante Chrétienne she made contact with the Amitié Chrétienne at Lyon and offered her services. She was exemplary among the dedicated youth whose militancy was forged by Abbé Glasberg.[36]

The ecumenism articulated by the Amitié Chrétienne was developed to include Jewish representatives in the Coordinating Committee for Relief Work in Internment Camps. Meeting in

Nîmes between November 1940 and March 1943 it became known simply as the Nîmes Committee. It brought together twenty-five organisations – Catholic, Protestant and Jewish – which were involved in relieving conditions in France's concentration camps. It was tolerated by, and also pressured by, Vichy but the most important aspect of its work was the dynamic one of concentrating the efforts of its different religious constituencies. Chairmanship was provided by the American Donald Lowrie, who had vast experience in international relief work for the YMCA and had himself visited Gurs.[37] It included Catholics Abbé Glasberg and Père Chaillet, Protestants Madeleine Barot and Quakers of the American Friends Service Committee, and for the Jewish OSE Dr Joseph Weill, who described the committee as 'a united front of moral and material resistance'.[38] It had sub-committees attending to hygiene, childcare and education in the camps, and managed to close down the worst camps such as Agde and Argelès, transferring their women and children to Rivesaltes. From here Andrée Salomon of OSE and the Irish Quaker refugee worker Mary Elms managed to extract children in Mary's car and get them to safe houses. In the winter of 1941–2 the head of Rivesaltes tried to have the children brought back to the camp under Vichy's policy of 'family regrouping', demanding their addresses from the relief organisations responsible. 'I replied,' said Andrée Salomon, 'that we do not have files to give you, we don't have the addresses and in any case it is not our duty to give them to you [. . .] All organisations agreed on this 'communion of resistance to orders.'[39]

Extracting inmates from the camps in small numbers was never going to be enough and in the summer of 1942 the Germans and the Vichy government, of which Pierre Laval was now premier, agreed to the deportation of foreign Jews from both the Occupied and Free Zones. Vichy police cooperated with what became known as the *rafle du Vel' d'Hiv*, when 13,000 Jews were rounded up in Paris on 16–17 July, and elsewhere in occupied

France shortly after. Many fled south but were soon caught in the net of 10,000 Jews the Vichy regime promised to deliver from the Free Zone. Most were arrested in the cities while others, conveniently held in the internment camps, were sitting targets.[40]

The response of the ecumenical networks was both open and public and also conspiratorial and underground. One of the most powerful responses to the round-up and deportation of Jews, which illustrated in poignant terms the horror of anti-Semitic persecution, were the pastoral letters condemning the inhumanity of the measures published by Monseigneur Salièges, Archbishop of Toulouse, on 23 August 1942, and by Monseigneur Théas, Bishop of Montauban, three days later. These pronouncements were pressed for by activists close to the reality of round-ups and deportations. Information about the round-ups was passed to Mgr Salièges both by Père Chaillet and by Charles Lederman of OSE.[41] The dissemination of this news, which was immediately censored by the Vichy authorities, also required the hard work of grass-roots militants. At Montauban, Marie-Rose Gineste, a social worker and disseminator of *Témoignage Chrétien*, duplicated copies and joined forces with a female friend and a young officer from Lorraine:

We set off on our bicycles along the roads of the department. We got to all the parishes and the following Sunday the letter was read simultaneously across the diocese. The huge joy I felt in having outwitted the prefect, the censor and the police vastly compensated for the exhaustion of travelling so many kilometres in record time under the August sun.[42]

In a similar way, Madeleine Barot gave news of the round-ups to her superior, Pastor Boegner, so that he also could protest to the authorities. She arrived in Nîmes at 11 p.m. on 12 August to report on deportations from Marseille, and warned of worse to come. On 18 August Boegner went to Lyon to meet Cardinal Gerlier, who was unwilling at this stage to go public like

Salièges but agreed with Boegner that they would each write personally to Pétain. Two days later Boegner noted in his diary, 'Telephone call from Madeleine Barot yesterday evening and this afternoon with dire predictions. She urged me to contact the prefect of Haute-Loire to try to save Le Coteau fleuri at Le Chambon [one of the safe houses], which I did at once.'[43]

Relief workers of all denominations working together were desperate to warn foreign Jews outside the camps of imminent round-ups and to extricate as many of those inside camps as possible. They concentrated first and foremost on children, who were the most vulnerable and innocent. Initially it seemed that the Germans did not wish to deport children, not least to maintain the illusion that deportees were bound for work camps, not for extermination. Laval, on the other hand, was keen to meet the German quotas for foreign Jews and to avoid painful public scenes of separation of parents and children. Germaine Ribière, at home in Limoges for the holidays, became a social worker for the Secours National in a nearby camp of Nexon, which was full of Strasbourg Jews. Finding out that all foreign Jews in Limoges were going to be rounded up at 5 a.m. the next morning, she warned Rabbi Deutsch, the head of the Jewish community and UGIF in Limoges. As a result only eighty of the 800 foreign Jews were arrested that morning, although many were captured later. Germaine also worked to get small children out of the camp, but nothing could be done for the adults. She promised the inmates that she would accompany them to the end and obtained the agreement of the Red Cross that she could go with them as a nurse. Her account expresses the solidarity of Christian activist and Jewish sufferer in contrast to the ignominy of the Vichy regime:

I went with people among whom were youths aged fifteen or sixteen. They were crammed into cattle trucks. They were all more or less dysenteric. I climbed into a truck and departed with them. At Limoges the head of the Red Cross ordered me to get out. I refused and did not step down. At Châteauroux a lieutenant in the French Army came to tell me to get out. I did not and we got to Vierzon. It was there that they were to be handed over to the Germans. In the train I had collected letters and jewels; people gave me everything that was precious to them. I won't dwell on the details of the journey. It was a convoy with all the attendant horrors.[44]

Vichy, however, was never a bloc and a few officials were prepared to make a stand against persecution. One instance occurred in the lead-up to the so-called Night of Vénissieux, a suburb of Lyon where a disused barracks was used as a processing centre for a convoy in the night of 26–27 August 1942. Frantic attempts were made by activists to use official instructions to take certain individuals, and in particular children, off the convoy, using a document leaked to Abbé Glasberg by Gilbert Lesage, head of the Foreigners' Control Service at Vichy. Lesage was a straightforward official except that at the age of nineteen he had walked into a Quaker bookshop in Paris where 'a beautiful, slender, charming young woman of the Scandinavian type smiled at me'.[45] Ella Barlow and her musician husband Fred ran a young people's international group dedicated to freedom, toleration and peace, and Lesage was immediately converted to Quakerism. He worked with the unemployed in Berlin and in Paris in the 1930s and after the war in 1940 he offered his services to Vichy to help refugees. He met Robert Gamzon who informed him of the special problems faced by Jewish refugees and he visited Gurs to see for himself. In July 1942 he tipped off Gamzon that the police were about to descend on his rural centres and sent Glasberg a Vichy police list of categories of Jews, such as pregnant women, couples with children under two, the war-decorated and the over 60s, who were exempted from deportation.[46]

With this document Abbé Glasberg went to Vénissieux and imposed himself as someone who would sort matters out. One advantage was his black Citroen with yellow-rimmed wheels, lent by a Lyon industrialist, which looked just like the prefect's, and carried his team into the barracks as the guards stood to attention. Another was his powerful personality. 'Immediately,' wrote Jean-Marie Soutou, 'he gave the order to summon the children. In his own way he intimidated the prefect's representative who was surprised to discover that his instructions were known.'[47] Glasberg's team included Catholics like Soutou, Protestants such as Madeleine Barot and Jews including Joseph Weill, Andrée Salomon, Charles Lederman and his friend Georges Garel.[48] Garel's real name was Grigori Garfinkel, a Russian Jew who had studied engineering at Zürich Polytechnique alongside Claude Bourdet.[49] They contested each case before a triage commission, which was hastily set up, and managed to exempt 550 people, including 108 children. Matters were not helped when the prefect arrived and Soutou found a document in his briefcases cancelling the exemptions that had hitherto been possible, so that the team had then to concentrate on getting children out of the camp.[50]

The main category of exemptions on which the team concentrated was of children under fourteen but success required persuading families in the barracks to entrust them to the relief organisations. Nothing could be said directly about the fate that awaited those who were deported, although Dr Weill had fairly good evidence about the gas chambers. Georges Garel described the terrors of that night that were not made easier by a power cut:

In the darkness we went from group to group of terrified people, asking their names [. . .] Some understood the situation and gave us their children. But other parents refused to be separated from their children [. . .] As time ran out we became stricter, and instead of asking whether parents wished to entrust their children to us, we announced, "We have come for your children" [. . .] When a mother clung on to her child we had to snatch it away from her [. . .] The whole camp echoed to cries and shouting.[51]

Joseph Weill observed that the women, old and sick were loaded onto wagons stamped '40 people, 20 horses', under the eyes of regional prefect Angeli and his police intendant. 'The coach carrying the children, the bigger ones hidden under the seats, drove out of the military camp without a fuss [. . .] and was taken to the headquarters of the Éclaireurs Israélites in Lyon,' which was in a former Carmelite convent on the hill of the Croix Rousse.[52] From there they were spirited away to a variety of schools, convents and private homes made available by the Catholic and Protestant communities.

A few days later the situation grew even more difficult. It became clear that the quota of 10,000 Jews demanded by the Germans from the Free Zone had not been met and that Laval had in fact ordered the deportation of children along with their parents. The convoy taking the adults north had stopped at the demarcation line and regional prefect Angeli telephoned Cardinal Gerlier in a fury, demanding the addresses where the children had been taken. On 2 September Gerlier summoned Chaillet, Glasberg and Soutou of Amitié Chrétienne to obtain this information. Glasberg was uncertain how to respond but Soutou said, 'Eminence, I will give them to you,' and told Glasberg afterwards, 'Calm down! We will give false addresses. I don't trust Gerlier.'[53] When Chaillet refused to give the children's addresses to the prefect he was placed under house arrest, but when the police commissioner asked for his particulars he replied, 'Colonel Chaillet, Hungarian Intelligence region', obliging the commissioner to stand to attention.[54]

As news of the incident spread, there were more public appeals to Vichy on the part of churchmen. Pastor Boegner, informed on 2 September by Madeleine Barot of the overruling of exemptions – she had seen an eight-month pregnant woman and an amputee of the Great War dragged away from Vénissieux – went to Vichy to meet Laval in person on 9 September. All that Laval would say was '"I cannot do anything else. It is prophylaxis." He does not want a single foreign Jew to remain in France.'[55] On 8 September, in Lyon, he had met Cardinal Gerlier, who gave him the text of a protest he had had read out in all the churches of the diocese two days before, a fortnight after that of Monseigneur Salièges.

Back in Nîmes he convened a meeting of the National Council of the Reformed Church to approve his own protest, which was read out in Protestant pulpits on 22 September.[56] All this was too late and mere words, for the Vichy government no longer had any bargaining power vis-à-vis the German authorities.

After the Vénissieux affair the public route to saving Jews from persecution effectively closed down. Quakers of the American Friends Service Committee tried to negotiate exit visas for 5,000 Jewish children who would be taken on a convoy to the United States, and their representative, Lindsley Noble, went to Vichy in mid-October 1942 to report that a thousand visas had come through. The Germans, however, feared the bad publicity that would arise in the United States over the rescue operation and a fearful premier Laval cancelled the whole scheme.[57] The Vichy authorities clamped down much more severely on relief organisations that were trying to save Jews and, when the Germans invaded the Free Zone in November 1942, the screw tightened even more. On 27 January 1943 Chaillet and Soutou of the Amitié Chrétienne were arrested and taken for questioning to the Hotel Terminus, the Gestapo headquarters in Lyon. Père Chaillet managed to eat compromising documents he had in his cassock, and Soutou recalled that Germaine Ribière went straight to the rue de Constantine to avert further arrests:

As soon as Germaine Ribière heard about our arrest she disguised herself as a cleaning lady and spend the day on the staircase on the floor beneath l'Amitié Chrétienne with a load of buckets, mops and brooms, telling anyone who looked like one of our protégés, 'Go away! The Gestapo has set a trap here!' That contributed a great deal to the fact that there was no incident.[58]

Soutou was imprisoned for three weeks at Fort Montluc until Cardinal Gerlier secured his release and he escaped to Geneva, where he set up a resistance facility behind a press office.[59] An arrest warrant was issued for Abbé Glasberg, who left for the

Montauban area. With the help of Mgr Théas, he reinvented himself there as Elie Corvin, curé of L'Honor-de-Cos and later joined an Armée Secrète *maquis* in the area, with responsibility for receiving and hiding parachuted weapons, and sat on the departmental liberation committee.[60] Germaine Ribière went to work with a new escape network to emerge from OSE, under the leadership of Georges Garel, who now played a key role in rescuing Jewish children.

At OSE Andrée Salomon rapidly concluded that their twenty homes for 1,600 Jewish children who had been extracted from the camps were now a prey to raids. The children would have to be reinvented as Aryans and scattered to the four winds.[61] Vichy was finished as a 'shield' and rumours of the mass killing of Jews in the East were filtering through. Georges Garel went to Toulouse to see Mgr Saliège, who had already been contacted by Charles Lederman, and concluded that Saliège had 'the makings of a saint'. Saliège offered him the cooperation of two Catholic charities, those of Sainte-Catherine and Saint-Étienne, which dealt with children's homes and foster care, and would provide families for Jewish children required to disappear.[62] Sabine Zlatin decided to move the children from the sanatorium of Palavas-les-Flots to the zone occupied by Italian forces and with her priest in Montpellier and the sub-prefect of Belley in the Ain she found a refuge hitherto used as a *colonie de vacances* for Catholic children at Izieu.[63] Meanwhile Garel and Andrée Salomon organised an escape line that took children to safety in Switzerland. This task was entrusted to Georges Loinger, of Strasbourg-Jewish origin, and Moscow-born Emmanuel Racine, who in turn enlisted the help of Jean Deffaugt, the mayor of Annemasse (Haute-Savoie) on the Swiss border. One of Loinger's tricks was to organise football matches with the children on the border, and when the ball went into Switzerland the children would scamper over the line.[64] On the other side the children were taken in hand by Joseph Weill, who himself escaped to Switzerland in 1943, and by his contacts,

Saly (*sic*) Mayer, director of the Swiss office of the American Joint Distribution Committee, and the Bishop of Fribourg. Funds from the Joint paid for escorts who came the other way across the border, ferried by (among others) a painter called Gabriel whose car had a false bottom and a priest who hid bank notes in his wooden leg.[65]

Another escape line was set up by the Zionist Youth Movement (MJS), which had been founded in Montpellier in May 1942. Children collected from Bordeaux or Toulouse made a stop at the chalet of Jeanne Latchiver, known as the Queen Mother, on the outskirts of Grenoble. Working with a refugee Viennese Jew, 'Toto' Giniewski, and his wife, nicknamed 'Tototte', they had contacts in various town halls that provided them with blank identity cards. Latchiver recalled that:

We began this work at about nine in the evening; the children had gone to bed. We were about a dozen and there were two typewriters. Somebody shouted, 'A name! A name for a Polish girl!' Someone replied, 'Léonidas', another 'Naphtali', whatever. We finished in the middle of the night and had the cheek to go up onto the mountain, to lie on the ground with the view of Grenoble at our feet, and to sing scouting and Hebrew sons. In the midst of the German occupation.[66]

During the night the children's real names were sewn into the lining of their clothes and the next morning they were taken by train to Annemasse, usually by young women, as if on a school or youth club outing. This part of the journey was extremely dangerous and two young escorts lost their lives. Twenty-year-old Mila Racine, Emmanuel's younger sister, was arrested by the Germans on 23 October 1943 and transferred to Drancy. She told the mayor of Annemasse, who saw her in prison before she left, to bring her rice powder and lipstick: 'I promise that I will not cry when I get into the lorry", she said, "but I want to be beautiful.'[67] Marianne Cohn, described by the mayor as 'a sweet brunette, not very tall, bright, full of faith and energy', was stopped at Annemasse with her convoy of children on 31 May 1943 and imprisoned with them. The mayor and Georges Loinger managed to get seventeen of the twenty-eight children out of the prison, but Marianne refused to leave those who remained. She was taken by the Gestapo in July and her body was found after the Liberation, on 21 August 1944, 'almost completely naked apart from a little blouse and the yellow shoes that [Emmanuel] Racine had bought for her [. . .] It seems that she was killed with a spade'.[68]

Protestants as well as Catholics rallied to help Jews on the run. One of the most important refuge centres was the Cévennes village of Le Chambon-sur-Lignon. This had been visited on 15 August 1942 by Vichy's Youth Minister, Georges Lamirand, who was given a meagre meal at the college and then, after a chapel service, was surprised to be presented by the older schoolboys with a petition protesting against the deportation of foreign Jews. One Saturday a fortnight later Vichy gendarmes raided the plateau to arrest foreign Jews. Pastor Trocmé was summoned to the town hall to provide their addresses but, like Père Chaillet, refused. Similarly, he refused to give the order that the Jews report to the town hall to be registered. The Jewish population had already been despatched from the boarding houses to individual farms, drawing on the fellow-feeling of a Huguenot population that had suffered its share of religious persecution in the seventeenth and eighteenth centuries. Now Trocmé told the local scouts to go from farm to farm telling the Jews to leave during the night and take refuge in the surrounding mountains and woods. When the police searched the village the next day they found only an Austrian-Jewish lawyer, M. Steckler, who believed that since his sister was a Protestant deaconess, he was not Jewish enough to be deported.[69]

Trocmé was arrested for his pains in February 1943, and spent five weeks in prison at St Paul d'Eyjeaux, near Limoges, until Laval ordered his release to avoid antagonising the British. Meanwhile 'the CIMADE', said Trocmé, 'had organised what was called an "underground railway" at the time of American Slavery, to get

Jews over the Swiss frontier'. Madeleine Barot was one of the escorts, now using the pseudonym of Monette Benoît. Staging-posts along the route in Haute-Savoie included the Protestant vicarage of Annecy and the Catholic vicarage of Douvine. At the frontier 'the priest pushed a big cement cylinder under the barbed-wire fence and the wretched people wriggled along the pipe. Switzerland was on the other side.'[70] The importance of camouflage and dispersal was illustrated by the round-up of twenty-five foreign Jewish students entrusted to André Trocmé's cousin Daniel at the Maison des Roches at Le Chambon on 29 June 1943. André tried to enlist the help of a German chaplain but discovered that 'though he said he belonged to the [anti-Nazi] Confessing Church, that did not stop him from hunting Jews'. Daniel Trocmé, although a Protestant, was deported with them and died in Poland at Majdanek on 4 April 1944, most likely gassed. 'That was very probably the fate of the "Jew" Daniel Trocmé,' said his cousin.[71]

Jews were both recipients of Gentile help and contributors in their own right to the wider strategy of resistance. One of these enterprising activists was a young forger Oscar Rosowsky, who produced thousands of false documents for those on the plateau of Le Chambon for those who needed them. He was born in Berlin in 1923 to a White Russian playboy who managed (or rather mismanaged) the Berlin office of the grandfather's Riga-based international timber business. When things became too hot in Germany the family came to Nice, which was a haven for Europe's Jewish élite under the much milder Italian occupation. Oscar was educated at the Lycée of Nice and passed the *baccalauréat* in 1941, but under the Statut des Juifs was not able to pursue medical studies. Instead, he got a job servicing and mending typewriters, not least those at the prefecture, which gave him access to official identity cards. In August 1942 the *rafles* struck; his father was arrested and deported a month later. Using the false identity of a baron of the Napoleonic Empire, he fled to the Swiss frontier with his mother, but he was refused access and his mother was arrested and sent to Rivesaltes. Oscar now forged a residence permit to get his mother out of Rivesaltes and, using the connections of his Protestant friends in Nice, went with her to Le Chambon in November 1942. First he lived in the college's boarding house, then for greater safety in an isolated peasant's farm, where he forged false identities not only for Jews in hiding but also for those dodging forced labour service and active resisters. He exploited the fact that there was no national identity card but that these – along with food, textiles and tobacco ration cards – were issued by each town hall which had its own size and colour of paper. Increasingly he forged papers issued in Algeria, as this was now in the hands of the Free French. His own papers were in the name of Jean-Claude Plunne, born in Algiers, issued at Le Puy (Haute-Loire) and made himself first two, then four years younger that he really was, in order to avoid the risk of forced labour service.[72] When Vichy's counter-insurgent *Milice* came on the prowl for resistance activity, he hid his material in one of the peasant's bee-hives.[73]

In September 1943 Italy dropped out of the war, concluding an armistice with the Allies. In response, Germans now marched into the former Italian-occupied territories, including Savoy and the Nice region, and a massive round-up of Jews in Nice rapidly followed. Under the Italian occupation from November 1942 foreign Jewish interests had been maintained by a Refugee Assistance Committee in the rue Debouchage, known commonly as the Debouchage Committee. Ignace Fink, a Polish Jew and secretary of the committee, was in constant negotiations with the Italian-Jewish banker, Angelo Donati, whose brother was King Victor Emmanuel's doctor, and was able to provide funds, moderate persecution orders and allow Jews an escape route to Italy.[74] All this changed with the fall of the Italian regime, the evaporation of the Debouchage Committee and a Gestapo raid on the OSE offices in Nice. Once again Jews and Catholics collaborated to organise hiding places and escape lines. Moussa Abadi was a Syrian Jew who spent his early years in the Damascus ghetto, studied medieval literature at the Sorbonne and became a successful actor.[75] After the German occupation he fled from Paris to Nice, and in the spring of 1942 was shocked by seeing a Jewish woman being beaten to death on the Promenade des Anglais by a booted *Milicien*, while her six-year-old child screamed, 'Maman, maman, maman!'[76] Approached with finance and ideas in July 1943 by Maurice Brener, the underground delegate of the American Joint Distribution Committee in Nice and connected to Amitié Chrétienne, he set up a network – the Réseau Marcel – to try to save Nice's Jewish children. His first colleague was his future wife, Odette Rosenstock, a qualified doctor who had been prevented from continuing her work as a school doctor by the Statut des Juifs.[77] As with the Garel network, the help of the Catholic Church was vital. Abadi approached no less than the Bishop of Nice, Mgr Rémond, who had good memories of working as a military chaplain with Jewish chaplains during the Great War.[78] Rémond lent him an office in the episcopal palace in which he could forge new identities and ration books and provided contacts with religious houses and Catholic families across the diocese where children could be hidden. Again, the task of the female escort was perilous; Odette was arrested in April 1944 and deported to Germany, from which she eventually returned.[79] In spite of these losses the Reseau Marcel claimed to have saved 527 Jewish children.[80]

These rescue stories cannot mask the stories of tragedy that accompanied them all too often. Sabine Zlatin had taken her Jewish children extracted from Rivesaltes to a children's home at Izieu, near Lyon. This was in the small part of France occupied in November 1942 by the Italians and taken over by the Germans in September 1943. In April 1944, while Zlatin was away in Montpellier trying to transport more children to greater safety, the SS discovered the refuge and deported the children to

Auschwitz. The account of the suffering of these children became one of the most powerful episodes of the Barbie trial in 1987 and the subject of Zlatin's memoir of 1992.[81] What was not mentioned in 1987 or 1992 was the fact that in an interview of 1947, Zlatin went on to talk about how she had gone on, after this tragedy, to fight with the Resistance, and following an attempt to free resisters from Rouen prison, was arrested and beaten up by the Gestapo, but eventually managed to give them the slip. Forty or forty-five years after the war, the story told about Jews was as victims or as rescuers; the question of Jews as resisters, which had been a source of legitimacy for them at the Liberation, had been eclipsed from memory. The story of resistance by Jews, especially foreign Jews, together with a wide spectrum of other foreigners, must now be told.

8

The blood of others

Trained in the hard school of Polish illegality, they were the Yiddishland revolutionaries.

(Henri Krischer, 2000)

When Charles de Gaulle announced in August 1944 that the French had liberated themselves he had two thoughts in mind. The first was that the French had contributed militarily to their own liberation, assisted by the Allies, by making a contribution important enough to re-qualify for great power status. The second was that, in spite of their divisions and long dalliance with the Vichy regime and Marshal Pétain, the French people came round in the end to supporting the Resistance and the General himself. What was entirely glossed over was the role of foreigners in the French Resistance. Many of those who became involved in resistance activity in France had come there in the inter-war period as economic migrants seeking work, as political exiles fleeing repressive regimes, or as a combination of both. Some were anti-fascists who began their battle defending the Spanish Republic against Franco and later continued resistance in France, others were Jewish refugees from Central and Eastern Europe who decided to fight back against persecution. The lightning advance of the German armies in 1940 only increased the flight of refugees to France. When resistance activity developed it was populated by a rainbow of foreign activists whose case studies suggest a reconsideration of what is understood by the French Resistance.

In 1934 Franz Dahlem fled to France from Nazi Germany with his wife Käthe Weber and was welcomed by friends in Ivry, in the communist 'red belt' around Paris. Born a Catholic in 1892 in Rohrbach, Lorraine, when it was part of Imperial Germany, he had joined the German Social Democratic Party in Cologne in 1913 and was drafted into the German Army during the First World War. Inspired by the Russian Revolution, he was active in a soldiers' committee during the German Revolution of 1918 and was later elected a communist deputy to the Prussian parliament and to the Reichstag in Berlin.[1] Because he did not return to Lorraine when it was restored to France after 1918 he was regarded by the French as a deserter, although he described himself more positively as 'an internationalist from Lorraine who is fighting for the liberty of both the German and French peoples'.[2] In France, after 1933, he contributed to the international anti-fascist movement and when the Spanish Civil War broke out he went to Spain for the international communist organisation Comintern to work with German communists. Returning to France in 1938 after the fall of Teruel he was interned as an enemy alien at the outbreak of war in 1939. He described his interrogation by the French police as 'a plot to court-martial me, to eliminate me as a deserter, as a German or Soviet spy, [or] as an agent of Comintern'.[3] Held initially in the Colombes stadium outside Paris, where the Football World Cup final had been played in 1938, he was then sent to the high-security camp of Le Vernet in the Pyrenees. This became a headquarters of international anti-fascist activity and Dahlem was officially head of the French, Belgian and Luxemburg anti-Nazi action committees in the camp. To put a stop to his resistance activity Dahlem was moved to the prison of Castres in November 1941. There he was arrested by the Gestapo in August 1942 and deported to Mauthausen.[4]

The route of Vicente López Tovar from the Spanish Civil War to French Resistance was more direct. Born in Madrid in 1909, he spent his childhood in Buenos Aires, where he was sent to a Jesuit school but was abused by a priest: 'After that incident I could never endure being near a priest, nor believe in what they claimed to stand for.'[5] Returning to Spain after his father died in 1921, he found work as an apprentice to a camera business. Imprisoned in Barcelona for failing to do his military service he spent time in the army before catching what he called the 'virus' of Marxism, living as a bohemian in Madrid and selling communist papers. When the Civil War began he joined the Thaëlmann Battalion, 'named in honour of the great German [communist] leader who was a prisoner in Nazi gaols'.[6] Promoted to major by 1937 he commanded the 18th Mixed Brigade and was involved in the prolonged defence of Madrid. This was a defining moment for López Tovar: 'I had the satisfaction to believe that with its training and discipline this Brigade was certainly one of the best in Madrid. With it I learned to be a good Marxist-Leninist, for I accept that until then some of my behaviour was a little anarchistic.'[7] He was part of the famous XV Army Corps of the Popular Army that fought in the Battle of the Ebro, and left Madrid at the last minute by plane on 7 March 1939. He had the good luck not to be interned by the French but laid low, hidden by communist comrades. One of these was a garagist at Varilhes, in the foothills of the Pyrenees, who offered cover to Spanish republican refugees as woodcutters and charcoal-burners. It was among this virtual army of charcoal-burners that the Spanish Communist Party began to organise armed groups from the end of 1941. They were the original *maquisards*, a step ahead of the French by their experience of battle and hardship. 'We Spanish refugees were toughened by our Civil War,' said López Tovar. 'We could get away more easily because we had nothing more to lose, with no home and not even a suitcase. We had already lost everything in Spain.'[8]

The apprenticeship of Léon Landini, born in 1926 at Saint-Raphaël in the Var to Italian immigrants, was a little slower. His father Aristide was a charcoal-burner by trade rather than as a cover, and a died-in-the-wool 'red' from Tuscany. He had clashed with local landowners in 1905 over their appropriation of common land, and had been imprisoned for deserting from the Italian Army when he was called up in 1915. He joined the Italian Communist Party when it was founded in 1921, battled with Fascist squads as deputy-mayor of his village and fled to France in 1922 to escape being murdered by them. There he joined the diaspora of Italian immigrants who had come to France both to escape fascism and to seek work. He worked in the iron mines of Lorraine and the coal mines of the Nord, before going south to do forestry work, and later opened a grocery store at Le Muy, near Saint-Raphaël. His older son Louis, born in 1914, wanted to join the International Brigades to fight in Spain but was instructed by the Communist Party to stay in France, escorting volunteers to the Pyrenean frontier. The grocery store was a hiding place for Italian fascists on the run and the family story had it that Palmiro Togliatti, secretary of the banned Italian Communist Party, hid from the police briefly with them in 1937. The younger son, Léon, dated his first act of resistance to standing guard at the age of sixteen while a group of resisters derailed a German train near Saint-Raphaël on 28 October 1942. Two weeks later the Italian Fascists occupied the south-east corner of France, where Landini's family lived, and the anti-fascist struggle began in earnest. In May 1943 his father and brother were arrested by the Italians and tortured at Nice. The Italians left the area after they dropped out of the war in September 1943 and the pair fell into the hands of the Germans. They escaped from a holding centre at Dijon and rejoined the Resistance. When his father saw Léon again he said, 'You were a boy when I left and now you are a man.' Louis was summoned to become political commissar of a group of foreign resisters set up in Lyon called Carmagnole and he invited Léon to join them. When Léon arrived in December 1943 he was told that the survival rate for resisters of this kind was three months.[9]

Henri Krischer, who was six years older than Léon Landini, came to France at the age of two in 1922. His father was a Polish-Galician Jew who had fought in the Austro-Hungarian Army in 1914–18 and then left for Germany to find employment in the industrial heartland of the Ruhr. He worked as a coal-hauler at Dortmund, where Henri was born in 1920, but soon died of tuberculosis. For protection his mother married a cousin who was fleeing conscription into the new Polish Army that was fighting a war with the Soviet Union. In 1922 they came to Nancy, where there was a significant colony of Polish Jews. At school Henri had to deal with being bullied as a 'Polack' by assimilated French Jews and later fought pitched battles with extreme-right-wing students at the Lycée Poincaré. His ambition was to train as a doctor but when the Germans invaded in 1940 he fled south with his mother and wept to see young German men of his own age brandishing weapons 'as in a conquered land'. After a while they decided to go back to Nancy, which was a 'desert'.[10] Under the Vichy regime he was prevented from studying medicine by the *numerus clausus*, and was humiliated by having to wear the Yellow Star. He escaped with his parents from Nancy ahead of the round-ups of July 1942 and found his way to Lyon, where he joined the Carmagnole resistance group and soon acquired the nickname 'Admiral'. Carmagnole was a genuinely international organisation but its largest components were Jews from Poland, Hungary and Romania, whose native language was Yiddish. Krischer later reflected that:

No generation of people were beaten as they were. Trained in the hard school of Polish illegality, they were the Yiddishland revolutionaries [. . .] and if they were internationalists the fate of the Jewish people was their main preoccupation. The destruction of fascism, but also the coming of a messianic time, of a socialism that would free the Jewish people.[11]

The careers of these four individuals can only be understood in the context of the conflicts into which Europe was plunged between the First and Second World Wars. Three great narratives played themselves out. The first was inaugurated by the Russian

Revolution of 1917, which founded the first socialist society and also provided a model of international communism that galvanised revolutionaries across Europe. Fascism and Nazism were extreme nationalist responses to this Bolshevik threat and joined battle with it in Italy in the 1920s, and Germany in the 1930s. In 1936 the cockpit of the struggle moved to Spain, where General Franco launched a coup to destroy the left-wing Republic. The coup failed because Spanish communists, socialists, anarchists and regionalists rose up in defence of the Republic. Fascist Italy and Nazi Germany sent Franco reinforcements and while France and Britain refused to intervene, the Comintern decided on 18 September 1936 to provide aid for Spain.[12] This included recruiting volunteers from all countries to form the International Brigades. Composed of 36,000 fighters under 4,000 Comintern cadres, they went to Spain to support the republican cause and halt the rise of international fascism. Among those who went were 9,000 French, 3,000–5,000 Germans and Austrians, 3,000–4,000 Poles, 2,000–4,000 volunteers from the Balkans, 3,000 Italians, and 2,000 each from Belgium, Britain and the United States. Of these were between 6,000 and 8,500 Jews, or around 20 per cent of the total.[13]

A second narrative is that of the immigration of foreign labour into France before the First World War, but in particular in the 1920s, when losses in the trenches and economic recovery created a massive shortage of workers. France became a magnet for economic migrants, many of whom were also political exiles. In 1931 there were 508,000 Poles, many of whom worked in the coal mines of the Nord and Pas-de-Calais and the iron mines of Lorraine; 808,000 Italians, who worked in Lorraine and the wine industry of the Midi; and 352,000 Spaniards, working in the coal mines of the Aveyron and the fields of south-west France.[14] The story of Aristide and Léon Landini was repeated in a multitude of cases. Cesare Titonel and his two brothers fled from Conegliano in the Veneto in 1925, after one of them was arrested and beaten up by Fascists, and established themselves as farmers in the Garonne valley around Agen. The Italians met at the local bistro on a Sunday afternoon and on one occasion broke up a meeting of the Croix de Feu with shouts of 'banda di fascisti'. Cesare's daughter Damira, born in 1923, reflected that 'our parents had fled fascism and now fascism was catching us up.'[15] The case of Henri Krischer was also echoed by other examples. One of his friends at the Lycée Poincaré in Nancy was Salomon (known to his French friends as Georges) Weinstein, whose father was, similarly, a Polish-Galician Jew who had come to France to escape Polish military service. He began work in the Lorraine iron mines but then set up as a stallholder specialising in women's lingerie on the main square of Nancy. Georges and his younger brother Max studied Hebrew but also went to state schools and Georges sat his *baccalauréat* in 1939. The father was mobilised for war work at the arsenal of Roanne, near Saint-Étienne. There he was joined there by his sons, who fled the bombing of Nancy in 1940. Since they were registered as Jews in Roanne, Georges and Max left for Lyon when the round-ups intensified in the summer of 1942, inventing for themselves new identities and new roles, and joining up again with Henri Krischer, who had also fled south.[16]

This story of foreign immigration intersected with a third narrative – that of the arrival in France of persecuted Jews from Central and Eastern Europe. The roots of strife may be traced back to opposition to the Tsarist regime and pogroms in the Pale of Settlement, where Jews were confined from the Baltic to the Black Sea, which drove radicals and Jews westwards in search of a livelihood and liberty. The successor states that replaced the Russian, Austro-Hungarian and Ottoman Empires after their defeat in 1918 – Poland, Czechoslovakia, Austria, Hungary, Romania, Bulgaria and Yugoslavia – gave no succour to Jews. The new states were keen to assert the hegemony one dominant nationality over national minorities; they persecuted the Jewish communities that they had inherited from the divided Pale of

Settlement and clamped down on communist movements that were seen as Soviet fifth columns often orchestrated by persecuted Jews.

Jews from Central Europe who had fled both economic hardship and anti-Semitism were among the most high-profile migrants in France. In the 1930s there were 90,000 East European Jews in Paris out of a total Jewish population of 150,000. Of these, 45,000 were Poles, 16,000 were Russians, 12,000 were Hungarians, 11,000 were Romanians and 2,000 Lithuanians or Latvians.[17] Many Hungarian and Romanian Jews, excluded from university by a *numerus clausus* in their own country, came to France to study medicine or engineering. Russian Jews who had come to France before the First World War and lived in the *Pletzel* (Place) of the Marais, generally worked as jewellers and clockmakers, furniture makers and furriers. The Russian Jews of the *Pletzel* tended to be traditional in their religious practice and Zionist in their politics. Zionist organisations, including schools and sports clubs like the Maccabi, grouped in the Federation of Jewish Associations and published the *Parizer Haïnt* (*Paris Today*) as their Yiddish mouthpiece. Meanwhile the left-wing Zionist youth organisation, Hashomer Hatzaïr, aimed to facilitate emigration to Palestine.[18]

Polish Jews, by contrast, were often powerfully influenced by the Bolshevik Revolution and driven out of the new Poland, which had fought the Red Army in 1920 and banned the Polish Communist Party. They tended to concentrate in the north-eastern suburb of Belleville and the 11th *arrondissement* between Nation and République and worked in the clothing trade as tailors, hat-makers, glove-makers, shoe-makers and fine-leather craftsmen.[19] Isaac Krasucki, aged thirteen, had fled east to Białystok with his family when the Germans invaded in 1915. It became a 'red capital', occupied by Russian Bolsheviks, but their defeat by Polish forces at the Battle of Białystok in 1920 made life untenable for Polish communists, who were regarded as a Soviet fifth column. Krasucki came to Paris in 1926 and set up a knitting shop in Belleville, soon to be followed by his wife Léa and two-year-old son Henri.[20] In Belleville they rubbed shoulders with David Erlich, known as David Diamant, whose older brother had taken part in the October Revolution and, having trained at technical school as an engineer, was forced as a communist to leave Poland. He arrived in Paris in 1930, at the age of twenty-six, and set up a bed-linen business.

The Polish-Jewish milieu in Belleville tended to be less religious in observance and more progressive. It was broadly under the umbrella of the French Communist Party's Main d'Oeuvre Immigrée (MOI), which brought together all immigrant workers in different language-speaking groups, organised around labour unions, community organisations and the press. The communist trade-union organisation permitted Yiddish-speaking sections of existing unions. A Yiddish-speaking textile union was formed by Isaac Krasucki, and the Jewish Inter Union Commission was founded in 1935 by Krasucki and Jewish-communist lawyer Charles Lederman.[21] Community organisations included the Belleville working-men's club founded by David Diamant, the Jewish Workers' Sports Club (YASK) and the Union of Jewish Women. The main Yiddish press forum was the *Naïe Presse* or *New Press*, launched in 1934. Its leading lights included the journalist Adam Rayski, also from Białystok, the barber Jacques Kaminski and Lajb (Louis) Gronowski, a Jewish communist who had fled to Paris after two years in prison in Poland, and worked in hotels while describing himself as one of the 'generation of the children of Red October'.[22] This Jewish-communist community was forged by the demonstrations against the fascist threat in February 1934 and support for the Popular Front and the strikes of May–June 1936. It also held meetings to send aid and volunteers to the International Brigades in Spain, which included the Yiddish-speaking Botwin Company of 120 Jews, formed early in 1938 and integrated with the Dombrowski Batallion of the International Brigades.[23]

At this point the narrative of persecuted Jewry and international anti-fascist struggle intersected with each other. Two of the most outstanding Polish-Jewish fighters in the International Brigades and then the French Resistance were Mendel Langer and Joseph Epstein. Langer was born in Russian Poland in 1903 but his father, a militant of the Bund of Jewish Socialists, emigrated to Palestine with the family in 1914 to flee the pogroms. Mendel worked on the railways as a fitter, but the Zionist project did not work out for him: 'Langer wanted to work towards the coming of a universal socialism,' recalled one of the Brigade militants. 'He thought the Zionist movement useless and even backward. For him the solution to the Jewish problem was a huge combat that would end all oppression: the liberation of all oppressed peoples.'[24] He arrived in France in 1933, was employed as a metal worker in Toulouse and joined the MOI. Soon after the outbreak of the Spanish Civil War he volunteered for the International Brigades, fought in a Polish brigade, was appointed lieutenant of the 35th Division of Machine-Gunners and even married a Spanish girl.[25] Born in 1911 to a left-wing bourgeois Jewish family in Zamość, the Russian-Polish home town of Rosa Luxemburg, Joseph Epstein was a law student in Warsaw when he joined the illegal Polish Communist Party. Having been arrested by the dictatorial Piłsudski regime in 1931 he fled to France. He took refuge in Tours, where he knew some Polish students, and met pharmacy student Paula Duffau, whom he married in 1932. While pursuing his law studies in Bordeaux and Paris, Epstein continued as a militant of the Communist Youth. Volunteering to fight in Spain in the summer of 1936, he was wounded and returned to France, only to go back again early in 1938. He was appointed political commissar to the International Brigades but insisted on going to the Ebro front, and commanded the Ana Pauker Battalion of the 35th International Division, named after a Romanian communist who had been imprisoned by the regime.[26]

The situation of foreigners in France was made much more difficult by the defeat of the Spanish republicans in January 1939, the Nazi-Soviet Pact of August 1939, and the defeat of France in June 1940. In January 1939 Catalonia fell to Franco's forces, the Civil War was over and columns of Spanish refugees streamed over the Pyrenees to France. They did not receive a heroes' welcome. The French Republic recognised the Franco regime and sent Marshal Pétain as an ambassador in March 1939. French police rounded up Spanish republicans at the frontier and herded 226,000 of them into internment camps at the Mediterranean end of the border, 77,000 at Argelès and 90,000 at Saint-Cyprien.[27] As full-scale European war approached, some Spanish republicans of military age were recruited from the internment camps – threatened that if they did not enlist they would be sent back to Franco's Spain. Others were drafted into Companies of Foreign Workers (CTE) and put to work as agricultural labourers or woodcutters, or sent north as fortification builders or powder-factory workers. Spanish republicans who were considered a political danger and veterans of the International Brigades, such as Marcel Langer and Joseph Epstein, were moved in April 1939 to the Gurs camp at the Basque end of the Pyrenean frontier.[28] Some of the internees made elaborate sculptures out of the mud of the camp for an exhibition in Paris to mark the 150th anniversary of the French Revolution. After the Nazi-Soviet Pact conditions in the camp became much harsher and right-wing Basque deputy Jean Ybarnégaray demanded that former members of the International Brigades, as agents of Comintern, should be machine-gunned in batches of fifty.[29] Spanish republicans were removed from the camps to join units such as the 13th Half Brigade of the Foreign Legion.[30] Those who had the misfortune to be taken prisoner in France were not treated as regular POWs by the Germans but deported to Mauthausen.[31] Some Spanish republicans who had served with the Foreign Legion in Narvik stayed in Britain and fought with the Free French; others were repatriated with other French forces via Morocco. There an unpleasant fate awaited them as they were interned in the camps of Vichy's North African gulag, including the punishment camp of Djelfa, and were put to work on high-mortality projects such as the building of the Trans-Saharan Railway.[32]

The Nazi-Soviet Pact and the outbreak of war in September 1939 brought a new crop of camp prisoners: communists, enemy aliens, and in the case of German communists, both rolled into one as dangerous fifth columnists. At the high-security internment camp of Le Vernet, one of the inmates was Hungarian-Jewish journalist Arthur Koestler, who had been a member of the German Communist Party and a war correspondent in Spain: 'In Liberal-Centigrade, Vernet was the zero-point of infamy,' he wrote: 'measured in Dachau-Fahrenheit it was still 32 degrees above zero.'[33] He was impressed by the prominence of the International Brigadists, 'once the pride of the European revolutionary movement [. . .] One half of the world regarded them as heroes and saints, the other half loathed them as madmen and adventurers.'[34] One of those heroes and madmen was Franz Dahlem, who described how Le Vernet, designed in theory to silence international communist opposition, paradoxically brought it together in a powerful cocktail on the verge of riot. He recalled:

> The French government made the mistake of concentrating the cadres of the International Brigades and the apparachiks of central committees of communist parties in countries with fascist regimes or occupied by the Nazis in the Le Vernet camp. They constituted a formidable force that the French could not subdue by hunger or cold or threats or arguments or provocation, neither by the danger of death or by gunfire. They were subdued in [August] 1940 only by a thousand armed police.[35]

When war finally broke out, the French government was torn between its hostility to foreigners and its need for additional manpower to fight. There was a hasty naturalisation of Belgians, Swiss, Italians and Spaniards who had been in the country for five years. Jews with French citizenship, such as Georges Boris and

Léo Hamon, were no problem and were recruited into regular French units.[36] Over 100,000 foreigners fought under the French flag, either in the Foreign Legion, or in foreign units, or in the Czechoslovak or Polish armies which, after the final annexation of Czechoslovakia in March 1939 and the rapid defeat of Poland in September–October 1939, were under the authority of governments-in-exile in Paris.[37] After the defeat of 1940 much of the Polish Army got to Britain to continue the fight, but that which remained in France was demobilised by Vichy in September 1940. A small kernel of Polish officers and NCOs based in Grenoble formed a resistance group, the POWN, in September 1941. This was loyal to the Polish government-in-exile, which had moved to London and was deeply anti-communist.[38] Linked to the POWN, a group of Intelligence Service officers including Major Roman Czerniawski (Armand), who later worked with Mathilde Carré, set up a resistance group called F2 at Toulouse. This group organised an escape line for Polish soldiers over the Pyrenees and developed intelligence antennae at Marseille and Nice.[39]

The experience of Polish Jews in the Polish and French armies was rather more mixed. Victor Bardach, known in the Resistance as Jan Gerhard, was a Polish-educated Jew who, aged eighteen, fought in the Polish Army in Poland in 1939. He continued the fight in France in the 1st Division of Polish Grenadiers. Taken prisoner by the Germans, he was sent back from his *Stalag* as war-wounded and recovered in a hospital in Lourdes before joining the Resistance in France.[40] Joseph Epstein, on the other hand, having escaped from Gurs, joined the Polish Army but then discovered that most Polish officers had 'a fascist, racist ideology and pursued all those who had fought in Spain'. He therefore organised 'a little mutiny' among soldiers who felt more Jewish or communist than traditionally Polish: they then returned their uniforms to the Polish military command and joined the French Foreign Legion, along with outsiders as marginal as they.[41] The 13th Half Brigade of the Foreign Legion, which included Spanish republicans and

Central European Jews, saw early fighting in Norway, where they were sent to counter the German invasion at Narvik.[42] Other East European Jews were recruited to Foreign Volunteers' Regiments (RMVE), hastily thrown together.[43] The family of Boris Bruhman – later known as Boris Holban – in Bessarabia spoke Yiddish and Russian when it was part of the Russian Empire, but they suffered discrimination when it was annexed by Romania in 1918. Holban joined the Young Communists, was imprisoned in 1930, and deserted from the Romanian Army when forced to do military service in 1932. After another bout of prison he escaped with the help of communist militants to Czechoslovakia in 1936 and to France in 1938. Arriving too late to fight in Spain, he joined one of the Foreign Volunteers' Regiments and was taken prisoner in the Ardennes, but escaped from the POW camp in Metz, eventually to join the Resistance.[44]

Once the German Occupation was established foreigners quickly became aware of the precariousness of their position. The community that was of course most at risk was that of the Jews. In the Occupied Zone, the German military issued an ordinance on 27 September requiring all Jews to register immediately with the French authorities, having their identity card stamped 'Jew' in red. By the end of October, 87,000 French and 65,000 foreign Jews had their names and addresses on the census. Jewish businesses had to display a yellow sign reading *Judisches Geschäft*, a prelude to their being Aryanised, or compulsorily sold off, in the course of 1940 and 1941. Vichy's Statuts des Juifs of 2 October 1940 and 3 June 1941, which applied in both Free and Occupied Zones, dismissed Jews from the public services, state education and the media, and imposed strict quotas in the liberal professions.[45] Foreign Jews were liable to internment by the administrative decision of the authorities. On 14 May 1941 foreign Jews in the 11th *arrondissement* of Paris were ordered to report to the police. They were arrested and sent to camps at Pithiviers and Beaune-la-Rolande near Orléans. Outside Paris Jews were rounded up in Nancy, Metz and Bordeaux and sent to other camps such as those of Troyes, La Lande, south of Tours, and Poitiers. Further arrests in Paris followed on 20 August 1941 and for the first time Jews were sent to the semi-finished housing estate of Drancy in the north-east suburbs of Paris, from which they would later be deported.[46] The Germans decided on further segregation under the ordinance of 29 May 1942, which required all Jews over six years of age in the Occupied Zone, whether foreign or French, to wear the Yellow Star. The arrest of foreign Jews reached its apogee in Paris on 16–17 July 1942, when 13,000 were rounded up and interned in the Vélodrome d'Hiver, and was replicated elsewhere in the Occupied and Free Zones that summer, the camps decanting their inmates into Drancy, from which the train convoys moved east.[47]

To deal with the accumulating threats of unemployment, hunger, ill-health, arrest, internment, and the breakup of families, the Jewish communities responded with organisations both to provide relief and to undertake rescue. The Russian-Jewish Zionist community set up a committee in the rue Amelot in the 11th *arrondissement*, not far from the place de la République. It provided a 'Mother and Child' dispensary, a home for abandoned children, and four soup-kitchens. The committee had a public side that provided welfare in conjunction with the Red Cross, the Oeuvre de Secours des Enfants (OSE) and even Vichy's Secours National, but was also engaged in underground activity. Thus, for example, the dispensary provided false diagnoses to get internees to hospital and false papers were manufactured in order to help Jews at risk to escape.[48]

One of the younger members involved in the committee was 21-year-old Henri Bulawko, a Jewish immigrant from Lithuania who was prominent in the Maccabi Jewish sports movement and Hashomer Hatzaïr. The anti-fascist demonstrations in Paris after the right-wing attempted coup against the Republic on 6 February 1934 had been formative for Bulawko: 'Although we were not communists, my friends from Hashomer Hatzaïr decided to demonstrate.' He was involved in providing assistance to German Jews fleeing to France and was shocked by the arrest and imprisonment of such people, including his friend Rudy Moscovici, a brilliant harmonica player, in the autumn of 1940, shut up in the Tourelles barracks in Belleville.[49] He offered his services to the Amelot Committee and began to produce false identity cards with the help of a young French woman whose father-in-law was the mayor of Pantin outside Paris and thus had access to blank identity cards.[50]

The increasing tempo of arrests and internments increased both the work of the Amelot Committee and its neighbourhood committees and the danger of those working for them. Bulawko had been able to get some friends out of Pithiviers and Beaune-la-Rolande but camp security became much tighter. Despite his suspicion of communist Jews, for the sake of effectiveness he began to work with the likes of Roger Trugnan, whose father, of Romanian-Jewish origin, was a cabinet-maker, trade unionist and communist in the Faubourg Saint-Antoine.[51] Trugnan procured leaflets that were hidden inside packets of matzo for distribution during Passover in 1942.[52]

Within the more left-wing Polish-Jewish community a meeting was held on 15 July 1940 in the rue Custine, near Montmartre. It included barber and MOI cadre Jacques Kaminski, the journalist Adam Rayski, who had fought in Polish Army in 1940 and escaped from POW camp, and Sophie Schwartz of the Union of Jewish Women. They set up an organisation called Solidarity, which soon sprouted fifty groups across Paris and its suburbs, and founded a clandestine Yiddish paper called *Unser Wort (Our Voice).*[53]

The purpose of Solidarity was to defend the Jewish community which, argued David Diamant, had to rely on its own resources to save itself. The whole community was at risk and had to go underground: 'to survive meant to fight. The mission of active resistance organisations was to lead the Jewish masses to safety either alongside French organisations or within them.'[54] The first task was to provide information, since Jews were obliged to hand in their radios: 'Our aim,' said Rayski, who was in charge of the underground press, 'was to inform and warn Jews of imminent danger [. . .] Some kind of propaganda and above all information press was a *sine qua non* of the organisation of resistance.'[55] Rayski argued that *Unser Wort* revealed the existence of 'Drancy, the Paris Dachau' in November 1941 and gave the first news about gas chambers in October–November 1942.[56] Although most Jews felt that it was best to remain legal, Solidarity urged them not to register themselves as Jews on the census, for fear of worse to come. When Jews were interned they organised demonstrations outside the camps and tried to get some individuals released, for example on medical grounds. Jacques Ravine, who was arrested on 26 July 1941 and sent to Pithiviers, organised protests and escapes within the camp.[57] Strike action, which was extremely dangerous under German occupation, was nevertheless tried as a form of protest. David Diamant, whose bedding business was confiscated and who went to work in a glove-making factory, organised a strike there in November 1941 and claimed that 160,000 gloves were lost to the *Wehrmacht*.[58] Isaac Krasucki also organised sabotage and strikes in factories working for the Germans before he was arrested in February 1942. Despite the call to arms the best defence in the end was to lie low or to escape across the demarcation line to the Free Zone. From February 1941 Solidarity provided false identities for Jews who opted for these solutions. Rayski himself went to the Free Zone in May–October 1941 to build contacts and set up a Marseille edition of *Unser Wort*. He also met a group at Marseille under Marcel Langer that was hoping to get International Brigade internees out of Gurs and Le Vernet with false papers.[59]

These activities were greatly assisted by the younger generation of Jewish activists in their late 'teens, who had been brought up in the Communist Youth and then, after it was closed down, in the Jewish Youth that was part of MOI. Isaac Krasucki's son Henri had belonged to the 'Crocodiles', the communist pioneers of Belleville, that was run by Pierre Georges before the latter went to fight in Spain in 1936. Henri was a good student at the Lycée Voltaire but with the coming of war he left at the age of fifteen to be apprenticed as a fitter. In the Jewish Youth, overseen by Adam Rayski of the MOI, he spread warnings by flyer and word of mouth denouncing Nazis and warning the community about imminent arrests.[60] A friend of Krasucki's, Paulette Sliwka, whose Polish-Jewish father was involved in the leather trade in Belleville, was still at school when she began to send parcels to internees at Pithiviers and make *papillons* with a children's printing set and distribute them outside factories and cinemas.[61] Another friend of Krasucki, Roger Trugnan, who had left school and got a job in a telegraph company, was one of a Jewish Youth group of three which met each evening in the Square Saint-Bernard, behind the church. They pasted up *papillons*, handed out tracts in metro stations and cinemas, where they cat-called when German newsreels were shown.[62]

The organisation of an underground information system made it possible to distribute tracts warning the community of impending round-ups, so that the *rafle* of 16–17 July 1942, organised by the Vichy police under the eyes of the Germans, only caught half the 27,000 Jews targeted. David Diamant told a symposium in 1974:

I can see in this hall several of our comrades who took part in this rescue operation. With leaflets and words we went from neighbourhood to neighbourhood, street to street, house to house, floor to floor, door to door, to warn people of the danger that was closing in. If 14 or 15,000 Jews escaped the tragedy of 16 July it is in large part because of the mobilisation of our forces to save them.[63]

At this point two forms of resistance came together. Jewish rescue and resistance was not isolated but operated as part of a general anti-fascist struggle alongside activists from other nationalities grouped under the umbrella of the MOI. The MOI leadership, in close contact with the underground leadership of the PCF, was a triangle of three formed by two Poles of Jewish origin, Jacques Kaminski (code name Hervé) and Louis Gronowski (Brunot), and the Jewish Czechoslovak, Artur London (Gérard). Each was responsible for a collection of language groups: London for the Czechoslovaks, Yugoslavs, Hungarians and Romanians; Kaminski for the Jews, Bulgarians and Armenians; and Gronowski for the Poles, Spaniards and Italians. In fact the majority of the Poles, Czechoslovaks, Yugoslavs, Hungarians and Romanians were Jewish.[64] That said, it was at this point that Jewish resisters of different nationalities began to work with other foreign nationalities as part of a wider anti-fascist struggle. These included Spanish republicans, Italian anti-fascists and indeed with German anti-Nazis linked to the MOI through the Travail Allemand network, which tried to persuade German soldiers to desert.

After the German invasion of the Soviet Union the French Communist Party developed its own armed wing – the Organisation Spéciale (OS), later the Francs-Tireurs et Partisans (FTP), and opened what it called a second front behind German lines.[65] Small commando teams were organised in 'triangles', with one individual in charge of military matters, one political (liaison) and an third with technical responsibilities, that is, providing weapons and explosives. Only the group leader knew the identity of its hierarchical superior so that, if anyone was arrested and tortured, they would not be able to betray more than a couple of comrades. Leadership was provided by the National Military Committee, headed by Charles Tillon. Joseph Epstein (code name Gilles) directed FTP operations in the Paris region from February–March 1943. Before throwing himself into armed resistance he sent his wife and eighteen-month-old son Georges from Paris to a village in the Yonne for safe keeping, visiting them at weekends when he could on the coach and known to Georges as 'papa-bus'.[66] In parallel with the main OS and FTP organisation the MOI developed first an OS-MOI, then an FTP-MOI. These were held somewhat at arm's length by the Communist Party, partly for security reasons, partly because the relationship of the Party with immigrants remained somewhat ambivalent. The OS-MOI and FTP-MOI involved young people but they relied for their effectiveness on the leadership of Jewish immigrants and other foreigners who had gained military experience in the International Brigades in Spain. Rayski reflected that 'the three or four OS groups were formed above all of Jews who had fought in the Spanish Civil War and thus had experience of guerrilla warfare. They were commanded above all by people who had escaped from Gurs and Le Vernet.'[67] At the head of the whole organisation was Ljubomir Ilić, who had been moved from Le Vernet to the prison of Castres, from which he escaped. A Croatian born in Split in 1905, he went to France in 1925 to study architecture. In Spain he served with Dombrowski Battalion of the International Brigades, which lost two-thirds of its forces in the defence of Madrid and then became a commander of the XIV Army Corps, which was involved in guerrilla rather than conventional warfare and equipped him to direct guerrilla warfare in France.[68] Boris Holban was in command of FTP-MOI operations in the Paris region. He organised four detachments: the first Romanian and Hungarian, which was mostly Jewish, the second Polish-Jewish, the third Italian and the fourth mixed.[69] To provide manpower, continued Rayski, 'We brought together many young Jews without parents or homes in action groups of three people. During the winter 1942–3 we had about 300 people, mostly young people, in the Jewish groups of the Francs-Tireurs et Partisans.'[70] One of those young people was Marcel Rayman, who had come to Paris from Warsaw in 1931, at the age of eight. A graduate of the 'Crocodiles' and the YASK, he joined the FTP-MOI proper while only eighteen and proved one of its most daring militants.

Meanwhile there was a good deal of resistance activity by immigrants in the Free Zone. This was dangerous, because the Vichy regime was waging war against communists, Jews and foreigners, but resisters had only Vichy police and justice to fear. Things became much more difficult when the Germans occupied the Free Zone in response to the Allied invasion of North Africa in November 1942. By this time, however, the round-ups of Jews in the summer of 1942 had driven Jews in large numbers to the south where they intensified the work of Jewish and anti-fascist resistance.

One of the foci of anti-fascist resistance in the Free Zone was the presence of exiled Spanish republicans. In December 1941 leaders of the underground Spanish Communist Party (PCE) met at Carcassonne and decided on a strategy of armed struggle. In Toulouse in April 1942 Spanish communist leader Jaime Nieto convened a dozen former commanders of the Civil War who had escaped from camps like Le Vernet and founded a XIV Corps of Spanish Guerrillas, named in honour of the unit that had excelled in the Spanish Civil War. The aim was first to liberate France from the Germans and then re-cross the Pyrenees to liberate Spain from Franco. In November 1942, fearing that the German Occupation of the Free Zone would lead to the mass drafting of Spanish workers to Germany, the PCE created a Union Nacional Española (UNE) on the model of the PCF's Front National, which combined communists, socialists, anarchists and other republicans.[71]

The nucleus of the XIV Corps was established at Varilhes, near a charcoal-burning works at Aston in the Ariège. Its muscle came from Spanish republicans who had been in internment camps along the Franco-Spanish frontier and were now requisitioned by Vichy to work as agricultural labourers, wood-cutters, dam-builders and miners. Threatened with having to work for the Todt Organisation, building fortifications against Allied invasion along the Atlantic coast or summoned to do forced labour in Germany, they often deserted. They found their way to clandestine forestry works or charcoal-burners, which served as day cover for night-time resistance activity.[72] Weapons and money were in short supply but Vicente López Tovar remembers ambushing tobacco smugglers making their way over the Pyrenees and using the proceeds to fund the cause.[73] A massive setback was suffered on 23 April 1943 when the Vichy police and *Milice* raided the camp and arrested thirty-four guerrillas. Bereft of manpower and confidence, it was decided that the purely Spanish strategy would have to become part of the wider FTP-MOI enterprise. Contact was made with the FTP-MOI leadership in Lyon, which was headed by a German anti-Nazi, Norbert Kugler, known as Albert. From a working-class Jewish family in Bavaria, Kugler had been inspired by the Bolshevik Revolution, fled Germany in 1933, fought in Thaëlmann Battalion in Spain, and escaped from a French internment camp at Récébédou near Toulouse, where he forged ties with Jews and revolutionaries of many nationalities.[74] Through the FTP-MOI Spanish republican leaders learned to work with resisters of many different backgrounds. López Tovar was sent to head the FTP-MOI in the Dordogne and Limousin areas. His second-in-command was a Romanian former International Brigadist, Pavel Cristescu, who had escaped from Le Vernet. Most curiously, Lopez made contact with Colonel Berger of the Armée Secrète, who was very interested in his Spanish military past, and who offered to share parachuted weapons. He also suggested that some of his men might be retained in a camp run by French officers: 'I rejected the offer laughing out loud,' said López Tovar, 'I knew enough about the abilities of French officers from having seen them at work in 1940.'[75] It turned out that Colonel Berger was none other than André Malraux, who had fought in Spain, although he did not join the French Resistance until March 1944.

More closely integrated with the MOI was the underground German Communist Party (KPD) and Travail Allemand (TA), the network it developed to infiltrate and win over elements from the German occupation forces. German émigré anti-Nazis who had evaded internment or escaped from camps set up an underground KPD at Toulouse and tried to make contact with comrades still in the camps. In the autumn of 1940 Käthe and Robert Dahlem – the wife and brother of Franz Dahlem, the KPD leader interned in Le Vernet – were sent from Ivry by the underground French Communist Party to try to get Dahlem out. In Toulouse they gathered other German anti-Nazis, notably Walter Beling, a communist who had taken part in the Kiel sailors' mutiny of 1918, and Otto Niebergall, a communist from the Sarre who had come to France when the Sarre was restored to Germany in 1935, and who had been active in the Lorraine miners' union. Links were made with Georges Marrane of the PCF's Front National but attempts to free Dahlem failed. Beling and later Niebergall were sent to Paris in 1941 to organise the Travail Allemand in conjunction with the MOI.[76] One of the recruits to this work in the Free Zone was Gerhard Leo, whose father Wilhelm, a Jewish lawyer, had demonstrated in a libel trial in 1927 that Goebbels' club foot was not the result of torture inflicted by the French during their occupation of the Rhineland. He was forced to flee Nazi Germany in 1933 and set up a German-language bookshop in Paris near the place de la République, which became a meeting point for German anti-Nazis. Interned in Gurs at the outbreak of war, he lived after his release under a false identity in the Gascon countryside. Gerhard, born in 1923 and schooled in France, was the perfect recruit for Franco-German resistance.[77] When he came to see his father in Gascony he was introduced to the KPD leadership in Toulouse, notably Werner Schwarze (Eugen), a turner by trade and former member of the International Brigades: 'I joined a group of German communists,' recalled Leo, 'who, under the orders of the central committee of the French Communist Party, undertook "political work" inside the *Wehrmacht*.'[78] Gerhard got himself employed in the German bureaucracy in Toulouse, first in an office rounding up young Frenchmen for forced labour for Germany, then in the transport offices, as a cover while seeking to subvert German troops. Warned that he was suspected in Toulouse by the Germans, he was sent by Schwartze to Castres to work alongside Yugoslav resisters to bring over Soviet POWs who had been drafted into the *Wehrmacht*. Making and distributing flyers with two communist workers, Noémie and Marcel Boussière, he said that he felt 'immediately at home' in the joint anti-Nazi struggle.[79]

The communist dimension of resistance among Germans, German Jews and Spanish republicans was powerful and spectacular, but it was not the only dimension. There was a Zionist profile to Jewish rescue and resistance as well as a communist one. In Paris it developed in Paris around the rue Amelot, while in the Free Zone it took shape in Toulouse, which was full of Jewish refugees, some trying to get to Spain, others to Marseille and America. The central figure here was Abraham Polonski, who was born in Białystok, but fleeing the pogroms emigrated with his parents to Palestine in 1910. Five years there, facing young Arabs who chanted, 'Jew, Jew, I'll cut off your head!' were enough to make him a 'convinced Zionist' with 'a readiness to resist all those who attacked Jews'.[80] In 1915 Palestine was occupied by the Ottoman Turks and the Polonski family was driven out as Russian subjects. They took refuge in Alexandria, where Abraham heard talk of a Jewish battalion that would fight alongside the Allies. After the 1917 Revolution the family returned to Russia hoping for better times and Abraham was briefly a member of the communist youth movement, Komsomol. However, when Soviet troops withdrew from what now became Poland, the family was again persecuted and came to France, where Abraham studied to become an electrical engineer. In 1939 he attended the Zionist congress in Basle which, as war threatened, was thinking urgently about a future Jewish state. There he met Lucien Lublin, who had been a Zionist in Russian Poland, the Russian-Jewish poet and journalist David Fiksman, known as David Knout, and his poet and journalist and his wife Ariane (Regine), who was the daughter of the Russian composer Scriabin.[81]

In 1940 Polonski was drafted into war production, working for the National Nitrogen Office outside Toulouse. Lublin was mobilised but taken ill and found himself convalescing at Toulouse when the armistice was signed. He remembered that:

Whereas for most soldiers the war was finished, it was not so for us Jews. The front no longer existed but it was replaced by an Occupation whose consequences were much more serious that a war between two armies face to face.[82]

Polonski, Lublin and Knout, who came to Toulouse as a refugee, founded a secret society called Main Forte or Strong Arm. Its first task was to try to get interned foreign Jews out of the camps where the Daladier government and Vichy had interned them. It recruited its membership through a legitimate Hebrew study group educating Jews for a future in Palestine. One of these was Albert Cohen, who was born in Argentina and in 1940 served as an NCO in the French Army in Levant. After the defeat he was told that as a Jew he would have to surrender his stripes if he wished to continue to serve. He refused and returned to France, arriving in Toulouse in December 1940. He described a conversion experience to a new Jewish identity:

There I met my brother Simon. We wondered what we could do, as already the anti-Jewish laws were beginning to have an impact. We asked at the synagogue, and there they directed us to a Hebrew class run by David Knout. There I discovered a whole Jewish world that I scarcely knew, for though I was a foreigner I was French in my heart.[83]

From the study group Cohen was introduced by Knout to Main Forte, which now had the aim of 'resisting the anti-Jewish laws'. Initiation involved a secret ritual: 'It was a very tight group,' said Cohen, 'I took the oath in a darkened room. Then one evening, I was taken to meet Polonski, without being told that he was the leader.'

Main Forte was the predecessor of the Armée Juive or 'Jewish Army' that was set up in August 1941. Lucien Lublin recalls that 'we adopted the general aims of the French Resistance, that is, to support the Allied war effort, to prepare materially and mentally for the moment France would be liberated.' That said, he clarified, 'we wanted first to define purely Jewish objectives which were to be our own.'[84] The Jewish Army was answerable not to the French Resistance but to the Haganah in France, which reported to the head of the Haganah in Europe, who reported to the paramilitary Haganah in Palestine.[85] It was linked to other Zionist organisations, such as the Éclaireurs Israélites de France under Robert Gamzon, and received funding via Switzerland from the American Joint Distribution Committee.[86] Based in Toulouse the Jewish Army had outposts in Nice and in Lyon, where Ernest and Anne-Marie Lambert ran operations from the back of a stationers' shop. On a train Ernest Lambert met a friend from Strasbourg, Jacques Lazarus, a career soldier who had been dismissed from the French Army in 1941, under the Statut des Juifs, and then in 1943 from an insurance company. Although heading for North Africa, he decided to stop and join the Jewish Army, since he now felt more Jewish than French. He provided much-needed military expertise for the next stage of the struggle.[87]

This struggle was transformed by the *rafles* or round-ups of foreign Jews in the summer of 1942 that took place in both the Occupied and Free Zones. These highlighted the priority to rescue Jews from deportation but also the need for them to resist. Rescue, of course, may be seen as a form of resistance. Since the Nazi project was to exterminate the Jews, to survive, as David Diamant had said, was itself to fight.[88] To obey the rules and regulations to which they were subject meant in the end that they would go like lambs to the slaughter. Vichy and the Nazis were openly destroying Jewish communities and the response was that this destruction must be resisted and indeed avenged. Adam Rayski defined the politics of Jewish resisters after the round-ups in Biblical terms: '"An eye for an eye, a tooth for a tooth" must be the cry of all French Jews in their desire to avenge victims.

The concept of a "war within the war" appeared very early in our writings.'[89] Jews were fighting the Nazis not only to liberate France but for the very survival of the Jewish people. For young Jews this was not an abstract question: they saw their parents, uncles, aunts and even siblings arrested, interned and deported. They were the 'generation of the *rafle*' that was driven by the shock of the deportations into joining resistance activity against the Nazis, a resistance that grew progressively more violent.[90]

After the *rafles* of July 1942 it became very difficult to operate rescue organisations in Paris, either Zionist or communist. Before long, said Henri Bulawko, the Amelot Committee had 'no organisers, no hiding places, no paramilitary structures'.[91] Increasing numbers of activists fled to the Free Zone. Bulawko, who stayed in Paris, was arrested on 19 November 1942, and sent to Beaune-la-Rolande and Drancy before being deported to Auschwitz on 18 July 1943. Small groups of Jewish Youth remained in Paris, not least to look after their families while resisting. Paulette Sliwka heard rumours about the round-up on 15 July and slept away from home with a friend; she came back to her street the next day to see people being dragged away. She removed her brother's Yellow Star and took him to a children's home in the suburbs. Then she hid her parents in her father's workshop and supplied them with food and cigarettes. She continued operations with the Jewish Youth group that included Henri Krasucki, whose father had been arrested in February 1942 and deported, and with Roger Trugnan, scattering resistance leaflets on the metro and in cinemas. All three young people were arrested in March 1943, taken to Drancy and deported the following June to Auschwitz.[92]

In the face of the policy of extermination a minority of committed Jews fought back through the FTP and FTP-MOI. Their armed struggle was improvised and extremely dangerous. Weapons were difficult to come by and sometimes even acquired from the Jewish flea-market traders of the northern suburb of Saint-Ouen. Explosives to put in grenades were manufactured in a home laboratory in the rue Geoffroy Saint-Hilaire, in the Marais, by two former members of the International Brigades, one Polish-Jewish, the other Ukrainian-Jewish. Unfortunately both were killed by an explosion in the flat on 25 April 1942.[93] Tactics were also improvised according to circumstance and debates between leaders. Early in 1943 FTP commander Joseph Epstein suggested ratcheting up the conventional three-man triangle by operations that would involve 'three or four grenade- or bomb-throwers, and ten or twelve fighters spaced out along the escape routes to provide protection'. This was approved by the FTP in the person of Albert Ouzoulias, the commissar in charge of military operations, and Charles Tillon of the National Military Committee. In July 1943 a German parade goose-stepping along the Champs-Élysées according to its daily routine came under Epstein's new style attack. Three activists threw their grenades while nine others with revolvers, given money to buy clothes so that they would look like any other *flaneurs* from the posh neighbourhoods, were organised in two ranks. Two gunmen in the first rank fired at the Germans and Vichy police who gave pursuit, and they were covered in turn by four gunmen in the second rank. So successful was the tactic that only one comrade was lightly wounded in the hand while the Germans thought they had been hit by a hundred partisans.[94]

Attacks by Jews in FTP-MOI units were likewise daring and often dramatic. Attacks against German military installations and personnel were commonplace but special missions were also carried out on the leading figures of the German Occupation. General von Schaumburg, military commander of Greater Paris, was targeted as the man who signed the orders to execute French Resistance fighters. For three weeks an officer was observed by young women of the group going for a morning horse-ride in the Bois de Boulogne and then returning to the Trocadéro in an official car. On 28 July 1943 Marcel Rayman was one of a group of three which threw a bomb into the car in the rue Nicolo, killing its occupant. It turned out, however, to be not Schaumburg but an air force general.[95] Amends were made on 28 September after the military direction of the FTP-MOI in Paris was taken over from Holban by the Armenian poet and activist Missak Manouchian. Manouchian favoured breaking down the barriers between foreign immigrants and forged a multi-national squad of the Pole Marcel Rayman, the Italian Spartaco Fontano, the German-Jew Leo Kneller and the Spaniard Celestino Alfonso, a former International Brigadist and excellent shot. This squad executed SS Colonel Julius von Ritter (whose mission was to draft young Frenchmen into forced labour in Germany) on 28 September 1943.

Increasing danger in the Occupied Zone after July 1942 prompted thousands of Jews to flee to the Free Zone. This was not a great deal safer, because round-ups of foreign Jews took place there too, but at least the Zone was free of Germans until November 1942. For those who wanted to engage in resistance the main centres were Lyon and Toulouse. For those who simply wanted to flee the main destination was Nice, which was occupied by the Italians in November 1942, but Italian Fascists did not operate the same destructive policies against Jews as the Nazis. All this changed when the Italians dropped out of the war in September 1943 and the Germans arrived in Nice.

One family group that joined up in Lyon in the summer of 1942 was the Fryds. In 1939 Rywka (Rosine) Fryd had married Francis Chapouchnik, a worker in the fur trade and still only nineteen, and they came to Lyon in December 1941. She had lost her father at the beginning of the war and her mother was arrested in the round-up of 16 July and sent to Auschwitz. Her young brother, Simon, who Francis remembered machine-sewing trousers in his parents' home in the Marais, as 'a calm, serious boy', was interned in Beaune-la-Rolande. He escaped from there and joined Rywka and Francis in Lyon in August 1942.[96] The Fryds and Chapouchnik met up with the Weinsteins and became involved in the Union of Jewish Youth (UJJ). They were instructed by the Jewish communist lawyer and MOI activist Charles Lederman, who had played a key role in the Night of Vénissieux and, according to Chapouchnik, gave them 'a clearer understanding of our commitment to fight Nazism'.[97] Initially their work was to distribute flyers and *papillons*, marking such moments as, for example in September 1942, the 150th anniversary of the French revolutionaries' victory at Valmy, in the hope of reconstructing a patriotic national community. Max Weinstein recalled coming out of a Villeurbanne cinema with flyers in his pockets as a German patrol went by and being pushed into a doorway for a kiss by a female comrade to avoid attracting attention.[98] On the day the Germans marched into Lyon on 11 November 1942 Simon Fryd and Francis Chapouchnik provided armed cover for Norbert Kugler, a veteran of Spain, who threw a grenade at a German convoy marching along the banks of the Saône. This exploded in the gutter but was declared to be the first symbolic attack on the Germans in the former Free Zone.[99]

Things grew more serious at the beginning of 1943, as news filtered through of the German defeat at Stalingrad and of the Warsaw Ghetto uprising. Georges Weinstein, the Fryds and Francis Chapouchnik became involved in an double-headed FTP-MOI combat group that was called the Carmagnole Battalion in Lyon and Liberté in nearby Grenoble. Like the FTP-MOI groups in Paris, Carmagnole-Liberté combined young resisters with veterans who had been trained in combat, notably in the Spanish Civil War. One triangle was formed by Simon Fryd, the group's 'technician', who obtained explosives from miners working outside Lyon, his sister Rosine, who acted a liaison agent and carried weapons, and her husband, Francis Chapouchnik. Francis finally left his family and went underground, scolded by his mother as an 'ungrateful son'. Although, said Chapouchnik, 'the vast majority of fighters were youths,' they were led by older resisters who had been battle-scarred in the International Brigades.[100] Norbert Kugler was thirty-eight, while one of his lieutenants, Polish-Jewish Ignace Krakus (Roman), a former plumber and Brigadist who had escaped from Le Vernet in a dustbin, was thirty-four. Krakus was a genuine cosmopolitan, a comrade commented: 'He was Jewish but he spoke Yiddish badly. He had fought in Spain but he spoke Spanish badly. French he massacred. He spoke a mixture of all those languages. The complete foreigner. But he had a sharp sense of organisation and an incredible force of character.'[101]

Carmagnole-Liberté was indeed a very international organisation. Of the sixty-four cadres at the Liberation, thirty-six or 56 per cent were Polish Jews, nine or 14 per cent were Hungarian or Romanian Jews, six or 9.5 per cent were Italian and the same number French, of whom two were Jewish.[102] Among the Italians were Louis Landini, called to Lyon from Saint-Raphaël to act as political commissar and his younger brother Léon. Léon had been warned that the average life of a militant was three months but he was not the first victim.[103] Resisters who went underground lacked ration books and tickets and were often driven to obtain them by robbing public offices. On 29 May 1943 such a trivial job organised by Simon Fryd and Francis and Rosine Chapouchnik led to a shoot-out with police, one of whom was wounded. Francis and Rosine escaped to Grenoble and the Vercors but Simon was arrested and the Vichy authorities decided to make an example of him as a terrorist. He was sent for trial before the Lyon Section Spéciale, one of the exceptional courts set up by Vichy in August 1941, in response to Pierre Georges' first killing of a German soldier, to deal with enemies of the state. He was sentenced to death and guillotined in St Paul's prison on 4 December 1943. His last note read, 'I die for the cause I fought for. Avenge me.'[104]

This was a major shock to the Resistance but one to which they responded decisively. The private house of Faure-Pinguely, the magistrate who had sentenced Fryd, was watched by female members of the group in order to establish the magistrate's movements. On 12 December 1943, on the orders of Kugler, his house was approached by Maurice Najman (Gilles) dressed as a Gestapo agent and Roman Krakus and another comrade disguised as German soldiers. Polish-Jewish Najman had come to Lyon from Paris in 1941, aged twenty-one, finding a job as a mechanic. He went to Vénissieux to try to get his uncle out in September 1942 only to see 'dozens of men, women and children taken off in buses to Drancy'. In February 1943 his father was deported from Drancy and 'again, we could do nothing'. He joined Carmagnole as Captain Gilles and was keen to wreak vengeance on the magistrate. Roman hit him with a baton and 'we finished him off with pistol shots. I had only one regret: it all happened too quickly and M. Faure-Pinguely never knew who we were and why we had come to kill him.'[105]

Toulouse was another centre of international resistance. There the sister organisation of Carmagnole-Liberté was the 35th Brigade. It was named after the Spanish unit of its founder, Marcel Langer, who had escaped from Gurs.[106] Langer's commanders were drawn mainly from Jewish militants who had come to France to study because of the *numerus clausus* in Hungary or Romania, and had served in the International Brigades or Foreign Legion. For example, Marc Brafman, born in Łódź, came to France in 1936 to study chemistry in Montpellier and at the Sorbonne, and fought in the Foreign Legion, then the Polish Army, in 1940. Escaping to the Free Zone he found work with a miller and then, ordered to report to an internment camp near Toulouse, decided to go underground.[107] In February 1943 Marcel Langer was arrested at a suburban station of Toulouse with a briefcase full of explosives. He was sent for trial before the Section Spéciale of Toulouse, where *avocat-général* Lespinasse, prosecuting, demanded and obtained the death penalty. Langer was guillotined on 23 July 1943 but not before he told Lespinasse, 'My blood will fall upon your head.'[108] The Brigade, which now took the name of Marcel Langer, was taken over by Jan Gerhard, the Polish-educated Jew who had fought in the Polish Army both in Poland and France. He was militarily effective and had a vision of urban guerrilla warfare in the post-Stalingrad landscape.[109] Gerhard led the team that undertook the execution of Lespinasse on 10 October 1943. As he walked to church that morning, his wife on his arm, Lespinasse was approached from behind by a lone cyclist who fired four shots into his back. 'My husband never got involved in politics and, I repeat, to my knowledge he had no personal enemies,' his widow innocently told police. The police understood at once that it was a vengeance attack but suspected Marcel Langer's wife or a random Jewish student. At this point they had no inkling of what became known as the 35th Brigade Marcel Langer.[110]

To broaden the base of the Brigade Gerhard recruited a tranche of younger resisters. These included former members of the Éclaireurs Israélites (EIF), which had been tolerated by Vichy until 1942, but whose members under threat of deportation were now forced underground. Claude and Raymond Lévy, smarting from the obligation to register as Jews, dreamed of crossing the Pyrenees and becoming air-force pilots – 'knights of the epoch' – with the RAF or Free French.[111] Failing and briefly imprisoned in Marseille, they joined the EIF's rural encampments at Lautrec, then Moissac. When these broke up in 1942 they went to Toulouse and were incorporated into the 35th Brigade, even though Claude professed 'a physical fear of shooting German soldiers'.[112] Also recruited were anti-fascist Italians from the Garonne valley. Damira Titonel was the elder sister of four brothers and felt excluded from secret political discussions in her father's house, but was brought into resistance by 'a beautiful young blonde girl', Rosine Bet. Rosine introduced her to the Polish-Jewish 'Commandant', Joseph (Robert) Wachspress, who told her, 'We need all available fighters,' and Damira became his courier in the 35th Brigade.[113]

The urban guerrilla warfare undertaken by groups like the 35th Brigade was highly dangerous and extremely costly. Disaster struck on 1 March 1944 when Rosine Bet, David Freiman and

Enzo Godéas tried to explode a bomb in the Cinéma des Variétés in Toulouse, where the *Jew Suss* was playing to an audience of German soldiers. The bomb went off accidentally; Rosine and David were killed, Enzo was badly wounded and arrested. At this point the police rounded up and interrogated a score of young people and discovered all that they wished to know about the group. Marc Brafman and Damira Titonel, who were stopped on a train waiting to leave Toulouse, claimed to be only lovers but their cover was soon blown.[114] Titonel's brothers and Claude and Raymond Lévy were also arrested. Enzo Godéas, who was only eighteen, was executed at the Saint-Michel prison, tied to a chair, witnessed by Claude Lévy through the bars of his cell.[115] The 35th Brigade was virtually eliminated. From this point on resistance by the survivors became more transnational, since they were forced to work with resisters from other backgrounds. The high-risk strategy of Jan Gerhard was disapproved of by the FTP-MOI leadership, and the Communist Party, and he was sent off to command a *maquis* in the Ardennes.[116] His replacement, Warsaw-born Claude Urman, only twenty-three, who volunteered for Spain but had been sent back as under age, was sent by Norbert Kugler from Lyon to Toulouse but arrived only in time to witness the mass arrests and – as rural guerrilla action took over from urban – to retreat to the Tarn *maquis*.[117] Brafman and the Lévy brothers were deported on the so-called 'ghost train', which collected prisoners from Toulouse, Le Vernet and Noé and set off on 2 July 1944 for Dachau. Damira Titonel was put on a train on 24 July destined for Ravensbrück.[118]

The French Resistance mobilised only a minority of French people. The vast majority learned to muddle through under German Occupation and long admired Marshal Pétain, even when they fell out of sorts with the Vichy government headed by Pierre Laval. Communists, Jews and foreigners were persecuted by the Germans, Vichy, and even by the French Republic in 1939. Spanish republicans and veterans of the International Brigades fleeing defeat in Spain were interned by the French in camps along the Spanish border, soon to be joined by communists after the Nazi-Soviet Pact and German anti-Nazis when war was declared. Persecution of what it called 'anti-France' was stepped up by Vichy. Germany unleashed lethal anger against communists when it invaded the Soviet Union and intensified its round-ups of foreign Jews. The majority of the Jewish population in France, which was progressively excluded from society and then faced destruction, fled or hid rather than resisted. But with less to lose and fewer hiding places, communists, Jews and foreigners had greater incentives to resist than the average French person. The MOI, which organised foreigners under the umbrella of the Communist Party, became a nursery of resisters who engaged in highly dangerous urban guerrilla warfare through the FTP-MOI and the FTP itself. Jews of a Zionist rather than communist persuasion formed the Armée Juive, which was secretly linked to the paramilitary Haganah in Palestine. All this suggests that it may be more accurate to talk less about the *French* Resistance than about resistance in France.

9

The hinge: North Africa

The 8 November was a Day of Dupes. It was a right-wing revolution made by left-wingers.

(Raphaël Aboulker, 1947)

On 8 November 1942, hearing the news of the Allied landings in French North Africa, an office worker from Lyon snatched up her pen and wrote to the BBC:

You can't imagine my delight when I woke to hear the radio announcing your arrival in Algeria. Truly I am mad with joy. I want to shout out my happiness. I can't wait to get to the office tomorrow to share my giddiness with my colleagues who feel just the same way as me. I am sending you my best wishes and when as I hope you soon arrive in France there will not be enough flowers to throw at your feet.[1]

Less than a month later, two women from Marseille wrote an entirely different letter. It was full of incomprehension and bitterness about the strange and brutal turn events had taken:

No, we do not understand. A government has established itself in Algeria under Darlan, taking decisions in the name of Vichy. Instead of bringing French people together this can only drive them apart. If the Americans want to use the Admiral for their war aims, so be it. But the Admiral should take decisions by his own authority and not as the Marshal's representative. We will not be humiliated by the Americans in this way, even for a moment. Patriots are extremely unhappy. American radio seems to think that the Marshal is popular in France. Big mistake. You should see cinema audiences when the newsreel shows the Marshal arriving or at the end of one of his messages. There is an icy silence. Not a single hand clap [. . .] The Americans really do not understand the French.[2]

So what had gone wrong? How could it be that hopes of liberation that were raised to such a pitch on 8 November were so dashed by what appeared to be a deal between the Americans and the Vichy regime?

The explanation was not, unfortunately, hard to find. The liberation of North Africa was undertaken not by French troops but by Americans. De Gaulle was not even told that the landings were about to take place. When awoken by his chief of staff on the morning of 8 November, to be given the news, he replied: 'Very well. I hope that Vichy's men throw them back into the sea. That is no way to come into France, like a burglar.'[3] Relations between Roosevelt's administration and de Gaulle were very poor. Because it did not enter the war until December 1941, the United States did not feel betrayed by France's 1940 armistice with Germany as Great Britain did. Instead it sent a naval man, Admiral William Leahy, to be ambassador to Vichy in January 1941, calculating that he would have influence with Admiral Darlan, who then headed the French government. Leahy dreamed of using Darlan to bring France over to the Allies, but Darlan was irredeemably hostile to Great Britain after Mers el-Kébir, and calculated that the restoration of French power would come through collaboration with Germany. Darlan told Leahy in July 1941 that 'if the Americans showed up with 500,000 men his attitude would be entirely different, and if we came with enough force to give the French a reasonable prospect of holding their colonies against an Axis invasion, he would join with us.'[4] Leahy therefore saw his task to 'keep the French on our side so far as possible' through the Vichy regime and to limit their collaboration with Germany. He had no time for what he called 'the de Gaullists' or 'the underground people' and claimed they were threatening to assassinate Vichy ministers. Moreover, he concluded that 'the de Gaulle movement has not the following indicated in the British radio or in the American press. Frenchmen with whom I can talk, even those completely desirous of a British victory, have little regard for General de Gaulle.'[5]

The hostility of Roosevelt and his administration was partly the outcome of global strategy and partly a hostile reaction to the man himself. The United States felt betrayed by the Free French's violation of an agreement concluded between Vichy and Washington, under which France would not challenge American power in its Atlantic sphere of interest. On Christmas Day 1941, in their bid to secure portions of the French Empire, the Free French antagonised the Americans by seizing from Vichy the islands of Saint-Pierre et Miquelon off Nova Scotia, only 500 miles from US territory.[6] For his part, Roosevelt had his eyes on Dakar in Senegal as a possible American base and had already been annoyed by de Gaulle's attempt to recover it in September 1940. On a personal level, Roosevelt's views may have been shaped by those of Alexis Léger, the former diplomat who had refused to join de Gaulle in London, in June 1940, and who had gone to Washington. The President and his administration regarded de Gaulle as an egoistic troublemaker whose personal ambitions divided a French people otherwise considered happy under Marshal Pétain, and who harboured Napoleonic fantasies about seizing power in France as a dictator.[7]

Once America joined the war against the Axis, its strategy had no place for the ambitions of the Free French. America was focussed on French North Africa, which was a bastion of Vichy both militarily and politically. It was the base of France's navy until it was sunk at Mers el-Kébir, and of the 140,000-strong Army of Africa which, it was hoped, would resume hostilities against the Axis at some time in the near future. The United States was prepared to do a deal with whichever military or naval commander at Vichy could deliver North Africa. A prime target was General Weygand, Vichy's delegate-general in North Africa. In February 1941 Roosevelt's representative in Algiers, Robert Murphy, concluded a deal with Weygand, whereby the

Americans would secretly supply oil and weapons to the Army of Africa to enable it to re-enter the war. However, the Germans caught a whiff of Weygand's infidelity and twisted Pétain's arm to recall him, which he did in November 1941. The Army of Africa was now entrusted to General Alphonse Juin, who had formerly been chief of staff to General Noguès, the Resident General of the Moroccan Protectorate, who had conspicuously failed to continue the fight in North Africa in 1940 and saved it for Vichy.

From the middle of 1942 things were heating up on the American side. General Eisenhower was appointed supreme commander of an Allied expeditionary force in the North African theatre of operations, and went to Gibraltar to plan Operation Torch. It was vital to find a Vichy general with whom business could be done when the Americans landed, but this was not easy. Robert Murphy flew to Washington and met Roosevelt on 16 September to discuss options.[8] He then flew back to North Africa and on 9 October 1942 sounded out General Noguès in Morocco. But when Murphy mentioned an Allied landing, Noguès' 'reaction was explosive. "Do not try that!" he cried. "If you do, I will meet you with all the firepower I possess. It is too late for France to participate in this war now."'[9] With no joy there, the Americans moved on to their next candidate, General Giraud, who had escaped from a German fortress and, having declared his loyalty to Pétain, was living quietly in the south of France. A secret meeting was arranged between the Americans and General Charles Emmanuel Mast, who had been with Giraud in the fortress of Königstein, was considered his representative, and now commanded the XIX Corps at Algiers. Eisenhower's second-in-command, General Mark Clark, was taken by submarine from Gibraltar and landed on Cherchell beach, near Algiers, during the night of 22–23 October 1942. He met General Mast in an isolated house at the top of the cliff, where Murphy acted as interpreter. The plan was that when the Americans landed they would bring Giraud to Algiers and use him to ensure that North Africa swung into the Allied camp. Unfortunately, Giraud was no different from de Gaulle in having personal ambitions and imagined he would be appointed Supreme Commander of the Allied forces in North Africa, for what did the Americans understand about war?[10]

All these negotiations took place between military men at the highest level. There was no question of involving the French Resistance, in whatever form it might be. In the event, there was very little resistance activity in North Africa. The French settler community of *pieds noirs* in North Africa were among the most enthusiastic supporters of the Vichy regime and anti-Semitism was rife. The Legion Française des Combattants, 100,000 strong, and its militant core, the Service d'Ordre Légionnaire (SOL), were the transmission belts of the regime's ideology and instruments for denouncing opponents of the National Revolution.[11] Jacques Soustelle, a brilliant ethnologist working for the Free French in London, remarked:

For many French citizens of North Africa, if the National Revolution had not existed, it would have been invented. Nowhere in France or the Empire was it flaunted with such insolence: enormous slogans daubed onto walls, gigantic portraits of the good dictator. Nowhere did the Legion or the SOL have more recruits with the fateful 'smoothing iron' in their buttonhole.[12]

What Soustelle did not see was that many of those graffiti were swastikas and that Algiers had had its own 'little *Kristallnacht*' to terrorise the Jewish community on 12 September 1940.[13] The policy of excluding communists, Jews and foreigners was pursued with alacrity in North Africa. Communist organisations were smashed and their leaders sent for trial and imprisoned. The Jewish community, which in 1931 made up 13 per cent of the European population in Algiers, 19 per cent in Oran and 28 per cent in Constantine, had been granted French citizenship under the Crémieux law of 1870 and was thoroughly assimilated.[14] Not only were the Statuts des Juifs imposed on Algeria, purging the public service and professions of Jews, but Jewish businesses were Aryanised and the Crémieux law was abrogated on 7 October 1940, depriving Jews of citizenship and making them internal exiles. In 1941 a *numerus clausus* was imposed, limiting the proportion of Jewish children to 14 per cent of the school population, lowered the following year to 7 per cent, and imposing a higher education quota of 3 per cent, which virtually eliminated Jewish students from university.[15] Exclusion often became confinement. Jewish volunteers and Spanish republicans who had fought in the 1940 campaign and were repatriated from Britain after the armistice were interned along with communists and other unwanted elements in a network of gulags and work camps that stretched into the Sahara.[16]

Despite the intense Vichy loyalism of North Africa, there was a small resistance movement that tried to link up with American forces. It might be truer to say resistance cells, for they were small, disparate and ill-connected. They were composed of three distinct elements: activist members of the persecuted Jewish community, a Gaullist network centred on the University of Algiers, and right-wing and indeed extreme-right-wing cabals that agreed with Vichy except on the point of its collaboration with Germany. Tenuous links held them together briefly in their bid to act as a fifth column to make contact with arriving American forces, neutralise the Vichy supreme command and bring the Army of Africa into the Allied camp, but their agendas were very different and it did not take long for them to turn on each other.[17]

The first cell of resisters gravitated around José Aboulker, a 22-year-old medical student who was unable to continue his studies because of the *numerus clausus*. His father, Henri Aboulker, had been one of Émile Zola's bodyguards in Paris during the Dreyfus Affair, became a surgeon and professor at the Algiers Medical Faculty, and led the Radical-Socialists on the *conseil général*. As a veteran of the 1914–18 war he was personally exempted from Vichy's anti-Semitic laws, but this was not the case for his son or for his nephew, Raphaël, in his late thirties, who had served as a doctor in the Foreign Legion in the Sahara and with the cavalry at Oran. Resistance for the Jews, said José, was 'a necessity, a fight for survival against those who wanted to destroy them'.[18] His group included other medical students and *lycée* students in Algiers who were also now shut out of university education.[19] Raphaël said that about a hundred of them formed 'a tribe which was very suspicious of outsiders. They came from a predominantly Jewish neighbourhood.'[20] They trained in a gym as a self-defence group under Raphaël in order to build solidarity and protect speakers at meetings of such organisations as the International League against Anti-Semitism (LICA) and themselves from fascist attacks.[21] Links were established with André Achiary, a police chief of Basque origin, who headed the Brigade de la Surveillance du Territoire (BST). This was supposed to clamp down on suspected resistance but in fact protected them to the extent that Achiary himself, suspected by the Vichy authorities, was moved from Algiers to Sétif in the middle of 1942.[22]

The second cell of resisters was comprised of Gaullists at the University of Algiers, who had links to the Liberté and later the Combat movement in metropolitan France. René Capitant had been a law professor at Strasbourg before the war, moved with the university after the defeat to Clermont-Ferrand, and then requested a professorship at Algiers, telling his students that 'the road to Strasbourg goes via Algiers.'[23] In Algiers he found an 'overwhelming Vichysme' except in the oasis of the university. Key to the operation was André Fradin, a young industrialist from Lorraine who had fought in 1940 with François de Menthon, and who was captured and later repatriated because of his wounds. He was sent by Combat as a link man to Algeria, under the cover of running a fruit plantation: 'The originality of Combat across the sea,' reflected Fradin, 'was that it was the only Gaullist movement in North Africa, while the other movements [. . .] were attracted by the ideology of General Giraud and were supported by our British and American Allies.'[24] This indeed went for the group around José

Aboulker, who kept the Gaullists at arm's length because he saw them as propagandists more than conspirators and because in the first instance he was ready to go along with the Giraud option.[25]

The Gaullists indeed suffered from an absence of links to people who could help them. Fradin knew Robert Murphy but Capitant complained they had very little out of him, since he was 'violently Francophobe and anti-Gaullist (a bigoted Catholic of Irish origin). Like all the American establishment Murphy had no time for the Gaullists. He always kept Combat at a distance and never helped them to communicate with London.'[26] In the later summer of 1942 Capitant returned to France to talk to François de Menthon and other members of Combat who had connections with London. He also visited another general, Jean de Lattre de Tassigny, who was in command of the Armistice Army at Montpellier, to persuade him to come to Algiers, but without success. Lacking wider contacts, Combat concentrated less on intelligence and more on propaganda, seeking to develop support for de Gaulle in North Africa.[27]

Much more influential and well-connected was a group of extreme-right-wing conspirators that was Vichyist in all but strategy. Its most flamboyant member was Henri d'Astier de la Vigerie, the elder brother of Emmanuel d'Astier de la Vigerie of Libération, who had come to Algeria in the spring of 1941 and took a leadership position in the Chantiers de la Jeunesse, which replaced military service for twenty-year-olds in defeated France. Henri d'Astier was a royalist, a member of Action Française who had broken with Charles Maurras over the latter's endorsement of Vichy's policy of collaboration. D'Astier argued that 'France must first recover from the slap received in '40, the humiliation of which was unbearable.' That said, it was 'impossible to call on de Gaulle and the British because of Mers el-Kébir' and he feared that the arrival of de Gaulle would provoke civil war.[28] D'Astier was introduced to José Aboulker in January 1942 and they met regularly in José's father's flat in Algiers.[29]

More important though was d'Astier's meeting via Achiary with the central figure of the extreme-right-wing resistance group, Jacques Lemaigre-Dubreuil. Lemaigre-Dubreuil was a former soldier and banker who had married into the Lesieur cooking oil firm and became chief executive of a peanut-oil business, whose empire stretched from Dunkirk to Dakar.[30] He headed a Taxpayers' Federation that campaigned against the Popular Front and had been a member of the Cagoule, a conspiratorial group that broke with Action Française in 1935 in order to undertake violent subversive activity against the Republic. His right-hand man Jean Rigault, also a Cagoulard, was described by José Aboulker, who met him in June 1942, as 'a young man of cadaverous appearance, perhaps a drug addict on the evidence of his nervous twitches, very astute but deliberately cold in manner'.[31] Lemaigre-Dubreuil's plan was to use an American landing to swing the Army of Africa into the Allied camp. He had established contact with Robert Murphy when the latter first arrived in North Africa at the end of 1940. After the Weygand option fell through Lemaigre was very quickly onto the case of Henri Giraud, known to him through the Cagoule in the 1930s. In June 1942 he went to see Giraud in the south of France and persuaded him to become involved in the Americans' campaign in North Africa. This Giraud was happy to do, but was already asserting his terms, which included being made supreme commander of the Allied forces.[32]

Since the most likely site for an American landing was the coast of Morocco, Lemaigre-Dubreuil made contact with General Béthouart who, since parting company with de Gaulle in London in 1940 to go to North Africa, had been appointed by Weygand commander at Rabat. Lemaigre-Dubreuil talked to Béthouart about discussions with Giraud and the possibility of resuming hostilities with Germany. As intelligence about an imminent American landing became clearer, Béthouart received a second visit from Rigault on 2 November 1942. He was asked to take command of French troops in Morocco, which would rally to the

Americans and open the way for them, arresting any Vichy officers who tried to oppose the landing.[33] At this point Béthouart's desire to be involved clashed with his deference to military hierarchy. He agreed to arrest any recalcitrant officers apart from General Noguès, on the grounds that Noguès 'had great authority in Morocco and was friends with the Sultan who had confidence in him. His arrest would divide the army and Morocco; I could not make such a serious mistake.'[34] In the event, Béthouart's mistake turned out to be that he did not arrest Noguès.

For the Americans Operation Torch was a purely military affair and the struggle for power of various French military leaders became an unwelcome embarrassment. General Giraud was taken off the French Mediterranean coast by a British submarine under a US commander and brought to Allied headquarters at Gibraltar on 6 November to meet Eisenhower and Clark. In person he again demanded the post of Supreme Allied Commander in North Africa and Clark recalled, 'I gasped, and I thought that Ike had probably never been so shocked and showed it so little. It was rather like a bomb explosion.'[35] Giraud threatened to return to France if he did not have his way, but there was no way back and it was eventually agreed that he would take command of all *French* forces in North Africa. Events, however, now took a dramatic and unexpected turn. Admiral Darlan had been inspecting French forces in North Africa since 23 October, talking to General Noguès in Fez, General Juin in Oran and Admiral Raymond Fenard, who had succeeded Weygand as delegate-general, in Algiers. In Algiers he watched a parade headed by General Mast on 29 October and visited his son, Alain, who was sick in an Algiers hospital with polio.[36] There is evidence that he met Murphy there that afternoon.[37] How much prior knowledge he had of an American invasion is unclear, and he was dismissive of the power of this new nation. He had told Leahy the year before than unless the Americans landed with 500,000 men he would resist them. In the event only 75,000 American troops landed in

Morocco, Oran and Algiers, and Darlan gave orders to fire on them. Vichy seemed to be at war with the Allies.

So long as the enemy was at sea military protocol dictated that the navy was in charge; only once they had landed did the army take command. When the Americans attempted to land in Morocco the French Navy under Admiral Michelier opened fire. At 7 a.m. American aircraft appeared at Rabat. General Béthouart was placed on the horns of a dilemma: to resist the Americans or to join them? 'Around 8 a.m.,' he recalled, 'General Noguès called me on the phone and in a fit of anger told me that I had been set up by the "group of idiots" who surrounded me.' Noguès said that fighting was going on at Port Lyautey north of Rabat, at Oran and Algiers, and if Béthouart did not send in his troops to fight the Americans he, Noguès, would have all the officers shot. Béthouart replied that his aim was to prevent blood being shed between French and Americans and above all between French soldiers on different sides. To reinforce his point he went with officers loyal to him to the Residence at Rabat to talk to Noguès, but Noguès refused to meet them. Indeed he had them arrested, imprisoned and sent before a court martial, where Béthouart was accused of intelligence with the enemy and sentenced to death. 'Our hopes collapsed,' recalled Béthouart, 'and we thought that even more than 24 June [1940] France was losing the war for a second time.'[38]

In Algiers the situation was rather different. Civilian resistance was well organised, if disparate, and the Americans took the view that since fewer troops would be available for the landing at Algiers than those further west in Morocco, some inside support from French civilian as well as military resistance would be welcome. In the evening of 7 November Murphy met José Aboulker and the other leaders in Henri Aboulker's flat to finalise plans by which the Resistance would paralyse the Vichy command in Algiers overnight to prevent military opposition, while the Americans secured a foothold on the nearby coast.

Aboulker had met Murphy on 30 October and been promised delivery of Sten guns by submarine, but three nights in a row the submarine had not appeared.[39] Resisters were equipped with the armbands of volunteers, Lebel rifles and forged written orders for the staff of key command centres, which they set off in vehicles to occupy. José Aboulker recalled that:

Between one and two o'clock in the morning 400 armed civilians arrested Darlan and Juin, commander-in-chief in North Africa, and a number of other Vichy generals and high officials. We occupied the general staff offices, post office, military and civil telephone exchanges, the governor-general's palace, the prefecture, and the main police stations. At 2 a.m. Algiers was in our hands.[40]

Even in Algiers, however, things did not go the resisters' way. What, again, went wrong? To begin with there were too few insurgents, since many failed to turn up. D'Astier was supposed to bring 2,000 young people from the Chantiers de la Jeunesse but came with only 100; when José Aboulker asked for reinforcements he was told that the Chantiers youth were only to form 'General Giraud's guard of honour'.[41] Combat seemed content to have provided fifty men.[42] Second, Lemaigre-Dubreuil had gone in his brightly polished military boots to await the arrival of General Giraud at nearby Blida airport, but Giraud never came. Indeed, he did not reach Algiers until 9 November, when the drama was over. Third, Murphy came during the night of 7–8 November to see General Juin in the villa des Oliviers, the governor-general's palace, where he was being held, to persuade him to countermand Vichy's orders to resist attack from wherever it might come. Juin said he could do nothing without consulting Darlan, and when Darlan was brought from Admiral Fenard's house, he flew into a violent rage. Humiliated as head of the military to have been taken by surprise he was determined to resist, if only to defend his honour.[43] A small American force in the port area was beaten off and regular Vichy forces gradually regained government buildings. José Aboulker reflected that despite their heroism, against overwhelming odds 400 men could not:

neutralise an army of 11,000 men and 2,300 SOL in Algiers where fascism was triumphant on favourable soil. But many of us were very young men and we had dreamed of that night, as one dreams of glory when one is twenty.[44]

Darlan maintained the order to resist in Algiers until 5 p.m. on 8 November, when a local ceasefire was concluded, allowing the Americans to enter the city. Fighting continued, however, in Morocco and at Oran, despite pressure from Mark Clark and Robert Murphy on Darlan on 10 November to order a general ceasefire. Clark remembered 'a little man with watery blue eyes and petulant lips. He seemed nervous and uncertain, obviously ill at ease. Again and again he pulled a handkerchief from his pocket and mopped his balding head.'[45] Darlan nevertheless refused to budge, saying that he was under orders from Marshal Pétain to resist, that Laval was away and that the Vichy council of ministers did not meet until that afternoon. Mark Clark was incensed by this prevarication and pounded the table to make Darlan see sense and end hostilities. Then Pétain broadcast a message to announce that Darlan was dismissed as head of the armed forces in North Africa and replaced by General Noguès. Darlan 'acted like a king who had suddenly had his empire shot under him,' said Clark, and concluded an armistice with the Americans on 13 November.[46] Grasping the opportunity, Darlan switched sides and had himself recognised by the Americans as High Commissioner of the French Empire. He took supreme command of all French forces in North Africa and direct control of the navy, leaving the latecomer Giraud in control of the Army of Africa and the air force. In return the Americans obliged Darlan not to execute General Béthouart and to release him for a mission to the United States.

Politically, the gulf between the three elements of resistance was now dramatically exposed. Darlan recruited some of the extreme-right-wing conspirators of 8 November to serve him. Lemaigre-Dubreuil was put in charge of relations with the Americans, Rigault took over the interior, Henri d'Astier was put in charge of the police. The republican resisters and notably the Jewish community were abandoned. The 1870 Crémieux law, which had granted Jews citizenship, was not reinstated and they were not allowed to serve in the army. Instead, a small African Free Corps was set up to include Jews and other resisters of 8 November. The Legion and SOL continued to flaunt their dominance of the streets. Raphaël Aboulker made a comparison with another political turnabout in 1630, when Louis XIII ousted his mother from the regency in order to take command with Cardinal Richelieu:

The 8 November was a Day of Dupes. It was a right-wing revolution made by left-wingers [. . .] They were double-crossed but they could not work out by whom, or how. Those in power looked like the American wing of the National Revolution.[47]

News of the armistice between Darlan and the Americans 'went off like a bomb in London, as much for the British as for ourselves,' said Jacques Soustelle.[48] De Gaulle wanted to protest on the BBC but this was vetoed by Churchill, who told Roosevelt that 'in view of impending operations I should not allow anything that might compromise arrangements made by Eisenhower with Darlan or prejudice the military situation.'[49] The Gaullist position in Algiers appeared doomed by Darlan's abandonment of Pétain for American protection, opening the possibility of liberating France while keeping the institutions and personnel of Vichy more or less intact. De Gaulle tried to save the situation by sending General François d'Astier de la Vigerie, the elder brother of Henri and Emmanuel d'Astier de la Vigerie, to Algiers on 19 December 1942, not to see Darlan, but to go right to the top and speak to General

Eisenhower. The General had been relieved of his command by Vichy and retired to the country before going to London on the plane that brought Emmanuel back to France on 17/18 November 1942, to be briefed about his mission to Algiers. He told Eisenhower, rather unconvincingly, that 'General de Gaulle has limited but not negligible military means. He would like to reach an agreement with you about putting them to best use.' Eisenhower was not impressed. He told d'Astier that on French military questions they were dealing with Giraud, who commanded the Army of Africa. He added that he was about to leave to fight the Axis on the Tunisian front and did not want any 'regrettable incidents' in his rear; the Gaullists in Algiers should therefore keep quiet.[50]

Frustrated in his plan, François d'Astier was persuaded by Admiral Fenard to meet Darlan himself. This he agreed to do, but only in a private capacity so as not to cede any legitimacy. He was taken to the villa des Oliviers, where Darlan held court, and pictured himself in a cloak-and-dagger Wars of Religion novel by Alexandre Dumas. He was taken to:

a Moorish villa with a central courtyard onto which many doorways gave. All were open, the rooms were brilliantly lit and in each were dozens of armed officers. [He] smelled an atmosphere of putsch. Half jokingly, half serious, he recalled the Duke of Guise and The Forty Five and asked himself, 'Are they going to assassinate me?'[51]

In these treacherous surroundings he was introduced to Darlan, Giraud and Rigault. He refused to shake hands and reminded Darlan of his commitment in 1940 that the fleet would fight on. Slightly more favourably disposed to Giraud, d'Astier persuaded the latter to agree at least to the principle of cooperation with the Free French.

Leaving the villa, François d'Astier met the Gaullist leaders, René Capitant and his friends in Combat, who, enthused by the visit of de Gaulle's emissary, were stepping up a propaganda campaign against Darlan. Their newssheet published 10,000–

20,000 copies per issue in order to broaden support.[52] François d'Astier urged the Gaullists, as Eisenhower had advised, to stay quiet but to be at the ready while military operations in the desert took their course. He nevertheless asked René Capitant and his brother Henri to co-ordinate anti-Darlan forces.[53] Henri d'Astier was playing a double game, serving Darlan as his chief of police but building up the African Free Corps that might be used against him. In the political impasse his fantastical solution was to bring out the royalist pretender, the Comte de Paris, who had been exiled from France like all heads of French royal families under a republican law of 1886, as a 'bridge between Algiers and London'. 'To combat the Darlanist right,' he reflected, 'we needed a voice with authority to proclaim the necessity of union.'[54] He persuaded the Comte to fly from his estate at Larache in Spanish Morocco to Algiers, and introduced him to François. The Comte was delighted to be 'treated like a king for perhaps the first time in his life'. François d'Astier, thoroughly unconvinced by the royalist option, asked the Comte de Paris to rally to de Gaulle. He left Algiers obsessed by Darlan's shameless opportunism and with only one thought about him, that 'there are three thousand French people who want to punish him'.[55]

This in fact was something that Henri d'Astier and his confessor, the Abbé Pierre-Marie Cordier, had already planned. They groomed a number of young members of the African Free Corps and twenty-year-old student Fernand Bonnier de la Chapelle, who was too young to join de Gaulle but took part in the 8 November uprising, drew the short straw. After confessing to a priest and receiving absolution, Bonnier armed himself with a revolver and shot Darlan with two bullets in the stomach on Christmas Eve 1942. Though Bonnier fully expected to be pardoned for his noble deed, General Giraud made it clear that public order and authority had to be upheld. Condemned to death the following day by a military court Bonnier was executed by firing squad at dawn on 26 December.[56]

The death of Darlan did not spell the end of the American patronage of Vichy. It simply moved on to another figurehead. General Giraud, who had got to Algiers on 9 November, and now emerged from Darlan's shadow into the bright light of day. Neither he nor the Americans had any desire to change anything, let alone to build bridges to de Gaulle. Giraud announced that he was taking power in the name of Marshal Pétain and continuing the État Francais. Lemaigre-Dubreuil became head of his civil cabinet and *éminence grise* and Rigault was kept on as interior minister with the task of arresting and imprisoning the republican leaders of the 8 November rising, including José and Raphaël Aboulker. The Gaullists were pursued and went underground. Henri d'Astier was himself arrested on 10 January 1943. There was a huge outcry in the British press and Gaullists still at large, such as Fradin, together with Harold Macmillan, Britain's minister in the Mediterranean, put pressure on the Americans to release many of those arrested, including the Aboulkers, which happened on 7 February 1943.[57]

Giraud's position seemed unassailable. He enjoyed the support of the Americans, which continued to be negotiated by Lemaigre-Dubreuil. He inherited Darlan's supreme command of the Armed Forces in Africa and his title as High Commissioner of the French Empire. He appointed Marcel Peyrouton, who before the war had been resident-general in Morocco and Tunisia, as governor-general of Algeria. Since then, as Vichy's interior minister, Peyrouton had been responsible for the first Statut des Juifs and the abrogation of the Crémieux law, and was not going to revoke those in a hurry. Giraud set up an Imperial Council of all the African governors-general who had remained in the Vichy camp, including Peyrouton and Pierre Boisson, governor-general of French West Africa. At the beginning of January 1943 Giraud went on an official visit to see Boisson at Dakar, jewel of French West Africa, where he was greeted by crowds as Pétain might have been. Monsieur You, a primary school inspector at Dakar, was struck by a general who for his sixty-three years seemed 'astonishingly young, almost without wrinkles. Physically vigorous and full of authority. At ease in his role as leader. Impression of a calm, peaceful personality sure of himself.' And yet, reported You, Giraud's authority was not uncontested. A Gaullist committee was at work in Dakar and 'photos of de Gaulle start to circulate. Messages are going from Dakar to London and France.'[58]

This diary entry picked up on a sea change in the story of the French Resistance. The American landing in North Africa had roused intense feelings that a second front was opened up and that liberation was imminent. The Lyon office worker who wrote to the BBC was not the only French person who was 'mad with joy'. The so-called 'Darlan deal' between the United States and Vichy's admiral and the shabby way in which the resisters of 8 November were dealt was therefore greeted with both disbelief and anger in resistance and Free French circles. Serge Ravanel, who had recently joined Libération in Lyon, said that resisters 'bombarded London with telegrams supporting de Gaulle'.[59] De Gaulle, as head of the Free French, now appeared to be the only legitimate option because he enjoyed the support of resistance movements within France. His status as the figure that united all strands of resistance was heightened at the beginning of January 1943 when a delegate of the French Communist Party arrived in London to join him. Fernand Grenier, who had escaped from Châteaubriant before the fatal shootings of October 1941 and then gone to ground, was sent to London by the central committee of the French Communist Party in hiding, headed by Jacques Duclos, who lived a quiet life disguised as a 'country doctor, 1900 style'.[60] Grenier was escorted to the Breton coast, for embarkation on a British ship, by the ubiquitous Rémy, who had a sudden damascene realisation about the contribution of communists to the Resistance.[61] Grenier, for his part, was less than impressed by his first meeting with de Gaulle when he arrived in London: 'I waited for him to ask me questions about the FTP's armed struggle, the deportations, life in prison, etc. Nothing, nothing.'[62] Yet on 15 January 1943 Grenier on the BBC declared that 'the immense mass of French people, all those who are fighting, all those who are resisting, all those who hope, are with General de Gaulle who had the virtue [. . .] of not despairing while everything around was collapsing.'[63]

De Gaulle required the declared support of the French interior resistance and French public opinion in order to assert his case for leadership against Giraud and the Allies. Encouraged by renewed support, he fired off a letter to Giraud on Christmas Day 1942, warning of 'the absence of a national authority in the midst of the greatest national crisis of our history'. He pressed Giraud for an urgent meeting in Algeria or Chad to discuss organising 'all the Free French forces within and outside the country under a provisional central power'.[64] Giraud, with his power base in most of the Empire and the Army of Africa and enjoying the full support of the Americans, was in no hurry to do business. This prompted de Gaulle to send further insistent letters on 1 and 7 January 1943. As it happened, a moment to do business arose with the forthcoming Casablanca Conference of Churchill and Roosevelt, together with Eisenhower and Giraud between 14 and 24 January. Learning of this, de Gaulle went into high dudgeon, furious that the American president should simply arrive on French territory without so much as a request, and refused to fly out from London. Roosevelt mocked the relationship between Giraud and de Gaulle as a 'shotgun marriage' and Robert Murphy recalled that 'at Casablanca there was a great deal of joking about bringing together the French "bride" and "groom" and the President rather enjoyed Churchill's discomfiture.'[65]

In the event Churchill threatened to cut off British support for the Free French if de Gaulle did not turn up, and on 22 January de Gaulle, according to Murphy, 'having deliberately delayed his arrival until the last moment, made a great entrance and stole the show'.[66] Several days of tussling ensued, both between de Gaulle and Giraud and between de Gaulle and the Allies. General Catroux was brought in as an intermediary to negotiate a rapprochement between the two Frenchmen and at a lunch for them on 22 January noted the problem that:

General Giraud was not in principle hostile to the politics of Vichy and of Marshal Pétain [. . .] His platform seemed to be "Vichy against Germany" [. . .] keep order and prevent revolution.[67]

Giraud was a military man, who could not fathom how someone who had merely been a colonel when he himself was a five-star general could have the nerve to demand equal rank with him. Politically, moreover, in so far as he had any ideas, Giraud had hardly entered the twentieth century: 'He is stuck in 1936,' before the experience of the Popular Front, observed Catroux, 'in absolute ignorance of the will and sentiments of the nation. He is retrenched behind a military authoritarianism that understands only seniority, stars and decorations.'[68] In response de Gaulle tried to impress on Giraud the significance of the Free French epic in Africa and the popular support he enjoyed in France and beyond: 'General de Gaulle said to him, "So you want to become First Consul. But where is your plebiscite? Where are your victories?"'[69]

At a dinner that evening in honour of the Sultan of Morocco, Churchill and Roosevelt, Murphy and Macmillan, tried to overcome what they saw as petty disputes at the rear so the Allies could get on with winning the war. Churchill, irritated because no drink was being served, wagged his finger at de Gaulle and said in his schoolboy French, 'Mon Général, il ne faut pas obstacle [sic] la guerre!' – 'Don't stand in the way of the war!' In response, said Murphy, 'de Gaulle vehemently asserted that he enjoyed the popular support of the citizens of French North Africa and should not have been excluded from the Allied landings.'[70] Despite a photo call at which the two generals shook hands in front of a seated Roosevelt, union at this stage was not possible. De Gaulle was reluctant to agree to any deal mediated by the Allies, who had so disrespectfully set up camp on French territory and treated him with such disdain. He returned to London while Giraud remained in place, backed by the Americans.

What looked like failure, however, was in fact a long game played by de Gaulle, as wise observers such as Jacques Soustelle and Robert Murphy observed. Soustelle reminded de Gaulle in confidence that 'as far as the Algerian problem is concerned we can have only one objective: the victory of *la France combattante* in North Africa. With Giraud if he comes over to us, against him if he does not.'[71] Murphy, on his side, later understood that de Gaulle was 'two jumps ahead of everyone else'. Certain after the intervention of the USA and the victory of the USSR at Stalingrad that the Allies would win the war, he 'decided it was his function to concentrate on restoring France as a great power, which he considered her rightful position'.[72]

The Allied landings in North Africa caused a great deal of excitement among the French people that liberation was just around the corner. A new front had been opened up to parallel the Eastern Front and it would only be a matter of time before the Axis was forced to surrender and Vichy France would come to an end. Small groups of resisters mobilised in Algiers to make contact with the Americans and bring the Army of Africa over to the Allied camp. Yet this was to reckon without the Americans, who distrusted or wrote off the Gaullists and were prepared to do business with whichever Vichy general or admiral could deliver North Africa to them. This was the basis of the 'Darlan deal' of 13 November 1942 and, after his assassination, of the deal with Giraud. Vichy was safe in American hands while Gaullists, Jews and communists were rounded up into gaols and camps or forced to go underground. The entry of the United States into the war forced Churchill to reassess how significant a player de Gaulle really was and that actually he had delivered very little.[73]

There were, nonetheless, signs that wind was beginning to move behind de Gaulle's sails. The internal resistance increasingly looked to him at least as the symbol of national liberation, if not as a post-war political leader. He gathered support from a broad spectrum of resistance groups from the moderate wing to the communists, whose star was rising after the surrender of German forces at Stalingrad. There would be battles between some of the internal resistance and the Free French, and the Americans would not be quick to love de Gaulle, but in six months de Gaulle would be back in Algiers staking his claim to be the head of a provisional government that would replace Vichy after the liberation.

10

Apogee

France is renewing itself! [. . .] This people has decided to sweep away the old idols, routines and doctrines that nearly destroyed it.
(De Gaulle, 1943)

The American landings in North Africa on 8 November 1942 had an immediate and dramatic impact on metropolitan France. The Germans replied to the opening up of a Mediterranean front and to Darlan's truce with the Americans by crossing the demarcation line into the Free Zone on 11 November and occupying the whole of France. This was a clear violation of the 1940 armistice, which allowed Vichy to govern the Unoccupied Zone as a fully sovereign power and gave Vichy France a legal justification for re-entering the war on the side of the Allies. Eyes turned towards Marshal Pétain to see whether he would bring France's Army of Africa and Armistice Army and a country reinvigorated by the National Revolution into a renewed war against Germany. Would the army raise its standard two-and-a-half years after the national humiliation of 1940, as the German Army had after Jena in 1806 or the Russians after Tilsit in 1807, or would it demonstrate that it was merely an instrument for imposing order in France, alongside the Germans if necessary? In this moment of crisis no call came from the Marshal. Apart from a feeble protest on the airwaves, Pétain accepted the fait accompli and, minded by the German military, became from now on no more than a puppet in its hands.[1]

The 100,000-strong Armistice Army, organised in eight divisions across unoccupied France, was ordered to remain in its barracks and not resist the German troops as they drove south. There were a few dissenters who took the view that patriotism lay in resisting, rather than obeying orders. Jean de Lattre de Tassigny, who commanded a division in Montpellier, had refused an invitation from René Capitant, Combat's man in Algiers, to go to North Africa ahead of the American landings.[2] He now decided to take his troops out of barracks and head for the Corbières hills near the Pyrenees, in anticipation of a possible conflict. Far from being credited for his courage he was immediately relieved of his command by Vichy and sent to a military prison in Toulouse: 'What I did was not dictated by disobedience,' he wrote to Pétain on 18 November, 'but by love of France and the army.'[3] He was nevertheless accused of deserting his post and in January 1943 sent before Vichy's Tribunal d'État. Again he argued that 'the only mystique of this little Armistice Army was to "resist against any aggressor"'. To stay put would have been 'contrary to Honour and the moral suicide of this army which for two years had been trying to revive'.[4] His judges were deaf to his defence and he was sentenced to ten years in prison for deserting his post. That September, however, he managed to escape from Riom gaol with the help of his son Bernard, and was spirited away by a resistance escape line to London, and then to Algiers.

The Armistice Army was duly disbanded and ceased to exist. A minority of former officers set up a secret organisation called the Organisation de Résistance de l'Armée (ORA), which was designed to manifest itself when the Allies came to liberate France. It would draw on stockpiles of weapons, ammunition and equipment that had been hidden from the Germans by the Armistice Army in caves, cellars and garages. It wanted nothing to do with any other resistance movements, which it disdained as not properly military in hierarchy and discipline, and feared as being tainted by communism. And yet there was another army in France, the Armée Secrète – the virtual army of the Resistance – composed of men who for the moment went about their normal lives but would be ready, when the time came, to rise up and help the Allies. Between now and then a number of obstacles would have to be conquered. The first was the acquisition of weapons. The second was the development of strategy. The third was the question of who was going to command the army. Formally speaking, and on the insistence of London, the army was commanded by General Charles Delestraint, who had come out of retirement to fulfil this duty. But this command was contested by the internal resistance, and notably by Henri Frenay of Combat, who took the view that the Armée Secrète was and must be the armed wing of the internal resistance movements.

The search for weapons exposed a powerful mistrust between the Armée Secrète and the former Armistice Army. In December 1942 Delestraint sent Raymond Aubrac, the Armée Secrète organiser in the Lyon area, to see 61-year-old General Aubert Frère, in order to negotiate a handover of weapons from the former Armistice Army. General Frère had refused an offer from Pétain to be his minister of war and was (whether or not Aubrac knew it) the first head of the Organisation de la Résistance Armée. In the event Aubrac found 'an old man, almost disabled, out of touch', and in any case someone who did not want to do business with him. Frère sent him to see General Georges Revers, ten years younger and a key member of the French General Staff, at Vichy. He received Aubrac in his dressing gown and when asked to hand over the army's weapons to the Resistance he replied:

Young man, you are asking me to betray my country. You are asking the impossible. I am a subordinate. I can do nothing without an order from Admiral Darlan. Let us await his return.[5]

Aubrac was thrown out but the next day learned of Darlan's assassination. He went back to Revers and told him: 'you are not longer a subordinate. I am asking you to give me an order.' Hesistant and playing for time, Revers said that he would ask his wife and came back saying that it was too risky.[6]

Ironically, following the arrest of General Frère by the Gestapo in June 1943, and of his successor, Revers became head of the Organisation de Résistance de l'Armée in September 1943 and a post-war recommendation for the Resistance Medal declared that: 'He earned the recognition of his country and must be counted among the principal artisans of its liberation.'[7]

The question of strategy was no easier to resolve. How and where could a virtual army translate itself into a military force? Out of the question in occupied France, it became just as difficult in the Free Zone after the German occupation of November 1942. Some thinking had nevertheless gone into this. Pierre Dalloz was an amateur rock climber who, having been seconded to Giraudoux's Information Ministry in 1939, had served as a lieutenant in the Alpine Chasseurs in 1940. In March 1941 he was felling a dead nut tree in his garden with his friend Jean Prévost, who was in Grenoble to research a thesis on Stendhal. Above them towered the Vercors plateau and it came to him in a flash that it might provide not only a place of refuge but a natural site to organise resistance behind enemy lines. He saw it as 'a natural fortress, a warlike Vercors. We could turn it into a Trojan horse for airborne commandos.'[8] Dalloz took a job with Vichy as a planning official, which enabled him to tour the region by car to explore possibilities.

A Vercors stronghold became materially possible when in June 1942 Pierre Laval announced the policy of the Relève, by which one POW would be brought back from Germany in return for three workers who 'volunteered' to go to work in a German factory. The call up was only voluntary in name and provoked both strike action and the disappearance from circulation of young men who became known as *réfractaires*. In November 1942, for example, young workers from the Grenoble area were summoned to report for labour service in Germany. Of 1,200 called up only sixty reported for duty and the Vichy police and *gendarmerie* were sent after them.[9] A system for spiriting them away was quickly set up. Aimé Pupin was 'a little man with dark hair and jet-black eyes', who kept a café on the rue du Polygone at Grenoble.[10] In the army in 1940 he had thought about fleeing to England from La Rochelle but was stopped by his 'love of his family and native soil'. At Grenoble he became a member of Franc-Tireur and his bar became a silent turntable for receiving Relève-dodgers who found their way to Grenoble and finding them hiding places for them in the Alps.[11] Meanwhile the backroom of an ironmongery was used to filter and recruit young men, a task undertaken by white-haired Eugène Chavant, who had been sacked by Vichy as mayor of Saint-Martin d'Hères and now also kept a café. Money was provided in the first instance by Léon Martin, a pharmacist and former socialist mayor of Grenoble. Young men were put onto buses and taken on the first leg to Villard-de-Lans, from where couriers took them to Ambel farm. This was the first base of *réfractaires* who took cover and made themselves useful by doing forestry work.[12]

In December 1942 Pierre Dalloz went to see Yves Farge, Franc-Tireur leader at the *Progrès de Lyon*, to talk about his plan to convert the Vercors into a fortress. Farge mentioned it to Jean Moulin, who was persuaded by the idea, and Farge came to visit Dalloz in Grenoble on 31 December 1942, bringing money from Moulin to develop the plan. What was also needed, however, was the input of the Armée Secrète. Farge and Dalloz duly met General Delestraint at Lyon's Gare Perrache on 10 January 1943. Delestraint advised them to recruit professional soldiers as soon as possible to provide training and leadership for the *réfractaires*. One of the first to be found was Alain Le Ray, son-in-law of the writer François Mauriac, who had escaped from Colditz: 'From now on,' said Delestraint for security reasons, 'we will forget that name [Vercors]. Your plan will be called the *Montagnard* plan.'[13] Early in April 1943 Delestraint himself visited the Vercors, where about 350 men were grouped in nine camps, and held a meeting of the organising committee.[14]

The congregation of young men in the wild was the beginning of an army-in-waiting – what became known as the *maquis* – immediately posed the problem of command. The remains of the Armistice Army, used to the conventions of military hierarchy and uniforms that were no longer required for underground activity, and conscious of the danger of being deemed to be 'terrorists', were generally reluctant to come forward as officers. This left responsibility with the cadres of resistance movements who had done their military service and fought briefly in 1940, but were political rather than military animals. Those found by Raymond Aubrac to be regional commanders of the Armée Secrète in the former Free Zone, had often belonged to the young communists who had battled against the extreme right in the Latin Quarter in the 1930s. Although some were still in contact with the Communist Party, they had by and large distanced themselves from it over the Nazi-Soviet Pact, and were therefore communist sympathisers working with movements like Libération Sud rather than obedient militants. Jean-Pierre Vernant, who was now teaching philosophy at the Lycée of Toulouse, was made head of the Armée Secrète in Toulouse and the surrounding department of Haute-Garonne. Vernant did not deny his contacts with the Communist Party: 'The guy who gave me orders was Marrane,' organiser of the Front National in the Free Zone. He nevertheless insisted that the Nazi-Soviet Pact had demonstrated that the Communist Party could make big mistakes, and 'so I did not act like a corpse. There was a solidarity but I kept my distance [. . .] I'm not a soldier in a marching column that turns right or left according to orders.'[15] Also recruited in Toulouse by Aubrac was Maurice Kriegel, whose brother David, a young Alsatian Jewish doctor, Aubrac had come to know when garrisoned at Strasbourg in 1939. Maurice had begun law studies in Paris and battled alongside Pierre Hervé in the communist-dominated student movement, but he married a Polish girl, argued with his parents, and dropped out of law to work for an insurance company. In 1938, having been sacked as a trade-union activist, he became secretary of the CGT union representing the white-collar employees of banks, insurance companies and large stores. He fought in the artillery in 1940 but realising his vulnerability as a Jew, left Paris in 1942 for Toulouse, where most of his family had gone as refugees. There he linked up again with Pierre Hervé and Jean-Pierre Vernant, and was given the job of military inspector in the former Free Zone, with the task of checking on the organisation and (often inflated) numbers of the Armée Secrète in different areas.[16]

Not all cadres of the Armée Secrète were communist sympathisers. Serge Asher, who was studying at the École Polytechnique, which had been moved to Lyon, was for a long time an admirer of Marshal Pétain. He was ultimately projected towards resistance by the American landings, the German occupation of the Free Zone, and the failure of Vichy to snap into action. He became a liaison agent for Libération Sud, providing contact between the various regional leaders of the Armée Secrète. He was also asked by Aubrac to collect weapons from the Armistice Army that had been hidden in a warehouse near Lyon. The owner, who ran a drug company, refused to hand them over, claiming 'the resistance is full of communists. I would prefer to give them to the Germans.'[17] Asher graduated to the Free Corps, which he considered 'men of the avant-garde and champions of resistance', and took the *nom de guerre* 'Ravanel', after one of the peaks he loved climbing above Chamonix.[18] On 15 March 1943 he was arrested by the Gestapo in Lyon in a secret meeting with Aubrac and Kriegel. He tried to fight his way free and get down the stairwell but without success. Lucie got Raymond out of prison by threatening the public prosecutor that he would otherwise be dealt with by the Resistance at the liberation; Asher and Kriegel faked illness and were transferred to hospital, from which they were released by a Free Corps led by Aubrac.[19]

While the Armée Secrète developed on the ground a fierce debate took place about who should control it at the top. The Free

French in London wanted to command it through the reliable general they had appointed for the job, Charles Delestraint. But the internal resistance, which was steadily acquiring coherence and maturity, wanted the Armée Secrète to be its military wing, under the leadership of the movements. On 26 January 1943 the three main resistance movements in the former Free Zone – Combat, Libération and Franc-Tireur – finally came together to found the Mouvements Unis de la Résistance (MUR).[20] As a compromise each retained its own publications but a *comité directeur* or steering committee was set up. Henri Frenay was made responsible for military affairs, Emmanuel d'Astier for political affairs, and Jean-Pierre Lévy for security and material resources. Frenay, who had lost out initially in his campaign to become head of the Armée Secrète, now used the MUR as a launch pad to renew his ambitions to become leader of the metropolitan resistance both politically and militarily.

In response to this challenge from the internal resistance and notably from Frenay, Moulin and Delestraint returned to London on 14 February 1943 for talks with de Gaulle. They sought approval for two measures: first, to separate the military functions of the Armée Secrète entirely from the resistance movements and to confirm the military leadership of Delestraint; and second, to run the political affairs of the Resistance through a National Council of Resistance (CNR) that would include representatives not only of the resistance movements but also of trade unions and political parties: this reflected the changed picture resulting from the arrival in London, the previous month, of the Communist Party representative Fernand Grenier. The Communist Party was not a resistance movement in itself but it closely controlled movements such as the Front National and Francs-Tireurs et Partisans, and was also recovering influence in the CGT labour union. The Party's embrace of de Gaulle was a major coup for the Free French and required recognition, but it also opened the way to representation by the Socialist Party and others further to the right. For Jean Moulin this would serve to dilute both the obstinacy of the internal resistance leaders and the unknown quantity constituted by the Communist Party. It would also – as de Gaulle returned from Casablanca having failed to agree with Giraud – demonstrate to the Allies that de Gaulle had a broad and effective political base in France, which Giraud had never had, and Pétain was steadily losing. [21]

With these measures approved by de Gaulle, Jean Moulin was parachuted back into France on 20 March 1943 and made his way to Lyon. At that point Louis and Simone Martin-Chauffier's house at Collonges was the central meeting point for resistance meetings. To keep unwanted visitors away, said Simone, 'I had resumed the role of Cerberus [mythical guardian of the Underworld], as in [19]40–1 at the time of the Musée de l'Homme.' She remembered Jean Moulin and 'I wondered why this little man intimidated me so, for he said very little.'[22] Moulin chaired a meeting of the MUR but immediately came into conflict with Henri Frenay. Frenay was opposed to London's strategy to split the military from the political functions of the internal resistance and to bring each under its control. Two weeks after the meeting Frenay fired off both barrels of a protest to Moulin, who had left for Paris on 30 March, and to Delestraint. To Moulin he denounced:

an attempt to bureaucratise the Resistance, whereas we created it as free agents [...] You and some of your colleagues want to make us the faithful executors of orders given by the French National Committee. You don't seem to understand what we really are, a military and a revolutionary political force. On the military side, and with the reservations I made at our last meeting, we consider ourselves to be at de Gaulle's orders, but politically we maintain our complete independence.[23]

In a second letter, sent the same day, Frenay told Delestraint that though he might be the head of the Armée Secrète, he was a conventional military man with no experience of underground resistance or guerrilla warfare and no real understanding of the role that he had, out of the blue, been called upon to play. More than that, Frenay claimed, the Resistance was a revolutionary army which had more passion than discipline and would obey only leaders they loved and trusted, like himself:

These men can in no sense [. . .] be compared to the soldiers of a regular army. The discipline that they observe, which is relative, is much more like that of a revolutionary army. The underground nature of our organisation and action has not fostered blind obedience to any leader but obedience only to the leaders they know. Our discipline is based on confidence and friendship. If you send in new officers to take over these people, I predict that in most cases it will not work. They will come up against the inertia and distrust of their subordinates. A revolutionary army elects its leaders, they are not imposed on it.[24]

One of the tasks of this Armée Secrète, argued Frenay, was the 'work of insurrection', an uprising to be launched in conjunction with Allied invasion. From this followed the 'priority of the political over the military' and at the very least a 'right of approval' of the MUR's steering committee over orders given to the Armée Secrète. Since he was responsible for military affairs on behalf of the steering committee, Frenay was explicitly contesting Delestraint's authority.

Delestraint struck back at a meeting in Paris on 12 April 1943 chaired by Jean Moulin. He ruled out any talk of immediate action preceding Allied intervention: 'the Armée Secrète must prepare to intervene on D-Day in accordance with [the Allies'] landing plans and should not at this stage attack enemy targets.'[25] Two FTP representatives invited to the meeting said that they could not abandon the immediate action policy of the Communist Party and would not retreat to 'a secret barracks'.[26] Frenay, though profoundly suspicious of communists, also used the rhetoric of immediate action by a revolutionary army as a stick with which to beat London and its agents.

In this game of poker Frenay now produced a flush. This was a link that Combat had negotiated with the American secret services based in Switzerland. The contact was provided by Philippe

Monod, lawyer and scion of the well-connected Protestant family with an American mother, who had been recruited by Claude Bourdet to run Combat and the Armée Secrète in the Alpes-Maritimes around Cannes. In Cannes in November 1942 he had met an American lawyer friend, Max Shoop, who knew Allen Dulles, the head of the Office of Strategic Services (OSS) in Berne. Frenay sent Monod to see Dulles in Berne in March 1943, and Dulles secured Washington's agreement for a very large payment in return for intelligence provided. Combat could now also communicate directly with London via the American embassy in Berne, bypassing Jean Moulin. When Monod returned with the deal Frenay exclaimed:

'Come here so that I can embrace you!' We hugged each other, full with joy. 'Our worries are over! [. . .] The *maquis* will be supported and soon armed with American help. And we will have danger-free radio contact with London, as in peacetime.'[27]

This deal posed a massive threat to the Free French in London. First, it afforded Combat and the MUR an income stream and possible weapons drops independent of what London was channelling via Jean Moulin, which would strengthen their bid for autonomy. Second, it built a bridge to the Americans who were supporting Giraud, not de Gaulle, in North Africa. Moulin radioed his concerns urgently to London, saying also that Frenay had asked for an American plane to take him to directly to Algiers to speak to General Giraud. At a meeting of the MUR on 28 April Moulin told Frenay: 'You are stabbing General de Gaulle in the back.' He would do everything in his power to prevent the Swiss connection. Frenay replied, combining his rejection of the military and political schemes of London:

You have tried to strangle us [. . .] You want to control the Resistance without having the means or the stature to do so. Right here, we are fighting. As for your National Council, I want no part of it. I will not accept, and we will not accept, to be bureaucratised by you.[28]

Jean Moulin's mission to set up the National Council of Resistance did not encounter opposition from Henri Frenay alone. The question of the representation of political parties provoked controversy in other quarters too. Pierre Brossolette arrived in Paris from England on 12 February 1943 in order to mount a parallel bid to frustrate Moulin's plan. Brossolette's mission to London in 1942 had been to convince de Gaulle of the political importance of the Resistance alongside the military dimension. This had, by and large, been achieved but Brossolette wanted the resistance movements alone to be the vehicles of France's political renewal. In his view, the old political parties of the Third Republic that had led France to defeat and had bowed to Pétain's dictatorship had forfeited their right to be players. In particular he was in bad odour with leaders of the Socialist Party, such as Daniel Mayer, who had been promoted ahead of him in the 1930s and was trying to reconstitute the Party for the post-war period. Having lost favour with de Gaulle, Brossolette made a strange alliance with Colonel Passy, the head of the BCRA, who followed him to Paris, parachuted in on 26 February. With Passy was Forest Yeo-Thomas, an Englishman brought up in France, who had liaised between the British and French air forces before joining SOE and providing a link to the BCRA. Their February mission was called the Brumaire-Arquebuse mission, 'Brumaire' being Brossolette's code name and 'Arquebuse' Passy's.[29] Although Passy was right-wing and only really interested in military resistance he was impressed by Brossolette. He later called him: 'the most intelligent man I have met in my life, with an extraordinary political acumen and political knowledge. I learned all I know about politics from him, because I had never dabbled in politics.'[30] Yeo-Thomas noted that Brossolette had a fine effect on Passy, who 'never gave such a remarkable performance as when he was flanked by Brossolette, who channelled and guided his efforts'.[31]

The aim of Brossolette and Passy was to bring together the whole spectrum of resistance organisations in the Occupied

Zone, where Brossolette felt at home, and of which Moulin had little experience. These would be federated in a North Zone Coordination Committee (CCZN), which would deliberately leave out representatives of the political parties and trade unions, and confront Moulin with a fait accompli when he got to Paris. Highly significant in the line-up was the Organisation Civile et Militaire (OCM) of Colonel Touny, which hoped through the CCZN to become the most important resistance movement in the country. At the other end of the spectrum was Pierre Villon of the Front National, who was scandalised by the way some resisters were interested not in the work of liberation but in arrangements afterwards, 'looking to be awarded the maximum number of posts as ministers and prefects. A real vipers' nest.'[32] On the other hand, it was crucial for the communist-dominated Front National to be brought in from the cold and to be accepted like any other resistance movement.

Jacques Lecompte-Boinet, who had slowly rebuilt Frenay's decimated Combat team as Ceux de la Résistance, remembers being summoned to a secret meeting with Passy and Brossolette in a small flat in Auteuil in March 1943: 'This new colonel seemed very young,' he said of Passy, 'dry and meticulous, talking figures, weapons, money, radios, parachute drops.' Initially he appeared far more persuasive than Brossolette with his socialist past, who gave the impression that 'the Popular Front was back in business.' And yet 'Passy seemed decided to involve his friend in the whole conversation [. . .] We concluded that the young colonel was a plaything in the hands of pre-war politicians, even a "socialist."' Then Brossolette began to speak and worked the charms that gave him the nickname 'Cleopatra'. Bringing 'holy word from London' he explained that 'civil action' would not involve party politics but unite all political, religious and trade-union groups that might take part in 'the Nation's uprising'. Vichy officials would be replaced and 'legal transition' to a provisional government under de Gaulle effected. Brossolette, he said, 'a seducer full of irony, seated on the floor, threw sharp ideas known only to himself into the debate as if to tame us, with a laugh that those who knew him will never forget'.[33]

The North Zone Coordination Committee (CCZN) was officially created on 23 March 1943, including the OCM, Ceux de la Résistance and Libé-Nord; Pierre Villon and the Front National joined a day or two later.[34] On 31 March, Jean Moulin arrived in Paris and met Brossolette in the Bois de Boulogne. Passy related that Moulin was 'furious. He had heard that Brossolette had been rude about him.'[35] A tremendous argument took place between two rivals who were battling for control of the internal resistance: Moulin accused Brossolette of cutting the ground under his feet by setting up the CCZN, and Brossolette attacked Moulin for allowing the old discredited parties back into the game. Moulin nevertheless had the sang-froid to chair a meeting of the CCZN on 3 April and took the opportunity to inform resistance leaders of his plans for the National Council of Resistance.[36]

In the end, Moulin had his way. Brossolette and Passy returned to England on the night of 15/16 April 1943 and Moulin convened the first underground meeting of the National Council of Resistance on 27 May 1943 in a small flat at 48, rue du Four, in the 6th *arrondissement*, near Saint-Sulpice. This was a landmark in the history of the Resistance. It symbolised not only the coming together of nearly all the internal resistance movements and many of the political parties, but their acknowledgement of the leadership of de Gaulle in London. Luckily for Moulin, Frenay was not at the meeting of 27 May; he sent Claude Bourdet instead. Frenay later said that he did not doubt 'Jean Moulin's intellectual brilliance, courage and tenacity, but [. . .] Moulin's tactic was to disaggregate the Resistance by using d'Astier against Frenay, and then to drown it by letting political parties, beginning with the Communist Party, into the CNR.'[37] As it happened, neither Emmanuel d'Astier nor Jean-Pierre Lévy were at the meeting either, both sending substitutes.[38] For the first time politicians made an appearance in their own right. Lecompte-Boinet, who represented Ceux de la Résistance, found the attitude to the Resistance of people like André Le Troquer (a socialist deputy for Paris who had refused full powers to Pétain in 1940 and acted as counsel for Léon Blum when he was put on trial at Riom in 1942) somewhat challenging. They were, he said, 'so happy to rediscover old colleagues, elected by the people, and affected to look down on the newcomers who had the nerve to claim that they were their equals'.[39] The right was even more difficult to integrate. Lecompte-Boinet had been asked by Moulin to find representatives from the two main conservative parties of the Third Republic, which had played almost no role in the Resistance: the Alliance Démocratique and the Fédération Républicaine.[40] The only major movement in the north not involved was Défense de la France. Although Robert Salmon wanted to bring the movement into the mainstream, Philippe Viannay was reluctant to abandon the Pétainist loyalties he had inherited from his father. In addition, Salmon reflected, Moulin thought that Viannay might be another 'spoilsport', like Henri Frenay.[41]

Despite these tensions, the rites of solidarity and loyalty were duly performed that day. Jean Moulin read a message from de Gaulle calling for the Resistance on French soil to join in support of La France Combattante to strengthen it both in France and in relation to foreign powers, so that 'liberation and victory will be French'. In reply a motion drafted by Georges Bidault, who represented Christian democrats, in consultation with Moulin, asked that the provisional French government due to be established in Algiers be entrusted to de Gaulle, 'who has been the soul of the Resistance in its darkest hours', while General Giraud became commander-in-chief of the reformed French Army to pursue victory with the Allies.[42] Villon wanted to amend the text to say that 'the struggle has already begun', in order to endorse the Front National's strategy of immediate action, but was told by Moulin that this was for another occasion.[43]

The dynamic between what was happening in metropolitan France and what was happening in the Empire was very dramatic in those last days of May 1943. The first meeting of the National Council of Resistance in Paris represented one high point in the story of the Resistance and the Free French. Another was the arrival of General de Gaulle in Algiers on 30 May, leading to the formation on 3 June of the French Committee of National Liberation (CFLN), which would become the provisional government of the Republic ready to take power in liberated France. This development, however, was far from the 'straight line' of progression suggested by the central Gaullist myth; it involved a long struggle for power between de Gaulle and Giraud for control of the Committee and also of the armed forces being built up in North Africa.

After Darlan's assassination General Giraud had assumed civil as well as military powers in North Africa, and set up an Imperial Council of North and West African governors. His regime was essentially Vichyist without Pétain, and in February 1943 he invited former Vichy interior minister Pierre Pucheu, who had not wished to serve under premier Laval, to come and join his forces in North Africa.[44] Giraud enjoyed the protection of the Americans who wanted North Africa as a base for the military offensive against the Axis, which could not be hampered by Franco-French disputes. They wanted to postpone the question of France's political future until after the country was liberated, arguing constitutionally that it was up to the French people to choose their next government but practically giving themselves a free hand to impose military rule and deal with the Frenchman of their choice. They liked Giraud's motto, 'A single goal, Victory', whereas de Gaulle they regarded as a troublemaker driven by political ambition. US secretary of state Cordell Hull later wrote:

If [de Gaulle], as an Army general, had thrown himself wholeheartedly into the fight against the Axis in a military sense, if he had actually led

French troops against the enemy wherever possible instead of spending most of his time in London, he could have rallied far more support to himself among the French and among the United Nations. Instead, his own dictatorial attitude, coupled with his adventures in the political field, inevitably inspired the thought that that he was trying to develop a political standing that would make him the next ruler of France.[45]

When Churchill visited Washington in May 1943 he came under intense pressure to abandon de Gaulle for Giraud. Cordell Hull added the further argument that 'de Gaulle has permitted to come under his umbrella all the most radical elements in France [. . .] the Communists in France, probably the most highly organised political group there today, have announced their insistence that de Gaulle be their leader.'[46] Churchill, while conceding that de Gaulle was difficult to deal with, refused to abandon him because he was the symbol of the French Resistance. Likewise he refused to pit de Gaulle and Giraud against each other and saw the formation of the French Committee of National Liberation as a way of handing power over to a collective French body that would oversee the liberation of France.

Attempts to achieve reconciliation between Giraud and de Gaulle had in fact been going on in North Africa throughout the spring of 1943. The key players were General Catroux, the Free French High Commissioner in the Levant, and Harold Macmillan, the British minister resident in the Mediterranean. Macmillan saw Catroux as 'a French snob (princesses and all that) and yet with a broad, tolerant, liberal view of life. He is a sort of French Whig.'[47] Much more difficult to deal with was Giraud, who combined obstinacy with complete insensitivity to changing political realities. Giraud told Macmillan that he had an army of 450,000 men, 120,000 of them French and the rest colonial forces, who would simply not accept the leadership of de Gaulle, who was 'fifteen years younger [and] only a general of the second grade'. He believed that the French people were more Giraudist than Gaullist, said that 'a certain colonel Passy was flirting with communists and ran a communist organisation in France supported by war material dropped by English parachutes. In his opinion, France would need a period of military dictatorship under himself as commander-in-chief.'[48] Back in London de Gaulle tried to increase the pressure in a Grosvenor House meeting on 4 May. He declared that the French Empire must shortly be united under a 'strong, united, popular power', which clearly meant under him and not Giraud.[49] In response Catroux had to remind de Gaulle that Giraud 'represents, whether we like it or not, a real force in himself. He wields authority over the most important colonies of the imperial bloc and leads the only army that will be equipped [by the Americans] and will only be so if he remains its commander'. Giraud must be accorded, he told de Gaulle 'a position of parity with you' or no deal would be possible.[50]

De Gaulle had acquired some much-needed clout as the result of the gallant showing of the Free French forces in Africa. Leclerc's small Free French force, three-quarters composed of black African forces, pushed north against the Italians in Libya, taking the oasis of Koufra in March 1941 and the Fezzan in January 1943.[51] Meanwhile the forces of Pierre Koenig held the line at Bir Hakeim in May–June 1942 and fought alongside the Eighth Army at El Alamein in July and October 1942. The Free French took part in victory celebrations at Tunis on 20 May 1943, dramatically coming up for the first time against their old enemy, the Army of Africa, which had done no fighting until the offensive in Tunisia earlier in 1943. Leclerc's aide-de-camp, Christian Girard, described the confrontation of the old guard and the Free French. There was, he wrote:

a whole load of generals from the Giraud camp. Clean-shaven and constipated faces, frightened by responsibility. Giraud arrives, behind Alexander and Eisenhower. He looks tired and annoyed. The march past is too long. After an hour and a half of infantry parading our old reconnaissance and combat vehicles appear. They attract a lot of applause. Loud shouts of 'Vive de Gaulle' ring out as they go past.[52]

Despite their scruffiness, the Free French had a certain mystique and the sweet smell of success. Recruits from Army of Africa began to desert to them in considerable numbers. To prevent this, Giraud sent Leclerc and his forces for a couple of months to swat flies in the Tripolitanian desert.

It was therefore with some of the trappings of a triumphal hero, but with all to play for, that de Gaulle flew from London to Algiers on Sunday 30 May 1943 with a few faithful Free French in what one of them, his chief of staff Pierre Billotte, called 'a very small aircraft, the ugliest in the English fleet'.[53] Initially the balance of power did not look favourable. Giraud did not send a car to fetch de Gaulle from the airport and made no arrangement for his accommodation.[54] Churchill had sent his personal friend, General Georges, to support Giraud on the military side, although he was sixty-seven years old and was teased by Billotte as 'the most beaten general in French history'.[55] Roosevelt had told Churchill, 'best of luck in getting rid of our mutual headache'. On his side he sent Jean Monnet, who had snubbed de Gaulle in 1940, been working on the United States' Victory Plan and was supposed to provide Giraud with an awareness of political affairs that he lacked.[56]

Undismayed, the afternoon he arrived, de Gaulle laid a wreath in the form of a Cross of Lorraine on the main square and savoured what he considered was the applause of the crowd in this still Pétainist city:

Thousands of patriots, alerted at short notice by the Combat movement, quickly gathered and welcomed me with a huge clamour. Having saluted those Algerians who had given their lives for France, I broke into the 'Marseillaise', which was taken up by innumerable voices.[57]

Billotte, by contrast, thought that agents provocateurs were trying to organise a riot against de Gaulle and was injured trying to protect him. Maurice Schumann, voice of the Free French, was knocked over in the crush but was delighted to see the General so popular in his first real communion with the French.[58]

Behind the closed doors of the Lycée Fromentin a tremendous power struggle took place. The Free French regarded the Vichyists in place as incarnating defeat and reaction, if not treachery, while those around Giraud saw de Gaulle and his crew as rebels and revolutionaries. The Gaullists feared that a coup d'état might be mounted against them by forces loyal to Vichy such as the 5th Chasseurs d'Afrique, known to them as the '5th Nazis'.[59] The *commissaires* or ministers of the French Committee of National Liberation were divided between the two camps: Billotte and socialist André Philip for de Gaulle, and General Georges and Jean Monnet for Giraud. André Philip described the Committee as 'two clearly separated powers', with the military under Giraud enjoying 'truly dictatorial powers' under a state of siege that remained in force from Casablanca to Tunis. The army effectively controlled the police and judicial system, ran the secret services and imposed censorship of the radio and press, while 'almost all the staff employed in these services are the same as were employed under the Vichy regime'.[60]

One breakthrough for de Gaulle, on the other hand, was the fate of Vichy's African governors who had opposed the Free French at every turn. General Leclerc, who came to Algiers, reported a standoff in talks:

General de Gaulle entered, placed his kepi on the table and with his deep voice listed the names of certain important people: 'Boisson, Noguès [. . .] Peyrouton. When you have removed them, I shall return.' Then he put his kepi back on and moved towards the door. After a moment's disbelief [General] Georges said, 'General de Gaulle. There are, among the names you have cited, people whose patriotism is as sincere as yours, only they have a different conception of patriotism.' General de Gaulle half turned and said, 'I regret that.' And left.[61]

The deadlock was resolved by Giraud agreeing to dismiss Noguès, Boisson and Peyrouton. Catroux replaced Peyrouton as governor-general of Algeria. In return, de Gaulle had to concede that Giraud would remain as commander-in-chief of the armed forces in Africa and co-president of the French Committee constituted on 3 June.

The continuation of military dictatorship and a good many Vichy personnel did not prevent an outburst of voices, prompted by the arrival of de Gaulle in Algiers, of those who had taken part in the failed uprisings of 8 November and had been subjected to renewed persecution. Among them were the usual suspects of Jews, trade unionists and communists. Vichy's abrogation of the Crémieux law that had given Algerian Jews citizenship in 1870 had not been repealed and was indeed re-promulgated on 18 March 1943. The Jewish community sent a hail of petitions demanding the restitution of their rights.[62] The trade union of the air industry workers of Algiers, which they described as the biggest factory in North Africa, petitioned de Gaulle to complain that nothing had changed in the six months since the Allied landings: 'the same collaborators who used to govern us are mostly still in place, the bureaucracy is infested with Hitlerians and the officer corps corrupt'.[63] Twenty-six communist deputies, including the deputy for Marseille François Billoux and the deputy for Nanterre Waldeck Rochet, who had been arrested in 1939 and held in Algiers' Maison Carré prison, were released on 5 February 1943 and formed a small but vociferous lobby. They demanded a purge of Vichy collaborators, including Pierre Pucheu, who they held responsible for the execution of communists at Châteaubriant, the liberation of anti-fascists from Algeria's camps and prisons, and a complete reform of the army as 'a people's army, a modern, passionate army on the model of the Sambre-et-Meuse, Valmy, 1793, the Marne, Bir-Hakeim and Stalingrad'.[64]

There were nevertheless tight limits to what reforms could be achieved, set both by the Vichyist conditions in North Africa and the domination exercised by the Americans. Pierre Pucheu was placed under house arrest, then imprisoned, in Morocco.

But the Americans would tolerate no challenge to the position of Giraud as commander-in-chief of the armed forces. Eisenhower summoned Giraud and de Gaulle on 19 June and told them that in the face of the difficult task of liberating German-occupied Europe the existing organisation of the French military command in North Africa would not change in any way.[65] In addition, the Americans required the amalgamation of the Army of Africa and the Free French in readiness for the campaigns to come. This took place formally on 31 July 1943, although it involved formidable difficulties: the two armies had made opposite choices in June 1940 and in November 1942; they belonged to rival political and ideological camps; and at Dakar and Damascus they had actually fought each other. Together they had taken part in the victorious Allied march past in Tunis on 20 May 1943, but while Christian Girard highlighted the applause for the Free French, Diego Brosset, who commanded the 1st Free French Division, recalled the shame felt by their small forces, exhausted after long African campaigns and sick with dysentery, as they came up against the pristine Army of Africa:

When they see Giraudist officers – some of whom had fought us in Syria – strutting round the streets of Tunis, nicely done up in uniforms that have scarcely been used, they felt that those in high places were ashamed of them because they were dirty. They were a bit like younger brothers envious of their elder siblings and depressed to boot.[66]

That said, the balance of power was slowly shifting from the failed reactionary generals of the Army of Africa to the Free French, who were in harmony with the new France that would emerge at the Liberation. De Gaulle declared in a speech in Tunis on 27 June that 'France is renewing itself! Superficial minds clinging to the ashes of the past may think that they will see our country as they once knew it', but 'this people has decided to sweep away the old idols, routines and doctrines that nearly destroyed it.'[67] Major Brunet de Sairigné, commander of the

First Battalion of the 13th Half-Brigade of the Foreign Legion, was delighted with the speech, 'the best I have heard to date; the big bad guys get a good dressing-down [. . .] The crusty old crabs in the front rank were crestfallen. They are tortured to see their men come over to us and would like us to leave this evening.'[68]

In the summer of 1943 the metropolitan resistance and the Free French seemed at the top of their game. The metropolitan resistance movements had been brought together by Jean Moulin with representatives of the parties and trade unions and declared their trust in de Gaulle. De Gaulle had flown to Algiers and imposed himself and the Free French on Giraud's Vichyist regime under Allied protection. Two institutions, the National Council of Resistance and the French National Liberation Committee, symbolised the unity and integration of the Resistance in France and the Empire. The Free French had a prominent place and a good deal of prestige in the new amalgamated army. The model of what the liberation of France might look like, both politically and militarily, was taking shape. And yet, under the impact of a few events in June 1943, the whole edifice threatened to fall apart.

11

Rupture

De Gaulle fell under the influence of a milieu very different from his former milieu in London, which distanced him from his former revolutionary attitude [. . .] This idea of the state, of authority, his respect for order and organisation made him very attached to Catholicism.

(Georges Boris, 1947)

The French Resistance was at an apogee in the early days of June 1943. As a result of the diplomatic skills of Jean Moulin, the internal resistance was united and had formally acknowledged the leadership of de Gaulle. Moulin was both delegate-general of the London Committee and chair of the newly formed National Council of Resistance (CNR) and held executive and representative, political and military powers in his hands. The General himself had flown from London to Algiers and set up the French Committee of National Liberation (CFLN), the embryonic government-in-waiting of liberated France, of which he and Giraud were co-presidents. He had beaten off a bid by the Allies to dump him in favour of Giraud and forced them to work with him too. The French Army, soon to reunite, was to be re-equipped and re-armed by the generosity of the Americans in anticipation of opening a second front against the Axis in Europe. Had this structure remained in place, France could have looked forward to a liberation that would keep internal resistance, external forces and the Allies in step for a broad-based political settlement.

Such plans, however, came crashing down after a series of catastrophic events. On 9 June 1943 General Charles Delestraint, head of the Armée Secrète, was arrested in Paris by the Gestapo.

He was interrogated, imprisoned in Fresnes, then sent to the concentration camp of Struthof in Alsace before being moved on to Dachau. Less than two weeks later, on 21 June, a meeting of resistance leaders chaired by Jean Moulin was organised in the Lyon suburb of Caluire, in order to discuss who would replace Delestraint. It is still unclear who betrayed them. The prime suspect for a long time was René Hardy, a former primary schoolteacher and member of Combat who was a specialist in railway sabotage. He was sent for trial twice after the war, in 1947 and 1950, but acquitted on both occasions. The lawyer Jacques Vergès later pointed the finger of blame at Raymond Aubrac, suggesting he had been recruited by the Gestapo after he had been arrested on 15 March 1943 and released on condition he betray others. This accusation was shown to be completely unfounded. The fact, nevertheless, is that the Gestapo burst into the meeting and arrested Moulin, Aubrac and other resisters. Moulin was taken to Montluc prison in Lyon, where he was tortured by Gestapo chief Klaus Barbie. He was then taken by train to Germany but died en route on 8 July.[1]

Jean Moulin's arrest snapped the link between the internal resistance and the Free French. Threads painstakingly woven between London and occupied France were suddenly cut. A succession crisis broke out as Moulin's rivals manoeuvred to be appointed, but in the meantime the internal resistance regained the autonomy many of its leaders had tried to preserve against what they saw as Moulin's take-over bid.[2] This refound independence coincided with resistance activity becoming much more of a mass movement, as the Third Reich, fighting for survival on the Eastern Front, stepped up demands for young Frenchmen to go as forced labourers to work in German war factories. Some went, many more disappeared from circulation, and a significant minority took to the *maquis* and became the rank and file of the Armée Secrète. The popularisation of resistance played into the hands of the Communist Party, which bathed in the aura of heroism surrounding the Red Army's success against the Nazis. It developed a range of organisations, from the Front National and the Francs-Tireurs et Partisans to the Communist Youth and the Women of France Union to gain control of that mass movement and guide it towards immediate action and national insurrection.

When Jean Moulin was arrested, Claude Bouchinet-Serreulles, de Gaulle's former batman and BCRA official, was initially the man in the right place. He met Moulin in Lyon's Parc de la Tête d'Or just before Moulin was arrested, and radioed back to say that if required he would serve as provisional delegate-general until a permanent successor could be found. His offer was endorsed and he went to Paris which was now the centre for resistance movements.[3] To assist him, two other individuals were parachuted into France on 15–16 August 1943. François-Louis Closon was seconded from the interior commissariat to begin the work of appointing prefects loyal to de Gaulle who would take office at the Liberation.[4] Jacques Bingen of the BCRA came as delegate of the French Committee of National Liberation and – given the size of the country – Serreulles's *alter ego* in the former Free Zone. The evening before he left, in case he did not return, he wrote a moving letter to his mother. He was keen to do his duty, he said, and live up to the example of his older brother Max, who had been killed in 1917. His patriotism had been heightened but so too was his Jewish identity in the face of the brutality of Nazism:

I would betray the ideal for which I left France in June 40 if I stayed in an armchair until we won. I want to serve dangerously the ideals of liberty for which Max died in the last war. I have gained a love of France that is stronger, more immediate and more tangible than what I felt when life was sweet and indeed easy [. . .] In addition I want to avenge so many Jewish friends who have been tortured or murdered by a barbarism we have not seen for centuries. I want one more Jew (and there are so many of us, if only you knew) to play his part – and more than his part – in the liberation of France.[5]

Such powerful ideals did not exclude power struggles between those who aspired to succeed Jean Moulin. Pierre Brossolette was desperate to become permanent delegate-general but had the misfortune to be in England when Moulin was arrested. In August he went to see de Gaulle in Algiers where, he told his wife, 'the agitation that was the rule here has become a frenzy [. . .] people are in an cloud of improvisation and permanent crisis.'[6] He did not secure the post, and the General's parting words to him were, 'don't brutalise the Resistance.'[7] Undefeated, Brossolette concocted a scheme to find an uncontroversial man who would take the title while he, the king-maker, exercised the real power. The front man selected was Émile Bollaert, who had been prefect at Lyon from 1934 until September 1940, when he had been dismissed by Vichy, after which he had gone to Paris and found work as an insurance agent. Colonel Passy recalled:

Pierre wanted to govern, that is true. He wrote to me about it twenty-five times. 'We could govern through a stooge [. . .] a figurehead like Bollaert. He was a great prefect at Lyon, he is a bit senile and he knows nothing about the Resistance but I will teach him and as he needs me I will lead him more easily towards the political line we are looking for.'[8]

There was something ironic, observed Jacques Lecompte-Boinet, in that Brossolette, who took the *nom de guerre* 'Brumaire', echoing Bonaparte's coup d'état of 18 Brumaire Year VIII, found 'the oldest and crustiest civil servant in France to lead the way to the authoritarian republic of which he dreamed'.[9] But since the job was not his, Brossolette had Bollaert officially appointed delegate-general by Algiers and returned to France on 19 September 1943 to find him.

Serreulles and Bingen also went to see Bollaert to brief him about the post and to make sure that he was not simply putty in Brossolette's hands. They found themselves obliged to 'give him a veritable history lesson about the Resistance, for which Bollaert thanked them warmly, since otherwise he would not have been able to discharge his new office'.[10] Bollaert also decided that he would have to go to Algiers to meet de Gaulle personally, and there receive a proper anointing from the General himself. Brossolette accompanied him but this trip proved to be their downfall. Two attempts to be taken off by Lysander plane in the full moons of December and January failed. They then tried to get away by boat from the Breton coast on 2 February 1944 but the boat hit rocks. Returning to shore they were betrayed by a villager, arrested and taken for questioning to Rennes. On 19 March Brossolette's identity behind his code name was formally established by a Gestapo agent sent from Paris, but Bollaert's was never discovered. Both were taken to Paris and Brossolette was brutally interrogated for three days at the Gestapo's Paris headquarters in the avenue Foch. At midday on 23 March the men were left in a fifth-floor maid's room and Brossolette threw himself out of the window. He died in hospital of his injuries late that evening. Bollaert was deported to Dora and Bergen-Belsen, which he survived.[11]

As a result of this drama ties between London and Algiers and the internal resistance were grievously stretched. Leaders of the internal resistance seized the opportunity to reclaim as much independence as they could. After the Occupation of the Free Zone many resistance leaders who had formerly been based there came to Paris. Confronted by the problem of Vichy rather than just dealing with German occupation, southerners were often more politically minded than resisters from the north. Jacques Lecompte-Boinet noted that 'leaders from the north had a certain inferiority complex vis-à-vis their colleagues from the south [. . .] "the Resistance has come of age" was a slogan that came from the south.'[12] One of the southern resisters he had to deal with was the unlikely figure of Jean de Vogüé, scion of a noble family and former naval officer from the Vivarais, whose fortune came from the sugar industry and who was heir to the château of Vaux-le-Vicomte. Sent to reinforce Ceux de la Résistance, which arose from the ashes of Combat in the former Occupied Zone, he planned to use it as a vehicle for his own political ambition. According to Lecompte-Boinet he had a ready-made plan for a 'seizure of power in Paris on the day of the insurrection', becoming 'prefect of the Seine'.[13] This exemplified a tension between his personal idea of 'military resistance seeking to remain apart from what we called "all political taint" and the new political resistance that considered military resistance as old hat'.[14]

The new politics of Resistance was immediately manifested in the battle for the chairmanship of the National Council of Resistance that followed Moulin's arrest. Another ambitious southerner, Emmanuel d'Astier de la Vigerie, was keen to be elected. However, on behalf of the Délégation Générale Serreulles and Bingen proposed Georges Bidault, who had acted as Moulin's second on 27 May, and Bidault was elected. Bidault had made his own preparations. His background was Christian democratic but he was in favour with the Front National, and he garnered their votes. Subsequently he was accused of being indebted to the communists and unable to resist their demands, something that he resolutely denied.[15]

Since full meetings of the National Council were bound to be few and far between, for both logistical and security reasons, a *bureau permanent* was set up to act as its power-house. It became the official representative of the interior Resistance vis-à-vis London and Algiers, the French people and the Allies. It was chaired by Georges Bidault and had a majority of non-communists[16] but the most dynamic force on the committee was Pierre Villon, who fought to keep Bidault under a communist spell. Villon as Front National leader was in touch with the Communist Party central committee, notably Jacques Duclos, who for security reasons met them on a farm in the distant suburbs of Paris. Villon was dedicated to the strategy of immediate action leading to national insurrection, which would make the liberation of France not just a transfer of power between Pétainists and Gaullists but a revolution in terms both of a mass movement and of the radical transformation of society, including the nationalisation of key industries. He was a driving force behind drafting a National Council charter along these lines, which was first put to the Council on 26 November 1943.[17] Yves Farge tried to explain the dramatic nature of his confrontation with colleagues less radical than he in terms of the persecution he had suffered both as a communist and a Jew, having endured prison and the deportation of his wife to Auschwitz:

I saw him at meetings of the National Council of Resistance, to which I had to report, wrapped up in his thoughts, inspired by his slogans for action, formulating orders with a fierce will that made his face hard and his look steely. Sometimes his lips trembled as he tried to control his voice [. . .] For Villon the battle against the enemy in occupied France, following its betrayal, was a stage in the emancipation of humanity, one ordeal among many, a twist in the history of peoples. The systematic murdering of the fatherland through that of a people whose extermination had only begun, required a coming together of all friends of France and Liberty.[18]

The influence of the Communist Party in organisations like the National Council flowed from the prestige of the Red Army, following the victory of Stalingrad in February 1943. It also derived from the evolution of resistance – from a few small organisations to a larger movement of protest triggered by German demands for French labour to go to Germany. Public opinion, much of which for so long had given the Vichy regime the benefit of the doubt, now turned against it, as its claim to protect the people was rendered hollow.[19] The communists were able to channel much of that popular protest into support for themselves and for their doctrines of immediate action and national insurrection. This provoked responses from non-communist resisters, the BCRA in London, and the French Committee of National Liberation in Algiers, designed to contain communist resistance and, by reinforcing the power of the state, to avoid the twin spectres of popular revolution and Allied occupation.

Mass resistance was provoked in France by the Relève, a scheme trumpeted by Premier Laval in June 1942 that would bring back one POW from Germany in return for three skilled workers who 'volunteered' to take their place: in the event only 60,000 workers went to Germany by the end of August, and difficulties on the Eastern Front obliged the Germans to dig ever deeper for troops. In response to intensified German pressure a Vichy law of 4 September 1942 made all men aged eighteen to fifty liable to labour conscription, and the round-up of workers from factories triggered a wave of industrial action. On Tuesday 6 October 1942, for example, a list of seventy-five workers required to go to Germany was posted at the Batignolles-Châtillon locomotive works at Nantes. Alerted by a tract distributed by the communist-inspired Popular Factory Committees urging 'Hold fast. Don't go. Not a single French worker for the Boches' the workers went on strike. The management was unable to persuade the workers' leaders to end the strike and the *Feldkommandant* threatened to arrest them. Vichy officials managed to calm matters down and the disruption lasted only three hours, but a symbolic step had been taken in defiance of the Germans.[20]

In the Free Zone, which did not have to deal with the Germans, opposition was even fiercer. On 13 October 1942, a list of thirty conscripted workers was posted in the railway engineering workshops of Oullins, in the suburbs of Lyon. J. Enjoly, an engineering worker, trade unionist and secretary of the Communist Party cell, was among the organisers of a strike at 10.20 a.m. precisely: 'It was something extraordinary. At the agreed time, in small groups, all 3,000 railway workers from the workshops assembled in front of the management offices, happy but also surprised to see each other there. The management was terrified . . .' and called in the Vichy authorities and police, who surrounded the factory.[21] The strike continued until 8 p.m., the workers singing the 'Marseillaise' with tears in their eyes. At that point the workers left the factory and proceeded to the town hall in front of a huge crowd. The regional prefect did not dare send in the police but twenty-four strike leaders were arrested in their beds during the night. Enjoly escaped that fate by following Party rules and not going home that evening; the incident was given wide publicity in the Resistance and Allied press.[22]

The trade union movement had been emasculated by Vichy, which had tried to control labour through the Charter of Labour of 4 October 1941. This measure banned strikes and forced workers' representatives to sit alongside managers in new organisations.[23] Trade unions began to reform underground, although many trade-union activists were more interested in protecting the material interests of workers than in resistance activity that could lead to arrest, prison or deportation. A fillip was nevertheless given to resistance activity in the labour movement by the return to Paris of André Tollet. Tollet had been arrested as a communist in October 1940 and tunnelled out of a camp at Compiègne on 22 June 1942, while Laval was making his speech nearby in favour of the Relève. He went underground in Normandy before being recalled to Paris at Christmas 1942 in order to start rebuilding the trade-union federation in the capital: 'Nowhere did I feel more at ease than in Paris,' he wrote, 'You understood popular reactions, you could even predict them.'[24] Communist trade unionists like Tollet had been expelled from the CGT after the Nazi-Soviet Pact, but in April 1943 he was one of the militants who negotiated their return to the fold in a reunified CGT. He met non-communist trade unionist Louis Saillant on the banks of the Marne at Le Perreux to the east of Paris and went to a secret location in a woodworker unionist's house, where the agreement was signed.[25] The evolving plan was to undertake sabotage in factories working for the German war effort, and to develop underground union organisations.

Communists worked through labour organisations and also through those formed by the Resistance. One of these was Action Ouvrière (AO), set up by Combat at the end of 1942 to organise resistance activity among workers. Its leader was Marcel Degliame, a former hosiery worker and communist trade unionist from Troyes, who had been a POW in Germany and escaped to join the army in Syria, where he joined the Free French. He re-established contact with trade unionist Robert Lacoste, who had signed the Manifesto of 15 November 1940, and with the underground labour movement in Lyon, but soon learned that conventional trade-union action was not enough and that sabotage was the order of the day.[26] He was put in touch with Claude Bourdet, who was drawn by this 'big lad, built like Hercules, "prolo" and intellectual at the same time', who could remedy the fact the Resistance was 'terribly short of leaders who had a real experience of the labour movement'.[27]

Lyon became one of the centres of working-class resistance, and communists organised workers to rebuild support that they had lost since the Nazi-Soviet Pact. Jean Gay, who had been secretary of the public transport drivers' union in Lyon and imprisoned as a communist in 1939, took over the leadership of AO in the Lyon area. Alban Vistel of Franc-Tireur and MUR leader at Lyon described his 'swarthy complexion, dark look, broad shoulders [. . .] like a hard element forged by a past that I could only guess [. . .] For him the fight to free the country could not be separated from the battle for the emancipation and dignity of the working class.'[28] The stronghold of Action Ouvrière was the underground metalworkers' union that organised strike action in the big Lyon engineering factories to undermine production for the German war economy, particularly in the autumn of 1943, until Gay's arrest in March 1944.

In Languedoc the profile of Action Ouvrière was rather different. Its leader was Gérald Suberville, who had studied law at Rennes and was a trainee lawyer when war broke out. As an officer cadet in 1940 he commanded Spanish republicans in the 23rd Regiment of Foreign Volunteers. Retreating south, he got to Morocco but was unable to find a boat bound for London and, back in France, alternated working in factories with working for the Food Ministry, writing a thesis on the lack of food in occupied France. Through his supervisor in Rennes he made contact in July 1942 with René Courtin, a law professor at the University of Montpellier and leading light in Combat. He became convinced that the working class was:

[a] bearer of hope. Having nothing to lose it was more likely to throw itself into the collective fight, and not draw back because of the gravity of the risks involved. In occupied France it seemed obvious that 'bourgeois' resistance would subscribe to *attentisme* whereas working-class resistance would embrace immediate action.[29]

Suberville joined the Communist Party in September 1942 and became regional head of Action Ouvrière in the Montpellier area in the spring of 1943.[30] Unlike Degliame and Gay he had discovered the virtues of the working class rather than being born into it and used Action Ouvrière as a vehicle for communist activity. One of his key allies was 'the magnificent railwayman Sainte-Cluque', who had been secretary of the locomotive drivers' union at Béziers and, arrested and interned as a communist, escaped to throw himself into resistance. With Suberville he sabotaged the narrow-gauge line that serviced the mines of Bédarieux, which supplied ore to a factory producing aluminium for German planes, and organised strikes in plants all over the region, including the Bousquet d'Orb coal mine, to mark Armistice Day on 11 November 1943.[31]

In the Toulouse region, west of Montpellier, the organiser of Action Ouvrière was Léo Hamon, who had fled with his family to the Free Zone in 1942. He was even more of an intellectual than Suberville, but came from a Russian revolutionary tradition and had been a communist until the Nazi-Soviet Pact. In the south-west he worked alongside Marie-Rose Gineste, a social worker involved in *Témoignage Chrétien* and the Catholic trade-union movement, who had distributed the pastoral letter of Mgr Théas, Bishop of Montauban, protesting against the deportation of Jews in August 1942. Now she typed leaflets urging young people not to go to work in Germany, while Hamon found hiding places, forestry jobs and false IDs for *réfractaires* and organised a large protest demonstration against labour deportations on 1 April 1943.[32]

The labour draft had intensified with Vichy's law of 16 February 1943 on the Service du Travail Obligatoire (STO), which required all young men of military age – that is, born in 1921, 1922 and 1923 – to report for war work in factories in Germany. Between 600,000 and 650,000 French workers were drafted for work in the Reich between the autumn of 1942 and summer of 1944. Industrial workers, white-collar workers and students were hit more than young farmers but even these were targeted in June 1943. Avoiding labour conscription was difficult in north-eastern France, more easily achieved in Brittany, the Massif Central and the Alps. Initially, the proportion of young men who responded to the call was quite high, but from the summer of 1943 it fell off dramatically and draft-dodgers accounted for nearly 70 per cent in the autumn of 1943.[33]

Faced with the prospect of war work in Germany, where conditions were harsh and the danger of bombing by the Allies extremely high, young men vanished from normal circulation as networks were established to move and hide them. If they remained in the towns and cities they were in constant danger from *rafles* or round-ups by Vichy or the German police that took place in railway stations, in cafés, or as people came out of cinemas. The only way to protect themselves in urban areas was to volunteer for work in so-called *Speer-Betriebe* – designated factories and mines working for the Germans in France, but even these were sometimes raided. Otherwise it was advisable to go to the country, to find work on farms or – even better – in forestry plantations as woodcutters. Outside the legal system that provided them with identity and ration cards, they were effectively outlaws.[34] In some isolated parts of the country, such as the mountains and forests of the Alps and Massif Central, *maquis* were beginning to form. That did not mean that all *réfractaires* became *maquisards*; some simply lay low: depending on the area, between 5 per cent and 25 per cent of *réfractaires* joined a *maquis*, about 30,000 to 40,000 in all.[35]

Given its isolation and inaccessibility, the Alps were one of the most popular destinations for *réfractaires*. From the police dossiers of those who were involved in the *maquis* of the Glières plateau in Haute-Savoie it is possible to follow the itineraries of the young men who, often quite randomly, finished up there. Many of them had been at the Chantiers de la Jeunesse, glorified scout camps where – since military service was banned under the German Occupation – Vichy trained its young men in the Free Zone. When STO was introduced, the Chantiers were a sitting target for recruitment, so many young men took their leave. Yves Jeudy (b. 1921) was a baker from the Var who lived with his mother. He had served eight months in the Chantier de la Jeunesse at Gap until June 1942, and was called up for STO in March 1943. To avoid it he left home and wandered around south-east France until arriving at Thorens (Haute-Savoie), where he worked unpaid but sheltered as a farmhand for a farmer, Léon Jourdan. There he met a forest guard aptly nicknamed 'Forestier', who was well-known for guiding young men to the *maquis* camps on the Glières plateau, and that is where he went around 15 March 1944 in order, he later told the police, 'to prevent M. Jourdan getting into trouble'. Pierre Pelletier (b. 1922), from Vanves outside Paris and whose parents were divorced, had also done his time in a Chantier de la Jeunesse and then worked as a labourer for a firm servicing the Kriegsmarine at Saint-Nazaire. Called up for STO in June 1943 he went back to Vanves for ten days and then to Annecy, where he was advised to go to Thônes: 'I met some young people from the *maquis* who invited me to join them,' he recalled, and was sent up to a camp at Entremont commanded by a Lieutenant Tom [Morel]. Jacques Beges (b. 1923) was a leather goods worker who escaped from a Chantier de la Jeunesse near

Lyon in November 1943 because he was threatened with STO in Germany. He went to work for a farmer he knew in Haute-Savoie until January 1944, when the farmer said it was too dangerous to employ him. Having met a contact nicknamed 'Chocolat', he was taken to the Entremont camp and introduced to 'Loulou' (Louis Vignol), the leader of a group of about thirty young men living in a chalet. To begin with they just did jobs on the camp and kept guard, but on 2 February they went up to the Glières plateau to receive a parachute drop of weapons. Beges, Pelletier and Jeudy were all enrolled in the Bayard section under 'Lieutenant Roger', given a rifle and considered ready for action.[36]

Another destination for *réfractaires* was the Massif Central. Jean-Olivier Eleouet was a lathe-operator in a Paris factory, and he was called up early in 1943, aged twenty, for STO: 'I did not answer the summons, then the warnings and threats that were addressed to me,' he later wrote. He left Paris with two mates and the address of parents of a friend who lived in the Corrèze, in the north-west of the Massif Central. There they were put in touch with the Legros family at Tulle. The father was a veteran of 1914–18, the mother a dressmaker, and the son a seminarist who acted as their guide: 'In his cassock,' said Eleouet, 'he looked like our monitor' at a *colonie de vacances*. They were directed towards a *maquis* run by the Francs-Tireurs et Partisans, called the Groupe Guy Môquet II, after the young communist hero. After questioning they were then taken to the camp near the village of Sédières, where Jean-Olivier adopted the pseudonym 'Sparrow-hawk'. They had only one machine-gun and a few Sten guns, pistols and grenades. The winter was hard and they raided a Chantier de la Jeunesse to get their hands on leather jackets, sheepskin-lined jackets, boots and blankets. Eleouet also attended a communist staff school in the Dordogne, where the instructors were Spanish republicans – the most experienced of European resisters and much in demand. Their first military outing on 2 March 1944 was to join an FTP attack on the prison of Tulle to free some of their comrades: 'The success of this bold operation had a considerable effect on our morale and on those around us,' reflected Eleouet. 'This important action affirmed our credibility.'[37]

This sample of *réfractaires* found *maquis* to join but not all were so daring or so lucky. Their ballooning numbers posed a huge problem for resistance organisations. To answer this, an Action Committee against Deportation (CAD) was set up on 14 July 1943. Centred on Paris but with regional antennae, it brought together the whole spectrum of resistance movements, including those of the communists. It was headed by Yves Farge, head of the MUR in the Lyon region, who was sent to Paris by Jean Moulin because things were getting too hot for him in the South. He was joined by Léo Hamon, who had been running Action Ouvrière in the Toulouse region, and also felt the Gestapo hard on his heels. Hamon was later replaced by Maurice Kriegel, which reinforced the communists' grip on the Action Committee. This already included Pierre Villon, head of the communist-led Front National, André Tollet, communist head of the trade-union movement in Paris, and Henri Tanguy, head of the FTP in Paris. It ran a large operation, building bridges to the CGT and Christian trade unions, collecting money from industrialists who did not want their skilled workers to go to Germany, manufacturing false identity papers, and infiltrating the ministries of Food and Industrial production. Their most dramatic coup on 25 February 1944 was the attack organised by Léo Hamon and undertaken by FTP on the STO offices on the place Fontenoy, which burned the files holding details of thousands of STO conscripts and severely affected the labour draft.[38]

The development of resistance activity across many parts of France meant that departmental and local liberation committees began to develop at the same pace as the national movements and organisations. Controversial, however, was the establishment of a liberation committee for Paris. Since the Revolution, and because of the Revolution, central governments in France – whether monarchical, imperial or republican – had been reluctant to concede autonomous government to Paris, and in particular ruled out the possibility of a mayor of Paris. The Paris Commune of 1871 demonstrated only too clearly what an autonomous government might get up to and was crushed by the republican government of Adolphe Thiers. Interim delegate-general Serreulles took the same view, stating that the presence of the National Council of the Resistance based in Paris made the formation of a Paris Liberation Committee redundant, a decision that led him into direct conflict with the communists. André Tollet, who was in charge of the clandestine Paris trade-union federation, argued on the contrary that Paris must have its own liberation committee. He found an unlikely ally in Jean de Vogüé, who wanted a strong government in Paris in order to become its head. A meeting was arranged of representatives of interested parties, including the Front National and FTP, in the southern Paris suburb of Villejuif, which was attended by Serreulles. Tollet pointed out that 'if they thought in London that the people of Paris had fought to bring back the ideas of Monsieur Thiers on the need to keep too-turbulent Paris on a tight leash one would have to say that the minutes of this meeting were not accurate'.[39] Two months after the setting up of the CAD, on 23 September 1943, the formation of a Paris Liberation Committee was agreed.[40]

Its first meeting was held on 27 October, attended on that occasion – much to the embarrassment of Serreulles – only by the Communist Party and their organisations: the CGT trade unions, the Front National, the FTP, the Women of France Union and Communist Youth. A second meeting brought in other non-communist movements, such as Ceux de la Résistance and Défense de la France, and the minutes recorded that 'it was easy to see immediately that Pellerin [Serreulles' code name] had prepared the ground in advance and launched a scarcely veiled attack on the communists' influence.' The communists fought back, pointing out that 'the vast majority of the population did not hide its support for them'.[41] A subsequent meeting of the Paris Liberation Committee was attended by further moderate and conservative elements including the socialists, Christian trade unions, Organisation Civile et Militaire (OCM) and the Alliance Démocratique. It was agreed to set up a permanent *bureau* that would balance equal numbers of communists and non-communists. The communists included Tollet for the trade-union federation as chair and André Carrel, tall and gaunt, it was said, like a Jesuit or Dominican, for the Front National.[42] The non-communists included the elegant socialist Roger Deniau for Libé-Nord, Catholic and conciliatory Marie-Hélène Lefaucheux for OCM and de Vogüé for Ceux de la Résistance.[43] He was later replaced by Léo Hamon, who, seeing Paris revolutionaries in terms of Victor Hugo's *Les Misérables*, described chairman Tollet as 'a typical worker-militant, committed, sharp-tongued [. . .] a reincarnation of the eternal Gavroche'.[44]

Differences between communists and non-communists remained entrenched and even deepened, although opinions did not always reflect the background of the individual in an obvious way. Marie-Hélène Lefaucheux was the wife of a director of Renault, but conceded that the upper bourgeoisie to which she belonged:

had behaved rather badly. They were not all "collaborators", they did not all make profits working for the Germans, but they were often cowardly and reluctant to place themselves in danger [. . .] The working class, on the other hand, behaved very well. Workers did not hesitate to act or to accept dangerous missions. They were full of courage, hope and confidence.[45]

Léo Hamon and André Carrel were both sons of revolutionary Russian-Jewish parents, born and brought up in France. Carrel's real name was Hoschiller; his father had deserted both the 1917 Revolution and his wife and as a journalist defended the Comité des Forges steel cartel. André never recovered from being called as a student the son of an arms dealer and became a hardline communist, accepting the Nazi-Soviet Pact.[46] As a student Hamon had also become a communist but rejected the pact and joined the non-communist resistance:

I had done what was in my power to build bridges between the communists and our movements. I was seen as their ally. Good people thought I was their agent. But two years later I was firmly resolved to do what was necessary to ensure that in liberated France, they would have their place, their whole place, but nothing but their place.[47]

The communists on the Paris Liberation Committee planned to draw on the growing discontent of the people of Paris and to prepare for national insurrection. The capital was teeming with *réfractaires* evading ever more intense round-ups. There were plans to collect funds for them from workers, employers and the French Committee in Algiers to provide the 'outlaws' with subsistence.[48] In addition, workers and their families were increasingly hard-pressed by food shortages and price rises in the fourth year of German occupation. Large numbers of factories went on strike on 11 November 1943 to mark the twenty-fifth anniversary of the armistice. The FTP was desperate for weapons to arm strikers and *réfractaires* for the insurrection to come. Tollet argued at the *bureau* on 3 December 1943 that:

Paris was the biggest *maquis* and with financial help for the Parisian *réfractaires* we could organise a real blow to stop the deportation of our compatriots. In conjunction with the labour movements in the factories this movement would quickly reach a higher stage.[49]

A week later, and inspired by partisan warfare in Yugoslavia, the communists on the bureau argued that 'through our own action we could perhaps rapidly create the conditions of an insurrection rather than wait for it to be sparked by the [Allied] landing'.[50]

Faced by the communists' ability to penetrate and shape popular organs of the Resistance, non-communist resisters in London and Algiers sought to check their influence. A think-tank, which went under the name of the Comité Général d'Études (CGE), had been secretly at work since June 1942, as a result of encounters between Jean Moulin and Alexandre Parodi, a jurist on the Conseil d'État, who had lost his brother René to suicide when he refused to talk in Fresnes prison. Its task was to select from likely figures those who would be on standby at the moment of Liberation to serve as ministerial permanent secretaries, regional *commissaires de la République* and prefects. It also thought about the organisation of justice to deal with collaborators and about economic reconstruction. The committee was composed mainly of jurists such as former law professors Henri Teitgen, François de Menthon and René Courtin, together with non-communist trade unionist Robert Lacoste.[51] Francis-Louis Closon from the interior commissariat in London had been parachuted in to France for a first time on 15 April 1943 in order to liaise with it.[52] That summer Parodi was forced to abandon the Conseil d'État and go underground, but another member of the Conseil d'État, Michel Debré, who was close to Lecompte-Boinet and Ceux de la Résistance and concerned about the 'furies of the Liberation' that threatened, met Serreulles in the grill room of the Médicis restaurant in Paris in July 1943. He learned that 'another life was about to begin for me [. . .] the civil preparation of the Liberation' but he continued under the cover of his day job, hiding lists of potential candidates for key posts in the dusty law tomes of the Conseil d'État.[53]

The high profile of communists in armed resistance was a particular concern. The Armée Secrète remained a virtual army, lacking men, weapons and command structures, and in its absence the FTP and FTP-MOI carried out increasingly dangerous actions, both to themselves and to innocents who might be massacred in reprisals. On 26 June 1943 a meeting had been held in London, chaired by General François d'Astier, and including his brother Emmanuel and Jacques Bingen. It decided to select and send in regional military delegates to organise emerging armed resistance groups and place them under the authority of London. Colonel Passy, who was in Algiers at the time, was furious when he discovered this challenge to the BCRA, but was obliged to accept the decision. Candidates were in short supply and a first drop of ten officers on 12–13 September 1943 covered only five of the twelve designated military regions. They included Colonel Pierre Marchal, aged forty-two, a brilliant army officer who had been close to Delestraint, appointed super-delegate for the former Occupied Zone, and Major Albert Mangin, General Mangin's eldest son and brother-in-law of Diego Brosset and Jacques Lecompte-Boinet, in the former Free Zone.[54]

Brilliantly conceived on paper, the system got off to a very poor start. Ten days after arriving, Marchal was arrested in his Paris flat by the Gestapo and immediately took a cyanide pill. Mangin took refuge in Switzerland for a month in October and November before taking over as provisional National Military Delegate. Marchal's flat was owned by the widow of a POW, Jacqueline d'Alincourt, who had been recruited by Daniel Cordier. She was duly arrested along with a secretary and two liaison agents of Delegate-General Serreulles. This led to the discovery of his office at 129b rue de la Pompe and the code names of fourteen individuals involved with the National Council. Serreulles was told by the BCRA that he was 'brûlé' and all agents were instructed to have no contact with him. Though he went underground and tried to continue working, he was isolated and without credibility and eventually escaped to London, where he was hauled over the coals for what became known as the 'rue de la Pompe affair'.[55] No support for the military delegates was forthcoming from BCRA and SOE, which felt challenged. As a result they had no access to weapons drops, and so had no authority with local resistance chiefs: 'Without men, without weapons, without orders, almost without money,' Mangin told Passy, 'they all feel that they have been put in the front line but abandoned by their leaders.'[56]

De Gaulle's own position was to be reinforced in relation to the internal resistance and the Allies by calling a national assembly to Algiers. The French parliament had been abolished after it had voted to transfer full powers to Marshal Pétain on 10 July 1940 and the Vichy regime, though it played with constitution-making, ruled without a national assembly. De Gaulle capitalised on this by summoning a Provisional Consultative Assembly that would signal a transfer of political legitimacy from Vichy to Algiers. The assembly was intended to demonstrate the political support enjoyed by de Gaulle that his rival Giraud lacked, and reinforce his authority in the sceptical eyes of the British and, above all, the Americans. In terms of composition, the assembly balanced forty representatives from resistance organisations within France, chosen by the National Council of Resistance, with forty-four from other constituencies. These included twelve Free French, twelve members of the *conseils généraux* of Algeria and other now liberated African colonies, and twenty deputies and senators who had refused to vote full powers to Pétain, chosen by the communists, socialist, radical and conservative parties.

Resisters and politicians made their way, often by way of London, to Algiers in time for the opening on 3 November 1943. It was a moment of revealing encounters and dramatic changes in the balance of power. The leaders of resistance movements came up against party politicians, as they had in the National Council, but in a setting where the politicians claimed the upper hand. The executive in the form of the French Committee of National Liberation strove to impose its will on both of them. This went on against the military background in North Africa, where the Free French were vying with the Army of Africa in the newly amalgamated army, in which those who had long been loyal to Vichy saw the opportunity to hold on to power.

The metropolitan resistance tried to organise itself to be ready for the party politicians. A meeting of all resistance delegates was called on 1 November and Henri Frenay, who had struggled so much to ensure the unity and independence of the metropolitan resistance, announced that 'the Resistance must join forces against the parliamentarians'. This was difficult because the Resistance delegates stretched from the Communist Party, including former deputies for the Paris region and Marseille, to moderates such as Jacques Lecompte-Boinet. In the event Lecompte-Boinet found himself more in sympathy with many of the Third Republic politicians than with communist resisters. Given the exclusion of all politicians who had seen Pétain as a saviour in 1940 he was struck by 'the total absence of reactionary or moderate elements' in 'this Popular Front assembly'.[57]

In a first run-off, the party politicians managed to get their man elected speaker of the Assembly against the candidate proposed by Henri Frenay. The politicians' man was Félix Gouin, a leading socialist from Marseille who had helped in the defence of Léon Blum at his Riom trial and then escaped to Britain. Meanwhile delegates from the trade union operated as a conciliating force between resisters and politicians: 'For the first time in the history of the labour movement,' observed Albert Gazier, who had signed the manifesto of 15 November 1940, 'trade unionists took part in their own right in a political assembly.' According to their own rules laid down in 1906, the CGT was required to maintain the autonomy of the labour movement and not become involved in party politics. But since the trade-union delegates were chosen by the CGT and were responsible to it alone they now made an exception. The CGT and the Christian democratic unions worked together and 'on many occasions,' continued Gazier, 'trade unionists prevented clashes and misunderstandings and acted as mediators.'[58]

The gathering of the Assembly in Algiers gave de Gaulle the democratic legitimacy to undertake a major reshuffle of ministers, still known as *commissaires*, and finally to ease Giraud out of the co-presidency of the French Committee. Giraud remained commander-in-chief of the armed forces and still posed a

Four contrasting images at war and at peace, before the defeat of 1940. Only one of these future resisters would survive the German Occupation.
Clockwise from top left: Henri Rol-Tanguy on the Spanish front, 1930; Jean Cavaillès as a soldier in 1940; Jeanine Sontag, boating; Guy Môquet with his bicycle.

While the Free French organised in London for combat in Africa and the
Near East, resisters within France went underground to challenge the German
occupation and Vichy, often with terrible results.
Top: De Gaulle and George V review French Foreign Legion in London.
Bottom: Châteaubriant quarry, the day after the execution of twenty-seven
hostages, including Guy Môquet, on 22 October 1941.

TOLLET *ANDRE CHARLES*

- né le 1er Juillet 1913 à Paris (14e)
- dernier domicile connu : 10 ter, rue
  Janssens - Paris.

Ex-secrétaire de la Région Parisienne
de la Fédération des Jeunesses Communistes.
Chargé de la Direction du journal "L'A-
vant Garde".
Ex-membre du Comité de Front Populaire
de la Région Parisienne.
Arrêté le 16 Avril 1940 pour infraction
au Décret du 26 Septembre 1939.
Condamné le 23 Octobre 1940 à 15 mois
de prison.
Interné le 25 Septembre 1941, s'est évadé
de Compiègne dans la nuit du 21 au 22 Juin
1942.

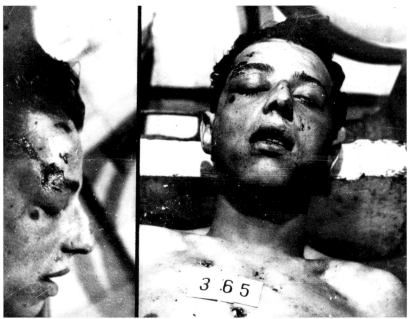

Disguises and cover stories were essential to underground resistance, ranged
against the ferocity of the Vichy and German authorities.
Top left: André Tollet police search file; *top right:* Pierre Georges/Colonel Fabien,
false ID as a priest; *bottom:* Executed Carmagnole militant.

Under the North African sun, de Gaulle and Giraud vie for supremacy while in the November gloom, resistance activists proclaim that the Republic is still a symbol of liberty and fraternity.

Top: De Gaulle and Giraud at Casablanca, as Roosevelt and Churchill look on, January 1943.

Bottom left and right: Marianne on a Bourg-en-Bresse plinth proclaiming the Fourth Republic, original photo and publicity mock-up, 11 November 1943.

The Germans were merciless against both young resisters caught red-handed and seasoned urban guerrillas, discredited as terrorists of foreign, communist and Jewish origin.
Top: Maquisards about to be executed at Lantilly, in Burgundy, 25 May 1943. *Right:* The *Affiche rouge* demonising resisters of the Manouchian group as 'the army of crime', February 1944.

August 1944. In Normandy, French forces land under General Leclerc, while in the capital, insurrection is debated in the Paris Liberation Committee.

Top: General Leclerc in Normandy, 1 August 1944.

Bottom: Paris Liberation Committee, posed after the Liberation. From the right: Georges Marrane, Marie-Hélène Lefaucheux, André Tollet (chair), Roger Deniau, André Carrel, Henri Rol-Tanguy and Léo Hamon.

For some, the Liberation meant triumph and reunion, but for others there was loss and tragedy.
Top left: Henri and Cecile Rol-Tanguy; *top right:* Madeleine Riffaud at the site of her triumph; *bottom:* Funeral of Pierre Georges/Colonel Fabien.

The memory of Resistance was contested by Gaullists, who saw it as victory in a Thirty Years War while ignoring the contribution of colonial troops, and by communists who saw it as an armed struggle, and were themselves divided over the contribution of foreigners and Jews.

Top: Gaullist march-past, 18 June 1945; *left:* Unveiling of the bust of Missak Manouchian at Ivry by his widow, Mélinée, in 1978.

political threat through some kind of coup. De Gaulle brought in resisters who had previously insisted on the autonomy of the metropolitan resistance both to reinforce that legitimacy and to control them. Henri Frenay wanted the War portfolio but this was given to André Le Troquer; instead, Frenay was put in charge of prisoners of war and deportees. Emmanuel d'Astier replaced André Philip as *commissaire* for the interior. René Capitant, the Algiers law professor who led Combat was put in charge of education and François de Menthon of the Comité Général d'Études was given the justice portfolio. The Crémieux law was finally put back onto the statute book, restoring citizenship to Algeria's Jews.[59] Lecompte-Boinet complained that resisters from the former Occupied Zone, considered less political than their colleagues in the former Free Zone, were not offered any posts: 'I waited in vain,' he said, 'for an invitation that never came.'[60]

There were limits to how far democratic legitimacy went in the hothouse atmosphere of Algiers. The first problem was the communists, with whose parliamentary group de Gaulle had been in tricky negotiations since the end of August 1943. They were keen to accept office but on two conditions: that they refer back to the central committee of the Party underground in France, and that they have some possibility of carrying through their own policies. Ferdinand Grenier arrived in Algiers from London on 30 October and on 8 November was offered either Food Supply or Production. After consulting the Party, he turned these down, on the grounds that he would be answerable to the governor-general of Algiers. Instead, he requested the Interior, Foreign Affairs or Colonies. This was clearly impossible and they were offered Information, but de Gaulle turned down their candidate. Finally, on 13 November, they were offered the portfolios for Health and Sports, but declined them.[61]

Jews, and in particular Jews of a communist persuasion, were another stumbling block. Raymond Aubrac, the leader of Libération who had escaped from France with his wife Lucie in

February 1944, came to Algiers and in April was proposed by d'Astier de la Vigerie to represent him as interior commissar on a standing committee that would oversee the work of the secret services. This was seen as a challenge to the power of the conservatives. Henri Frenay said in a ministerial meeting that there were 'too many Jews' in the Interior Ministry. Aubrac offered his resignation, as did Georges Boris, another Jewish member of the Interior Ministry who had visited Algiers in November 1943. Boris was appalled that there should be a *numerus clausus* in the services of the provisional government, and that in Algiers frankly Pétainist ideas should have so much sway.[62] He observed that de Gaulle, who had been surrounded by progressive as well as reactionary elements in London, was surrounded by only reactionary elements in Algiers. These allowed him to return to his own background of a French Catholic bourgeoisie close to Action Française, which worshipped order and hierarchy. In Algiers, explained Boris, de Gaulle encountered:

the Army of Africa [. . .] and the inhabitants of North Africa who were extremely Pétainist. He wanted to win everyone over and thus had to compromise with people he had previously detested [. . .] De Gaulle fell under the influence of a milieu very different from his former milieu in London, which distanced him from his former revolutionary attitude. He elaborated an authoritarian conception of the state, and had a fear of anarchy [. . .] This idea of the state, of authority, his respect for order and organisation made him very attached to Catholicism.[63]

Any right turn by de Gaulle was nevertheless limited by his power struggle with General Giraud and the remnants of Vichy. The secret services in Algiers were a particular problem. When the assembly was convened Giraud's secret services were still powerful and Colonel Passy feared they were plotting to take Giraud back to France in order to replace Laval as head of government, do a deal with the Americans, and force de Gaulle out of the picture.[64] Passy came from London to deal with the situation and a measure was pushed through the Assembly in late November, which set up a General Delegation of Special Services (DGSS) that combined the Giraudist secret services with the BCRA. This was entrusted to Jacques Soustelle, who in 1939 had been in charge of French secret services in Mexico, which the Germans used as a base to spy on the USA, and had been *commissaire* for Information with the Free French in London. He was a hardline Gaullist who could be trusted to be entirely loyal.

The army was another headache for the Gaullists. The Americans insisted on backing Giraud as commander-in-chief and the Army of Africa was the bedrock of the new model army amalgamated with the Free French. It remained superior to the Free French both in numbers and equipment supplied to them by the Americans. That said, certain parts of the army were spearheaded by the Free French. In Morocco, the 2nd Armoured Division (2nd DB) was being built up around General Leclerc and his forces after their exile by Giraud to the Tripolitanian desert. This involved an initial *blanchiment* or 'whitening' of the Free French. Leclerc was anxious to get rid of many of the Africans who had fought with him across the Sahara, and had numbered 2,700 alongside 550 Europeans for the attack on Fezzan. On 2 August 1943 he asked de Gaulle for 'white reinforcements to replace black soldiers who are unsuited to war in Europe: 1,500 French of whom 190 officers and 2,370 indigenous North Africans'.[65] He was happier with North Africans than with Sub-Saharans, but given the shortage of French soldiers, the white contingent was made up by Spanish republicans who had escaped to North Africa after defeat by Franco and had been kept in camps by Vichy and Darlan. They had been released to form the African Free Corps for the recovery of Tunisia and were then incorporated into the 3rd Chad Regiment which became part of the 2nd DB. The regiment's 9th company, commanded by captain Dronne, was known as 'la Nueve', the Ninth, because it was almost entirely composed of Spaniards.[66] That said, the 2nd DB included significant numbers from the Army of Africa, whom Leclerc's soldiers tried to force to wear the Cross of Lorraine, provoking violent clashes. In turn, officers of the Army of Africa tried to stop young people arriving clandestinely from France across Spain to join the new army from doing so: 'Does the fact of having four or five stars on the sleeve, of having fired on the Americans or having collaborated with Pétain,' asked Leclerc's aide-de-camp Christian Girard sarcastically, 'give the right to frustrate what remains of these young people's enthusiasm?'[67]

Matters were also facilitated by the arrival of a new general who would take command of the so-called the 'B Army', which included most of the Army of Africa and Diego Brosset's 1st Free French Division. On 20 December 1943 General Jean de Lattre de Tassigny, having escaped from a Vichy prison and been taken to London by the Resistance, finally arrived in Algiers and was appointed by Giraud to operational command. When he visited the 2nd DB on 2 January 1944 he told them that General Giraud 'has been my friend, my commander. I will obey him unconditionally.' But, he added, 'I will seek to be the common denominator between General de Gaulle, General Giraud and the War Minister. I am a soldier, not a politician.'[68] A former general of the Armistice Army who had tried to resist the German occupation of the Free Zone in November 1942 and had been punished by Vichy for his pains, he had no association with North Africa or Giraudism and was a leader who in time could make amalgamation serve the Gaullist cause.

In the spring of 1944 de Gaulle felt strong enough in North Africa to flex his political muscle, call for national unity and finally end the troublesome diarchy with Giraud. On 18 March 1944 he offered a reworking of his appeal of 18 June 1940. He called on French soldiers, sailors, airmen and 'all those fighting in the *maquis* and in towns and factories' to 'fight all together'. Political consequences followed. The provisional government, he said:

wants people of all – I repeat, all – origins and all political alignments, and notably those who have taken a major part in the efforts and sacrifices of combat to be associated with its actions and even its composition, on condition that with it they pursue the general interest of which all are only servants, without exceptions or privileges. It is my honour to summon all French people to a national union.[69]

Having announced the line, de Gaulle moved against Giraud by using his association with former Vichy minister Pierre Pucheu against him. Pucheu had been invited to North Africa to do business with Giraud but had been imprisoned by the French Committee. Now he was sent before a military tribunal and on 11 March sentenced to death. De Gaulle refused to pardon him and he was shot on 20 March.[70] Giraud, tainted by the relationship with Pucheu, was deprived of his post as commander-in-chief and disappeared from the scene for good. He would be airbrushed out of the Gaullist account of resistance and liberation as if he had never existed.

The communist group, which had campaigned to punish Pucheu for executing communist resisters, was again approached by de Gaulle. Grenier and Billoux met him on 28 and 31 March and duly accepted the Air ministry and a ministry without portfolio.[71] This opening of the executive to the communists upset conservative resisters such as Henri Frenay. Referring explicitly to de Gaulle's speech of 18 March on the need to bring together people from all political traditions, he lobbied for a ministerial position to be given to his friend Pierre-Dominique Dunoyer de Segonzac, who had been his dormitory companion at Saint-Cyr. As a soldier Frenay, like Dunoyer, had initially been seduced by the promise of Pétain and Dunoyer had tried to train a chivalric élite for Vichy at Uriage, but his illusions had now been dashed and he had found his way to Algiers. Frenay argued in support of Dunoyer:

Though in an official capacity, this man fought against the Hun, collaboration, totalitarianism and Vichy's exceptional laws. He has continued that fight underground for the last fourteen months and will return to it. He has publicly disavowed the Marshal in whom he had the weakness to believe. Is he going to be treated like a second-class Frenchman while he has risked his life, rallied to the Resistance and is preparing to return to the fight?[72]

De Gaulle, however, trod a very tight rope between opening the possibility of office to those who had served Vichy for a time and those who had too much of Vichy about them ideologically. Dunoyer was not made an offer and Frenay complained that Gaullism, far from melting into the nation, 'is folding back on itself and becoming isolated', so that the General was now surrounded only by 'a handful of men'.[73]

Relations between the Free French and metropolitan resistance had been ruptured by the arrest of Charles Delestraint and Jean Moulin and the failure to re-establish London's control in any convincing way. This enabled metropolitan resistance leaders to seize the initiative and coincided with a popularisation of resistance activity in response to German demands for labour and the flight of young men to the woods and mountains, and sometimes to the *maquis*. Communist and also some non-communist leaders developed a rhetoric and strategy of immediate action and national liberation as a way to contest the leadership of London and Algiers and their insistence on doing nothing until the Allies landed. De Gaulle was also faced by the military and political primacy of Giraud in North Africa, commanding as he did the remnants of the Vichy regime there. Slowly but surely de Gaulle regained control through his friends on the National Council of Resistance and by plans to give the levers of the state to men he could trust. In North Africa he squeezed Giraud off the French Committee of National Liberation and built a political power-base in the Provisional Consultative Assembly. He was obliged to make concessions to the communists who had publicly rallied to his cause but suspected that they harboured a revolutionary agenda which they might try to implement through such bodies as the Paris Liberation Committee. That said, the power struggle did not only involve de Gaulle, the Free French, the metropolitan resistance and elements in North Africa who were still nostalgic for Marshal Pétain. The Allies – both British and American – would ultimately play a huge part in the eventual outcome.

12

Skyfall or guerrilla

A wider and wider mass of young réfractaires *and indeed all Frenchmen need to be brought into the immediate action of guerrilla warfare that we are waging.*
(Charles Tillon to de Gaulle, 1943)

The tussles and conflicts between resisters in metropolitan France and between the Free French and Vichyites in North Africa were of very limited interest to the Allies. Their concern was the defeat of Germany and to that even the liberation of France was of secondary importance. Moreover the liberation of France, it was felt, could be delivered from the sky, in the shape both of Allied bombs and SOE agents parachuted in to work with select groups of French resisters. There was, however, another vision of resistance that was held by some resisters in metropolitan France and especially communists. This was modelled on the French revolutionary idea of the *levée en masse*, the people in arms who would rise up to free themselves from foreign oppression through guerrilla warfare. The battle between these two options began a long time before a second front was opened up and only intensified after D-Day.

Allied strategy was, in the first place, to bomb military-industrial installations in France that were contributing to the German war effort. Ideal from their point of view, they could prioritise military aims, exclude political considerations, and have nothing to do either with the internal French Resistance nor with the Free French. Bombing had considerable support from the population, at least in the early days, since the RAF benefitted from a heroic status gained during the Battle of Britain. That said, however precise it might be, it could not avoid inflicting civilian casualties, and this was mercilessly exploited by Vichy propaganda to turn public opinion against the Allies. An alternative Allied approach was therefore to organise the sabotage of military-industrial installations by agents who were parachuted into France to work with emerging resistance circuits. These circuits operated across wide areas but involved only an élite of French resisters on the ground. Weapons and explosives drops were guided in by agents and their radio operators and used to arm only select groups. At all costs it was felt necessary to keep weapons out of the hands of communist partisans. Yet the Resistance was independently gaining strength on the ground. The Armée Secrète had been developed as an army-in-waiting of people going about their normal lives but ready to support the Allied offensive when D-Day finally came. Free Corps or commandos were taking action to get comrades out of jail, take out collaborators and even kill Germans. Most important, the imposition of STO provided the raw material of the *maquis*, which planned to undertake guerrilla warfare against the occupying forces.

The first dramatic bombing raid of the Allies was on the Renault factories in Boulogne-Billancourt in the western suburbs of Paris on 3 March 1942. A Paris high-school student 'who listens to you every day like most girls at my *lycée*', wrote to the BBC in London:

I visited the vicinity of the Renault plant; that was great work! It is a pity that there have been some casualties among the civilian population. We mourn them but we do not blame the English. We know that they are doing it on purpose in order to deliver us.[1]

Local people demonstrated their solidarity by burying downed pilots with full honours. A veteran of the Great War in Nantes told the BBC about the funeral of four British airmen there in 1941:

Their graves are covered in flowers. The first wreath laid on the airmen's grave carried the inscription: 'A group of metalworkers'. Every Sunday in the cemetery a large and reverential crowd processes in front of our dear English friends. Three-quarters of them are working-class people.[2]

Not all Allied pilots who were brought down by German anti-aircraft fire died; many bailed out over in Belgium and northern France and, if lucky, were hidden by locals. Escape lines were organised by a few courageous local resisters to spirit these airmen to a neutral country so that they could resume the fight with the Allies. These circuits were purely military in purpose, to assist the Allied war effort. They had no political agenda and did not undertake political propaganda. Initially they functioned with very little Allied help, apart from diplomatic help in Spain or Switzerland, although in time Allied agents and servicemen linked up with the internal resistance.

The Comet line was originally devised by a young Red Cross nurse, Andrée de Jonghe, and her father Frédéric, a primary-school teacher from an industrial suburb of Brussels. They began by hiding and smuggling out British soldiers stranded in Belgian military hospitals after Dunkirk.[3] Later they concentrated on airmen who had been brought down, escorting them first from the Brussels-controlled Forbidden Zone of the Nord/Pas-de-Calais into France – sometimes forced to swim across the Somme – then across France to the Pyrenees and to neutral Spain. There Andrée negotiated a deal with the British authorities in Bilbao to keep them out of Spanish prisons and get them to England.[4] As British raids grew more intense and more airmen fell in France a turntable was created in Paris in the spring of 1942. It was a bourgeois Catholic network that included the Jesuit father Michel Riquet, a veteran of the Great War and chaplain to Catholic doctors, who was linked to Henri Frenay, and Robert and Germaine Aylé, who were in business and close to the Dominicans. The group organised safe houses and false papers for Allied pilots in transit.[5] Stanislas Fumet, who had moved to Paris from Lyon, dined at the Aylés' flat with Riquet, 'a joyful and most friendly evening', one Friday in June 1943 four days before the Aylés and Frédéric de Jongh were arrested.[6] Frédéric de Jongh and Robert Aylé were shot at Mont Valérien on 28 March 1944.

Germaine Aylé was deported, as was Andrée de Jonghe, who had been arrested in the Pyrenees in January 1943; both survived.

After these arrests the Comet operation was organised on the Belgian side by an industrialist of aristocratic stock, Baron Jean de Blommaert, and on the French side by Philippe d'Albert Lake, a publicist for P&O whose mother was English, and by his American wife, Virginia, from Dayton, Ohio, who went to France to avoid having to teach at her mother's private school and married Philippe in 1937. They had a flat in Paris and a country cottage at Nesles-la-Vallée, 40 kilometres north-west of the capital. She recalled an autumn evening in 1943 when the local baker drove up to ask them to help with three American airmen who had been shot down:

The dark-haired, slanting-eyed Willy was from Hawaii. He was an oculist. There was serious, love-lorn Bob from California and Harry, a jolly factory worker from Detroit. They seemed so happy to be able to relax for a few hours and to talk with us who spoke and understood English.[7]

She decided there and then to 'work for the Underground', hiding airmen in their Paris flat or walking arm-in-arm around the Trocadéro Gardens, under the noses of sightseeing Germans, before it was time to take the train. When from the end of May 1944 Allied bombing disrupted the rail network they took airmen to a *maquis* in the Fréteval Forest near Châteaudun, the 'Sherwood' plan masterminded by Colditz escapee Airey Neave, who worked for MI9. About 150 airmen were hidden there by mid-August 1944. Unfortunately, Virginia was arrested near there with a downed airman on 12 June 1944 and deported to Ravensbrück, which she survived.[8]

The Comet line ferried Allied airmen to Spain via the Free Zone, but after the Germans occupied the whole of France in November 1942 the South lost its attraction and escape routes via Brittany were organised. The Shelburn network, active from 1943, escorted airmen to the Breton coast from which they were picked up at night by a British boat. The meeting-point was the Café de Biarritz on the Boulevard Saint-Michel, run by Georges Labarthe, a veteran of two wars from south-west France, and his wife. They had links to resistance organisations such as Libé-Nord and ORA, although they did not see themselves as 'members'. The café was frequented by young men from the nearby École Polytechnique, Saint-Cyr, École Navale and the École de l'Air, so that Allied military men passing through were less likely to be recognised.[9] At first the Labarthes advised them on how to get to the demarcation line, then teamed up with Mme Labarthe's dressmaker and organised their own escape line. Marie-Rose Zerling, a young Alsatian woman and science teacher who knew Jean Cavaillès at Libé-Nord, organised accommodation for escaping airmen, who were then taken in small groups by courier, boarding the night train to Brittany from the Gare Montparnasse. Arriving at the last moment in order to avoid undue attention, they often encountered hostility from passengers in crowded trains obliged to vacate seats booked for the airmen but the latter were unable to give themselves away by talking. One of the couriers learned the trick of warning grumblers, 'These gentlemen are Todt engineers. They are pretending not to understand but I'm sure that at least one of them does.'[10]

Once at the station of Saint-Brieuc the key contact on the north coast of Brittany was Georges Jouanjan. An escaped POW, he hoped to find a way to join the Free French in Britain by talking to pilots shot down in aerial combat. When a Halifax crashed after bombing Lorient on 13 February 1943 he and a local miller sheltered half a dozen surviving airmen and got them taken off the coast. One of the airmen, Gordon Carter, who subsequently married Jouanjan's sister, was debriefed by British secret services, which sent in an agent to make contact with the Breton group and set up a regular escape line. This was Vladimir Bouryschkine, an American basketball champion of Russian origin who went under the name of Val B. Williams. As the trainer of the Monaco basketball team, he had begun his resistance career by persuading the local Italian commander that Allied POWs at the nearby Fort de la Revère had a right under the Geneva Convention to enjoy one afternoon of sport per week. In this way he spirited fifty-three men away by boat to Gibraltar. Having met Jouanjan, he went to Paris to establish a link there, which he did via Marie-Hélène Lefaucheux's OCM.[11]

Back on the north Breton coast, the villagers of Plouha gathered at the café-tobacconist shop of François Le Cornec and organised the ferrying of airmen from the local train station to villagers' houses. Then, in response to a BBC message, 'Tout va bien à la Maison d'Alphonse,' they were walked to a small house on the cliff-top, the same Maison de l'oncle Alphonse, and thence onto the beach. They used a creek, the Anse Cochat, from which signals were flashed to British ships but could not be seen by German lookouts. They were taken off on a launch bound for Dartmouth commanded on a regular basis by corvette captain David Birkin.[12] Sixteen airmen were packed off on the night of 28–29 January 1943 and 128 altogether – including ninety-four Americans and thirty-two British and Commonwealth servicemen – until the Germans left the area early in August.[13] Unfortunately, back in Paris, the Gestapo came for the Labarthes on 5 June. Georges got away but his wife and daughter were deported and did not return from the camps.

Allied bombing of military targets in France was generally supported by French public opinion until 1943, when the US Air Force joined the bombing campaign and regularly bombed from high altitude by day, much less accurately than the RAF. Civilian deaths rose to about 60,000 – about the same number as British victims of German air raids. Those who worked in shipyards and factories that were harnessed to the German war effort were potential targets, as were civilian populations in the same ports and cities.[14] In Brittany the port of Lorient was attacked in January and February 1943, Saint-Nazaire in February and March 1943 and Nantes on 16 and 23 September 1943.[15] Over 800 were killed and 1,800 were injured in the first raid, while 1,300 were killed in the second.[16] A high-school student from Nantes who had witnessed the bombing and managed to make his way to England was debriefed in February 1944. He said that the raids had killed 3,000 people and another 3,000–4,000 were missing. He said that:

He himself was not particularly bitter about these raids, one of which did a great deal of damage to the docks. He had, however, seen a good deal of bitterness among his fellow-citizens [. . .] people might not have been so bitter, he thought, if the BBC or rather the Allied Air Forces through the BBC had said just one word of excuse [. . .] instead of pretending that the raid had been 100 per cent successful, when everyone in Nantes could see that this was not so.[17]

After these disasters, Vichy claimed alone to be protecting the lives and interests of French people. An alternative strategy was to sabotage military-industrial installations on the ground, avoiding the downside of collateral damage. This might be undertaken in the first place by small numbers of French resisters fed up with the political infighting of resistance who wanted only to contribute to military solutions. It was also undertaken by SOE agents parachuted into France and making contacts with resisters on the ground. Their ideal profile was that they were bilingual and while totally loyal to the Allies could pass for French men or women.

A prime example of the first kind of resister was Jean Cavaillès. A brilliant mathematician and friend of Lucie Aubrac, he was one of the founders of Libération in Clermont-Ferrand in 1941. Appointed to a post at the Sorbonne, he very soon went to Paris and became involved in Libé-Nord, along with the likes of Christian Pineau. When Pineau went to London in March–April 1942, he persuaded de Gaulle that the Free French must become more political, but in return Colonel Passy asked him to set up his own intelligence network called 'Phalanx' in the Free Zone and 'Cohors' in the Occupied Zone. Cohors was entrusted to Cavaillès, who built up his network from Belgium to Brittany around two very different groups: first, young teachers such as his former pupil Jean Gosset, who had taught at the *lycées* of Brest and Vendôme, and second, an artistic 'society' of former students of the École du Louvre, such as Mme Tony-Robert and her former teacher and curator there, Robert Rey.[18] Mme Tony-Robert's tall, shy and bespectacled nephew, who was ashamed to have been invalided out of the army, redeemed himself by becoming Cavailles' personal courier.[19] Gosset, like Cavaillès, used the vaults of the Louvre as a hiding place in Paris and also returned to Brittany to set up a network with a friend, Yvonne Queffurus, who was bursar at the college of Quimperlé, which reported on the movement of German troops and ongoing work on the Lorient submarine base.[20]

Pineau and Cavaillès were due to go to London to discuss their intelligence network and perhaps become more involved in sabotage. However they were arrested during the night of 5–6 September 1942, while trying to get off the French coast at Narbonne to a waiting submarine. Although they were acquitted by a Vichy military court at Montpellier, they were immediately interned by the prefect as undesirables in the Saint-Paul d'Eyjeaux camp near Limoges. Pineau managed to escape from the train on the way there and Cavaillès escaped from the camp on 29 December 1942.[21] In January orders came from London that Cavaillès should split Cohors between an intelligence arm and a sabotage arm, to be headed up by Gosset. Cavaillès finally got to London from the Breton coast via a fishing boat that took him to a British launch. His sister recorded that:

He admired the calmness with which the British people accepted the danger of bombing raids. But he was quickly deceived by contact with the Free French. The soldier he remained was shocked by the triviality of the gossip – what he disdainfully called 'the émigré mentality' – the cliquishness of the Gaullist clan, women even wearing the cross of Lorraine on their hats, and above all the machinations, the ambitions and the politicking that ended up with the Committee in Algiers.[22]

Yves Farge observed a similar change in Cavaillès on his return to France. The young man was disillusioned by the tensions between the Free French in London – about to move to Algiers – and the metropolitan resistance and by the amount of energy that was taken up by politics rather than defeating the enemy. He decided to work on sabotage with the Allies far from the world of political intrigue:

Cavaillès came back from London a disappointed man. When I recall what he said I believe that he picked up astonishingly early the drama that is evident in French politics today that set the internal resistance against the external resistance. In my mind's eye I see him nervous. He needed explosives. This clear-thinking Huguenot always gave me the impression that he carried a great sorrow in his breast.[23]

Cavaillès resigned from the leadership of Libé-Nord and devoted himself entirely to military action. He had been given two missions in Brittany, one to destroy German radio beacons on the Brittany coast which could be used to detect Allied bombers and the other to sabotage the infrastructure of U-boat bases.[24] This last task he entrusted to Jean Gosset, who – as fiction aped extraordinary reality – is believed to be the model for Philippe Gerbier in Joseph Kessel's *Armée des ombres*. Gosset investigated the possibility of sabotaging the Lorient U-boat base with the help of a New Zealand commando team. Cavaillès went to Lorient at Easter 1943 and managed to get inside the base in overalls with the help of a local man who worked there with a German pass. He confirmed that sabotage was a better option than bombing, if they could find a landing ground for the New Zealand commandos.[25] The mission, however, was never accomplished by Cavaillès, who was arrested in Paris on 28 August 1943. He was interrogated by the same *Abwehr* officer who he imagined to be responsible for the death of his comrade René Parodi, found hanged in his prison cell at Fresnes on 16 April 1942. Questioned as to why he had become involved in such desperate resistance, Cavaillès riposted that it was to avenge the death of Parodi. Cavaillès was himself shot in the fortress of Arras on 17 February 1944.[26]

The sabotage work was taken over by Jean Gosset, who duly destroyed pylons near Hennebont on 21–22 September 1943, the railway from Hennebont to Lorient, and transformers at the Lorient submarine base on 14 October. Gosset then went to London for two months' training, where he was described by the commanding officer as 'a nervous and rather intellectual type. He has very poor physique, making him awkward at weapons training. His great interest seems to be Demolitions' – i.e. explosives. He was parachuted back on 30 December 1943 to head Cohors, now called 'Asturies', and undertook successful sabotage operations both in Lorient and on the Hotchkiss-Borsig and Timken ball-bearing factories in Paris.[27] He was arrested in Rennes on 25 April 1944 and deported to Neuengamme, where he died on 21 December 1944.[28]

More common in the work of sabotage were British agents with French backgrounds who were trained for SOE work back in France. These were generally officers who had fought in 1940 but women were often involved too. The latter were recruited into the auxiliary services and started as couriers but sometimes took over command roles when their commanding officer was arrested. Agents worked with small groups of French resisters on sabotage, which required the parachuting-in of weapons and explosives, extreme care being taken that they did not fall into the wrong hands.

Maurice Southgate was British but had been educated in France, was married to a French woman and ran a luxury upholstery business in Paris. He fought in France in 1940 and was one of the survivors of the *Lancastria*, which was evacuating British troops to England when it was sunk by the Germans off Saint-Nazaire on

17 June, a disaster that the British government attempted to cover up. He trained with SOE and was parachuted into the Auvergne on 25 January 1943 with courier Jacqueline Nearne. She recorded the initial confusion and panic of their landing:

I saw three shadows, of which one was pointing a revolver at me. I thought that my mission was already finished. A few moments later I realised that one of the shadows was my boss who had been parachuted in with me and whom I had not recognised. The other two shadows were trees. As we went along we met a peasant on a bicycle and twice my companion asked him the way in English.[29]

Southgate's instructions were to 'undermine the Hun in every way possible, with the least inconvenience for French people. Avoid all contact with French political groups (this was an absolute dogma for our minders in the UK; they had a real thing about it)'.[30] He put together a sabotage circuit which had two main regional leaders. In the Indre, near Châteauroux, he worked with Auguste Chantraine (Octave), the former mayor of the village of Tendu who had been dismissed because he was a communist. Chantraine commanded a group of Francs-Tireurs et Partisans with whom SOE would not normally have worked, but did so because of their effectiveness. In the Pyrenees, near Tarbes, Southgate worked with a former POW, Charles Rechenmann ('Julien'), who had been released by the Germans as a Lorrainer on condition that he lived in annexed Lorraine or Germany, which he promptly fled.[31] His group was made up former POWs like himself, on whom he could rely. Their sabotage successes included the Hispano-Suiza aircraft factory at Tarbes, a foundry at Bergerac, and a bridge-making factory at Châteauroux. SOE chief Maurice Buckmaster described Southgate as 'the uncrowned king of five large departments in France'.[32]

That September Pearl Witherington arrived to act as Southgate's courier. She tried to persuade the management of the Michelin factory in Clermont-Ferrand, which was working for the Germans, to undertake sabotage onsite or to suffer Allied bombing. Unfortunately the Michelin bosses refused to believe that they would be bombed so Pearl cabled back, 'I hate to suggest the bombing of Michelin but [. . .] I think it would teach the management a lesson and force their hand if Clermont-Ferrand were bombed.'[33] More successful as a case of sabotage to avoid bombing was that undertaken at the Peugeot works at Sochaux, on the Swiss border, by Harry Rée. Born in Manchester to a Danish-Jewish father whose business had been in Hamburg, he was educated at Shrewsbury School and Cambridge and was teaching modern languages at Beckenham County School when war broke out. Left-wing and a conscientious objector, he nevertheless realised that the war was 'much more than a capitalist business' but an 'anti-Jewish business' too and volunteered as an anti-Nazi rather than an anti-German. His trainers at SOE described him as 'highly strung and nervy', worried about his 'school standard' French, and as 'uncompromising [. . .] very tactless and hates authority as such'.[34] In April 1943 he was dropped near Tarbes, and met by Southgate who was alarmed by Rée's accent. He was taken by courier Jacqueline Nearne to Clermont-Ferrand to attempt once again to sabotage the Michelin factory; when that did not work out he set to work on the Peugeot factory at Sochaux, which was making tracks and engines for German tanks. This had been bombed by the RAF on 14 and 16 July 1943, killing 110 and seriously injuring 154. Harry Rée made contact with Rodolphe Peugeot, who was keen on sport and pro-British, and persuaded him that sabotage within the factory would be preferable to the RAF returning. Between 3 and 5 November key workers recruited to the circuit used plastic explosives that had been parachuted in to blow up the turbine compressors and electricity transformers. It was, reflected Rée, 'a wonderful job for an ex-conscientious objector to stop bombing by blowing up machinery'.[35]

Even more dramatic were the SOE activities of Michael Trotobas, who undertook sabotage in northern France. With a French father and Irish mother, his unstable childhood was spent variously in Brighton, Dublin and the Toulon area. He worked in turn as a cook, waiter, electrician and debt collector, and thought about joining the French Navy before volunteering for the British Army in 1933. Wounded at Dunkirk, he was commissioned and joined SOE. Described by his trainers as quick-thinking but hot-tempered and liable to depression, he was parachuted in in November 1943 to organise sabotage in the heavily industrialised Lille area, 'the Hell of the North'.[36] He made contact with French colleagues, including a Denise Gilman, who became his liaison agent and a police officer who gave him a police identity. Known as 'Capitaine Michel', he organised a series of commando raids such as that of the night of 26–27 June 1943, which virtually destroyed the huge locomotive factory of Fives-Lille. In October he undertook a series of train derailments, a train carrying aircraft oil was blown up at Roubaix station on 5 November and another carrying dynamite and munitions exploded between Lille and Valenciennes on 23 November, which also put the line out of action. Unfortunately a parachute team coming in to lend support was captured by the Gestapo and information extracted led to Trotobas's lodgings. At 7 a.m. on 28 November, it was reported:

Michel was up and ready to go out, dressed in police uniform. Finding himself confronted by Germans, he immediately knocked down the lieutenant in charge of the detachment. The soldiers retaliated with machine-gun fire. In the ensuing brawl, Captain Michel and a young girl belonging to the organisation who was there [Denise Gilman] were killed, along with another German soldier.[37]

Trotobas was recommended for the Victoria Cross but did not receive it as his death was not witnessed by a senior officer, but Buckmaster noted that 'his heroic death has become legendary'.[38]

This sabotage activity in urban and industrial sites ignited a certain number of fireworks but it did not deal with the reality that the forced labour draft (STO) had driven young men of military age into the wilds of forest and mountain to escape going to Germany.[39] Some simply lay low while others joined camps of *maquisards*. These were initially concerned with finding food and shelter and frequently acquired a bad reputation when they raided farms for food, town halls for false papers and tobacconists for cigarettes. However, they formed a reserve army that could be called upon to act behind German lines when the Allies finally landed on French soil. Until then they were beset by three fundamental problems: lack of weapons, lack of training and lack of leadership.[40]

Since the Resistance had failed to persuade the disbanded Armistice Army to part with its hidden weapons, and German weapons could only be acquired by force in unequal combat, the only other source of arms was the sky. This source was limited and skewed. Limited because the Allies only had so much to offer and skewed because they did not want weapons to fall into the wrong hands, by which they meant those of communists. Key relationships were formed between SOE agents and small groups of non-communist resisters often commanded by former officers of the Armistice Army.

In November 1942 SOE agent George Reginald Starr was landed from a felucca on the south coast of France. He had trained as a mining engineer in Scotland before learning French while working on the Belgian coalfield at Liège. Originally supposed to go to Lyon, he heard that it was infested by police and went to Agen in Gascony. He set up his headquarters in the village of Castelnau-sur-l'Auvignon and recruited a team from among refugees from Alsace-Lorraine in order to receive parachute drops. This became the Wheelwright Circuit, which had tentacles from the Pyrenees to Vierzon. Unfortunately he was without regular radio contact with London until the arrival in August 1943 of Yvonne Cormeau, whose father was a Belgian consular official, and who had decided to continue the war fought by her husband when he was killed in an air raid in London in 1940. Under the code name 'Annette' she worked as Starr's radio operator, travelling widely to avoid detection, and orchestrated the delivery of 147 arms drops to the circuit.[41] SOE agent Harry Despaigne, usually known as Major Richardson, made a similar impact on south-west France, into which he was parachuted in September 1943. Born in London to a French father and a Belgian refugee from the 1914–18 German occupation of Belgium, he worked for a shipbroker before the outbreak of war in 1939, when he joined the Light Infantry. Recruited to SOE he was described as having 'a curious and enigmatical personality and is altogether rather a dark horse'.[42] In Toulouse he met Roger Mompezat, who had fought in the colonial infantry in 1918 and been a civil servant in Madagascar between the wars. Together they organised the parachuting of weapons into the Ariège, Aude and Tarn, and in April 1943 set up the Montagne Noire Free Corps. Heavily armed and highly effective, this group attracted the envy and hostility of less well-provided *maquis*, who regarded them as little better than mercenaries working for the Allies.[43]

Even more significant than the south-west as an area of *maquis* activity were the foothills of the Jura and Alps. It was there that two of the most famous *maquis* formed on the Glières and Vercors plateaux, but the help of SOE agents was crucial. Richard Heslop was dropped into the Ain, north-east of Lyon, in September 1943. Born in France but brought up in England after his father's death, he was educated like Rée at Shrewsbury and at London University before going into the shipping business. A lieutenant in the Devonshires in 1940 he joined SOE and, dropped into France, became the second-in-command of Major Henri Petit, a veteran of the Great War and of 1940, known in the Resistance as 'Romans-Petit'. In January 1944 Heslop reported that Romans-Petit had '3,500 fully trained and armed men under his direct orders'.[44] This made an impact symbolically long before it did militarily. On 11 November 1943 a group of well turned-out *maquisards* processed down from the Jura hills to lay a wreath on the war memorial of the small town of Oyonnax. Homage was rendered to the heroes of the First World War by those who aspired to be the heroes of the Second. More important, it was the staging of the liberation of a French town, designed to counter the image of the *maquisards* as outlaws, and to dramatise their fitness to receive weapons. Romans-Petit recalled that 'the magnificent appearance of our young men, the guard of honour in white gloves, bore witness to the facts that were not looters but soldiers. The underground press all talked about it and we received many congratulations. The British, American and Canadian press dedicated long columns to it and carried photographs of the procession.'[45]

Staging a symbolic liberation was not the same thing as carrying it out militarily. On the Vercors plateau the situation did not look good down to the end of 1943. The Italians extended their zone of occupation in November 1942 to cover the Vercors, and on 27–28 May 1943 surprised a lorry carrying petrol to the *maquis*. This led to the arrest of twenty men, including Aimé Pupin: 'The *maquis* are disorganised, communications have been cut and funds are not getting through,' reported Pierre Dalloz, who went underground and escaped from France to Algeria via Barcelona and Gibraltar that November.[46] The *maquis* was reorganised and a second organising committee was set up in June 1943, headed on the military side by Alain Le Ray, who had escaped from Colditz, and on the civilian side by Eugène Chavant, a Great War *poilu* and former socialist mayor in the Grenoble suburbs. Together they celebrated a festival of unity of the plateau on 10 August 1943. On 6 January 1944 an Allied mission, code-named 'Union', landed on the plateau to help train and organise the growing *maquis*. It was composed of Henry Thackthwaite, a British former schoolteacher, Peter Julien Ortiz, an American marine with a French father who had earlier served in the French Foreign

Legion, and a French wireless operator. They found a *maquis* about 3,000 strong, of whom only 500 were properly organised into groups of ten and armed with Sten guns. Four RAF pilots – who bailed out of a Halifax on 7 February and were sheltered for seven weeks by the Vercors *maquis* – were impressed by the bravado of Ortiz, who drove around in his marine's uniform, in a car stolen from the Gestapo and 'practically lives on benzedrine'. However, they expressed concern about the 'poor quality' of the *maquisards*, some of whom were only fifteen or sixteen, and were 'willing enough to fight the *Milice* but the majority were scared of the Germans, who used all kinds of weapons against them, such as armoured cars, tanks and mortars'.[47]

One way of ensuring the efficacy of the *maquis* while maintaining outside control was to develop the idea of a local rising co-ordinated with airborne troops. Under the 'Plan Caïman' or 'Alligator Plan' devised by Free French General Billotte, *maquisards* would be mobilised in the Massif Central with outside support to pin down the Germans in the South while landings got under way on the Channel coast. The plan was not adopted by the Allies, partly because of its impracticality, partly for fear of encouraging national insurrection. Nevertheless SOE leader Maurice Southgate contacted the charismatic resistance leader in the Auvergne, Émile Coulaudon ('Gaspard'), on 15 April 1944, and asked him, 'Could you hold a position for a few days in an area of the Massif Central to be decided on and control the access roads? In that case we could parachute in semi-heavy weapons and also commando forces to lead your corps francs.' Gaspard agreed for the four departments under his control, and this was approved both by London and by a meeting of the Regional Liberation Committee called to a farm in the Haute-Loire by Henri Ingrand, the *commissaire de la République*-in-waiting. Unfortunately Southgate was arrested by the Gestapo in Montluçon on 1 May 1944. Coulaudon nevertheless went ahead on 20 May, publishing a call to a *levée en masse* that resulted in 2,700 individuals in fifteen companies gathering on Mont Mouchet by the end of the month.[48]

Well into 1944 supplies of weapons from the air were limited and restricted to non-communist fighting groups. This of course infuriated the communists, who increased pressure on the Free French to intercede with the Allies on their behalf. In London Fernand Grenier went several times a month in the summer of 1943 to see Colonel Passy to request weapons for the FTP but without success; he also wrote a pamphlet on the glorious achievements of the FTP but Soustelle at the Information Ministry gave him no money to publish it and he had to turn to British communists for help.[49] Charles Tillon, head of the Francs-Tireurs et Partisans (FTP) in France, who later described the BCRA as 'driven by the narrowest anti-communist mentality that was entirely contrary to the interest of the Resistance',[50] wrote directly to de Gaulle in Algiers in August 1943. He underlined the significance of the flux to isolated areas of *réfractaires*, who with a little help could be trained by the communists in a whole new strategy of guerrilla warfare:

You know that for two years the FTP have conducted an armed struggle against the invader. They are part of the Armée Secrète and without qualification they are under your orders and those of the CFLN [. . .] A wider and wider mass of young *réfractaires* and indeed all Frenchmen need to be brought into the immediate action of guerrilla warfare that we are waging [. . .] But we lack the necessary weapons, food coupons and money to provide security and material existence to the Francs-Tireurs and *réfractaires* for whom we are responsible.[51]

Tillon reinforced his point by sending a delegate to London early in September 1943 to discuss the question of parachuted weapons with both the BCRA and the Allies. The delegate was interrogated for a week by the British secret services and asked to reveal the names of his leaders, which he refused to do for their protection. Eventually he got to see Colonel Passy only to be himself persuaded of the 'corrupt milieu of the BCRA'. He also saw British and American officers who expressed surprise that the

Francs-Tireurs were receiving no weapons. Free French and Allies each blamed the other for failure to support them: 'According to the Allies it was the BCRA that wanted to deny us weapons while for the BCRA it was the Allies who were refusing to give them to us.'[52] In truth, neither the BCRA nor the Allies wanted to arm the communists lest the national insurrection they desired became a communist revolution. The communists nevertheless did not give up. Waldeck Rochet, one of the twenty-six communist deputies who had been held at the Maison Carrée of Algiers in 1941–3, travelled to London to lobby for the French communist position. He was well connected with Tom Bell and Harry Pollitt of the Communist Party of Great Britain and, in the rather vain hope of persuading the British establishment, attended the Armistice Day celebrations of 11 November 1943 in the ranks of the 'Français de Grande Bretagne' and gave fortnightly talks on the BBC.[53]

Although the travails of the communists were obvious, other elements of the internal resistance were also frustrated by London. Pierre Dalloz, architect of the original plan to use the Vercors as a natural fortress to pin down the Axis, who arrived in Algiers in November 1943, wrote a report on the Vercors project which, he claimed, had been endorsed by both Jean Moulin and Delestraint. Like the communists he could garner no interest from Colonel Passy. He found the BCRA 'strongly infiltrated by fascists and Cagoulard elements' who thought that 'French people arriving from France were hotheads' and were convinced that the only viable resistance was that organised by themselves.[54]

Some difference was made by the appointment of Emmanuel d'Astier as commissar for the interior. For him, the interior meant a metropolitan France that was destined to be a major force in the liberation. The 'French army of the interior' would enable the French to 'acquire a strong, patriotic and popularly based government headed by the man who at first was only a symbol but is now the leader of the Fatherland in toil'. He realised that arms drops were only going to circuits under the direct control of British officers, greatly demoralising most *maquisards*. The conclusion might legitimately be drawn that 'the British government does not wish to arm the French Resistance.'[55]

D'Astier embarked on a mission to persuade the British to arm that resistance. At a press conference in Algiers on 15 November 1943 he announced that only 4,000–5,000 out of 30,000 *maquisards* in the former Free Zone were armed.[56] In December 1943 he was in London and met Waldeck Rochet, who extracted a promise that if d'Astier managed to persuade the British to make more arms drops, some of them would go to the FTP.[57] Flying back to North Africa d'Astier managed to arrange an interview on 14 January 1944 with Churchill in Marrakech. Churchill was surrounded by the likes of Harold Macmillan, the diplomat Duff Cooper (biographer of the devious Talleyrand), and the beautiful Lady Diana Cooper in 'a straw hat with a veil, as seen in Egypt'. Churchill received him in his bedroom, and appeared to d'Astier less like a bulldog than like 'a newborn child that has aged'. After Churchill had complained how difficult de Gaulle was – 'how can we get on with each other? He hates England' – he told d'Astier that 'We must make war. We will help you,' and invited him to a meeting of the War Cabinet in London.[58] D'Astier was privileged enough to attend this meeting on 27 January 1944. In the teeth of objections from Lord Selborne, Minister of Economic Warfare, and Sir Charles Portal, Chief of the Air Staff, that the British simply did not have enough planes to drop arms to the French, and to d'Astier's argument that 'If air support is not stepped up rapidly, it will be too late,' Churchill ruled that as he was supplying Tito he would now supply weapons to enable south-east France to become a second Yugoslavia.[59]

Arms drops did increase but they did not in themselves lead to greater military success. On 14 February 1944 a first supply of fifty-four containers of weapons was parachuted onto the Glières plateau. This had a practical aim, to pin down the Germans away from the landing beaches, but also a symbolic one, as a demonstration that the French Army, humiliated in June 1940 and November 1942, was now rising from the ashes. On 6 February 1944 Maurice Schumann on the BBC ordered members of the Armée Secrète in waiting to join the *maquis* while at the same time workers went on strike and resisters sabotaged railways. To counter this Philippe Henriot, the new strident voice of Radio Paris, attacked 'terrorists' who were fomenting civil war. Vichy and German forces closed in during the night of 9/10 March. The raw recruits were soon rounded up. Jacques Beges, the *réfractaire* from Lyon, admitted to the police having taken part in an attack by about 150 *maquisards* in a hotel in Entremont, where Vichy police were holed up – an attack in which their leader Tom Morel was killed. A final Vichy-German offensive was launched on 23 March as calls went out in vain for more parachuted weapons and a bombing of German positions. On 25 March the order came to disperse. Captured *maquisards*, such as Pierre Pelletier from Vanves and Yves Jeudy from the Var, denied they had fired a shot, and claimed that as soon as Vichy and the Germans launched their offensive the *maquis* leaders disappeared. These stories were to save their own skins but the real significance of the Glières was hotly debated. Vichy propaganda mocked it as a military disaster but the BBC fought back early in April, creating a legend that 500 men had held off 12,000 Germans and had 'brought Bir Hakeim to France'.[60]

These events gave grist to intense debates that went on among French resisters and the Free French about the best strategy for the French to adopt. For the Free French who worked closely with the Allies, arms drops were payments on account while awaiting D-Day. Weapons were to be squirreled away until the moment came to attack the enemy rear; to move too soon was simply to invite brutal repression and reprisals. For others in the internal resistance, especially communists, such thinking was a manifestation of *attentisme*, of wait-and-see, which would do nothing to energise or galvanise the people of France, who had suffered occupation for nearly four years and wanted nothing more than to be up and at 'em. Their strategy was one of immediate action, on however small a scale, gearing up to what was imagined as national insurrection and guerrilla warfare after the Allied landings.

One platform for the communists to develop their strategy was the National Council of Resistance (CNR) and above all of its military committee, the COMIDAC (or COMAC as it became on 15 May 1944). The driving force on the National Council was the leader of the Front National, Pierre Villon. One resister reported back to Interior commissar Emmanuel d'Astier, that Villon's fanaticism in the cause of popular insurrection gave him a charismatic authority. He was 'the real mouthpiece of the Party and the communist wing of the CGT [. . .] a proponent of direct action, he emphasised the need for national insurrection, which attracted a great many supporters and gave him a very strong position'.[61] Against Colonel Touny of the OCM, who argued that the FFI should simply execute Allied orders, Villon had a plan of immediate action and secured a formal condemnation of *attentisme* by the National Council on 15 March 1944.[62] Villon was also the driving force of COMAC, whose other permanent members were Maurice Kriegel for the Southern Zone and Jean de Vogüé for the Northern Zone. That gave a balance of two communists to one non-communist, who seemed increasingly to side with them. Lecompte-Boinet, who returned to Paris from Algiers in February 1944, was shocked to hear from General Revers, who sat on COMAC as a technical advisor without voting powers, that Jean de Vogüé, Lecompte's former colleague in Ceux de la Résistance, 'is finding it difficult to stand up to the communists, who are gaining the upper hand'.[63] Villon, on the other hand, took the view that the non-communists had only themselves to blame. Revers, he said, 'never expressed any opinion or offered any advice. More than once he simply fell asleep in his armchair.'[64]

A second platform of the communists, which became increasingly more important, was the Paris Liberation Committee (CPL). Its OCM representative, Marie-Hélène Lefaucheux, warned that the 'ferocious reprisals' inflicted by the Waffen SS and Vichy's police and *Milice* after risings like the Glières setback forced a reconsideration of immediate action. The communist lobby took the opposite line, demanding that guerrilla war should continue and if necessary move from the Alps to Paris. Georges Marrane for the PCF 'demanded that the provisional government in Algiers support the *maquis* and *réfractaires* effectively so that from now on war could waged against the Hun as in Yugoslavia'. For the Front National Villon 'intervened to underline the need to arm patriots and mobilise the masses in the Paris region'.[65] A few weeks later André Tollet, chair of the Paris Liberation Committee and leader of the organised workers in the capital, proclaimed that 'in the armed struggle we must rely on unionised and non-unionised workers and on *réfractaires*, both for immediate action and for D-Day.'[66]

To counterbalance this communist surge in resistance organisations the provisional government in Algiers tried to reinforce the effectiveness of its own agents both military and civil. It was still trying to catch up and realise the union between internal resisters and Free French that had snapped when Jean Moulin was arrested almost a year earlier. The presence of the internal resistance was necessary to demonstrate to the Allies how much support de Gaulle had, but at the same time it was necessary to clip the wings of a national insurrection that might be exploited by the communists for their own ends.

The first piece of this jigsaw puzzle was the new delegate-general of the provisional government from March 1944. Alexandre Parodi was a key member of the Comité Général d'Études of experts who were choosing the new rulers of France. Since the arrest of Jean Moulin the provisional government had struggled to find a single, effective and dutiful delegate-general to do its work but in Parodi it had a solution. This was not a complete remedy to the situation. On 6 May 1944 Jacques Bingen, who was sent to the former Free Zone to represent Parodi, wrote a long letter in which he accused London and Algiers of not supporting delegates in the field like himself. For six months, he said, he had received no personal letter and no official or unofficial encouragement. He complained of 'scandalous and inhuman shortcomings' in London and Algiers and of 'castration in the field' that was provoking the arrest of too many agents. Without wishing to criticise Parodi he regretted the recall of Serreulles, who 'alone knew something about something', and warned de Gaulle about the quality of 'establishment' advisers with whom he was surrounding himself: 'Beware of docile loyalists who are only ambitious, crafty devils of no value. They could easily topple him.'[67] Less than a week later, on 12 May, Bingen was himself arrested by the Gestapo on Clermont-Ferrand railway station and swallowed his cyanide capsule rather than talk under torture. Another key intermediary between the internal and external resistance had been lost.

A second piece of the puzzle took the form of military delegates sent to work with local and regional resistance chiefs, in order to keep them on side. When they had first arrived in September 1943 they had too little backing, too few weapons to distribute, and encountered major catastrophes.[68] Between March and May 1944, however, nine new military delegates arrived in France. The increased tempo and volume of Allied arms drops, over which the military delegates had some control, gave them much greater authority vis-à-vis resistance chiefs in desperate need of weapons.[69] To cap the hierarchy a national military delegate was sent in. This was Jacques Chaban-Delmas, a young Inspecteur des Finances who had been working as a mole in Vichy's Ministry of Industrial Production and had been proposed by Jacques Bingen. Although only twenty-nine years old and a sub-lieutenant in 1940 he was given the rank of general in order to have the necessary military authority. This team was given the full support of General Koenig, the hero of Bir Hakeim, who, on 4 April 1944, was appointed delegate of the provisional government to the Supreme Allied Command in London and chief of the internal resistance forces, which in theory established a direct line of command from the Allies to the *maquis*.

The effectiveness of this command depended on the degree to which resistance forces on French soil were brought into some kind of unified army of the shadows. In the lead up to D-Day, the internal resistance suffered not only from a lack of weapons, training and leadership but from deep divisions that were political and generated by different views of what resistance might be. At one extreme were the communist-led Francs-Tireurs et Partisans, which had undertaken armed struggle since June 1941 and were committed to national insurrection, and yet who felt marginalised, even ostracised, by the other forces of resistance and by the Allies. At the other extreme was the Organisation de Résistance de l'Armée (ORA), which was Giraudist if not Pétainist except in its refusal to accept Germany's violation of the armistice in November 1942. In the middle were the Mouvements Unis de la Résistance, composed of Combat, Libération and Franc-Tireur, which in February 1944 broadened out into the Mouvement de Libération Nationale (MLN) to include a wider non-communist front, including Défense de la France, which had long nurtured the idea that Pétain would turn patriotic, together with Combat's branch in the Occupied Zone, Ceux de la Résistance.[70]

The first task of the MLN was to bring together all the military forces under its control – the Armée Secrète, the Free Corps and the various *maquis* units – in something called the Liberation Free Corps (CFL). It was easier to undertake this kind of unification in theory than on the ground. Serge Ravanel was only twenty-four years old and, though a Polytechnician, had not actually fought in 1940. He was nevertheless sent by night train to Toulouse on 7 April 1944 with orders from Alfred Malleret, chief of the Liberation Free Corps' general staff, to unify the rival resistance military units there. There was a standoff between Aubier, the Armée Secrète leader, who was not a local man, and the *maquis* leader, a petty Tarn nobleman called Albert Sarda de Caumont, who lacked the common touch. Neither Aubier nor Sarda commanded a majority and the MLN was powerless to decide between them. To break the deadlock, Ravanel eventually suggested himself as the provisional leader. He took the train back to Paris, fully expecting to be dressed down by Malleret. Instead, Malleret said with 'a naughty look, "What you have done is very smart."'[71] Ravanel's provisional leadership of the CFL in Toulouse was accepted and soon became permanent.

The second stage was to bring together the Liberation Free Corps, the Francs-Tireurs et Partisans and the ORA in the French Forces Françaises de l'Intérieur or French Forces of the Interior (FFI) that were set up in February 1944 in order to complete this work of unification from extreme left to extreme right. This involved dealing with both communists and former soldiers of the Armistice Army. In the Toulouse area a Free Corps had been put together after November 1942 by a former officer in the Armistice Army, Major André Pommiès.[72] He had not been able to assemble all former soldiers in the Armistice Army, since many preferred to join the Army of Africa, which was more conventional and less risky, or 'wanted to ignore everything that was happening beyond the narrow horizon of family life'.[73] By May 1944 the Free Corps nevertheless boasted about 9,000 men who were well supplied with weapons and vehicles belonging to the former Armistice Army and by parachute drops from the Allies. Pommiès stuck to what he called the 'hard line' of purely military activity, sabotage and harassment of the Germans, refused to have anything to do with what he called politics and rejected any orders that did not come from a hierarchical superior. He would thus take no orders from Ravanel, whom he saw as his hierarchical inferior and a political animal to boot, and was surprised to find himself criticised as a

Giraudist, Vichyist, royalist or even fascist.[74] Despite his military efficiency, Ravanel thought that Pommiès 'never understood that because the Resistance had to fight against Vichy it had to use political arguments and get involved in politics'.[75] Equally difficult to contact and manage were the Francs-Tireurs et Partisans, with their 'iron Bolshevik discipline'.[76] Ravanel tried to use Jean-Pierre Vernant, who commanded the CFL in the Haute-Garonne, and was a communist but with the MLN, as a bridge to the FTP. He and Vernant were both graduates of *grandes écoles* and Ravanel was moving to the left politically, but was unable to persuade the FTP leader who came from a different class and culture. Ravanel reflected that the FTP leader had 'a terrible inferiority complex' based on a sense of being excluded by the Allies and Free French. Moreover, he said patronisingly, 'I had an education that he lacked. He was always a prole. He was not at ease with me, he thought that he was going to get screwed over.'[77]

What was going on in a region like Toulouse was one thing, but what really mattered was the national command of the FFI and the extent to which it shared a vision with and obeyed orders from London and Algiers. The first national commander of the Forces Françaises de l'Intérieur, Pierre Dejussieu ('Pontcarrel'), a professional soldier, was arrested in May 1944 and deported to Buchenwald. It would have been ideal for the provisional government if this command had been in Koenig's gift, but in this instance the Conseil National's military committee, COMAC, held the reins of power. It decided to appoint Alfred Malleret ('Joinville'), a communist and head of the Liberation Free Corps general staff. This gave communists the power to appoint men they favoured to regional FFI commands. Political considerations would triumph over conventional military concerns, youth would triumph over age and communists would defeat non-communists. The FFI regional chief of the Paris region, Pierre Lefaucheux, who had come from Renault and OCM, was not to the taste of the communists. He was questioned by COMAC on

17 May for hostile comments he was alleged to have made about the Paris Liberation Committee, on which his wife struggled to defend a non-communist viewpoint. In June Lefaucheux was fortuitously arrested by the Germans, which laid the way open to his replacement by a communist, Henri Tanguy, now known as 'Rol-Tanguy'. He would play a critical role in the liberation of Paris two months later.

As D-Day approached, the tension between two models of liberation had yet to be decided. The model favoured by the Allies and the provisional government was for the internal resistance to be entirely subordinated to the Allied landings and strategic priorities, in order to avoid the sudden release of pressure that might generate a national insurrection and possible communist seizure of power. The model favoured by the communists was that the landings must indeed provoke a national insurrection and that this must be supported by the provisional government and the Allies. It was not clear whether the plan involved a communist seizure of power but it certainly envisaged an embrace of power by the people and the sweeping away of old élites and institutions in some kind of brave new world. Which model would triumph would be shaped by the storm of forces at work in the weeks after D-Day.

13

D-Day

Maximum slowdown, repeat, maximum slowdown of guerrilla activity.

(General Koenig, 14 June 1944)

At dawn on Monday 5 June 1944 Roger Lefèvre, a 21-year-old primary school teacher at Viriat near Bourg-en-Bresse, was revising his medieval history for a degree examination he was due to take in Lyon the following Saturday. His wife was pregnant and he was staying in Bourg with his in-laws, who kept a typewriter and sewing-machine shop. Lefèvre was the leader of a local Free Corps and had taken a famous photo of the bust of Marianne on the plinth belonging to the vanished statue of Edgar Quinet at Bourg on 11 November 1943.[1] There was a knock at the window. It was Roland Chanel, an eighteen-year-old lathe operator, who was also his courier, with news that orders had arrived for all Free Corps to take to the *maquis*. He entrusted Chanel with instructions for the Free Corps members to meet at the market garden of the parents of Roger Trontin on the outskirts of the town. He then wrote to his history teacher, asking to take his examination at a later date, and phoned the GP, who was sympathetic to the Resistance, for a sick note to explain his absence from school. The *Milice* had established checkpoints on roads leading out of the town so his wife packed his rucksack with maps, binoculars, stripped-down machine-gun and first aid into the bicycle trailer, covered it with gardening tools, boots and overalls, and wheeled it past the guards. Lefèvre was joined by his group – Chanel and Trontin together with a mechanic, a baker and two pork

342

butchers, aged between eighteen and twenty-one – who went up by car and then on foot to the *maquis* headquarters, where André Lévrier ('Lévêque') was waiting for them. The group of eighty were issued with FFI armbands in the hope that if they were taken prisoner they would be treated as POWs rather than terrorists. There, on 6 June, they heard of the Normandy landings and prepared for action.[2]

Similar events occurred in thousands of places all over France as coded messages came over the BBC airwaves to *maquis* groups. The moment had arrived for the virtual army to emerge from the shadows and join the fight to liberate France. Plans had been devised whereby the Resistance would provide support for the main Allied offensive, sabotaging railways (the Green Plan), main roads (the Tortoise Plan) and telecommunications networks (the Purple Plan), in order to impede the redeployment to Normandy of German forces from other fronts or other parts of occupied France. These plans had been endorsed by General Koenig, Algiers' delegate to the Supreme Allied Command, and by Colonel Passy, who was now his chief of staff. On the other hand BBC messages broadcast on 5 June carried coded instructions to the Resistance not only to activate the Green, Tortoise and Purple Plans but to commence guerrilla activity.[3]

Those who now entered the fray with great hope and enthusiasm had every reason to believe that they would be powerfully supported by both the Allies and the French forces of the French Committee of National Liberation. Unfortunately, things were not as simple as that. The goal of the Allied Supreme Command was to drive German forces back into Germany with a minimum of political complications and no political disorder in France. The US government had not excluded establishing an Allied Military Government in Occupied Territory (AMGOT), as they had in Italy. The progress of the Allied offensive, moreover, was much slower than anticipated. Caen was supposed to fall eight days after D-Day but it took twenty days, until 26 June. Cherbourg was not taken until 30 June and the allies did not force their way out of the Cotentin peninsula towards the Loire and Brittany until the end of July. The first contact resisters had from the Allies were skeletal Jedburgh missions, which landed trios of French, British and American officers, together with fighting equipment, to organise and command French *maquis*. Even arms drops were slow to arrive and a substantial drop across the south of France did not take place, symbolically, until Operation Cadillac on 14 July.[4]

Neither did French forces immediately appear to support the brave but often foolhardy actions of the *maquisards*. Relations between de Gaulle and the Allies, always at best difficult, reached crisis point on the eve of D-Day. Churchill summoned de Gaulle and told him that the French would not be taking part in the Normandy landings. When the General protested, Churchill said that these were Roosevelt's orders. He added that if he had to choose between Roosevelt and de Gaulle he would always choose Roosevelt, and if he had to choose between Europe and the wider world he would always choose the wider world.[5] General Leclerc's 2nd Armoured Division did not land on the Normandy coast until 1 August, while the main French landing was that of the B Army, that amalgamation of the Free French and Army of Africa, in Provence as part of Operation Anvil on 15 August. In the absence of military activity de Gaulle's concerns were mainly political. He needed to convince the Allies that he commanded the broad support of the French people, who would liberate themselves with the help of the Allies, in order to cast aside the threat of an Allied Military Government. The Committee of National Liberation had voted on 5 May 1944 to call itself the Provisional Government of the French Republic beginning 3 June but the American government still refused to accept this. President Roosevelt and Secretary of State Cordell Hull took the view that the French people would decide in free elections after liberation what government and leader they wanted.[6] Secretary of War Henry Stimson registered that Hull 'hates de Gaulle with such fierce feeling that he rambles into almost incoherence whenever we talk about him'. But Stimson realised that the Americans could not involve themselves in supervising elections in France, that the British would never accept an AMGOT, and that de Gaulle had become 'the symbol of the deliverance of the French people'.[7] This was amply demonstrated when de Gaulle made a lightning visit to the liberated town of Bayeux on 14 June 1944 to be welcomed by a rapturous crowd.[8] This he used to persuade the Allies of his popular legitimacy. He flew for the first time to Washington to meet Roosevelt on 7 July and for the first time received a civil welcome.[9] There remained, however, the task of showing that while the French people were behind him and were makers of their own liberation, there would be no question of a national insurrection and certainly not a communist seizure of power.

This ambiguity was thrown into sharp relief by D-Day.[10] Although de Gaulle had declared in 1942 that national liberation was inseparable from national insurrection, he meant this only in a figurative sense. He did not anticipate the French people coming out of the shadows to take up arms. Where they did it had to be in order to support military activity by regular forces. Speaking on the BBC at 5.30 p.m. on 6 June, he asked 'that our action behind enemy lines be linked as closely as possible to the front line action of the Allied and French armies'. Other leaders of the Resistance, in particular communists, had a very different vision of what national insurrection and liberation meant. For them, the words of the 'Marseillaise', 'Aux armes, citoyens', were to be taken literally, as they had been against the Germanic invaders in 1792 and 1871. Waldeck Rochet, London delegate of the central committee of the French Communist Party, speaking on the BBC on 7 June, appealed to 'all French people to unite, arm themselves and fight to drive the invader from the soil of the *patrie* and restore its liberty, greatness and independence. Long live the Allies! Death to the Boches and to traitors!'[11]

The decisive point of this conflict was who would give orders to the interior resistance, now more or less united in the Forces Françaises de l'Intérieur (FFI), and what those orders were to be. The French Provisional Government took the view that the chain of command went from General Koenig in London to the National Military Delegate, Jacques Chaban-Delmas, who would instruct the chief of the FFI general staff, and down to the regional military delegates who would instruct the regional FFI commanders in different parts of France. The communists, however, who controlled the Military Committee of the National Council of Resistance (COMAC) through Pierre Villon and Maurice Kriegel-Valrimont, with Jean de Vogüé following in their wake, took the view that it was *their* task to send orders to the chief of the FFI general staff and regional FFI commanders. The fact that the chief of the FFI general staff, Alfred Malleret ('Joinville'), was a communist, as was the FFI chief in the Paris region, Henri Rol-Tanguy, gave them powerful leverage. Léo Hamon, from his viewpoint of the Paris Liberation Committee, described Rol-Tanguy as 'brutal, dynamic, fanatical, clear and effective – in the direction his Party has defined for him, of course'.[12]

The fact that the initial commands to the *maquis* involved the question of guerrilla action as well as sabotage played into the hands of those who felt liberated from years of pent-up frustration and were keen to attack German forces now presumed to be on the defensive. Unfortunately, the enthusiasm of the *maquisards* was not sustained by having sufficient weapons, adequate training or effective command, either by Frenchmen with military experience or by Allied agents and commandos dropped into combat zones. Against them, the German occupying forces were committed not only to resist the Allied invasion but to eliminate the threat from those they saw as 'terrorists' operating behind their lines. Though many FFIs wore armbands in lieu of uniform to show that they were soldiers and entitled to be treated as such under the laws of war, for the Germans they were still terrorists and would be dealt with as such. The result was that for ten long weeks between 6 June and 15 August the *maquis* suffered a series of disastrous setbacks. Savage reprisals were unleashed on towns and villages across France suspected of harbouring resisters, from isolated villages to major cities and, above all, in the 'redoubts' where *maquis* had set up strongholds in anticipation of Allied help that came too little and too late.

Immediately after 6 June the local FTP *maquis* in the Corrèze, a region of wooded plateau and hills in the Limousin, on the north-west of the Massif Central, planned an attack on the Vichy police barracks and Gestapo base in Tulle, the departmental capital. Their number included Paris metalworker Jean-Olivier Eleouet, who had come there in the spring of 1943 to flee the STO and joined an FTP *maquis* that took the name of Guy Môquet.[13] They also included Gerhard Leo, a young German-Jewish refugee who a few days earlier had escaped from a train taking him to trial in Paris as a traitor working for the CALPO in Toulouse, which had been attacked by FTP *maquisards* at Allansac as it crossed the Corrèze.[14] In the attack during the night of 7/8 June, Eleouet was wounded in the face and forty Germans were killed. The *maquisards* beat a hasty retreat to the woods but the Das Reich division, moving up from the south-west, arrived at Tulle.

The Germans took the view that the 'terrorists' had accomplices in the town who must be punished as an example. Early on 9 June the male population of Tulle was assembled on the square. Many of them were workers at the town's armaments factory, precision engineering factory and gas works. Papers were inspected in the presence of the mayor and key workers such as railwaymen, electricians, doctors and pharmacists were let go. The mayor asked for other categories to be released: the staff of the prefecture and town hall, post office and gas workers, artisans, garagists and butchers. Some were allowed to go, others driven back. Some five hundred, mainly young men, were left on the square and sorted into three columns. The local schoolteacher, Antoine Soulier, describes how 'the sinister Walter', head of the Gestapo in Tulle, 'bareheaded, long hair scraped back, his eyes half closed, gutless, wearing a large fringed great-coat with no other identification than the SS badge on his right sleeve', went from group to group, questioning individuals in impeccable French, and 'from time to time, with a wave of his index finger, sent some unfortunate person to the middle column'.[15]

While this was going on German soldiers were collecting ropes and ladders from local shops, and attached the ropes to balconies along the main street, overlooking the River Corrèze. At midday a notice was posted, saying that since forty Germans had been assassinated by communist bands, 120 *maquisards* and their accomplices would be executed. The executions began about 5 p.m. The middle column, 'a tight and compact bloc like a rugby scrum', was quickly propelled towards the ladders, which the men, hands tied behind their backs, were forced to climb. Soulier continued:

A ladder topples, a shot rings out, a being falls into the void. The scene unfolded like a local fête. An accordion played accompanying music. In the Tivoli café, under the shade of the plane trees, the German officers refreshed themselves and flirted with a woman well known in Tulle, the interpreter of the armaments factory.[16]

In the event, ninety-nine men were hanged, including Soulier's own son, a mathematics student at the Lycée Louis-le-Grand in Paris. The others were workers from the armaments and engineering factory, artisans, shopkeepers, white collar workers and students. Twenty-five were aged eighteen to twenty-five and seven under eighteen.[17] The remaining men on the square, 'frozen with horror', were kept in the arms factory overnight and the next day over 300 of them were taken to Limoges, from where 149 were deported to Germany.

Over 450 miles away, in the French Ardennes near the Belgian border, another *maquis* was forming with disastrous consequences. The so-called 'Paul plan' devised by former leaders of the Armée Secrète was supposed to establish a net of *maquis* from Nancy in Lorraine and Charleville-Mézières in the Ardennes to Reims and the south of Paris that would slow down the advance of German forces from the East to Normandy. One of these *maquis* was established at Revin in the Ardennes forest and was the targets of a Jedburgh mission, code-named 'Citronelle', on 12 April 1944. Jacques de Bollardière, who had joined the Free French in 1940 and had been wounded in the Libyan campaign, was parachuted in with an American and a British officer. The local *maquis* commander was Robert Charton, aged twenty-four, an employee of the Société Générale bank who had served briefly in 1940. Swept up by the excitement on 6 June, he brought 200 inexperienced young men into the core *maquis*, pushing numbers up to 300: 'It was madness,' one of his superiors later said, 'for the young men had no proper clothing, no weapons. The *maquis* had not the means to accommodate them all at once,' but now had to equip, feed and train them as best they could.[18] Lacking discipline, one of the *maquisards* went home to tell his sick wife where he was, and was captured and interrogated by the Germans. The forest was now surrounded by 3,000 Germans of a Panzer Division, which attacked the *maquis* on 12 June. Some *maquisards*, led by Jacques de Bollardière, managed to find an escape route that night through the enemy lines. Others, less fortunate, lost and separated from their officers, were rounded up by the Germans, beaten with sticks and rifle butts, and then shot: 106 bodies were shovelled into shallow graves.[19]

It is not clear how much detail of these early disasters filtered back to London, but on 14 June Koenig sent an order to the military delegates in France: 'Maximum slowdown, repeat maximum slowdown of guerrilla activity.'[20] This was read to COMAC by Chaban-Delmas, who attended its meetings, and added that to calm the situation arms drops would be interrupted until the August full moon. The communists howled in protest. Kriegel-Valrimont was incensed that orders were being sent directly to

FFI chiefs, bypassing the COMAC, and challenged this attempt to break the national insurrection. He immediately drafted a COMAC order to FFI leaders to the effect that they should seize enemy arms depots to arm patriots, occupy public buildings, railway stations, post offices and power stations, free political prisoners from prisons and execute traitors. It trumpeted:

There can be no insurrection without the masses. And the masses cannot join an insurrection without the support of the FFI armed forces [. . .] Stepping up guerrilla action galvanises the popular will to fight and is one way to launch national insurrection.[21]

Villon added the argument that if France was to 'prevent the establishment of an Anglo-Saxon military administration, it had to provide the Algiers government with a powerful resistance proving by its strength the importance of its contribution and making possible the country's liberation'.[22] On 15 June, Waldeck Rochet wrote from London to his comrade François Billoux in Algiers to say that French patriots were massively contributing to slowing the progress of German forces to the front, and that he had opposed whoever said that guerrilla action was premature: 'It is not a question of criticising those who are fighting in France from the safety of London but of helping them [patriots] by sending them weapons and ammunition.'[23]

All of this may have had some effect, because the COMAC meeting on 19 June heard that Koenig had revised his order to 'slow down guerrilla activity' to make it read: 'continue maximum elusive guerrilla activity with armed units against lines of communication'.[24] Other members of the National Council of Resistance, however, were increasingly worried by the demagogy of the COMAC communists and the absence of de Vogüé, who had gone off to organise a *maquis* in the middle of France like a new Tito. 'The drama,' confided CNR president Georges Bidault to Jacques Lecompte-Boinet on 20 June, 'is that Vogüé is preoccupied with other things, the Southern Zone has delegated a communist [Kriegel-Valrimont] and the FFI chief of general staff, Joinville, is sectarian, kneejerk, not very intelligent, and also on the extreme left'.[25] A few days later Lecompte concluded that Villon's ambition was to 'get rid of Chaban and the regional military delegates, and behind them Koenig, all to the advantage of Thorez'.[26]

One solution to the danger of untrained and impetuous *maquis* emerging into daylight and having themselves and innocent bystanders massacred, was to concentrate resistance fighters in redoubts that would be supplied from the air with weapons and a commando leadership, in order to hold up German forces moving to fronts established by regular forces. Even these, however, were liable to go wrong, given the lack of training of raw young *réfractaires*, the acute lack of weapons, and especially of heavy weapons capable of dealing with German metal and firepower, and the lack of effective command. In addition there were frequently conflicts on the ground between *maquisards* of different political persuasions, between *maquisards* and regular soldiers and between French units and Allied missions.

Two obvious areas where redoubts might be established were the Alps and the Massif Central. For the Massif Central, a Plan Caïman or Alligator Plan had been devised by Colonel Pierre Billotte, de Gaulle's chief of staff, although the Allies had not endorsed it.[27] Charismatic local resistance leader Émile Coulaudon ('Gaspard') from Clermont-Ferrand was nevertheless fired up about the idea and organised it with SOE agent Maurice Southgate and the Auvergne *commissaire de la République*-in-waiting, Henri Ingrand. Southgate was arrested on 1 May but contact was made with another SOE mission, 'Freelance', which included Captain John Hind Farmer (Hubert) and the New Zealander Lieutenant Nancy Wake. They had to wait some time for the arrival of the radio operator, Denis Rake, who made a detour via a boyfriend in Châteauroux: 'Even in the days when homosexuality was illegal he had never concealed the fact that he was queer,' said Wake. 'We were both fond of him but knew he could be completely unreliable.'[28] On 20 May the order was issued for a *levée en masse* of *maquisards* to gather on Mont Mouchet, at the frontier between the Haute-Loire, Lozère and Cantal. Ingrand recalled that:

There was so much enthusiasm that it was impossible to stop the mobilisation. News spread everywhere, people were impatient to get going. There was a sort of rivalry and amour propre. All of the Auvergne was soon in the loop, and people talked about it openly, even in the shops of Clermont. Men left for the Cantal in large numbers. There were special trains to which families accompanied a son, a brother or a friend, in response to the official mobilisation.[29]

The first tentative German attack on the *maquis* occurred on 2 June. It was repulsed and a group of inspired *maquisards* went down to the nearest village, Paulhac, and stretched a banner across the road that read, 'Ici commence la France libre'.[30] Meanwhile D-Day brought more patriots onto Mont Mouchet, including significant numbers of Spanish republicans. One newcomer was Jacques Monod, scion of a famous Protestant family, who had been an infantry lieutenant in 1940 and taught philosophy at the Lycée of Marseille, where he joined Combat. In September 1943 he was forced to flee with his wife and children to the Lozère, where his brother was a country doctor. On 6 June 1944, Monod decided to go up to Mont Mouchet to resume the fight, seeing the *maquisards* as latter-day Camisards, and left two days later.[31]

The Germans, coming up from Saint-Flour, attacked the *maquis* again on 10 June. They put the villages of Ruines and Clavières to fire and sword. At Clavières sixty-one *maquisards* were killed along with the mayor and nine villagers considered to be harbouring terrorists. At Ruines twenty-six people were shot, including the *instituteur*. Hélène Odoul, a retired headteacher who lived in the village, said that she gathered together 'the little boys abandoned in the school, where the *instituteur*'s wife was mad with grief [. . .] All over the village men were seized and shot, as was a young woman', the wife of a prisoner of war.[32] Ingrand noted that the Germans inflicted 'terrible reprisals on the villages they took back; isolated farms and whole villages were destroyed and peasants shot. At Ruines one person per household was shot, including a child of seven.'[33] The *maquisards* retreated to Chaudes-Aigues, fortified the Réduit de la Truyère, a promontory surrounded by deep gorges, and were supplied by Allied arms drops brought in by the Freelance team. The SOE team was concerned about the concentrated nature of the force. Nancy Wake said that 'Hubert [John Farmer] tried diplomatically to get him to form his men into smaller groups, but Gaspard waved aside the suggestion. He was rightly proud of the way he and his men had faced up to the German attack but he was a stubborn man and very self-opinionated.'[34] A massive attack by 22,000 German soldiers, supported by tanks and armoured cars, was launched on 20 June, resisted by about 2,000 *maquisards*. Denis Rake's commanding officer later reported, 'On each occasion that we were attacked, by his personal behaviour and apparent fearlessness, he contributed to a large extent to the good morale of the poorly trained *maquis*.'[35] Jacques Monod, at the head of a section drawn from Michelin car workers, was killed, as were thirty-five Spanish republicans of an FTP company who covered the French retreat.[36] Rake was forced to abandon his radio transmitter in the retreat, and to get urgent messages back to London Nancy Wake cycled to Châteauroux, where Rake knew there was another SOE operator, covering 500 kilometres in seventy-two hours.[37] A massive arms drop from a fleet of Flying Fortresses on 14 July came too late to save them.

A second area selected as a possible redoubt was the Vercors plateau near Grenoble. As early as 1941 Pierre Dalloz had imagined it a 'natural fortress' to pin down German forces away from landing areas and to serve as a springboard for the liberation of French territory. He had been unable to interest Colonel Passy and the BCRA in Algiers in November 1943 and went to work for Emmanuel d'Astier in the Interior Commissariat in London. It was from there that he was summoned by the BCRA on 5 June 1944, and by chief of staff General Béthouart on 8 June, who suddenly wanted to see his plans for the Alps. On 15 June he was told by Colonel Billotte, 'your Vercors is engaged'.[38]

The Vercors was a volcano waiting to erupt. STO *réfractaires* and other enthusiasts had been going up to the *maquis* since the autumn of 1942, grouped in scattered camps. D-Day increased the rate of mobilisation and concerns were expressed that these were forcing the hand of military leaders. Alban Vistel, head of the Mouvements Unis de la Résistance in the Lyon area, feared that popular mobilisation and activity was getting out of hand but that any touch on the brakes now would expose the local population to reprisals. He cabled COMAC on 12 June to say that the inhabitants of the Rhône-Alps area:

have gone beyond the objectives set out in the Plan. Stop. We are trying to contain their activity. Stop. Impossible to go into reverse in these departments. Stop. Can't pull back otherwise surrounding population is in danger. Stop. Retreat means disaster. Stop. Beg you for big parachute drops on these territories.[39]

On the plateau tension developed between enthusiastic young *maquisards* and career officers who had been brought in from the former Armistice Army, whose ideas about military discipline and tactics were extremely conventional. Joseph Gilbert, a local youth who had come up onto the Vercors, described being reviewed on 5 June by Colonel François Huet ('Hervieux'), who had commanded Moroccan cavalry in the Army of Africa in the 1930s, had been a tank commander in 1940 and served in the Armistice Army until it was disbanded:

Obligatory salute, respect for hierarchy, standing to attention with finger on the trouser seam, marching in time in properly spaced ranks, the officer being the superior and the *maquisard* the subaltern.[40]

While Gilbert was persuaded by ideas of guerrilla warfare, Huet was wedded to notions of pitched battles on the plateau. This was tested by the Germans' initial attack on the village of Saint-Nizier, the northern gateway to the Vercors plateau, on 13 June. The assault was initially checked by three *maquis* companies, one led by writer Jean Prévost. But on 15 June a thousand Germans and French *Milice* attacked Saint-Nizier at dawn and finally established a foothold on the plateau, killing twenty-four *maquisards* and wounding fifty. The Germans themselves lost six killed and fifteen wounded, and set fire to Saint-Nizier in reprisal.[41]

Koenig's change of tactic in his message of 19 June may have been a response to this setback, and to those on Mont Mouchet. When he spoke of 'elusive guerrilla action' he was criticising the tactic of gathering substantial *maquis* forces at strongpoints with the aim of holding down large numbers of German forces away from the coast. On the Vercors Joseph Gilbert came to his own conclusion that the static approach was now discredited: 'Rooting us to the spot [. . .] this defensive strategy was a complete denial of our mission and raison d'être: guerrilla warfare.'[42] At this point two Allied missions came to the Vercors in order to give it additional command, contacts and weapons. The Eucalyptus mission, which arrived during the night of 26–27 June, did not have the same Franco-British expertise of earlier SOE teams. It was led by Major Desmond Longe, who had worked for a bank in Jamaica before the war and had done most of his wartime service in West Africa and India. He was described as 'perhaps a little lacking in personality and the power of inspiring confidence in his subordinates'; his French was described as 'very poor'.[43] His second-in-command, Major John Houseman, had been a surveyor and land agent in High Wycombe, Buckinghamshire, and served in the Middle East; he too had a 'limited working knowledge of French'.[44] The mission included a French captain who arrived two weeks late, a French-speaking American wireless operator who provided a link to London and British and French wireless operators linking to London and Algiers. Longe immediately got on well with Colonel Huet, who invited the mission to take its meals at his headquarters in the village of Saint-Martin. Then, during the night of 28–29 June, an American secret services (OSS) mission, code-named 'Justine', was parachuted in – thirteen men led by Lieutenants Vernon Hoppers and Chester Myers. It was to provide modern leadership and develop guerrilla tactics such as ambushes on German convoys on the plateau. They were less impressed by Colonel Huet, reflecting that he 'had been in the regular French Army and it was easy to see the effects of his training in the organisation of the personnel of the Vercors'. Significantly, however, they were asked by Huet on 12 July to train some of the men in guerrilla tactics.[45]

The Allied missions facilitated the delivery of weapons from the sky. A first parachute drop arrived on 25 June and the US Flying Fortresses Operation Cadillac mission on 14 July, dropping weapons across the south, also took in the Vercors. One enduring problem, however, was that heavy weapons such as mortars and anti-tank weapons could not be parachuted in. On 29 June and 7–8 July Algiers therefore sent a commando force to prepare an airstrip for planes to land at Vassieux. On 21 July planes appeared in the sky above the Vercors. For some time *maquisards* imagined that airborne support had arrived. In fact it was a German attack using gliders, which released two batches of eighty paratroopers. Joseph Gilbert described the German troops who 'drove down towards Vassieux yelling and seemed to spin on themselves to machine-gun and exterminate everything living they found'.[46] At the same time German mountain troops assaulted the plateau from four sides, including up the seemingly impregnable south-east face of the plateau, hoisting up heavy weapons after them.[47]

The Vercors redoubt was on the verge of being overrun. Eugène Chavant, who was the civilian *maquis* chief alongside the military chief Huet, was in charge of food supply, transport, parachuting and security. On 21 July he sent a desperate message to Algiers: 'If no help is forthcoming we will judge Algiers to be criminals and cowards. I repeat: criminals and cowards.' Colonel Huet sent a radio message to London on 23 July:

Have been holding out for 56 hours against three German divisions. Forces fighting courageously but desperately because exhausted physically and have almost no ammunition. Despite our repeated requests we are alone and have received no support or help since the beginning of the battle. Situation could become desperate any moment resulting in terrible suffering on the Vercors plateau. Have done all our duty but full of sadness about the heavy burden of responsibility of those who, from far away, committed us to such a risky adventure.[48]

Appeals from the plateau were reinforced by a direct appeal of the National Council of Resistance in Paris to Churchill, begging him to 'get support in equipment, munitions and airborne troops to the internal resistance as soon as possible, without which the effort they are making will result in a painful and perhaps dreadful fate'.[49] These pleas fed directly into a row taking place in Algiers over airborne support. Communist Air Commissioner Fernand Grenier pressed for air support to be sent in under a French commander. Ranged against him, however, was Jacques Soustelle, secretary-general of the National Defence Committee (CDN), who had the ear of de Gaulle. Although the CDN approved the air support plan in principle on 28 June, and Grenier drafted two decrees to implement the plan and to appoint a French commander, de Gaulle refused to sign them. It may be that he wanted to put pressure on the Allies to commit, given that the French themselves had very little air potential, or that he preferred to appoint Billotte to the post. The upshot was that Grenier unleashed an explosive letter to de Gaulle 27 July: 'I do not personally wish to be associated with the criminal policy of having the means of support but not using them when our brothers in France call for help.'[50] At the ministerial council the next day de Gaulle flew into a rage and demanded that Grenier withdraw the letter. This he did, while considering that it was 'always necessary to do everything possible to get the Allies to agree to the broadest support we can give tactically to the FFIs'.[51]

Resistance on the Vercors collapsed. Huet gave the order for the *maquis* to disperse into the woods and mountains of the plateau. The Germans controlled the escape routes and organised a manhunt, killing anyone they thought was implicated in the fighting, setting fire to villages and massacring their inhabitants. A wireless operator came across a nineteen-year-old French secretary from the HQ: 'Her legs had been pulled up behind her back. She was opened from top to bottom and had her guts around her neck.' He also had 'pictures of the battered bodies' of others, including Jean Prévost, who were killed trying to escape from the Vercors.[52] All in all, 639 *maquisards* and 201 civilians were killed, and 500 houses destroyed.[53] Desmond Longe led a group back down to the plateau in search of food and water, and on 31 July led a retreat some 300 kilometres towards Switzerland.[54] The American section remained in hiding on the plateau from 26 July till 6 August: 'For 11 days we ate nothing but raw potatoes and occasionally a little cheese,' stolen from a farmer, they reported. After a forced march of 40 kilometres 'the section arrived in the Belledone mountains in very poor shape. I had lost 37lbs myself, three of the men were not able to walk for almost two weeks and some of the men had cases of dysentery which lasted a month.'[55]

At the opposite end of France, in Brittany, there were also terrible mishaps. Spontaneous and premature mobilisation as a result of what seemed to be calls to arms from the BBC took place there as in the Massif Central and the Alps. The *maquis* of Saffré, 20 miles inland from Nantes, was Brittany's answer to the disasters of Tulle and Revin. A *maquis* had been operating in the nearby village of Bouvron from the end of 1943, but on Saturday 17 June 1944 a decision was made to convene in the nearby forest of Saffré, in anticipation of an arms drop. The abbé Henri Ploquin, curate of Bouvron, regretted how amateur they were and how little attention was paid to security. Local inhabitants out for a Sunday stroll asked, 'What are you doing there?' and 'Are you in the Resistance?' Two young women thought to be the mistresses of German officers were captured and brought to the *maquis* leaders. It was discussed whether to shoot them but they were let go and the camp itself was struck in case the women betrayed them, and reconvened two days later, on 22 June, two or three hundred strong. One of the leaders then had a shoot-out with two *Feldgendarmes*, who raised the alarm, and the Germans attacked the camp at dawn on 28 June. In the fighting twenty-three *maquisards* were killed and thirty, including the abbé Ploquin, taken prisoner. They were taken to a château outside Nantes, where a military court went swiftly into action. Twenty-seven of the *maquisards*, all under twenty-six and five under twenty, were condemned to death as terrorists. Ploquin, who escaped the death penalty, was able to confess the young men, give them communion, and collect their last wishes and mementoes for their families:

I embraced all of them and then we were separated. The 27 victims were tied two by two. At this point Lucien Corgnet, aged 26, founder and leader of the 'Richelieu' *maquis* of Fay-de-Bretagne, said a wonderful thing, 'Lads, we are going to sing the "Marseillaise" to show that we are Frenchmen.' And he started up the 'Marseillaise' as they were given the order to go out. Everyone joined in like a choir as they went into the park. It was night-time. It was raining. It was 10.50 p.m. Ten minutes later we heard a volley. The first ones were being shot by German bullets, a hundred metres away, in the park. We fell to our knees and said the rosary. I heard seven or eight volleys, from 11 p.m. to 11.43 p.m. and a few rare coups de grace.[56]

Of the three *maquisards* who remained, two were executed in July and Ploquin was deported to a concentration camp in Germany on 10 August. Sixteen other *maquisards* who had fled were tracked down in the surrounding countryside and executed, and farms were burned down.[57]

Sixty miles west, in the Morbihan, the *maquis* of Saint-Marcel fared rather better because of the presence of regular French and Allied forces. The local FFI commander, Paul Chenailler, a former sea captain, had gathered about him a *maquis* numbering 3,000 men after D-Day. He urgently requested weapons drops and military command. An advanced guard from the 4th Regiment of Chasseurs parachutistes arrived on 7 June under Lieutenant Pierre Marienne, four out of the nine of whom survived a German attack on them. They were followed on 10 June by fifty of the rest of the regiment under Lieutenant-Colonel Pierre Bourgoin. Both Marienne and Bourgoin were French Algerians who had joined the Free French; Bourgoin had lost his right arm in the Tunisian campaign. These paratroopers oversaw the supply and training of the French *maquis*, which was attacked by the Germans on 18 June. On this occasion, unlike on the Vercors, Allied support was forthcoming as four US fighter planes strafed the German columns advancing on the *maquis*. After a fierce battle in which the FFIs lost thirty killed and sixty wounded, and claimed to have killed 500 Germans (though the real figures were more like fifty killed and fifty wounded) the *maquis* scattered, claiming victory. Marienne was captured and shot by the Germans on 12 July while the one-armed Bourgoin was pursued with a price on his head.[58]

In the south of France the situation was even more confused. The Allied presence was reduced and occurred later, with the landing in Provence on 15 August of American and French forces, many of which had fought their way up through Italy. Tensions between former officers of the Armistice Army and resistance organisations that were left-wing, even communist, dated back to the German occupation of the Free Zone in November 1942, when the Armistice Army refused to hand over weapons to the Resistance and kept them with its own Organisation de Résistance de l'Armée (ORA). In addition, apolitical or right-wing resistance groups were often favoured by Allied agents in terms of parachuted weapons and they kept their distance from the main

FFI command structure. Resistance in the south was extremely diverse and fragmented from both the national and religious angle, including Spanish republicans and anti-fascist Germans and Italians, and Jewish resisters, communist and Zionist alike, who were battling the Holocaust as well as German occupation.

Some order and coherence might have been brought to this fractured resistance by the leadership of General Cochet, who had escaped from France to London in November 1942 and on 8 July 1944 was appointed commander of the FFI in the Southern Zone under the authority of General Sir Henry Maitland Wilson, Supreme Allied Commander in the Mediterranean Theatre. His main responsibility was to prevent German forces coming from the south-west into the Rhône Valley, which would be needed by troops driving north after landing in Provence. But Cochet, who had always been a one-man resistance band opposed to Vichy's collaboration with Germany rather than to Vichy itself, found it difficult to be accepted, either by the Free French who surrounded de Gaulle, or by the internal resistance that wanted political renewal as well as liberation.[59] Cochet had very little sympathy with the cocktail of military and political ambitions in the internal resistance and looked to former officers of the Armistice Army, whom he called the *ci-devants*, to take control.[60] He expressed horror that one of the Resistance movements had proclaimed, 'The resistance volunteers are like the brothers of the volunteers of 1793 [. . .] They refuse to serve under the *ci-devants* of the Ancien Regime and think only of "generalised insurrection".'[61] As far as he was concerned the internal resistance should not meddle in politics. He had heard that 'some Resistance leaders had asked for political commissars to be created in the *maquis*', which was unacceptable. 'The FFI are militarised,' he argued, 'and as in regular mobilised units involvement in political activity should be formally prohibited.'[62]

Serge Ravanel, who was appointed chief of the FFI in the Toulouse area by General Koenig on D-Day and raised to the rank of colonel, was precisely the sort of internal resister who was anathema to Cochet. Ravanel had met Cochet once in 1941, when the General was lecturing in Lyon, and they spoke about the possibilities of resistance while walking on the banks of the Saône. Since then, Ravanel had fallen in with Libération and his politics had shifted steadily to the left, espousing the doctrine of national insurrection. His team included former communist sympathisers such as Jean-Pierre Vernant, who was appointed chief of the FFI in Toulouse and the surrounding department of the Haute-Garonne, commanding a *maquis* of about a thousand men, and was also a member of the underground Departmental Liberation Committee (CDL), on which he had responsibility for military affairs.[63] Ravanel managed to assert his authority at the expense of the regional military delegate, Bernard Schlumberger, who never managed to bring him into line. He also encountered little opposition from Jean Cassou, veteran of the Musée de l'Homme group and now *commissaire de la République* waiting to take power in Toulouse. Cassou was a fervent supporter of the Spanish republican cause and not concerned to rein in the Spanish – or other – guerrillas who were extremely active in the Toulouse area.

On the other hand, Ravanel found it difficult to assert his authority over the *ci-devants* of whom Cochet so manifestly approved. Colonel Pommiès, who had built up his own Free Corps of 9,000 men, drawn mostly from the former Armistice Army, simply refused to accept that Ravanel was his military superior. He claimed that Ravanel's letter of appointment as regional FFI commander from Koenig, of which he finally got wind on 21 June, was a forgery. He could not accept that a young man who, though a graduate of the École Polytechnique and a regular officer, could give orders to a hardened soldier like himself whose rank had been earned through combat rather than awarded for political reasons. He insisted on calling Ravanel by his family name Asher and indeed, much to Ravanel's annoyance, spelled it with a Jewish inflection, Ascher. In his own eyes Pommiès was a purely military man and had no truck with what he called politics, and even less with what he called the 'fiasco' of the doctrine of national insurrection.[64] Cassou was also concerned about the behaviour of Pommiès. He wrote to Interior commissar d'Astier de la Vigerie of the need to eliminate 'pretorian separatism, dissident groups answering more or less to the IS [Intelligence Service], a sort of feudalism of armed bands that tries to take possession of a part of the *maquis* and keep itself in readiness for who knows what kind of risky eventuality'.[65] Pommiès received a rap over the knuckles from Malleret-Joinville, chief of the FFI general staff, and was instructed to conform to FFI discipline. He still refused to budge however and a compromise reached on 4 August allowed him considerable autonomy for his Free Corps and the right to liaise directly with London and Algiers.[66]

Ravanel also had difficulties with resistance leaders who were working with the British and were effectively a law unto themselves. SOE agent George Starr's Wheelwright mission had received a hundred drops of parachuted weapons from the British between February and May 1944 and he behaved like a warlord in Gascony. 'I compared him to Lawrence of Arabia,' said Serge Ravanel, 'a died-in-the-wool Intelligence Service professional, probably the AMGOT officer appointed to the South-West by the Inter-allied General Staff.'[67] The fact that such warlords remained self-contained and better armed did not necessarily make them more effective militarily when the Germans attacked. During the night of 6–7 June Starr's 150-strong group retrieved their weapons, ammunitions and vehicles from a local château and took to the *maquis* at Castelnau-sur-l'Auvignon. Soon they were joined by 150 men of the 35th Brigade of Spanish Guerrillas, but on 21 June, they were attacked by 2,000 Germans, losing nineteen men while claiming 247 German dead, and forced to withdraw. On 2 July they were again attacked from the air and decided to link up at Maupas with the *maquis* of Maurice Parisot, a manager of large estates in Algeria before the war and now in Gascony. They combined their forces as the Armagnac Battalion, 3,500 strong, which was able to take the offensive to the Germans at Estang on 3 July and at Aire-sur-Adour in the Landes on 12 August.[68] Starr's courier, Anne-Marie Walters, whom he sent off to England on 1 August to report back, duly pronounced:

> Hilaire [Starr] is strictly an agent and neither a politician nor a military strategist [...] the guerrilla action he commanded was most unsuccessful up to the time he joined the Maupas *maquis* and worked with a staff of regular French Army officers amongst which I must mention Capitaine Parisot and Capitaine Monnet. Hilaire had great difficulties managing the political entanglements of our region. It was absolutely impossible to keep out of politics after D-Day. We had to be in contact with the surrounding *maquis* in order to carry out united action.[69]

The Montagne Noir Free Corps, led by SOE agent Harry Despaigne, alias Major Richardson, and former colonial administrator Roger Mompezat, also refused to integrate with the FFI and turned away volunteers judged to be communist in leaning.[70] Gérald Suberville, FFI chief in the Hérault, who drew on the railway workers and miners of the Languedoc involved in Action Ouvrière, did not mince his criticisms. Armed to the teeth, 700 strong, Richardson's men enjoyed parading for the local population but, said Suberville, 'as far as military activity was concerned they were involved in nothing apart from a few skirmishes'. At the same time 'they spread calumnies and accused the FFI workers' *maquis* of Cabardès [Aude] of being a band of deserters and pillagers'. However, the separatism of these Free Corps did not make them any more effective militarily. When the Germans launched an air assault on 20 July 1944, it shattered them, inflicting large casualties. Ironically, sixty of the survivors then joined the workers' *maquis* of Cabardès.[71] At least, reflected Ravanel, Colonel Pommiès understood the principles of guerrilla warfare, whereas the entrenched camp of the Montagne Noire was 'our Vercors'.[72]

Spanish republicans were heavily involved in *maquisard* activity in the south-west, sometimes in strictly Spanish groups, on other occasions well integrated into the FTP-MOI or units such as the Armagnac Battalion. The XIV Corps of Spanish Guerrillas was organised into a large number of divisions, functioning quasi-independently. Vicente López Tovar, for example, commanded the 15th Division in Dordogne, Lot and Corrèze from December 1943, operating with a range of FTP-MOI and Armée Secrète groups, and claimed to receive few orders from the general staff in Toulouse. In May 1944 the XIV Corps reorganised itself as the Agrupación de los Guerrilleros Españoles. Its general staff was closely connected with the Spanish Communist Party and asserted some autonomy from the French Resistance with a view to the next stage of the anti-fascist combat, since the liberation of France from the Germans would be followed by the liberation of Spain from Franco.[73] On this basis an agreement was concluded in Foix in June between the Union Nacional Española and the Mouvement de Libération Nationale, represented by *commissaire de la République*-in-waiting, Jean Cassou. Each side affirmed its common goal of 'the liberation of peoples oppressed by international fascism' and the view that 'the re-establishment of liberty in France and Spain is one and the same problem'.[74] That said, López Tovar was troubled by the communist cronyism that seemed to define the general staff of the Agrupación. He wondered, for example, how Luis Fernandez, who had once been a muleteer providing water for the republican forestry workers hidden in the Pyrenees, and with little combat experience, was now head of the general staff in Toulouse. Fernandez and others on the general staff were equally concerned that guerrilla leaders in the field like López Tovar, had lost their republican innocence by working with Frenchmen and foreigners of many different kinds, communist and non-communist.[75]

The rainbow of foreign anti-fascists involved in the struggle against German occupation in the region included a small number of German anti-Nazis. An underground centre near

Toulouse, where German and Austrian anti-Nazis worked for CALPO, mobilised on 6–7 June and thirty-six of them later joined the Armagnac Battalion. They took part in the fighting at Estang on 3 July, in which their oldest member, Johann Haffner, a 53-year-old socialist from Düsseldorf, was killed.[76] Meanwhile a group of German veterans of the International Brigades, under former Reichstag deputy Otto Kühne, escaped from French camps and took refuge in small foundry and forestry works in the Cévennes. When German forces invaded the Free Zone they took to the *maquis* and made contact with the German Communist headquarters in Lyon and with CALPO. They worked with French *maquis* such as the Bir Hakeim of Jean Capel ('Barot'), but there was rivalry for control and disaster struck with a massacre at La Parade on 28 May. Kühne now took command of survivors and was appointed FTP-MOI chief in Cévennes, commanding an exotic force of Germans, Poles, Italians, Spaniards and Armenians.[77]

There was a significant Jewish contingent to the Resistance in the Toulouse area, including Zionist Jews grouped around Polonski's Armée Juive and Robert Gamzon's Éclaireurs Israélites de France (EIF) at Moissac (Tarn-et-Garonne). One of Polonski's group, Pierre Loeb, was born at Thionville in the Moselle and as a French Jew had served in the French Air Force 1940: 'For weapons,' he recalled, 'we really only had whistles, and we could do nothing in the way of armed action at that point.'[78] In the spring of 1944 things became too hot in Toulouse and Loeb organised a Jewish *maquis* at L'Espinassier in the Tarn. Just before D-Day, the Jewish group was ordered to join a larger *maquis* on the Montagne Noire. Of three platoons, one was composed of Frenchmen, the second of Spanish republicans and former Russian POWs who had been drafted into the *Wehrmacht* but deserted, and the third was a Jewish platoon, which highlighted its identity by wearing blue-and-white shoulder flashes. It was called the Trumpeldor platoon in honour of a Zionist hero killed in Palestine in 1920. Although the Jewish platoon was a model from the military point of view its distinctiveness upset one

French commander, Captain Kervanoël, who announced, 'Your Jewish problem gets up our noses. Change your names, marry some Christian girls, and in a generation there will be no Jewish problem.'[79] Meanwhile, at Moissac, the EIF was forced to disperse in May 1944 after three years under Vichy and eighteen months under German occupation. Robert Gamzon gave his young men the choice between making their way to Spain and joining a *maquis* at Vabre in the Tarn. This was called the Marc Haguenau Company, in honour of an EIF activist who had been arrested by the Gestapo in Grenoble in February 1944 and shot while trying to escape. A German attack on 7–8 August left three Jewish and four non-Jewish *maquisards* dead. Subsequently, the company was brought under the leadership of General Dunoyer de Segonzac, the former director of Vichy's élite training school at Uriage, who had broken with the regime, made contact with Pommiès in Toulouse, and now commanded a *maquis* in the Tarn.[80]

These groups, it is clear, were many, varied, and often operated with little control from above. The most effective communist-Jewish resistance network in Toulouse was the 35th FTP-MOI Brigade, named after Marcel Langer. Serge Ravanel later reflected that 'my movement had little contact with them. Underground activity required rigorous isolation. But we knew of their existence and often of their exploits. We recognised their trade mark by the kind of operations they undertook.'[81] One of those was the assassination in October 1943 of *avocat-général* Pierre Lespinasse, who had demanded the death penalty for Marcel Langer. Another, unfortunately, was the bomb explosion in the Cinéma des Variétés in Toulouse on 1 March 1944 that led to the mass arrests of 4 April.[82] The Brigade's ambitious chief, Jan Gerhard, was promptly reined in by the FTP-MOI leadership and sent to command a *maquis* in the Ardennes. A replacement, 23-year-old Warsaw-born Claude Urman, who had volunteered for Spain but had been turned back as under age, was sent by FTP-MOI leader Norbert Kugler in Lyon to Toulouse, but arrived only in time to witness the disaster and – as rural guerrilla action took over from more dangerous urban guerrilla attacks – retreated to the Tarn *maquis*.[83] Militants of the Brigade who had finished up in prison – Marc Brafman, Sewek Michalak and the Lévy brothers – were deported on the so-called 'ghost train', which collected prisoners from Toulouse, Le Vernet and Noé, and set off on 2 July 1944 for Dachau. Interrupted by Allied bombing, its progress was slow and Brafman and the Lévy brothers managed to escape from the train in the Lyon area on 26 July.[84]

The Lyon area was almost as anarchic as the Toulouse area in the ten weeks that followed after D-Day. The control exercised from London and Algiers through the delegate-general of the French Committee of National Liberation and his deputy was sorely compromised by the arrest and suicide of his deputy in the former Free Zone, Jacques Bingen, on 12 May. The key figure at Lyon was Alban Vistel, who was both chief of the Mouvements Unis de la Résistance (MUR) and chair of the Departmental Liberation Committee. He worked together with Albert Chambonnet, codename Didier, a miner's son from the Alès coalfield who had made a career in the air force and become FFI chief in the Lyon region. They had to face the combined challenges of warlords, popular revolt and the diversity of anti-fascist resistance.

Dominant in the foothills of the Jura was Major Romans-Petit, aided by British SOE agent Richard Heslop, who had staged the symbolic liberation of Oyonnax on 11 November 1943 and was fiercely jealous of his autonomy.[85] Chambonnet, backed by Vistel, wanted to get rid of Romans-Petit and replace him with a much less controversial general who had made contact with the Armée Secrète.[86] Unfortunately, Chambonnet was arrested by the Gestapo in Lyon on 10 June 1944, and Alban Vistel took over his military responsibilities. This only provided Roman-Petit with more opportunity to take risks. On 10–11 July 1944 the Germans launched a powerful attack on his *maquis*. Battles were fought for the possession of Nantua and Oyonnax, but after three days

Romans-Petit ordered a retreat to the hills, which exposed local populations to German wrath. Pauline Mercier, whose pharmacist husband had been shot by the Germans the previous December, took on the role of a nurse and organised the evacuation by lorry of twenty-two wounded *maquisards* from Nantua hospital to a Jura village: 'The Germans were ten minutes away from us,' she remembered, 'and the local people knew that they would be shot without mercy and the village burned if the Germans discovered that they had given us cover,' so they moved uphill to the Crêt de Chalam.[87] The Germans, indeed, reoccupied Nantua and Oyonnax and inflicted severe reprisals on the inhabitants of the towns and surrounding villages. Marcelle Appleton, a key resistance figure at Bourg, said that the difference between the communities of the Vercors and the Ain was that 'on the Vercors, they knew that if they had suffered, the *maquis* had suffered more than them, and had always sacrificed itself to defend them. In the Ain, there was the opposite feeling, that the *maquis* had abandoned them, alone, to reprisals.'[88] Confirmed in their view that Romans-Petit would have to go, Vistel went to see him on 15 August, but by that stage he had reconstituted his forces and strengthened his position; so Vistel did not have the authority or backing to dismiss him.

Meanwhile, among the working classes of Lyon, pressure was building up for arming the people and some sort of commitment to national insurrection. The driving force behind this idea was Action Ouvrière, which enjoyed strong support among the railway and engineering workers of the big factories in the suburbs of Lyon. Their leader, Jean Gay, had been arrested in March 1944 but the organisation became no less combative. Action Ouvrière groups at the railway workshops of Oullins, the railway depot at Vénissieux and the Berliet lorry factory wrote to Alban Vistel on 17 June 1944. They denounced what it called the *attentisme* of the Resistance leadership, pressed for a common front with communist organisations and demanded weapons for the *milices patriotiques* of six or seven men that were being formed among workers to police factories and neighbourhoods and supplement the FFIs. Alban Vistel could only reply weakly that they had not been able to put their hands on arms held by the former Armistice Army, and that they continued pressurising French and Allied authorities to arm the French people.[89] On 10 July Action Ouvrière at Oullins rammed home the message:

We urge you to tell Marshal [*sic*] Koenig that we do not understand the sense of his telegram, in which he gives the order for the maximum slowdown of guerrilla activity. Shouldn't the example of Marshal Tito inspire us? [...] The D-Day order has chloroformed the will to act of the population and of the workers in particular.[90]

Other resistance groups in Lyon were also struggling to make an impact. At the university students of the Jeunesse Étudiante Chrétienne had divided over whether or not to refuse or respond to the STO. Jean-Marie Domenach and his friend Gilbert Dru led a minority opposition, which found support among their elders in *Témoignage Chrétien*, such as Pierre Chaillet and André Mandouze. Domenach maintained close links with Dunoyer de Segonzac, director of Uriage, which was dissolved after the Germans occupied the Free Zone. He joined a *maquis* founded on the Vercors in July 1943 by a group from Uriage and worked with the 'flying teams', which went from *maquis* encampment to an encampment providing instruction and entertainment. After a German attack in December 1943 they scattered and Domenach followed Dunoyer de Segonzac to the Tarn in June 1944 and took command of the Bayard Free Corps, musing on this new incarnation of chivalry.[91] Meanwhile, Gilbert Dru went to Paris in October 1943 to meet Christian resistance leaders and returned to Lyon to set up a Coordination Committee for Christian Action (CCAC) in Lyon that would link Christians in local and departmental liberation committees and build bridges to the CGT and Christian trade unions. Unfortunately, Dru was arrested after a meeting of the CCAC on 17 July 1944, along with a comrade from Savoy named Francis Chirat, and imprisoned in Montluc.[92]

Underground in the same city but poles apart from these middle-class Christian resisters was the FTP-MOI network Carmagnole-Liberté. It was composed not of locals but of disparate groups that had fled to Lyon for safety: young Jews of Polish origin who had escaped the round-ups in Paris – the so-called 'génération du rafle' – young Hungarian or Romanian Jews studying in France because of the *numerus clausus* in their own country, Italian immigrants of anti-fascist persuasion, and Spanish republicans, commanded by older resisters who were veterans of the International Brigades.[93] A Carmagnole-Liberté group under Roman Krakus had retreated from the city for a *maquis* outside but some younger activists remained in the city to continue urban guerrilla action against German forces. The only weapons they had were those they seized from the Germans by attacking either individual soldiers or garages used to repair and shelter German vehicles. On 3 July a squad of five attacked a garage in the rue Félix-Faure in Lyon: it included Italian immigrant Léon Landini, whose elder brother was Carmagnole's political commissar, and Jeanine Sontag, of Polish-Jewish origin, who had dropped out of university to join the Resistance. As they made their move several lorries arrived bristling with Vichy police and Germans. They tried to escape up a ladder and through a skylight at the back of the garage but Jeanine twisted her ankle and was unable to follow: 'Frightened, not knowing what to do,' Landini remembered, 'feeling guilty that we had not fulfilled our role as protectors, we very slowly left the scene of fighting.'[94] Later they were themselves captured but did not suffer Jeanine's fate.

All those imprisoned for resistance activity were treated as hostages who might be executed at any time. During the night of 26–27 July a bomb exploded in the Moulin à Vent café at the corner of the place Bellecour in the centre of the city, a favourite haunt of German soldiers. The next day a truck arrived outside the café from Montluc prison and pulled up. Five men were unloaded, shot one after the other and left in the gutter. They were Léon Pfeffer, twenty-one, a German-Jewish militant in Carmagnole-Liberté, whose parents had been deported from Paris in 1942; René Bernard, a boilermaker and activist in the Communist Youth; the regional FFI leader Albert Chambonnet and Christian resisters Gilbert Dru and Francis Chirat. Drawn from diverse strands of the Resistance in Lyon, they were closer in death than they ever had been in life. For fear of antagonising the Germans, Cardinal-Archbishop Gerlier refused to officiate at their funerals.[95]

Even more savage was the massacre at Saint-Genis-Laval, south-east of Lyon. As the net closed around them, the Germans dealt with their political prisoners either by deporting them or by simply killing them. On the morning of 20 August, the Germans loaded about 100 prisoners from Montluc into lorries and took them to a disused fort called Côte-Larette. Six by six, hands tied behind their backs, they were led to the guard house and up to the first floor, where they were shot. Blood trickled through the ceiling. When the room was full of bodies the butchery continued on the ground floor. Then the building was set on fire. Yves Farge, newly appointed *commissaire de la République*, continued:

A victim appeared at a window and was immediately targeted by sustained machine-gun fire. 'At that moment – said a witness – riddled with bullets and under the effects of the heat, the face stopped moving, seized up and, as the temperature intensified, melted like wax.' Two other unfortunates who had only been wounded jumped from the window. They were shot down and their bodies thrown onto the furnace. The monsters left the fort with their clothes soiled by blood and brains.[96]

One of the dead was Jeanine Sontag.

The battle for control of the metropolitan resistance took place with even greater ferocity in Paris. There the problem was not so much warlords beyond the reach of the FFI command but who would give orders to that FFI command in the debate over national insurrection. The situation was complicated by the fact that Paris was again the centre of national government and the conduit for orders from the Allied Supreme Command as well as the focal point of a possible national insurrection as Parisians engaged once again with their revolutionary past.

In the National Council of Resistance and its military committee COMAC struggle continued over who should be sending orders to the FFI. Alexandre Parodi, delegate of the French Committee of National Liberation, and National Military Delegate Jacques Chaban-Delmas fought to persuade COMAC that orders came from General Koenig, who alone knew what Allied strategy was, and that COMAC was there to pass these on to FFI chiefs. On 21 June, however, the Front National leader Pierre Villon proposed to the Conseil National that only COMAC understood the realities of resistance in France and its authority should be superior to that of Koenig. The same day he told COMAC that Koenig's orders only took account of Allied strategy and made no mention of the Resistance. The Conseil National supported Parodi but the majority view on COMAC, in spite of Chaban-Delmas, was that 'action within the country has to be directed by resistance within the country'.[97]

Views of delegates from London and the shadow of the Allies had much less influence on the Paris Liberation Committee, which was dominated by communists and asserted itself as the mouthpiece and instrument of revolutionary Paris. It was chaired by the diminutive André Tollet, head of the Paris trade-union federation, backed by the journalist André Hoschiller (André Carrel) and more recently by Georges Marrane, the pre-war mayor of Ivry-sur-Seine, who for three years had furrowed the roads of France on his bicycle on behalf of the Front National. Against them were ranged Roger Deniau, a socialist and trade unionist representing Libération-Nord, Marie-Hélène Lefaucheux, wife of the arrested Pierre Lefaucheux, for OCM, and above all by Léo

Hamon of Ceux de la Résistance, the northern branch of Combat. The influence of the Committee depended on how much power it could carve out. Since the Revolution of 1789, Paris had been kept very much under the thumb of the centralised French authorities. There was no mayor of Paris and state power in the capital was wielded by the prefect of the Seine and the prefect of police. The communists on the Paris Committee were keen to reassert the power of the representatives of the people in a way that had not been seen since the 1871 Paris Commune. Throughout June 1944 they waged a campaign to seize from the French Committee of National Liberation the right to appoint the new prefect of the Seine. In mid-July, at a CPL meeting attended by Parodi, Tollet read out a letter received from the PCF in hiding in the Paris region, which proposed for prefect no less than Georges Marrane, pointing out that in the Popular Front era he had been chair of the Conseil général of the Seine, abolished by Vichy. Tollet added that they needed:

an administrator who would also be a man of the masses, having the ear of the population and able to communicate its aspirations to the government. In the past the people [of Paris] has been bullied by representatives imposed on them by the government, but democratic spirit requires that account is taken of the popular will and mass movements.[98]

The non-communist members of the Paris Committee argued in response that the prefect must be appointed – as he had been since Napoleonic times – by the government. Marcel Flouret, a former official of the Cour des Comptes, who had also directed the private office of Vichy's Air Minister in June and July 1940, was nominated prefect, much to the fury of the communists.

In the absence of executive power, the Paris Committee found ways to build up people power as the Germans' grip began to weaken. Just as the people of Paris had risen up in 1789 to demand more bread, so on 1 July 1944 a protest march demanding bread formed in the Faubourg Saint-Denis and moved east towards the place de la République. Considering it only a hunger march, the Germans did not intervene. An eyewitness observed:

Young people led the way, forming a chain at the front and distributing leaflets as they went along. A large crowd immediately formed. Housewives left queues to join the procession [. . .] The neighbourhood was soon black with people and a powerful column moved up the street shouting slogans [. . .] 'We want bread!' 'Down with the hunger-merchants!', 'Milk for our babies!', 'Food!' were the main slogans at the beginning, soon followed by 'Death to the Milice!', 'Death to Darnand!', 'Execute Pétain!', 'Execute Laval!' [. . .] At the rue Lancry German forces with machine-guns arrived, along with police vans. The police vans followed the cortege for a long while but without intervening [. . .] At the corner of the rue du Château d'Eau a comrade began to speak, saying, 'Parisians, in spite of the Boches and the bandits of the Milice, the streets of Paris are yours!'[99]

Another major opportunity for the Paris Committee was the celebration of 14 July in 1944. This celebration, together with flying the tricolour, had been banned under the German occupation and sporadic attempts to mark the day had been marked by repression, both by the German and Vichy authorities. Now it was called for over the BBC and the people of Paris were keen to manifest their presence, even though the Germans were never as repressive as when they felt cornered. Local committees of the main Paris Committee organised strikes in the factories, marches in the street and flying the tricolour. And after a procession to the war memorial in the Salpêtrière Hospital in the 13th *arrondissement*, a group of staff decided to fly a tricolour flag from the chapel tower. A passing German tank burst in and its crew forced the staff to take it down but one of the nurses recorded that 'we were all happy, as our flag had flown for over an hour and had been seen all over the neighbourhood.'[100] At the Paris Committee it was reported that 100,000 people had come onto the streets, 'which must encourage all resistance organisations and movements to step up their activity in order to draw the masses into resistance and struggle against the invaders and their valets'.[101] The working-class suburbs of Paris, the so-called red belt where the communists had been strong, were particularly active. Pierre Georges, aka Colonel Fabien, who commanded the FTP on the left bank and southern suburbs of Paris, protected from possible attack a procession to the cemetery of Ivry, where the Germans had buried the bodies of resisters shot at Mont Valérien or Vincennes.[102] The crowd then joined striking railway workers from Vitry-sur-Seine and Villeneuve-Saint-Georges, marching to the municipality that lay between them, Choisy-le-Roi (which was graced by a statue of Rouget de Lisle, who had composed the 'Marseillaise' in 1792). On the way back, seven railwaymen from Vitry and nine from Villeneuve were arrested by the Germans. This provoked a strike by railway workers to liberate the men across southern and eastern Paris and hinder the German retreat, which spread from Vitry and Villeneuve and to Noisy-le-Sec. Strikers held meetings in factory canteens at which speakers were protected from possible arrest by *milices patriotiques*, security teams which formed the nucleus of a neighbourhood revolutionary force under communist control.[103]

Strike action spread in the Paris region during the first fortnight of August from the railways to engineering works, the building trade, banks, insurance companies, the Galeries Lafayette and public services.[104] Electricity and gas supplies were cut off; cinemas and restaurants closed.[105] The burning question, however, was whether demonstrations and strikes would or should be geared towards insurrection. On 3 July Colonel Rol-Tanguy, FFI chief in the Paris region, reported that he had only 1,750 men under arms but with help from resistance movements could mobilise about 60,000 men, except that weapons were lacking. Given the shortage of FFIs, numbers could be made up only by the formation of *milices patriotiques*, which COMAC ordered on 26 July to be set up in factories, neighbourhoods and villages and which might become the instrument of national insurrection. A week later, however, a telegram came through from Koenig that Eisenhower had declared that what he called 'the FFI army' under Koenig's command was 'considered an integral part of the Inter-allied Expedionary Forces' under Eisenhower's command.[106] At this point the non-communists felt they had regained the initiative and vented their spleen on the prophets of national insurrection. Léo Hamon did not mince his words about Maurice Kriegel-Valrimont of COMAC: 'always that emphatic pathos drowning his insinuations that perfectly imitates solemn pontification. When the bugger does not deceive he exasperates.'[107] Jacques Lecompte-Boinet took a similar view of Pierre Villon, his colleague on the National Council of Resistance: 'He is highly intelligent but simplistic and violent. When he speaks about French interest I can't forget, in spite of myself, that he is a communist loyal to Moscow.'[108]

D-Day was the signal for thousands of young French people to come out of the shadows and take to the *maquis*, ready for action in support of the Allies and French forces that returned to fight on the mainland after a long four years. For a long time still, however, Allied and French help did not materialise. The Allies had their own strategic priorities and scarcely rated regular French forces, let alone the rag-tag army of the FFIs, capable of serious action. They did not want to become involved in French politics, especially when it involved a communist threat. National insurrection was the slogan on many French lips but it meant different things to different people. When de Gaulle mentioned it in 1942 it was to gain authority over the metropolitan resistance and to demonstrate his popular legitimacy to the Allies. Two years later, having done deals with Vichyists and Giraudists in North Africa, the term was no longer part of his lexicon. Instead it was trumpeted by communists and their allies as a way of beating non-communist resisters and encouraging the FFI to action. It was also a tool to criticise General Koenig in London and his orders, which were modelled on what the Allies wanted rather than on the aspirations of the French people.

In the event, who gave orders to the FFI was almost an academic point. The ties between the internal and external resistance established by Jean Moulin had not been fully reconstituted since his arrest, and a delegate-general like Alexandre Parodi did not have the persuasive authority of Moulin. At the regional level FFI commanders had difficulty disciplining the diverse constituencies of the Resistance, from warlords like Pommiès, Starr and Romans-Petit, to popular insurgents in Paris and Lyon, to the bright palette of anti-fascist resisters, Polish Jews and Spanish republicans, Italians and Germans. In the end these resistance groups went their own way, organising their own operations as the opportunities presented themselves. In the first ten weeks the results were dramatic but often catastrophic. The Germans regarded *maquisards* and urban guerrillas as terrorists to be shot summarily on arrest. Villagers who harboured them were also liable to ferocious reprisals. The cost of resistance activity was extremely high. Not until after 15 August 1944 did the tide begin to change and liberation finally come into sight.

14

Liberation

The charcutier, full-length in the gutter, gave free rein to his sub-machine gun, as in 1914.
(eyewitness account by Mme Lamontellerie, Paris XVIII)

On 16 August 1944, a day after the Allied landings began in Provence, General Diego Brosset himself came ashore with his First Free French Division after over four years' absence from French soil. He noted that:

The landing was astonishingly successful. Almost no [enemy] resistance, good FFI support, bridgehead immediately established and quickly put to use, outskirts of Hyères reached on D + 3, Draguignan taken on D + 2. We are pushing towards Aix, but . . .[1]

The success story was not complete. The French forces were very much the junior partners of the American Seventh Army and under their orders.[2] The French were ordered to deal with German resistance on the coast and take a major port – either Toulon or Marseille – by D + 25 while the Americans themselves drove north to Grenoble and Lyon. In the event, Brosset entered Toulon only a week later on 23 August, 'circled by women's arms and men's hands' and on 27 August there was a triumphal parade there of the B Army, of which he was a part. This pointed up a second problem, the enduring tension between the hardened Free French who had fought their way up through Africa since 1941 and those who had joined much later from the Armistice Army or Army of Africa. General de Lattre, who had come over from the Armistice Army and commanded the B Army that amalgamated all those forces, was disdained by Brosset as more of a showman than a soldier hardened by years of fighting in Africa. 'He [. . .] thinks only of his glory like the Sun King except that he has the cinema too, which he uses and abuses.'[3] Similarly, he disdained units of the Army of Africa such as the 9th Colonial Infantry Regiment: 'Still too young,' grumbled Brosset, 'that division marches past better than it fights, which is the contrary of mine.' The Toulon review also demonstrated that while all French people were delighted that the liberators had finally landed, some were still under the spell of the mystique of Marshal Pétain and were not uniformly supporters of de Gaulle: 'A large and enthusiastic crowd,' wrote Brosset, 'not many shouts of "de Gaulle", a few "Long live the Army!" but in truth the accent was on "Long live France!"'[4]

The superiority of the Americans and the legacy of Vichy were compounded by a third problem: relations between the FFIs who had been involved in resistance against the Germans for months and the French armies, which now returned to metropolitan soil for the first time since 1940. The landings in Provence also provoked strike action on the part of workers to jam what remained of the German war machine and the emergence of liberation committees composed of representatives of resistance organisations, political groups and trade unionists that tried to seize power from the Vichy authorities in almost every town, village and department. All this dramatised an intense and ongoing debate between those who saw national liberation as coterminous with national insurrection and those who wanted to avoid insurrection at all costs and, while abolishing Vichy, to ensure that state power passed as smoothly as possible into the hands of the republican provisional government.

Conflict flared up very sharply in Marseille, 60 kilometres to the west of Toulon, a major trading and industrial city with a revolutionary past. Raymond Aubrac was appointed *commissaire de la République* for the Marseille region on 6 August 1944 and, flying from Algiers via Naples and Ajaccio, landed at Saint-Tropez on 18 August. His task was to ensure that the provisional government took control of events there. However, the day he arrived a general strike was declared by workers in Marseille and the following day the Departmental Liberation Committee of the Bouches-du-Rhône announced a full-scale insurrection. Barricades went up all over the city, forcing German troops back to a few defendable points. On 24 August Aubrac had lunch with General de Lattre at Aubagne, to the east of Marseille, symbolising the unity of civil and military powers. But he was then fetched in an FFI car to be taken to the prefecture where the Liberation Committee was directing what looked like a revolutionary situation.[5] He relied on the Communist Party and the trade unions to restore order, and dealt with the Vichy police and collaborationist *Milice* by setting up Republican Security Forces drafted from FTP and *milices patriotiques*. To keep up the war effort he took under public control fifteen port and transport firms employing 15,000 workers whose bosses were arrested for collaboration. To some it looked as if the *commissaire* had gone native and legitimised a new revolutionary order.[6]

Seven hundred miles away in Brittany the balance of power between the Allies, French forces and the Resistance was very different. On 30 July American forces under General Bradley burst through the German lines at Avranches, near Mont Saint-Michel. The Americans were keen to drive east, to roll the Germans towards the frontier. A limited American force under General Patton thus drove into Brittany and the Loire Valley, happy enough to cooperate with French commanders drawn from the regular army and with FFIs. Command of the FFIs in Brittany was exercised not by a communist but by the unlikely figure of Colonel Albert-Marie Eon, aged forty-nine, an artillery officer who had served in the Army of Africa and in the Tunisian campaign under Giraud, before deciding to go to England by slow boat from Algiers in order to train with the secret services ahead of the landings.[7] He argued strongly that the Resistance was of much more use to the Allies in areas close to their theatre of operations than far away from the Normandy coast in the Alps or Massif Central and on 25 July was appointed by Koenig chief of the FFI in Brittany. This he achieved in preference to Colonel Passy, who coveted the job and tried to strengthen his case by spreading rumours that Eon was 'a neurotic, a madman', but was nonetheless reduced to serving as Eon's chief of staff.[8] Eon assembled around him a team of officers who were mostly veterans of the Tunisia campaign. He was also given the support of eleven Jedburgh teams formed of a French, British and US serviceman who would supervise drops of weapons for 30,000 men, train them in their use and co-ordinate their resistance with the strategy of the Allied armies. Eon visited them and told them about the Breton *bocage* of hedged farmland and sunken lanes that had given cover for the Chouans or royalist guerrillas who had fought against the French Revolution in the 1790s.[9]

Colonel Eon was dropped into France during the night of 4–5 August and established his headquarters near Guingamp in the Côtes-du-Nord. His priority was to provide intelligence about German positions and FFI combat support for the US offensive into Brittany. Initially, General Bradley was sceptical about the usefulness of the FFIs and keen that they should surrender or bury their weapons as soon as American soldiers had established their superiority. However, Koenig resisted this and in any case events happened too fast for this to be realistic.[10] On 17 August around Paimpol, Eon recalled that:

for the first time organised French forces about 2500 strong, serving under a united command and working with American tanks and artillery and the Technical Air Force, took responsibility for breaking an important pocket of enemy resistance in particularly brilliant circumstances.[11]

Effective FFI support for US military action led to the liberation of Rennes on 4 August, Angers on 10 August, and Nantes on 12 August. The Germans were driven back to pockets in Saint-

Nazaire, Lorient and Brest, ports that they had strongly fortified. The main American forces now swung east to drive for the Seine. On 3 September American planes attacked German positions on the Crozon peninsula outside Brest, and hit Eon's headquarters and the nearby village of Telgruc, turning it into 'an inferno and a pile of ruins' and shattering Franco-American relations in Brittany.[12] Eon protested to US General Middleton for this mistake and for the underestimation of the contribution of the FFIs and local inhabitants in Brittany. By this time, though, Eon had also been informed that de Gaulle had dissolved the FFIs, which were now to be sent home or incorporated into the regular army, and he duly left for Paris.

Meanwhile the transfer of power between Vichy and the republican provisional government was complicated by the American presence. The Americans had still not recognised the French provisional government and there was still an outside chance that they would ditch de Gaulle by doing a deal with what was left of the Vichy regime. On 10 August, as American troops approached and German forces retreated, Michel Debré, who had been appointed *commissaire de la République* for the Angers region, entered the prefecture by showing his Conseil d'État pass and then declared that he was taking over in the name of de Gaulle. He shook hands with the Vichy regional prefect, who quietly withdrew, and sat himself behind the empty desk declaring, 'I had become the state.'[13] His authority ran from Tours to Nantes but in Nantes the American colonel in charge of the city still preferred to do business with the Vichy prefect. Debré had to hasten to Nantes on 15 August for a showdown with the American colonel, lecturing him on the fact that Vichy was finished and de Gaulle was now in charge. He endeavoured to install the prefect who had been vetted by the Comité Général d'Études but who was cold-shouldered by the Pétainist establishment in Nantes, headed by the bishop, and scarcely tolerated by the Departmental Liberation Committee which was controlled by communists.[14]

These events highlighted powerful obstacles that stood in the way of the liberation of France by the French people themselves. The relationship of the French with the Allies was still very difficult. French forces came under the overall leadership of General Eisenhower, who was committed to a strategy that placed the defeat of Germany above the liberation of France. This, for example, explained the ruthlessness with which the Allies had bombed the German war machine in France, at the cost of 60,000 French lives. In the summer of 1944 French forces had the impression of playing a minor role in the great drama, consigned to tasks for which the Americans themselves had no time. In addition, the Americans were very suspicious of the FFIs; not only were they untrained and poorly armed, but they seemed to be controlled by communists and bent on national insurrection. After the war Eisenhower conceded that the French Resistance saved the Allies both time and losses and enabled them to pursue their main strategy of driving east, but in 1944 compliments were not as fulsome.[15] There was still a nagging suspicion in many French minds that the Allies intended to set up a military government in France rather than allow them to arrange their own affairs democratically.

The Roosevelt administration had a pronounced dislike for de Gaulle and even after the latter's visit to Washington in July 1944 it seemed possible the Americans might conclude an eleventh-hour deal with Vichy. This was certainly in the mind of premier Pierre Laval who, on 30 July, tried to persuade Pétain to leave Vichy for Paris, form a new government and welcome the Allies. Pétain refused to budge, feeling that in Vichy at least he had the remnants of symbolic power. Laval, therefore, went to Paris alone on 9 August and on 12 August to Nancy, where Édouard Herriot, speaker of the Chamber of Deputies until 1940, was under house arrest in a clinic. The plan was to bring him to Paris, either to form a new government or to preside over a meeting of a reconvened National Assembly, both Chamber and

Senate.[16] 'There is a rumour,' Lecompte-Boinet noted in his diary on 14 August, 'that Herriot, fetched from Nancy by Laval, has set up permanently in the Hôtel de Ville and that Pétain himself will come to Paris to welcome the Americans [. . .] We are going to be shafted.'[17]

A lunch was held at Matignon, the prime minister's residence, on 17 August, attended by Laval, his daughter, Josée de Chambrun, Herriot and the German ambassador, Otto Abetz. Herriot, however, had no intention of pulling Laval's chestnuts out of the fire. He was in nostalgic mood, remembered Josée de Chambrun:

Herriot told how he had been given a doctorate honoris causa at Oxford at the same time that the German scientist Max Planck, famous for his refutation of the theory of spontaneous generation, had been similarly honoured. Everything is in Latin during these ceremonies and president Herriot wondered how Planck managed to prepare an address that would necessarily be full of scientific words.[18]

In the event the project of a Laval-Herriot government under American protection was still-born. Abetz, with new orders, told Laval to take his government to Belfort on the Swiss border. When Laval refused he was arrested and taken via Nancy to Belfort anyway, where he was joined on 20 August by Pétain.[19] The Vichy regime would live out its final weeks not in France but in the castle of Sigmaringen, where its remaining dignitaries were taken.[20]

Meanwhile, Allied and French landings in Provence entirely changed the relationship between partisans of national insurrection and supporters of orderly regime change. For Serge Ravanel, the FFI commander in the Toulouse region, 15 August was a 'thunderbolt' that confronted German forces with a choice of being thrown into the sea or blockaded in the South.[21] After an attempt to contain the invasion German forces began to retreat north and east towards the German frontier, leaving the Resistance to take possession of the towns and cities they left behind. This was particularly the case in the south-west, where the presence of Allied and regular French forces was extremely limited, the FFI were numerous and confident, and officials loyal to de Gaulle had to deal with a revolutionary situation on the ground.

As the German garrisons left Toulouse, the city was liberated on 19 August by a variegated force of FFIs, dominated by communists and led by Jean-Pierre Vernant, together with Spanish republicans, the Pommiès Free Corps and George Starr's Armagnac Battalion. Power was assumed by the Comité Départemental de la Libération and by Jean Cassou as *commissaire de la République*. Unfortunately Cassou was knocked unconscious in the streets of Toulouse that night by a retreating German vehicle and left in a coma. A replacement was found in Pierre Bertaux, who had welcomed Cassou to Toulouse when he first arrived and ran an early resistance group, now defunct. The fact that he was not immediately invested by the provisional government made it difficult for him to assert his authority over the charismatic Ravanel. Meanwhile the powerless regional military delegate reported that 'extremist elements have taken over since the liberation of Toulouse': Ravanel had dissolved the Vichy police forces and 'only the FTP is now controlling the city'. With the French Army and Allies far away in Normandy and the Rhône Valley, this intensified the fear in Gaullist circles that Toulouse was becoming the capital of a Red Republic.[22]

After the liberation of Toulouse, the rest of the region was liberated by a rainbow of FFIs, which confirmed the truly multinational profile of the Resistance in the south-west of France. On 22 August, a hundred of Gérald Suberville's Hérault FFIs held up a German force of 1,500 for several hours at Colombières (Hérault) as it tried to force its way east towards the Rhône.[23] Spanish republicans were active from the Dordogne to the Pyrenees. Forces under López Tovar liberated Périgueux on 19 August and Agen, 100 kilometres to the south, two days later.[24] Foix, near the Spanish border, was liberated on 18 August by

Spanish republicans under Brigadier Royo, in conjunction with a French officer, Marcel Bigeard. Bigeard had escaped from a POW camp in 1941 and joined the Army of Africa before volunteering, like Eon, to work with the BCRA, and was parachuted into the Ariège as military delegate on 8 August.[25] French FFIs and Spanish guerrillas then attacked the German garrison at Saint-Girons, from which they were forced to withdraw. A German column, reinforced by a 'Turkestan legion' of ex-Soviet POWs recruited in Central Asia, was ambushed by fifteen Spaniards at Rimont on 21 August. The Germans set fire to the village and shot six inhabitants before Spanish reinforcements arrived under Royo. Some 1,200 German prisoners surrendered and were taken to the camp at Le Vernet, where so many Spanish republicans had languished years before.[26]

The Jewish *maquis* also played their part. Fighting alongside Dunoyer de Segonzac's *maquis* de Vabre, the Compagnie Marc Haguenau ambushed a German train on the Mazamet-Castres line on 19 August. Battle continued all night as the *maquisards* machine-gunned the train, 'stopped like a fish immobilised by a harpoon', as one of their number later wrote. 'The train gave up a hundred men and cannon and the prestige of warriors to those comrades who took part in the upsurge of liberation.'[27] The *maquis* then went on to take the German garrison of Castres, where 4,200 men and seventy-one officers surrendered, and the Jewish company was proud to join the victory parade in Castres on 21 August.[28] Meanwhile, the FTP-MOI of the Cévennes under Otto Kühne attacked the mining town of Alès with seventy men, including Germans, Spaniards, Czechs, Slovaks, Yugoslavs, and deserters from *Wehrmacht*. A battalion of five companies, including the 104th or 'German company' was concealed in goods wagons with the help of French railwaymen, and descended during the night of 23–24 August to Nîmes, which they then liberated. The anti-Nazi German company marched proudly at the head of the liberation parade.[29]

None of this was to the taste of General Cochet, who in theory had supreme command of the FFI in the Southern Zone. On 19 August, the day Toulouse was liberated, he issued an order that betrayed a very different vision of FFIs from the way they saw themselves. FFIs who were under eighteen or over forty-five years old should be immediately disarmed and 'volunteers' aged eighteen to forty-five should carry weapons 'only when on duty and on orders from their superiors'. France, he said, needed to show their Allies that they were 'a great nation, strong and disciplined. To wage war is to fight with all means available and those means may be expressed in a single motto: TO SERVE.'[30] Cochet's fears were confirmed when he arrived in Toulouse in early September. He found Ravanel 'an absolute master', obliging Bertaux to sign orders dissolving the *gendarmerie* and police and entrusting public order to the '*milices patriotiques*, that is to say, the FTP'. He claimed that Ravanel said that they had no need for people from London or Algiers and were going to 'establish the Republic of Toulouse'. In response Cochet threatened to bring an armed division to the city to restore order. Things calmed down when Ravanel met Cochet, recalled that he had attended the General's lecture in Lyon in 1941 and spoken on the *quais* of the Saône, and agreed to defer to *commissaire* Bertaux.[31]

As German power crumbled and the Resistance grew in strength, so the new authorities of the Republic found themselves with greater leverage. While the Germans perpetrated the massacre of Saint-Genis-Laval, the FFI in Haute-Savoie took 752 Germans prisoner and the FFI in the Loire captured a contingent of German police. On 21 August *commissaire* Farge, backed by a delegate of the French Committee of National Liberation and the military delegate in the Southern Zone, sent a strongly worded letter to the Vichy regional prefect, Red Cross and Swedish consul in Lyon. It warned Colonel Knapp, the German police chief at Lyon, that these prisoners would be considered hostages at risk of execution should any more French patriots be executed. Two days later, the Vichy prefect handed over the keys of Montluc prison.[32]

In Lyon, a strike had originally been planned for 10 August 1944, the symbolic date of the fall of the French monarchy in 1792. The local Action Ouvrière leader wrote to Alban Vistel to say they were working to ensure that 'this movement succeeds, gains strength and becomes an insurrectional strike, ushering in the national insurrection, which is inseparable from national liberation'. This, he said, also required the FFI to create a 'climate of war', not only by sabotaging electricity pylons but by 'visible actions, harassing the enemy, guerrilla warfare, spectacular gestures that will draw the masses into action against the Boches'.[33] The strike did not go ahead on 10 August but at 10 a.m. on 24 August, in response to the massacre of Saint-Genis-Laval and events in Paris, a strike began at the railway workshops at Oullins, where an organising committee called for an insurrectionary strike. The ringleaders were immediately sacked by their employers but were replaced by a resistance committee. The next day Action Ouvrière expanded their *milices patriotiques* to squads of ten and thirty each, which would link up with the FFI, and sent two men on a mission to find the *maquis* of Chamelet in the Beaujolais north-west of Lyon and invite it to occupy Oullins. It did so at dawn on Sunday 27 August, as the local population threw up barricades and installed a new municipality there.[34] Its hand forced by the momentum of events, the Departmental Liberation Committee at Lyon under Alban Vistel gave an official order during the night of the 24–25 August to begin a general strike.[35]

Meanwhile, the lesson of Saint-Genis-Laval had not been lost on other resisters in Lyon. They were anxious to get their comrades out of other prisons in the city, such as Saint-Paul, before they too could be massacred. These attacks now took place under cover of the strike and insurrection. One of the prisoners at Saint-Paul was Nathan Saks ('Raymond') of Carmagnole-Liberté, who had been wounded in a resistance operation on 9 March 1944 and taken to a clinic by a trio of Hungarian-Jewish comrades, who had then been captured and shot at the Fort de la Duchère on 27 March. Saks had been handed over to the police and was under sentence of death in the prison infirmary. Carmagnole executed a daring attack and helped Saks and nine other resisters to scale the prison wall. While Saks was cared for by Carmagnole's Polish-Jewish doctor, the other escapees joined *maquis* outside the city commanded by Roman Krakus or fell back with other members of Carmagnole to the working-class suburb of Villeurbanne, where many of them had their roots.[36]

Wearing FFI arm-bands, the Carmagnole fighters were welcomed by the Villeurbanne population as liberators and decided to try to meet their expectations. Led by 24-year-old Henri Krischer on 23 August, they occupied the town hall, set up a liberation committee and built barricades to defend themselves. Léon Landini, who had been arrested on 25 July, escaped on 24 August in time to take part in the insurrection. Max Weinstein of the Union of Jewish Youth, the adolescent version of Carmagnole, headed a detachment with only a revolver and expressed gratitude to 29-year-old Malfada Motti ('Simone'), an Italian immigrant and 'an authentic heroine of the Resistance', who acted like a big sister and championed his right to have a machine-gun ahead of another resister who was older but a newcomer: 'Alone, armed with a machine-gun,' recalled Weinstein, 'she held up a whole enemy detachment during the fighting at Villeurbanne.'[37] On 29 September, after three days, the Germans returned in force to Villeurbanne and dislodged the Carmagnole resisters. They escaped east to Pont de Chéruy and linked up with some Savoyard *maquisards* to form the FFI Bataillon Henri Barbusse, engaging the Germans at Pusignan.

During the night of 2–3 September the Germans finally left Lyon, blowing up the bridges over the Rhône and Saône to cover their retreat. At dawn on 3 September the FFIs moved into the city: 'An army surged from the earth,' wrote Yves Farge. 'Carried by a popular will, dressed in poor uniforms and with weapons acquired in bazaars, it went to meet the armoured Allied forces that were coming up the Rhône.'[38] The French forces were led by General Brosset, who set himself up in the Hôtel de Ville in order, he said:

to restore order to the house. Shooting was going on in the city, and an order was necessary to put an end to this fancy-dress parade. Then the inevitable review [of troops] had to be organised, a mass at Fourvières, a ceremony in front of the Fort de la Duchère where executions had taken place. Then contact with the civilian authorities.[39]

Brosset was unimpressed by the civil authorities. Yves Farge had occupied the prefecture as *commissaire de la République,* and met Brosset at the Hôtel de Ville. Brosset noted that the commissaire was 'a man whom I would have to get to know more to analyse' but did not record his name.[40] On his side Farge was struck by the powerful man with the Croix de la Libération on his chest and who 'smells of the desert, sweat and bravery'.[41] It was a classic encounter between the sunburned Free French warrior who had battled through Africa and Italy, and the bespectacled conspirator of the shadows, only now emerging into the daylight. They quarrelled. Brosset demanded powers of police to impose order in the city; Farge declared that he exercised full powers as *commissaire de la République* but did not have a copy of the decree to back it up. In the end, the matter was settled by Brosset's charisma:

A few moments later I was contemplating Brosset in the middle of the road, standing in his command car, kepi thrust back, chest sticking out, shouting, 'Band of idiots, are you finished?' And like a miracle, the rifles and machine-guns fell silent.[42]

Meanwhile, in Paris a new German military governor had been put in charge with orders to defend it to the last against both Allies and insurgents. General Dietrich von Choltitz had served on the Eastern Front, taking Sebastopol, and had been moved to Normandy after D-Day. On 7 August he was summoned to meet Hitler in his bunker near Rastenburg in East Prussia. He found 'an old man, stooping, puffy, with thin grey hair that bristled, trembling and extenuated'. When Hitler spoke about the execution of the generals who had tried to kill him there on 20 July, 'his language became bloodthirsty, saliva dripped from his mouth, and his body shook'. Von Choltitz learned that a Sippenhaft law had been signed ordering that the family of any officer guilty of faltering would be arrested and if necessary executed. He said farewell to his own family before he returned to Paris on 9 August and set up his headquarters at the Hôtel le Meurice on the rue de Rivoli.[43]

There, as the Allies drew closer and the temperature of revolt rose in Paris, the Germans increased the tempo of emptying prisons and camps. There were fears of a prison massacre, but instead the inmates of Fresnes and Drancy were herded onto a final convoy that left Paris for more secure camps in Germany on 15 August. Among those on the train were Pierre Lefaucheux, the Organisation Civile et Militaire resister and former commander of the FFI in the Paris region, who had been arrested and imprisoned in Fresnes, and François Girard, aged nineteen, who had been arrested for his role in Défense de la France. Marie-Hélène Lefaucheux was desperate to follow her husband and took leave from her responsibilities on the Paris Liberation Committee. Travelling with a friend who had a side-car attached to her bicycle, she saw them loaded at Fresnes onto ten coaches:

For some time, on bicycles, a few women managed to follow the terrible route. I imagine that they had the same anxiety as me, terrified that they would take the road for Mont Valérien or Vincennes.[44]

The coaches, however, went to the goods station at Pantin and the prisoners were crowded into wagons that were 'hermetically closed, apart from two narrow openings covered with barbed wire'. Marie-Hélène managed to persuade the guards to get a parcel of food to her husband and, as the train left at 11.30 p.m., her resistance friend Claire Girard arrived by car, looking for her brother François. Together they followed the convoy east and glimpsed her husband at Châlons-sur-Marne, where the wagons were opened to give the prisoners some water. At Bar-le-Duc, they heard from the Red Cross that, following news of a deal arranged by the Swedish consul Raoul Nordling, the train should stay on French soil. They woke the local sub-prefect, and then went to Nancy to persuade the prefect to telephone the Swedish consulate to have the train stopped, but to no effect. Fortuitously, the rump of the Vichy government had arrived in Nancy and Marie-Hélène used her husband's business connections to try to persuade Jean Bichelonne, the former minister of Industrial Production, and Laval to intervene, but they admitted they were powerless.

The train crossed the German frontier at 2 p.m. on 18 August, and Marie-Hélène Lefaucheux decided at this point to return to the capital to resume her work with the Paris Liberation Committee. Claire Girard was also keen to see her mother, who was unwell. Arriving at dawn on the 19th, Marie-Hélène went to the Hôtel de Ville, which, she said, 'I would scarcely leave during the week that would follow.'[45] Events had moved swiftly in the three or four days she had been away. The strike movement that had been spreading across Paris since early August took a critical turn when it came to involve the Paris police forces. Although the police were naturally Vichy's force of repression, the Préfecture de Police had been infiltrated by resistance networks, notably the Front National, NAP-Police and a group called Honneur et Patrie, whose leaders were arrested in December 1943 and deported to Mauthausen. The police were acutely aware of the shifting balance of power as the German and Vichy powers crumbled and regime change became inevitable; they saw the advantage of patriotic gestures in order not to be pilloried as collaborators. A key player in this respect was Yves Bayet, who had been secretary-general of the prefecture of Nantes in 1942 and deeply implicated in enforcing the Relève and hunting communists. He went missing from Nantes in 1943 and reappeared in Paris as Jean-Marie

Boucher, a force in NAP-Police.[46] A meeting on 15 August 1944 decided to launch a police strike. The next day an eyewitness in the 17th *arrondissement* noted that all the police stations were shut while the Germans were leaving in greater numbers 'under the ironic gaze of the Parisians. The Germans were throwing luggage, furniture, weapons, archives and even "souvenirs" pillaged right up to the last minute pêle-mêle into every sort of car or lorry.'[47]

Meanwhile, on 17 August, while Laval was trying to win Herriot over at lunch in Matignon, an intense debate took place in the Paris Liberation Committee on whether to issue an order to launch an insurrection to drive out the Germans and seize power for the Resistance before the Americans arrived. A first question was whether the FFI had enough armed men to launch a rising. A second was whether the Paris Committee could agree on a course of action and bring over the National Council of Resistance (CNR), or whether the communists would go it alone. Behind the debates were the fantasies and fears of another Paris Commune or of another Warsaw Uprising that was even then being abandoned by the Soviets and strangled by German repression. Although laconic, the minutes of the meeting dramatise the debate between the enthusiasts – Tollet as chair, Rol-Tanguy for the FFI, Carrel for the Front National – and the sceptics, Deniau for Libération-Nord and Hamon for Ceux de la Résistance:

Rol: The Germans and Allies are playing for time. We have to take responsibility. Thousands of armed men, including police and FFI. Possible to have a real army capable of resistance. Some buildings occupied by FFI, skirmishes. Atmosphere of combat. Propose motion: Means for guerrilla action and possibility to start insurrection.
Deniau: What do you have in the way of armed forces?
Rol: 600 armed men, stocks of weapons at certain points and police forces.
Deniau: Rather small numbers to go into action.
Rol: All under FFI command.
Deniau: Small numbers. We have to think.
Hamon: Rol motion OK, but not for an insurrection. Small numbers.

We need to talk to CNR. Need to appoint a delegation to talk to CNR. *Carrel*: More optimistic on the possibilities of insurrection. FFI have occupied buildings. Forces are together [. . .] Incidents, shootings. We must reply. We must crush German forces [. . .] Americans afraid of people of Paris. If they wanted to they could enter Paris. Must trigger insurrection.

Hamon: Not OK for triggering it today.

Carrel: CPL solidarity preferable. If not, FN will issue the order.

Hamon: Discipline. Not go it alone. Not a fait accompli.

Tollet: Can't allow [American] entry without insurrection. Need rapid agreement tomorrow.

Deniau: Warsaw example. Need opinion of CNR. No useless shedding of Parisian blood.[48]

The next day, 18 August, at a secret meeting of the Paris Liberation Committee at Vanves, the communist group launched an offensive, saying that if the Committee did not endorse the call to insurrection, the Front National, the CGT trade-union federation and Communist Party would go it alone. The *bureau* of the National Council of Resistance, dominated by Villon, seconded the demand for a call for insurrection and put it to a plenary meeting of the Council, which met in the rue de Naples, near the Parc Monceau. In the absence of Georges Bidault it approved the trade unions' call for a general strike and the call for insurrection, but only in the Paris region.[49]

That afternoon, the Paris Liberation Committee and the National Council of Resistance, constantly on the move to avoid detection, met together in the rue de Bellechasse, off the Boulevard Saint-Germain, and formally endorsed the call for insurrection. 'At the Education Ministry,' noted Hamon, 'the staff have raised tricolour flags and the crowd is singing the "Marseillaise".'[50] Rol-Tanguy, who had established his headquarters in the catacombs under the place Denfert-Rochereau, went to see Delegate-General Parodi to obtain his agreement to an insurrection order to the people of Paris. This order was posted all over the city at dawn on Saturday 19 August.[51]

The first response was that at 7 a.m. that morning, as Marie-Hélène Lefaucheux was returning to Paris, a force of 2,000 striking police in civilian clothes got into the Préfecture de Police and seized it for the Resistance. The tricolour was raised in the courtyard, Yves Bayet pronounced it independent of Vichy, and Vichy's prefect of the Seine and prefect of police were arrested.[52] Francis-Louis Closon of the Interior Ministry arrived with a new prefect of police, Charles Luizet, whom he had been chaperoning for the past six weeks. 'Below, in the vast central courtyard,' noted Closon, 'improvised cooks with tricolour armbands were roasting quarters of beef on enormous spits [. . .] On the top floor, shots were being fired on Germans who ventured onto the boulevard du Palais.'[53]

Away from the city centre, the town hall of the 17th *arrondissement* in the rue de Batignolles was occupied by FFIs, who ran up the tricolour and Allied flags to cheers from the crowd. A recruitment office was set up in the town hall and weapons requisitioned from a German garage and the local police station. A seventeen-year-old who claimed to be the youngest FFI in the 17th said that no more than 100–150 FFIs provided the core of fighters in the *arrondissement* on 19 August.[54] 'Barricades were being erected all round the town hall,' noted eyewitness M. Lassalle. 'Now the FFI are patrolling in cars requisitioned or even stolen from the Boches, on which they have painted Lorraine crosses and FFI in big letters. They are attacking all the Germans they find.'[55] FFIs drawn from the working-class 'Épinettes lads' in the 17th then moved down to seize the town hall of the more elegant 8th around the Parc Monceau, hoisted the tricolour, took the Marshal's picture out of its frame, and claimed power in the name of the local liberation committee.[56]

The French Committee of National Liberation in Algiers, now the provisional government, was not impressed by this anarchy. Fearing either a Paris Commune or a Warsaw bloodbath it appealed to the workers of Paris on 20 August, saying that 'disorder, looting and mindless destruction serve only to impoverish the nation and inflict additional suffering on the population. Maintaining order is in the general interest.' This immediately provoked conflict with the communists over the old question of immediate action versus *attentisme*, national insurrection or state power. The communist deputies for the Paris region, still in North Africa, pointed out that 'looting' was actually the seizure of German weapons, 'destruction' meant attacks on German bases, weapon stockpiles and prisons, and that the 'order' against which they were fighting was 'the Hitlérian order, the so-called New Order against which France is fighting a war'. The French National Committee, they insisted, would do better to encourage the national struggle of the people of Paris 'in the face of *attentiste* orders that are too often repeated by the radio of the provisional government'.[57]

Meanwhile, an attempt to organise a ceasefire was being mediated by the Swedish consul, Raoul Nordling, who went to see Governor von Choltitz on 19 August. Von Choltitz was torn between orders to fight to the last and increased terrorist activity and the imminent arrival of the Allies. His problem was to find partners on the French side that would impose such a ceasefire. A key mediator was Edgard Pisani, the 25-year-old head of the private office of the new prefect of police Charles Luizet. Pisani contacted Léo Hamon and told him that Nordling would see him at 7 a.m. the following morning, 20 August, to agree truce conditions. Hamon, effectively leader of the non-communists on the Paris Liberation Committee, was afraid of a communist seizure of power and equally worried that the Germans, while leaving the city, were capable of the most brutal atrocities, as in Warsaw.[58] He was keen to arrange a truce but not before the Resistance had secured one more building. At 5 a.m. on 20 August, with Yves Bayet and the socialist Henri Ribière, he led an assault on the Hôtel de Ville. Entering the main offices he went to the prefect's chair and declared: 'I am taking possession of this Hôtel de Ville in the name of the Paris Liberation Committee, of the provisional government and of the people of Paris.' Then, seeing a bust of Pétain, he ordered, 'Take away this bust which has no more place here.'[59]

The Hôtel de Ville in the right hands, Hamon went to see Nordling about the truce. They agreed to a text by which the German command would recognise the Resistance's possession of the public buildings they had occupied and would treat French prisoners under the laws of war, not as terrorists, in return for a ceasefire until the Germans had evacuated Paris. Not having a uniform, all FFI would wear armbands to show they were legitimate fighters who, if captured, would be treated as prisoners of war.[60] This truce now had to be sold to the National Council of Resistance, which was not a foregone conclusion. A meeting at 9 a.m. was dominated by Parodi, Chaban, Bidault and Ribière, who were in favour of the truce and Villon, who was against, but there were not enough present to make the meeting quorate. Another meeting was scheduled for the afternoon, but in the meantime Parodi was arrested by the Germans and brought before von Choltitz. The German commander was prepared to have him shot, since he had a copy of the insurrection order in his pocket, but Parodi declared that he was a minister of General de Gaulle and had unique authority to make a ceasefire hold.[61] He was released and arrived exhausted at the meeting of the National Council at 5 p.m., where National Military Delegate Chaban, returning from a mission to London for updated orders, reported that General Koenig was 'absolutely against street fighting in Paris. Moreover,' he continued, 'General Patton has no intention to change his plans in order to hasten the taking of Paris.'[62] It became clear that the Allies would not reach the capital soon enough to avoid a bloodbath if no truce was declared. Villon was still leading opposition to the truce in the name of the revolutionary honour of the people of Paris. Lecompte-Boinet observed that:

sometimes he smiled in commiseration when his adversaries were speaking, sometimes adopted a cold attitude, full of menace [. . .] He said in effect, 'It is not about the lives of 50,000 Parisians. It is about the people of Paris taking part in the victory. For my part, I would prefer to sacrifice 50,000 Parisians.'[63]

André Tollet, who was invited to the meeting as chair of the Paris Liberation Committee, saw the truce as no less than a stitch-up against communist insurrection between the Junker von Choltitz and the 'reactionary capitalist' Nordling, who was a major shareholder in the Swedish SKF ball-bearing company.

In the event a compromise was accepted whereby the truce would remain in place for twenty-four hours, giving time for the Allies to draw nearer; meanwhile posters calling for insurrection would not be put up in the streets. The next day, 21 August, on the Paris Liberation Committee, Hamon tried to defend the truce, saying that the Germans had requested it and the government endorsed it. In response Tollet demanded a 'union in the Resistance to fight on. The Germans have committed many crimes. We can have no confidence in them.'[64] The Paris Committee caved in and announced that the fight would continue. Rol-Tanguy asked Parodi to endorse the order to continue the insurrection, which he did, despite opposition from Chaban. Georges Marrane called for barricades to be built to prevent the circulation of tanks, as they had done successfully, made of felled trees, in the Corrèze, which had long been his base. He later noted that barricades went up only in the working-class neighbourhoods of Paris and the suburbs, proving that 'Paris has been liberated by the people.'[65] Tollet explained this in terms of the heritage of the people of Paris, for whom barricade-building was part of a revolutionary culture going back to the Commune of 1871 and the Revolutions of 1848 and 1789:

Barricades were being thrown up with fervour. The science of insurrection had been passed down between the generations. We were very close to the Faubourg Saint-Antoine. I remember an old upholsterer who, as he took tacks from his mouth, was humming Pottier's old song, 'L'insurgé, son vrai nom c'est l'homme'.[66]

In the 17th *arrondissement* FFI patrols on bicycles spread the news that the truce was broken. German soldiers began firing at windows from which tricolours were hanging. FFIs occupying the Batignolles town hall fanned out and seized several German lorries and two tanks: 'They have built such road blocks with overturned lorries and barricades with paving-stones and the wrought-iron grills from the foot of trees,' observed M. Lassalle, 'that the Germans cannot get near the Batignolles town hall.'[67] In the 8th *arrondissement*, an attack on the German barracks that had been resisted on 19 August, began again on the 22nd. An eyewitness, Lamontellerie, reported that:

Around 4.15, an attack was mounted by two FFI lorries armed with sub-machine guns, machine-guns and carbines [. . .] Contrary to expectation, the defence was weak. There were only a score of armed and determined men. There was a very lively exchange of fire. The charcutier, full-length in the gutter, gave free rein to his sub-machine gun, as in 1914. The FFI took the barracks. The Germans lost five men; the others were wounded or taken prisoner.[68]

Madeleine Riffaud, captured and tortured after killing a German NCO on 23 July, had been sentenced to death and should have been executed on 5 August. Instead, she was put aboard a deportation train that left Paris on 15 August. Miraculously, she and a British intelligence agent known as Anne-Marie were taken off the train and brought back to Fresnes prison. Then, under the truce negotiated by Nordling, they were released, and Madeleine rejoined the FFI. She was sent by Rol-Tanguy on 23 August, the day of her twentieth birthday, to lead a three-man grenade attack on a German train at the Belleville–La Villette bridge, which forced it to take refuge in the tunnel under the Buttes Chaumont, where it surrendered. Later, in fighting round the place de la République, she received an army commendation to the effect that, 'always at the head of her men and throughout the combat [she] gave a remarkable example of physical courage and moral fortitude'.[69]

Paris appeared to be in the grip of a popular revolution in the tradition of 1789 or 1871, but this was as far as the national insurrection got. It had been made possible by the Allies' bearing down on Paris, but the arrival of French and Allied forces also meant that any idea of a popular seizure of power was rapidly and unceremoniously eliminated from the agenda. It was not, in the end, a choice between national insurrection and Allied liberation.[70] Despite Rol-Tanguy's desire for the FFI to be the spearhead of the liberation of Paris before the Americans arrived, he was fully aware of the FFI's limited numbers and weaponry, and of the risk of a Paris insurrection being crushed by the Germans for lack of Allied support, as in Warsaw. On 18 August he therefore sent a member of his staff, Major Brécy, out of Paris to make contact with American forces under Bradley and Patton, which drove across the Seine north and south of Paris on 21 August. Unfortunately Brécy was killed when his vehicle was attacked by an American plane 30 miles south of the capital, at Étampes. A second mission by his chief of general staff, Major Cocteau-Gallois, crossed German lines and met up with Bradley and Leclerc on 22 August.[71] A parallel mission was headed by Raoul Nordling's brother Ralf, who set out in a car under the Swedish flag on 22 August to make contact with Generals Bradley and Patton.[72] That same day von Choltitz was given personal orders from Hitler to destroy Paris. He hesitated, preferring to become an American POW rather than face a war crimes tribunal, and the Allies, together with Leclerc's 2nd Armoured Division, swung towards Paris.[73]

De Gaulle was insistent that French forces should be the first into Paris to ensure its liberation: 'Any number of American divisions,' General Bradley considered wryly, 'could more easily have spearheaded our march into Paris. But to help the French recapture pride I chose a French force with the tricolour on their Shermans.'[74] Leclerc's division, moreover, had battled valiantly alongside Patton at Argentan earlier in the month. It arrived in the city outskirts on 23 August and reached the Paris prefecture around 9 p.m. on 24 August as church bells rang out to greet them. Lecompte-Boinet noted that:

The advanced guard of the Leclerc Division is on the square of the Hôtel de Ville. There is a huge to-do. A French captain, a real one, is almost carried in triumph and seems dumbstruck under the prefect's chandeliers. He is sunburned and bearded and has tears of joy in his eyes. Chad and the CNR have finally joined hands.[75]

The bearded captain was Captain Raymond Dronne, of the Régiment de Marche du Tchad, whose 9th Company was called 'la Nueve' because it was composed mainly of Spanish republicans; their half-track armoured cars bore inscriptions recalling Civil War battles: 'Guadalajara', 'Teruel', 'Ebro' and 'Madrid'. Communists were also prominent in the liberation of Paris. Colonel Fabien, who had been active in the insurrection in the 13th *arrondissement*, linked up with three tanks of Leclerc's forces to take possession of the Palais du Luxembourg, where the Senate usually sat, on 24 August.[76] Such details were soon forgotten as the moment was transformed into the Gaullist legend of Paris liberated by regular French forces. Not forgotten, by contrast, was the acclamation of the people of Paris, who poured into the streets to give voice to their pleasure and relief. Eyewitness M. Lassalle from the Parc Monceau confided in his diary that:

in spite of nightfall, the Parisians came to the Hôtel de Ville. They came out to express their joy. In the rue de Prony a huge red firework was lit and two verses of the 'Marseillaise' were sung by a wonderful voice. It was that of Marthe Chenal, reprising thirty years later her singing of the national anthem on the steps of the Opéra as she had in 1914.[77]

This was also the moment at which the internal and external resistance met physically for the first time.

Given the long and acrimonious conflict between national insurrection and state power, the ritual of coming together was highly charged. The National Council of Resistance and the Paris Liberation Committee met at 10.30 that evening and it was agreed that the Councils' charter would be given to de Gaulle as the blueprint for the new order. It went almost without saying that de Gaulle would proclaim the Republic, abolished in 1940, as in so many revolutions, from the balcony of the Hôtel de Ville. But when de Gaulle arrived the next day, Friday 25 August, he avoided the Hôtel de Ville and went first to the Préfecture de Police to meet the new prefect of police Luizet and Delegate-General Parodi, and high-ranking civil servants along with Georges Bidault, chair of the National Council. Lecompte-Boinet captured the silent and almost effortless hijacking of the revolution by the servants of the state:

There is a striking contrast between the dishevelled, enthusiastic and heroic FFIs in the courtyard of the Préfecture and the calculated prudence, composure and good manners of those who only have to sit down in the Louis XVI armchairs in order to come into their inheritance.[78]

Eventually, around 5 p.m., de Gaulle did go to the Hôtel de Ville where he was greeted by Bidault for the National Council and Marrane for the Paris Committee. Marrane, who was still on the revolutionary script, proclaimed that 'worthy of its noble traditions [Paris] has been liberated by the Forces Françaises de l'Intérieur, the *milices patriotiques* and the whole of its population, men, children, and old people'.[79] De Gaulle replied, initially mesmerising the communist group, according to Lecompte:

He is very pale and his features particularly drawn. [Auguste] Gillot and Villon are in the front row, drinking in the General's words as if they were listening to the gospel being read. It is the first time I have seen these communists moved and shedding the carapace the Party has given them to rediscover their humanity.[80]

Lecompte-Boinet was also gratified by 'the fusion of the two Resistances', but was quickly disillusioned when he learned de Gaulle had left down the stairs without proclaiming the

Republic. A rumour spread that he refused to do this because in his eyes the Republic had never been abolished, but at the same time he did not want to pose as a demagogic revolutionary. The National Council was hastily reconvened 'in an atmosphere of disappointment. Politics has come into its own again and I have to say that I too was shocked by the fact that this gesture was not made.'[81]

Meanwhile, Governor von Choltitz, presiding over the collapse of German power in the Hôtel Le Meurice, was asked if he was ready to sign a ceasefire by an Allied officer that afternoon of 25 August. Bundled into a car that took him to the Préfecture de Police, he was threatened by crowds and defended by a woman with a Red Cross armband: 'Madame, like Joan of Arc,' he told her. At the Préfecture de Police he was introduced to General Leclerc and signed a cease-fire order. He was then escorted by Leclerc in an armoured vehicle to the Gare Montparnasse where, his heart failing, he signed a document of surrender in the presence of General Bradley.[82] On behalf of the FFI, Colonel Rol-Tanguy insisted on adding his signature nearly an hour later.[83]

The next day, Saturday 26 August, de Gaulle headed the famous victory parade down the Champs-Élysées. This has been described as his 'apotheosis', a 'coronation' by the people who turned out in their tens of thousands.[84] The fight for precedence between the internal and external Resistance was already intense. There was no André Tollet for the Paris Committee but rather Le Troquer, the socialist minister of war from Algiers, who would become chair of the provisional municipal council in his place.[85] Lecompte-Boinet, as one of the representatives of the National Council, was 'concerned to stick close to de Gaulle and above all to process in front of the men from London. De Gaulle had Le Troquer on his right and Bidault on his left; I was just behind, next to Koenig and Leclerc.'[86] Hamon reflected that only four members of the National Council accompanied the General but, he reflected, 'this man has the heart of the people of Paris.'

The Council met again at the Hôtel de Ville and hoped that the General might reappear, but the General, thinking more of Church and nation, went to a service at Notre-Dame. Bidault was criticised for not having persuaded de Gaulle to declare the Republic but de Gaulle was now next to a king and Louis Saillant teased, paraphrasing Henri IV, 'the CNR is worth a mass.'[87]

The liberation of Paris was not the end of the liberation of France, nor of its people, so many of whom were still in camps and prisons in Germany. But it was the end of the dream of a national insurrection, which impinged on many French people both as a historic failing and in their private lives. Two odysseys pinpoint this: that of the so-called Schneider Column's race to sever the German retreat, and that of Marie-Hélène Lefaucheux to make contact with her husband in Buchenwald concentration camp.

After the liberation of the south-west of France, a plan was hatched to send a mobile force north-eastwards from the south-west to cut off the retreat of a German column of 25,000 men (under the command of Prussian General Botho Elster), which was moving towards Dijon, the Belfort gap and south Germany. If it got to Dijon it would threaten the left flank of French and Allied armies that were moving up north from Lyon. The mobile force was organised rapidly under the eyes of General Cochet. It represented the triumph of regular officers of the Armistice Army and the Army of Africa over the revolutionary cadres of the FFI. In order to achieve this, a special mission flown in from Algiers on 1 September composed of Maurice Chevance, alias 'Bertin', who had served in the Army of Africa until 1940 and become Frenay's right-hand man in Marseille; and Colonel Jean Schneider, who had fought in the Great War and then in the Army of Africa.[88] Selected for the mobile force were not the FFIs of a communist disposition but rather those of the old school that had fitted reluctantly into the FFI framework. These were the Pommiès Free Corps and a regiment from Mazamet and Castres under Dunoyer de Segonzac.

A force of 32,000 men was thrown together under reliable officers in a couple of days and loaded onto trains on 3 September. Schneider himself flew to Clermont-Ferrand on 4 September. Pommiès' and Segonzac's forces came together at La Palisse on 6–7 September and Autun on 7–8 September.[89] Elster's column had been harassed all the way by FFI forces, notably by the Brigade Charles Martel of Colonel Raymond Chomel, a former officer in the Armistice Army who had joined the ORA and was now an FFI commander in the Indre. SOE agent Pearl Witherington commanded the *maquis* of the Wheelwright network in the Gâtines Forest, under the orders of Chomel.[90] A battle took place for the control of Autun on 9–10 September and bridges across the Loire and Allier were cut to prevent the German column crossing them. General Elster and 18,000 troops were encircled and surrendered. Despite having been defeated by the French, Elster insisted on surrendering to a high-ranking Allied officer, preferably American, and at the surrender ceremony in Issoudun on 11 September the FFI commanders were not invited by the Americans to sign.[91] Thus the most tangible contribution of the FFIs to the liberation was not even registered in the annals.

The civilian population, meanwhile, was left to tie up the manifold threads of their own lives. Marie-Hélène Lefaucheux, who had returned from following the convoy taking her husband to Germany to serve with the Paris Liberation Committee, set off again on 27 August in a car lent by the Red Cross, catching up with the advance guard of the American Army at Troyes. She went to see a Gestapo officer in Metz, and explained that her husband had been arrested as a reserve officer and taken to Buchenwald, but that he was entirely innocent. Since the Germans were retreating and thinking of future outcomes, an order was issued entrusting her husband to the *Sicherheitsdienst* at Metz. Marie-Hélène paid an Italian entrepreneur who worked for the Germans to take her to Saarbrücken, passing lorries of retreating Germans, piled high with plunder. At Saarbrücken the Gestapo officer arrived and got in when he was told that there was cognac in the car. They passed through Frankfurt, Fulda and Weimar before arriving at Buchenwald on 3 September. The German went into the camp to negotiate and four hours later Marie-Hélène saw that:

the tall thin vagabond walking next to the Boche was actually my husband. He was wearing the coat my sister-in-law had managed to pass to him at Fresnes and a hat that fell over his nose because his head was shaved. When the car door opened I said, 'Hello, how are you?' And he found it quite natural to sit down next to his wife.

They left the Gestapo officer at Neustadt, where he rejoined his unit. When they got back to Paris Marie-Hélène rang Claire Girard, who had come with her on the initial voyage to the frontier after 15 August. Her mother, whom Claire had returned on 19 August to see, answered the phone and said that Claire, 'on whose tender gladness I counted on our return', had been shot by the Germans a week before in the Oise, while taking food to a *maquis*.[92]

Four forces converged in this story of the liberation of Paris: the Allied and French armies, the internal resistance and the people. They could not all come out on top but there were some surprises and some disappointments. De Gaulle extracted from the Allies that French forces would be the first into Paris and founded the myth that the French liberated themselves. The internal resistance was invited briefly to the reception and thanked but then marginalised as the Gaullist state-in-waiting slipped almost effortlessly into position. The people of France were there on cue to acclaim their liberators and fulsomely to provide the legitimacy that de Gaulle needed to persuade the Americans in particular that he must head the new state. But joy in liberation was only one emotion to be expressed by French people: along with the joy and often instead of it went pain, suffering and loss.

15

Afterlives

We have not finished paying for all this.

(Genia Gemähling, 1985)

On Sunday 27 August 1944 at 6 p.m., de Gaulle invited about twenty leaders of the Resistance in Paris to the War Ministry, where he had set up his headquarters. Maurice Kriegel-Valrimont, one of the leaders of the National Council's military committee (COMAC), was flabbergasted by the dismissive way in which the General treated those who had masterminded events over the past weeks:

He made a solemn entrance. The performance was of a military concision. He dismissed each officer with a, 'Good, next!' [. . .] Immediately it was about restoring order, then talk or rewards and decorations that he wants to confer as soon as possible [. . .] Suddenly he got up, made his thanks and left with a 'Goodbye, madame, goodbye, gentlemen.'[1]

The 'Madame' was Cécile, the wife and liaison officer of Colonel Rol-Tanguy. Rol had been asked what he did before the war. When he said that he had been in the International Brigades the General had merely said, 'Good!' and shaken his hand. Cécile had managed to procure a blue dress from a friend, Dédée, who was a sales assistant on the Champs-Élysées, and told the General that she had worked in the Resistance with her husband. She too was shocked by his attitude: 'Personally I did not find it very welcoming. It was a very small reception, without even a glass of wine to finish with.'[2]

For many French people the expulsion of the Germans and

the restoration of liberty was enough. The tyrant expelled, people came together to kiss the Allied soldiers who paraded through their towns, to dance in the streets, to participate in impromptu carnivals. Traitors were summarily shot and women who had slept with Germans were taunted by crowds and had their heads shaved. As de Gaulle said, only 'a handful of scoundrels' behaved badly under the German Occupation; the rest could look each other confidently in the eyes as patriots. Those who had fought in the Resistance, however, wanted something more: to sweep away the remains of Vichy and indeed of the Third Republic that had failed, and to bring in a brave new world of greater equality and fraternity. In the weeks and months following the Liberation conflicts were played out between activists in the internal Resistance, who wanted liberation to lead to revolution, and ambitious men around the provisional government in Algiers and London who wanted to restore order and authority.

One dimension of this conflict was the question of the French Army. Many FFI commanders of a left-wing persuasion saw the regular army as that which had failed to fight in 1940 and failed to resist in 1942. They imagined a new army, voluntary, democratic and patriotic, along the lines of the armed *sans-culottes* who had defeated the invading Prussian Army at the Battle of Valmy (1792) and were a force in the revolutionary armies of the Year II. Against them, more conservative commanders, many of whom had belonged to the Armistice Army or Army of Africa, wanted a rapid return to the conventional army, professional and hierarchical, that would drive the remains of the *Wehrmacht* back to Germany and reassert social order and French greatness.

It was decided as early as 29 August 1944 – two days after de Gaulle had received the leaders of the Paris uprising – that those elements of the FFIs who wished to fight on would be integrated into the First Army proper, while others would be free to go home. On 5 September troops paraded in Lyon before de Lattre de Tassigny, '*maquisards* mixed with the Army of Africa', as *commissaire de la République* Yves Farge described it.[3] Following the review, General de Lattre gave an interview to Madeleine Braun, who had worked with Georges Marrane in the Front National, for a Lyon newspaper. He was fully aware of the rival ambitions of different factions in the First Army that was now being assembled:

Some think they are qualified – uniquely qualified – to give France a new army, made in the image of the *maquis* [. . .] Some newspapers controlled by the FFI breathe a whiff of anti-militarism fanned by the rancour left by the defeat of 1940 and the failure to act in November 1942.[4]

De Lattre was of the opinion that, in the short term at least, concessions had to be made to the FFIs: 'It is indispensable that they keep their names, their mystique and the pride of their units,' he continued. 'The FFI boys can form additional units that will fight alongside our regular army.' In the longer term, however, these units would have to be absorbed into the regular army, whose commanders were bemused by the diversity and indiscipline of FFIs and their readiness to promote commanders very rapidly in the heat of battle:

The 'regular' army was 'proud of its turn-out, its discipline and its strength. As a general rule ranks had been dearly acquired and rewards were rare. The sense of duty was exceptionally strong and a deep fraternity in arms went closely with a respect for hierarchy [. . .] For the regiments that landed [in Provence], the extreme variety of FFI organisations, their highly original concept of discipline, the poverty of their equipment, the crying inadequacy of their weaponry, the ease with which they had awarded themselves higher ranks and the overtly political nature of many of their aspirations, clashed with the classic military views of many officers.[5]

De Gaulle, for his part, was also determined to restore order and hierarchy in the army as soon as possible, and to dress down those FFI commanders who had been promoted out of necessity when the French Army and the Allies had required effective forces behind German lines in the weeks before and after D-Day. Particularly in a city like Toulouse, which had gained a reputation as capital of the 'Red Republic', FFI leaders and the Resistance had to be put in their place. Landing at Blagnac airport on 16 September, de Gaulle was presented to Serge Ravanel, still only twenty-four years old. Ravanel was wearing the Croix de la Libération that d'Astier de la Vigerie had awarded him when he came to Toulouse as minister of the interior on 28 August. De Gaulle asked, 'Who authorised you to wear the Croix de la Libération?' and when Ravanel said, d'Astier, the General snapped, 'That's not true,' and ordered him to remove it. Ravanel then introduced his FFI officers to de Gaulle. Their hopes of recognition was soon dashed:

The officers felt desperately humiliated. They were not officers of the 'real' army. They had usurped their ranks. One remark said it all. 'What?' the head of state challenged Berthet-Deleule, 'You were a private in 1939 and now you are a lieutenant-colonel?' [...] In the stairwell, Captain Viltard, a pure hero of the Resistance, was in floods of tears.[6]

Another concern of de Gaulle was to reclaim the story of the Resistance for the French and the French alone. That the French had liberated themselves had to be asserted both against the Allies and against foreign anti-fascists who had contributed to the French Resistance. Colonel George Starr of the Armagnac Battalion was invited to the official lunch with de Gaulle, but *commissaire* Bertaux told him that he was not welcome. Summoned by de Gaulle that afternoon, he was asked what he was doing in Toulouse and said that he had organised FFI battalions in the region: 'You, a foreigner, have no right to form battalions,' shouted de Gaulle. 'You have done nothing!' Starr was ordered to leave Toulouse at once, but replied that he was responsible for Jedburgh teams and Allied missions that included French officers. 'Take them with you,' continued the General, 'they are traitors, mercenaries. Take them with you!'[7] Next morning there was a review of the FFI troops, among whom were Spanish republicans who were proud to march before de Gaulle, although they had no uniforms and wore German helmets repainted blue. Ignorant of the international dimension of the Resistance, de Gaulle asked Ravanel, 'Why have these Spaniards come to bother us, marching with the FFIs?'[8]

The balance of power had shifted. The moment of insurrection was over, and military hierarchy and professionalism were now back in the saddle. The army was to be a French army, not mixed up with unreliable foreign elements. Ravanel later reflected on his change of fortune:

I was a subordinate and when I asked a question I was told that it was not my business. Little guy on the block, I was not concerned. The big boys were there to decide. 'I will send you a general who will take command. You will return to the ranks.'[9]

The general sent to command the 17th military region at Toulouse was Algerian-born Philibert Collet, who had made a reputation in the 1920s putting down the Druzes in Syria and had come over to the Free French in Syria in 1941. Ravanel left for Paris and was seriously hurt in a car accident on 20 September. He was officially awarded his Croix de la Libération on 14 July 1945, but he concluded that at Toulouse de Gaulle 'had wanted to make an example. No doubt because the Resistance there was well organised, active and dynamic. In fact he wanted to emasculate the Resistance as a whole.'[10]

Soldiers reacted in very different ways to the shift from a revolutionary to a traditional army. When de Lattre's army arrived in France, soldiers who had belonged to the Armistice Army and had been stood down in November 1942, but had not joined the *maquis*, now re-emerged to join what they saw as the regular army. One of these was Jean Le Châtelier, who had remained in an army desk job in Grenoble and had three children during the war. In the spring of 1944 he cycled up to the Vercors to offer intelligence, but quarrelled with the *maquis* commander who demanded he leave his family and refused to recognise his official rank. He was relieved when de Lattre's army came through Grenoble: 'When I saw troops arriving that were organised traditionally, with regiments, battalions, companies, officers and comrades whom I knew at least in part, I said to myself, "At last!"' In 1946, at the general staff college, he found himself in the same promotion as three former *maquisards*, including 'the famous colonel [Ravanel] from Toulouse'. On one occasion Ravanel asked him to fetch his pipe from his bedroom and he was scandalised to find 'a book, which when I looked, turned out to be Karl Marx's *Capital!*'[11] Le Châtelier went on to have a distinguished military career in the regular army, endeavouring to re-impose French greatness in the colonies, first in Indochina, then in Algeria.

Some individuals joined up because it seemed to be the best way of covering the tracks of dubious behaviour under the Occupation. Roland Farjon, who had been a key figure in the Organisation Civile et Militaire (OCM), had been arrested by the Gestapo in 1943 and was thought to have betrayed a number of his comrades. He escaped from prison just before D-Day with what appeared like help from a sympathetic German. He reinvented himself as a resister, fighting as an FFI captain under Maurice Clavel, who liberated Chartres.[12] He entered Paris and took part in the victory parade in front of de Gaulle and Churchill on 11 November 1944. He volunteered for the 1st Regiment of Fusiliers Marins, which fought in Alsace and was then sent to the Alps. He was wounded on 1 April 1945 and recommended for the Croix de Guerre.[13] Within a month or two, however, Farjon's shady past would be revealed.

Very different was the experience of Claude Monod, a 28-year-old surgeon in Paris who had worked with Défense de la France, became an FFI chief in Burgundy and was involved in the liberation of Châtillon-sur-Seine north of Dijon. He signed up for the First Army and did two months at an officers' training school in the Nièvre. He nevertheless retained a powerful nostalgia for the FFIs who, in a revolutionary tradition, had made up for the disaster of 1940. He reported that:

The FFIs really embody the *levée en masse* of the French people against the invader. Anyone who spent only a few days in the *maquis* could not but be struck by the energy, enthusiasm and combative spirit of these men [. . .] They had exactly what the French Army lacked in 1940: the will to fight, faith in victory, a clear sense of what they were fighting for, and total devotion to their country.[14]

At the training school, Monod was concerned that the commanders of the First Army wanted to break up the FFI units and award promotion for long service rather than for talent and charisma. He wrote to an officer who had been in an FFI *maquis* in the Jura on the blinding differences which oppose the FFI and the Army of Africa: 'We are in 1944, yet paradoxically we have been brought back to the century of Louis XIV: the *Armée du Roy*, an army of mercenaries, is fighting on the marches of the kingdom and the country does not give a damn.'[15] Monod continued the patriotic fight beyond the marches of the kingdom until he was killed at Graben in southern Germany on 2 April 1945.

Many FFIs accepted the offer to demobilise and go home. They had been involved in resistance movements whose profile, mainly communist and immigrant, bore no resemblance to that of the new army. Often they were exhausted by years of living underground, avoiding arrest and deportation, and wanted only to return to some kind of normal life. Max Weinstein, who had taken part in the Villeurbanne insurrection as one of the Union of Jewish Youth (UJJ), initially joined the 1st Rhône Regiment, which was composed 'essentially of resisters'. It had a Jewish company, of which he was secretary, as some of the older Jews of foreign origin could only speak Yiddish, and he attended a training course for NCOs. However, the regiment was soon reorganised as part of the regular army under officers who were 'Pétainists or had lain low', rechristened the 127th Alpine Land Forces and sent to the Alpine front. Max decided not to follow them. He returned to the elevator factory where he had been working, collected four months' back pay, and blew it all with his friends on a meal in a black market restaurant. He then discovered that since he was under eighteen he would get a premium of 3,000 francs if he left the army, so he did, training for work in the radio industry and joining the Communist Party.[16]

Other FFIs, on the other hand, were keen to volunteer for the army proper and to finish the job of driving Germans out of France. Despite the good intentions of de Gaulle and de Lattre, the re-professionalisation of the French Army was slow in coming. Colonel Fabien threw together a 'Paris battalion' or 'Paris regiment' from his FFIs and set off for the frontier with a flag donated by the Paris Liberation Committee but very little in the way of vehicles, equipment, uniforms or even helmets. They were cold-shouldered by the French First Army, which wanted nothing to do with these Bolshevik ragamuffins, but were placed under the command of the US V Corps, which used them to secure their rear as they advanced on Germany.[17] They were accompanied by two Polish infantry units, together 3,000-strong, who were kitted out in American uniforms, carried Allied weapons and wore an armband inscribed 'Allied Expeditionary Forces'. That said, many pledged allegiance to the Lublin government in Nazi-free Poland, which was loyal to Moscow rather than to the Polish government-in-exile in London. They included Jan Gerhard, who had commanded the Brigade Marcel Langer in Toulouse and then a *maquis* in the Meuse, and Ignaz (Roman) Krakus, one of the leaders of Brigade Carmagnole in Lyon.[18]

These forces, however variegated, were crucial to the French military effort. In the autumn of 1944, as the armies approached the German border in the Vosges and Alsace, it became clear that the black forces of the Army of Africa would find it hard to weather the continental winter. In addition, the US command, which had black troops but also operated a segregation policy, was hostile to the use of African soldiers in Allied armies. The result was the so-called *blanchiment* or 'whitening' of the French Army. It had the secondary effect of providing more equipment to the likes of Fabien's men and integrating them into the command structure of the French Army. This usually occurred behind the lines but might also happen at the front: 'We watched an extraordinary sight,' said de Lattre, 'that even went on shell holes a few hundred metres from the enemy. Boys came to take the place of the Senegalese, acquiring greatcoats, helmets, weapons and orders all at the same time.'[19]

Parallel to this process was another, to remove women in the military from the frontline. Madeleine Riffaud had commanded the FFI Saint-Just company in the liberation of Paris, but she was not allowed to join the regular army: 'Not only are you not of adult age,' said the commanding officer, 'but you don't have your father's permission and you are spitting blood into your handkerchief,' since she had not recovered fully from TB.[20] The case of one of the few women to see action in the French Army came to light only in 1984. Colette Nirouet, also known as Evelyne, had fought with *maquisards* in the Auvergne and had then joined the 152nd Infantry Regiment as a nurse. Desperate to go to the front, she persuaded her commanding officer on 29 October 1944 to issue her with a khaki uniform and machine-gun. On 10 November female personnel were ordered to the rear but she refused to comply. On 26 November, in the Oberwald, she tried to persuade a German unit to surrender, telling them in German that they would be treated as POWs: 'She advanced, upright, towards the enemy post. The answer came, sudden and unexpected: a short crack of gunfire in the silence. Without a sound, Evelyne collapsed among the dead leaves and broken branches.'[21]

Shortly afterwards, the epic of Colonel Fabien and his men came to an end. General Béthouart, who had preferred the Army of Africa to following de Gaulle in 1940, was given command of

Fabien's Paris regiment in December 1944. Rather to his surprise he found in Fabien 'an intelligent, energetic man with real authority as a commander. His men have a magnificent enthusiasm.' That said, when he visited them on 15 December, he detected a 'lack of experience, naturally, but also a lack of organisation. I saw a young woman typing in a shell hole.' He also noted that 'Fabien had retained an immoderate love of explosives from his past.'[22] On 27 December Fabien and a number of his command were testing an anti-tank mine for use against the Germans. It blew up, killing Fabien, four other officers and a secretary. Rumours spread in the regiment that the mine had been booby-trapped and that this was an assassination. Debate has raged about whether this was truly an accident or whether some in the traditional army were happy to see the end of this alternative model of a French army. In any case, Fabien's regiment was renamed the 151st, after that once commanded by de Lattre at Metz. This was a tribute, but also the end of an era. The funeral of Colonel Fabien and two of the other officers killed with him was held in Paris on 3 January 1945, in the pouring rain.[23]

The army was one body in which the struggle was played out between those who wanted a return to order and normality, and those who looked to more revolutionary solutions. Another was the world of politics. Many in the Resistance imagined that after years of struggle and inspired by manifestoes such as the programme of the National Council of Resistance, France would become a fairer and more equal society. They hoped resistance movements would transmute fairly easily into political movements that would act as forces for these changes. However, they failed to recognise two factors: first, that the only ambition of de Gaulle was to strengthen the state and to secure his leadership role within it; and second, that the political parties (which had failed lamentably in 1940 but had regained a foothold in the National Council and even more in the Provisional Consultative Assembly, which decamped from Algiers to Paris after the Liberation), intended to resume business as usual and to defeat any challenge by resistance movements.

An early inkling of this was experienced by Jacques Lecompte-Boinet who, as a member of the National Council of Resistance, attended the same meeting at the War Ministry on 27 August 1944 as Maurice Kriegel and the Rol-Tanguys. He described how de Gaulle pulled up the drawbridge separating the internal Resistance, whose job he considered finished, and the external Resistance, which now took over the reins of government. The General, he discovered, claimed a new source of legitimacy – the Nation – which he mobilised against the minority of active resisters:

We are in a fortress, the fortress of Gaullism outside France. It is a Troy with no way in for our horse. [De Gaulle] thanks us and advises us to be calm and reasonable, advice that is more like an order. Our spokesman, Bidault, is very intimidated.[24]

The only delegate who felt able to speak was the communist Villon, who asked whether de Gaulle had approved the truce of 20 August, and when he would permit their leader Maurice Thorez, still in Moscow, to return to France: 'The General, clearly exasperated, got up. "I hope to see you soon, gentlemen." The schism between the two Frances, the two new Frances was complete.'[25] At the National Council meeting on 29 August Bidault reported that de Gaulle was not interested in their programme: 'I talk to him of "Resistance". He answers, "Nation". He believes he is the Nation incarnate.'[26]

This schism was equally evident in de Gaulle's dealings with the Paris Liberation Committee. It was dominated by the communists and chaired by André Tollet, a communist himself and head of the trade-union movement in Paris. De Gaulle could not abide the prospect of giving the Croix de la Libération to Paris while Tollet was chair. So the committee was enlarged as a provisional municipal council by two-fifths, including the likes of medical professor Robert Debré, the father of Michel Debré, and a canon of the church of Saint-Germain-des-Prés. Léo Hamon, architect of the truce of 20 August, manoeuvred to secure a new chair, André Le Troquer, the former socialist deputy who had been *commissaire* for war in Algiers. Paris was duly awarded the Croix de la Libération.[27] A knife was turned in the wound when Gaston Palewski, head of de Gaulle's private office, made a speech suggesting that Parisians had taken advantage of the insurrection in August 1944 to loot and pillage. Tollet replied forcefully that the honour of the people of Paris had been impugned and drew comparisons with the suppression of the Commune in 1871:

Indignation is not enough in the face of so many insults hostile to the people and to the French. The people of Paris must call for an apology. If they could have their say they would spew up this imitator of Thiers, who also insulted the Parisians.[28]

De Gaulle set his cards squarely on the table when he formed his provisional government on 10 September. The internal resistance was not gratified with places, although Henri Frenay, who became minister for Prisoners, Deportees and Refugees, claimed that five members of Combat's organisation committee were in the government.[29] That said, they had long since gone their separate ways, not least as a result of the row over his approach to Pierre Pucheu in 1942. His rival Emmanuel d'Astier, who had been *commissaire* for the Interior, heard on the radio while he was on tour in Toulouse, that he had been sacked. He was offered the embassy in Washington by de Gaulle, fobbed off with the explanation that in a few months he would be ready for the Foreign Office, but turned it down.[30] The Foreign Office went to Georges Bidault, who had been chair of the National Council and was thus a bridge to the Resistance but while politically astute was not seen as a threat by de Gaulle. Lecompte-Boinet thought that people would be disappointed when they discovered that 'this famous Resistance leader was now only the beadle'.[31]

Philippe Viannay, leader of Défense de la France, had met de Gaulle at Rambouillet in July 1944 and sincerely believed that he was in line for ministerial office: 'France is ripe for all kinds of change,' he had said. 'France has a valiant elite that has emerged spontaneously and is ready to become involved again.' In reply, de Gaulle said caustically, 'France is not a country that is beginning. It is a country that is continuing.'[32]

Given their role in the Resistance and support for him since 1943, de Gaulle was obliged to have two communists in his government. That said, he would not accept Pierre Villon because of his vociferous opposition to the truce, and Maurice Thorez was not allowed back to France until 27 November, after he had approved the dissolution of the *milices patriotiques*, seen as a dangerous manifestation of the people in arms. Fernand Grenier as air *commissaire* had argued with de Gaulle about the failure adequately to arm the Vercors, and was replaced by FTP leader Charles Tillon, who was divided by his resistance activism from party bosses Thorez and Duclos. François Billoux, who had been minister of state in Algiers, became the second communist minister, at Public Health. They were heavily outvoted over the dissolution of the *milices patriotiques* and were kept well contained by trade unionists and SFIO stalwarts Robert Lacoste at Industrial Production and – when he returned from the camps – Christian Pineau at Food.

The backbone of de Gaulle's government was composed of the Free French who had already provided service in London and Algiers. These included René Pleven, who had masterminded the Brazzaville conference and became colonial secretary, then finance minister. He saw off Pierre Mendès-France, who had been impressed by Keynes at Bretton Woods and wanted to step up monetary controls, nationalisation and economic planning in ways that were considered far too radical. The Free French core also included Jacques Soustelle as minister of Information, the same job he had done in Algiers, René Capitant, the leader of Combat in North Africa, at Education, and the faithful General Catroux as minister for North Africa. Another element was provided by members of the Comité Générale d'Études (CGE), which had seen to the peaceful transfer of power from Vichy to the Republic, while avoiding both an AMGOT and an insurrection by appointing to key posts in the administration and judiciary. These included Robert Lacoste but above all the jurists Alexandre Parodi, who had been head of the Délégation Générale and became minister of Labour and Social Security, and François de Menthon who became minister of Justice with responsibility for ensuring that the purging of traitors was legally organised. He was replaced when he became a prosecutor at the Nuremberg trial in June 1945 by his colleague from Liberté, the information minister Pierre-Henri Teitgen.[33]

One of the key functions of the Comité Général d'Études was the appointment of *commissaires de la République*, who replaced Vichy's regional prefects in order to oversee a peaceful transition of power in the provinces. They were proconsuls with far-reaching powers to deal with pressing problems of food supply, the punishment of collaborators and restoring order. These included Raymond Aubrac in Marseille, Yves Farge in Lyon, Henri Ingrand in Clermont-Ferrand, Francis-Louis Closon in Lille and Michel Debré, a member of the Conseil d'État and the CGE, in Angers. The *commissaires* had to deal on the one hand with collaborators, who were often being punished summarily by FFIs and other vigilantes, by putting into place Cours de Justice that would undertake this legally. On the other hand they had to deal with the liberation committees that had sprung up in towns and departments and were competing for power with mayors and prefects. Composed of representatives of resistance organisations, political parties, trade unions and women's organisations, they filled a role that had been vacated by the *conseils généraux*, which had been replaced by Vichy's appointed *conseils départementaux*. In general, relations between Departmental Liberation

Committees and prefects was good, but in a minority of cases there was strain, if not conflict.[34] To assert their continuing role, these committees held a series of congresses in the autumn of 1944 to demand far-reaching reforms along the lines of the charter of the National Council of Resistance. The first, on 5 September 1944, met symbolically at the château of Vizille, where delegates of the three Ancien Regime orders – clergy, nobles and Third Estate – had met in July 1788, the mythic beginning of the French Revolution. These were followed by other meetings at Valence on 22 September and the so-called Estates General of French Renaissance at Avignon on 7–8 October. De Gaulle was invited to attend but refused, since he could not accept the Resistance as a 'constituted body'.[35]

Commissaires came from different backgrounds and saw their responsibilities in different ways. Those who had been involved in the Comité Générale d'Études regarded their main task as restoring order and averting any revolutionary threat. In Lille, Francis-Louis Closon built a bridge to the cardinal-archbishop and vied with the communists and socialists who dominated the liberation committees in the Nord and Pas-de-Calais and who looked to the Estates General as a way of knocking down new Bastilles, such as the employers.[36] At Angers, Debré recycled officials from Vichy who were prepared to rally to the new regime, made peace with local bishops and in Nantes was able to balance communists by encouraging socialists, Christian democrats and indeed conservatives.[36] In other areas, by contrast, *commissaires* were more inclined to negotiate with radical forces. In Lyon, Yves Farge was sympathetic to the *cahiers* drawn up by the CDL in advance of the Estates General, echoing 1789, as evidence that 'in the silence of oppression a whole people had meditated on the country's destiny [. . .] There are noble perspectives, a keen will to work and a deep sense of the realities confronting us.'[38] In Marseilles, which reverted to chaos at the Liberation, Raymond Aubrac made an alliance with the Communist Party and CGT trade unions to keep order, deal with collaborationists and take much of the local economy into public ownership. But he was vigorously opposed by the socialists under Gaston Defferre, who controlled the town hall, considered Marseille their fief and appealed to de Gaulle to have Aubrac recalled in January 1945.[39]

As provincial France returned to business as usual the experiment of the *commissaires de la République* came to an end. The four or five prefects they supervised in each region demanded their own autonomy, as did a whole range of local departments. Elections in 1945 brought back municipal councils, *conseils généraux* and parliamentary deputies, each of whom wanted to control their own fiefs, from communists in the Nord-Pas-de-Calais to Catholics in the west of France. Prefects and deputies soon began working hand in glove, as they had under the Third Republic, in pursuit of patronage, jobs, contracts and subsidies.[40] Frustrated by the erosion of his power, Yves Farge resigned in August 1945 in order to stand in the elections to the Constituent Assembly. Henri Ingrand protested vigorously the following month and resigned not long afterwards. Michel Debré had already accepted an invitation from de Gaulle in April 1945 to oversee a reform of the public administration. This would involve the creation of the École Nationale d'Administration to train future servants of the state, which he envisaged being run by a 'republican monarch' like de Gaulle.[41]

This fundamental conflict between the state, which remained powerfully in place at the Liberation, and the forces of democracy and change, was sharply expressed by the communist Pierre Hervé in his 1945 book on *The Liberation Betrayed*:

It was said that there were two powers in France. There was the metropolitan Resistance and its *comités de libération* that was up against the civil and military apparatus imported onto French soil from London and Algiers [. . .] Conflict was inevitable between the democratic and revolutionary aspirations expressed in the charter of the National Council of Resistance and the authoritarian, clerical and conservative tendencies that held sway in ministerial offices.[42]

The conflict between these two visions now shifted from the organisation of the bureaucracy to local and national elections. One of the aims of the liberation committees was to organise common Resistance lists for forthcoming elections. After they disappeared from the scene, this campaign was taken up by resistance movements that were keen to transform themselves into a political force. Most important here was the Mouvement de Libération Nationale (MLN), which grouped together all non-communist resistance movements and claimed a membership of 2 million, and the communist-led Front National (FN), which claimed 500,000 members.[43] Denise Domenach was chosen to represent young people on the CDL in Lyon, and then sent to Paris by the MLN to take part in youth debates there. She recalls the rise and fall of a moment of great hope from both political and personal perspectives:

Our hearts and eyes were full of love. We spoke at congresses and wrote in the papers. We felt invested with great power and with my comrades I had a huge desire to transform life. We were going to change the world. But it did not last long. By the end of December 1944 that MLN had no more money to pay us and my parents were ringing the alarm for me to come back to Lyon to continue my studies and my life as a proper young woman.[44]

Some leading resisters on the left hoped for a merger of the MLN and FN that would form a progressive union, a great party of the Resistance. Among them were members of Libération who had either always been close to the communists, such as Pierre Hervé or Maurice Kriegel-Valrimont, or had been seduced by them later, such as Emmanuel d'Astier. Hervé, for example, believed that 'a powerful movement lifting the whole people' might be translated into a 'humanist or liberal socialism, labour and western' that would also be inspired by 'the Soviet people that is battling heroically today to make socialism more than an abstract concept'.[45] Other resisters, by contrast, feared the ambition of the communists and those they called the 'cryptos' to penetrate and control such a party. They included leaders of Franc-Tireur such as Antoine Avinin and Jean-Pierre Lévy, intellectuals of Défense de la France such as Robert, Salmon and Combat heavyweight Henri Frenay.[46] After passionate debates at a congress at La Mutualité in Paris in January 1945, the opponents of the merger won majorities. The road was in principle open for a French-style Labour party, but it was already too late. Municipal elections had been called for April and May and the political parties, both old and new, seized the moment to dictate political terms.

On the centre-right, a new party was set up by resisters of a Christian Democratic persuasion. This was the Mouvement Républicain Populaire (MRP), which was conceived by the likes of Georges Bidault, Maurice Schumann, François de Menthon and Pierre-Henri Teitgen. Given the discredit into which conservatives associated with Vichy had fallen, it tended to attract votes from the Right, from supporters who were strongly anti-communist and indeed anti-socialist: 'We are building the MRP with women and priests,' Bidault admitted.[47] It was also attractive to de Gaulle before he left power in January 1946 and in 1947 founded his own party, the Rassemblement du Peuple Français (RPF), and was a very successful machine for creating ministers.

Socialists had attempted to reform under the Occupation as the Libé-Nord of Henri Ribière and as the Comité d'Action Socialiste, led by Daniel Mayer. But the idea of a humanist socialism embodied by Léon Blum on his return from deportation was contested by Guy Mollet, who had been involved to a small extent in the OCM but was above all a machine politician. He believed that the SFIO had to compete as a Marxist party of the working class with the Communist Party and beat Mayer to the secretary-generalship of the SFIO in August 1946.[48] This combination of opportunism and ideology drove away resisters who wanted far more from politics. Robert Salmon, formerly of Défense de la France, criticised:

something unbearable, intolerable. The atmosphere of meanness, envy, spinelessness in congresses and sections [. . .] To make a career there you had to have the soul of a demagogue and hypocrite that I could not manage.[49]

This did not prevent Salmon from pursuing a brilliant career after the Liberation. He was briefly a deputy in the Constituent Assembly and a Paris municipal councillor. He went into journalism, transforming *Défense de la France* into the popular daily *France Soir*, which sold a million copies in 1953. Doing well, he looked back favourably on the period, saying, 'We never laughed as much as in the Resistance.'[50]

In one way more favourable to the Resistance but in another suspicious of it was the Communist Party, which, when elections were held, turned out to be the largest party at the Liberation. It claimed to be the leading party of the Resistance, with 75,000 of its members shot by Vichy or the Germans. But the Party's links to the Resistance had always been indirect, through organisations such as the Front National and FTP, while Thorez was in Moscow and Duclos in hiding in France. Moreover, it had to answer for the two years it had spent under the Nazi-Soviet Pact, formally in alliance with Hitler. That said, its kudos as the party of resistance heroes, basking in the light of the Soviet Union's role in defeating Nazi Germany, attracted resisters and intellectuals to it. Emmanuel d'Astier was persuaded to stand as a communist in elections to the Constituent Assembly in the seemingly unwinnable conservative constituency of Ille-et-Vilaine. He was accompanied by Pierre Hervé when he addressed railway workers at Rennes station. Rumblings of discontent about his aristocratic background were met by the riposte of one of his team: 'Don't forget that Lenin was noble and so was Mirabeau.'[51] But as Claude Bourdet noted, the Communist Party bosses always controlled an agenda that had little to do with the Resistance: 'The PCF led its resisters to the Rubicon,' he said, 'to go fishing.'[52]

The liberation of France has to be seen in transnational and international perspective. Foreigners who had fought in the French Resistance were fighting for the liberation of France, and for many the experience of fighting in that resistance deepened their French identity. At the same time, however, the liberation of France was only a prelude to the liberation of their own homeland. Thus Spanish republicans wanted to return to liberate Spain from Franco, German anti-fascists wanted to establish a free Germany, and Zionist Jews wanted to go to Palestine and establish an independent Jewish state. Unfortunately, international politics and diplomacy fought out between the Allies did not always afford these resisters the liberation they craved.

Some Jews of foreign origin were entirely assimilated and had become even more French as a result of their careers in the Resistance. Léo Hamon, who had been born in Paris to Russian-Polish parents, had played a leading role in the liberation of Paris, and by negotiating the truce of 20 August, prevented it from falling into the hands of the communists. He decided to keep the French name he had adopted rather than going back to Goldenberg: 'I am not a Jew as a noun whose French nationality is described by an adjective describing a non-essential. I am a Frenchman to whom the adjective "Jewish" applies, alongside other adjectives.'[53] He was appointed to the Provisional Consultative Assembly, was elected to the Paris municipal council in May 1945 on a Resistance list, and was then elected to Conseil de la République or the upper house for the MRP. Continuing his career in the law, both practising and academic, he had a prominent political career in the Fourth and Fifth Republics.

Many young Jews of the *génération du rafle* had been raised in France but brought closer to the reality of their Jewishness by persecution and the deportation of members of their family. They had fought in the Resistance as 'the war within the war'. Once the country was liberated, however, they wanted to return to Paris to resume interrupted studies and careers and integrate fully into French society. Oscar Rosowsky, the young forger of Le

Chambon-sur-Lignon, went to Paris to begin the medical studies that Vichy had prevented him doing. His father did not return from the camps but his mother reopened her fashion shop. He married a fellow Jewish student and once qualified as a doctor he dedicated himself to working-class families who had greater access to medical care thanks to the new Social Security regime.[54] For many Jews of immigrant origin the Communist Party was a powerful vehicle of integration into French society. After the liberation the MOI and its affiliated organisations were abolished and merged into organisations that made no distinction between French and foreigners, such as the Union des Femmes Françaises and the Union de la Jeunesse Républicaine de France. Max Weinstein became secretary of the communist section in the 1st *arrondissement* of Paris and for a long time was perfectly happy to let his Jewish identity be eclipsed by his French one.[55]

For other resisters of foreign origin, the happy end was not reached at the liberation of Paris or even by the entry of French forces into German territory. After the liberation of Toulouse Spanish republicans from a range of parties and unions gathered there in great numbers, holding meetings, publishing newspapers and talking openly of invading Spain to reverse the defeat they had suffered in 1939. They would foment national insurrection and promote the guerrilla warfare that they had perfected in France in order to bring down the Franco regime. Spanish republicans who had fought in the FFIs were directed to the Pyrenean frontier and exploratory missions were made into Spain to test the insurrectionary pulse of the people. Unluckily for them, the Franco regime had intelligence of the attack, furnished not least by French and Allied authorities, who were opposed to this attempt to reopen the Spanish Civil War and encourage communism. The British and Americans exerted great pressure on the French not to let the situation get out of hand and the French government set up a regional military command to deal with it.[56] In Spain, despite a wave of strikes in late September 1944, there was no mood for insurrection. Within Spanish republican ranks there were also differences between the military commanders of the invasion, notably Colonel López Tovar, and the political leadership of the Agrupación de los Guerrilleros Españoles, which was very much controlled by the Spanish Communist Party. On 19 October 1944 López Tovar led an attack by about 2,500 men through the Val d'Aran. The Spanish republican flag was raised in a number of towns and villages but the Francoist regime was ready for them and the invaders were captured or beaten back by 29 October. Scores were executed or imprisoned for long years.[57] Those who managed to get back to France were persecuted after 1950 when the Franco regime was fully integrated into the Western camp as a player in the Cold War, Spanish republican activities in France were closed down and 150 activists were arrested. López Tovar, who had been awarded the Legion of Honour in 1946, was placed under house arrest and was unable to work. He complained that he received no help from the French Communist Party: 'the only people who helped me were not in the Party.'[58]

German anti-fascists had been active in the French Resistance through groups affiliated to the MOI and various *maquis*. Highly significant too was the Comité Allemagne Libre (CALPO), the French antenna of the Freies Deutschland organisation set up in Moscow in July 1943 to induce desertions from the *Wehrmacht* to anti-Nazi resistance movements. Russian POWs who had been drafted into the *Wehrmacht* were particularly good targets and on 5 September 1944 Ukrainians fighting with the French Resistance helped liberate Pontarlier in the Jura.[59] Members of the CALPO were also active encouraging desertions from the Pockets along the Atlantic coast such as Saint-Nazaire, Lorient and Royan, where German troops, isolated by the retreat, were still holed up. They entered POW camps around Toulouse and Limoges to negotiate the liberation of German anti-fascists and identify Nazi war criminals to the French authorities.[60] On 13 November 1944 the first public meeting of the CALPO was held in Paris, under its president, Otto Niebergall, attended by Pierre Villon for the Front National, Pascal Copeau for the MLN and Père Chaillet of *Témoignage Chrétien*.[61] Niebergall wrote to the French Ministry of War to suggest sending former FFIs into Germany to recruit partisans from POW camps, foreign workers and the civilian population in order to establish 'veritable *maquis*' to undertake 'direct action against the Nazi war machine', leading to the establishment of a free and independent Germany.[62] The Allies, however, did not want the work of regular armies in Germany to be challenged by partisan warfare and were imposing zones of occupation that would later be concretised in the country's division. Links to the CALPO were rapidly closed down.

Anti-fascist resisters, both Jewish and non-Jewish, who had fled to France from persecution in Central and Eastern Europe in the 1930s, returned to their countries now liberated from Nazism in order to help build a brave new socialist world. Niebergall went back to the Sarre, which was now under French occupation, and began work again for the German Communist Party (KPD). In the new German Democratic Republic (GDR) returning anti-fascists were promoted to leading positions in the Communist Party and to the army, police, administration and universities it controlled. Franz Dahlem, who had headed the underground KPD in France and ran Travail Allemand from prison before being deported to Mauthausen, became a politbureau member of the Socialist Unity Party that combined communists and socialists.[63] Anti-fascists also reached influential positions in other Peoples' Democracies. Artur London returned to Czechoslovakia and was appointed deputy minister of foreign affairs in 1948. Louis Gronowski, one of the Polish-Jewish leaders of the FTP-MOI, went back to Poland in 1948 to pay homage at the remains of the Warsaw Ghetto, and definitively in 1949.[64] Boris Holban, who had been Manouchian's predecessor in the Paris FTP-MOI, and Mihail Florescu, who had fought in the south-west alongside López Tovar, returned to Romania to pursue careers in the army.[65]

The integration of these former resisters into brave new worlds did not always go according to plan. At the onset of the Cold War strife broke out in many communist parties between the 'Muscovites' who had weathered the war in Moscow and were seen to be faithful to the Stalinist order, and those who had fought in the international anti-fascist movement in Spain, France, Italy or Yugoslavia and came to be seen as Titoists, Zionists or US spies. One of Gronowsky's comrades was tried in Hungary with Lazlo Rajk, who was hanged in 1949. Artur London was sent for trial with Rudolf Slansky in November 1952; Slansky was hanged while London was sentenced to life imprisonment but released in 1955.[66] In East Germany former members of the International Brigades fell under suspicion. Franz Dahlem was expelled from the politbureau of the Socialist Unity Party and would have been tried if the GDR had orchestrated a show trial.[67] In Poland, Ignaz Krakus ('Roman') was dismissed from the army and unable to find alternative work except in an engineering factory. Further difficulties came with the wave of officially sponsored anti-Semitism that swept through the Eastern Bloc during the 1967 Six Day War between Israel and the Arab states. It was particularly harsh in Poland, where Gronowski called it a 'dry pogrom'.[68] He left Poland permanently for France in August 1968. Krakus left in 1969 and found work in a nylon factory on the French-Belgian border until his death the following year.[69] Jan Gerhard was murdered in his Warsaw flat in mysterious circumstances on 20 August 1971, perhaps because he was about to make revelations about the massacre of striking shipyard workers at Gdańsk and Gdynia by militia forces the previous December.[70]

For Jews of a Zionist affiliation, some of whom had been involved in the Armée Juive, the goal was not the liberation of France but escorting Jews to safety and a new life in Palestine. After the expulsion of the Nazis the main obstacle was the British, who opposed the mass exodus of Jews to Palestine. Abraham Polonski renamed the Armée Juive the Organisation Juive de

Combat, to make it more acceptable to the British. He used it to escort fleeing Jews to boats in the Marseille from where they set sail to begin a new life in Palestine, soon to become Israel.[71] One of those who left was Anne-Marie Lambert, whose husband Ernest had been taken by the Germans from Montluc prison and shot on 8 July 1944. Widowed at twenty-four and pregnant, she dreamed of a new life. Jacques Lazarus described her departure:

They left one fine morning from old Europe. They lead a tough existence as Palestinian pioneers on a collective farm [. . .] In this country of Hope she wants to forget the terrible things that afflict her spirit. But she will raise her daughter in the memory of her father, a hero shot one day in July.[72]

The return home did not follow immediately for the vast number of resisters, both Jewish and non-Jewish, who had been deported to German concentration camps. The war continued as Allied troops battled towards Germany, but the Germans fought back in December and January in the Battle of the Bulge.[73] The liberation of the camps had to await the arrival of the Allied armies in Germany in the spring of 1945. Before that, the last winter of the war was extremely difficult. Christmas united less than it separated families that were nominally liberated in France from those who were still in the forces or languishing in camps. Teresa Szwarc, now a second lieutenant in the Corps des Volontaires françaises, learned that George Torrès, whom she had married in Kensington on 15 June 1944 before he went to fight with General Leclerc, had been killed while on night patrol on 8 October. An army chaplain recovered his wedding ring and identity plaque. Pregnant with his child, who would be born in February, Teresa wrote on Christmas Eve that she was spending:

Christmas without Georges. All that remains is you, Dominique, our rings together on my finger and his identity plaque on my wrist. Outside there is night and there is war. Tonight my suffering communes with the innumerable beings who are suffering on the earth, the prisoners, the deportees, the martyrs in the camps, the prisons and the battlefields, all those who are suffering tonight from cold and hunger and loneliness. It is not right to be happy this Christmas night of 1944.[74]

The pain of that night was also felt by Jean Bertin, who had resisted with Rémy's Confrérie Notre-Dame and in a POW resistance movement, had been arrested on 1 June 1944 and sent to Buchenwald. On Christmas Eve 1944 he wrote a short piece, which he later sent to Rémy, poignantly contrasting their brutalised existence, without news of family or friends, with his vision of liberated France:

Tonight it is Christmas, Feast of Joy and Hope. Far away, in liberated France, the families of us prisoners are weeping. Are my family alive? And the others? [. . .] Christmas! The bells of France! Midnight mass in the snow. Tomorrow we will have the factory, hunger, cold, the shouting of our executioners, the ugly faces of the damned race against which I rose up. What would I not give to spend a single day in our France without Boches, without swastikas, without Gestapo, and then come back here to die?[75]

The last months of the camps were the most murderous. The SOE agent Maurice Southgate was one of thirty-six other British, French and Belgian agents accused of spying and deported to Buchenwald at the end of June 1944. Fourteen of these were hanged in September, and another fourteen in October. These included Charles Rechenmann, who had run a sabotage group in the Tarbes area under Southgate.[76] Of the rest, three Frenchmen were shot, two were sent to factory work that meant death in a matter of weeks, and two Englishmen escaped. Southgate was the only one of the thirty-six who survived in the camp.[77] As the Red Army approached prisoners in camps to the east were taken west by forced marches and shot by the roadside if they gave up. Old people were disposed of. Germaine Tillion's mother, aged sixty-nine, was gassed at Ravensbrück on 2 March 1945. The advance of the Anglo-Americans also provoked reactions. General

Delestraint, the former commander of the Armée Secrète, who proudly bore himself as a general at Dachau, was shot by the Germans in the back of the neck on 19 April 1945.[78]

News of the horrors of the camps arrived very quickly. Marie-Hélène Lefaucheux returned to Germany to visit a number of camps in the hope of extracting other comrades as she had extracted her husband. She reported back to Consultative Assembly's commission on deportees on 27 April. Lecompte-Boinet who was in the audience, followed her gaze as she discovered Bergen-Belsen:

in the middle of a great forest, in a clearing and there, behind the barbed wire, in sheds exposed to the wind, is the extermination camp with 60,000 racial deportees. The only ones still standing are those who managed to decide to eat the corpses. Madame Lefaucheux remarked that the Jews tended to eat the livers while the others ate what remained of the flesh.[79]

The liberation of the camps in April 1945 did not necessarily bring happiness. Former inmates were slowly brought home and processed at the Hôtel Lutetia in Paris. Families came to see if their loved ones had turned up. Those who returned hoped to be reunited with their families. Paulette Sliwka had been deported to Auschwitz and when she finally got back to Paris on 29 May her family were not at the welcoming point. She walked home, up to Belleville, where she found her father shaving and her mother preparing his lunch-box for work. 'I was pampered and fussed over' by family and then by friends who rushed round.[80] Roger Trugnan was not so lucky. He recalled singing the 'Marseillaise' when Buchenwald was liberated on 19 April 1945. Only five of his group of thirty-five or thirty-six returned. He arrived at the Hôtel Lutetia and 'waited until 2 a.m. Nobody came to fetch me. I had a sort of premonition about what had happened.' Eventually he heard from his aunt about the fate of his parents and little sister.[81] In a reversal of roles Maurice Lubczanski waited in vain for his deported family to reappear and sank into a depression: 'After the insurrection and everything that happened,' he said, 'I had my first depression. A very deep depression, because I was not expecting the Liberation like that.'[82]

The liberation of the camps triggered a settling of accounts as surviving resistance deportees, like the Furies, returned to demand justice for those who had betrayed them. Malefactors who had lain low were finally exposed and reaped the reward of their treachery. In May 1946 Germaine Tillion testified to an examining magistrate against Robert Alesch, the false curate from Luxemburg who had betrayed dozens of resisters fighters, including her own mother and Anise Girard. He had fled to Belgium but was arrested by the American authorities in July 1945 and sent back to France to face justice. He was condemned to death by the Cour de Justice de la Seine on 26 May 1948 and shot on 25 January 1949.[83]

Justice also came to another traitor who had attempted to reinvent himself as a resister and soldier, Roland Farjon. The Organisation Civile et Militaire (OCM) was devastated in January 1945 that one of the bodies found in unmarked graves in the citadel of Arras, where they had been shot by the Germans, was that of Colonel Alfred Touny.[84] On 13–14 July 1945 surviving deportees of the OCM testified to police commissioner Georges Descroisettes. Each told the story of having been arrested and then told by fellow prisoner Farjon that the Germans knew everything and it was pointless not to talk: 'We have played and we have lost' was his refrain. Exchanging glances and words with each other they realised that he was a mole and a traitor.[85] Farjon tried to justify himself, appealing to OCM leader Maxime Blocq-Mascart, but without success. He also tried to see de Gaulle, but the General would not receive him. On 21 July 1945 he threw himself into the Seine. In his briefcase was found a letter to Blocq-Mascart: 'Please God that you and my comrades in the Resistance see that this suicide is a gesture of courage, for that is how I am acting.'[86]

The settling of accounts with British resisters alleged to have committed crimes was much less severe. It may be said, indeed, that grim episodes in the life of the Resistance were covered up by the establishment in order to preserve the narrative of British heroism. When Maurice Southgate was arrested and taken to the Paris headquarters of the Gestapo, avenue Foch, he was surprised to see SOE agent 'Bob' Starr – George Starr's younger brother – in relaxed mood with the Germans, smoking and chatting with the Germans. It occurred to him, and to others who saw Starr there, that he was working for the Germans. Starr was later deported to Sachsenshausen as a POW, not as a spy. Interrogated on his return, he argued that he had decoded BBC messages that the Germans already possessed and, as an artist, drew maps from information they also had. He was not pursued, either under the 1940 Treachery Act or the 1901 Army Act.[87] Meanwhile George Starr was criticised by his courier, Anne-Marie Walters, whom he had sent home. She alleged that with his bodyguard, a Russian and former member of the Foreign Legion, called Buresie, 'a dangerous and bloodthirsty character also slightly mad', Starr had delighted in torturing captured *Miliciens*: 'One man's feet were held in the fire for twenty minutes until his legs were slowly burned off to the knees; other tortures are too horrible even to mention. A good number of people were also shot.'[88] At this point the SOE closed ranks. When Walters applied to go back to France to work for the SOE, Maurice Buckmaster refused to see her and later told her father that she had 'behaved with the scantest courtesy. In fact old-fashioned people like myself might call it sheer rudeness.'[89] She found a new outlet for her ambitions in giving interviews and writing a lightly fictionalised account of her adventures, *Moondrop to Gascony*.[90] In the meantime a rather perfunctory court of enquiry met in February 1945 to assess the allegations made against Starr. No action was taken and indeed he was awarded the DSO.

The liberation was at one level about the expulsion of the tyrant and the reunion of families. But after the celebrations were over it was not easy to return to normal life. People returned back from the front, or from fighting behind German lines, or from camps and prisons, having encountered moments of exhilaration but also terrible suffering. The families to which they returned were often broken by exile, deportation or death – partners without spouses, mothers without children, children without parents or siblings. Society too was scarred by mass displacement, food shortages, Allied bombings, German reprisals and conflict verging in some parts of the country on civil war.

Defeat, occupation, resistance and liberation inflicted a heavy toll on private lives. The intense experience of resistance created new relationships and left old ones meaningless. Individuals were brought together from very different backgrounds who would never have met if the social conventions of peacetime had prevailed. Resistance created a fraternity or sorority of heroism and suffering that only those who had experienced it could share. These new relationships, however, were created in dramatic and artificial conditions which often left them troubled and did not always last.

Maurice Lubczanski had worked closely in Carmagnole with Jeanne Regal during the Occupation. They came from very different backgrounds – he a Polish-Jewish immigrant, she from an assimilated French-Jewish family. Her father had died during the war and she had not attended his funeral for security reasons. When they decided to get married her mother opposed her marriage to a foreigner and claimed that the communists had kidnapped her daughter. Maurice, meanwhile, trained in theatre in Lyon and set up a theatre company. They went to Paris to start a new professional life and a family.[91] Philippe Viannay had been challenged by Hélène Mordkovitch in 1940 to become involved in resistance and the look they exchanged became a love that was at the heart of Défense de la France.[92] After the war, however, Philippe did not make a career out of his resistance past. He concentrated on charity work and refused to be paid.

This impacted on his family and Hélène Viannay later admitted that their condition was 'abominable, indescribable. How did we manage to survive? I was deeply depressed, unable to think. I was undernourished for years, the children too.'[93]

The reunification of families sometimes brought as much grief as joy. Damira Titonel had been deported to Ravensbrück for her work with the 35th Marcel Langer Brigade. When she returned her close-knit Italian immigrant family was in tatters. She was greeted by her mother in tears and her father, limping, having been injured on a deportation train leaving for the camps. Her brother Titan also returned from the camps, and Armand from prison, while Mathieu had fought with the *maquis* at the Battle of Castelnau under Robert Wachspress. Damira broke up with her fiancé who now meant nothing to her after her time in the camps and married a local young man, Gilles. But she named her child Robert after the man of her life, 'the commandant I admired so much so that the boy would grow up to be like him'. She hoped for a better world and joined the Communist Party but this only made her life more difficult. When she went on strike in 1947 she was called a 'layabout' by the butcher who refused to give her credit. The local priest refused to confirm her children and the government rejected her application to run a newsagent-tobacconist because she was a communist. Not until 1983 did she meet up with her comrades from the Brigade Marcel Langer and found an association to bring them together.[94]

The return from Ravensbrück was a little easier for three women who had supported each other through trial and tribulation, willing each other to survive. The most meaningful relations they now had were with those who had experienced the camps with them. Germaine Tillion came home without her elderly mother, who had been gassed. Her ethnography research archives had been lost or destroyed, and in any case what obsessed her now was not North African tribes but the camps. She began to research and write about Ravensbrück, and about the last deportation convoy to leave on 15 August 1944. Shortly after the publication of her book, and on behalf of former inmates of the camp, she attended the trial in Hamburg of those Germans held responsible for the atrocities of Ravensbrück.

The second woman was Geneviève de Gaulle, who had joined Défense de la France, had been arrested in July 1943 and deported in February 1944. She returned to discover that 'no-one was bothered with us. Life went on'. She married another former resister, Bernard Anthonioz, who had published underground works in Switzerland during the war. He rose to become a founding member of de Gaulle's Rassemblement du Peuple Français and became artistic director of André Malraux's Ministry of Culture in 1958. Geneviève, however, tragically marked by Ravensbrück, wanted nothing to do with high-profile politics after the war. Rather she devoted herself to the cause of families who had suffered bereavement or deprivation through their involvement in resistance through the Comité des Oeuvres Sociales de la Résistance (COSOR). She also helped the immigrant populations of the shanty towns around Paris, whose expressions reminded her of those in the camps, through ATD Fourth World, founded in 1957.[95] Fifty years on, she also returned to meditate on the horrors of Ravensbrück.[96]

The third of the trio who returned from Ravensbrück was Anise Girard. She came home to find that her sister Claire had been shot by the Germans the previous August. When Mlle Merlat of what became the Commission for the History of the Second World War came to interview the Girard family in February 1946 she found Dr Louis Girard, 'quite old and diminished by his long period of deportation' and Mme Girard, who had been involved in the Comet escape line, 'rather thin and wearing no makeup', broken by the family trauma. Their daughter Anise was there as well as their son, François, 'a tall blond boy, somewhat listless', aged only nineteen, who had been involved in Défense de la France and been arrested in May 1944. It was the train carrying him that

Claire had followed fruitlessly with Marie-Hélène Lefaucheux before her death. Attached to the interview notes was a black-rimmed card announcing Claire's funeral on 4 September 1944 in the church of Courdimanche, close to where she had been shot by the Germans.[97] Anise Girard subsequently married André Postel-Vinay, the 'madman' who escaped from the Saint-Anne asylum in Paris with the help of his sister, Marie-Hélène Lefaucheux. He had got to London and joined the Free French, where as Inspecteur des finances he was well equipped to take charge of the finances of Free France and later of the colonies. But Anise returned to the question of the concentration camps, and in particular the gassings, both in Germaine's 1973 book on Ravensbrück, and in historical works published jointly in the 1990s.[98]

Personal disappointment was also the lot of some of those who had fought in SOE alongside the French Resistance, or their loved ones. The wartime experience of some agents was so dramatic that they were unable to return to a conventional life. Richard Heslop flew back from France at the end of August and began a relationship with a women called Violet. A year later, however, the Air Ministry received a letter from a Susan Heslop in Keighley, who had borne Heslop a daughter in 1941 and who wanted to know where he was in order to take out a maintenance order. Heslop had told Susan that he was already married, and she hoped that he would divorce his first wife, Beryl, and marry her: 'I had no idea that Heslop was a married man,' she said. 'He gave me every reason to believe he was single and very much in love with me, [but] when I wanted to know why we were not marrying, he wrote to tell me he was already married.' Now Susan found out to even greater distress that there was a third woman, Violet, with whom he had had two babies and was now marrying.[99]

Pearl Witherington, on the other hand, had joined the SOE in part to be reunited with her French boyfriend, Henri Cornioley, whom she rediscovered on mission and recruited into her circuit. She was given an honorary commission in the WAAF in July

1944 but resigned it the following May. In October 1944 she had married Cornioley and they settled in Paris. She took pride in her war record and was incensed in September 1945 to be offered an MBE (civil), since women were evidently not considered for military decorations. She declined the honour, which she described as 'puny', explaining:

The work which I undertook was of a purely military nature in enemy occupied territory. I spent a year in the field and had I been caught I would have been shot or, worse still, sent to a concentration camp. Our training, which we did with the men, was purely military, and as women we were expected to replace them in the field. Women were parachuted as w/t operators etc., and I personally was responsible for the training and organisation of nearly three thousand men for sabotage and guerrilla warfare. The men have received military decorations. Why this discrimination with women when they put the best of themselves into the accomplishment of their duties?[100]

The depression faced by many former resisters meant that relationships were often forged in sanatoria where they spent time recovering physically and mentally after the war. Those who had been in the Resistance in France often met up with people who had returned from the camps. Denise Domenach, suffering physical and mental exhaustion after her moving experience with the MLN in Paris, was summoned home, but her brothers had left: Jean-Marie had got married, René had joined up. She was unable to focus on her studies. She was sent by her doctor to Combloux, a sanatorium in the Alps, where she met a young Yugoslav, Bernard Lallich, who had been involved in a French intelligence network, been tortured by the Gestapo and escaped from the deportation convoy that left on 15 August 1944. She remembers young people coming in from the concentration camps like 'zombies'. She did not understand and for a long time did not want to know. She preferred to sing in the choir organised by Lallich. 'We decided to confront our future together and we went back to resume our studies,' she wrote. 'Together we decided to live.'[101]

The pathway of Madeleine Riffaud was somewhat more tragic. She had not been allowed to join up after the liberation of Paris and then heard that her communist comrades in Fabien's brigade had been sent across the Rhine in rubber boats to allow the command to gauge where enemy fire was coming from, and did not return. She had escaped from the 15 August convoy and went often to the Hôtel Lutetia to see if any of the women who had gone on that journey came home, but none did. Her fiancé from the Resistance movement was dying and she had fought with her parents: 'I wanted to kill myself as I was lonely. I had no friends.' Suffering from a recrudescence of TB, she went to the Combloux sanatorium where she met the young communist militant Pierre Daix, a returnee from Mauthausen. He saw her as Delacroix's *Liberty leading the people* and she saw him as a resistance hero, but 'on the inside he was in pieces and I was in pieces too'. Together they had a child, but Madeleine was told that it had been infected by the disease she carried. It was taken from her and kept in an incubator for two years.

There was, however, one ray of hope. On 11 November 1944, after a sleepless night and with 'a terrible depression', she attended the victory parade and then went to a café for something hot with a group of poets she knew through the Communist Party: 'The one person who saved me was Paul Eluard,' who in effect adopted her and launched her career. Eluard wrote the preface for a volume of poems, obsessed with death, called *Le Poing fermé*, and Picasso did a pen portrait of her for the frontispiece. She met Vercors who was fascinated by her and she decided that she would have rather written *Le Silence de la Mer* than wielded a machine-gun. She fought back through journalism, writing about the miners' strike of 1947. In the mining basin she discovered the exploits and journal of Charles Debarge and published an edition of it in 1951. The high point of her career came later as a war correspondent in Vietnam.[102]

While some former resisters used their credentials to carve a political, journalistic or artistic career for themselves, others gave much of their lives through organisations like the Centre d'Orientation Sociale des Étrangers (COSE), founded by the Abbé Glasberg, to sorting out some of the cases of broken families and broken lives. This gave rise at times to resentment between the 'losers' in the Resistance story who remained with the shipwreck and the 'winners' of the Resistance, who tuned it to their advantage. Such contradictions of the aftermath of Liberation were nicely illustrated by the case of Genia Deschamps. The daughter of Russian Jewish immigrants, she had married just before the war but her husband was killed in Champagne on 12 September 1944. In truth, she had drifted away from him because they did not share a common experience in resistance, and it was through the Resistance, and notably the Mouvement de Libération Nationale, that she met and married Jean Gemähling of Combat. The Resistance had extracted her from her 'little world of Russian immigrants' and integrated her into French society; without that, she told her husband, 'I would not have known you'. For all that, however, she remained identified with those who suffered the travails of being refugees, deportees, and having their lives ruined by war and resistance to oppression. She helped returning deportees from the camps find jobs and the benefits to which they were entitled. She assisted refugees and immigrants through COSE and, knowing Russian, Polish and Spanish, she worked for eight months in Germany in 1946 for the health department of the Allied Control Commission. The Resistance, she saw, had made the careers of a small minority but many more had suffered materially and morally from their dedication to a cause, and those handicaps were transmitted to the next generation, whose education became another priority:

[Robert] Salmon made himself a launch pad. He had no trouble walking over other people's corpses to advance his career. The Resistance served him, as it did [Michel] Debré for example. [But] most people lost three or four years from their career. They were shattered physically or mentally and that often impacted on the next generation, which is often forgotten. Because if the parents were not mentally strong, nine times out of ten their children were not either [. . .] And so we have not finished paying for all this.[103]

Genia Gemähling's verdict catches a general mood of disappointment. There was a powerful tension in post-Liberation France between the images of women embracing American tank crews or cheering de Gaulle's victory promenade on the Champs-Élysées and the realities encountered by ordinary men and women and recorded in their testimony. Volunteers who had joined the Forces Françaises de l'Intérieur for the battles after D-Day were either sent home or enrolled into the new French Army, which had no time for revolutionary posturing and took many of them to their deaths. Members of resistance organisations who hoped to form a broad reforming movement were disappointed as party politicians and bureaucrats restored a very familiar political order. Many resisters of foreign origin returned to parts of Europe liberated from Nazism but which soon fell under the grip of Stalinism or sailed to Palestine, despite energetic attempts by the British to keep them out. Those who returned from the camps, finally, found too often that their families had been torn apart, that traitors were still running free and that time-servers had carved out power and influence for themselves.

Conclusion:
Battle for the Soul of the Resistance

We are giving the country the impression that the Resistance is divided, that former resisters are opposed to each other, whereas thirty years ago we were united.

(Christian Pineau, 1977)

The story of the French Resistance is central to French identity. It is not, however, a static and given narrative but one that has been powerfully contested and revised over time. Rival resistance groups developed their own collective memories that they fought to impose as the dominant narrative of 'the Resistance'. That dominant narrative was rewritten over time under the influence of external events such as the Cold War, Algerian War and 1968, as well as changing perspectives on the Second World War, notably the tendency to see it primarily through the lens of the Holocaust. Witness accounts allow us to explore the construction of group memory and the challenges they offered to dominant narratives. Ultimately it helps us to understand what those memories meant to a small band of comrades, particularly the memory of those who were lost in the minds of those who survived.

At the Liberation, de Gaulle administered a sharp rebuke to the French Forces of the Interior (FFIs) and liberation committees and asserted supremacy of the regular army and the state.[1] This was accompanied by a succession of ceremonies that highlighted the role of the élite Compagnons de la Libération, the regular military army and of course the General himself.[2] The contribution of those who had been close to Vichy, particularly in the Army of Africa, was written out of the story. The straight line drawn in the

445

Gaullist narrative between June 1940 and August 1944 excluded the detour via North Africa and the role of General Giraud, who had been de Gaulle's rival from November 1942 to April 1944: 'De Gaulle felt the need to impose himself as the sole liberator,' Giraud reflected bitterly in 1949. 'An immense arrogance, with violence or cunning added according to circumstance.'[3]

The Communist Party, which emerged in 1945–6 as the largest political party in France with 5 million voters (26 per cent of the total) and over 800,000 members, tried to contest the Gaullist version. It asserted a counter-narrative of resistance as part of the French revolutionary tradition since 1789 and liberation as an act of national insurrection, the triumph of the people in arms.[4] To mark the first anniversary of the liberation of Paris, communists held a ceremony on 24 August 1945 to name the place Stalingrad in the presence of the Soviet ambassador and unveiled a plaque to mark the catacombs under Paris where Colonel Rol-Tanguy had made his headquarters during the insurrection of August 1944. The next day, however, an official ceremony was orchestrated at the Hôtel de Ville where the Gaullist contingent asserted their precedence. Speeches were given by General de Lattre de Tassigny, commander of the French First Army who had received the German surrender in Berlin, by former delegate-general Alexandre Parodi and by André Le Troquer, now president of the Paris municipal council. Colonel Rol-Tanguy was pointedly refused a place in the front rank of the official stand and dramatically walked out with his staff.[5]

Conflict between Gaullists and communists was at first muted since they cohabited in government. It became sharper after de Gaulle resigned as head of government in January 1946, largely as a result of conflict with the Communist Party, and after communist ministers were forced out in May 1947 under pressure from the United States as the Cold War began to bite and they were seen as a threat to Western security.[6] This reopened quarrels about the commitment to fight of the internal resistance versus the *attentisme* of the decision-makers in London and Algiers, and about the liberation as national insurrection for new society versus national liberation to restore the state. In October 1947 Gilbert Renault, code name 'Colonel Rémy', former leader of the Confrérie Notre-Dame resistance network, attacked the communist former Air commissioner Fernand Grenier in the press for failing to arm the Vercors. Just as Stalin had stood back and watched the Warsaw Uprising being crushed by the Germans because it was not led by communists, so Colonel Rémy suggested that for partisan reasons Grenier had let the Vercors burn. Grenier had quarrelled with de Gaulle in July 1944 about the lack of French and Allied air support for the Vercors, but had been forced to observe collective ministerial responsibility and climb down. Now out of office he called for a mass protest meeting in Paris that day, 13 November 1947 on 'The Tragedy of the Vercors'. He argued passionately that the disaster had been caused by:

the whole policy pursued by London and Algiers. The aim was to use the resistance of the French people to give de Gaulle authority vis-à-vis the Allies, but at the same time to do everything necessary to ensure that this resistance did not come to mean *social liberation at the same time as national liberation.*[7]

The Gaullist and communist narratives of resistance and liberation were both – in their different ways – positive. Former Vichy supporters had been silenced by purge and punishment at the Liberation but the onset of the Cold War afforded them an opportunity to articulate a black legend of resistance that indicted communists and drove a wedge between them and the Gaullists. In 1948 Abbé Jean-Marie Desgranges, who in the 1930s had been a deputy from Brittany, revealed what he called 'the masked crimes of *résistantialisme*'. His account focussed on the banditry of the *maquis*, stirred up by Spanish republican brigands, the *épuration sauvage* or settling of scores that had killed 80,000 French people after the Liberation, and the confiscation of citizen's rights from

600,000 honest French people.[8] *Résistantialisme* for him was no different from the atrocities inflicted on Catholics and royalists by the revolutionary Terror of 1793. The power of this critique led to a rehabilitation of Marshal Pétain, who had been sentenced to life imprisonment in 1945 and lived out his sentence on the Île d'Yeu off the Vendée coast until his death in 1951. An argument was developed that the French people had been loyal both to Marshal Pétain, who had kept them safe while waiting for help to arrive, and to de Gaulle who co-ordinated that help. There was even a story that, despite appearances, Pétain and de Gaulle had been secretly working together. In 1950 Colonel Rémy quoted de Gaulle as saying, 'France, remember, must always have two strings to her bow.' In 1940 she needed the Pétain 'string' as well as the de Gaulle 'string'.[9]

Such a reconsideration of the wartime past made it possible for politicians who had been associated with Vichy to return to power for the first time since 1944 and for amnesty laws to be passed in 1951 and 1953. These made peace with those who had been sentenced for collaboration with the Germans, restored confiscated civil and political rights, reduced prison terms and released some individuals altogether. Those who had been fully engaged in resistance at the time now felt sidelined. Jean Cassou had campaigned for aid to the Spanish Republic, worked with the Musée de l'Homme network and was nearly killed while serving as *commissaire de la République* in Toulouse. Now director of the Musée National d'Art Moderne at the Jeu de Paume, he turned around Pétain's complaint in June 1941 that French people had 'short memories' to complain in 1953 that 'nothing is left of the spirit of the Resistance', which had been forgotten.[10]

Meanwhile, under the impact of the Cold War the Communist Party turned in on itself and examined the question of resistance in the glare of dictates of party unity and loyalty to Moscow. There was a tension between the leadership under Maurice Thorez, who had accepted the Nazi-Soviet Pact, deserted from the army and taken refuge in Moscow, and militants who had been at the forefront of the anti-fascist struggle from the Spanish Civil War, were opposed to the Nazi-Soviet Pact, had fought in the French Army in 1940 and been at the sharp end of French Resistance as Francs-Tireurs et Partisans (FTP). The leadership asserted its own resistance credentials by republishing in December 1947 the so-called appeal of 10 July 1940, which was supposed to be Maurice Thorez's call to resistance but in fact called for no such thing. It then dealt with the 'internationalists' who were criticised for going too far in the international anti-fascist struggle and for failing to obey party orders. What happened in France was a local version of the Stalinist show trials that purged the Communist Parties of Eastern Europe in the period 1948–52. Communist resisters who had been active in non-communist organisation like Libération, such as Jean-Pierre Vernant and Pierre Hervé, were purged from the Party or broke with it. In 1952 Charles Tillon, who had been active in the International Brigades and FTP, was accused of claiming that the FTP had operated virtually independently of the Party during the Occupation, not least during the Paris insurrection. Instead of endorsing the official line that Thorez's desertion in 1939 had been the trigger of communist resistance, confirmed by his appeal of 10 July 1940, Tillon was alleged to have told Thorez's wife, Jeannette Vermeersch, 'The fight against war? I began it when you were not even there!' As a result of this arrogance and indiscipline, Tillon was expelled from the Central Committee of the PCF, left his Paris base of Aubervilliers and retired to the Provence countryside.[11] He was rehabilitated by the Party in 1957 but after another quarrel attacked the Party in *A Moscow Trial in Paris* (1971).[12]

In turn the Gaullist myth of Resistance tore itself apart over the Algerian War, which lasted from 1954 to 1962. France had been liberated in 1944 from the platform of its African Empire and North Africa in particular was the hinge that permitted an amalgamation of the Free French and the Army of Africa into an army equipped not only to free France but then to reconquer the Empire. De Gaulle told a conference of colonial governors at Brazzaville in the French Congo in January 1944 that 'France found a resource and a springboard for its liberation in its overseas territories and because of this there is henceforth an indissoluble link between the metropolis and the Empire.'[13] The Algerian War was fought to prevent Algeria seceding from France, but the methods used by the French Army and authorised by French politicians to interrogate captured rebels appeared to many as no different from the methods that had been used by the Nazis to interrogate French resisters: in a word, torture.[14]

This conflict divided the army itself, an army that had had different experiences of resistance and liberation. Jacques de Bollardière and Jacques Massu were contemporaries from Saint-Cyr and had both fought in Africa with the Free French. But while Massu had landed in France with Leclerc's 2nd Armoured Division, Bollardière had fought with the *maquis* in France and had a formative experience when fellow *maquisards* were captured by the Germans, tortured and shot.[15] Even more powerful was his reaction when two Germans were later taken prisoner and he realised that he had the power of life and death over them: 'We were not Nazis!' he said, remembering that 'In the *maquis* I had sung, with a flame in my heart, the great and passionate *Song of the Partisans*: "Friend, if you fall, a friend will come from the shadows to take your place".'[16] In January 1957, meanwhile, Massu and his paratrooper regiments were given full powers to deal with 'terrorists' in what became known as the Battle of Algiers: 'I scorn your action,' Bollardière told Massu and asked to be moved back to France, where he was shut up in a military prison.[17] Later he became involved in a range of peace protests such as opposing French nuclear testing in the Pacific and the extension of a military camp on the Larzac plateau.[18]

Similar conflicts broke out among civilians. Jacques Soustelle, who had run the secret services in Algeria in 1943–4, returned there as governor-general in 1955 along with fellow ethnographer Germaine Tillion, who had been involved in the Musée de l'Homme resistance network and deported to Ravensbrück. To begin with they agreed that Algeria could be properly integrated into France through economic development and education. However, confronted by the violence of the Algerian National Liberation Front (FLN), Soustelle authorised a policy of repression and torture. Germaine Tillion, on the other hand, returned to Algeria in 1957 as part of an International Commission against the Concentration Camp Regime in order to investigate claims of torture: 'Among the witnesses of the sufferings of this foreign people,' she said, 'were some French people who had endured the same crushing ordeals fewer than twenty years before.'[19]

De Gaulle returned to power in 1958 to bring the Algerian War to an end. His decision to grant Algerian independence alienated not only former generals of the Army of Africa who staged a military coup against him in 1961 but also former resistance colleagues Jacques Soustelle and Georges Bidault. They claimed that de Gaulle had betrayed the legacy of resistance and became involved in the extreme-right-wing Secret Army Organisation (OAS) to hold on to Algeria by terror. Soustelle argued that those who had backed de Gaulle in 1958 to save Algeria could not imagine that 'the liberator would become the liquidator'.[20] In 1962 Bidault founded a National Council of Resistance to save French Algeria, a reincarnation of the original CNR he had chaired in 1943. He argued that de Gaulle did not have a monopoly of appeals to continue fighting in the face of defeat, telling a Belgian newspaper:

Twenty years ago, General de Gaulle appealed to the nation to reject the armistice and the defeat. [He] reproached the Vichy government for not having carried on the struggle in North Africa. He underlined the importance of the Empire for the defence of the fatherland. Now we are being asked to do the opposite of what many laid down their lives for. The Resistance is not the private property of 'the man of 18 June', who is not qualified to ask others to demonstrate a passive obedience that he did not.'[21]

It now becomes clear how important the myth of resistance was to the restoration of peace and unity in France after the end of the Algerian War in 1962. It required a resistance story that would unite rather than divide the country and reassert Charles de Gaulle as its originator and unifying force.

In December 1964, in advance of the presidential elections of 1965, the remains of Jean Moulin were solemnly translated to the Panthéon. A rousing speech was made by the veteran writer and latter-day resister André Malraux, who praised Moulin only to pay homage to the watching general. 'Alone,' he declared, de Gaulle 'could summon the Resistance movements to union among themselves and with all the other combats, for only through him did France wage a single combat.'[22] This ceremony, broadcast to the nation, was the apotheosis of the Gaullist narrative, as the head of state and delegate in France basked in mutually reflected glory. The message of the event was perpetuated by a national competition on Resistance and Deportation that was launched in 1964 by resisters' associations and the Education Ministry in order to engage young people with the Resistance story of heroism and suffering. Each year, high-school students would be given an essay question on some aspect of the Resistance and prizes awarded for the best answers. Together these marked the culmination of what Henri Rousso called the 'resistancialist myth' that celebrated a people united in resistance behind de Gaulle.[23]

The resignation of de Gaulle in 1969 and death the following year opened a new phase in the battle for the soul of the Resistance. The Gaullist myth lost its grip on the popular imagination. President Pompidou had not been involved in the Resistance and told the *New York Times Magazine*, 'I hate all that business. I hate medals, I hate decorations.' This was later interpreted on a television debate by journalist Maurice Clavel, who was said to have 'liberated' Chartres cathedral, to say that the Resistance episode indeed filled Pompidou with 'revulsion and irritation'.[24] Pompidou wanted to heal the divisions it left in French society and made a gesture to the silent majority that had elected him after the turmoil of 1968 by quietly pardoning Paul Touvier, the leader of Lyon's counter-insurgent Militia during the Occupation. However, *Le Chagrin et la Pitié*, which opened in French cinemas in 1971, shook to the ground one of the pillars of the Gaullist myth that the French had behaved honourably under the Occupation. On the contrary, it suggested, they had been supine, cowardly and only too frequently given to collaboration.[25]

The disappearance of de Gaulle effectively orphaned former leaders of resistance organisations. Without their leader they fell to quarrelling amongst themselves. Unable or unwilling to attack the General himself they attacked his alter ego in the Resistance, Jean Moulin. Henri Frenay, the former head of Combat and minister for Prisoners, Deportees and Refugees at the Liberation, had long nurtured the view that Jean Moulin, who had been his rival in 1943, was not in fact de Gaulle's loyal servant but a communist agent. This he now publicised in his 1973 memoirs, *La Nuit finira*, and rammed home the accusation in 1977 with an even more explicit broadside, *L'Énigme Jean Moulin*.[26] His argument was that since Moulin had headed the private office of Pierre Cot, the Popular Front's Air Minister in the late 1930s, and since Cot had become a fellow traveller of the Communist Party after the war, Moulin must therefore have been a communist. These accusations caused a rift with former colleagues such as Francis-Louis Closon and Christian Pineau.[27] The quarrel came to a head in 1977 on the television programme, *Les Dossiers de l'Écran*, which brought together a galaxy of former resisters to debate the question: Colonel Passy, Christian Pineau, Francis-Louis Closon, Raymond Aubrac, Pierre Villon and Jean Moulin's radio operator, Daniel Cordier. They all criticised Frenay's action for soiling the memory not only of Jean Moulin but of the Resistance in general.

Christian Pineau argued piously – and not quite candidly – that if they disagreed now, that was not the case then:

It is a mistake of historical proportions to trace our current disagreements back thirty years. Jean Moulin died a hero, he can't answer back, so let us leave him to sleep in peace. We are giving the country the impression that the Resistance is divided, that former resisters are opposed to each other, whereas thirty years ago we were united.[28]

Daniel Cordier became more and more agitated during the programme, as his master's honour was called into question. He finished up by challenging Frenay's use of evidence. 'You have not done your homework. *La Nuit finira* was a testimony, not the work of a historian.' Leaving the studio he decided to undertake ten years' work in the archives in order to clear the name of Jean Moulin.[29]

A further consequence of the disappearance of de Gaulle was to open up the field to a number of players who sought to promote their collective memory as the dominant narrative. These included the Communist Party, which endeavoured to make a comeback after the setbacks of the early Cold War. They also included a new generation of 1968 *gauchistes* who had felt unable to attack the man of 18 June 1940 too much when he was alive, but now made contact with former resisters and revived the memory of Resistance for their own radical purposes. They also included foreign resisters whose story had been marginalised by the 'nationalisation' of the Resistance myth after the Liberation, and Jewish resisters, in particular those of immigrant origin who, unlike assimilated Jews, had not been part of the mainstream Gaullist and communist resistance movements.

The story of the Resistance as a popular movement and the liberation as a national insurrection by the people in arms had recently been retold in René Clément's 1966 film, *Is Paris Burning?* Moreover the 25th anniversary of the Liberation in 1969 provided an opportunity for communists to denounce as partial the celebrations organised by the government. Georges Marrane, apostle of the Front National in the Free Zone and the communists' candidate for prefect of the Seine in 1944, complained that the government had 'honoured the memory of General Leclerc and his 2nd Armoured Division' but that Paris had already liberated itself by the time he arrived. He also criticised the television, then a state monopoly, on which 'not once was mention made of the contribution of the people of Paris and barricades'.[30] On 18 May 1969 Jacques Duclos, running in the presidential elections, laid the first stone of a Musée de la Résistance at Ivry, Marrane's fief, which was to be the site of a populist, communist view of events. He turned the difficult question of communists' behaviour under the Nazi-Soviet Pact of 1939–41 into an advantage:

It is because we were hunted, insulted, persecuted and threatened with the death penalty and because our persecutors had brought France to the abyss that there was in our momentum an enthusiasm, a spirit of sacrifice and a confidence in the future that other resisters did not have.[31]

The prime mover behind the museum was André Tollet, who saw himself in the tradition of Paris *sans-culottes*, had been chair of the Paris Liberation Committee in 1944 and had just published a book to highlight the role of the working class in the Resistance.[32] When the municipality of Ivry ran out of money Tollet found alternative accommodation in a large house in the eastern Paris suburb of Champigny-sur-Marne, where it is still located.[33]

In the wake of 1968, however, the Communist Party was unable to monopolise an alternative view of the Resistance to that of the Gaullists. The *gauchistes* of 1968 criticised the Party for refusing to back them during the events of May. Many of their leaders were Trotskyists or Maoists who had broken from the communist youth movement as too 'Stalinist' in the lead-up to 1968. In the 1960s they were less likely to be inspired by stories of the Resistance than – following the victory of the Algerian National Liberation Front – by Third World wars of liberation against

Western colonialism and American and Soviet imperialism that were sweeping the globe from Cuba and Latin America to Africa, Vietnam and the China of Mao's Cultural Revolution.[34] Some *gauchistes*, it is true, developed the cult of those who had resisted in the FTP-MOI, notably the Manouchian group who had been used by the German authorities in the notorious *Affiche rouge* to discredit the Resistance as the work of communists, foreigners and Jews, and who had been executed on 21 February 1944.[35] Similarly Pierre Goldman, whose father had been an activist in the Jewish Union for Resistance and Mutual Aid (UJRE) in Lyon, recalled that 'I grew up around memories of the Resistance, of a certain resistance – that of communist Jews – and before I even knew the meaning of the words Alésia, Saint-Louis, Napoleon and Verdun, I knew of Marcel Rayman and his comrades.'[36]

After the failure of May 1968 some activists went home, and some became involved in experiments of personal liberation. A hard core, however, regrouped in clandestine organisations such as the Gauche Prolétarienne (GP) in order to rekindle the revolution. The Pompidou government clamped down hard on these and in 1970 a good many young revolutionaries were languishing in French prisons. This brought about a novel connection between former resisters and the generation of 1968. Former resisters such as Charles Tillon and intellectuals including Jean-Paul Sartre, troubled by this brutal repression, set up a Secours Rouge network, modelled on the Secours Rouge International that had supported communist and anti-fascist exiles who had come to France in the 1930s. A new row was provoked between Tillon and the French Communist Party, which had accepted him back in 1957. Tillon did not hesitate to go public, criticising Duclos for his lack of resistance activity during the Occupation and the Communist Party in general for falling into line behind the Soviet clampdown in Czechoslovakia in 1968.[37] In July 1970 he was expelled from the Party by his local branch in Aix-en-Provence, but he seemed not to care.[38] He was now fêted by the *gauchistes* who in turn embraced his reading of the Resistance that argued that the Francs-Tireurs et Partisans operated more or less independently from the underground leadership of Duclos and all the more so from the Thorez in Moscow. In 1970 Tillon was contacted by a former comrade from the FTP, Denis Le Dantec, whose son, Jean-Pierre Le Dantec, editor of the Gauche Prolétarienne's paper, *La Cause du Peuple,* was in prison. Tillon replied to him:

I feel very emotional to learn that your son has taken up my fight in a world where things are made so much more difficult by people abandoning their principles, betraying each other and taking the wrong path. But great things now belong to your son and to his generation.[39]

Inspired by his new freedom, Tillon abandoned all trace of his previous party loyalty. He rewrote the story of his time on the Resistance in a more autobiographical way, telling the Trotskyist Krivine brothers that 'I did not want to mix up the history of the FTP and that of the Stalinist PC.' His 1977 account, *On Chantait rouge*, highlighted his own appeal to resist on 17 June 1940, while under the Nazi-Soviet Pact the Party in Paris was negotiating with the Germans to publish *L'Humanité*, a story which – he claimed – the likes of Duclos had been trying to cover up ever since. Tillon's line was now that in June 1940 there were 'virtually two communist parties', one collaborating with the Nazis under the pact and one 'which was already thinking that the fight against the invader had to be carried on'.[40]

When he came out of prison, Jean-Pierre Le Dantec also returned to heroic stories of the Resistance. However, he fastened not on Tillon but on the journalist Maurice Clavel, who was said to have 'liberated' Chartres cathedral. He recalled that:

Clavel had an almost Christ-like vision of us. He thought that we were bearers of ideals of sharing and generosity that were like those of the Resistance. That echoed our own idea that was that we were undertaking a new resistance, because the process of resistance had never been finished in France.[41]

Le Dantec was not alone among the young generation of revolutionaries seeking inspiration from older resisters who were uncompromised by association with the Communist Party. Alain Raybaud, another member of the Gauche Prolétarienne, had been involved in exploits to rekindle revolution among northern miners. There he met Roger Pannequin, twenty-six years his senior, who had resisted in that area under the Occupation as a young schoolteacher alongside miners such as Charles Debarge. In 1976 Raybaud wrote the preface to Pannequin's memoirs, *Ami, si tu tombes*, explaining that he had learned two things from Pannequin, 'the heroism of ordinary people' and 'solidarity. When things go badly, when there are arrests and even executions, there are mates, comrades, friends and even bourgeois to defend you, help your family [. . .] sometimes even to take your place.'[42]

At this point resisters of foreign origin made a serious challenge to insert their story into the dominant narrative. It had been essential to the Gaullist myth that to recover their honour after the defeat of 1940 the French had liberated themselves. The contribution of the Allies was mentioned as little as possible and the role of foreigners who were fighting a pan-European anti-fascist struggle was deliberately ignored. The Communist Party was just as guilty of nationalising the Resistance story. A communist ceremony at Père Lachaise cemetery on 30 June 1946 to bury an urn of ashes brought from Auschwitz honoured 180,000 French 'victims of Nazi barbarism' gave the impression they were communist deportees such as Danielle Casanova because no mention was made of the fact that most of them were Jewish.[43] Slowly, however, foreigners who had taken part in the French Resistance made their voices heard and began to receive recognition.

In Moscow on 3 September 1964 a former FTP commander who had gone there to join a commemoration of the 25th anniversary of liberation movements in Europe, died of a heart attack. Boris Matline was the son of Russian Jews and two years old in 1904 when his parents fled from the pogroms to Paris. He worked as a mechanic on the Paris buses and during the Occupation was active in the underground trade-union movement and MOI, concealing his foreignness under the pseudonym Gaston Laroche. Fortunately he left behind the manuscript of a book, *They Called them Foreigners*, on the role of immigrants in the French Resistance, arguing that 'the participation of immigrants in the struggle against Hitlerisme and in the liberation of France should not be condemned to oblivion.'[44]

Spanish political and trade-union groups, including veterans' associations, had been banned in France since 1950 as the price of good Cold War relations with the Franco regime. Yet Toulouse was the capital of the Spanish republican emigration, and after Franco's death in 1975 an association of former Spanish guerrillas was finally approved by the French authorities. Unfortunately its emergence served to trigger a row between military leaders such as López Tovar, who had fought alongside the FTP-MOI and political leaders such as Luis Bermejo, closer to the Spanish Communist Party and the Agrupación de los Guerrilleros Españoles. López Tovar went as far as to accuse Bermejo of being a deserter who had escaped the firing squad and an imposter who had invented his military rank.[45] This did not prevent the association launching a subscription for a national monument to the memory of Spanish guerrillas who had died for France. Sculpted by the Spanish republican Manolo Valiente, it was unveiled by French president François Mitterrand and Spanish premier Felipe Gonzales at Prayols near Foix in June 1982 and became the focus for annual celebrations.[46] Spaniards of la Nueve, the 9th Company, which had been the first into liberated Paris were commemorated much later, perhaps because such recognition dramatically punctured the Gaullist myth of national liberation. To mark the 60th anniversary of the Liberation in 2004 the socialist mayor of Paris, Bernard Delanoë, unveiled a series of medallions along the route taken from the Porte d'Italie by Spanish republicans in the French Army whose contribution was honoured in a more cosmopolitan climate.[47]

As early as the 1960s French communists were remaking connections with German anti-fascists who had fought against Hitler in the French Resistance and had returned after 1945 to build the German Democratic Republic. Albert Ouzoulias, the French FTP leader, took part in festivities to honour victims of the Nazi regime in East Berlin in 1964 and cited the last words of the metalworker Pierre Timbaud before being shot by the Germans at Châteaubriant: 'Long live the German Communist Party!'[48] Gerhard Leo, who had come to France as a German Jewish exile, worked for Travail Allemand to encourage desertion from the *Wehrmacht* and joined the Corrèze *maquis*, translated into German the speech of a former *maquisard* comrade who attended an international Resistance meeting in East Berlin in September 1969. Living in Paris between 1973 and 1985 as correspondent of the DDR paper *Neues Deutschland*, he wrote up his own story for *L'Humanité* in 1984. In 1986 he completed his mission by persuading the municipality of Uzerche to erect a monument to pay generous tribute to 'my liberator and friend', his FTP commander in the Corrèze who had been hanged by the SS after the events in Tulle.[49]

The role of Jewish immigrants in the French Resistance had been highlighted after the end of the war in a number of publications by former Jewish resisters including David Knout and Jacques Lazarus. These focussed on the role of foreign Jews of Zionist affiliation rather than communists.[50] The story of Jews as heroes was soon eclipsed by that of Jews as victims of the Holocaust, which came to occupy centre stage in the representation of the Second World War.[51] Even former Jewish resisters who wanted to find out the truth about the deportation of their families were swept up in this. In 1967 Claude Lévy, a former member of the Brigade Marcel Langer who lost his father in the Shoah and escaped from a train deporting him in 1944, published a first book on the round-up of the Vel' d'Hiv on 16 July 1942. He established that over 27,000 non-French Jews had been rounded up in Paris and its suburbs on that date, but complained that his research had been frustrated by 'not only a veil of oblivion but indeed a carefully woven tissue of counter-truths that had been carefully thrown over these events'.[52] After this, however, a new wave of publications returned to the role of Jews in the French Resistance. Anny Latour undertook a series of interviews with Jewish resisters and Jewish and non-Jewish rescuers, which she used for her work on *Jewish Resistance in France, 1940–1944*, published in 1970. The élite she was studying, she said, was 'that which, in response to the agony of shame and humiliation, became aware of their Jewishness and rose up as Jews against their Nazi oppressors'.[53] David Diamant published his *Jews in the French Resistance* in 1971, demonstrating the high proportion of Jews in FTP-MOI detachments, including the Manouchian group, and also the importance in rescue and resistance of groups such as the UJRE.[54] With Jacques Lazarus and Claude Lévy, Diamant organised a conference on Jewish resistance in November 1974, for the 30th anniversary of the Liberation, and an exhibition to go with it.[55]

The rise of Jean-Marie Le Pen's National Front after 1974 (quite different from the Resistance organisation) and above all after the defeat of the centre right in 1981 brought a violent racist and anti-Semitic rhetoric into French politics, and triggered a great debate about the place of immigrants in French society. One of the outcomes of this was a *prise de conscience* of activists in the Resistance who were both Jewish and immigrants, and more often than not communist. Under attack, they began to speak out in order to establish their patriotic past. In January 1982 the historian Annette Wieviorka received a letter from a group of former immigrant Jewish resisters, including Henri Krischer, 'the Admiral' of Carmagnole, requesting that she interview them and tell their story. She responded positively and four years later published *They were Jews, Resisters, Communists*, in which these young people were characterised as the 'generation of the round-up', whose immigrant parents had often been arrested in 1942 and who themselves had fled to the Free Zone to become involved in Jewish resistance – the war within the war.[56] Meanwhile these immigrant resisters' groups organised themselves into associations and lobbied local and national government to commemorate their contribution to the Resistance. That of Carmagnole-Liberté emerged as a force under the guidance of the Italian anti-fascist Léon Landini and that of the 35th Brigade Marcel Langer under the Polish-Jewish resister Claude Urman. When Charles Hernu, socialist mayor and deputy for Villeurbanne, became Mitterrand's Defence Minister in 1981, he contacted Landini and honoured those who had taken part in the liberation of Villeurbanne in 1944. Ninety former members of Carmagnole-Liberté were decorated in 1982 and their history was engraved in the stones of the capital of the Resistance. Plaques were unveiled at Saint-Genis-Laval to commemorate the massacre, not least of Jeanine Sontag, a street at Vénissieux was named after Norbert Kugler and another one in Lyon after Simon Fryd, who had been guillotined.[57] Similar recognition was accorded to the veterans of the 35th Marcel Langer Brigade in Toulouse. At a ceremony there in September 1983, former FTP commander Serge Ravanel admitted that he had not known much about the group at the time, apart from hearing about its deeds. But he now acknowledged that 'Marcel Langer was a pioneer. His blood shed by a French guillotine nurtured the growth of generations of resisters in the region.'[58] Claude Urman highlighted the special role in the brigade of Italian immigrants such as the Titonel and Bet families and Rosine Bet was celebrated as a very special martyr.[59] In July 1985, finally, former veterans of the 35th Brigade gathered for the award of a resistance medal to Cecilia, widow of Marcel Langer, in front of the stele marking his grave in Toulouse.[60]

Public recognition of the role of foreigners in the Resistance had an impact on historical scholarship between the mid-1980s and mid-1990s. Rolande Trempé, a historian at the University of Toulouse, highlighted the role of Spanish republican guerrillas in the *maquis* of the south-west in 1986.[61] Denis Peschanski, a CNRS researcher, organised a conference on the role of Central European immigrants and refugees in the Resistance and in 1989 published the influential *Le Sang de l'Étranger* with Stéphane Courtois and former resister of Polish-Jewish origin, Adam Rayski.[62] In 1992 François Marcot and the historian of Camisard memory Philippe Joutard organised a conference on foreigners in the French Resistance, while Jean-Marie Guillon and Pierre Laborie included articles on the Jewish resistance and immigrant resistance in a 1995 collection on history and memory.[63] Finally, in 1996, a Franco-German conference was held on the part of anti-Nazi Germans in the French Resistance.[64]

The emerging story of foreign and Jewish resistance damaged the French Communist Party, which had never been candid about the role of these kinds of resisters in the FTP and FTP-MOI. In the mid-1980s the Party was in any case struggling for survival. It had been embraced by François Mitterrand in the Common Programme of 1972 the better to asphyxiate it. It shared power with him in 1981 but was again ejected from government in 1983 when Mitterrand executed a U-turn, moving towards the centre ground. The Party's reputation was not helped by allegations that its general secretary, Georges Marchais, had gone to work in a German factory during the war not because he was forced to but because he volunteered. Neither was it helped by the story of Jewish immigrant resistance highlighted by Serge Mosco's 1985 film, *Des Terroristes à la Retraite*. Using interviews with survivors of the Manouchian group, Mosco set out to convey the message that in 1943 the clandestine leadership of the French Communist Party and commanders of the communist FTP propelled the immigrant fighters of the FTP-MOI into the most dangerous operations, such as attacks on German columns and German generals, and then betrayed them. These activists were almost all arrested and shot at Mont Valérien. The Communist Party tried to prevent the film from being broadcast on television, but in vain. In the *Dossiers de l'Écran* debate following the film, a former member of the Manouchian group, Arsène Tchakarian, detailed their numerous exploits while Annette Kamieniecki demonstrated how many of these had been subsequently credited to the FTP.[65] The Communist Party tried to point the finger of blame for the betrayal of Manouchian at FTP-MOI commander Boris Holban, who had gone back to Romania after the war. FTP-MOI leader Adam Rayski blamed another agent, Joseph Davidovich, while Holban now began to write his memoirs in order to exculpate himself.[66] The story underlined the fact that communist leaders such as Jacques Duclos had lived out the war in secret locations while immigrants with no hiding place had sacrificed themselves for France, and their deeds had been appropriated to gild the reputation of the Party.

Meanwhile, the breakthrough of the new narrative, that Jews were now seen as victims of the Holocaust rather than as resistance heroes, had a negative impact on the reputation of the non-communist resistance. The key moment was the Barbie trial of 1987 and the key figure that of Serge Klarsfeld, president of the Association of Sons and Daughters of Jewish Deportees from France, who had hidden in a cupboard aged eight to escape discovery while his father had been deported to Auschwitz. Klarsfeld chronicled the names of each of the 75,000 Jews – 24,000 of them French Jews and 51,000 of them foreign – who had been sent on convoys to the death camps and from which only 2,500 returned.[67] He also exposed the role of the Vichy government in rounding up Jews in a 1983 book brutally entitled *Vichy-Auschwitz*.[68] A qualified lawyer, he now acted as prosecuting counsel in the Barbie trial, arguing that the 'butcher of Lyon unleashed himself on his victims both by the sadism of the physical and psychological tortures he inflicted and by the fanaticism that drove him to assume personal and total responsibility for sweeping murderous operations such the round-up at Izieu.'[69] In a powerful challenge to the Resistance narrative which gave pride of place to those who had taken up arms against Hitler, he declared that 'the fact of being a Jewish child condemned you to death more surely than any act of resistance.'[70]

Ranged against Klarsfeld as defence counsel was Maître Jacques Vergès, a showy yet inscrutable figure who had made his reputation defending Algerians accused of acts of terrorism against France during the Algerian War, and now took up the challenge of defending a Nazi. He suggested that putting Barbie on trial was the French way of dealing with the shame of their defeat in 1940 and their occupation by the Germans: 'We all know,' he said, 'that the French feel intensely ashamed about the disaster of 1940 and what followed. This trial is their way of covering their embarrassment by projecting responsibility and punishment onto Barbie, who becomes a scapegoat.'[71] He summoned Raymond Aubrac as a witness for the defence and hoped, even if he could not save Barbie, to discredit the Resistance community as a whole by exposing Aubrac as the man who betrayed Jean Moulin. Faced by this accusation, Aubrac began not with his own story but with the fate of his parents. Aubrac, he made clear, was only his *nom de guerre*; his real name was Samuel and his parents, Albert and Hélène Samuel, had been arrested in November 1943 and 'handed over to the Gestapo, which was run by Klaus Barbie. On 4 January [1944] they were transported to Drancy, and they were both in convoy number 66 to Auschwitz, where they were murdered on arrival.'[72]

Those who spoke for the central memory of the Resistance learned at this juncture that the best way to save its honour was to underline not its heroism but its suffering. Thus the embodiment of the true resister at the Barbie trial was not Raymond Aubrac but a frail but still handsome woman aged eighty-six called Lise

Lesèvre. The wife of an engineering professor, she had joined the Resistance movement Combat and organised the recruitment to the Resistance of members of France's élite *grandes écoles*. She was arrested in March 1944 and Barbie and his henchmen set to work on her. First of all she was beaten. Then she was fitted with handcuffs that had spikes on the inside, which were tightened each time she refused to answer:

At midday, I was hung up by my wrists [. . .] I don't know how long for. My arms were stretched out and I could not breathe. As I still didn't talk, Barbie threatened, 'We are going to fetch your husband and your son and you will speak in front of them' [. . .] We were able to say 'be brave' to each other but when I saw them arrive the situation was unbearable for me.

She was interrogated for nineteen days in a row, underwent water torture and a mock trial. 'They read me the sentence in German. I heard the word "terrorist" three times. Thus I was condemned to death.' In the event she was deported to Ravensbrück, while her husband died of typhus at Dachau. Her sixteen-year-old son survived Neuengamme but was drowned when the ship carrying him home was accidentally torpedoed by the Allies: 'From Jean-Pierre's friends I knew of his heroic conduct,' she said. 'He did not flinch for a second.' And yet the message of Lise Lesèvre was not so much one of heroism as suffering, reminding the audience that, like Jews, resisters had been tortured and deported, and had also died.[73]

In the wake of the Barbie trial came a major rewriting of the Resistance narrative. The emphasis was placed on resistance to Nazi ideology and practices rather than on patriotic resistance to German power. It stressed resisters' commitment to humanity and the universal rights of man and their suffering rather than their heroism. This revised narrative gave voice to constituencies whose story had not to date been adequately heard, namely women resisters and French people who had dedicated themselves to rescuing the victims of Nazi persecution, especially Jewish children. Attention was also paid to passing on the narrative to younger generations. Former resisters interviewed at this time often made the point that while they had not really discussed their past with their own children, almost by common consent, their grandchildren showed much more interest in what they had done during the war: 'We are being asked questions about the Resistance by our grandchildren,' said Robert Salmon in 1985.[74] 'I have only begun to talk about it in the last two or three years,' echoed Hélène Viannay in 1986, 'and only to the grandchildren.'[75]

Organisations dating from the war that had been charged with looking after the interests of former resisters had to come to terms with the fact that their members were dying out and that their new purpose must be to hand on a positive memory of the Resistance. The statutes of a new Resistance Foundation were accordingly approved in 1992 by a meeting chaired by Jean-Pierre Lévy, founder of Franc-Tireur, now aged eighty-one. The mission taken up by the Foundation was to 'combat the falsifiers' of the Resistance story and to pass on 'the common heritage championed by all resisters'. Its work was supported by a sister organisation, Memory and Hopes of the Resistance, set up in 1993 and chaired by Jacques Vistel, son of the former head of the Lyon Liberation Committee, Alban Vistel. This took special responsibility for putting the children and grandchildren of resisters in contact with young people to spread the good word and to help them, for example, with the essays they might be writing for the annual competition on Resistance and Deportation. In Lyon a Centre for the History of Resistance and Deportation opened its doors in 1992. Its first director was not a male veteran but a young female academic, Sabine Zeitoun, who had published studies on the rescue of Jewish children under the Occupation.[76] She underlined the redemptive importance of locating the Centre in the premises once occupied by the Gestapo, Klaus Barbie's headquarters and 'the place where Jean Moulin was tortured'.[77] The Centre immediately organised an exhibition dedicated to Jean Moulin but also inaugurated a large-scale oral history programme videotaping interviews with former resisters connected with Lyon, and notably with resisters of Jewish immigrant origin who had hitherto been overlooked.

The search for a more humanitarian image of the French Resistance opened a space for women resisters that had long been virtually closed. From the outset resistance had been presented as a very masculine exercise, the continuation of the war abroad and underground in France, with the highest accolades given to armed struggle. The military conception of resistance was embedded in the rules governing the allocation of awards such as the Combattant Volontaire de la Résistance, which brought membership of an élite group and material benefits. Very few women qualified and many were rejected. Andrée Ponty, who had been involved in the communist-inspired *comités populaires* and the rue Daguerre demonstration, was told in 1975 that there was not enough evidence in her application of 'an adequate presence in a fighting unit or of adequate activity'.[78] Julia Pirotte, a resister of Polish-Jewish origin, who had been involved in intelligence and propaganda work in Marseille, used her photographic skills to produce false IDs and stormed Marseille police prefecture on 21 August 1944, 'flag in hand'. She nevertheless had her application rejected in 1973 and again in 1978: 'I am tired of it all,' she told a former FTP leader, 'but I have the satisfaction of knowing that I did something for France. If France does not want to recognise it, that's her business.'[79]

There were, of course, women resisters who were greatly acclaimed, such as Berty Albrecht, one of the six female Compagnons de la Libération, buried at Mont Valérien, and Danielle Casanova. These were secular saints and martyrs who were celebrated for their ultimate sacrifice. The original citation for Berty Albrecht as Compagnon said that she had been shot by the Germans; only later did it transpire that she had hanged herself rather than betray her comrades under interrogation. Danielle Casanova, who had been deported from Fort Romainville outside Paris and died in Auschwitz, was effectively canonised by the communists as a contemporary Joan of Arc. A statue of her was unveiled at Fort Romainville in May 1956, but to emphasise the saintly analogy the procession began at the rue Danielle-Casanova near the Opéra and went via the place Jeanne d'Arc.[80] Other women attained a symbolic notoriety, although in a less exalted way. Rosine Bet, who had blown herself up in a bomb attack on Germans in a Toulouse cinema in 1944, was publicly recognised by the community of resisters in the cemetery where she lay in 1987.[81] The case of Colette Nirouet, who was killed in action in Germany on 26 November 1944, did not come to light until *L'Humanité*'s survey on 'Les Inconnus de la Résistance' in 1984. Antonin Cubizolles wrote in to say, 'It took me years to discover that the "Joan of Arc" of the 152nd was in fact Ginette or Colette Nirouet, born in Paris on 25 May 1926, and to find her family. Who will help me to find her grave? Who will help me to have her honoured as she deserves?'[82] She was duly recognised as Morte pour la France in 1985 and awarded the Croix de Guerre in 1987.[83]

Of course not all women resisters could die in action. The feminist movement of the 1970s began to credit women's particular contribution to the Resistance and to express frustration at being marginalised. As late as 1977 Christian Pineau spoke of 'The Resistance that was born of the initiative of certain men'.[84] That same year, however, the communist-sponsored Union des Femmes Françaises organised a conference on *Women in the Resistance*. Lucie Aubrac told delegates that women had been 'important hinges' in the Resistance, although they had been squeezed out of leadership positions when resistance organisations became more structured and out of political positions at the Liberation as a result of 'male atavism'.[85] In 1984 she published her best-selling memoirs *Ils Partiront dans l'Ivresse*. The title derived from the

BBC message on 21 February 1944 that indicated that, having master-minded a plan to release Raymond from prison, she, Raymond and their unborn child would be flown out of France.[86] Two years later Geneviève de Gaulle argued that she had not done anything heroic in a macho way but that she still claimed the title of resister:

I never blew up a bridge or derailed a train or shot at a German. I made a small contribution, that of a young student. I did a certain number of operations [. . .] and so quite rightly I consider myself to be a resister.[87]

Increasingly, women spoke out and were listened to. A series in 1989, *Women at War*, interviewed a range of women resisters. Some, like Micheline Eude-Altman, said that they had mainly typed messages and cycled miles as a liaison agent before being arrested. Others, such as the explosives expert Jeanne Bohec and Madeleine Riffaud, who had shot a German, talked about their involvement with violence.[88] Claude Berri's 1997 film was called *Lucie Aubrac*, not *Raymond Aubrac*, and was based on her memoirs. Interviewed at the time, she said that 'women were the essential links in the Resistance' and that as far as the Aubrac couple were concerned, 'it's often about me that people talk.'[89] In a 2002 programme featuring three women who survived Ravensbrück – Germaine Tillion, Anise Postel Vinay and Geneviève de Gaulle, Germain Tillion announced squarely that in 1940 'men were nowhere to be seen. It was women who kick-started the Resistance.'[90] The coming to power in Paris of socialist mayor Bernard Delanoë also made a difference to the memory of women resisters. In 2004 two women deputy mayors with responsibility for gender equality and memory hosted a conference dedicated to the six female Compagnons de la Libération. One of them, Simone Michel-Lévy, a resister within the Post Office who had been hanged at Flossenburg ten days before the camp was liberated in April 1945, had a road named after her in Paris in 2007.[91] Ultimate recognition came on 27

May 2015 when the coffins of Germaine Tillion and Geneviève de Gaulle were transferred to the Panthéon with the remains of Pierre Brossolette.

The feminisation of the Resistance story did not, in the end, make it invulnerable to the criticisms that had surfaced during the Barbie trial. This was particularly the case because attacks on Raymond Aubrac now included his wife Lucie, who was accused of fictionalising events in her memoirs. When Klaus Barbie died in 1992 it was said he had left a 'will' in the possession of Jacques Vergès that allegedly provided proof that when he had first been arrested in March 1943, Raymond Aubrac was interrogated by the Gestapo, recruited by them, and released in order to betray Jean Moulin. This was used by a journalist Gérard Chauvy, who made these allegations in *Aubrac. Lyon 1944* and provoked a furious controversy.[92] Rather than rejecting it out of hand some journalists and historians felt that the Aubracs should be questioned on the matter. The newspaper *Libération* organised a Round Table on 17 May 1997 at which the Aubracs were confronted by a panel of historians. Much of the debate turned on the historical accuracy of Lucie Aubrac's memoirs. François Bédarida warned her of the danger of embellishing the past as fiction while Daniel Cordier criticised 'an exciting adventure novel that you unwisely passed off as your memoirs'.[93] Historians Maurice Agulhon, Jean-Pierre Vernant and Laurent Douzou were more favourable to the Aubracs but were on the defensive. In the end the Aubracs were 'cleared' of any wrongdoing but Lucie was furious at having been subjected to such an inquisition and Douzou decided to work with Lucie on a highly accurate biography that would be published after her death.[94]

The women's story of the Resistance, highlighting a devotion to others rather than to their own glory, was one way in which the Resistance narrative came to be rewritten. Another was the coming of the story of the Righteous, whose dedication was above all to rescue Jews threatened with deportation and extermination.

This challenged the original discourse of the Resistance as military and patriotic and replaced it with one more humanitarian and more ecumenical.

The memory of the Righteous was promoted in two separate quarters. First, there was a group of former Jewish scouts, the Éclaireurs Israélites de France, who had set up a secret network, known as the Sixième or Sixth, to rescue Jews in danger. Among them were Jacques Pulver, who was born in Brussels to Polish parents, and the Strasburger Lucien Lazare. They discovered that numerous dossiers of French individuals who had been recommended to Yad Vashem, the Jerusalem organisation responsible for memorialising the Holocaust, for the accolade of Righteous among Nations were gathering dust in the drawers of the Israeli embassy in Paris.[95] Germaine Ribière, who had travelled part of the way on a deportation convoy of Jews from Limoges, had been named Righteous in 1967. Pierre Chaillet and Gilbert Lesage, who had been involved in the Vénissieux rescue, were honoured respectively in 1981 and 1985. Marie-Rose Gineste, who had carried the appeal against the deportations by the Bishop of Montauban across the diocese, was also recognised in 1985. However the campaign by Pulver and Lazare resulted in a spike of recognition of the French Righteous, which rose from thirty-three in 1987 to 153 in 1989.[96] Among the honoured in 1988 were Madeleine Barot of CIMADE and Pastor Boegner. Monseigneur Rémond of Nice was recognised in 1991, André Dumas of CIMADE and Jean-Marie Soutou of Amitié Chrétienne in 1994 and belatedly Alexandre Glasberg of Amitié Chrétienne in 2003.

A second driver of recognition was the Plateau of Le Chambon-sur-Lignon which, drawing on the Resistance past of the Protestants of the Cévennes, had played a dramatic role in hiding Jews during the Occupation.[97] Their memory had been revived by Anny Latour, who interviewed Pasteur Trocmé and Oscar Rosowsky, the Russian-Jewish expert in counterfeit papers, who had become a doctor in the Paris region. A plaque in homage to the Protestant community was unveiled at Le Chambon in June 1979. This memory received much wider recognition as a result of a 1979 best-seller by Philip Hallie, based on Trocmé's memoirs, *Lest Innocent Blood be Shed*. It was further publicised by Pierre Sauvage, who had been born on the plateau during the war and returned to make the film *Weapons of the Spirit*, which triumphed at Cannes in 1987. His interpretation, which featured a 'good' German officer who disliked persecuting Jews, was criticised by Rosowsky and others in the Le Chambon community, but it gave an international profile to the story.[98] Daniel Trocmé, who had been deported and gassed in Poland, had been honoured as Righteous in 1976. André and Magda Trocmé were in turn recognised in 1984 and the people of Le Chambon were collectively recognised as Righteous among Nations in 1988. Jacques Chirac visited the plateau in July 2004 and praised its inhabitants: 'They chose tolerance, solidarity and fraternity,' he said. 'They chose the humanist values that unite our national community and found our common destiny.'[99]

Less than three years later, on 18 January 2007, Chirac honoured the Righteous of France as a whole in a magnificent ceremony at the Panthéon. Those interviewed by the media said that they were ordinary people who did not consider themselves to be heroes or heroines but were human beings, educated in French and universal values to do good: 'I am not a heroine,' said former actress Hélène Duc-Catroux, who was recognised as Righteous in 2005 at the age of eighty nine, 'but someone who was motivated by her own nature and by her upbringing also, to be an honest and upright person.' Édouard (Bouli) Simon, a former Jewish scout, declared these gestures of rescue to be acts of resistance as finer if not finer than blowing up a train:

People so often say that the French behaved scandalously [under the Occupation]. They must know that very many of them, known and unknown, were on the contrary extremely brave. To prevent children and old people from being deported just because they were Jewish was a kind of resistance like any other.[100]

This new way of looking at the Resistance permitted a reconsideration of the behaviour of the French people in general under the Occupation. Their honour had been dealt a blow by *Le Chagrin et la Pitié* thirty-five years earlier, but the concept of rescue-as-resistance allowed this to be restored.

The veteran historian Jacques Sémelin was asked by Simone Veil in 2008 to think about why three-quarters of the 330,000 Jews in France during the war, that is 250,000, had survived the Holocaust. He calculated that only a proportion escaped the country or were saved by organised rescue networks. This therefore left 200,000 who 'found complicity in the heart of French society'. Using the testimony of Jews who were saved, Sémelin argued that the difference was made by the generous 'little gestures' of the French population, providing them with food, hiding and help to escape. More controversially, argues Sémelin, they were helped by the presence of the Vichy state that was sometimes able to cushion German demands.[101] Sémelin's thesis was powerfully criticised by historians for downplaying the force of anti-Semitism both of the French people and the Vichy regime, but it responded to the search for rehabilitation of the French so far as their conduct under the Occupation was concerned and therefore reinforces the redeeming myth of the 'good French'.[102]

This humanitarian narrative of resistance as rescue, celebrating the brave actions of the chosen Righteous and the 'little gestures' of a much wider population, has become the dominant narrative or myth of the Resistance. Myth again, not in the sense of a fiction but as a story that gives meaning and identity to a society. A response to the guilt felt in France about the country's role in the Holocaust, it is also a new and powerful way of presenting the behaviour of French people in the Second World War. It has pushed out of the spotlight other dominant myths of the Resistance, both the Gaullist myth of national liberation and the communist myth of popular insurrection. These cults have their own shrines, ceremonies and faithful. The

Gaullist narrative is now embodied in a museum opened to mark the 50th anniversary of the Liberation in 1994, dedicated to the joint memory of Marshal Leclerc and Jean Moulin and located at the Gare Montparnasse, where Leclerc took the surrender of General von Choltitz. The communist narrative is cultivated further out from central Paris, having failed to gain a foothold in Ivry, at the Musée de la Résistance nationale at Champigny-sur-Marne, opened in 1985, and at a number of provincial sites, such as the Resistance museum of Châteaubriant, where twenty-seven communist hostages were shot in October 1941. None, however, is as powerful as the Memorial of the Shoah, a few hundred yards from the Paris Hôtel de Ville, where the inscribed names of 3,400 Righteous of France echo the 76,000 names of the Jews deported from France.

These narratives are dominant in the sense that they have emerged triumphant in the battle of memories that is the legacy of the Second World War in France, as in other countries. They have marginalised if not silenced other memories sustained by particular groups of resisters. These fight as much as they can for the soul of resistance but they do not have the reach or resonance in society of those more powerful stories. They are, nevertheless, what remains of the multitude of different resistance networks that were active, many of which were devastated by arrest, imprisonment and deportation, and most of which tell a story which is less appealing to contemporary audiences.

The Memorial of the Shoah, unsurprisingly, has been more interested in the memory of the Holocaust than in that of the Jewish resistance. This was discovered by Max Weinstein, who took part in the liberation of the Lyon suburb of Villeurbanne at the age of seventeen. He was too young to join the Carmagnole-Liberté group and instead joined the Union of Jewish Youth (UJJ). After the war he became a communist but later criticised the Party for glossing over the contribution of Jewish resisters to the cause. He collected a file of documents to assert the contribution of the

UJJ to the Resistance and to have it recognised. The Memorial of the Shoah in Paris seems to have shown little interest in his work but he managed, with the help of a friend who was going to Washington in 1997, to persuade the US Holocaust Memorial Museum to take a copy for their archives.[103] That year he also published his memoirs.[104] In 2008 he created an association for the Memory of the Jewish Resisters of the MOI, which would represent all resistance groups of foreign Jewish origin.[105] Whereas the Vercors had its site and museum on the spot, he said, these groups were scattered all over France. He had his eyes on the headquarters of the progressive Jewish movement in Paris, at 14 rue de Paradis in the 10th *arrondissement*, as a site for the museum. In the event the premises were never secured and the museum remained virtual.[106]

The Communist Party also marginalised stories it did not welcome, usually those of communist resisters who were active on the ground in France and strayed too far from the control of the Party leadership which was either in Moscow, like Thorez, or in hiding in France, like Duclos, or escaped to London, like Grenier, or was released from Vichy's prisons in Algiers. Charles Tillon, who claimed to have issued his own appeal to resist on 17 June 1940 while the Party followed the line of the Nazi-Soviet Pact, and took control of the Francs-Tireurs et Partisans in France, was expelled from the Central Committee in 1952 and finally broke with the Party in 1977. PCF general secretary Georges Marchais, who far from joining the Resistance had gone as a voluntary worker to Germany during the war, tried to gag Tillon in 1984, only to be told that he was 'an accomplice of the Stalinist trials' and 'not to divide resisters over their victory while you were on the side of the defeated'.[107] Tillon duly left his personal archives not with those of the Party in Saint-Denis but, curiously, in the Centre d'Histoire of Sciences-Po. French leaders of the FTP were not, however, above marginalising communist freedom fighters of foreign and Jewish origin and threatened the claims of the *French*

Communist Party. Henri Rol-Tanguy, leader of the FTP and later Forces Françaises de l'Intérieure in the Paris region who were at the heart of insurrection of August 1944, was a comrade but also rival of Joseph Epstein, the brilliant Polish-Jewish national FTP commander shot at Mont Valérien in 1944. Léon Landini, head of the Carmagnole-Liberté association, has argued that Rol-Tanguy was reluctant to acknowledge that Epstein was his superior and would have received von Choltitz's surrender if he had still been alive. Equally, Landini accused Rol-Tanguy of being reluctant to support a campaign to have a road named after Epstein in Paris, although a square was finally named after Joseph Epstein in the 20th *arrondissement* of Paris in 2004, two years after Rol-Tanguy's death.

The memory of communist resisters, in turn, has still had to contend with the dominant Gaullist narrative of national resistance. This may be seen in the rivalry between Rol-Tanguy and the cult of General, later Marshal, Leclerc which symbolises the debate between liberation by popular insurrection and national liberation by the tanks of the 2nd Armoured Division. Although Rol-Tanguy featured prominently in the 1966 film *Is Paris Burning?* played by Bruno Crémer, at various events sponsored by Jacques Chirac, mayor of Paris between 1977 and 1995, Cécile Rol-Tanguy recalled that 'la Maréchale', the widow of General Leclerc, and her sons, looked down their noses at them.[108] When the Museum dedicated to Leclerc and Jean Moulin opened in 1994, Rol-Tanguy attended a conference on Resistance and Liberation in Paris along with André Tollet, former head of the Paris Liberation Committee, to put the case for liberation from below: 'The success of the insurrection,' he declared, 'was that the whole population rose up at the call of the Resistance and that all the forces of the Resistance were united under a single command' – his own.[109] After Rol-Tanguy's death the memory of Paris insurrection was maintained by Cécile Rol-Tanguy and by the Musée de la Résistance nationale, founded by Tollet, a man who deserves greater recognition in the annals of the Resistance.

The Gaullist narrative that imposed itself after 1944 no longer has the influence it one enjoyed. It has been overtaken in recent years by that of the Holocaust and the Righteous among Nations. But it holds on, asserting a story of national liberation that arose from 'the one France, the true France, eternal France'. It is also that of the Free French whose epic began with prising French Equatorial Africa from Vichy in the 'three glorious days' of 26–28 August 1940, which included Leclerc's seizure of power in Douala, Cameroon. Although the Order of Liberation was created at Brazzaville in November 1940 and 140 of the 1,038 Compagnons came from French Equatorial Africa, only eight of these were black Africans.[110] Since Cameroon's independence in 1961 the Free French story, symbolised by the statue of General Leclerc in Douala, has come to represent the stifling of a national Cameroonian memory by a colonial French memory. A Cameroonian veteran, Womondje Barnabé, interviewed for a 1998 thesis said that 'Leclerc was bad for the Cameroonians. He declared that however good a black soldier might be, he could not be promoted above the rank of warrant officer.'[111] The statue of Leclerc was defaced in 2009 by a Cameroonian nationalist, Mboua Massock, who scrawled 'our own heroes and martyrs first' and 'fifty years after independence is too much'. In 2013 the statue was overturned by another activist, André Blaise Essama, who explained: 'I smashed this monument so that General Leclerc could return to the land of his ancestors in France [. . .] The square where it stood covers us in shame' and should be replaced by 'national heroes'.[112]

In the thick of the battle to impose a dominant narrative of the Resistance group memories of the Resistance continue to be cultivated. A memory that was once dominant may indeed continue as a collective memory that gives identity and solidarity to a particular group. Max Weinstein struggled to develop a group memory of the UJJ, the adolescent wing of Carmagnole-Liberté, but Carmagnole-Liberté itself established a powerful group memory thanks to the work of former militants such as Henri Krischer and Léon Landini. The latter donated its rich archives, with biographies and photographs of scores of former members, some taken by the Vichy authorities after torture, to the Musée de la Résistance nationale. Landini has spoken in the name of the group on many public occasions, describing at the annual commemoration of the Glières *maquis* in May 2010 that some resisters from the Glières escaped to fight with Carmagnole-Liberté.[113] These group memories have a public face but also a private one. They sustain among the survivors of the group the memory of its hopes and fears, triumphs and tragedies. It is an inward-looking memory of those who were shunned by Vichy, the German authorities and by French society in general as foreigners, Jews and communists, even as criminals and terrorists. They now fight to assert their heroism and legitimacy in the French revolutionary tradition in the face of a humanitarian discourse that bears little relation to the violence of their cause. What bound together his group, Landini reflected in an 2012 interview, was 'love, fraternity, a solidarity and respect for each other'. Above all he still regretted the death of the beautiful young Jewish girl, Jeanine Sontag, whom his team was forced to abandon in a failed operation and who died in the massacre of Saint-Genis-Laval. After the tape machine stopped recording he confided:

I don't really believe in heaven, but if I did, I would be able to look my old comrades in the eye and say, 'Until the end of my days, I continued to fight for the cause for which you died.'[114]

What, it may be asked, happens to group memories once the last member of the group has died? One way of preserving the memory is through the families of the resisters. Claire Rol-Tanguy, daughter of Henri and Cécile Rol-Tanguy, became general secretary of the Friends of Combatants in Republican

Spain (ACER). She is committed to the memory of volunteers like her father who joined the International Brigades in Spain and of Spanish republicans who fought in the French Resistance. This 'hereditary resistance' is, however, not always as straightforward as it might appear. Resisters who had suffered arrest, torture and deportation were not always minded to tell their story to their partners or children, for fear of stirring up the pain or of not being understood. They were often more ready towards the end of their lives to tell their grandchildren, whom they saw as more open to share their past than their own children had been. Julien Blanc, the historian of the Musée de l'Homme resistance network, spent long hours interviewing Germaine Tillion, the guardian of the group's archives and memory. But he was also the grandson of Jean-Pierre Vernant, leader of Libération and the FFI in the Toulouse area. Vernant, a brilliant ancient historian, went on to become a professor at the Collège de France. He did not take part in the many commemorations of the French Resistance and only ever spoke about his experiences to a small number of comrades who had been through the same ordeal. Not until shortly before his death did he speak to his grandson about his resistance past, a powerful and painful story that Julien Blanc shared for the first time at a conference to mark the 70th anniversary of the Liberation in London in June 2014.[115]

The nurturing of group and individual memories threatened with silencing cannot, however, be left to their own families. It is up to historians to recover these testimonies, published and unpublished, filmed, recorded or transcribed. An archive of interviews from the French Resistance and from other resistance movements round the world is being established at the University of Sussex. Only by heeding these voices and tracing the groups that gave rise to them can the historian offer an authentic picture of the breadth and diversity of resistance activity that developed in hidden corners of France, in immigrant communities that had taken refuge in France and in the furthest reaches of the French Empire among colonial peoples as well as the Free French. The story of the French Resistance is central to French identity. If the story changes, it is an invitation to re-examine that identity.

List of Abbreviations

AEF, Afrique Équatoriale Française/French Equatorial Africa

AMGOT, Allied Military Government for Occupied Territories

ATS, Auxiliary Territorial Service

BCRA, Bureau Central de Renseignements et d'Action/Central Bureau for Information and Action

CAD, Comité d'Action contre la Déportation/Action Committee against Deportation

CALPO, Comité Allemagne Libre pour l'Ouest/Free Germany Committee in the West

CCZN, Comité de Coordination Zone Nord/North Zone Coordination Committee

CDL, Comité Départemental de Libération/Departmental Liberation Committee

CFL, Corps Français de Libération/French Liberation Corps

CFLN, Comité Français de Libération Nationale/French National Liberation Committee

CGE, Comité Général d'Études/General Planning Committee

CGT, Confédération Générale du Travail/General Confederation of Labour

CHDGM, Comité d'Histoire de la Deuxième Guerre Mondiale/Committee for the History of the Second World War

CHG, Comité d'Histoire de la Guerre/Committee for the History of the War

CHOLF, Commission d'Histoire de l'Occupation et de la Libération de la France/ Commission for the History of the Occupation and Liberation of France

CIMADE, Comité Inter Mouvements Auprès Des Évacués/Inter-movement Committee for Evacuees

CNR, Conseil National de la Résistance/National Council of Resistance

COMAC, Comité d'Action Militaire/Military Action Committee

COSE, Centre d'Orientation Sociale des Étrangers/Foreigners' Social Advice Centre

COSOR, Comité d'Oeuvres Sociales de la Résistance/Resistance Social Services Committee

CPL, Comité Parisien de la Liberation/Paris Liberation Committee

CVF, Corps de Volontaires Françaises/French Women's Volunteer Corps

DB, Division Blindée/Armoured Division

DGSS, Délégation Générale des Services Spéciaux/Special Services General Delegation

EIF, Éclaireurs Israélites de France/French Jewish Scouts

FFI, Forces Françaises de l'Intérieur/ French Forces of the Interior

FN, Front National/National Front

FTP, Francs-Tireurs et Partisans/Free-Shooters and Partisans

IHTP, Institut d'Histoire du Temps Présent/Institute for the History of the Present Time

List of Abbreviations

JEC, Jeunesse Étudiante Chrétienne/Christian Student Youth

KPD, Kommunistische Partei Deutschlands/German Communist Party

MLN, Mouvement de Libération Nationale/National Liberation Movement

MOI, Main d'Oeuvre Immigrée/Immigrant Labour

MUR, Mouvements Unis de la Résistance/United Resistance Movements

NAP, Noyautage des Administrations Publiques/Public Services Infiltration

OCM, Organisation Civile et Militaire/Civil and Military Organisation

ORA, Organisation de Résistance de l'Armée/Army Resistance Organisation

OSE, Oeuvre de Secours aux Enfants/Children's Rescue Programme

PCF, Parti Communiste Français/French Communist Party

RMVF, Régiment de Marche de Volontaires Étrangers/Foreign Volunteers Infantry
Regiment

SOL, Service d'Ordre Légionnaire/Legion's Security Service

STO, Service du Travail Obligatoire/Compulsory Labour Service

UGIF, Union Générale des Israélites de France/General Union of French Jews

UJJ, Union de le Jeunesse Juive/Union of Jewish Youth

UJRE, Union des Juifs pour la Résistance et l'Entraide/Jewish Aid and Resistance
Union

WAAC, Women's Army Auxiliary Corps

WAAF, Women's Auxiliary Air Force

YASK, Yiddisher Arbeter Sport Klub/Jewish Workers Sports Club

Cast List

Abadi, Moussa (1910–97), rescuer with Réseau Marcel in Nice

Aboulker, José (1920–2009), Jewish medical student and resister in Algiers

Albert Lake, Virginia d'(1910–97), American resister with Comet line

Albrecht, Berty (1893–1943), resister with Combat, companion of Henri Frenay

Alesch, Robert (1906–49), priest of Luxemburg origin, traitor

Appleton, Marcelle (*b.* 1895), Gallia resistance, Bourg-en-Bresse

Asher, Serge, *see* Ravanel

Astier de la Vigerie, Emmanuel d'(1900–69), head of Libération, *commissaire* for the Interior

Astier de la Vigerie, François (1886–1956), Free French general

Astier de la Vigerie, Henri d' (1897–1952), royalist resister in North Africa

Aubrac, Lucie (1912–2007), resister with Libération

Aubrac, Raymond (1914–2012), resister with Libération, *commissaire de la République* in Marseille 1944

Avinin, Antoine (1902–62), resister with Franc-Tireur, Lyon

Barot, Madeleine (1909–95), general secretary of Inter-movement Committee for Evacuees (CIMADE)

Beling, Walter (1899–1988), German communist resister with Travail Allemand and CALPO

Bernard, Lucie, *see* Aubrac, Lucie

Bertaux, Pierre (1907–86), *commissaire de la République* in Toulouse, 1944

Béthouart, General Antoine (1889–1982), commander in Norway, with Army of Africa and with First Army

Bidault, Georges (1899–1983), Christian democrat, chair of National Council of Resistance

Billotte, Pierre (1906–92), head of de Gaulle's general staff

Bingen, Jacques (1908–44), deputy delegate-general of CFLN

Blocq-Mascart, Maxime (1894–1965), resister with Organisation Civile et Militaire and on CNR

Boddington, Nicholas (1904–74), SOE deputy to Maurice Buckmaster

Bohec, Jeanne (1919–2010), member of Corps des Volontaires françaises, BCRA agent

Boisson, Pierre (1894–1948), Vichy governor-general of French West Africa

Bollaert, Émile (1890–1978), prefect of the Rhône, delegate-general of French Committee of National Liberation

Bollardière, Jacques Pâris de (1907–86), Free French soldier, *maquis* chief in Ardennes, 1944

Boris, Georges (1888–1960), Free French link to BBC and director of Interior commissariat

Cast List

Bouchinet-Serreulles, Claude (1912–2000), head of de Gaulle's civil cabinet, delegate-general of CFLN

Bourdet, Claude (1909–96), resister with Combat

Brinon, Fernand de (1885–1947), Vichy's ambassador to occupied Paris

Brosset, Diego (1898–1944), Free French general

Brossolette, Pierre (1903–44), resister with Musée de l'Homme, Confrérie Notre-Dame and BCRA

Brunet de Sairigné, Gabriel (1913–48), Free French soldier

Brustlein, Gilbert (1919–2009), communist resister

Buckmaster, Maurice (1902–92), head of SOE France

Bulawko, Henry (1918–2011), Jewish rescuer, organiser of the Amelot committee

Capitant, René (1901–70), law professor and leader of Gaullist resistance in Algiers

Casanova, Danielle (1909–43), communist women's organiser and resister

Cassou, Jean (1897-1986), resister with Musée de l'Homme, *commissaire de la République* in Toulouse, 1944

Catroux, General Georges (1877–1969), governor-general of Indochina, High Commissioner in the Levant, governor of Algeria

Cavaillès, Jean (1897–1986), philosophy lecturer, resister with Libération and Cohors-Asturies

Chaillet, Pierre (1900–72), Jesuit priest, resister with *Témoignage Chrétien* and Amitié Chrétienne in Lyon

Chavant, Eugène (1894–1969), civil commander of the Vercors

Chomat, Claudine (1915–95), communist women's organiser and resister

Clark, General Mark (1896–1984), Eisenhower's second-in-command in North Africa

Closon, François-Louis (1910–98), official with interior commissariat, *commissaire de la République* in Lille, 1944

Cochet, Gabriel (1888–1973), Air force general, lone resister, commander of FFIs in Southern Zone

Cohen, Albert (*b.* 1916), resister with Armée Juive

Cordier, Daniel (*b.* 1920), Jean Moulin's wireless operator

Coulaudon, Émile (Gaspard) (1907–77), *maquis* leader in the Auvergne

Courcel, Geoffroy de (1912–92), head of de Gaulle's military cabinet

Dahlem, Käthe (1899–1974), German communist resister with Travail Allemand and CALPO

Dahlem, Franz (1892–1981), German communist resister, organiser of Travail Allemand

Dalloz, Pierre (1900–82), visionary of the Vercors

Darlan, Admiral François (1881–1942), naval commander, head of French government 1941-2, brought Vichy North Africa over to Americans

Debarge, Charles (1909–42), miner, resister with FTP in Pas-de-Calais

Debré, Michel (1912–96), jurist, member of Comité general d'Études, *commissaire de la République* in Angers, 1944

Degliame, Marcel (1912–89), resister with Combat and Action Ouvrière

Delestraint, General Charles (1879–1945), head of Armée Secrète

Deschamps, Genia, *née* Kobozieff, *see* Gemähling, Genia

Despaigne, Harry, *see* Richardson, Major

president of the French Committee of National Liberation

Glasberg, Abbé Alexandre (1902–81), Lyon curate, rescuer with Amitié Chrétienne, *maquisard* in Tarn-et-Garonne

Gosset, Jean (1912–44), agent with Cohors-Asturies

Gronowski, Louis (Lajb) (1904–87), Polish-Jewish resister with FTP-MOI

Hall, Virginia (1906–82), American journalist and intelligence agent

Hamon, Léo (Lew Goldenberg) (1908–93), resister with Ceux de la Résistance, member of Paris Liberation Committee

Hautecloque, Philippe de, *see* Leclerc, General

Hervé, Pierre (1913–93), resister with Libération

Heslop, Richard (1907–73), SOE agent

Holban, Boris (Bruhman) (1908–2004), Romanian-Jewish resister with FTP-MOI

Hull, Cordell (1871–1955), US secretary of state

Humbert, Agnès (1894–1963), resister with the Musée de l'Homme

Ilić, Ljubomir (1905–94), Yugoslav resister, on national military committee of FTP

Ingrand, Henri, surgeon (1908–2003), resister with Combat, *commissaire de la République* in the Auvergne

Jonghe, Andrée de (1916–2007), Belgian organiser of the Comet line

Juin, Alphonse (1888–1967), General in Army of Africa, commander of French expeditionary force in Italy

Kessel, Joseph (1898–1979), journalist and novelist

Knout, David (1900–55), Russian-Jewish resister with Armée Juive

Koenig, Pierre (1898–1970), Free French general, commander of FFIs, French delegate to Supreme Allied Command

Krasucki, Henri (1924–2003), Polish-Jewish resister, later general secretary of CGT

Kriegel, Maurice (1914–2006), communist resister with Libération, member of COMAC

Krischer, Henri (1920–2000), Polish-Jewish resister with Carmagnole-Liberté

Kugler, Norbert (1906–82), German anti-Nazi resister with Carmagnole-Liberté

Kühne, Otto (1893–1955), German anti-Nazi resister, *maquis* leader in the Cévennes

Lacoste, Robert (1898–1989), trade unionist, member of CNR and CFLN

Landini, Léon (*b.* 1926), resister with Carmagnole-Liberté

Langer, Mendel (1903–43), organiser of FTP-MOI resistance in Toulouse

Lattre de Tassigny, Jean de (1889–1952), general in Armistice Army, commander of B Army and First French Army

Laval, Pierre (1883–1945), French politician and head of government, 1942–4

Lazarus, Jacques (1916–2014), resister with Armée Juive

Leahy, Admiral William (1875–1959), US ambassador to Vichy

Leclerc, General Philippe (1902–47), commander of the 2nd Armoured Division

Lecompte-Boinet, Jacques (1905–74), resister with Combat and Ceux de la Résistance, member of CFLN

Lederman, Charles (1913–98), Polish-Jewish lawyer, rescuer and resister with OSE, UJRE and Carmagnole

Lefaucheux, Marie-Hélène (1904–64), resister with Organisation Civile et Militaire, member of Paris Liberation Committee

Lefaucheux, Pierre (1898–1955), resister with Organisation Civile et Militaire, FFI commander in Paris region

Lemaigre-Dubreuil, Jacques (1894–1955), industrialist and link to Americans in North Africa

Leo, Gerhard (1923–2009), German communist, resister with Travail Allemand and CALPO

Le Ray, Alain (1910–2007), escaped POW, military organiser of Vercors

Le Troquer, André (1884–1963), socialist politician, *commissaire* for war with CFLN, head of Paris municipal council

Lévy, Jean-Pierre (1911–96), leader of Franc-Tireur

London, Artur (1915–86), Czechoslovak-Jewish resister, leader of FTP-MOI

López Tovar, Vicente (1909–98), Spanish republican resister

Macmillan, Harold (1894–1986), British minister resident in the Mediterranean

Malleret, Alfred (Joinville) (1911–60), communist, national commander of FFI

Manouchian, Missak (1906–44), resister of Armenian origin, leader of FTP-MOI in Paris

Marrane, Georges (1888–1976), mayor of Ivry-sur-Seine, leader of Front National in Free Zone

Martin-Chauffier, Simone (1902–75), resister with Musée de l'Homme and in Lyon

Mayer, Daniel (1909–96), socialist militant, resister with Comité d'Action Socialiste

Menthon, François de (1900–84), Christian democratic resister with Liberté

Monod, Claude (1917–45), surgeon, FFI commander in Burgundy, joined First Army

Monod, Jacques (1903–44), philosophy teacher, resister on Mont-Mouchet

Monod, Philippe (1900–92), resister with Combat

Monnet, Jean (1888–1979), envoy to USA, promoter of CFLN, later architect of French planning and European Union

Môquet, Guy (1924–41), young communist resister

Mordkovitch, Hélène, *see* Viannay, Hélène

Moulin, Jean (1899–1943), French administrator, de Gaulle's emissary to France, founder of the National Council of Resistance

Murphy, Robert (1894–1978), US representative in North Africa

Nearne, Jacqueline (1916–82), SOE agent

Niebergall, Otto (1904–77), German communist, resister with Travail Allemand and CALPO

Noguès, General Charles (1876–1971), Resident-general in Morocco, commander of North African forces

Oddon, Yvonne (1902–82), resister with Musée de l'Homme

Ouzoulias, Albert (1915–95), leader of young communist resisters, national military commissar of FTP

Pannequin, Roger (1920–2001), schoolteacher, resister with FTP in Nord

Parodi, Alexandre (1901–79), jurist, delegate-general of CFLN

Passy, Colonel (1911–98), head of Free French secret service

Pétain, Marshal Philippe (1856–1951), French head of state 1940–44

Petit, Major Henri (Romans-Petit) (1897–1980), *maquis* leader in the Ain

Philip, André (1902–70), socialist politician, *commissaire* of the Interior

Pineau, Christian (1904–95), trade unionist, resister with Libé-Nord

Pinton, Auguste (1901–84), resister with Franc-Tireur in Lyon

Pleven, René (1901–93), Free French head of foreign affairs, CFLN *commissaire* for Economy, Finances and the Colonies

Polonski, Abraham (1913–?1990), organiser of the Armée Juive

Pommiès, Major André (1904–78), commander of Pommiès Free Corps

Postel-Vinay, André (1911–2007), resister with Organisation Civile et Militaire

Pucheu, Pierre (1899–1944), industrialist, Vichy Minister of the Interior

Rake, Denis (1902–76), SOE agent

Ravanel, Serge (1920–2009), resister with Libération, head of FFIs in Toulouse region

Rayski, Adam (1913–2008), Polish-Jewish rescuer and resister

Rée, Harry (1914–91), SOE agent

Rémy (1904–84), resister with Confrérie Notre-Dame

Renault, Gilbert, *see* Rémy

Revers, Georges (1891–1974), general in Armistice Army, resister with ORA

Ribière, Germaine (1917–99), rescuer with Amitié Chrétienne and OSE

Ribière, Henri (1897–1956), socialist militant, resister with Libé-Nord

Richardson, Major (1917–92), SOE agent in south-west France

Ricol, Lise (1916–2012), communist women's resistance, partner of Artur London

Riffaud, Madeleine (*b.* 1924), resister with FTP, journalist

Rivet, Paul (1876–1958), director of Musée de l'Homme

Rochet, Waldeck (1905–83), London delegate of PCF central committee, later general secretary of PCF

Rol-Tanguy, Cécile (*b.* 1919), liaison agent of Henri Rol-Tanguy

Rol-Tanguy, Henri (1908–2002), communist, FTP leader in Paris region

Roosevelt, Franklin D. (1882–1945), US President

Rosenstock, Odette (1914–97), rescuer with Réseau Marcel, wife of Moussa Abadi

Rosowsky, Oscar (1923–2014), forger at Le Chambon-sur-Lignon

Salomon, Andrée (1908–85), rescuer of Jewish children with OSE

Salmon, Robert (1918–2013), resister with Défense de la France

Samuel, Raymond, *see* Aubrac, Raymond

Schumann, Maurice (1911–98), Free French spokesman on the BBC

Sivadon, Jeanne (1901–95), social worker, resister with Combat

Soustelle, Jacques (1912–90), head of Free French intelligence in Algiers

Southgate, Maurice (1913–90), SOE agent

Starr, George Reginald (1904–80), engineer, SOE agent, resistance leader in SW France

Suberville, Gerald (*b.* 1917), head of Action Ouvrière in Languedoc

Szwarc, Tereska, *see* Torrès, Tereska

Teitgen, Pierre-Henri (1908–97), law professor, resister with Liberté, Minister of Justice

Terré, Hélène (1903–93), chief of Corps des Volontaires françaises

Thorez, Maurice (1900–64), general secretary of PCF

Tillion, Germaine (1907–2008), anthropologist, resister with Musée de l'Homme and Gloria

Tillon, Charles (1897–1993), FTP leader, Air minister 1944

Titonel, Damira (1923–2011), resister of Italian origin with 35th Brigade FTP-MOI in Toulouse

Tollet, André (1913–2001), communist resister, chair of CPL

Torrès, Tereska (1920–2012), resister with Corps des Volontaires françaises

Touny, Alfred (1886–1944), resister with Organisation Civile et Militaire

Trocmé, André (1901–71), Protestant pastor and rescuer at Le Chambon-sur-Lignon

Trotobas, Michel (1914–43), SOE agent in Lille

Vernant, Jean-Pierre (1914–2007), resister with Libération, FTP commander in Toulouse region

Viannay, Hélène (1917–2006), Russian-Jewish resister with Défense de la France

Viannay, Philippe (1917–86), resister with Défense de la France

Vildé, Boris (1908–41), White Russian, resister with Musée de l'Homme

Villon, Pierre (Roger Ginsburger) (1901–80), communist head of Front National, member of CNR and CPL

Vistel, Auguste, 'Alban' (1905–94), head of MUR, chair of CDL and FFI commander in Lyon

Vogüé, Jean de (1908–72), naval officer, resister with Ceux de la Résistance

Vomécourt, Pierre de (1906–86), agent of British Intelligence Service

Vomécourt, Philippe de (1902–64), agent of British Intelligence Service

Wake, Nancy (1912–2011), New Zealand SOE agent

Walters Comert, Anne-Marie (1923–98), SOE agent

Weinstein, Max (b. 1927), resister with UJJ

Witherington Cornioley, Pearl (b. 1914), SOE agent

Weygand, General Maxim (1867–1965), Vichy defence minister and delegate-general in French Africa

Yeo-Thomas, Forest (1902–64), SOE agent

Zlatin, Sabine (1907–96), rescuer with OSE, director of orphanage of Izieu

Notes

Introduction

1 www.lemonde.fr/politique/article/2008/04/30/allocution-de-nicolas-sarkozy-lors-de-la-ceremonie-d-hommage-aux-martyrs-du-bois-de-boulogne-le-16-mai-2007_1040045_823448.html

2 Charles de Gaulle, *Discours et messages I* (Paris, Plon, 1970), pp. 439–40

3 Gérard Namer, *La Commémoration en France, 1944–1982* (Paris, S.P.A.G./Papyrus, 1983), p. 84

4 Vladimir Trouplin, *Dictionnaire des Compagnons de la Libération* (Bordeaux, Elytis, 2010), pp. 12–17; Guillaume Piketty & Vladimir Trouplin, *Les Compagnons de l'Aube. Archives Inédits des Compagnons de la Libération* (Paris, Textuel, 2014)

5 Olivier Wieviorka, *La Mémoire désunie. Le Souvenir politique des années sombre, de la Libération à nos jours* (Paris, Seil, 2010), pp. 42–9

6 Serge Barcellini and Annette Wieviorka, *Passant, souviens-toi! Les lieux du souvenir de la Seconde Guerre mondiale en France* (Paris, Plon, 1995), pp. 332, 383; Robert Gildea, *Marianne in Chains: In Search of the German Occupation, 1940–1945* (London, Macmillan, 2002), pp. 386–7

7 Pierre Laborie, *Le Chagrin et le Venin. La France sous l'Occupation, memoires et idées recues* (Montrouge, Bayard, 2011), pp. 26, 60–8

8 Marcel Ophüls, *The Sorry and the Pity. Chronicle of a French City Under the German Occupation* (St Albans, Paladin), p. 118

9 René Rémond, *Paul Touvier et l'Église* (Paris, Fayard, 1992), p. 381; Henry Rousso, *The Vichy Syndrome. History and Memory in France Since 1944* (Cambridge, Mass., 1991), pp. 114–55

10 AN BB 30/1891, *Procès Klaus Barbie, 13e audience, 27 mai 1987*, pp. 13–14. See also Sabine Zlatin, *Mémoires de la 'Dame d'Izieu'* (Paris, Gallimard, 1992)

11 *Procès Klaus Barbie, 21e audience, 11 juin 1987*, pp. 6–11

12 Sarah Gensburger, *Les Justes de France. Politiques publiques de la mémoire* (Paris, FNSP, 2010), p. 80; Rebecca Clifford, *Commemorating the Holocaust. Dilemmas of Remembrance in France and Italy* (Oxford, OUP, 2013), pp. 194–200

13 BN Inathèque, Hommage de la nation aux Justes de France, FR2, 18 Jan. 2007

14 See for example, Eric Hobsbawm and Terence Ranger (eds.), *The Invention of Tradition* (Cambridge, CUP, 1983), and Raphael Samuel and Paul Thompson (eds.), *The Myths We Live By* (London, Routledge, 1990)

15 Laurent Douzou, *La Résistance française: une histoire périlleuse* (Paris, Seuil, 2005), pp. 53–62; Douzou (ed.) *Faire l'histoire de la Résistance* (Rennes, Presses Universitaires de Rennes, 2010), pp. 15–78

16 AN 72AJ675, Comité d'Histoire de la Guerre, 1 Jul. 1946. Report by Édouard Perroy, pp. 49–50. The interviews are collected in the Archives Nationales 72AJ series

17 Henri Michel, *Histoire de la Résistance* (Paris, PUF, Que sais'je? 1950); *Les Idées politiques et sociales de la Résistance: documents clandestins, 1940–1944* (Paris, PUF, 1954); *Les courants de pensée de la Résistance* (Paris, PUF, 1962); Henri Michel and Marie Granet, *Combat. Histoire d'un movement de résistance* (Paris, PUF, 1957)

18 Marie Granet, *Défense de la France, histoire d'un mouvement de résistance, 1940–1944* (Paris, PUF, 1960); *Ceux de la Résistance, 1940–1944* (Paris, Éditions de Minuit, 1964); *Cohors-Asturies: histoire d'un réseau de résistance, 1942–1944* (Bordeaux, Édition des 'Cahiers de la Résistance', 1974)

19 Henri Noguères, Marcel Degliame-Fouché and Jean-Louis Vigier, *Histoire de la Résistance en France* (Paris, Robert Laffont, 1967), I, p. 15; Bruno Leroux, 'Des historiographies parallèles et concurrentes du Comité d'histoire de la Deuxième Guerre mondiale: *L'Histoire de la Résistance en France d'Henri Noguères* et *La Résistance d'Alain Guérin*', in Douzou (ed.), *Faire l'histoire de la Résistance*, pp. 95–115

20 Jean-Louis Crémieux-Brilhac, *Ici Londres: les voix de la liberté, 1940–1944* (5 vols., Paris, la Documentation française, 1975–6)

21 Agnès Humbert, *Notre guerre* (Paris, Emile-Paul frères, 1946)

22 Yves Farge, *Rebelles, soldats et citoyens: carnet d'un commissaire de la République* (Paris, Grasset, 1946); Emmanuel d'Astier de la Vigerie, *Sept fois sept jours* (Paris, Les Éditions de Minuit, 1947); Colonel Passy, *Souvenirs. 1. 2e bureau, Londres; Souvenirs. 2, 10, Duke Street, Londres. le B.C.R.A.* (Monte-Carlo, R. Solar, 1947–8); Rémy, *Mémoires d'un agent secret de la France libre (juin 1940–juin 1942)* (Monaco, Raoul Solar, 1947); *Le Livre du courage et de la peur (juin 1942–novembre 1943)* (2 vols, Monaco, Raoul Solar, 1946); *Comment meurt un réseau (novembre 1943–août 1944)* (Monaco, Raoul Solar, 1947); *Une affaire de trahison (novembre 1943–février 1944)* (Monaco, Raoul Solar, 1947); *Les Mains jointes (1944)* (Monaco, Raoul Solar, 1948); *Mais le temple est bâti (1944–1945)* (Monaco, Raoul Solar, 1950)

23 Dwight D. Eisenhower, *Crusade in Europe* (New York, Doubleday, 1948); Winston Churchill, *The Second World War* (6 vols., Cassell, 1948–54); General de Gaulle, *Mémoires de Guerre* (3 vols., Paris, Plon, 1954–9)

24 See for example, General Béthouart, *Cinq années d'espérance. Mémoires de guerre, 1939–1945* (Paris, Plon, 1968); Jacques de Bollardière, *Bataille d'Alger, bataille de l'homme* (Paris & Bruges, Desclée, De Brouwer, 1972); Roger Pannequin, *Ami si tu tombes* (Paris, Sagittaire, 1976); Charles Tillon, *On chantait rouge* (Paris, R. Laffont, 1977); Simone Martin-Chauffier, *A bientôt quand même* (Paris, Calmann-Lévy, 1976)

25 Henri Frenay, *La Nuit finira* (Paris, Robert Laffont, 1973)

26 Henri Frenay, *L'Énigme Jean Moulin* (Paris, Robert Laffont, 1977)

27 Daniel Cordier, *Jean Moulin I. Une ambition pour la République. L'inconnu du Panthéon, juin 1899–juin 1936* (Paris, Lattès, 1989); *Jean Moulin II. Le choix d'un destin. L'inconnu du Panthéon, juin 1936–novembre 1940* (Paris, Lattès, 1989); *Jean Moulin III. De Gaulle, capital de la Résistance. L'inconnu*

du Panthéon, novembre 1940–décembre 1941 (Paris, Lattès, 1993); *Jean Moulin. La République des catacombes* (Paris, Gallimard, 1999)

28 François Marcot, *La Résistance dans le Jura* (Besançon, Cêtre, 1985); Jean-Marie Guillon, *La Libération du Var, Résistance et nouveaux pouvoirs* (Paris, Centre national de la recherche scientifique/IHTP, 1990); and Jacqueline Sainclivier, *La Résistance en Ille-et-Vilaine, 1940–1944* (Rennes, PU de Rennes, 1993)

29 Laurent Douzou, *La Désobéissance: histoire d'un mouvement et d'un journal clandestins, Libération-Sud, 1940–1944* (Paris, O. Jacob, 1995), Olivier Wieviorka, *Une certaine idée de la Résistance: Défense de la France: 1940–1949* (Paris, Seuil, 1995); Alya Aglan, *La résistance sacrifiée: le mouvement Libération-Nord* (Paris, Flammarion, 1999)

30 Guillaume Piketty, *Pierre Brossolette. Un héros de la Résistance* (Paris, O. Jacob, 1998)

31 Daniel Virieux, 'Le Front National de lutte pour la liberté et l'indépendance de la France. Un movement de résistance, période clandestine (mai 1941–août 1944) (thesis, Paris VIII, 1996)

32 Jean-Marie Guillon and Pierre Laborie (eds.), *Mémoire et histoire; la Résistance* (Toulouse, Privat, 1995), Christian Bougeard and Jacqueline Sainclivier (eds.), *La Résistance et les Français. Enjeux stratégiques et environnement social* (Rennes, Presses Universitaires de Rennes, 1995); François Marcot (ed.), *La Résistance et les Français: lutte armée et maquis* (Paris, les Belles Lettres, 1996); Laurent Douzou, Robert Frank, Denis Peschanski, Dominique Veillon (eds.), *La Résistance et les Français: villes, centres et logiques de décision* (Paris, IHTP, 1995)

33 François Marcot, Bruno Leroux and Christine Levisse-Touzé, *Dictionnaire historique de la Résistance* (Paris, Robert Laffont, 2006)

34 AN 72AJ2217, Fonds Brossolette. Interviews by Gilberte Brossolette; Gilberte Brossolette, *Il s'appelait Pierre Brossolette* (Paris, A. Michel, 1976)

35 Les Cahiers de l'IHTP, 4 (Jun. 1986). *Questions à l'histoire orale. Table ronde du 20 juin 1986*, 104. Another IHTP round table in 1992 – Les Cahiers de l'IHTP, 21 (Nov. 1992) *La Bouche de Vérité? La recherche historique et les sources orales* – elicited similar misgivings about oral testimony

36 Mémorial de la Shoah, DVXI-77, Fonds Anny Latour. Anny Latour, *La Résistance juive en France, 1940–1944* (Paris, Stock, 1970)

37 Musée de la Résistance Nationale, 'Les Inconnus de la Résistance'. Extracts were published in Florian Benoît & Charles Silvestre, *Les Inconnus de la Résistance* (Paris, L'Humanité/Messidor, 1984)

38 Irène Nemirowsky, *Suite française* (Paris, Denoel, 2004), translated (London, Chatto & Windus, 2006)

39 Agnès Humbert, *Notre guerre. Souvenirs de Résistance: Paris 1940–41, le bagne, occupation en Allemagne* (Paris, Tallandier, 2004), translated as Agnès Humbert, *Résistance: memoirs of Occupied France* (London, Bloomsbury, 2008)

40 Judy Barrett Litoff (ed.), *An American heroine in the French Resistance. The diary and memoir of Virginia d'Albert-Lake* (New York, Fordham UP, 2006)

41 Laurent Douzou, *La Résistance française: une histoire périlleuse* (Paris, Seuil, 2005), pp. 275–6

42 Georges Waysand, *Estoucha* (Paris, Denoël, 1997)

43 Claude Lévy, *Les Parias de la Résistance* (Paris, Calmann-Lévy, 1970)

44 Marc Lévy, *Les Enfants de la liberté* (Paris, Robert Laffont, 2007)

45 Guillaume Piketty (ed.), *Français en Résistance. Carnets de guerre, correspondance, journaux personnels* (Paris, Robert Laffont, 2009)

46 Bruno Curatolo and François Marcot, *Écrire sous l'Occupation. Du non-consentement à la Résistance. France-Belgique-Pologne* (Rennes, Presses Universitaires de Rennes, 2011)

47 Daniel Cordier, *Alias Caracalla* (Paris, Gallimard, 2009), back cover

Chapter 1

1 On the *exode*, see Hanna Diamond, *Fleeing Hitler. France 1940* (Oxford, OUP, 2007); Nicole Dombrowski Risser, *France under Fire: German Invasion, Civilian Flight, and Family Survival During World War II* (New York & Cambridge, CUP, 2012)

2 Interview with Madeleine Riffaud, conducted by RG, Paris, 15 Apr. 2012

3 On the defeat see Andrew Shennan, *The Fall of France, 1940* (Harlow, Longman, 2000), Julian Jackson, *The Fall of France. The Nazi Invasion of 1940* (Oxford, OUP, 2003), Jean-Louis Crémieux-Brilhac, *Les Français de l'an 40* (Gallimard, 1990), and Ernest May, *Strange Victory. Hitler's Conquest of France* (London, Tauris, 2000)

4 Julian Jackson, *The Popular Front in France. Defending Democracy, 1934–38* (Cambridge, CUP, 1988); Julian Jackson, *France. The Dark Years, 1940–1944* (Oxford, OUP, 2001), pp. 97–111; Robert Soucy, *French Fascism. The Second Wave, 1933–1939* (New Haven and London, Yale UP, 1995)

5 Philippe Pétain, *Actes et Écrits* (Paris, Flammarion, 1974), pp. 448–9

6 Charles de Gaulle, letter to his mother from Wülzburg near Weissenburg, Bavaria, 1 Nov. 1918 in *Lettres, Notes et Carnets, 1905–18* (Paris, Plon, 1981), p. 525

7 Edward Spears, *Assignment to Catastrophe II. The Fall of France, June 1940* (London, Heinemann, 1954), p. 145

8 Charles de Gaulle, *Discours et messages I, juin 1940–janvier 1946* (Paris, Plon, 1970), p. 4

9 Jean-Louis Crémieux-Brilhac, *La France libre: de l'appel du 18 juin à la Libération* (Paris, Gallimard, 1996), pp. 59–60, 83–4

10 AN 72AJ220, testimony of Denis Saurat, Sept. 1951; Denis Saurat, *Watch over Africa* (London, Dent, 1941), p. 3

11 Lionel Gossman, *André Maurois (1885–1967). Fortunes and Misfortunes of a Moderate* (New York, Palgrave Macmillan, 2014), pp. 44–5

12 Jean Monnet, *Mémoires* (Paris, Fayard, 1976), pp. 168–79

13 Mireille Sacotte, *Saint-John Perse* (Paris, Pierre Belfond, 1991), pp. 157–74

14 Martin Gilbert, *Winston S. Churchill VI. Finest Hour, 1939–1941* (London, Heinemann, 1983), pp. 590–1; Nicholas Atkin, *The Forgotten French. Exiles in the British Isles, 1940–44* (Manchester, Manchester UP, 2003), pp. 143–4

15 Jean-Louis Crémieux-Brilhac, *Georges Boris. Trente ans d'influence. Blum, de Gaulle, Mendès France* (Paris, Gallimard, 2010), pp. 20–1, 27–85

16 AN 72AJ220/II, testimony of Georges Boris, 27 May and 3 Jun. 1947. See also

account of Geoffroy de Courcel in Georges Boris, *Servir la France. Textes et témoignages*, p. 286

17 General Béthouart, *Cinq années d'espérance. Mémoires de guerre, 1939–1945* (Paris, Plon, 1968), p. 92

18 Béthouart, *Cinq années d'espérance*, p. 92

19 Jean-Louis Crémieux-Brilhac, *La France Libre. De l'appel du 18 juin à la Libération*, pp. 62–3

20 Capt P.O. Lapie, *La Légion Étrangère à Narvik* (London, John Murray, 1941), p. 30; Douglas Porch, *The French Foreign Legion* (London, Macmillan, 1991), pp. 448–54; André-Paul Comor, *L'Épopée de la 13e demi-Brigade de la Légion Étrangère, 1940–1945* (Paris, Nouvelles Éditions Latines, 1988)

21 Jean-Louis Crémieux-Brilhac, *La France libre: de l'appel du 18 juin à la Libération*, pp. 86–9

22 Comor, *L'Épopée de la 13e Demi-Brigade*, pp. 86–96

23 Jean-François Muracciole, *Les Français Libres. L'autre résistance* (Paris, Tallandier, 2009), pp. 145–7

24 Nicholas Atkin, 'France in Exile: the French Community in Britain, 1940–1944', in Martin Conway and José Gotovitch (eds.), *Europe in Exile. European Exiles in Britain, 1940–1945* (Oxford, Berghahn, 2001), pp. 219–20

25 Jean Toulat, *Combattants de la non-violence. De Lanza del Vasto au Général de Bollardière* (Paris, Cerf, 1983), p. 175. See also Guy Bourbault, Benoît Gauchard & Jean-Marie Muller, *Jacques de Bollardière, Compagnon de toutes les liberations* (Montargis, Non-Violence-Actualité, 1986)

26 Général de Bollardière, *Bataille d'Alger, bataille de l'homme* (Paris & Bruges, Desclée De Brouwer, 1972), p. 22

27 Gabriel Brunet de Sairigné, 'Carnets et lettres, 1940–45' in Guillaume Piketty (ed.), *Français en Résistance. Carnets de guerre, correspondances, journaux personnels* (Paris, R. Laffont, 2009), pp. 466–7

28 Colonel Passy, *Souvenirs I. 2e Bureau, Londres* (Monte-Carlo, Raoul Solar, 1947), p. 26; Albertelli, *Les Services Secrets*, pp. 24–5

29 Claude Bouchinet-Serreulles, *Nous étions faits pour être libres. La Résistance avec De Gaulle et Jean Moulin* (Paris, Bernard Grasset, 2000), p. 38

30 AN 72AJ421, Bingen note, 6 Jul. 1940

31 AN 72AJ220/III, testimony of Claude Bouchinet-Serreulles, 12 Dec. 1948, 20 Mar. & 7 Nov. 1949, 12 Feb. 1950. See also AN 72AJ234/1, testimony of Claude Bouchinet-Serreulles, 21 Apr. 1948

32 AN 72AJ4231, Papiers Bingen, reports on reorganising the Free French merchant fleet, 12 & 27 Aug. 1940

33 AN 72AJ238/III, Hélène Terré, 'Nous entrerons dans la carrière. Une histoire de l'AFAT (typescript, 229p), p. 5

34 Tereska Torrès, *Une Française Libre. Journal, 1939–1945* (Paris, France-Loisirs, 2000), p. 34. Entry for 25 Jan. 1940

35 Torrès, *Une Française Libre*, p. 53. Entry for 19 Jun. 1940.

36 Anthony Clayton, *France, Soldiers and Africa* (London, Brassey's Defence Publishers, 1988), pp. 209–69

37 General Catroux, *Deux actes du Drame indochinois. Hanoi: juin 1940. Dien Bien Phu: mars–mai 1954* (Paris, Plon, 1959), pp. 47–91

38 Christiane Rimbaud, *L'affaire du Massilia, été 1940* (Paris, Seuil, 1984)

39 Charles de Gaulle, *Mémoires de Guerre I* (Paris, Plon, 1954), p. 229; Jean Lacouture, *De Gaulle. The Rebel, 1890–1944* (London, Harvill, 1993), p. 229; Jean-Louis Crémieux-Brilhac, *La France libre: de l'appel du 18 juin à la Libération*, p. 52

40 Charles de Gaulle, *Mémoires de Guerre. I* (Paris, Plon, 1954), 72; de Gaulle, *Lettres, Notes et Carnets. Juin 1940–Juillet 1941* (Paris, Plon, 1981), p. 15, has this text of the letter.

41 AN 72AJ210/A1, interview with General François d'Astier de la Vigerie, 22 Feb. 1948

42 AN 13AV61, interview with José Aboulker, 16 Mar. 1990

43 François Garbit, *Dernières lettres d'Afrique et du Levant (1940–1941)* (Saint-Maur des Fossés, Éditions Sépia, 1999), pp. 33–4. Republished in Piketty (ed.), *Français en Résistance*, p. 531

44 AN 72AJ225/1, Blanche Ackerman-Athanassiades, 'A l'ombre de la Croix de Lorraine' (MS, 1961), p. 35

45 Raoul Salan, *Mémoires* (Paris, Presses de la Cité, 1970), p. 11

46 Jean-François Muracciole, *Les Français Libres. L'Autre Résistance* (Paris, Tallandier, 2009)

47 Eric Jennings, *La France libre fut africaine* (Paris, Perrin, 2014), pp. 28–31

48 François Garbit, letter to his mother, 15 Sept. 1940, in Piketty (ed.), *Français en Résistance*, p. 547

49 AN AJ225/I AEF, testimony of governer Henri Laurentie, 19 Oct. 1948

50 Garbit, *Dernières lettres*, 51; Piketty (ed.), *Français en Résistance*, p. 547

51 Piketty (ed.), *Français en Résistance*, p. 675

52 Jennings, *La France libre fut africaine*, pp. 45–50

53 AN 72AJ217/A IV 1, AOF. Maurice Maillat, 'Dakar sous la flame de la guerre, 1939–1945' (MS, 1975)

54 Charles de Gaulle, *Lettres, Notes et Carnets*, de Gaulle to his wife, 28 Sept. 1940, p. 127

55 Martin Gilbert, *Winston S. Churchill VI*, p. 812; Jackson, *France. The Dark Years*, p. 391; Jean-Louis Crémieux-Brilhac, *La France libre: de l'appel du 18 juin à la Libération*, pp. 120–6

56 Henri Frenay, *La Nuit finira. Mémoires de la Résistance, 1940–1945* (Paris, Robert Laffont, 1973), p. 42

57 AN 72AJ46/I, testimony of Henri Frenay, Feb.–Mar. 1948

58 Henri Frenay, *La Nuit finira* (Paris, Robert Laffont, 1973), p. 38. See also Michèle Cointet, *Pétain et les Français, 1940–1951* (Paris, Perrin, 2002), p. 151, and Jean-Paul Cointet, *La Légion Française des Combattants* (Paris, Albin-Michel, 1995)

59 AN 72AJ46/I, testimony of Henri Frenay, Feb.–Apr. 1948, pp. 5, 48–9

60 Philippe Viannay, *Du Bon Usage de la France* (Paris, Éditions Ramsay, 1988), pp. 18–20; See also AN 6AV639 Interview of Hélène Viannay with Olivier Wieviorka, 6 May 1987

61 AN 450AP1, Journal Lecomte-Boinet, 9 (2 Sept. 1939), p. 46

62 AN 450AP1, Journal Lecomte-Boinet, 9 (2 Sept. 1939), p. 46 (letter to his wife of 28 Jun. 1940), p. 123 (10 Apr. 1942)

63 Francis Crémieux, *Entretien avec Emmanuel d'Astier* (Paris, Pierre Belfond, 1966), pp. 16, 20

64 Crémieux, *Entretien avec Emmanuel d'Astier*, p. 79; Emmanuel d'Astier, *Sept Fois Sept Jours* (Paris, les Éditions de Minuit, 1947), pp. 9–24

65 Agnès Humbert, *Resistance. Memoirs of Occupied France* (London, Bloomsbury, 2009), pp. 5–7. This was originally published as *Notre guerre. Souvenirs de Résistance* (1946) and re-edited by Tallandier in 2004

66 Gabrielle Ferrières, *Jean Cavaillès. Un philosophe dans la guerre, 1903–1944* (Paris, Seuil, 1982), p. 133

67 Gabrielle Ferrières, *Jean Cavaillès*, pp. 17–18

68 Guillaume Piketty, *Pierre Brossolette. Un Héros de la Résistance* (Paris, Odile Jacob, 1998)

69 AN 72AJ2217, interview of Louis Joxe with Gilberte Brossolette, 1973

70 AN 72AJ2217, interview of Pierre Bertaux with Gilberte Brossolette, 1973

71 AN 72AJ2215, account by sub-lieutenant Rozzi, 16 Mar. 1945

72 Eugen Weber, *Action française: Royalism and Reaction in Twentieth Century France* (Stanford, Stanford UP, 1962); William Irvine, 'Fascism and the strange case of the Croix de Feu', *Journal of Modern History* LXIII (1991); Robert Soucy, *French Fascism. The First Wave, 1924–1933* (New Haven and London, Yale UP, 1986); *French Fascism. The Second Wave, 1933–1939* (New Haven and London, Yale UP, 1995); Sean Kennedy, *Reconciling France Against Democracy: The Croix de Feu and the Parti Social Français, 1927–1945* (Montreal, McGill-Queen's University Press, 2007)

73 AN 72AJ58 V, testimony of Colonel Alfred Heurtaux, 7 Jan. 1946

74 Gilles Perrault, *La Longue traque* (Paris, Lattès, 1975), pp. 48–55

75 Allen Middlebro', 'Choices and Actions of Members and Former Members of the French Communist Party, 1939–1941' (Oxford D.Phil thesis, 2011)

76 On the French Communist Party see Stéphane Courtois and Marc Lazar, *Histoire du Parti Communiste Français* (2nd edn., Paris, PUF, 2000); Annie Kriegel, *The French Communists. Profile of a People* (Chicago & London, U of Chicago Press, 1972); Daniel Brower, *The New Jacobins. The French Communist Party and the Popular Front* (Ithaca, NY, Cornell UP, 1968); Nicole Racine and Louis Bodin, *Le Parti communiste français pendant l'entre-deux guerres* (Paris, FNSP, 1972)

77 Léo Hamon, *Vivre ses choix* (Paris, Robert Laffont, 1991), pp. 13, 28–37, 51–7, 76, 79, 91

78 Pierre Villon, *Résistant de la première heure* (Paris: Éditions sociales, 1983), pp. 44–5

79 Fonds Douzou, interview with Jean-Pierre Vernant, 10 Jan. 1985

80 CHRD Lyon, interview with Lucie Aubrac, 26 Sept. 1996

81 Raymond Aubrac, *Où la Mémoire s'attarde* (Paris, Odile Jacob, 1996), pp. 31, 33, 358

82 Vernant interview

83 Raymond Aubrac, *Où la Mémoire s'attarde*, pp. 55–8

84 Lise London, *La Ménagère de la rue Daguerre. Souvenirs de Résistance* (Paris, Seuil, 1995), pp. 7–8; Artur London, *On Trial* (London, Macdonald, 1970), pp. 23–5; see also London, *L'Espagne* (Brussels, Tribord, 2003)

85 Lise London, *La Ménagère de la rue Daguerre*, pp. 27-58

86 André Tollet, *Ma Traversée du Siècle. Mémoires d'un syndicaliste révolutionnaire* (Paris, VO Éditions, 2002), pp. 10–11

87 Tollet, *Ma Traversée du Siècle*, pp. 28–39

88 Roger Bourderon, *Rol-Tanguy* (Paris, Tallandier, 2004), pp. 35–93; Interview with Cécile Rol-Tanguy, conducted by RG, Paris, 20 Jun. 2012

89 Bourderon, *Rol Tanguy*, p. 138

90 Bourderon, *Rol Tanguy*, p. 143

91 Interview with Cécile Rol-Tanguy

92 Musée de la Résistance, Champigny. Fonds Monique Georges. Biographie de la Famille Georges de 1887 à 1945 (9p); Monique Georges, *Le Colonel Fabien était mon père* (Paris, Mille et Une Nuits, 2009), pp. 19–61

93 Pierre to Andrée Georges, 20 Feb. 1940, cited in Monique Georges, *Le Colonel Fabien était mon père*, p. 92

94 Biographie de la Famille Georges de 1887 à 1945

95 Charles Tillon, *On chantait rouge* (Paris, R. Laffont, 1977), p. 301

96 Tillon, *On chantait rouge*, p. 301

97 Madeleine Riffaud, *On l'appelait Rainer* (Paris, Julliard, 1994), p. 20

98 AN 6AV520, interview of Geneviève Anthonioz de Gaulle with Olivier Wieviorka, 11 Feb. 1985

99 AN 6AV637, interview of Hélène Viannay with Olivier Wieviorka, 15 Sept. 1986

Chapter 2

1 Interview with Christian de Mondragon, conducted by RG, Nantes, 29 Apr. 1997; Gildea, *Marianne in Chains*, pp. 146–7

2 Rita Thalmann, *La Mise au pas: idéologie et stratégie sécuritaire dans la France occupée* (Paris, Fayard, 1991); Éric Alary, *La ligne de demarcation, 1940–1944* (Paris, Perrin, 2003, 2010)

3 Philippe Burrin, *Living with Defeat. France Under the German Occupation, 1940–1944* (London, Arnold, 1996), pp. 191–209; Julian Jackson, *France the Dark Years*, pp. 142–65; Robert Gildea, *Marianne in Chains*, pp. 65–88; Richard Vinen, *The Unfree French. Life Under the Occupation* (London, Allen Lane, 2006), pp. 99–132, 155–80

4 Jean-Paul Cointet, *La Légion Française des Combattants* (Paris, Albin-Michel, 1995)

5 Michael Marrus and Robert Paxton, *Vichy France and the Jews* (New York, Basic books, 1981); Renée Poznanski, *Jews in France During World War II* (Hanover, N.H. & London, University Press of New England, 2001); Julian Jackson, *France the Dark Years*, pp. 354–81; Robert Gildea, *Marianne in Chains*, pp. 223–42, 65–88; Richard Vinen, *The Unfree French*, pp. 133–54

6 Gildea, *Marianne in Chains*, pp. 109–33; Vinen, *The Unfree French*, pp. 213–45

7 Burrin, *Living with Defeat*, pp. 228–61; Gildea, *Marianne in Chains*, pp. 285–304; Vinen, *The Unfree French*, pp. 247–93

8 See François Bédarida, 'L'histoire de la Résistance: lectures d'hier, chantiers de demain', *Vingtième siècle* 11 (Jul–Sept. 1986), pp. 75–89; Olivier Wieviorka, 'A

la recherche de l'engagement', *Vingtième siècle* 60 (Oct.–Dec. 1998), pp. 58–70; Jacques Sémelin, 'Qu'est-ce résister?', *Esprit* (Jan. 1994), pp. 50–63; Pierre Laborie, 'L'idée de Résistance. Entre définition et sens. Retour sur un questionnement', in *Les Français des années troubles* (Paris, Points-Seuil, 2003); Pierre Laborie, 'Qu'est-ce que la Résistance?' in Marcot (ed.), *Dictionnaire historique de la Résistance*, pp. 29–38; Olivier Wieviorka, *Histoire de la Résistance, 1940–1945* (Paris, Perrin, 2013), pp. 15–18

9 François Marcot, *La Résistance dans le Jura* (Besançon, Cêtre, 1985), p. 72, cited by Olivier Wieviorka, *Histoire de la Résistance, 1940–1945* (Paris, Perrin, 2013), p. 106; Robert Gildea, 'Lettres de correspondants français à la BBC (1940–1943): une Pénombre de la Résistance', *Vingtième Siècle*, 125 (Jan.–Mar. 2015), pp. 61–76

10 Gildea, *Marianne in Chains*, p. 146

11 Benoîte and Flora Groult, *Journal à Quatre mains* (Paris, Denoël, 1962), pp. 558–9. Entry of 18 Nov. 1940

12 Aurélie Luneau, *Je vous écris de France: lettres inédites à la BBC, 1940–1944* (Paris, L'Iconoclaste, 2014)

13 Renée Poznanski, *Propagandes et persecutions*, p. 103; Wieviorka, *Histoire de la Résistance*, pp. 23–4

14 BBC Written Archives Caversham (WAC), French Service. Anonymous letters from France, no. 7, 2 Aug. 1940

15 Anonymous letters No. 61, 7 Sept. 1940

16 Jean-Louis Crémieux-Brilhac, *Les Voix de la Liberté. Ici Londres, 1940–1944* (5 vols., Paris, La Documentation Française, 1975), I, p. 205; Aurélie Luneau, *Radio Londres, 1940–1944. Les Voix de la Liberté* (Paris, Perrin, 2005), pp. 101–2

17 Anonymous letters, no. 554, 28 Mar. 1941

18 Anonymous letters, no. 208, 7 Jan. 1941

19 Paula Schwarz, 'The politics of food and gender in occupied Paris', *Modern and Contemporary France* 7/1 (1999), pp. 35–45; Jean-Marie Guillon, 'Les manifestations ménagères. Protestation populaire et résistance feminine spécifique' in Gilzmer, Levisse-Touzé and Maertens, *Les femmes dans la Résistance en France* (Paris, Tallandier, 2003), pp. 107–33

20 Musée de la Résistance. Fonds Roussel. Résistance. Attestations Zones Nord et Sud. Certification of activity of Claudine Chomat, 18 Dec. 1958

21 Albert Ouzoulias, *Les Bataillons de la Jeunesse* (Paris, Les Éditions sociales, 1967), p. 47

22 Roger Bourderon, *Rol-Tanguy* (Taillandier, 2004), pp. 151–175

23 Lise London, *La Mégère de la rue Daguerre. Souvenirs de Résistance* (Paris, Seuil, 1995), p. 107

24 AN 72 AJ 69 III. Parti Communiste. Testimony of Nicole Barry, 16 Nov. 1946; Lise London, *La Mégère de la rue Daguerre*, pp. 158–63

25 Germaine Tillion, 'Première résistance en zone occupée. Du côté du réseau Musée de l'Homme-Haut-Vildé', *Esprit* 261 (Feb. 2000), p. 112. Julien Blanc, historian of the network, prefers an astronomical analogy, calling the network a 'nebula' or interstellar cloud of dust, the best term he could imagine for 'a grouping that was being put together but was still fragmented, if not anarchic'. Julien Blanc, *Au Commencement de la Résistance. Du côté du Musée de l'Homme, 1940–1941* (Paris, Seuil, 2010), p. 125

26 AN 72AJ66/I, Germaine Tillion, Rapport d'activité sur le secteur Hauet (réseau Hauet-Vildé), n.d.; Musée de l'Homme. Généralités sur l'UNCC, n.d.

27 Julien Blanc, *Au Commencement de la Résistance*, pp. 78–100; Boris Vildé, *Journal et Lettres de Prison, 1941–1942*, Institut d'Histoire du Temps present, Cahier no. 7, 1988, introduction

28 AN 72AJ66/I, Yvonne Oddon, Réseau Hauet-Vildé. Rapport sur mon activité de Résistance, 1940–41, n.d.

29 Jean Cassou, *Une Vie pour la liberté* (Paris, Robert Laffont, 1981), p. 114. See also Cassou, *La Mémoire courte* (1953) (Paris, Mille et une Nuits, 2001), p. 10

30 Agnès Humbert, *Resistance* pp. 11–12. Entry of 6 Aug. 1940. The Carbonari were a secret society opposed to Austrian occupation and reactionary government in early nineteenth-century Italy

31 AN 72AJ66/I, testimony of Claude Aveline, 19 Jan. 1957; testimony of Jean Cassou, 8 Feb. 1946

32 Simone Martin-Chauffier, *A Bientôt quand même* (Paris, Calmann-Lévy, 1976), p. 79

33 Germaine Tillion, 'Première résistance en zone occupée', p. 117

34 AN 72AJ66, Résumé de la deposition faite par Gaveau, agent de la Gestapo, le 5 nov. 1945, avec les commenatires de Mlle Tillion, 2 Mar. 1946; AN 13AV60, interview with Germaine Tillion, 13 Mar. 1990

35 AN 72AJ2215, Brossolette lecture notes, 1941

36 Jacques Lusseyran, *Et La Lumière fut* (Paris, Éditions de Félin, 2005), pp. 115, 150, 169

37 Olivier Wieviorka, *Une certaine idée de la Résistance. Défense de la France, 1940–1949* (Paris, Seuil, 1995)

38 AN 6AV622, interview of Robert Salmon by Olivier Wieviorka, 7 Feb. 1986

39 AN 72AJ50/II, Additional testimony of Robert Salmon, 22 May 1957

40 AN 6AV622, interview of Robert Salmon by Olivier Wieviorka, 7 Feb. 1986; see also AN 72AJ50/IV, testimony of Philippe Viannay, 24 Nov. 1947, 16 Mar. 1957, 4 May 1959

41 AN 6AV637, interview of Hélène Viannay conducted by Olivier Wieviorka, 15 Sept. 1986

42 Philippe Viannay, *Du Bon Usage de la France* (Paris, Éditions Ramsay, 1988), p. 27

43 AN 72AJ50/IV, testimony of Robert Salmon, 13 Feb. 1947

44 AN 6AV526, interview of Genia Gemähling conducted by Olivier Wieviorka, Nov. 1985

45 AN 6AV622, interview of Robert Salmon conducted by Olivier Wieviorka, 23 May 1986; Robert Salmon, 'Défense de la France' in *Il y a 45 ans. Témoignages pour l'histoire* (Paris, Senate, 1986), p. 95; AN72AJ50/II, Additional testimony of Robert Salmon, 22 May 1957

46 AN 72AJ50/III, testimony of Geneviève Anthonioz-de Gaulle, 11 Jan. 1957

47 The Confédération Générale du Travail (CGT) and the Confédération Française des Travailleurs Chrétiens (CFTC)

48 Jean-Pierre Le Crom, *Syndicats nous voilà. Vichy et le corporatisme* (Paris, Les Éditions de l'Atelier/Éditions ouvrières, 1995)

49 These included Louis Saillant, secretary of the trade unions in the Drôme and

Ardèche, Albert Gazier of the Paris Employees' Union, Christian Pineau of the Bank Employees' Union, Robert Lacoste of the civil servants' union and Gaston Tessier, secretary general of the CFTC

50 AN 580AP25/1, Fonds Christian Pineau, article in *Syndicats*, 3 Aug. 1938

51 AN 580AP25/1, Fonds Christian Pineau. Allocations prononcées au restaurant du Sénat lors du diner commemorative donné en l'honneur de centenaire de Christian Pineau, le 14 octobre 2004, 3. Speech of Alya Aglan

52 AN 72AJ59/V, testimony of Christian Pineau, 25 May 1950

53 See above, pp. 44–5

54 Maxime Blocq-Mascart, *Chronique de la Résistance* (Paris, Corréa, 1945), p. 32; see also AN 72 AJ 67/III, testimony of Maxime Blocq-Mascart, n.d.

55 Testimony of André Postel-Vinay, 20 Jan. 1951; testimony of Pierre Lefaucheux, 20 Jan. 1951; André Postel-Vinay, *Un fou s'évade. Souvenirs de 1941–42* (Paris, Éditions du Félin, 1997)

56 AN 72AJ67/II, testimony of Marcellin Berthelot, n.d.

57 Maurice Rajsfus, *La police de Vichy: les forces de l'ordre françaises au service de la Gestapo, 1940–1944* (Paris, le Cherche midi, 1995)

58 Laurent Douzou, 'La Résistance à Lyon (1940–1944)', Colloque *Lyon dans la Seconde Guerre mondiale. Métropolis à l'Épreuve du Conflict*, Lyon, 6–7 Nov. 2013

59 Simone Martin-Chauffier, *A Bientôt quand même*, pp. 119–20

60 AN 72AJ55/II, testimony of Yves Farge, 17 May 1946

61 AN 72AJ55/II, testimony of Yves Farge, 17 May 1946

62 AN 72AJ181BII, Antoine Pinton, Contribution à l'histoire de la Résistance à Lyon et principalement du movement Franc-Tireur, n.d., p. 8.

63 AN 72AJ55/I, testimony of Antoine Avinin, 14 Jan. 1947

64 AN 72AJ55/I, testimony of Joseph Hours, 14 Jan. 1947

65 BBC Written Archives, Caversham. French Service. Anonymous letters from France, no. 268, 26 Feb. 1941; Laurent Douzou and Dominique Veillon, 'La résistance des mouvements: ses débuts dans la région lyonnaise (1940-42), in Jean-Marie Guillon, Pierre Laborie (eds.), *Mémoire et Histoire: la Résistance* (Toulouse, Privat, 1995), pp. 154–5. I am indebted to Laurent Douzou for advice on this point

66 CHRD Lyon, interview with Micheline Altman, 16 Jul. 1997

67 AN 72AJ55/I, testimony of Jean-Pierre Lévy, 1 Nov. 1946; Jean-Pierre Lévy, *Mémoires d'un franc-tireur. Itinéraire d'un résistant, 1940–1944* (Paris, Éditions Complexe/IHTP, 1998), pp. 36–57

68 In general see Dominique Veillon, *Le Franc-Tireur. Un journal clandestin, un movement de Résistance* (Paris, Flammarion, 1977); H.R. Kedward, *Resistance in Vichy France. A Study of Ideas and Motivation in the Southern Zone, 1940–1942* (Oxford, OUP, 1978), pp. 146–9

69 Laurent Douzou (ed.) *Souvenirs inédits d'Yvon Morandat, Cahiers de l'IHTP* 29 (Sept. 1994), p. 63

70 Stanislas Fumet, *Histoire de Dieu dans la Vie. Souvenirs choisis* (Paris, Fayard, 1978), p. 453; Charles d'Aragon, *La Résistance sans héroisme* (Paris, Seuil, 1977), p. 23

71 Marie-Odile Germain (ed.), *Stanislas Fumet ou la Présence au Temps* (Paris, Éditions du Cerf/BNE, 1999)

72 CHRD Lyon, interview with Jean-Marie Domenach, 16 Apr. 1997; Jean-Marie Domenach and Denise Rendu, 'Une vie', in Bernard Comte, Jean-Marie Domenach & Christian Rendu (eds.), *Gilbert Dru. Un Chrétien resistant* (Paris, Beauchesne, 1998), pp. 59–127

73 AN 72AJ73/VI, testimony of Père Chaillet. 5 Feb. 1962; Chaillet's account of the origins of the paper is in *Témoignage Chrétien*, 21 (21 Oct. 1944); Renée Bédarida, *Les Armes de l'Esprit* (Paris, Etions Ouvrières, 1977), pp. 38–53; Renée Bédarida, *Pierre Chaillet. Témoin de la résistance spirituelle* (Paris, Fayard, 1988); Kedward, *Resistance in Vichy France: A Study of Ideas and Motivation in the Southern Zone, 1940–1942* (Oxford, OUP, 1978), pp. 28–9, 175–80

74 Laurent Ducerf, *François de Menthon. Un Catholique au service de la République, 1900–1984* (Paris, Cerf, 2006), pp. 16–69; Kedward, *Resistance in Vichy France*, pp. 29–32

75 AN 72AJ46 III, testimony of François de Menthon, 28 Nov. 1945

76 AN 72AJ48, témoignage de Pierre-Henri Teitgen, 13 Jan. 1947

77 AN 72AJ126BI, testimony of Léo Hamon, 7 Mar. 1946

78 Emmanuel d'Astier, *Sept Fois Sept Jours* (Paris, Éditions de Minuit, 1947), pp. 31–2; Fonds Douzou, interview with Charles d'Aragon, 5 Mar. 1986

79 AN 72AJ60/I, testimony of Mme Samuel, née Lucie Bernard, dans la clandestinité Catherine, maintenant Lucie Aubrac, 26 Sept. 1945. See also AN 13AV89, interview with Lucie Aubrac, 14 Mar. 1984; Laurent Douzou, *La Désobéissance. Histoire du Mouvement Libération* (Paris, O. Jacob, 1995), pp. 38–41

80 *Gringoire* was a newspaper that preached collaboration with Germany

81 Laurent Douzou (ed.), *Notes de Prison de Bertrande d'Astier de la Vigerie (15 mars–4 avril 1941), Cahiers de l'IHTP* 25 (Oct. 1993)

82 Gabrielle Ferrières, *Jean Cavaillès. Un Philosophe dans la guerre* (Paris, Seuil, 1982), p. 154. See also Alya Aglan, 'Le Résistance', in Aglan and Azéma, *Jean Cavaillès, resistant, ou la pensée en actes* (Paris, Flammarion, 2002), p. 85

83 Raymond Aubrac, *Où la Mémoire s'attarde*, p. 60

84 Fonds Douzou and AN 13AV96, interview of Georges Canguilhem with Laurent Douzou. 6 Feb. 1985

85 Fonds Douzou and AN 13AV105, interview of Jean-Pierre Vernant with Laurent Douzou, 10 Jan. 1985

86 AN 13AV106, interview of Jean-Pierre Vernant with Laurent Douzou, 10 Jan. 1985

87 AN 72AJ59/V, testimony of Henri Ribière, 26 Jun. 1946

88 Daniel Mayer, *Les Socialistes dans la Résistance* (Paris, PUF, 1968), 14; Olivier Wieviorka, *Histoire de la Résistance*, pp. 56–61

89 AN 72AJ170/BI, testimony of Albert van Wolput, 21 Feb. 1947

Chapter 3

1 Musée de la Résistance, Carton 126A, Témoignages III. Testimony of Paul Dubois on miners' strike, 1941, n.d., p. 5

2 Maurice Dommanget, *Histoire du premier Mai* (Paris, Société universitaire d'édition et de librairie, 1953)

3 Auguste Lecoeur, 'Les Grèves des Mineurs du Nord-Pas-de-Calais' in Institut d'Histoire des Conflits Contemporains, *Séance Solennelle des Témoignages 1941* (Paris, Sénat, 1986), pp. 139–48

4 Musée de la Résistance, Carton no. 124, Témoignages I. Testimony of Joseph Bricourt, n.d., p. 2

5 Roger Pannequin, *Ami, si tu tombes* (Paris, Babel, 2000), p. 127

6 Musée de la Résistance, Carton no. 126, Témoignages III. Journal de Charles Debarge (1942, 172pp), pp. 14–18

7 Journal de Charles Debarge, pp. 22–3

8 Auguste Lecoeur, 'Les Grèves des Mineurs, p. 146. Musée de la Résistance, Carton 126A, Témoignages I. Interview with Joseph Bricourt, n.d.; Carton 126A. Témoignages III. Paul Dubois text on the miners' strike, n.d.

9 Journal de Charles Debarge, 28 Aug. 1941, p. 50

10 Musée de la Résistance, Champigny. Fonds Guy Môquet. Juliette Môquet to Guy, 25 Apr. 1941; Guy Môquet to his mother, 16 May 1941

11 Musée de la Résistance, Champigny, Carton 129, Témoignages III. Interview with Léon Mauvais, 1964.

12 See above, pp. 54–5

13 Stéphen Courtois, *Le PCF dans la guerre. De Gaulle, la Résistance, Staline.* (Paris, Ramsay, 1980), pp. 125–40

14 Roger Bourderon, *Rol-Tanguy*, pp. 151–75

15 Albert Ouzoulias, *Les Fils de la Nuit* (Paris, Grasset, 1975), p. 53; see also Ouzoulias, *Les Bataillons de la Jeunesse* (Paris, Éditions sociales, 1967), pp. 86–8

16 Ouzoulias, *Les Bataillons de la Jeunesse*, p. 120

17 Musée de la Résistance, Champigny, Carton 124, Témoignages I, Gilbert Brustlein, Souvenirs, n.d., p. 18

18 Ouzoulias, *Les Bataillons de la Jeunesse*, p. 118

19 Musée de la Résistance, Champigny, Carton 124, Témoignages I, Gilbert Brustlein, Souvenirs, n.d., p. 19

20 Louis Oury, *Rue du Roi Albert. Les Otages de Nantes, Châteaubriant et Bordeaux* (Pantin, Le Temps des Cerises, 1997), pp. 107–19; Robert Gildea, *Marianne in Chains*, pp. 243–50

21 Charles de Gaulle, *Discours et messages I, 1940–1946* (Paris, Plon, 1970), pp. 122–5

22 AM Nantes, decree of 11 Nov. 1941

23 AD Loire-Atlantique 132 W 54, report of prefect, 1 Dec. 1941

24 Centre d'Histoire, Sciences Po, Fonds Tillon, CT100, interview, 28 Nov. 1979, p. 7. See also Charles Tillon, *On Chantait rouge*, pp. 345, 348

25 Journal de Charles Debarge, Entry for 23–25 Dec. 1941, p. 82

26 Journal de Charles Debarge, pp. 112–16; Pannequin, *Ami si tu tombes*, pp. 143–50

27 Journal de Charles Debarge, pp. 152

28 AM Ivry, 15W16, Declaration of Front National, 15 May 1941

29 AM Ivry, Marrane. Guerre. Undated account by Marrane of the meetings in Lyon

30 Yves Farge *Rebelles, soldats et citoyens. Carnet d'un commissaire de la République* (Paris, Grasset, 1946), p. 58

31 AM Ivry. Marrane. Guerre. Mémoires de Madeleine Braun concernant Georges Marrane p. 16. Vercingétorix was a Gallic chief who resisted Julius Caesar and was executed on his orders in 46BC

32 Simone Martin-Chauffier, *A Bientôt quand même*, p. 151

33 Charles d'Aragon, *La Résistance sans héroisme*, p. 62

34 See above, pp. 77–8

35 AN 72AJ73, Louis Cruvillier, Quelques notes sur la formation de Témoignage Chrétien, 1957; testimony of André Mandouze, Sept. 1946; 'Déclaration d'activité de Marie-Rose Gineste', 13pp, n.d.

36 See above, p. 76

37 CHRD, interview with Micheline Altman, 16 Jul. 1997

38 AN 72AJ181 BII, Auguste Pinton, 'Contribution à l'histoire de la Résistance à Lyon et principalement du movement Franc-Tireur', n.d., pp. 19–20

39 AN 72AJ435/I.3, Le premier Appel du Général Cochet, 6 septembre 1940

40 Jean-Pierre Lévy, 'France-Liberté. Franc-Tireur' in *Il y a 45 ans. L'année 1941. Témoignages pour l'histoire* (Paris, 1986), p. 104

41 AN 72AJ435/I.3, Conférence faite aux Étudiants catholiques à Lyon en mai 1941

42 AN 13AV46, interview with Serge Ravanel, 26 Feb. & 4 Mar. 1991

43 Antoine Delestre, *Uriage, une communauté et une école dans la tourmente, 1940–1945* (Nancy, PU of Nancy, 1989); Bernard Comte, *Une utopie combattante: l'École des cadres d'Uriage, 1940–1942* (Paris, Fayard, 1991); John Hellman, *The Knight-monks of Vichy. Uriage, 1940–1945* (Montreal and Kingston, McGill-Queens UP, 1993)

44 Dominique Missika, *Berty Albrecht* (Paris, Perrin, 2005)

45 Jacques Baumel, *Résister. Histoire secrète des années d'occupation*, p. 109; Albin Vistel, *La Nuit sans ombre*, p. 56

46 Claude Bourdet, *L'Aventure incertaine* (Paris, Stock, 1975), pp. 27–8

47 AN 72AJ46/I, testimony of Claude Bourdet, 6 Jun. 1946; Bourdet, *L'Aventure incertaine*, pp. 28–33; Renée Bédarida, *Père Chaillet*, p. 120

48 Frenay, *La Nuit finira*, pp. 73–4

49 Bourdet, *L'Aventure incertaine*, p. 33

50 Frenay, *La Nuit finira*, pp. 103, 118–19

51 AN 72AJ47III, Entretien avec le Général Cochet. Propos recueillis par Henri Michel, 31 Jan. 1956

52 AN 72AJ46/I, testimony of Claude Bourdet, 6 Jun. 1946; testimony of Henri Frenay, Feb.–Mar.–Apr. 1948

53 AN72AJ80/I, testimony of Jeanne Sivadon, 14 Feb. 1946; testimony of Elisabeth Dussauze, 21 Feb. 1946; AN 72 AJ 46, testimony of Henri Ingrand, 25 & 31 Mar. 1949

54 AN 450AP1, Journal Lecompte-Boinet, 1939–1942 (1946), pp. 86–91. 4 Feb. 1941

55 AN 72AJ2026, Résumé de la conversation entre MM Rollin, directeur general adjoint de la Sûreté Nationale et le capitaine Frenay, le 28 janvier 1942

56 AN 72AJ2026, Résumé de la conversation entre le capitaine Frenay et M. Pucheu, Ministre de l'Intérieur, le 29 janvier 1942

57 Frenay, *La Nuit finira*, p. 161

58 AN 72AJ60/I, Témoignage de E. d'Astier de la Vigerie, 8 Jan. 1947; Wieviorka, *Histoire de la Résistance*, pp. 175–7

Chapter 4

1 Philippe de Vomécourt, *Who Lived to See the Day* (London, Hutchinson, 1961), pp. 24–5

2 AN 72AJ39/I, Note de Pierre de Vomécourt sur la constitution par les Anglais des réseaux d'action en France, dits plus tard 'Réseaux Buckmaster' (Sept. 1945); AN 72AJ40/VII, testimony of Pierre de Vomécourt, 31 Oct, 2, 6 & 9 Nov. 1946

3 AN 72AJ40/VII, testimony of Pierre de Vomécourt, 31 Oct, 2, 6 & 9 Nov. 1946

4 MRD Foot, *SOE in France. An Account of the Work of the Special Operations Executive in France, 1940–1944* (London, HMSO, 1966; 2nd edition, Frank Cass, 2004); Maurice Buckmaster, *They Fought Alone. The Story of British Agents in France* (London, Odhams Press, 1958)

5 Nicholas Atkin, *The Forgotten French. Exiles in the British Isles, 1940–44* (Manchester, Manchester UP, 2003), p. 148

6 Jean Lacouture, *De Gaulle. The Rebel, 1890–1944* (London, Harvill, 1993), pp. 344–6; See above, pp. 24–5

7 Martin S. Alexander, 'Dunkirk in military operations, myths and memories' in Robert Tombs and Emile Chabal (eds.), *Britain and France in Two World Wars* (London, Bloomsbury, 2013), pp. 93–118

8 Robert Gildea, *Children of the Revolution. The French, 1799–1914* (London, Penguin, 2008), plate 41

9 Martin Gilbert, *Winston Churchill VI. Finest Hour*, p. 668

10 See above, pp. 36–7

11 Audrey Bonnery, 'La France de la BBC, 1938–1944' (doctoral thesis, University of Burgundy, 2005), pp. 239–40. Transcript of *The Week in France* by Thomas Cadett

12 Jean-Louis Crémieux-Brilhac, *La France Libre*, p. 88; in general, see Jean-Françis Muracciole, *Les Français Libres. L'Autre Résistance* (Paris, Tallandier, 2009)

13 James Barr, *A Line in the Sand. Britain, France and the Struggle that Shaped the Middle East* (London, Simon & Schuster, 2011), pp. 207–17

14 AN 72AJ428, Telegrams of Catroux to de Gaulle, 10 & 14 May, 1941; de Gaulle draft proclamation, 28 May 1941

15 Jean-Louis Crémieux-Brilhac, *La France libre: de l'appel du 18 juin à la Libération*, pp. 156–61

16 Gilbert, *Winston S. Churchill VI*, p. 1157

17 Henri de Wailly, *Syrie 1941. La Guerre occultée. Vichystes contre Gaullistes* (Paris, Perrin, 2006), p. 433

18 Wailly, *Syrie 1941*, pp. 441–7

19 Bonnery, 'La France de la BBC', pp. 283–92; Martin Conway and José Gotovitch (eds.), *Europe in exile: European exile communities in Britain 1940–1945* (New York and Oxford, Berghahn, 2001)

20 Albertelli, *Les Services Secrets du Général de Gaulle. Le BCRA, 1940–1944* (Paris, Perrin, 2009), pp. 51–2

21 Albertelli, *Les Services Secrets*, pp. 52–3

22 Albertelli, *Les Services Secrets*, pp. 90–99

23 AN 13AV75, interview of André Dewavrin with Olivier Wieviorka, 7 Apr. 1991

24 Claude Bourdet, *L'aventure incertaine*, pp. 95–7

25 NA HS9/647/4, letter of Virginia Hall, 25 Nov. 1941

26 Denis Rake, *Rake's Progress* (London, Leslie Frewin, 1968), p. 104

27 Passy, *Souvenirs I*, p. 88. The street in question was Old Barracks Yard

28 AN 72AJ51/VII. Abbé Georges Bernard, vicaire à Saint-Martin, Conférence donné à la Société Archéologique de Nantes, 7 May 1951

29 AN 72AJ51/VII, testimonies of M. et Mme Lacasse, 26 Jun. 1946

30 AN 72AJ51/VII, testimony of Max André, Oct. 1945

31 Rémy, *Mémoires d'un Agent secret de la France Libre I. 18 juin 1940–18 juin 1942* (Paris, France-Empire, 1959), p. 48

32 Rémy, *Mémoires d'un Agent secret*, p. 51

33 Passy, *Souvenirs I*, p. 71

34 Rémy, *Mémoires d'un Agent secret*, p. 103

35 AN 72AJ49, testimony of M. de la Débuterie, Rochetrejoux (Vendée), n.d.

36 See above, p. 69

37 AN 72AJ2217, interview of Colonel Passy with Gilberte Brossolette, 19 & 26 Jun. 1973

38 Rémy, *Mémoires d'un Agent secret de la France Libre I*, p. 365

39 Rémy, *Mémoires d'un Agent secret de la France Libre I*, p. 366. See also AN 72AJ59/IV, testimony of Louis Vallon, 25 Mar. 1947; Guillaume Piketty, *Pierre Brossolette*, pp. 165–74

40 Passy, *Souvenirs I*, pp. 49–52

41 Christian Pineau, *La Simple Vérité, 1940–1945* (1st edn. 1960) (Geneva, Editions de Crémille, 1972), vol. I, pp. 103–4, 128–30. See also AN 72AJ2217, interview of Christian Pineau with Gilberte Brossolette, 1973

42 Pineau, *La Simple Vérité*, p. 153

43 Pineau, *La Simple Vérité*, p. 156–7. See also AN 72 AJ59/V, testimony of Christian Pineau, 25 May 1950

44 Pineau, *La Simple Vérité*, p. 190. For successive drafts of this text see AN 580AP25/3, Fonds Christian Pineau

45 Charles de Gaulle, *Discours et messages* vol. I, p. 182

46 Rémy, *Mémoires d'un Agent secret de la France Libre I*, p. 491; Piketty, *Brossolette*, p. 175

47 AN 72AJ49, Confrérie Notre Dame, précis, pp. 23–5

48 Yves Farge, *Rebelles, soldats, citoyens. Carnets d'un commissaire de la République* (Neuilly, Editions St Clair, 1975), pp. 29–30; Alya Aglan, 'La Résistance', in Aglan, *Jean Cavaillès* (2002), pp. 92–4

49 AN 72AJ59/V, testimony of Louis Vallon, 25 May 1947

50 Passy, *Souvenirs II. 10, Duke Street, Londres* (Monte-Carlo, 1947), p. 66

51 AN 72AJ2215, original of report entrusted to Siriex, London (28 Apr.) 1942; Guillaume Piketty, *Pierre Brossolette. Un Héros de la Résistance* (Paris, Odile Jacob, 1998), p. 179

52 AN 72AJ2215, original of report entrusted to Siriex, London (28 Apr.) 1942; Guillaume Piketty, *Pierre Brossolette*, p. 187

53 AN 72AJ58/XII, testimony of Gilberte Brossolette, 27 Jan., 7 & 14 Feb. 1947. Worth about 250 euros at current prices

54 AN 72AJ49, exchange of letters Brossolette-Passy-Rémy (Dec. 1942). Communicaed by Serreulles.

55 Jean-Pierre Azéma, *Jean Moulin: le politique, le rebelle, le resistant* (Paris, Perrin, 2003), pp. 102–4

56 Daniel Cordier, *Jean Moulin, l'inconnu du Panthéon I. Une ambition pour la République, 1899–juin 1936* (Paris, Lattès, 1989), p. 36; Azéma, *Jean Moulin*, pp. 167–75; Jackson, *France. The Dark Years*, p. 429

57 Passy, *Souvenirs II. 10, Duke Street*, p. 104

58 Emmanuel d'Astier de la Vigerie, *Sept fois sept jours*, p. 76

59 Passy, *Souvenirs II. 10, Duke Street*, p. 81

60 Emmanuel d'Astier de la Vigerie, *Sept fois sept jours*, pp. 76–7, 80

61 Frenay, *La Nuit finira*, p. 146

62 See above, pp. 104–5

63 AN 72AJ55/I, testimony of Jean-Paul Lévy, 1 Nov. 1946

64 Frenay, *La Nuit finira*, p. 201–2; Charles d'Aragon, *La Résistance sans héroisme*, pp. 91–4

65 Frenay, *La Nuit finira*, p. 347

66 Claude Bourdet, *L'aventure incertaine*, p. 140

67 Claude Bourdet, *L'aventure incertaine*, pp. 141–2

68 Passy, *Souvenirs II. 10, Duke Street*, p. 350; Arthur Calmette, *L'OCM. Organisation Civile et Militaire. Histoire d'un movement de résistance de 1940 à 1946* (Paris, PUF, 1961), p. 38; Piketty, *Brossolette*, p. 243

69 AN 72AJ2026, Frenay to Giraud, 14 Aug. 1942; Frenay, *La Nuit finira*, p. 219

70 Passy, *Souvenirs II. 10, Duke Street*, p. 247

71 Passy, *Souvenirs II. 10, Duke Street*, pp. 261–81; Frenay, *La Nuit finira*, pp. 230–5

Chapter 5

1 Jeanne Bohec, *La Plastiqueuse à bicyclette* (Paris, Mercure de France, 1975), pp. 14–29

2 See above, pp. 67–9

3 Agnès Humbert, *Résistance. Memoirs of Occupied France*, p. 25

4 Laurent Douzou, La Résistance, une affaire d'hommes?' Cahiers de l'IHTP 31 (Oct. 1995); Claire Andrieu, 'Women in the French Resistance. Revisiting the historical record', *French Politics, Culture and Society* 18/1 (spring 2000), pp. 13–27; Dominique Veillon, 'Les Femmes anonymes dans la Résistance', in Gilzmer, Levisse-Touzé and Maertens, *Les femmes dans la Résistance en France* (Paris, Tallandier, 2003), p. 101

5 AN 72AJ238/III, Hélène Terré, 'Nous entrerons dans la carrière. Une histoire de l'AFAT (typescript, 229p), pp. 4–6. See also above, pp. 30–31

6 Hélène Terré, 'Nous entrerons dans la carrière, pp. 35, 45–55, 127

7 Tereska Torrès, *Une Française Libre, 1939–1945* (Paris, France Loisirs, 2000), p. 135, diary entry 20 Jul. 1941

8 Torrès, *Une Française Libre*, pp. 171–2, diary entry 2 Jan. 1942

9 Torrès, *Une Française Libre*, pp. 189–92, diary entries 18 Jun. & 14 Jul. 1942

10 Mémorial Leclerc/Musée Jean Moulin, Teresa Torrès archive, cutting from an unspecified newspaper, Sept. 1942

11 Torrès, *Une Française Libre*, p. 249, diary entry 11 Dec. 1943

12 CHRC, interview with Micheline Altman, 16 Jul. 1997

13 Denise Domenach Lallich, *Demain il fera beau. Journal d'une adolescente (1939–1944)* (Lyon, BGA Permazel, 2001), p. 24

14 Denise Domenach Lallich, *Demain il fera beau*, pp. 24, 115–16

15 Denise Domenach Lallich, *Demain il fera beau*, pp. 24, 32–5; CHRD Lyon, interview with Denise Domenach, 6 Feb. 1996

16 CHRD, interview with Jeannette and Maurice Lubczanski, 12 Feb. 1999

17 AN 72AJ60/II, testimony of Anne Hervé, 7 Jan. 1947; AN 72AJ69/IV, testimony of Pierre Hervé, 29 Mar. 1950

18 AN 72AJ188A III. Haute-Savoie. Testimony of Mme Lamouille of Vougy, 2 Jan. 1946; on the Glières *maquis*, see below, pp. 297–8, 333–4

19 AN 72AJ92C1 Ain. Testimony of Marcelle Appleton, 14 Nov. 1945; AN 72 AJ 1899, testimony of Hean Villaucher, vice president of CDL, Ain, 16 Dec. 1944

20 AN 72AJ45/IV, testimony of Germaine Aylé, 26 Dec. 1946; Odile Vasselot, *Tombés du ciel*, pp. 15–27

21 Olwen Hufton, 'Women in Revolution', *Past & Present* vol. 53(1) (1971), pp. 90–108; Dominique Godineau, *The Women of Paris and their French Revolution* (Berkeley, University of California Press, 1998)

22 Musée de la Résistance. Fonds Roussel. Attestation for Claudine Chomel by liquidateur national for FN, 18 Dec. 1958

23 Musée de la Résistance Carton 126 A. Témoignages III. Yvonne Dumont, secretary-general of UFF, former senator, 1968; Musée de la Résistance, Carton 129. Témoignages VIII. Léon Mauvais, 1964, p. 18

24 BBC Written Archives Centre, Caversham, Anonymous letters, no. 796, 23 Aug. 1941

25 AN 72AJ87/I. Vercors. Rapport de Pupin, 15 Oct. 1947, p. 5 (The woman was probably Geneviève Gayet)

26 Musée de la Résistance. Inconnus de la Résistance (1984), account of Claude Pascal, Béziers

27 Musée de la Résistance, Carton 125. Témoignages II. Marie-José Chombart de Lauwe, 4 May 1967

28 AN 72AJ49, testimony of Marguerite Blot, 3 Feb. 1947. Dumont himself, however, was arrested by the Germans and shot at Mont Valérien on 13 May 1943

29 Laurent Douzou (ed.), *Notes de Prison de Bertrande d'Astier de la Vigerie (15 mars–4 avril 1941), Cahiers de l'IHTP* 25 (Oct. 1993), p. 46

30 Robert Gildea, 'Lettres de correspondants français à la BBC (1940–1943). Une pénombre de la Résistance', *Vingtième siècle. Revue d'histoire*. Vol. 125 (Jan.-Mar. 2015), p. 63

31 Anonymous letters, no. 472, 17 avril 1941. See also above, p. 64

32 Anonymous letters, no. 186, 26 mai 1941

33 AN 6AV622, interview of Robert Salmon with Olivier Wieviorka, 7 Feb. 1986. See above, p. 70

34 AN 6A591 interview of Jacqueline Pardon with Olivier Wieviorka, 21 Jan. 1987

35 CHRD Lyon, interview of Charlotte Nadel, 17 Apr. 1998

36 AN 6A527 interview of Genia Gemähling with Olivier Wieviorka, Nov. 1985

37 AN 6A527 interview of Genia Gemähling with Olivier Wieviorka, Nov. 1985

38 CHRD Interview with Micheline Altman, 16 Jul. 1997

39 AN 72AJ68/V, testimony of Marie-Hélène Lefaucheux, n.d.; Renée Bedarida, *Pierre Chaillet, Témoin de la Résistance spirituelle* (Paris, Fayard, 1988), pp. 217–21

40 AN 72AJ170 B1, testimony of Mme Alloy, directrice de l'école maternelle, Hellemmes, 30 Jan. 1947

41 Charles Monier, *Les Chemins de la Résistance à Bollène et dans Le Canton, 1939–1944* (Bollène, 2002), p. 112, cited in Christiane Guldenstadt, *Les Femmes dans la Résistance* (Herbolzheim, Centaurus Verlag, 2006), p. 94

42 Musée de la Résistance. Inconnus de la Résistance (1984), account of Joseph Rossi, Vif (Isère), 13 Aug. 1984

43 Interview of Cécile Rol-Tanguy with RG, 20 Jun. 2012; Roger Bourderon, *Rol-Tanguy* (Paris, Tallandier, 2004), pp. 182–3, 223, 233

44 *L'Humanité*, 31 Aug. 1944, cutting in Musée de la Résistance. Fonds David Diamant. UJRE Carton 12/24

45 Musée de la Résistance, Carton 127bis, Témoignages V. Nicole Lambert-Philippot (1975), p. 2

46 Musée de la Résistance, Carton 127bis, Témoignages V. Nicole Lambert-Philippot (1975), pp. 3–9

47 *Les Inconnus de la Résistance* (1984), p. 34.

48 Torrès, *Une Française Libre,* diary entries 11 Dec. 1943, p. 249, Apr. 1944, p. 262, 15 Jun. 1944, p. 264

49 NA HS9/1089/4, finishing report of Jacqueline Nearne, 25 Aug. 1942

50 See below, pp. 324–5

51 NA HS9/982/4, report on Anne-Marie Comert née Walters, 26 Oct. 1943

52 NA HS9/982/4, report on Anne-Marie Comert née Walters, 4 Nov. 1944

53 Pearl Witherington Cornioley, *Code Name Pauline. Memoirs of a World War II Special Agent* (Chicago, Chicago Review Press, 2013), pp. 32, 36

54 Pearl Witherington Cornioley, *Code Name Pauline,* pp. 81–93

55 SHD Vincennes 16 P 67268, Jeanne Bohec épouse Couty, STS reports of 5 & 19 Oct. 1943

56 AN 72AJ220/1, testimony of Jeanne Couty-Bohec, 29 Oct & 4 Nov. 1949, pp. 13–14

57 AN 72AJ220/1, testimony of Jeanne Couty-Bohec, 29 Oct & 4 Nov. 1949, p. 15

58 See below, p. 360

59 Jeanne Bohec, *La Plastiqueuse à bicyclette,* p. 226

60 AN 72AJ50/II. Défense de la France. testimony of the Girard family, 1 Feb. 1946

61 Claire Girard to her brother Augustin, Oct. 1942, *Lettres (1939–1944),* in Guillaume Piketty (ed.), *Francais en Resistance,* 653.

62 Claire Giraud, *Lettres (1939–1944),* 660, spring 1944

63 Claire Giraud, *Lettres (1939–1944),* 662, Jun. 1944

64 Claire Giraud, *Lettres (1939–1944),* 664, Jun. 1944

65 Madeleine Riffaud, *On l'appelait Rainer* (Paris, Julliard, 1994), p. 56

66 AN 72AJ56/III FTPF. Testimony of Madeleine Riffaud, 4 Jul. 1946

67 Madeleine Riffaud, *On l'appelait Rainer,* p. 96

68 Interview with Madeleine Riffaud, conducted by RG, Paris, 15 Apr. 2012

69 Madeleine Riffaud, *On l'appelait Rainer*, pp. 93–8
70 See below, p. 400

Chapter 6

1 Simone Martin-Chauffier, *A Bientôt quand même*, pp. 105–6
2 See above, pp. 67–9
3 Martin-Chauffier, *A Bientôt quand même*, p. 52
4 Madeleine Riffaud, *On l'appelait Rainer* (Paris, Julliard, 1994), pp. 26–7
5 Denise Domenach-Lallich, *Demain il fera beau. Journal d'une adolescente, 1939–1944* (Lyon, Lyon: Éditions BGA Permezel, 2001), p. 26
6 Denise Domenach-Lallich, *Demain il fera beau.* p. 26
7 See above, pp. 97–8
8 AN 13AV135, interview with Serge Ravanel, 26 Feb. 1991
9 See above, p. 40
10 AN 450AP1, Journal Lecompte-Boinet, 1939–1942 (1946), 6 Oct. 1941, p. 69
11 See above, p. 102
12 AN 450AP1, Journal Lecompte-Boinet, 1939–1942 (1946), 5 Mar. 1943, p. 62
13 AN 450AP1, Journal Lecompte-Boinet, 1939–1942 (1946), 6 Oct. 1941, p. 71. This section was added in retrospect
14 See below, pp. 218–19
15 See above, pp. 87–8
16 Albert Ouzoulias, *Les Fils de la Nuit* (Paris, Grasset, 1975), p. 55
17 Nina Gourfinkel, *Aux Prises avec mon temps 2. L'Autre patrie* (Paris, Seuil, 1953), pp. 284–5; Gourfinkel, *Théâtre russe contemporain* (Paris, la Renaissance du Livre, 1931)
18 CDJC CMXCIV-9 (I) Fonds Abadi. Moussa Abadi, Allocution, Colloque des enfants cachés, Palais du Luxembourg, 21 May 1995
19 See below, p. 203
20 See below, pp. 327–8
21 Gerhard Leo, *Un Allemand dans la Résistance. Le train pour Toulouse* (Paris, Editions Tirésias, 1997), pp. 260–1
22 Christian Pineau, *La Simple Vérité, 1940–1945* (1st edn. 1960), Geneva, Editions de Crémille, 1972,vol.I, pp. 103–4, 128–30. See also AN 72AJ2217, interview of Christian Pineau with Gilberte Brossolette, 1973
23 Charles d'Aragon, *La Résistance sans héroisme* (Paris, Seuil, 1977), pp. 57–8
24 See above, p. 128
25 NA HS9/1539/6, draft report, 7 Mar. 1942, Selborne to Churchill, 21 Mar. 1942. See above, pp. 106–7
26 AN 7241/7, testimony of André Girard, Aug. 1950
27 André Gillois, *Ce Siècle avait deux ans. Mémoires* (Paris, Mémoire du Livre, 2002), p. 398
28 AN 7241/7, testimony of Maurice Diamant-Berger, 10 Oct. 1946
29 NA H56/327, report of Boddington to SOE, 11 Aug. 1942
30 Gillois, *Ce Siècle avait deux ans*, pp. 413–14
31 Germaine Tillion, 'Première résistance en zone occupée. Du côté du réseau Musée de l'Homme-Haut-Vildé', *Esprit* 261 (Feb. 2000), p. 117

32 AN 72AJ39, testimony of Philippe de Vomécourt, Dec. 1946; Jan & Feb. 1947

33 Mathilde Carré, *I was 'the Cat'* (London, Souvenir Press, 1960), p. 107

34 AN 72AJ40/VII, testimony of Pierre de Vomécourt, 31 Oct, 2, 6 & 9 Nov. 1946; AN72AJ627, reports to London of Pierre de Vomécourt, 15 Jul., 8 Aug. 1942.

35 Gilles Perrault, *La Longue traque* (Paris, Lattès, 1975), pp. 16–45

36 NA HS9/1539/6, preliminary interrogation of Pierre de Vomécourt, 21 Apr. 1945

37 Monique Georges, *Le Colonel Fabien était mon père*, p. 183

38 André Postel-Vinay, *Un fou s'évade. Souvenirs de 1941–1942* (Turriers, Transfaire, 1996), p. 168

39 Dominique Missika, *Bert Albrecht*, pp. 208–66

40 Raymond Aubrac, *Où la Mémoire s'attarde*, p. 92

41 Raymond Aubrac, *Où la Mémoire s'attarde*, pp. 107–10. Lucie Aubrac, *Ils partiront dans l'ivresse* (Paris, Seuil, 1984), pp. 120–1; Laurent Douzou, *Lucie Aubrac*, p. 136

42 AN 450AP/1, Lecompte-Boinet, Journal 1939–42, p. 118. Entry Apr. 1942

43 Monique Georges, *Le Colonel Fabien était mon père*, p. 196

44 AN 6AV527, interview of Genia Gemähling with Olivier Wieviorka, Nov. 1985

45 Laurent Douzou, *Lucie Aubrac*, pp. 110–14, 139–46

46 NA HS9/1539/5, interrogation of Philippe de Vomécourt, 25 Jan. 1945, p. 12

47 NA HS9/1240/3, finishing report of Harry Rée, 1 Jan. 1943

48 NA HS9/1240/3, interrogation of Harry Rée, 24–27 Jul. 1944

49 NA HS9/701/1, Richard Heslop, 'False Identities', script for a BBC talk, 28 Oct. 1945

50 Pearl Witherington Cornioley, *Codename Pauline. Memoirs of a World War II Special Agent* (Chicago, Chicago Review Press, 2013), p. 57

51 NA HS9/982/4, interview with Anne-Marie Walters 16 Jan. 1945, released by the censor, 8 Mar. 1945; interview in *Daily Telegraph*, approved by censor 18 Mar. 1945

52 NA HS9/1407/1, interrogation of George Reginald Starr, 20–1 Nov. 1944

53 NA HS9/987/I, cover story and list of goods for 'Riquet', 10 Sept. 1943

54 See below, p. 304

55 Musée de la Résistance, Carton 130, Témoignages III. Testimony of Renée Quatremaire, n.d.

56 AN 72AJ181 BII, Auguste Pinton, 'Contribution à l'histoire de la Résistance à Lyon et principalement du movement Franc-Tireur', n.d., pp. 22–3

57 Philippe Viannay, *Du Bon Usage de la France* (Paris, Editions Ramsay, 1988), p. 67

58 Roger Lefèvre, *Souvenir de maquisards de l'Ain* (St Cyr-sur-Loire, Alan Sutton, 2004), pp. 8–9; Musée de la Résistance, Champigny, NE 3832, testimony of Roger Lefèvre, proviseur honoraire de Lycée, ancien chef de corps franc des maquis de l'Ain, to president of Fondation de la Résistance, 9 Oct. 2009

59 Joseph Kessel, *L'Armée des ombres* (Paris, Plon, 1963), Preface, pp. 5, 8

60 Laurent Douzou, *Lucie Aubrac*, p. 145

61 Kessel, *L'Armée des ombres*, p. 132. See Anne Simonin, 'La Résistance sans fiction? *L'Armée des ombres* (1943) in Bruno Curatolo and François Marcot (eds.), *Écrire sous l'Occupation. Du non-consentement à 1a Résistance, France-Belgique-Pologne* (Rennes, PU Rennes, 2011), pp. 233–53

Chapter 7

1 André Jacques, *Madeleine Barot. Une indomptable énergie* (Paris, Cerf/Labor et Fides, 1989), p. 12–46; *Les Clandestins de Dieu. Cimade, 1939–1945. Textes rassemblés par Jeanne Merle d'Aubigné et Violette Mouchon* (Paris, Fayard, 1968), pp. 62–4

2 Nicole Dombrowski Risser, *France under Fire. German Invasion, Civilian Flight and Family Survival during World War II* (Cambridge, CUP, 2012), pp. 34–53

3 Hanna Diamond, *Fleeing Hitler. France 1940* (Oxford, OUP, 2007); Dombrowski Risser, *France under Fire*, pp. 86–137

4 Philippe Burrin, *Hitler and the Jews* (London, Edward Arnold, 1994), pp. 53–64

5 Burrin, *Hitler and the Jews*, pp. 84–92, 115–31

6 Jean-Louis Clément, *Les évêques au temps de Vichy. Loyalisme sans inféodation. Les relations entre l'Église et l'État de 1940 à 1944* (Paris, Éditions Beauchesne, 1999), pp. 37–8

7 Maurice Rajsfus, *Des Juifs dans la Collaboration: l'UGIF 1941–1944* (Paris, EDI, 1980)

8 Jan Sigurd Kulok, 'Trait d'union: the history of the French relief organisation Secours national/Entr'aide française under the Third Republic, the Vichy regime and the early Fourth Republic, 1939–1949' (Oxford DPhil thesis, 2003); Jean-Pierre Le Crom, *Au secours, Maréchal! l'instrumentalisation de l'humanitaire, 1940–1944* (Paris, PUF, 2013)

9 CDJC DLXI-94, interview of Andrée Salomon with Anny Latour, n.d.; Georges Weill, 'Andrée Salomon et le sauvetage des enfants juifs (1933–1947), in *French Politics, Culture and Society* 30/2 (summer 2012), pp. 89–96

10 CDJC DLXI-55, interview with Shimon Hammel, n.d.

11 Daniel Lee, *Pétain's Jewish Children. French Jewish Children and the Vichy Regime* (Oxford, OUP, 2014); Denise R. Gamzon, *Mémoires* (Jerusalem, 1997), pp. 32–5, 55–75

12 Compagnies de Travailleurs Étrangers

13 Sabine Zlatin, *Mémoires de la 'Dame d'Izieu'* (Paris, Gallimard, 1992), pp. 14–38

14 Le Comité Inter-Mouvements auprès des Évacués. See Patrick Cabanel, *Histoire des Justes en France* (Paris, Armand Colin, 2012), pp. 124–5

15 BDIC FΔ 2149/1081, 'Notes sur la Cimade' (Jul. 1952), 16pp.

16 BDIC FΔ 2149/1081, letter of Suzanne de Dietrich to 'chers amis', 25 May 1940

17 BDIC FΔ 2149/1081, Violette Mouchon, 'Parlons de la Cimade', *Lien* (Nov–Dec. 1944), pp. 256–61; *Les Clandestins de Dieu. CIMADE 1939–1945*; Cabanel, *Les Justes de Dieu*, pp. 126–30

18 Philippe Boegner (ed.), *Carnets du Pasteur Boegner, 1940–1945* (Paris, Fayard, 1992), p. 96

19 BDIC FΔ 2149/5001, Conférence de Mlle M. Barot, 4 Dec. 1941

20 BSHPF DT TRO, Journal André Trocmé (1960), pp. 367–72

21 Journal André Trocmé, p. 383–5; Cabanel, *Les Justes de Dieu*, pp. 172–87

22 BDIC FΔ 2149/5005, André Dumas to Madeleine Barot, 18 Mar. 1942

23 BDIC FΔ 2149/5005, André Dumas to Madeleine Barot, 26 Mar. 1942

24 Lucien Lazare, *L'Abbé Glasberg* (Paris, Editions du Cerf, 1990), pp. 19–34; Christian Sorrel (ed.), *Alexandre Glasberg, 1902–1981. Prêtre, Résistant, Militant. Chrétiens et Sociétés.* Documents et Mémoires no. 19 (Lyon, 2013), pp. 15–35

25 Nina Gourfinkel, *Aux Prises avec mon Temps II. L'Autre Patrie* , pp. 231–2

26 Gourfinkel, *Aux Prises avec mon Temps II*, pp. 233, 240

27 Gourfinkel, *Aux Prises avec mon Temps II* cix; Cabanel, *Les Justes de France*, pp. 137–40

28 Anne Grynberg, *Les Camps de la Honte. Les Internés juifs dans des camps français* (Paris, Editions de la Découverte, 1991), pp. 184–5

29 Lazare, *L'Abbé Glasberg*, p. 41

30 BDIC FΔ 2149/5001, report of M. Toureille of Aumônerie protestante pour les Réfugiés étrangers en France, ECCO, Geneva, 27 Jan. 1942

31 AN 72AJ71/XI, testimony of Abbé Glasberg, 16 Aug. 1946

32 Jean-Marie Soutou, 'Souvenirs des années noires', *Les Cahiers de l'Alliance Israélite Universelle*, 201 (Oct–Nov. 1979), 10; Jean-Marie Soutou, *Un Diplomate engagé. Mémoires, 1939–1979* (Paris, Éditions de Fallois, 2011), pp. 25–9; Cabanel, *Histoire des Justes*, pp. 153–5

33 See above, p. 78

34 *Témoignage Chrétien*, no. 23, 4 Nov. 1944

35 *Témoignage Chrétien*, no. 24, 11 Nov. 1944

36 CDJC DLXI-85, interview of Germaine Ribière with Anny Latour, n.d.

37 Donald Lowrie, *The Hunted Children* (New York, Norton, 1963), pp. 83–7, 128–31

38 Joseph Weill, *Contribution à l'Histoire des Camps d'Internement dans l'Anti-France* (Paris, Éditions du Centre, 1946), p. 109

39 CDJC DLXI-94, interview of Anny Latour with Andrée Salomon, n.d.

40 Renée Poznanski, *Les Juifs en France pendant la Seconde Guerre mondiale* (Paris, Hachette, 1997), pp. 307–46; Asher Cohen, *Persécutions et sauvetages. Juifs et français sous l'Occupation et sous Vichy* (Paris, Cerf, 1993)

41 CDJC DLXI-28, interview of Georges Garel with Anny Latour, n.d.; See also Jean-Louis Clément, *Mgr Solages, archévêque de Toulouse* (Paris, Beauchesne, 1994); François Drouin & Philippe Joutard (eds.), *Monseigneur Théas, évêque de Montauban, les Juifs, les Justes* (Toulouse, Privat, 2003) and Sylvie Bernay, *L'Église de France face à la persécution des Juifs, 1940–1944* (Paris, CNRS, 2012)

42 AN 72AJ73, testimony of Marie-Rose Gineste, n.d. Since 1790 departments and dioceses in France have mapped onto each other

43 P. Boegner (ed.), *Carnets du Pasteur Boegner*, 12, 14, 18 & 19 Aug. 1942, pp. 191–3

44 CDJC DLXI-85, interview of Germaine Ribière with Anny Latour

45 CDJC DCLXXXIII-17 Fonds Gilbert Lesage, 'Ella Barlow'

46 CDJC DCLXXXIII-7 Fonds Gilbert Lesage, Témoignage; DCLXXXIII-4, certificate by Abbé Glasberg, 2 Feb. 1970; Lucien Lazare, *L'Abbé Glasberg*, p. 15

47 Soutou, 'Souvenirs des années noires', p. 12

48 Cabanel, *Les Justes de France*, pp. 157–60; Madeleine Comte, 'L'abbé Glasberg au secours des Juifs', in Sorrel (ed.), *Alexandre Glasberg, 1902–1981. Prêtre, Résistant, Militant*, pp. 52–4

49 Valérie Perthuis, *Le Sauvetage des Enfants Juifs du Camp de Vénissieux, août 1942* (Lyon, Editions Lyonnaises d'Art et d'Histoire, 1997), pp. 17–39
50 Lucien Lazare, *L'Abbé Glasberg*, p. 15
51 CDJC DLXI-28, interview of Georges Garel with Anny Latour
52 CDJC DLXI-104, interview of Dr Joseph Weill with Anny Latour, n.d.
53 Lucien Lazare, *L'Abbé Glasberg*, 11–17; Interview with Georges Garel, n.d.
54 Joseph Weill, *Le Combat d'un Juif*, p. 180
55 P. Boegner (ed.), *Carnets du Pasteur Boegner*, 9 Sept. 1942, p. 199; 15 Sept. 1942, p. 206
56 P. Boegner (ed.), *Carnets du Pasteur Boegner*, 8 Sept. 1942, p. 199; BSHPF DT BAR/4, 'Rapport de M. le Pasteur Boegner à l'Assemblée Générale du Protestantisme', pp. 14–16
57 CDJC RG 67.007, Box 61/86, minutes of meeting of American Friends Service Committee, Marseille, 7, 14 & 21 Oct. 1942
58 Soutou, *Un Diplomate engagé*, p. 39
59 AN 72AJ73/VI, testimony of Père Chaillet, 5 Feb. 1962; AN 72AJ 71/XI, testimony of Abbé Glasberg, 16 Aug. 1946; Soutou, 'Souvenirs des années noires', p. 14; Jean-Maris Soutou, *Un Diplomate engagé*, pp. 37–40; Lazare, *L'Abbé Glasberg*, pp. 17–18, 58–9
60 Norbert Sabatié, 'L'Abbé Glasberg et la Résistance dans le Tarn-et-Garonne, 1943–44', in Sorrel (ed.), *Alexandre Glasberg, 1902–1981. Prêtre, Résistant, Militant*, pp. 59–69
61 Interview with Andrée Salomon
62 Interview with Georges Garel
63 Zlatin, *Mémoires de la 'Dame d'Izieu'*, pp. 40–2
64 Interview with Andrée Salomon
65 CDJC DXLI-103, interview with Joseph Weill, 1974
66 CDJC DXLI-55, interview of Jeanne Latichiver, 'La Reine Mère', with Anny Latour, n.d., p. 8
67 CDJC DXLI-55, interview with Anny Latour of Jean Deffaugt, mayor of Annemasse, n.d., p. 6
68 Jean Deffaugt interview, pp. 13–14.
69 BSHPF DT TRO, Journal André Trocmé, pp. 387–96
70 Journal André Trocmé, p. 431. On Barot, see BDIC FΔ2149/15002, Passages en Suisse, 1939–45, handwritten note, n.d.
71 Journal André Trocmé, pp. 418–19 bis
72 Memorial de la Shoah/Ina, Interview with Oscar Rosowsky, 5 Jun. 2006; Rosowky private papers
73 CDJC DXLI-55, interview of Oscar Rosowsky with Anny Latour n.d.; BN Inathèque, Mémorial de la Shoah, interview with Oscar Rosowsky, 5 Jun. 2006
74 CDJC DXLI-25, interview of Ignace Fink with Anny Latour n.d.
75 See above, pp. 160–61
76 Moussa Abadi, Allocution, 2
77 Miranda Pollard, 'A Question of Silence? Odette Rosenstock, Moussa Abadi and the Réseau Marcel', in *French Politics, Culture and Society* 30/2 (2012), p. 126
78 CDJC Fonds Abadi CMXCIV-11, Mgr Rémond, *Pourquoi* (1948), pp. 2–3;

Ralph Schor, *Un Évêque dans le siècle, Monseigneur Paul Rémond, 1873–1963* (Nice: Serre, 1984)

79 Moussa Abadi, Allocution, pp. 4–5
80 CDJC Fonds Abadi CMXCIV-9(1), Odette Rosenstock, 'Pourquoi j'ai été arrêtée', n.d.
81 AN 72AJ71/XI, testimony of Sabine Zlatin, 4 Feb. 1947; Zlatin, *Mémoires de la 'Dame d'Izieu'*, p. 57

Chapter 8

1 Franz Dahlem, *Am Vorabend des zweiten Weltkrieges* (Berlin, Dietz Verlag, 1977), vol. I, pp. 19–24
2 Musée de la Résistance, Champigny. Fonds Ouzoulias, carton 2, dossier 2. Résistance allemande, Dahlem handwritten memoirs (1974), p. 2; Florimond Bonte, *Les Antifascistes allemands dans la Résistance* (Paris, Éditions sociales, 1969), pp. 96–8
3 Dahlem handwritten memoirs (1974), p. 4
4 Musée de la Résistance, Champigny. Fonds Ouzoulias, carton 2, dossier 5, note on Franz Dahlem by Service Liquidateur of Front National, 12 May 1972
5 AD Haute-Garonne 16J222, Vicente Lopez Tovar, 'Autobiographie' (typescript, 1991), p. 1
6 Vicente López Tovar, 'Autobiographie', p. 12
7 Vicente López Tovar, 'Autobiographie', p. 20
8 Vicente López Tovar, 'Autobiographie', p. 47
9 Interview with Léon Landini, conducted by RG, Bagneux, 20 Apr. 2012
10 CHRD Lyon, interview with Henri Krischer, 6 Jul. 2000
11 RHICOJ, *Les Juifs dans la Résistance et la Libération* (Paris, Scribe, 1985), pp. 174–84
12 E.H. Carr, *The Comintern and the Spanish Civil War* (New York, Pantheon Books, 1984), pp. 20–3
13 P. Dan Richardson, *Comintern Army. The International Brigades and the Spanish Civil War* (Lexington, UP of Kenticky, 1982); Michael Jackson, *Fallen Sparrows: the International Brigades in the Spanish Civil War* (Philadelphia, American Philosophical Society, 1994), pp. 69, 75, 84; Rémi Skoutelsky, *L'Espoir guidait leurs pas. Les Volontaires français dans les Brigades Internationales, 1936–1939* (Paris, Grasset, 1998); David Diamant, *Combattants juifs dans l'Armée républicaine espagnole* (Paris, Le Pavillon, 1971), pp. 127–8
14 Gérard Noiriel, *Le Creuset français. Histoire de l'Immigration, XIXe-XXsiècles* (Paris, Seuil, 1988), annexe statistique; Janine Ponty, *Polonais méconnus. Histoire des Travailleurs immigrés en France dans l'entre-deux-guerres* (Paris, Publications de la Sorbonne, 2005), pp. 7–176; Denis Peschanski, 'La Résistance immigrée' and Genevièvre Dreyfus-Armand, *Les Espagnols dans la Résistance: incertitudes et spécificités*, both in Jean-Marie Guillou and Pierre Laborie (eds.), *Mémoire et Histoire. La Résistance* (Toulouse, Privat, 1995), pp. 202, 218
15 Damira Titonel Asperti, *Écrire pour les autres. Mémoires d'une résistante. Les antifascists italiens en Lot-et-Garonne sous l'Occupation* (PU de Bordeaux, 1999), pp. 21–2, 31

16 Max Weinstein, *Souvenirs, souvenirs* (Nice, Éditions du Losange, 1997), pp. 19–20, 42–3, 51; Interview with Max Weinstein, conducted by RG, Paris, 24 Apr. 2012; Interview with Felicie Weinstein, George's widow, conducted by RG, Sevran, 16 May 2012

17 David H. Weinberg, *Les Juifs de Paris de 1933 à 1939* (Paris, Calmann-Lévy, 1974), p. 20

18 Weinberg, *Les Juifs de Paris*, pp. 48–53

19 Weinberg, *Les Juifs de Paris*, pp. 20–36

20 Nicholas Tandler, *Un Inconnu nommé Krasucki* (Paris, la Table Ronde, 1985), pp. 15–27

21 Weinberg, *Les Juifs de Paris*, pp. 58–9; Tandler, *Un Inconnu nommé Krasucki*, pp. 30–9

22 Louis Gronowski, *Le Dernier Grand Soir. Un Juif de Pologne* (Paris, Seuil, 1980), p. 59

23 Diamant, *Combattants juifs dans l'Armée républicaine espagnole*, pp. 146–9; Weinberg, *Les Juifs de Paris*, pp. 171–4

24 Claude Lévy, *Les Parias de la Résistance* (Paris, Calmann-Lévy, 1970), p. 61

25 Greg Lamazères, *Marcel Langer. Une Vie de combats. Juif, communiste, resistant et guillotiné* (Toulouse, Privat, 2003)

26 Musée de la Résistance, Champigny. Fonds Ouzoulias, carton 5, biography of Joseph Epstein by Paula Duffau (22pp), pp. 1–12

27 Geneviève Dreyfus-Armand, *L'Exil des Républicains Espagnols en France. De la Guerre civile à la mort de Franco* (Paris, Albin Michel, 1999), pp. 35–7; Geneviève Dreyfus-Armand and Émile Temine, *Les camps sur la plage. Un exil espagnol* (Paris, Éditions Autrement, 1995)

28 Denis Peschanski, *La France des Camps. L'Internement, 1938–1946* (Paris, Gallimard, 2002), pp. 58–9

29 AD Haute-Garonne 16J199, General Ilic, 'Interbrigadistes dans les camps français' (1986), pp. 8–11

30 See above, pp. 26–7

31 José Borras, *Histoire de Mauthausen. Les cinq années de deportation des républicains espagnols* (Choisy en Brie, La Bochetière, 1989)

32 Dreyfus-Armand and Temine, *Les camps de la plage*, pp. 38–44; Evelyn Mesquida, *La Nueve. 24 août 1944. Ces républicains espagnols qui ont libéré Paris* (Paris, Cherche-Midi, 2011), pp. 48–9

33 Arthur Koestler, *Scum of the Earth* (London, Jonathan Cape, 1941), p. 85

34 Koestler, *Scum of the Earth*, p. 111

35 Dahlem handwritten memoirs (1974), p. 5. See also Sybille Hinze, *Antifascisten im Camp Le Vernet* (Berlin, Militärverlag des Deutschen Demokratischen Republik, 1988), pp. 30–2, 44

36 See above, pp. 25–6, 46–7

37 Jean-Louis Crémieux-Brilhac, *Les Français de l'An 40. I. La Guerre oui ou non* (Paris, Gallimard, 1990), pp. 492–4

38 Janine Ponty, 'La résistance polonaise: le POWN. Contribution à l'histoire de la résistance non-communiste', in Karel Bartosek, René Gallissot, Denis Peschanski (eds.), *De l'exil à la Résistance: réfugiés et immigrés d'Europe centrale en France: 1933–1945* (Saint-Denis, Presses Universitaires de

Vincennes/ Arcantère, 1989), pp. 173–83

39 AN 72AJ543–4, 'Le Réseau F2', published by *Revue historique de l'Armée* (1952), pp. 81–6; Translation of interview with Roman Czerniawski in *Syrena-Ozelbialy*, 127 (Mar. 1975), pp. 1–2. See above, pp. 165–6

40 AN 72AJ73, Renseignements donnés par Jan Gerhard, Feb. 1963; Gerhard Verbizier, *Ni Travail, ni famille, ni patrie. Journal d'une Brigade FTP-MOI. Toulouse, 1942–44* (Paris, Calmann-Lévy, 1994), pp. 89–90

41 Biography of Joseph Epstein by Paula Duffau , p. 14

42 See above, p. 27

43 Technically known as Régiments de Marche de Volontaires Étrangers (RMVE)

44 Boris Holban, *Testament. Apres quarante-cinq ans de silence le chef des FTP-MOI de Paris parle* (Paris, Calmann-Lévy, 1989), pp. 15–78

45 Renée Poznanski, *Les Juifs en France pendant la Seconde Guerre mondiale* (Paris, Hachette, 1997), pp. 97–117, 138–59; Michael Marrus and Robert Paxton, *Vichy France and the Jews* (New York, Basic Books, 1981); Paul Webster, *Pétain's Crime. The Full Story of French Collaboration in the Holocaust* (London, Macmillan, 1990)

46 Renée Poznanski, *Les Juifs en France*, pp. 55–96, 257–9; Renée Poznanski and Denis Peschanski, *Drancy. Un camp en France* (Fayard/ Ministère de la Défense, 2015), pp. 52–6

47 Poznanski, *Les Juifs en France*, pp. 290–339; Poznanski and Peschanski, *Drancy*, pp. 122–36

48 Diamant, *Les Juifs dans la Résistance* française, p. 55

49 CDJC MDXVIII/9, Fonds Bulawko, Henry Bulawko, 'Du Courage. Réflexions et témoignage', n.d., pp. 2–6, 9

50 CDJC DLXI-12, interview of Henry Bulawko with Anny Latour, n.d.; CDJC MDXVIII/6, Fonds Bulawko, Henry Bulawko, 'Le Centre Amelot tel que je l'ai vécu' (Jun. 1994), pp. 2–4

51 CHRD Lyon, interview with Roger Trugnan, 23 Feb. 2000

52 Bulawko, 'Le Centre Amelot tel que je l'ai vécu', p. 5

53 David Diamant, *Les Juifs dans la Résistance française, 1940–1944* (Paris, Le Pavillon, 1971), p. 54; Ravine, *La Résistance organise des Juifs en France*, p. 55; Cukier, Dominique Decèze, David Diamant, Michel Grojnowski, *Juifs révolutionnaires*, p. 150

54 AD Seine-Saint-Denis 335 J5, Fonds Diamant, 'Les Juifs de France dans la guerre contre le Nazisme', MS, n.d. but 1960s, p. 18

55 DLXI-84, interview of Adam Rayski with Anny Latour, n.d.

56 Adam Rayski, 'Diversité et unite de la Résistance juive; RHICOJ, *Les Juifs dans la Résistance et la Libération* (Paris, Scribe, 1985), p. 166

57 Musée de la Résistance, Fonds Roussel, Résistance, Attestations diverses, Jacques Ravine, 28 Jun. 1950

58 AD Seine-Saint-Denis 335 J7, Fonds Diamant, David Diamant, 'Les Juifs dans la Résistance et la Résistance juive en France', Symposium du 23 nov. 1974, p. 7

59 CDJC DLXI-84, interview of Adam Rayski with Anny Latour, n.d.

60 Tandler, *Un Inconnu nomé Krasucki*, p. 81

61 CHRD, interview with Paulette Sarcey, 22 Feb. 2000

62 CHRD, interview with Roger Trugnan, 23 Feb. 2000

63 AD Seine-Saint-Denis 335 J7, Fonds Diamant, David Diamant, 'Les Juifs dans la Résistance et la Résistance juive en France', Symposium du 23 Nov. 1974, p. 8

64 Gronowski, *Le Dernier Grand Soir*, pp. 79, 122, 137

65 See above, pp. 89–90, 92–3

66 Musée de la Résistance, Champigny. Fonds Ouzoulias, carton 5, biography of Joseph Epstein by Paula Duffau , p. 22

67 CDJC DLXI-84, interview with Anny Latour of Adam Rayski, n.d., p. 10

68 Musée de la Résistance, Champigny, Fonds de l'Amicale des Anciens FTP-MOI du Bataillon Carmagnole Liberté/2, Ljubomir Ilitch

69 Holban, *Testament*, pp. 86–115

70 CDJC DLXI-84, interview with Anny Latour of Adam Rayski, n.d., p. 13

71 AD Haute-Garonne 16J182, Sixto Agudo, 'Participation des Espagnols à la Résistance dans la 4e Région', n.d., pp. 68–70

72 AN 72AJ126CII7, Historique du XIVe Corps de Guerrilleros Espagnols (Sept. 1976); Claude Delpla, 'Les origines des guerrilleros espagnols dans les Pyrénées (1940–43) in Jean Ortiz (ed.), *Rouges Maquis de France et d'Espagne* (Biarritz, Atlantica, 2006), pp. 163–73; Geneviève Dreyfus-Armand, *L'Exil des Républicains espagnols en France*, pp. 163–9

73 Vicente López Tovar, 'Autobiographie', pp. 55–6

74 Musée de la Résistance. Fonds des Anciens FTP-MOI du Bataillon Carmagnole-Liberté. Carton 2. Biography of Norbert Kugler

75 Vicente López Tovar, 'Autobiographie', pp. 73–5

76 Bonte, *Les Antifascistes allemands dans la Résistance française*, pp. 137–9; Otto Niebergall, 'Der antifasciste deutsche Widerstandkampf in Frankreich – seine Leitung und Entwicklung', in Dora Schaul, *Erinnerungen deutscher Antifascisten* (Berlin, Dietz Verlag, 1973), pp. 25–34; Musée de la Résistance. Fonds thématique 111B. Résistance allemande, Maurice Kriegel to COMAC, 23 Jan. 1946, on Niebergall; Musée de la Résistance, Fonds Ouzoulias, Carton 2, dossier 5, on Käthe Weber, 12 May 1972; Musée de la Résistance. Liquidation OS-FN-FTP. 281. Allemagne, on Beling, 3 Apr. 1971

77 Gerhard Leo, *Un Allemand dans la Résistance* (Paris, Éditions Tirésias, 1997), pp. 36–44

78 Leo, *Un Allemand dans la Résistance*, p. 117

79 Leo, *Un Allemand dans la Résistance*, p. 133

80 CDJC DLXI-77, interview of Abraham Polonski with Anny Latour, Tel Aviv, 1968

81 CDJC –DCCCXCV, Hélène Menegaldo, 'Ariane Scriabina, Héroïne de la Résistance Française à Toulouse', *Slavica occitania* 7 (1998), pp. 173–6

82 CDJC DLXI-67, interview of Lucien Lublin with Anny Latour, Sept. 1968, p. 2

83 CDJC DLXI-17, interview of Albert Cohen with Anny Latour, 1973

84 CDJC DLXI-67, interview of Lucien Lublin with Anny Latour, Sept. 1968, p. 7

85 Polonski interview, p. 11

86 Lublin interview, p. 10

87 Jacques Lazarus, 'Sous le drapeau bleu-blanc', in RHICOJ, *Les Juifs dans la Résistance*, p. 132

88 See above, pp. 220–21

89 Rayski, 'Diversité et unite de la Résistance juive', p. 167

90 Annette Wieviorka, *Ils étaient Juifs, résistants, communistes* (Paris, Denoël, 1986), pp. 140–59

91 Bulawko, 'Le Centre Amelot tel que je l'ai vécu', p. 6

92 Tandler, *Un Inconnu nommé Krasucki*, pp. 96, 113, 204; CHRD, interview with Paulette Sarcey, 22 Feb. 2000, and Roger Trugnan, 23 Feb. 2000

93 CDJC DLXI-84, interview of Adam Rayski with Anny Latour, n.d., p. 11

94 Musée de la Résistance, Fonds Ouzoulias. Ouzoulias, 'Le Dombrowski de la Résistance française' (MS, 31pp), pp. 18–19

95 CDJC DLXI-84, interview with Anny Latour of Adam Rayski, n.d., pp. 13–15

96 Musée de la Résistance. Fonds des Anciens FTP-MOI du Bataillon Carmagnole-Liberté, Carton I. Testimony of Francis Chapouchnik, 20 May 1985

97 CHRD Lyon, interview with Francis Chapouchnik, 11 Jun. 1997. On the Night of Vénissieux, see above, pp. 194–7

98 Max Weinstein, *Souvenirs, souvenirs* (Nice, Éditions du Losange, 2007), pp. 95–6

99 Musée de la Résistance. Fonds des Anciens FTP-MOI du Bataillon Carmagnole-Liberté. Carton I. Testimony of Francis Chapouchnik, 20 May 1985

100 CHRD Lyon, interview with Francis Chapouchnik, 11 Jun. 1997

101 Fonds des Anciens FTP-MOI du Bataillon Carmagnole-Liberté, Carton 2, Interview with Jeannine Krakus, Paris, 2 Oct. 1986; testimony of Jacquot Szmulewicz in Annette Wieviorka, *Ils était juifs, résistants, communistes* (Paris, Denoël, 1986), pp. 203–4

102 Claude Collin, *Carmagnole et Liberté. Les Étrangers dans la Résistance en Rhône-Alpes* (Grenoble, Presses Universitaires de Grenoble, 2000), pp. 24–5

103 Fonds des Anciens FTP-MOI du Bataillon Carmagnole-Liberté, Carton 2, Biography of Léon Landini; Interview with Léon Landini, conducted by RG, Bagneux, 20 Apr. 2012

104 Fonds des Anciens FTP-MOI du Bataillon Carmagnole Liberté. I, letter of Francis Chapouchnik, 3 Dec. 1968

105 Ezer Najman, 'Capitaine Gilles du Groupe Carmagnole' in RHICOJ, *Les Juifs dans la Résistance et la Libération* (Paris, Scribe, 1985), pp. 170–2; Fonds des Anciens FTP-MOI du Bataillon Carmagnole Liberté, Carton I, Testimony of Gilles Najman, n.d., p. 12; CHRD Lyon, interview with Maurice Najman, 13 Apr. 1999

106 See above, p. 214; Jean-Yves Boursier, *La Guerre des partisans dans le Sud-est de la France, 1942–1944. La 35e Brigade FTP-MOI* (Paris, l'Harmattan, 1992)

107 Gérard Verbizier, *Ni Travail, ni famille, ni patrie. Journal d'une Brigade FTP-MOI. Toulouse, 1942–1944* (Paris, Valmann-Lévy, 1994), pp. 27, 114–16

108 Lévy, *Les Parias de la Résistance*, p. 157

109 Gérard Verbizier, *Ni Travail, ni famille, ni patrie*, pp. 91–2, 119–20

110 AD Haute-Garonne 5795W574, commissaire de police de Sûreté, Toulouse, interview with Mme Lespinasse, 10 Oct. 1943 and report, 18 Nov. 1934; Lévy, *Les Parias de la Résistance*, pp. 157, 168, 184–8

111 Verbizier, *Ni Travail, ni famille, ni patrie*, p. 65

112 Verbizier, *Ni Travail, ni famille, ni patrie*, p. 117

113 Damira Titonel, *Ecrire pour les autres*, pp. 31, 40–1

114 AD Haute-Garonne 5795W574, commissaire de police de Sûreté, Toulouse, interrogations, 3, 4 Apr. 1944

115 Verbizier, *Ni Travail, ni famille, ni patrie*, p. 219

116 AN 72AJ73, Renseignements donnés par Jean Gerhardt à Mme Kahn, Feb. 1963

117 Testimony of Claude Urman, 3 Nov. 1988, in David Diamant, *250 Combattants de la Résistance racontent* (Paris, L'Harmattan, 1991), pp. 222–4.

118 Verbizier, *Ni Travail, ni famille, ni patrie*, pp. 236–9; Titonel, *Écrire pour les autres*, pp. 46–53; Marc Lévy, *Les Enfants de la Liberté* (Paris, Robert Laffont, 2007), pp. 275–361

Chapter 9

1 BBC Written Archives Caversham (WAC), French Service. Anonymous letters from France, no. 1428, signed 'Nany 1902', Lyon, 8 Nov. 1942

2 Anonymous letters from France, no. 1439, signed '22 Deux Cocottes', Marseille, 3 Dec. 1942

3 AN 72AJ220/1, testimony of General Pierre Billotte, 4 & 11 July 1950, p. 15

4 William D. Leahy, *I was there* (London, Gollancz, 1950), p. 161; Jacques Raphaël-Leygues and François Flohic, *Darlan* (Paris, Plon, 1986), p. 154

5 Leahy, *I was there*, p. 56

6 Jean-Louis Crémieux-Brilhac, *La France libre*, pp. 278–86

7 Mireille Sacotte, *Sant-Jean Perse* (Paris Pierre Belfond, 1991), pp. 164–6; Colin Nettelbeck, *Forever French. Exile in the United States, 1939–1945* (New York and Oxford, Berg, 1991), pp. 132–3

8 Arthur Layton Funk, *The Politics of Torch. The Allied landings and the Algiers Putsch, 1942* (Lawrence, University Press of Kansas, 1974), pp. 100–3

9 Robert Murphy, *Diplomat among Warriors* (London, Collins, 1964), p. 100

10 Mark Clark, *Calculated Risk* (New York, Harper & Brothers, 1950), pp. 68–89; Funk, *The Politics of Torch*, pp. 149–64

11 Jacques Cantier, *L'Algérie sous le régime de Vichy* (Paris, Odile Jacob, 2002), pp. 59–61, 197–218

12 Jacques Soustelle, *Envers et contre tout 2. De Londres à Alger, juillet 19–février 1943* (Genève, Editions de Crémille, 1970), p. 96. Legionnaires wore a shield-shaped metal badge in their button-hole popularly known as the 'smoothing iron'

13 Benjamin Stora, *Les Trois Exils. Juifs d'Algérie* (Paris, Stock, 2006), pp. 78–80

14 Stora, *Les Trois Exils*, p. 76

15 Michel Ansky, *Les Juifs d'Algérie. Du décret Crémieux à la Libération* (Paris, Éditions du Centre, 1950); Michel Abitbol, *The Jews of North Africa during the Second World War* (Detroit, Wayne State UP, 1989), pp. 59–74; Stora, *Les Trois Exils*, p. 81–7

16 Michel Ansky, *Les Juifs d'Algérie*, pp. 261–9; Cantier, *L'Algérie sous le régime de Vichy*, pp. 315–20

17 Christine Levisse-Touzé, *L'Afrique du Nord dans la Guerre, 1939–1945* (Paris, Albin Michel, 1998), pp. 208–18

18 AN 13AV61, interview with José Aboulker, 16 Mar. 1990

19 José Aboulker, *La Victoire du 8 novembre 1942. La Résistance et le débarquement des Alliés à Alger* (Paris, le Félin, 2012), pp. 433–41

20 AN 72AJ210, testimony of Raphaël Aboulker, 27 Jun. 1947, p. 6

21 Yves-Claude Aouate, 'Des patriotes oubliés' in RHICOJ, *Les Juifs dans la Résistance et la Libération* (Paris, Éditions du Scribe, 1985), p. 32; Aboulker, *La Victoire du 8 novembre 1942*, p. 433

22 AN 72AJ211/AIV, testimony of José Aboulker, 14 Feb. 1947, p. 5; Aboulker, *La Victoire du 8 novembre 1942*, pp. 443–4, 452

23 AN 72AJ47II, testimony of René Capitant, 21 Mar. 1957, p. 2

24 AN 72AJ46III, testimony of André Fradin, 26 Mar. 1957, p. 2

25 Louis Joxe, *Victoires sur la Nuit, 1940–1946. Mémoires* (Paris, Flammarion, 1981), pp. 10–48; Aboulker, *La Victoire du 8 novembre 1942*, p. 566

26 AN 72AJ47II, testimony of René Capitant, 21 Mar. 1957, p. 6

27 AN 72AJ47II, testimony of René Capitant, 21 Mar. 1957, pp. 6–7

28 AN 72AJ210/AI, testimony of Henri d'Astier de la Vigerie, 27 Jan. 1947, p. 1

29 Aboulker, *La Victoire du 8 novembre 194*, pp. 478–9

30 William A. Huntingdon, *The Assassination of Jacques Lemaigre Dubreuil. A Frenchman between France and North Africa* (London & New York, Routledge Curzon, 2005)

31 AN 72AJ211/AIV, testimony of José Aboulker, 14 Feb. 1947, p. 2; Aboulker, *La Victoire du 8 novembre 1942*, p. 503

32 Murphy, *Diplomat among Warriors*, pp. 149–53; Claude Bourdet, *L'aventure incertaine*, p. 141

33 AN 72AJ213, General Béthouart, 'Les Événements du 8 novembre 1942,' n.d. but probably 1944, p. 2

34 Général Béthouart, *Cinq Années d'Espérance. Mémoires de guerre, 1939–1945* (Paris, Plon, 1968), p. 129

35 Mark Clark, *Calculated Risk*, p. 96

36 Funk, *The Politics of Torch*, pp. 178–80

37 Raphaël-Leygues and Flohic, *Darlan*, p. 160

38 AN 72AJ213, General Béthouart, 'Les Événements du 8 novembre 1942', pp. 10–12; See also Béthouart, *Cinq Années d'Espérance*, pp. 155–70

39 Aboulker, *La Victoire du 8 novembre 1942*, pp. 522–7

40 Musée de la Résistance, Champigny, 124. Témoignages I. José Aboulker, 'Nous qui avons arrêté le général Juin', *La Nef*, Paris, no. 25 (Apr. 1959), p. 15; Aboulker, *La Victoire du 8 novembre 1942*, pp. 573–84

41 AN 72AJ211/AIV, testimony of José Aboulker, 14 Feb. 1947, p. 9

42 AN 72AJ47II, testimony of René Capitant, 21 Mar. 1957, p. 3

43 Aboulker, *La Victoire du 8 novembre 1942*, pp. 585–94

44 José Aboulker, *La Nef* (Apr. 1959), p. 16

45 Mark Clark, *Calculated Risk*, p. 106

46 Mark Clark, *Calculated Risk*, pp. 109–16; Maréchal Juin, *Mémoires I* (Paris, Fayard, 1959), pp. 80–104; Funk, *Politics of Torch*, pp. 235–48; Raphaël-Leygues and Flohic, *Darlan*, pp. 167–203

47 AN 72AJ210, testimony of Raphaël Aboulker, 27 Jun. 1947, pp. 12–13

48 Soustelle, *Envers et contre tout*, p. 137

49 Churchill to Roosevelt, 22 Nov. 1942, in *Churchill and Roosevelt. The*

Complete Correspondence, ed. Warren F. Kimball (Princeton, Princeton UP, II, pp. 29–30

50 AN 72AJ210/A1, testimony of General François d'Astier de la Vigerie, 22 Feb. 1948

51 Testimony of General François d'Astier de la Vigerie, 22 Feb. 1948, p. 10

52 AN 72AJ47II, testimony of René Capitant, 21 Mar. 1957, p. 9

53 Soustelle, *Envers et contre tout*, p. 202

54 AN 72AJ210/AI, testimony of Henri d'Astier de la Vigerie, 27 Jan. 1947, pp. 8, 10

55 Testimony of General François d'Astier de la Vigerie, 22 Feb. 1948, pp. 13, 16

56 Mario Faivre, *Nous avons tué Darlan. Alger 1942* (Paris, La Table Ronde, 1975), pp. 26, 66–8, 141–52

57 AN 72AJ211/AIV, Supplementary testimony of José Aboulker, 21 Feb. 1947, p. 2

58 AN 72AJ217/AIII, AOF. Journal de M. You, Inspecteur primaire a Dakar, 1942–44, pp. 23, 39

59 AN 13AV41, interview with Serge Ravanel, 2 Apr. 1991

60 Fernand Grenier, *C'était ainsi. Souvenirs* (Paris, Éditions sociales, 1959), p. 120

61 Rémy, *Mémoires d'un agent secret de la France libre II. Juin 1942-Nov. 1943* (Paris, France-Empire, 1960), pp. 172–3

62 Grenier, *C'était ainsi*, p. 133

63 AD Seine Saint-Denis, Archives Grenier 299J. Londres 1943. Fernand Grenier, 'Appel à l'union', 15 Jan. 1943

64 AN 72AJ1923, de Gaulle to Giraud, 25 Dec. 1943

65 Murphy, *Diplomat among Warriors*, pp. 215–16; Arthur Layton Funk, *Charles de Gaulle. The Crucial Years, 1943-1944* (Norman, University of Oklahoma Press, 1959), pp. 54–100; Jean-Louis Crémieux-Brilhac, *La France libre*, pp. 454–9

66 Murphy, *Diplomat among Warriors*, p. 219

67 AN 72AJ429II, Catroux report of 29 Jan. 1943, pp. 1–2

68 AN 72AJ429II, Catroux report of 29 Jan. 1943, p. 6

69 AN 72AJ429II, Catroux report of 29 Jan. 1943, p. 3

70 Murphy, *Diplomat among Warriors*, p. 219

71 AN 72AJ1923, 'Top secret' note of Soustelle to de Gaulle, 17 Feb. 1943

72 Murphy, *Diplomat among Warriors*, p. 222

73 Churchill to Roosevelt, 16 Dec. 1941, in *Churchill and Roosevelt. The Complete Correspondence*, ed. Warren F. Kimball (Princeton, Princeton UP, 1984), pp. 297–8

Chapter 10

1 Marc Ferro, *Pétain*, pp. 441–2

2 See above, p. 247

3 Jean de Lattre, *Ne Pas Subir. Écrits 1914-1952* (Paris, Plon, 1984), p. 245

4 Jean de Lattre, *Ne Pas Subir*, p. 256

5 AN 72AJ60/I, testimony of Raymond Aubrac, 9 & 16 Jan. 1947, p. 6; Raymond Aubrac, *Où la mémoire s'attarde*, p. 85

6 AN 72AJ60/I, testimony of Raymond Aubrac, 9 & 16 Jan. 1947, p. 7

7 SHD 16P 507141, Revers file, report for 'médaille de la Résistance', n.d.

8 Pierre Dalloz, *Vérités sur le Drame du Vercors* (Paris, Fernand Lanore, 1979), p. 11

9 AN 72AJ87/I, Dr Martin, 'Naissance du Vercors,' n.d., p. 7

10 Pierre Dalloz, *Vérités sur le Drame du Vercors*, p. 24

11 AN 72AJ87/I, Rapport de Pupin, 15 Oct. 1947

12 AN 72AJ87/II, testimony of Pierre Dalloz, 12 Apr. 1946, pp. 2–4; Dalloz, *Vérités*, p. 26; AN 72AJ87/I, Rapport de Pupin, 15 Oct. 1947, pp. 11–14

13 Pierre Dalloz, *Vérités sur le Drame du Vercors*, p. 58

14 AN 72AJ87/II, testimony of Pierre Dalloz, 12 Apr. 1946, pp. 4–6; AN72AJ625, Alain Le Ray, 'Chronique sommaire de développement du Vercors', p. 4

15 Fonds Douzou, interview with Jean-Pierre Vernant, 10 Jan. 1985

16 AN 72AJ60/III, testimony of Maurice Kriegel-Valrimont, 17 Jan. 1947

17 AN 13AV41, interview with Serge Ravanel, 2 Apr. 1991.

18 AN 13AV46, interview with Serge Ravanel, 16 Apr. 1991; see above, p. 157

19 AV 13AV93, interview of Raymond Aubrac by Laurent Douzou, 21 Mar. 1984; AN 13AV46, interview with Serge Ravanel, 11 Apr. 1991; Kriegel, *Mémoires rebelles*, p. 50

20 John F. Sweets, *The Politics of Resistance in France, 1940–1944. A History of the Mouvements Unis de la Résistance* (DeKalb, Northern Illinois University Press, 1976), pp. 62–3

21 Daniel Cordier, *Jean Moulin. L'Inconnu du Panthéon*, pp. 126–41

22 Simone Martin-Chauffier, *A bientôt quand même*, p. 247

23 AN 72AJ2026, Frenay (Gervais) to Moulin (Max), 8 Apr. 1943

24 AN 72AJ2026, Frenay to General Delestraint (Valentin), 8 Apr. 1943

25 Daniel Cordier, *Jean Moulin. La République des catacombes* (Paris, Gallimard, 1999), p. 334; Sebastien Albertelli, *Les Services secrets*, p. 284

26 Cordier, *Jean Moulin. La République des catacombes*, p. 335

27 Henri Frenay, *La Nuit finira*, 307; AN 72 AJ 46/I, testimony of Claude Bourdet, 6 Jun. 1946; AN 72 AJ 48, testimony of Philippe Monod, 18 Jun. 1955

28 Robert Belot and Gilbert Karpman, *l'Affaire Suisse. La Résistance a-t-elle trahi de Gaulle?* (Paris, A. Colin, 2009), pp. 125–6

29 Daniel Cordier, *Jean Moulin, l'inconnu du Panthéon. I*, pp. 112–14; Piketty, *Pierre Brossolette*, pp. 250–96

30 AN 13AV75, interview of André Dewavrin/Colonel Passy conducted by Olivier Wieviorka, 7 Jun. 1990

31 AN 72AJ220/I, testimony of F. Yeo-Thomas, 4 Jul. 1947

32 Pierre Villon, *Résistant de la première heure* (Paris, Éditions sociales, 1983), p. 71

33 AN 450API, Lecompte-Boinet, Journal, Jan.–Oct. 1943, pp. 84–9; For a very similar account see AN 72AJ2217, interview of Lecompte-Boinet with Gilberte Brossolette, 4 Jul. 1943

34 Guillaume Piketty, *Pierre Brossolette*, pp. 281–4

35 AN 13AV75, interview of André Dewavrin/Colonel Passy with Olivier Wieviorka, 7 Jun. 1990

36 Passy, *Souvenirs*, III, p. 180; Piketty, *Pierre Brossolette*, p. 289; Jackson, *France: the Dark Years*, p. 452

37 AN72AJ46/I, testimony of Henri Frenay, Feb./Mar./Apr. 1948, pp. 10–12

38 Pascal Copeau and Claudius-Petit. The two main trade-union federations were represented by the non-communist Louis Saillant (CGT) and the Catholic trade unionist Gaston Tessier.

39 AN 450API, Lecompte-Boinet, Journal, Jan.–Oct. 1943, p. 169

40 AN 450API, Lecompte-Boinet, Journal, Jan.–Oct. 1943, pp. 165–7. For the first he found Joseph Laniel, a Norman industrialist who had in fact voted full powers to Pétain in 1940, and for the second, the writer and politician Jacques Debû-Bridel, who had a past with Action Française.

41 AN 6AV625, interview of Robert Salmon with Olivier Wieviorka, 23 May 1986

42 René Hostache, *Le Conseil National de la Résistance* (Paris, PUF, 1958), pp. 142–3; Georges Bidault, *D'une Résistance à l'autre* (Paris, 1965), p. 40

43 Pierre Villon, *Résistant de la Première heure* (Paris, Editions sociales, 1983), pp. 72–4

44 Fred Kupferman, *Le Procès de Vichy. Pucheu, Pétain, Laval* (Brussels, Complexe, 1980), pp. 29–33

45 Cordell Hull, *Memoirs II* (New York, Macmillan, 1948), pp. 1163–4

46 Cordell Hull, *Memoirs II*, p. 1217; Gabriel Kolko, *The Politics of War. Allied Diplomacy and the World Crisis of 1943–1945* (London, Weidenfeld & Nicolson, 1969), p. 70

47 Harold Macmillan, *War Diaries. Politics and War in the Mediterranean, January 1943–May 1945* (London, Macmillan, 1984), p. 73

48 Macmillan, *War Diaries*, pp. 69–71. Note of a conversation of 26 Apr. 1943

49 Charles de Gaulle, *Discours et messages I. 1940–1946* (Paris, Plon, 1971), p. 289

50 AN 72AJ429 II. Négociations d'Alger. Catroux to de Gaulle, 11 May 1943

51 Eric Jennings, *La France libre fut africaine* (Paris, Perrin, 2014), pp. 129–40

52 Christian Girard, *Journal de Guerre, 1939–1945* (Paris, L'Harmattan, 2000), p. 69. Entry of 21 May 1943

53 AN 72AJ220/I, testimony of General Billotte, 4 & 11 Jul. 1950, p. 9

54 AN 450API, Lecompte-Boinet, Journal de Guerre. Mission à Londres et à Alger, Oct. 1943–Feb. 1944, 1 Dec. 1943, p. 104

55 Testimony of General Billotte, 4 & 11 Jul. 1950, p. 20; Churchill, *The Second World War. Vol. V. Closing the Ring*, p. 154

56 Jean Monnet, *Mémoires* (Paris, Fayard, 1976), pp. 220–1; Nettelbeck, *Forever French*, pp. 161–2

57 Charles de Gaulle, *Mémoires de Guerre II. L'Unité, 1942–1944* (Paris, Plon, 1956), p. 104

58 Testimony of General Billotte, 4 & 11 Jul. 1950, p. 20

59 Testimony of General Billotte, 4 & 11 Jul. 1950, p. 21

60 AN 72AJ243/I, André Philip, Note du Comité de Libération nationale (Sept. 1943), p. 3; Arthur Layton Funk, *Charles de Gaulle. The Crucial Years, 1943–1944*, pp. 101–49; Jean-Louis Crémieux-Brilhac, *La France libre*, pp. 553–8

61 Christian Giraud, *Journal de Guerre, 1939–1945* (Paris, L'Harmattan, 2000), p. 78

62 Benjamin Stora, *Les Trois Exils. Juifs d'Algérie* (Paris, Stock, 2006), p. 100

63 AN 72AJ1923, letter from Syndicat de l'Atelier de l'Air d'Alger to de Gaulle's personal general staff, 8 Jun. 1943

64 AN 72AJ243/II, 'Texte complet de la Déclaration des 26 Députés communistes

français fait à Alger le 12 juin 1943', pp. 2–3

65 AN 72AJ243/I, Résumé de l'entretien du 19 juin 1943 chez le Général Eisenhower; Cordell Hull, *Memoirs II*, p. 1221

66 AN 450AP2, J. Lecompte-Boinet, Journal de Guerre. Mission à Londres et à Alger, oct. 1943–fév. 1944, pp. 100–1. Entry of 29 Nov. 1943

67 Charles de Gaulle, *Discours et messages I. 1940–1946*, pp. 306–9

68 André-Paul Comor (ed.), *Les Carnets du lieutenant-colonel Brunet de Sairigné* (Paris, Nouvelles Editions Latines, 1990), p. 152. Entry for 3 Jun. 1943

Chapter 11

1 Daniel Cordier, *Jean Moulin. La République des catacombes* (Paris, Gallimard, 1999), pp. 456–66; Jean-Pierre Azéma, *Jean Moulin. Le Rebelle, le Politique, le résistant* (Paris, Perrin, 1943), pp. 400–430

2 Jackson, *France: the Dark Years*, pp. 462–4; Wieviorka, *Histoire de la Résistance*, pp. 289–307

3 Claude Bouchinet-Serreulles, *Nous étions faits pour être libres* (Paris, Grasset, 2000), pp. 291–314

4 Francis-Louis Closon, *Le temps des passions. De Jean Moulin à la Libération, 1943–1944* (Paris, Presses de la Cité, 1974), pp. 211–38

5 AN 72AJ234/IV, Jacques Bingen to his mother, Paris XVI, 15 Aug. 1943

6 Pierre Brossolette, 'Lettres à son épouse (1939–1943), in Guillaume Piketty (ed.), *Français en Résistance* (Paris, Laffont, 2009), pp. 449, 451

7 AN 72AJ2217, interview with Lecompte-Boinet conducted by Gilberte Brossolette, 4 July. 1973, p. 6

8 AN 72AJ2217, interview with Colonel Passy, conducted by Gilberte Brossolette, 19 & 26 Jun. 1973, p. 14

9 AN 72AJ2217, interview with J. Lecompte-Boinet, conducted by Gilberte Brossolette, 4 Jul. 1973, p. 7

10 AN 72AJ234/I, Notes sur Jacques Bingen recueillis par Mme Granet d'apres les indications de Claude Serreulles, 21 Apr. 1948, p. 3

11 AN 72AJ220/I, testimony of Émile Bollaert, 4 Jun. 1946; AN 72AJ2217, interview with Bollaert, conducted by Gilberte Brossolette, 1973, p. 6; Piketty, *Pierre Brossolette*, pp. 335–9

12 AN 450API, Lecompte-Boinet, Journal, Jan.–Oct. 1943, pp. 197, 202. Entry for Jun. 1943

13 AN 72AJ42, testimony of Jean de Vogüé, 17 Nov. 1947; AN 450API, Lecompte-Boinet, Journal, Jan.–Oct. 1943, p. 93. Entry for Apr. 1943

14 AN 450API, Lecompte-Boinet, Journal, Jan.–Oct. 1943, p. 269. Entry for Aug. 1943

15 AN 72AJ65/II, testimony of Georges Bidault, n.d.

16 It included Debû-Bridel for the Fédération Républicaine, the trade unionist Louis Saillant, and Pascal Copeau of Libération for the MUR

17 Pierre Villon, *Résistant de la première heure*, pp. 77–9

18 Yves Farge, *Rebelles, soldats et citoyens*, pp. 43–4

19 Pierre Laborie, *L'Opinion française sous Vichy* (Paris, Seuil, 1990), pp. 282–92

20 Robert Gildea, *Marianne in Chains*, pp. 271–3

21 Musée de la Résistance, Champigny, Carton 126A, Témoignages III. J. Enjoly, 18 Nov. 1964

22 Raphaël Spina, 'La France et les Français devant le Service du Travail Obligatoire (1942–1945)' (Thesis, ENS Cachan, 2012), pp. 262–8

23 Jean-Pierre Le Crom, *Syndicats, nous voila! Vichy et le corporatisme* (Paris, les Éditions de l'Atelier/les Éditions ouvrières, 1995)

24 André Tollet, *La Classe ouvrière*, p. 135

25 André Tollet, *La Classe ouvrière*, pp. 150–2, 166; AN 72AJ43/III, testimony of Robert Bothereau, 14 Jun. 1948

26 Henri Noguères, Marcel Degliame-Fouché and Jean-Louis Vigier, *Histoire de la Résistance en France II. Juillet 1941–octobre 1942* (Paris, Robert Laffont, 1969), pp. 546–7

27 Bourdet, *L'aventure incertaine*, pp. 83–4

28 AN 72AJ626, Alban Vistel, 'Action Ouvrière,' n.d., p. 281. See also Vistel, *La Nuit sans ombre. Histoire des Mouvements Unis de la Résistance, leur rôle dans la libération du Sud-Est* (Paris, Fayard, 1970), p. 271

29 Gérald Suberville, 'L'action ouvrière du Languedoc,' in Jules Maurin (ed.) *Les lendemains de la Libération dans le Midi. Actes du Colloque de Montpellier 1986* (Université Paul-Valéry-Montpellier III, 1997), p. 167

30 Musée de la Résistance, Champigny, Fonds Suberville Carton 12. Fiche concernant l'activité de Suberville, n.d.

31 Gérald Suberville, *L'Autre Résistance* (Aiou, Saint-Étienne Vallée Française, 1998), pp. 25–31. This book was drafted in 1963; H.R. Kedward, *In Search of the Maquis. Rural Resistance in Southern France, 1942–1944* (Oxford, Clarendon Press, 1993), pp. 218, 282

32 AN 72AJ126B1, testimony of Léo Hamon, 7 Mar. 1946; AN 72AJ73, testimony of Marie-Rose Gineste, n.d; see above, p. 192

33 Jean Quellien, 'Les Travailleurs forces en Allemagne. Essai d'approche statistique,' in B. Garnier & J. Quellien (eds.), *La main d'Oeuvre française exploitée paer le III Reich* (Caen, centre d'Histoire Quantitative, 2003), pp. 67–84; Spina, 'La France et les Français devant le Service du Travail Obligatoire,' p. 775

34 Rod Kedward, 'The Maquis and the Culture of the Outlaw,' in Rod Kedward and Roger Austin (eds.), *Vichy France and the Resistance. Culture and Ideology* (London and Sydney, Croom Helm, 1985), pp. 232–51

35 Spina, 'La France et les Français devant le Service du Travail Obligatoire,' pp. 937–8; H.R. Kedward, *In Search of the Maquis. Rural Resistance in Southern France, 1942–1944* (Oxford, Clarendon Press, 1993)

36 AN 72AJ119CI, Procès-verbaux d'interrogatoires de maquisards des Glières: Jacques Beges (16 Apr. 1944), Pierre Pelletier and Yves Jeudy (17 Apr. 1944)

37 Musée de la Résistance, Champigny, 126A, Témoignages III. Jean-Olivier Eleouet, alias Lieutenant Yvon, 'Mémoires d'un Franc-Tireur et partisan Français pour servir à l'histoire de la Résistance en Corrèze' (1981), pp. 2–7, 10–12

38 AN 72AJ55/II, testimony of Yves Farge, 17 May 1946; AN 72AJ42 and 72AJ126BI, testimony of Léo Hamon, 7 Mar. 1946; Léo Hamon, *Vivre ses choix* (Paris, R. Laffont, 1991), pp. 163–5; André Tollet, *La Classe ouvrière dans la*

Résistance, p. 142

39 André Tollet, *La Classe ouvrière dans la Résistance*, p. 172

40 Andre Tollet, 'Intervention' in Comité d'histoire de la Deuxième guerre mondiale, La Libération de la France. Actes du Colloque international tenu à Paris du 28 au 31 Octobre 1974 (Paris, CNRS, 1976), pp. 545–9,

41 Musée de la Résistance. CPL. Fonds Legendre. Procès-verbaux du CPL et son bureau, 3 Nov. 1943

42 Henri Denis, *Le Comité Parisien de la Libération* (Paris, PUF, 1963), pp. 34–5; André Carrel, *Mes Humanités. Itinéraire d'un homme engagé* (Paris, l'Oeil d'Or, 2009)

43 Denis, *Le Comité Parisien de la Libération*, p. 35–6

44 André Tollet, *La Classe ouvrière*, 173–4; AN 72AJ, p. 42, testimony of Jean de Vogüé, 17 Nov. 1947, p. 8; Léo Hamon, *Vivre ses choix*, p. 170

45 An 72AJ68/V, testimony of Marie-Hélène Lefaucheux, n.d.

46 André Carrel, *Mes Humanités*, pp. 12–84

47 Léo Hamon, *Vivre ses choix*, p. 158

48 Procès-verbaux du CPL et son bureau, 26 Nov. & 10 Dec. 1943

49 Musée de la Résistance, Champigny. Fonds Legendre. Procès-verbaux du CPL et bureaux, 3 Dec. 1943

50 Procès-verbaux du CPL et bureaux, 10 Dec. 1943

51 AN 72AJ45/VI, testimony of René Courtin, 27 May 1946

52 Francis-Louis Closon, *Le Temps des passions*, pp. 60–2. See above, p.287

53 AN 72AJ42, testimony of Michel Debré, 13 May 1946; Sciences-Po, Centre d'Histoire, Témoignages sur la Guerre d'Algérie, interview with Michel Debré conducted by Odile Rudelle, 1981, pp. 65–9

54 Philippe André, *La Résistance confisquée? Les Délégués militaires du Générale de Gaulle à la Libération* (Paris, Perrin, 2013)

55 AN72 AT45/I, Serreulles, 'Affaire de la rue de la Pompe', London, 14 Mar. 1944; NA HS9/982/4, interrogation of Serreulles, 15 Mar. 1944

56 Report of Mangin, 31 Jan. 1944, cited by Philippe André, *La Résistance confisquée*, p. 75

57 AN 450AP2, J. Lecompte-Boinet, Journal de Guerre. Mission à Londres et à Alger, oct. 1943–fév. 1944, pp. 60, 64. Entry of 10 Nov. 1943

58 Musée de la Résistance 126A, Témoignages III. Albert Gazier, 'Les Syndicalistes à l'Assemblée Consultative d'Alger et de Paris' (Nov. 1972), pp. 3–5

59 Michel Ansky, *Les Juifs d'Algérie*, pp. 317–20

60 AN 450AP2, J. Lecompte-Boinet, Journal de Guerre. Mission à Londres et à Alger, oct. 1943–fév. 1944, p. 38. Entry of 9 Nov. 1943

61 AD Seine Saint-Denis, 307 J 154. Dossiers conservés dans les archives de Gaston Plissonnier. Relations de la delegation du Comité central à Alger avec le Général de Gaulle. Summary 25 Nov. 1943; Archives Grenier 299 J. Alger 1944. Interview of Grenier and Paul Barette, 16 Feb. 1944

62 AN 72AJ410, Boris to de Gaulle, 12 Apri. 1944; Boris to d'Astier, 12 Apr. 1944; Raymond Aubrac, *Où la mémoire s'attarde* (Paris, O. Jacob, 1996), pp. 119–31

63 AN 72AJ220/II, testimony of Georges Boris, 27 May & 3 Jun. 1947

64 AN 72AJ220/III, testimony of Jacques Soustelle, n.d., p. 21

65 Eric Jennings, *L'Afrique noire fut africaine* (Paris, Perrin, 2014), pp. 169–70

66 Raymond Dronne, *Carnets de route d'un croisé de la France libre* (Paris, France-Empire, 1984), pp. 249–54; Evelyn Mesquida, *La Nueve, 24 août 1944. Ces Républicains espagnols qui ont libéré Paris* (Paris, Cherche-Midi, 2011)

67 Girard, *Journal de Guerre*, pp. 108, 110. Entries of 24 Oct. & 15 Nov. 1943. See also Paul de Lagarde, *En suivant Leclerc* (Paris, Au fil d'Ariane, 1964), pp. 19–20, 40–3

68 Girard, *Journal de Guerre*, p. 115. Entry of 2 Jan. 1944; General de Lattre, *Histoire de la Première Armée Française. Rhin et Danube* (Paris, Plon, 1949), pp. 3–12

69 Charles de Gaulle, *Discours et messages* vol. I, p. 390

70 Fred Kupferman, *Le Procès de Vichy*, pp. 34–40

71 François Billoux, *Quand nous étions ministres* (Paris, Éditions sociales, 1972), p. 55

72 AN72 AJ243/II and AN 72AJ2006, Frenay to de Gaulle, 27 Mar. 1944

73 AN 72AJ243/II and AN 72AJ2026, Frenay to de Gaulle, 27 Mar. 1944

Chapter 12

1 BBC Written Archives, Caversham, Anonymous letters from France, no. 938, Apr. 1942

2 Anonymous letters, 207, 10 Feb. 1941

3 See above, pp. 137–8

4 Cécile Jouan, *Comète, histoire d'une ligne d'évasion* (Furnes, Editions du Beffroi, 1948); Colonel Rémy, *Le Réseau Comète* (3 vols, Paris, Perrin, 1966–71); Odile de Vasselot, *Tombés du ciel. Histoire d'une ligne d'évasion* (Paris, Editions du Félin, 2005)

5 AN 72AJ45/IV, testimony of R.P. Riquet, 30 Mar. 1946; AN 72AJ45/IV, testimony of Germaine Aylé, 24 Nov. & 26 Dec. 1946

6 Stanislas Fumet, *Histoire de Dieu dans ma vie. Souvenirs choisis* (Paris, Fayard-Mame, 1978), p. 477

7 Judy Barrett Litoff (ed.), *An American Heroine in the French Resistance. The Diary and Memoir of Virginia d'Albert-Lake* (New York, Fordham UP, 2006), p. 96

8 Judy Barrett Litoff (ed.), *An American Heroine*, pp. xviii–xix, 102; Airey Neave, *Saturday at MI9. A History of Underground Escape Lines in Northwest Europe in 1940-1945 by a Leading Organiser of MI9* (London, Hodder & Stoughton, 1969), pp. 250–60

9 AN 72AJ80/VIII, testimony of Georges Labarthe, 24 Jun. 1946

10 AN 72AJ80/VIII, testimony of Jean Pivert, 21 June. 1946

11 AN 72AJ80/VIII, testimony of Georges Jouanjean, 16 Apr. 1962; AN 72AJ115A1, testimony of Val B. Williams (Vladimir Bouryschkine), 18 Sept. 1961. See also Neave, *Saturday at MI9*, pp. 217–18

12 AN72AJ115 AIII, testimony of Marie-Thérèse Le Calvez, n.d.; *Ouest-France*, 19 Mar. 1967

13 AN 72AJ115AI, J. Manguy, 'Le Réseau d'Evasion 'Shelburn. Pat O'Leary' à l'Anse-Cochat en Pluha' (1965)

14 Simon Kitson, 'Criminals or Liberators? French public opinion and the Allied

bombing of France, 1940–1945', in Claudia Baldoni, Andrew Knapp and Richard Overy (eds.), *Bombing, States and peoples in Western Europe, 1940–1945* (London & New York, Continuum, 2011), pp. 279–90; Andrew Knapp, *Les Français sous les Bombes Alliées, 1940–1945* (Paris, Tallandier, 2014), pp. 33–152

15 Eddy Florentin, *Quand les Alliés bombardaient la France, 1940–1945* (Paris, Perrin, 1997), pp. 88–98, 178–84

16 Robert Gildea, *Marianne in Chains*, p. 308

17 BBC Written Archives, Caversham. Interview with Civilian Escapers: 'D', 19 Feb. 1944

18 AN 72AJ44, testimony of Mme Tony-Robert, 15 Jan. 1946, Daniel Appert, 19 Feb. 1946 & Robert Rey, 6 Apr. 1946

19 Gabrielle Ferrières, *Jean Cavaillès*, p. 186

20 AN 72AJ166 Morbihan AIII, 'Le Réseau Cohors-Asturies à Quimperlé et dans le Morbihan, communiqué par M. Leroux le 15 Sept. 1969', based on interviews with Mlle Queffurus, p. 1

21 Gabrielle Ferrières, *Jean Cavaillès*, p. 170

22 Gabrielle Ferrières, *Jean Cavaillès*, p. 194

23 Yves Farge, *Rebelles, Soldats et Citoyens*, p. 29

24 Gabrielle Ferrières, *Jean Cavaillès*, pp. 182–6; Alya Aglan, 'La resistance' in Aglan and Azema, *Jean Cavaillès* (2002), pp. 123–33

25 'Le Réseau Cohors-Asturies à Quimperlé et dans le Morbihan', p. 3

26 Gabrielle Ferrières, *Jean Cavaillès*, pp. 191–204; Alya Aglan, 'La résistance' in Aglan and Azema, *Jean Cavaillès*, pp. 132–4

27 NA HS9/603/1, report by commanding officer on Gosset, 17 Dec. 1943; recommendation by Major-General Gubbins for the Military Cross, 23 Aug. 1945

28 AN 72AJ166, 'Le réseau Cohors-Asturies à Quimperlé et dans le Morbihan', pp. 5–8

29 NA HS9 1089/4, report by Jacqueline Nearne, n.d. but 1945

30 AN 72AJ39, testimony of Maurice Southgate, 18 Jun. 1946

31 NA HS9/1238/1, Charles Rechenmann file

32 NA HS9/1395/3, Buckmaster report, 8 Apr. 1944. See also M.R.D. Foot, *SOE in France. An Account of the Work of the British Special Operations Executive in France, 1940–1944)* (London, Frank Cass, 2004), pp. 253–4

33 NA HS9/355/2, report by Pearl Witherington, 11 Mar. 1944

34 NA HS9/1240/3, finishing report of Harry Rée, 1 Jan. 1943

35 Imperial War Museum 8720, interview with Harry Rée, 18 Jan. 1985; François Marcot, 'La direction de Peugeot sous l'occupation: Pétainisme, réticence, opposition et résistance', *Le Mouvement social* 189 (Oct.–Dec. 1999), pp. 27–46

36 NA HS9/1487/1, report of 30 Apr. 1941; Pierre Seailles, 'Bref historique du réseau Sylvestre,' n.d.

37 NA HS9/1487/1, 'The Death of Captain Michel', unsigned, 16 Feb. 1944

38 NA HS9/1487/1, Buckmaster report, 28 Jun. 1945

39 See above, pp. 296–9

40 Rod Kedward, *In Search of the The Maquis. Rural Resistance in Southern France, 1942–1944* (Oxford, Clarendon Press, 1993)

41 AD Haute-Garonne 16J58, Philippe de Gunzbourg, 'Le Reseau Wheelwright.

De Vierzon aux Pyrénées' (1977), pp. 1–4

42 NA HS9/427/9, report on Harry Despaigne, 10 Mar. 1942

43 NA HS9/427/9, report by Captain Despaigne, 27 Sept. 1944

44 NA HS9/701/1, Heslop file

45 AN 72AJ92 CIV. Ain, Rapport d'activité de H. Petit, alias Colonel Romans, sur son rôle dans la Résistance, communiqué à Mme Appleton en août 1946, p. 3. See also Henri Romans-Petit, *Les Obstinés* (Ceignes, ETD, 1995), pp. 41–47, and H.R. Kedward, *In Search of the Maquis*, pp. 65–6

46 AN 72AJ87/II, testimony of Pierre Dalloz, 12 Apr. 1946, p. 6

47 NA HS9/1126/3, report of interview with four RAF officers, 14 Apr. 1944. See also M.R.D. Foot, *SOE in France*, pp. 357–8, 391

48 AN 72AJ106 AI, E. Coulaudon, 'Le Mont Mouchet'; Robert Gildea, 'Resistance, Reprisals and Community in Occupied France', *TRHS* 13 (2003), pp. 170–1

49 Fernand Grenier, *C'est ainsi. Souvenirs*, pp. 138–44, 152–8

50 Centre d'Histoire, Sciences-Po, Fonds Tillon, CT100/I, interview with Tillon conducted by Pierre Boutang, 28 Nov. 1979

51 Centre d'Histoire, Sciences-Po, Fonds Tillon CT3, dossier 1, Tillon to de Gaulle, 6 Aug. 1943

52 Centre d'Histoire, Sciences-Po, Fonds Tillon CT3, dossier 1, R. Houzé to Tillon, 15 Sept. 1943

53 AD Seine Saint-Denis, 314J7, Waldeck Rochet, Emploi du Temps à Londres, 1943–44, 11 Nov. & 7 Dec. 1943

54 AN 72AJ87/II, testimony of Pierre Dalloz, 12 Apr. 1946, pp. 8–9, 13; Pierre Dalloz, *Vérités sur le Drame du Vercors*, pp. 151–5. See also Pierre Bolle (ed.), *Grenoble et le Vercors. De la Résistance à la Libération* (Grenoble, Presses Universitaires de Grenoble, 2003)

55 AN 72AJ409, 'Note spéciale sur les parachutages d'armes à la Résistance française', 31 Oct. 1943

56 Sébastien Albertelli, *Les Services secrets*, pp. 440–1

57 AD Seine Saint-Denis, 314J7, Waldeck Rochet, Emploi du Temps à Londres, 1943–44, 8 Dec. 1943; Waldeck Rochet to Grenier, 13 Dec. 1943

58 Emmanuel d'Astier de la Vigerie, *Sept fois sept jours*, pp. 162–5

59 Emmanuel d'Astier, *Le Dieux et les hommes, 1943–1944* (Paris, Julliard, 1952), pp. 43–8

60 J-L Crémieux-Brilhac, 'La Bataille des Glières et la Guerre psychologique', *RHDGM* 99 (1975), pp. 45–72; Claude Barbier, *Le Maquis des Glieres; mythe et réalité* (Paris, Perrin, 2014)

61 AN 72AJ234/V, report by Yvon Morandat to Emmanuel d'Astier, 29 Feb. 1944

62 Pierre Villon, *Résistant de la première heure*, pp. 82–3

63 AN 450AP2, Lecompte-Boinet, Journal, Feb.–Jul. 1944, p. 53. Entry for 11 Mar. 1944

64 Musée de la Résistance, Fonds Pierre Villon, Carton 3. Article for *France d'abord,* 15 Dec. 1947

65 Musée de la Résistance, Fonds André Tollet IIII. CPL Bureau, procès-verbaux des séances, 19th séance, 31 Mar. 1944

66 CPL Bureau, procès verbaux des séances, 22e séance, Apr. 1944

67 Musée de l'Ordre de la Libération, Bingen file. Letter and will of Bingen, 14 Apr. 1944. I am indebted to Guillaume Piketty for this reference

68 See above, pp. 303–4

69 Philippe André, *La Résistance confisquée?*, pp. 137–50

70 John F. Sweets, *The Politics of Resistance in France*, pp. 122–9; Wieviorka, *Histoire de la Résistance*, pp. 342–5

71 AN 13AV50, interview with Serge Ravanel, 26 Jun. 1991

72 Dominique Lormier, *L'Épopée du Corps Francs Pommiès, des Pyrénées à Berlin* (Paris, Jacques Grancher, 1990)

73 AD Haute-Garonne 16J 271, General André Pommiès, 'Le Corps Franc Pommiès et l'ORA de Toulouse dans la Résistance, 1964), p. 3

74 Pommiès, 'Le Corps Franc Pommiès', p. 10

75 AD Haute-Garonne 16J 263, Ravanel to Daniel Latapie, 6 Dec. 1992

76 AN 13AV52, interview with Serge Ravanel, 26 Jun. 1991

77 AN 13AV53, interview with Serge Ravanel, 17 Dec. 1991

Chapter 13

1 See above, pp. 177–8

2 Roger Lefèvre, *Souvenirs de Maquisards de l'Ain* (Saint-Cyr-sur-Loire, Alan Sutton, 2004), pp. 13–21

3 Jean-Louis Crémieux-Brilhac (ed.), *Les Voix de la Liberté. Londres, 1940–1944* V (Paris, La Documentation Française, 1976), pp. 41–2

4 See below, pp. 353, 356

5 Jean-Louis Crémieux-Brilhac, *La France libre*, p. 836; Robert Gildea, 'Myth, Memory and Policy in France Since 1945' in Jan-Werner Müller, *Memory and Power in Postwar Europe* (Cambridge, CUP, 2002), p. 61

6 Jean-Louis Crémieux-Brilhac, *La France libre*, pp. 819–24

7 Vere Harmsworth Library, Oxford, Stimson Papers, reel 127, 'Re: de Gaulle. From the Record of the Day, Jun. 14, 1944'

8 Jean-Louis Crémieux-Brilhac, *La France libre*, pp. 843–8; Jackson, *France: the Dark Years*, pp. 551–2; Philippe Buton, *La Joie douloureuse. La Libération de la France* (Paris, Complexe, 2004), pp. 69–71

9 Arthur Layton Funk, *Charles de Gaulle*, pp. 279–82; Jean-Louis Crémieux-Brilhac, *La France libre*, pp. 850–4

10 The best recent account of this is Olivier Wieviorka, *Normandy: the Landings to the Liberation of Paris* (Cambridge, Mass., Belknap Press, 2008)

11 Crémieux-Brilhac (ed.), *Les Voix de la Liberté. Londres, 1940–1944 vol.* V, pp. 48, 52

12 AN 72AJ42, Journal de Léo Hamon, 23 Jun., 1944, p. 145; 30 Jun. 1944, p. 139

13 Musée de la Résistance, Champigny, Carton 126A, Témoignages III. Jean-Olivier Eleouet, alias Lieutenant Yvon, 'Mémoires d'un Franc-Tireur et partisan Français pour servir à l'histoire de la Résistance en Corrèze' (1981), see above, p. 298

14 Musée de la Résistance, Champigny. Liquidation OS-FN-FTP. Allemagne. Letter of Gerhard Leo, 25 May 1984. Gerhard Leo, *Un Allemand dans la Résistance. Le Train pour Toulouse* (Paris, Éditions Tirésias, 1997), pp. 245–59

15 AN 72AJ112A1 Corrèze. Antoine Soulier, 'Le Drame de Tulle', p. 4

16 Antoine Soulier, 'Le Drame de Tulle', pp. 6–7

17 AN 72AJ112A111 Corrèze. Liste des 99 martyrs du 9 juin 1944 à Tulle

18 AN 72AJ99. Ardennes. Testimony of General Nérot, 10 Feb. 1951

19 Philippe Leclerc, L'Affaire des Manises (Langres, Dominique Guéniot, 2004)

20 Maurice Kriegel-Valrimont, La Libération. Les archives du COMAC (mai–août 1944) (Paris, les Éditions de Minuit, 1964), p. 40

21 Kriegel-Valrimont, La Libération, pp. 45–6

22 Pierre Villon, Résistant de la première heure, p. 93

23 AD Seine Saint-Denis, 307 J 154, Dossiers conserves dans les archives de Gaston Plissonnier, Waldeck Rousseau to central committee delegation of PCF, 15 Jun. 1944

24 Kriegel-Valrimont, La Libération, p. 52

25 AN 450AP2, Lecompte-Boinet, Journal, Feb.–Jul. 1944, pp. 212–3, entry for 20 Jun. 1944

26 Lecompte-Boinet, Journal, Feb.–Jul. 1944, 219, entry for 24 Jun. 1944

27 See above, pp. 330–3

28 Nancy Wake, The White Mouse (London, Macmillan, 1985), p. 117; Denis Rake, Rake's Progress; the Gay – and Dramatic – Adventures of Major Denis Rake, MC, the Reluctant British War-Time Agent, with a foreword by Douglas Fairbanks (London, Leslie Frewin, 1968)

29 AN 72AJ63/IV, testimony of Henri Ingrand on the Mont Mouchet maquis, n.d.

30 Rod Kedward, 'Ici commence la France libre', in H.R. Kedward and Nancy Wood, (eds.), The Liberation of France. Image and Event (Oxford, Berg, 1995), pp. 1–11

31 AN 72AJ106 A1. Cantal. Récit fait par Jean Rothé, professeur à l'Université de Strasbourg des combats du Mont Mouchet et de Chaudes-Aigues en juin 1944, pp. 8–10

32 AD Puy-de Dôme 908W150, report of Hélène Odoul, mayor of Ruines, 8 Aug. 1945

33 AN 72AJ63/IV, testimony of Henri Ingrand, p. 4

34 Nancy Wake, The White Mouse, p. 124

35 NA HS9/1648, recommendation of Denis Rake for the Military Cross, n.d. but before Jun. 1945

36 AN 72AJ142 A1. Haute Loire. Capitaine Volle, 'Les Combattants de la Libération de la Haute Loire' (1963), p. 13

37 Nancy Wake, The White Mouse, p. 135

38 Pierre Dalloz, Vérités sur le Drame du Vercors, pp. 155, 174–5, 187–94

39 AN 72AJ624, Alban Vistel cable to COMAC, 12 Jun. 1944

40 Joseph Gilbert, Combattant du Vercors (Paris, Fayard, 1972), p. 163

41 Peter Lieb, Vercors 1944. Resistance in the French Alps (Oxford, Osprey, 2012), p. 36; Paddy Ashdown, The Cruel Victory. The French Resistance, D-Day and the Battle for the Vercors, 1944 (London, HarperCollins, 2014), pp. 192–216

42 Joseph, Combattant du Vercors, p. 147

43 NA HS9/937/8, finishing report of Desmonde Longe (b. 8 Aug. 1914), 11 Aug. 1942

44 NA HS9/749/1, SOE record of service of John Vincent Houseman (b. 22 Sept.

1914), 19 Aug. 1943

45 AN 72AJ84/1, OSS Aid to the French Resistance in World War II. Operations in Southern France, pp. 29–32

46 Joseph, *Combattant du Vercors*, p. 226

47 Lieb, *Vercors 1944*, pp. 46–59; Ashdown, *The Cruel Victory*, pp. 296–335

48 NA HS9/937/8, report on 'Interallied Mission Eucalyptus to the Vercors', by Lieutenant André E. Paray, 17 Oct. 1944, p. 4

49 AN 72AJ624, CNR to prime minister Churchill, 21 Jul. 1944

50 Delloz, *Vérités sur le Drame du Vercors*, pp. 255, 263–4. For an alternative view see Jacques Soustelle, *Envers et contre tout,* III, pp. 239–42

51 Delloz,*Vérités sur le Drame du Vercors*, pp. 264–6; AD Seine Saint-Denis, Archives Grenier 2995 Grenier to de Gaulle, 28 Jul. 1944. The letter of 27 Jul. is not on file

52 'Interallied Mission Eucalyptus to the Vercors', by Lieutenant André E. Paray, p. 8

53 Lieb, *Vercors 1944*, p. 71. These figures are accepted by Paddy Ashdown, *The Cruel Victory*, p. 355

54 NA HS9/937/8, Houseman to General Gubbins, 19 Sept. 1944

55 OSS Aid to the French Resistance in World War II. Operations in Southern France, p. 32

56 AN 72AJ146 BIV. Loire Atlantique. Abbé Henri Ploquin, 'Souvenirs' (1970), p. 17

57 See also Gildea, *Marianne in Chains*, pp. 325–6

58 AN 72AJ166 Morbihan AII. General Eon,' Histoire des FFI du Morbihan', n.d. 15pp, pp. 5–8; Gérard Le Marec, *La Bretagne dans la Résistance* (Rennes, Ouest-France, 1983), pp. 245–53; Jean Paulin, *La rage au cœur* (1958)

59 Sébastien Albertelli and Johanna Barasz, 'Un résistant atypique: le général Cochet, entre vichysme et gaullisme', *Histoire et Politique*, 5 (May–Jun. 2008), www.histoire-politique.fr

60 The term 'ci-devants' was applied to former nobles whose hereditary titles were abolished by the French Revolution

61 AN 72AJ438, Cochet to de Gaulle, 20 Jul. 1943

62 AN 72AJ446, Cochet to Comité d'Action en France, Algiers, 11 Jul. 1944

63 AN 72AJ60/III, Rapport d'activite de J-P Vernant, n.d., pp. 2–5

64 AN 72AJ125/II, Pommiès to professeur Ressignac, Montauban, 26 Aug. 1963; AD Haute-Garonne 16 J 271, General Pommiès, 'Le Corps Franc Pommiès', pp. 12–13; AD Haute-Garonne 16 J 263, Ravanel to Daniel Latapie, 6 Dec. 1992

65 AN 72AJ126 CVI, Report of Cassou to Emmanuel d'Astier de la Vigerie, mid-Jul. 1944, p. 6

66 General Pommiès, 'Le Corps Franc Pommiès', pp. 15–16

67 AN 13AV53, interview with Serge Ravanel, 17 Jan. 1992

68 AN 72AJ129 BII. Gers, Journal de Route du Bataillon de Guerrilla Armagnac, tenu par le Cl. Monnet (Oct. 1965); AD Haute-Garonne 16J 58, 'De Vierzon aux Pyrénées. Le Réseau Wheelwright', pp. 6–8

69 NA HS9/982/4, Anne-Marie Comert née Walters, Report on mission in France, 18 Sept. 1944

70 Roger Mompezat, *Le Corps franc de la Montagne noire, journal de marche, avril–septembre 1944* (4th edn. Castres, les Anciens du Corps franc de la Montagne noire, 1994); Kedward, *In Search of the Maquis*, pp. 183–5

71 Musée de la Résistance, Champigny. Fonds Suberville, 11. Rapport sur le maquis des Corps Francs de la Montagne Noire, 30 Jul. 1944

72 AD Haute-Garonne 16J36, Serge Ravanel, Intervention au Colloque de la Résistance, 28–31 Oct. 1974, p. 3

73 AN 72AJ126 C II 7, Haute Garonne. Historique du XIV Corps de Guerrilleros Espagnols (1976); Claude Delpla, 'Les origins des guerrilleros espagnols dans les Pyrénées (1940–43) and Fabien Garrado, 'Les "memoires" du Général Luis Fernández, chef de la Agrupación de los Guerrilleros Españoles', in Jean Ortiz (ed.), *Rouges Maquis de France et d'Espagne* (Biarritz, Atlantica, 2006), pp. 172–9, 193–209

74 AN 72AJ100 Ariège. Robert Fareng, 'La Libération de l'Ariège (1940–1944), DES d'Histoire modern, 1946, pp. 298–9

75 AD Haute-Garonne 16J222, Vicente López Tovar, 'Autobiographie' (1991), pp. 2–3, 81–5

76 AD Haute-Garonne 16J14, Calpo, 'Union dans la lutte. La condemnation à mort de l'Allemagne nazie', n.d., pp. 36–8

77 Eveline and Yvan Brès, 'Des Allemands maquisards dans les Cévennes des Camisards', in Philippe Joutard, Jacques Poujol, Patrick Cabanel (eds.), *Cévennes, Terre de Refuge, 1940–1944* (Montpellier, Les Presses du Languedoc, 1987), pp. 91–7

78 CDJC DLXI-65, interview with Pierre Loeb, n.d.

79 CDJC DLXI-66, interview with Pierre Loeb, conducted by Anny Latour, 1973, p. 13

80 Denis Gamzon, *Mémoires* (Jerusalem, 1997), p. 90

81 AD Haute-Garonne, 16J300, 35e Brigade Marcel Langer, Cérémonies en homage à la 35e Brigade FTP-MOI, Toulouse, Sept. 1983, introduction

82 See above, p. 238

83 Testimony of Claude Urman, 3 Nov. 1988, in David Diamant, *250 Combattants de la Résistance témoignent* (Paris, L'Harmattan, 1991), pp. 222–4

84 Verbizier, *Ni Travail, ni famille, ni patrie,* pp. 236–9; Marc Lévy, *Les Enfants de la Liberté* (Paris, Robert Laffont, 2006), pp. 319–61

85 See above, p. 329

86 AN 72AJ 92CI. Ain, testimony of General Bousquet, Bourg, 15 Jul. 1946

87 AN 72 AJ92CI. Ain, testimony of Mme Émile Mercier, née Pauline Perrotet, 16 Jul. 1946

88 AN 72AJ90 AI Ain, Madame Appleton, 'Note sur les Différends entre le Directoire et le Colonel Romans', n.d. but 1946

89 AN 72AJ626, Action Ouvrère letters of 17 Jun. 1944; Alban Vistel reply of 21 Jun. 1944

90 AN 72AJ626, Action Ouvrère, Oullins, to Alban Vistel, 10 Jul. 1944

91 CHRD Lyon, interview with Jean-Marie Domenach, 16 Apr. 1997

92 Bernard Comte, Jean-Marie Domenach, Christian Rendu, Denise Rendu, *Gilbert Dru. Un Chrétien resistant* (Paris, Beauchesne, 1998), pp. 76–124

93 See above, pp. 234–5

94 Musée de la Résistance. Fonds de l'Amicale des Anciens FTP-MOI du Bataillon Carmagnole-Liberté. I. Testimony of Léon Landini, Bagneux, Feb. 1991; Interview with Léon Landini, conducted by RG, Bagneux, 20 Apr. 2012;

Claude Collin, *Carmagnole-Liberté. Les Étrangers dans la Résistance en Rhône-Alpes* (Grenoble, PU de Grenoble, 2000), pp. 103–15, 146–8

95 Comte et al., *Gilbert Dru*, pp. 124–5

96 Yves Farge, *Rebelles, Soldats et Citoyens. Souvenirs d'un Commissaire de la République* (Paris, Grasset, 1946), pp. 147–8

97 Maurice Kriegel-Valrimont, *La Libération. Les Archives du COMAC (mai-août 1944)* (Paris, Les Éditions de Minuit, 1964), pp. 56–65

98 Musée de la Résistance, Fonds André Tollet. 1.1.1.1. CPL Bureau, procès-verbaux des séances, 31st session (14 Jul. 1944)

99 Musée de la Résistance, Fonds André Tollet, 2. Note sur la manifestation du 1er juillet 1944 sur le Ravitaillement, signed 'Villa'

100 Musée de la Résistance. Les Inconnus de la Résistance. Testimony of Suzanne Neige, Montrouge, 16 Jul. 1984

101 Musée de la Résistance, Fonds André Tollet. 1.1.1.1. CPL Bureau, procès-verbaux des séances, 31st session (14 Jul. 1944)

102 Monique Georges, *Le Colonel Fabien était mon père*, pp. 217–9

103 Musée de la Résistance, Fonds André Tollet, 2, Union des Syndicats ouvriers de la Région parisienne. 'Comment doit-on conduire une greve? A la lumière des mouvements des cheminots', n.d., Tollet, *La Classe ouvrière dans la Résistance* (Paris, Editions sociales, 1969), pp. 221–7

104 Tollet, *La Classe ouvrière*, pp. 231–4

105 AN 7261/I, M. Lassalle, 'La Libération de Paris, vue de la Plaine Monceau', p. 2

106 Kriegel-Valrimont, *La Libération*, p. 140

107 AN 72AJ42, Journal de Léo Hamon, 7 Aug. 1944, p. 197

108 AN 450AP2, Lecompte-Boinet, Journal, Aug. 1944, 1 Aug. 1944, p. 2

Chapter 14

1 Diego Brosset, *Carnets de guerre, correspondence et note (1939-1944)*, in Guillaume Piketty, *Français en Résistance* (2009), p. 383. Entry for 20 Aug. 1944

2 Arthur Layton Funk, *Hidden Ally. The French Resistance, Special Operations and the Landings in Southern France, 1944* (New York, Greenwood Press, 1992), pp. 95–136

3 Brosset, *Carnets de guerre*, p. 385. Entry for 21 Aug. 1944

4 Brosset, *Carnets de guerre*, p. 389. Entry for 27 Aug. 1944

5 Raymond Aubrac, *Où la Mémoire s'attarde* (Paris, Odile Jacob, 1996), pp. 124–9

6 Raymond Aubrac, *Où la Mémoire s'attarde*, pp. 124–41; David Scott Bell, 'Politics in Marseille since World War II with special reference to the political role of Gaston Defferre' (Oxford DPhil thesis, 1978), pp. 11–16

7 AN 72AJ220/I, Résistance extérieure. Testimony of General Eon, 27 Dec. 1948

8 Service historique de la Défense, Vincennes, 16P 209959, personal file of Albert-Marie Eon, reference of André Rous, Feb. 1946

9 Centre d'histoire, Sciences Po. Fonds Charles Tillon, CT3, dossier 2. Colonel Eon, Journal de Marche et Opérations du commandement des FFI en Bretagne, n.d., 18p, p. 2

10 NA H57/127, Participation of the FFI in the Liberation of France, pp. 611–2

11 Eon, Journal de Marche, p. 8

12 Centre d'histoire, Sciences Po. Fonds Charles Tillon, CT3, dossier 2, Eon to General Middleton, 7 Sept. 1944

13 Michel Debré, *Trois Républiques pour une France. Mémoires I. Combattre* (Paris, Albin Michel, 1984), p. 295

14 Gildea, *Marianne in Chains*, pp. 330–4

15 Dwight D. Eisenhower, *Crusade in Europe* (London, Heinemann, 1948), pp. 324–5

16 *France during the German Occupation, 1940–1944* (Stanford, Hoover Institution, 1957), II, pp. 1052–81; Walter Stucki, *La Fin du regime de Vichy* (Neuchâtel, Editions de la Baconnière, 1947), pp. 72–4

17 AN 450AP2, Lecompte-Boinet, Journal, Aug. 1944, 14 & 17 Aug. 1944, pp. 43–53

18 *France During the German Occupation, 1940–1944*. II (Stanford, Hoover Institution, 1957), pp. 1023

19 Stucki, *La Fin du regime de Vichy*, p. 106–28

20 Henry Rousso, *Un Château en Allemagne: la France de Pétain en exil, Sigmaringen 1944–1945* (Paris, Ramsay, 1980)

21 AN 13AV56, interview with Serge Ravanel, 17 Jan. 1992

22 AD Haute Garonne 16J275, regional military delegate Brice (Schlumberger) to 'Constant', 27 Aug. 1944; AN13AV56, interview with Serge Ravanel, 17 Jan. 1992; Jackson, *France: the Dark Years*, p. 574

23 Suberville, L'Autre Resistance, pp. 68–9; Gilbert de Chambrun, *Journal d'un militaire d'occasion* (Avignon, Aubanel, 1982), p. 172

24 AD Haute Garonne 16J222, Vicente Lopez Tovar, 'Autobiographie', pp. 87–8

25 SHD Vincennes 16P 59351, Marcel Bigeard file

26 AN 72AJ100/A1, testimony of Albert Fernandez, 10 Nov. 1950; AN 72 AJ 100 Ariège. Robert Fareng, 'La Libération de l'Ariège, pp. 353–71

27 AD Haute Garonne 16J66, René Soucasse, 'Souvenir encore. Le Train de Mazamet' (2pp, handwritten, 6 Nov. 1979).

28 *Organisation juive de combat. France 1940–1945*, p. 269

29 Dora Schaul, *Resistance. Erinnerungen deutscher Antifascisten* (Berlin, Dietz Verlag, 1973), p. 446

30 AN 72AJ446/IV.2, Note from Cochet's headquarter copied to Generals Patton and de Lattre de Tassigny, 19 Aug. 1944

31 AN 72AJ446/IV.6, 'Le Général Cochet à Toulouse. Témoignage', n.d.

32 Farge, *Rebelles, Soldats et Citoyens*, pp. 143–4

33 AN 72AJ626, Action Ouvrère, Ladoumègue to Alban Vistel, n.d. but before 10 Aug. 1944

34 AN 72AJ180 BI. Rhône. Extracts from René Laplace, 'Le Combat d'Oullins', *Dauphiné Libéré*, 24 Aug.–5 Sept. 1965

35 F. Rude, *La Libération de Lyon et de sa région* (Paris, Hachette, 1974), p. 85.

36 Musée de la Résistance. Fonds de l'Amicale des Anciens FTP-MOI du Bataillon Carmagnole-Liberté. 2. Fiche on Josel Koenigsberg. 3. Testimonies of 'Paul' and 'Jacquot' (Jacques Szmulewicz) on Nathan Saks, n.d. (1985)

37 Max Weinstein, *Souvenirs, souvenirs* (Nice, Éditions du Losange, 1997)

38 Yves Farge, *Rebelles, Soldats et Citoyens*, p. 174

39 Diego Brosset, *Carnets de guerre, correspondence et note (1939–1944)*, in Guillaume Piketty, *Français en Résistance* (2009), p. 392. Entry for 6 Sept. 1944

40 Brosset, *Carnets de guerre*, p. 392. Entry for 6 Sept. 1944

41 Farge, *Rebelles, Soldats et Citoyens*, p. 202

42 Farge, *Rebelles, Soldats et Citoyens*, p. 202

43 Sciences-Po, Centre d'Histoire, Fonds A. Parodi PA 10, Mémoires de Dietrich von Choltitz (1949), pp. 6–7, 14–21. This is a MS copy of von Choltitz, *Un Soldat parmi des soldats* (Avignon, Aubanel, 1965), the French translation of his *Soldat unter Soldaten* (Konstanz, 1951)

44 AN 72AJ67/4, M.H. Lefaucheux, 'L'évasion de M. Lefaucheux', p. 1

45 AN 72AJ67/4, M.H. Lefaucheux, 'L'évasion de M. Lefaucheux', pp. 1–5

46 Luc Rudolph (ed.), *Au Coeur de la Préfecture de Police de la Résistance à la Libération III. La Libération de Paris* (Paris, 2011), pp. 16–19; Gildea, *Marianne in Chains*, pp. 289, 317–18

47 AN 72 61/I, M. Lassalle, 'La Libération de Paris, vue de la Plaine Monceau', pp. 1–2

48 Musée de la Résistance, Fonds André Tollet. 1.1.1.1. CPL Bureau, procès-verbaux des séances, 37th session (17 Aug. 1944)

49 AN 450AP2, Lecompte-Boinet, Journal, Aug. 1944, 19 Aug. 1944, p. 67

50 AN 72AJ42, L'insurrection parisienne. Extrait des souvenirs inédits de Léon Hamon, 18 & 19 Aug., pp. 5–6

51 Sciences-Po, Centre d'Histoire, Fonds A. Parodi PA11, draft text on Liberation of Paris, pp. 4–6; *Le Monde*, 24–5 Aug. 1969, account by Rol-Tanguy

52 Rudolph (ed.), *Au Coeur de la Préfecture de Police de la Résistance à la Libération III. La Libération de Paris*, pp. 26–8

53 Francis-Louis Closon, *Le temps des passions*, p. 228

54 AN 72AJ61/I, Libération de Paris. Témoignage de M. Heinemann, 19 avenue de l'Esperance, Bobigny (Seine), n.d (1958), p. 3

55 AN 7261/I, M. Lassalle, 'La Libération de Paris, vue de la Plaine Monceau', p. 3

56 AN 72AJ62/III, 'L'insurrection dans le XVIIIe'. Reportage de Mme Lamontellerie, rue Capitaine Lagache, pp. 6–11

57 AN 72AJ409/7, protest of communist deputies, 20 Aug. 1944, in files of d'Astier de la Vigerie

58 AN 72AJ42, L'insurrection parisienne. Extrait des souvenirs inédits de Léon Hamon, p. 11

59 AN 72AJ42, L'insurrection parisienne. Extrait des souvenirs inédits de Léon Hamon, p. 15

60 AN 72AJ42, L'insurrection parisienne. Extrait des souvenirs inédits de Léon Hamon, p. 17

61 Mémoires de Dietrich von Choltitz (1949), pp. 67–70; Fonds Parodi PA11, draft text on Liberation of Paris, 7, IIb

62 AN 450AP2, Lecompte-Boinet, Journal, Aug. 1944, 20 Aug. 1944, p. 81

63 AN 450AP2, Lecompte-Boinet, Journal, Aug. 1944, 20 Aug. 1944, p. 74

64 Musée de la Résistance, Fonds André Tollet. 1.1.1.1. CPL Bureau, procès-verbaux des séances, 38th session (21 Aug. 1944); Tollet, *La Classe ouvrière*, pp. 250–56

65 Musée de la Résistance, p. 129, Témoignages VII. Georges Marrane, le Comité

Parisien de Libération (1969), pp. 1–3

66 Tollet, *La Classe ouvrière*, p. 245. Eugène Pottier (1816–87) was a composer of revolutionary songs, including the 'Internationale'

67 AN 72 61/I, M. Lassalle, 'La Libération de Paris, vue de la Plaine Monceau', p. 4

68 AN 72 AJ 62/III, 'L'insurrection dans le XVIIIe'. Reportage de Mme Lamontellerie, rue Capitaine Lagache, p. 11

69 Musée de la Résistance. Fonds André Tollet 2. Résistance – Après Guerre. Rol to Tollet, 21 Aug. 1969; Madeleine Riffaud, *On l'appelait Rainer*, p. 146

70 Buton, *La Joie douloureuse*, pp. 87–91

71 Musée de la Résistance, p. 130. Témoignages VIII. Colonel Rol-Tanguy n.d., pp. 2–3; Roger Bourderon, *Rol-Tanguy*, p. 378

72 Sciences-Po, Centre d'Histoire, Fonds Parodi, alexandre de Saint-Phalle, 'Rapport concernant la mission plénipotentiaire envoyée auprès du Haut Commandement Allié le mardi 22 août 1944'

73 Musée de la Résistance, p. 130. Témoignages VIII. Colonel Rol-Tanguy n.d., pp. 2–3; Roger Bourderon, *Rol-Tanguy*, p. 378

74 Omar N. Bradley, *A Soldier's Story* (New York, Henry Holt, 1951), p. 392

75 Lecompte-Boinet, Journal, Aug. 1944, 24 Aug. 1944, p. 113

76 Monique Georges, *Le Colonel Fabien était mon père*, pp. 229–32

77 AN 72 61/I, M. Lassalle, 'La Libération de Paris, vue de la Plaine Monceau', p. 6

78 450 AP 2, Lecompte-Boinet, Journal, Aug. 1944, 25 Aug. 1944, p. 109

79 Archives Municipales, Ivry. Marrane. Guerre. 'Allocations pronounces à l'Hotel de Ville le 25 aout, lors de la reception du General de Gaulle'

80 450 AP 2, Lecompte-Boinet, Journal, Aug. 1944, 25 Aug. 1944, p. 128

81 450 AP 2, Lecompte-Boinet, Journal, Aug. 1944, 25 Aug. 1944, p. 129

82 Mémoires de Choltitz, pp. 99–105

83 Philippe Buton, *La Joie douloureuse*, p. 91

84 Jean-Louis Crémieux-Brilhac, *La France libre*, pp. 903–6

85 Andé Tollet, *Ma Traversée de siècle. Mémoires d'un syndicaliste révolutionnaire* (Paris, 2002), p. 61

86 450 AP 2, Lecompte-Boinet, Journal, Aug. 1944, 26 Aug. 1944, p. 137

87 AN 72AJ42, L'insurrection parisienne. Extrait des souvenirs inédits de Léon Hamon, pp. 32–4. Henri IV is said to have declared in 1594 that 'Paris is worth a mass', meaning that it was worth converting to Catholicism to become king

88 AD Haute Garonne 16J 465, Colonel Schneider, 'La Colonne Légère de Toulouse', n.d., pp. 8–18

89 AN 72AJ226 IV/4. Colonel Schneider, 'Rapport d'Opération du groupement Schneider. 1er septembre–10 novembre 1944 (29pp), pp. 3–17; Notes on Colonel Schneider by General Bertin-Chevance, 1 Feb. 1945

90 Pearl Witherington Cornioley, *Codename Pauline*, pp. 95–101

91 NA H57/127, Participation of the FFI in the Liberation of France, 1944. Pt II, pp. 523–5; Michel Jouhanneau, *L'Organisation de la Résistance dans l'Indre* (Franconville, 1975)

92 AN 72AJ67/4, Marie-Hèlène Lefaucheux, 'L'évasion de M. Lefaucheux', pp. 6–16; *Lettres de Claire Girard, fusillée par les Allemands le 27 août 1944* (Paris, Roger Lescaret, 1954), pp. 13–14

Chapter 15

1 Maurice Kriegel-Valrimont, *La Liberation. Les archives du COMAC*, pp. 227–8

2 Cited in Roger Bourderon, *Rol-Tanguy*, pp. 460–1; Interview of Cécile Rol-Tanguy with RG, Paris, 20 Jun. 2012

3 Farge, *Rebelles, Soldats et Citoyens*, p. 213

4 Interview in *Patriote* of Lyon, 9 Sept. 1944, cited in General de Lattre, *Histoire du Première Armée Française* (Paris, Plon, 1949), p. 182

5 De Lattre, *Histoire du Première Armée Française*, p. 181

6 'Le récit du colonel Ravanel', *L'Express*, 29 Mar. 1959, cutting in AN 72 AJ 125/II. See also 72 AJ 125/IV, interview with Ravanel, 10 Sept. 1969; Pierre Bertaux, *La Libération de Toulouse et de sa région*, pp. 88–93

7 AD Haute Garonne 16J58, 'De Vierzon aux Pyrénées. Le Réseau Wheelwright', 10. Starr duly flew back to Britain on 26 Sept. 1944

8 AN 13AV58, interview with Serge Ravanel, 26 Feb. 1992

9 AN 13AV58, interview with Serge Ravanel, 17 Jan. 1992

10 Serge Ravanel, *L'Esprit de Résistance* (Paris, Seuil, 1995), p. 16

11 Sciences Po, Paris, Centre d'Histoire, Témoignages sur la Guerre d'Algérie, interview with General Le Châtelier, Feb. 1981, pp. 3, 10–11

12 See above, p. 167

13 SHD 16P216468, file of Roland Farjon

14 Claude Monod, *La Région D. Rapport d'activité des maquis de Bourgogne-Franche Comté* (St Etienne-Vallée Francaise, AIOU, 1993), pp. 80–1

15 Monod to Lieutenant-Colonel Lagarde, 12 Dec. 1944, in Monod, *La Région D*, p. 107

16 Interview with Max Weinstein, conducted by RG, Paris, 24 May 2012

17 Monique Georges, *Le colonel Fabien était mon père* (Paris, Mille et Une Nuits, 2009), pp. 252–4

18 AN 72AJ73. Résistance étrangère. Renseignements donnés par Jean Gerhard à Mme Kahn, Feb. 1963; Musée de la Résistance, Fonds de l'Amicale des Anciens FTP-MOI du Bataillon Carmagnole-Liberté.2, notes on interview with Jeannine Krakus, Paris, 2 Oct. 1986; Claude Collin, 'L'attitude des résistants face aux « libérateurs » américains: un mélange d'admiration et de méfiance', *Annales de l'Est* 44 (1992 no. 2), pp. 126–7

19 General de Lattre, *Histoire du Première Armée Française* (Paris, Plon, 1949), pp. 180–2. See also Claire Miot, 'Le retrait des tirailleurs sénégalais de la Première Armée française en 1944. Hérésie stratégique, bricolage politique ou conservatisme colonial?' *Vingtième Siècle* no. 25 (jan.–mars 2015), pp. 77–89

20 Interview with Madeleine Riffaud, conducted by RG, Paris, 15 Apr. 2012

21 Letter of Antonin Cubizolles, Paris (1984), in Floriane Benoit et Charles Silvestre (eds.), *Les Inconnus de la Résistance* (Paris, L'Humanité/Editions Messidor, 1984), pp. 19–20

22 General Béthouart, *Cinq années d'espérance. Mémoires de guerre, 1939–1945* (Paris, Plon, 1968), pp. 303–5

23 Monique Georges, *Le colonel Fabien*, pp. 268–77, 289–90

24 450 AP 2, Lecompte-Boinet, Journal, Aug. 1944, 27 Aug. 1944, pp. 147–8

25 450 AP 2, Lecompte-Boinet, Journal, Aug. 1944, 27 Aug. 1944, pp. 149–51

26 450 AP 2, Lecompte-Boinet, Journal, Aug. 1944, 29 Aug. 1944, p. 168

27 Léo Hamon, *Vivre ses choix*, pp. 227–8; AN 6AV 624, interview with Robert Salmon, conducted by Olivier Wieviorka, 7 Feb. 1986

28 *La Marseillaise*, 21 Sept. 1945

29 Henri Frenay, *La Nuit finira*, p. 460

30 Emmanuel d'Astier de la Vigerie, *Sept Fois Sept Jours*, pp. 206–7

31 450 AP 2, Lecompte-Boinet, Journal, fin 1944, 25 Sept. 1944, p. 123

32 Philippe Viannay, *Du bon Visage de la France* (Paris, Editions Ramsay, 1988), p. 152

33 Pierre-Henri Teitgen, *Faites entrer le Témoin suivant, 1940–1958. De la Résistance à la Ve République* (Rennes, Ouest-France, 1988), pp. 145, 208–38

34 Jacqueline Sainclivier, 'Le pouvoir resistant (été 1944)' in Philippe Buton and Jean-Marie Guillon, *Les pouvoirs en France à la Libération* (Paris, Belin, 1994), pp. 20–37; Buton, *La Joie douloureuse*, pp. 139–42, 145–6

35 AN 6AV624, interview with Robert Salmon, conducted by Olivier Wieviorka, 11 Apr. 1986

36 Francis-Louis Closon, *Commissaire de la République du Général de Gaulle* (Paris, Julliard, 1980), pp. 19–21, 156–63

37 Robert Gildea, *Marianne in Chains*, pp. 330–5

38 Yves Farge, *Rebelles, Soldats et Citoyens*, p. 268

39 Charles-Louis Foulon, *Le pouvoir en province à la Libération. Les commissaire de la République* (Paris, FNSP/Armand Colin, 1975), pp. 233–4

40 Foulon, *Le pouvoir en province à la Libération*, pp. 247–57

41 Sciences Po, Centre d'Histoire, Témoignages sur la Guerre d'Algérie. Michel Debré, 1981, p. 102; Michel Debré, *Refaire la France* (Paris, Plon, 1945), p. 122

42 Pierre Hervé, *La Liberation trahie* (Paris, Grasset, 1945), pp. 104–5

43 Buton, *La Joie douloureuse*, pp. 175–6

44 Denise Domenach Lallich, *Demain il fera beau*, p. 39

45 Pierre Hervé, *La Liberation trahie* (Paris, Grasset, 1945), p. 78; AN 13 AV 78, interview with Pierre Hervé, conducted by Olivier Wieviorka, 20 Dec. 1990

46 Henri Frenay, *La Nuit finira*, p. 478; Jean-Pierre Lévy, *Mémoires d'un franc-tireur*, pp. 136–7

47 AN 13AV68, interview with Claude Bourdet conducted by Olivier Wieviorka, 9 Jan. 1987

48 Martine Pradoux, *Daniel Mayer, un socialiste dans la Résistance* (Paris, Les Éditions ouvrières, 2002), pp. 238, 244–5

49 AN6AV624, interview with Robert Salmon, conducted by Olivier Wieviorka, May 1986

50 AN 6AV629, interview with Robert Salmon, conducted by Olivier Wieviorka, 20 Jun. 1986

51 Francis Crémieux, *Entretiens avec Emmanuel d'Astier* (Paris, 1966), p. 132

52 AN 13AV68, interview with Claude Bourdet conducted by Olivier Wieviorka, 9 Jan. 1987

53 Leo Hamon, *Vivre ses choix*, p. 220

54 Mémorial de la Shoah/INA, interview with Oscar Rosowsky, 5 Jun. 2006

55 Interview with Max Weinstein, conducted by RG, Paris, 24 May 2012

56 NA FO 1049/9, Telegram from Madrid to British Foreign Office, 7 Oct.

1944; Colonel Pedron to Allied supreme Headquarters, 17 Oct. 1944; AD Haute-Garonne 16J180, Daniel Latapie, Guerrilleros Espagnols, Documents vol. 1 (1990), record of conversation between General Koenig and General Harold Redman of SHAEF, 19 Sept. 1944; report of DGSS, 10 Oct. 1944, FFI general staff, 16 Oct. 1944, US telegram 24 Oct. 1944

57 AN 72AJ126/II. Haute-Garonne, testimony of Daniel Latapie for Henri Michel, 2 Jan. 1976; AD Haute-Garonne 16J139, Sixto Agudo, 'Les Résistants Espagnols après la Libération', 1976; AD Haute-Garonne 16J222, Lopez Tovar, 'Autobiographie', pp. 106–17

58 AD Haute Garonne 16J222, Lopez Tovar, 'Autobiographie', pp. 146–9

59 Mémorial de Caen, TE 693, Jacques Filardier, 'Peur ne connais pas' (typescript, 1983), pp. 10–26

60 Musée de la Résistance, Fonds thématique 111B, report by Niebergall on visits to POW camps, 28 Oct. 1944

61 Musée de la Résistance, Fonds thématique 111B. Press confererence of CALPO, 13 Nov. 1943

62 Musée de la Résistance, Fonds thématique 111B, Niebergall to General Joinville, 24 Nov. 1944

63 Josie McLellan, *Antifascism and memory in East Germany: remembering the International Brigades, 1945–1989* (Oxford, Clarendon Press, 2004), pp. 46–8

64 Louis Gronowski, *Le Dernier Grand Soir*, pp. 200–6

65 Gavin Bowd, 'Romanians in the French Resistance', *French History* (2014) 28 (4): pp. 541–59

66 Artur London, *The Confession* (New York, Morrow, 1970); French version, *L'Aveu* (Paris, Gallimard, 1972)

67 Josie McLellan, *Antifascism and memory in East Germany*, pp. 57–64

68 Louis Gronowski, *Le Dernier Grand Soir*, pp. 263–75, 289

69 Musée de la Résistance, Fonds de l'Amicale des Anciens FTP-MOI du Bataillon Carmagnole-Liberté.2, notes on interview with Jeannine Krakus, Paris, 2 Oct. 1986

70 Jean-Yves Boursier, *La Guerre des partisans dans le Sud-Ouest de la France, 1942–1944. La 35e Brigade FTP-MOI* (Paris, L'Harmattan, 1992), p. 146

71 Memorial de la Shoah, Fonds Anny Latour, DLXI-77, interview with Abraham Polonski, n.d., pp. 10–13

72 Jacques Lazarus, *Juifs au combat*, pp. 112–3, 149

73 Guillaume Piketty, *La Bataille des Ardennes. 16 décembre 1944–31 janvier 1945* (Paris, Tallandier, 2013)

74 Teresa Torrès, *Une Française Libre*, p. 311

75 Mémorial de Caen, Fonds Colonel Rémy, 106. Jean Bertin, 'Noël 1944'

76 NA HS9/1238/1 Rechenmann file

77 NA HS9/1395/3, press cutting n.d. but Apr.–May 1945

78 AN 580 25/3. Fonds Christian Pineau. Robert Shepard, 'Le general Charles Delestraint. La dernière Étape', n.d., pp. 8–9

79 450 AP 2, Lecompte-Boinet, Journal, 1945. 27 Apr. 1945, p. 133

80 CHRD Lyon, interview with Paulette Sarcey, 22 Feb. 2000

81 CHRD, interview with Roger Trugnan, 23 Feb. 2000

82 CHRD, interview with Maurice Lubczanski, 12 Feb. 1999

83 AN Z/6/597/5014, Germain Tillion deposition 31 May 1946; Julien Blanc, *Au commencement de la Résistance*, pp. 394–8

84 AN 72AJ67/I, OCM. Maxime Blocq-Mascart to Min. Interior, 30 Jan. 1945

85 AN Z6NL475, Roland Farjon. Testimony of André Velut, 14 Jul. 1945; Fernand Lhermitte, 13 Jul. 1945; Georges Foudrinoy, 14 Jul. 1945; Madeleine Baumel, n.d.; report of commissaire Descroisettes, 5 Nov. 1945

86 AN 72 AJ 67II. OCM. Affaire Farjon. Pencil letter stamped 22 Jul. 1945 by commissaire de police, forwarded by Min. Justice to Blocq-Mascart, 10 Oct. 1945

87 NA HS9/1406/8, note of Captain Starr's interrogation, 13 Jun. 1945

88 NA HS9/1407/1, report by Miss A.M. Walters, 18 Sept. 1944, p. 3

89 NA H9/982/4, Buckmaster to Mr Walters, 27 Jan. 1945

90 Anne-Marie Walters, *Moondrop to Gascony* (London, Macmillan, 1946)

91 CHRD, interview with Jeannette Lubczanski, 12 Feb. 1999

92 See above, p. 70

93 AN 6AV639, interview with Hélène Viannay, conducted by Olivier Wieviorka, 6 May 1987

94 Damira Titonel Asperti, *Écrire pour les autres*, pp. 64–71

95 AN 72AJ50/III., testimony of Geneviève de Gaulle, 11 Jan. 1957; AN 6 AV 521, interview with Geneviève de Gaulle, conducted by Olivier Wieviorka, 12 Dec. 1986

96 Geneviève de Gaulle Anthonioz, *La Traversée de la Nuit* (Paris, Seuil, 1998), translated as *God Remained Outside. An Echo of Ravensbrück* (London, Souvenir Press, 1998)

97 AN 72AJ50/II, testimony of the Girard family collected by Mlle Merlat, Feb. 1946. See above, pp. 168–9, 407

98 Anise Postel-Vinay, 'Les exterminations par gaz à Ravensbrück, in Germaine Tillion, *Ravensbrück* (1973), appendix 1, pp. 305–30; Eugen Kogon, Hermann Langbehn, Adalbert Rückert, *Nazi Mass Murder. A Documentary History of the Use of Poison Gas* (New Haven and London, Yale UP, 1993), pp. 50–1, 186–90; Anise Postel-Vinay and Jacques Prévotat, 'La Déportation', in J-P Azéma and François Bédarida (eds.), *La France des années noires* (Seuil, 1993), II, pp. 429–61

99 NA HS9 701/1, Susan Heslop to Air Ministry, 14 Sept. 1946

100 NA HS9 356, Pearl Cornioley to Vera Atkins, Air Ministry, 20 Oct. 1945

101 CHRD Lyon, interview with Denise Domenach-Lallich, 6 Feb. 1996; *Demain il fera beau*, pp. 39–42

102 Madeleine Riffaud, *On l'appelait Rainer*, pp. 153–8, 193–7. *Les Carnets de Charles Debarge*, ed. Madeleine Riffaud. Préface by Charles Tillon (Paris, Éditions sociales, 1951)

103 AN 6AV527, interview with Genia Gemähling, conducted by Olivier Wieviorka, Nov. 1985

Conclusion

1 See above, pp. 408–12, 418–22

2 See above, pp. 2–4

3 Général Henri Giraud, *Un Seul but, la victoire. Alger, 1942–1944* (Paris, Julliard, 1949), p. 282

4 On the statistics see Stéphane Courtois and Marc Lazar, *Histoire du Parti communiste français* (2nd edn., Paris, PUF, 2000), pp. 230, 248

5 Gerard Namer, *La Commémoration en France, 1944–1982* (Paris, S.P.A.G./Papyrus, 1983), p. 121; interview with Cécile Rol-Tanguy conducted by RG, Paris, 20 Jun. 2012

6 Olivier Wieviorka, *La Mémoire désunie*, pp. 99–102

7 AN 72AJ87/I. Vercors, F. Grenier, 'Le Vercors les accable', *Les Lettres Françaises*, 13 Nov. 1947; Philippe Barrière, *Histoire et Mémoires de la Seconde Guerre mondiale. Grenoble et ses après-guerre, 1944–1964* (PU Grenoble, 2004), pp. 430–1

8 Abbé Desgranges, *Les crimes masqués du 'Résistantialisme'* (Paris, L'Élan, 1948), pp. 9–16, 69–74

9 Rémy, 'La Justice et l'opprobre', *Carrefour* 11 Apr. 1950

10 Jean Cassou, *La Mémoire courte* (1953) (Paris, Mille et une nuits, 2001), p. 51

11 AD Seine Saint-Denis, 261 J 6/5, Affaire Tillon, rapport du Bureau politique présenté au Comité Central, 3–4 Sept. 1952, par le camarde Léon Mauvais; Sciences-Po, Centre d'Histoire, Fonds Tillon CT35, declaration of Tillon to bureau politique, 3 Sept & 14 Oct. 1952; *L'Humanité*, 4 Oct. 1952; *Candide*, 24 May 1962

12 Charles Tillon, *Un 'Procès de Moscou' à Paris* (Paris, Seuil, 1971)

13 *La Conférence Africaine Française, Brazzaville* (30 janvier 1944–8 février 1944) (Algiers, Commissariat aux Colonies, 1944), p. 27

14 Raphaëlle Branche, *La torture et l'armée pendant la guerre d'Algérie, 1954–1962* (Gallimard, 2001)

15 See above, p. 349

16 Jacques Pâris de Bollardière, *Bataille d'Alger, bataille de l'homme* (Paris & Bruges, Desclée De Brouwer, 1972), pp. 84, 98

17 Massu, *La Vraie bataille d'Alger* (Paris, Plon, 1971), p. 225

18 Jean Toulat, *Combattants de la Non-Violence. De Lanza del Vasto au Général de Bollardière* (Paris, Cerf, 1983), pp. 201–12

19 Germaine Tillion, *Les Ennemis Complémentaires* (Éditions de minuit, 1960), pp. 151–2

20 Jacques Soustelle, *L'Espérance trahie* (Paris, Éditions de l'Alma, 1962), pp. 8, 218

21 *OAS parle* (Paris, Julliard, 1964), p. 275. See also Bidault, *D'une Résistance à l'autre* (Paris, Les Presses du siècle), pp. 248, 283

22 André Malraux, 'Transfert des Cendres de Jean Moulin au Panthéon. Discours prononcé à Paris le 19 décembre 1964', in *La Politique, la Culture. Discours, articles, entretiens* (Paris, Gallimard, 1996), p. 297

23 Rousso, *The Vichy Syndrome. History and Memory in France since 1944* (Cambridge, CUP, 1991), pp. 16–18, 303

24 Rousso, *The Vichy Syndrome*, pp. 114–5

25 See above, pp. 5–6

26 Henri Frenay, *La Nuit Finira* (Paris, Robert Laffont, 1973); *L'Énigme Jean Moulin* (Paris, Robert Laffont, 1977)

27 AN 72AJ233/II, Francis Closon to Henri Frenay, 13 Oct. 1974; AN 72 AJ 2217, interview of Christian Pineau with Gilberte Brossolette, 1973

28 BN Inathèque. Les dossiers de Écran, 11 Oct. 1977. 'Jean Moulin, 17 juin 1940–21 juin 1943'.

29 Daniel Cordier, *Jean Moulin. L'Inconnu du Panthéon* I (Paris, J.-C Lattès, 1989), p. 279

30 Musée de la Résistance, 129. Témoignages VIII. Georges Marrane, 'Le Comité parisien de la Libération' (1969), p. 4

31 AN 72AJ693, *Notre Musée* 34 (Apr.–May 1969), p. 1–2

32 André Tollet, *La Classe ouvrière dans la Résistance* (Paris, Éditions sociales, 1969)

33 André Tollet, *Ma Traversé du Siècle. Mémoires d'un syndicaliste révolutionnaire* (Montreuil, VO Éditions 2002), pp. 97–9

34 Robert Gildea, James Mark and Niek Pas, 'European Radicals and the 'Third World': Imagined Solidarities and Radical Networks, 1958–1973', *Cultural and Social History* 8:4 (2011), pp. 449–72; Robert Gildea, James Mark and Annette Warring (eds.) *Europe's 1968. Voices of Revolt* (Oxford, OUP, 2013), pp. 88–103

35 Interview with Tiennot Grumbach, conducted by RG, Paris, 18 Apr. 2008

36 Pierre Goldman, *Souvenirs obscurs d'un Juif polonais né en France* (Paris, 1975), p. 33. Alésia was the site of a great battle between the Gauls and Julius Caesar; Louis IX or Saint-Louis was a great crusading king of France

37 *Le Nouvel Observateur*, 29 Jun. 1970; *Le Monde*, 21 & 24 Jul. 1970,

38 AD Seine Saint-Denis, 261 J6/5. Boîte I, Dossier 6, PCF bureau federal, Aix-en-Provence, to Comité central, 18 Jul. 1970; *L'Humanité*, 18 Jul. 1970

39 Sciences Po, Centre d'Histoire, Fonds Tillon, CT 31, Denis Le Dantec to Tillon, 28 Sept. 1970 and draft reply n.d.

40 Sciences Po, Centre d'Histoire, Fonds Tillon, CT 100, interview with Jean-Michel and Alain Krivine for *Rouge*, Oct. 1977; Charles Tillon, *On chantait rouge* (Paris, R. Laffont, 1977), p. 40. Sciences Po, Centre d'Histoire, Fonds Tillon, CT 100/2, interview with *Histoire-Magazine*, 9 Oct. 1980

41 Interview with Jean-Pierre Le Dantec, recorded by RG, Paris, 24 May 2007

42 Roger Pannequin, *Ami si tu tombes* (Paris, Babel, 2000) pp. 11–13

43 Annette Wieviorka, *Déportation et genocide: entre la mémoire et l'oubli* (Paris, Plon, 1992), pp. 136–9

44 Gaston Laroche, *On les nommait les Étrangers. Les Immigrés dans la Résistance* (Paris, Éditeurs Français Réunis, 1965), p. 16

45 AD Haute Garonne 16J 47, Lopez Tovar note on the Amicale des Anciens Guerrilleros Espagnols and Bermejo, 5 May 1975

46 Barcellini and Wieviorka, *Passant, souviens-toi. Les lieux du souvenir de la Seconde Guerre mondiale en France* (Paris, Plon, 1995), p. 279

47 *La Colonne du Capitaine Dronne. Les hommes de la Nueve entrent dans Paris le 24 août 1944* (Paris, IME, 2005)

48 Musée de la Résistance. Fonds Ouzoulias. Carton 21. Dossier 5. Résistance allemande. Speech of Ouzoulias, Berlin, 7 Sept. 1964

49 Musée de la Résistance, Liquidation OS-FN-FTP. Allemagne, Michel Lissansky to Rouquet, 14 & 15 Aug. 1984; Musée de la Résistance. Les inconnus de la Résistance, p. 170. Michel Lissansky, 15 Aug. 1984; Gerhard Leo, *Un*

Allemand dans la Résistance (1997), pp. 260, 287

50 David Knout, *Contribution à l'histoire de la Résistance juive en France 1940–1944* (Paris, Éditions du Centre, 1947); Jacques Lazarus, *Juifs au combat: témoignage sur l'activité d'un mouvement de résistance* (Paris, Éditions du Centre 1947)

51 Eric Conan and Henry Rousso, *Vichy, un passé qui ne passé pas* (Paris, Fayard, 1994), pp. 13, 269–73

52 Claude Lévy and Paul Tillard, *La Grande Rafle du Vel d'Hiv (16 juillet 1942)* (Paris, Robert Laffont, 1967), avant-propos

53 Anny Latour, *La Résistance juive en France, 1940–1944* (Paris, Stock, 1970), p. 11

54 David Diamant, *Les Juifs dans la Résistance française, 1940–1944. Avec armes et sans armes* (Paris, Le Pavillon, 1971)

55 AD Seine Saint-Denis 335 J7, symposium du 23 novembre 1974

56 Annette Wieviorka, *Ils étaient juifs, résistants, communistes* (Paris, Denoël, 1986)

57 SHD Vincennes, IKS 60 Urman, 35e Brigade, *Carmagnole-Liberté, Francs-Tireurs et Partisans de la Main d'Oeuvre Immigrée* (1982); interview with Léon Landini, conducted by RG, Bagneux, 20 Apr. 2012

58 SHD Vincennes, 19P 31/24, *35e Brigade Marcel Langer et 3402e Compagnie FTPF* (Toulouse, 1983), n.p.

59 Memorial de la Shoah, Fonds Claude Urman. Commemorations 4.3, *La Dépêche du Midi*, 18 Aug. 1984; see below, p. 469

60 AD Haute Garonne 16J272, cuttings from *La Dépêche de Toulouse*, 18 Jul. 1985, and *Le Journal de Toulouse*, 22 Jul. 1985

61 Rolande Trempé, 'Le Rôle des Étrangers MOI et guerrilleros', in Trempé (ed.), *La Libération dans le Midi de la France* (Toulouse, Éché, 1986), pp. 63–78

62 Karel Bartosek, René Gallissot, Denis Peschanski (eds.), *De l'exil à la Résistance: réfugiés et immigrés d'Europe centrale en France: 1933–1945* (Paris, Presses universitaires de Vincennes/ Arcantère, 1989); Stéphane Courtois, Denis Peschanski and Adam Rayski, *Le Sang de l'étranger: les immigrés de la MOI dans la Résistance* (Paris, Fayard, 1989)

63 Philippe Joutard and François Marcot (eds.), *Les étrangers dans la Résistance en France* (Besançon, Université de Franche-Comté, 1992); Jean-Marie Guillon et Pierre Laborie (eds.), *Mémoire et histoire, la Résistance* (Toulouse, Privat, 1995)

64 Christine Levisse-Touzé et Stefan Maertens (eds.), Des Allemands contre le nazisme: oppositions et résistances, 1933–1945 (Paris, Albin Michel, 1997)

65 *Des Terroristes à la Retraite/Les dossiers de l'Écran*, 2 Jul. 1985

66 *L'Histoire*, 81 (Sept. 1985), interview with Adam Rayski, p. 98; Boris Holban, *Testament* (1989)

67 Serge Klarsfeld, *Le Mémorial de la déportation des juifs de France* (Paris, the author, 1978)

68 Serge Klarsfeld, *Vichy-Auschwitz: le rôle de Vichy dans la solution finale de la question juive en France, 1943–1944* (Paris, Fayard, 1983)

69 AN BB 30/1892 *Procès Klaus Barbie, 25e audience, 17 June 1987*, pp. 5–6

70 *Procès Klaus Barbie, 25e audience, 17 June 1987*, p. 19

71 AN BB30/1893, *Procès Klaus Barbie, 37e audience, 3 July 1987*, A 50.

72 AN BB30/1892, *Procès Klaus Barbie, 23e audience, 15 June 1987*, pp. 36–8

73 AN BB30/1891, *Procès Klaus Barbie, 10e audience, 22 May 1987*, pp. 12–24

74 AN 6AV619/1, interview with Robert Salmon conducted by Olivier Wieviorka, 23 Dec. 1985

75 6 AV 521, interview with Hélène Viannay conducted by Olivier Wieviorka, 12 Dec. 1986

76 Sabine Zeitoun, *Ces Enfants qu'il fallait sauver* (Paris, France Loisirs, 1990) and *L'Oeuvre de Secours aux Enfants* (Paris, L'Harmattan, 1990)

77 Sabine Zeitoun, 'Mémoire. Des Outils pour la transmission au CHRD de Lyon', *Cahiers d'histoire* 39 (1994), p. 318

78 AD Seine Saint-Denis 274 J3, Fonds Andrée Ponty, decision by secrétaire d'État aux Anciens combatants, 21 Apr. 1975

79 Musée de la Résistance. Liquidation OS-FN-FTP. Pologne, Julia Pirotte, application of 12 Sept. 1971; letter to Gaston Beau, 5 May 1978

80 Sandra Fayolle, 'Danielle Casanova et les enjeux de mémoire' in Gilzmer, Levisse-Touzé and Maertens, *Les Femmes dans la Résistance française* (Paris, Tallandier, 2003), pp. 357–9

81 Memorial de la Shoah, Fonds Urman 4.8, *Sud Ouest. Lot-et-Garonne*, 27 Feb. & 2 Mar. 1987

82 Letter of Antonin Cubizolles, Paris (1984), in Floriane Benoit et Charles Silvestre (eds.), *Les inconnus de la Résistance* (Paris, L'Humanité/Editions Messidor, 1984), pp. 10, 19–20.

83 SHD Vincennes 16P 445423, dossier of Colette/Ginette Nirouet

84 *Les Dossiers de l'Écran*, 11 Oct. 1977

85 Lucie Aubrac, 'Présence des femmes dans toutes les activités de la Résistance', in *Actes du Colloque Les Femmes dans la Résistance, tenu à l'initiative de l'Union des femmes Françaises* (Paris, Editions du Rocher, 1977), pp. 19–21

86 Lucie Aubrac, *Ils partiront dans l'ivresse* (Paris, Seuil, 1984)

87 AN 6AV520, interview with Olivier Wieviorka, 12 Dec. 1986

88 Guylaine Guidez, *Femmes dans la Guerre 4. Femmes résistantes ou le temps du courage*. 18 Aug. 1989

89 Lucie Aubrac, *Cette exigeante liberté. Entretiens avec Corinne Bouchoux* (Paris, L'Archipel, 1997), pp. 115, 127

90 BN Inathèque, *Soeurs en résistance*. France 2. 25 Oct. 2002

91 Guy Krivopissko, Christine Levisse-Touzé and Vladimir Trouplin, *Dans l'Honneur et par la Victoire: les femmes Compagnons de la Libération* (Paris, Tallandier, 2008), p. 77

92 Gérard Chauvy, *Aubrac. Lyon 1944* (Paris, Albin Michel, 1997)

93 An account of the processings was published in *Libération*, 9 Jul. 1997. See also Pierre Péan, *Vie et morts de Jean Moulin* (Fayard, 1998), pp. 659–60; Laurent Douzou, *La Résistance française: une histoire périlleuse* (Paris, Seuil, 2005), pp. 262–72; Olivier Wieviorka, *La Mémoire désunie*, pp. 248–51

94 Laurent Douzou, *Lucie Aubrac* (Paris, Perrin, 2009)

95 Sarah Gensburger, *Les Justes de France. Politiques publiques de mémoire* (Paris, Presses de la FNSP, 2010), pp. 53–7

96 Sarah Gensburger, *Les Justes de France*, p. 66

97 François Boulet, 'Mémoires et histoire de la montagne-Refuge du Chambon-sur-Lignon, 1940–1944–1994', *Cahiers d'Histoire* 39 (1994), pp. 299–316;

Marianne Ruel Robins, 'A Grey Site of Memory: Le Chambon-sur-Lignon and Protestant Exceptionalism on the Plateau Vivarais-Lignon', *Church History* 82 (2013), pp. 317–52; Caroline Moorehead, *Village of Secrets* (London, *The Spectator*, 2014)

98 Magda Trocmé, Madeleine Barot, Pierre Fayol & Oscar Rosowsky, 'Le mythe de commandant SS protecteur des juifs', *Le Monde juif no.* 130 (Apr.–Jun. 1988), pp. 61–6

99 http://www.crif.org/fr/lecrifenaction/Allocution-de-Jacques-Chirac-au-Chambon-sur-Lignon-le-8-juillet-20043301

100 Inathèque, Hommage de la nation aux Justes de France, FR2, 18 Jan. 2007

101 Jacques Sémelin, *Persécutions et Entraides dans la France occupée. Comment 75% des Juifs en France ont échappé à la mort* (Paris, les Arènes-Seuil, 2013), p. 797

102 For criticisms see Robert Paxton, 'Vichy made it worse', *New York Review of Books*, 6 Mar. 2004; Renée Poznanski, intervention at workshop on 'the Rescue of Jews in Western Europe during the Holocaust', Queen Mary University of London, 7 Jul. 2014

103 http://collections.ushmm.org/search/catalog/irn501789

104 Max Weinstein, *Souvenirs, souvenirs* (Nice, Editions du Losange, 1997)

105 http://ujre.pagesperso-orange.fr/PDF/MRJ-MOI_STATUTS.pdf

106 http://www.mrj-moi.com; interview with Max Weinstein, conducted by RG, Paris, 24 Apr. 2012

107 Centre d'histoire, Sciences-Po, Fonds Charles Tillon CT101, communiqué, 12 Jan. 1984

108 Interview with Cécile Rol-Tanguy, conducted by RG, Paris, 20 Jun. 2012

109 *Résistance et Libération. Actes du Colloque des 25 mai 1994 et 17 mai 1995* (Paris, Académie de Paris, 1995), p. 23

110 Eric Jennings, *La France libre fut africaine*, p. 274

111 Léonard Sah, 'Le Cameroun sous mandat français dans la Deuxième Guerre mondiale' (University of Provence thesis, 1998), p. 304, cited by Jennings, *La France libre fut africaine*, p. 131

112 http://rue89.nouvelobs.com/2014/02/21/cameroun-tete-general-le-clerc-rouvre-les-plaies-decolonisation-250151

113 https://www.youtube.com/watch?v=FCfLWaJt_ek

114 Interview with Léon Landini, conducted by RG, Bagneux, 20 Apr. 2012

115 http://lfhm2014.com/

Bibliography

Primary

a) Archives
(i) Archives départementales de la Haute-Garonne, Toulouse
  16J Fonds Daniel Latapie
    29, 179–84 Guerrilleros espagnols
    36, 263 Serge Ravanel
    58 Wheelwright circuit
    139 Val d'Aran invasion
    14, 145 Comité Allemagne libre
    190–210, 272, 275, 300 archives of 35th Marcel Langer Brigade
    222 Vicente Lopez Tovar, autobiography
    271 Corps Franc Pommiès
    465 Colonel Schneider, 'La colonne légère de Toulouse'

  5795W574 Police dossier on assassination of magistrate Lespinasse, 1943

(ii) Archives départementales de la Seine Saint-Denis
  Archives of the French Communist Party
    229 J Fonds Fernand Grenier
    261 J6 Tillon Affair, 1952
    274 J3 Fonds Andrée Ponty
    307 J 154 Archives de Gaston Plissonnier: PCF delegations in London and Algiers, 1943–4
    314 J7 Fonds Waldeck Rochet
    335 J Fonds David Diamant

(iii) Archives municipales, Ivry
  Fonds Georges Marrane

(iv) Archives Nationales, Paris
  72 AJ Comité d'histoire de la Deuxième Guerre mondiale
    35–89 Metropolitan resistance: movements, networks, political parties, trade unions
    90–209 Metropolitan resistance by departments
    210–19 Resistance and events in the French Empire
    220–48 Resistance outside France and central organizations of the Resistance
    Private archives collected by the Committee, including

408–10 Emmanuel d'Astier de la Vigerie
428–30 General Catroux
435–60 General Cochet
518–19 Jean Gemähling
521–4 Henry Ingrand
543–44 Paule Letty-Mouroux (Franco-Polish F2 network)
586–7 Georges Szekeres (Comité d'action et de défesne des immigrés)
588 Comité Allemagne Libre pour l'Ouest (CALPO)
624–6 Alban Vistel
627 Philippe de Vomécourt
1899–1900 Marcelle Appleton
1923 Jacques Soustelle
2026–7 Henri Frenay
2215–18 Pierre et Gilberte Brossolette

450 AP 1–3 Fonds Lecompte-Boinet
580 AP 25–6, Fonds Christian Pineau

BB30 1891–3 Trial of Klaus Barbie before Assize Court of Lyon,
11 May–3 July 1987

Z6 Cour de justice of Seine department

597/5024 Robert Alesch
NL 475 Roland Farjon

(v) BBC Written Archives, Caversham, French Service
Anonymous letters from France 1940–3
Interviews with civilian escapers, 1941–4

(vi) Bibliothèque de Documentation Internationale Contemporaine (BDIC),
Nanterre
BDIC FΔ 2149, Archives of CIMADE

(vi) Bibliothèque Nationale, Paris, Inathèque
Les dossiers de Écran, 11 Oct. 1977, 'Jean Moulin'
Les dossiers de Écran, 2 July 1985, 'Des Terroristes à la retraite'
Soeurs en résistance. France 2, 25 Oct. 2002
Hommage de la nation aux Justes de France, FR2, 18 Jan. 2007

(vii) Bibliothèque de la Société de l'histoire du protestantisme français, Paris
DT BAR. Archives of Madeleine Barot
DT TRO André Trocmé, Journal [1960]

(viii) Centre de documentation juive contemporaine, Mémorial de la Shoah, Paris
CMXCIV Fonds Abadi
DCLXXXIII, Fonds Gilbert Lesage

DLXI, Fonds Anny Latour
MDXVIII, Fonds Bulawko
Fonds Claude Urman

(ix) Centre d'Histoire de Sciences-Po, Paris
PA 7, 10–11 Fonds Alexandre Parodi
CT3, 31, 100 Fonds Charles Tillon
Témoignages sur la Guerre d'Algérie, collected by Odile Rudelle

(x) Mémorial de Caen
Fonds Colonel Rémy
TE 693, Jacques Filardier, 'Peur ne connais pas'

(xi) Musée de l'Ordre de la Libération, Paris
Fichier Bingen

(xii) Musée de la Résistance Nationale, Champigny-sur-Marne
Cartons 124–131 Têmoignages
Fonds du Bataillon FTP-MOI Carmagnole-Liberté
Fonds David Diamant
Fonds Monique Georges
Fonds Legendre
Fonds Guy Môquet
Fonds Ouzoulias
Fonds Suberville
Fonds Roussel
Fonds André Tollet
Fonds Pierre Villon
Fonds thématique 111B
Liquidation OS-FN-FTP

(xiii) Musée du Général Leclerc de Hautecloque et de la Libération de Paris-Musée Jean Moulin
Fonds Teresa Torrès

(xiv) National Archives, Kew
HS9, files of SOE agents
H57/129 Participation of FFI in the liberation of France
FO 1049/9 Val d'Aran affair

(xv) Service historique de la Défense, Vincennes
IK 560 Urman papers, 35th Marcel Langer Brigade
16P files of individual soldiers
19P 31/24 35th Marcel Langer Brigade

(xvi) Vere Harmsworth Library, Oxford
Stimson Papers

Bibliography

b) Recorded Interviews
(i) Archives Nationales, Paris

a) *Interviews conducted by Olivier Wieviorka*:
6AV 520–1 Geneviève de Gaulle, 12 Dec. 1986, 11 Feb. 1995
6AV 526–7, Genia Gemähling, Nov. 1985
6AV 591 Jacqueline Pardon, 21 Jan. 1987
6 AV 619–30 Robert Salmon, 23 Dec. 1985–20 Jun. 1986
6 AV 637–9 Hélène Viannay, 15 Sept. 1986, 6 May 1987
13 AV 67–8 Claude Bourdet, 9 Jan. 1987
13 AV 75 André Dewavrin, Colonel Passy, 7 Jun. 1990, 7 Apr. 1991
13 AV 78 Pierre Hervé, 20 Dec. 1990

b) *Interviews conducted by Laurent Douzou*:
13 AV 89 Lucie Aubrac, 14 Mar. 1984
13 AV 93 Raymond Aubrac 21 Mar. 1984
13 AV 96 Georges Canguilhem 6 Feb. 1985
13 AV 105, Jean-Pierre Vernant, 10 Jan. 1985
13 AV 135 Serge Ravanel, 26 Feb. 1991
These have been complemented by transcripts of these interviews and others in
  Laurent Douzou's archive

Other interviews:
13 AV 41–59 Serge Ravanel, 2 Apr. 1991–26 Feb. 1992
13 AV 60 Germaine Tillion, 13 Mar. 1990
13 AV 61–3 José Aboulker, 16 Mar. 1990
16 AV 66 Roger Pannequin, n.d.

(ii) Imperial War Museum, London
  8270 Interview with Harry Rée, 18 Jan. 1995

(iii) Centre d'Histoire de la Résistance et de la Déportation, Lyon
  239 Denise Domenach-Lallich, 6 Feb. 1996
  309 Lucie Aubrac, 26 Sept.1996
  318 Jean-Marie Domenach, 16 Apr. 1997
  327 Francis Chapouchnik, 11 Jun. 1997
  342 Micheline Altman, 16 Jul. 1997
  421 Jeanette Lubczanski, 12 Feb. 1999
  422 Maurice Lubczanski, 12 Feb. 1999
  438–9 Maurice Najman, 13 Apr. 1999
  520 Berthe Weinstein, née Zarnowieck, 21 Feb. 2000
  524 Paulette Sarcey, 22 Feb. 2000
  527 Roger Trugnan, 23 Feb. 2000
  577 Henri Krischer, 6 Jul. 2000

(iv) Bibliothèque Nationale, Paris, Inathèque
  Oscar Rosowsky, 5 Jun. 2006
(v) Interviews conducted by the author
  Christian de Mondragon, Nantes, 29 Apr. 1997
  Jean-Pierre Le Dantec, Paris, 24 May 2007
  Tiennot Grumbach, Paris, 18 Apr. 2008
  Denise Guillaume, Suberville, 14 Apr. 2012
  Madeleine Riffaud, Paris, 15 Apr. 2012
  Léon Landini, Bagneux, 20 Apr. 2012
  Max Weinstein, Paris, 24 Apr. 2012
  Bernard Zouckerman, Paris, 26 Apr. 2012
  Felicie Weinstein, Sevran, 16 May 2012
  Cécile Rol-Tanguy, Paris, 20 Jun. 2012

Secondary

Abitbol, Michel, *The Jews of North Africa During the Second World War* (Detroit, Wayne State UP, 1989).

Aboulker, José, *La Victoire du 8 novembre 1942. La Résistance et le débarquement des Alliés à Alger* (Paris, Editions du Félin, 2012).

Aglan, Alya, 'La Résistance', in Alya Aglan and Jean-Pierre Azéma, *Jean Cavaillès, résistant, ou la pensée en actes* (Paris, Flammarion, 2002).

———, *La Résistance sacrifiée. Le mouvement Libération-Nord* (Paris, Flammarion, 1999).

Alary, Éric, *La Ligne de démarcation, 1940–1944* (Paris, Perrin, 2003, 2010).

Albertelli, Sébastien, *Les Services Secrets du Général de Gaulle. Le BCRA, 1940–1944* (Paris, Perrin, 2009).

——— and Johanna Barasz, 'Un résistant atypique. Le général Cochet, entre vichysme et gaullisme', *Histoire et Politique*, 5 (May–June 2008).

Alexander, Martin S., 'Dunkirk in Military Operations, Myths and Memories', in Robert Tombs and Emile Chabal (eds.), *Britain and France in Two World Wars* (London, Bloomsbury, 2013), pp. 93–118.

André, Philippe, *La Résistance confisquée? Les Délégués militaires du Général de Gaulle à la Libération* (Paris, Perrin, 2013).

Andrieu, Claire, 'Women in the French Resistance: Revisiting the Historical Record', *French Politics, Culture and Society*, 18/1 (Spring 2000), pp. 13–27.

Ansky, Michel, *Les Juifs d'Algérie. Du décret Crémieux à la Libération* (Paris, Éditions du Centre, 1950).

Aouate, Yves-Claude, 'Des patriotes oubliés', in RHICOJ, *Les Juifs dans la Résistance et la Libération* (Paris, Editions du Scribe, 1985)

Ashdown, Paddy, *The Cruel Victory: the French Resistance, D-Day and the Battle for the Vercors, 1944* (London, HarperCollins, 2014).

Atkin, Nicholas, *The Forgotten French: Exiles in the British Isles, 1940–44* (Manchester, Manchester UP, 2003).

———, 'France in Exile: the French community in Britain, 1940–1944', in Martin Conway and José Gotovich (eds.), *Europe in Exile: European Exiles in Britain, 1940–1945* (Oxford, Berghahn, 2001).

Bibliography

Aubrac, Lucie, *Cette exigeante liberté. Entretiens avec Corinne Bouchoux* (Paris, L'Archipel, 1997).

____, *Ils partiront dans l'ivresse* (Paris, Seuil, 1984).

____, 'Présence des femmes dans toutes les activités de la Résistance', in *Actes du Colloque Les Femmes dans la Résistance, tenu à l'initative de l'Union des femmes Françaises* (Paris, Editions du Rocher, 1977), pp. 19–21.

Aubrac, Raymond, *Où la Mémoire s'attarde* (Paris, Odile Jacob, 1996).

Azéma, Jean-Pierre, *Jean Moulin. Le politique, le rebelle, le résistant* (Paris, Perrin, 2003).

Barbier, Claude, *Le Maquis des Glières. Mythe et réalité* (Paris, Perrin, 2014).

Barcellini, Serge and Wieviorka, Annette, *Passant, souviens-toi. Les lieux du souvenir de la Seconde Guerre mondiale en France* (Paris, Plon, 1995).

Barr, James, *A Line in the Sand: Britain, France and the Struggle that Shaped the Middle East* (London, Simon & Schuster, 2011).

Barrett Litoff, Judy (ed.), *An American Heroine in the French Resistance: the Diary and Memoir of Virginia d'Albert-Lake* (New York, Fordham UP, 2006).

Barrière, Philippe, *Histoire et Mémoires de la Seconde Guerre mondiale. Grenoble et ses après-guerre, 1944–1964* (Grenoble, PU de Grenoble, 2004).

Bartosek, Karel, René Gallissot and Denis Peschanski (eds.), *De l'exil à la Résistance. Réfugiés et immigrés d'Europe centrale en France: 1933–1945* (Paris, PU de Vincennes/Arcantère, 1989).

Baumel, Jacques, *Résister. Histoire secrète des années d'occupation* (Paris, Livre de Poche, 2003).

Bédarida, François, 'L'Histoire de la Résistance. Lectures d'hier, chantiers de demain', *Vingtième siècle*, 11 (July–September 1986), pp. 75–89.

Bédarida, Renée, *Les Armes de l'Esprit. Témoignage Chrétien* (Paris, Editions Ouvrières, 1977).

____, *Pierre Chaillet, Témoin de la Résistance spirituelle* (Paris, Fayard, 1988).

Bell, David Scott, 'Politics in Marseille since World War II with Special Reference to the Political Role of Gaston Defferre' (D.Phil thesis, University of Oxford, 1978).

Belot, Robert and Gilbert Karpman, *L'Affaire Suisse. La Résistance a-t-elle trahi de Gaulle?* (Paris, A. Colin, 2009).

Benoit, Floriane and Charles Silvestre (eds.), *Les Inconnus de la Résistance* (Paris, L'Humanité/Editions Messidor, 1984).

Bernay, Sylvie, *L'Église de France face à la persécution des Juifs, 1940–1944* (Paris, CNRS, 2012).

Bertaux, Pierre, *La Libération de Toulouse et de sa région* (Paris, Hachette, 1973).

Béthouart, Antoine, *Cinq années d'espérance. Mémoires de guerre, 1939–1945* (Paris, Plon, 1968).

Bidault, Georges, *D'une Résistance à l'autre* (Paris, Les Presses du Siècle, 1965).

Billoux, François, *Quand nous étions ministres* (Paris, Éditions Sociales, 1972).

Blanc, Julien, *Au Commencement de la Résistance. Du côté du Musée de l'Homme, 1940–1941* (Paris, Seuil, 2010).

Blocq-Mascart, Maxime, *Chronique de la Résistance* (Paris, Corréa, 1945).

Boegner, Philippe (ed.), *Carnets du Pasteur Boegner, 1940–1945* (Paris, Fayard, 1992).

Bohec, Jeanne, *La Plastiqueuse à bicyclette* (Paris, Mercure de France, 1975).

Bollardière, Jacques de, *Bataille d'Alger, bataille de l'homme* (Paris and Bruges, Desclée De Brouwer, 1972).

Bolle, Pierre (ed.), *Grenoble et le Vercors. De la Résistance à la Liberation* (Grenoble, PU de Grenoble, 2003).

Bonnery, Audrey, 'La France de la BBC, 1938–1944' (doctoral thesis, University of Burgundy, 2005).

Bonte, Florimond, *Les Antifascistes allemands dans la Résistance* (Paris, Éditions Sociales, 1969).

Boris, Georges, *Servir la France. Textes et témoignages* (Paris, Julliard, 1963).

Borras, José, *Histoire de Mauthausen. Les cinq années de deportation des républicains espagnols* (Choisy-en-Brie, La Bochetière, 1989).

La Bouche de Vérité? La recherche historique et les sources orales, Cahiers de l'IHTP, 21 (Nov. 1992).

Bouchinet-Serruelles, Claude, *Nous étions faits pour être libres. La Résistance avec De Gaulle et Jean Moulin* (Paris, Bernard Grasset, 2000).

Bougeard, Christian and Jacqueline Sainclivier (eds.), *La Résistance et les Français. Enjeux stratégiques et environnement social* (Rennes, PU de Rennes, 1995).

Boulet, François, 'Mémoires et histoire de la montagne-refuge du Chambon-sur-Lignon, 1940–1944–1994', *Cahiers d'Histoire*, 39 (1994), pp. 299–316.

Bourbault, Guy, Benoît Gauchard and Jean-Marie Muller, *Jacques de Bollardière, Compagnon de toutes les libérations* (Montargis, Non-Violence-Actualité, 1986).

Bourderon, Roger, *Rol-Tanguy* (Paris, Tallandier, 2004).

Bourdet, Claude, *L'Aventure incertaine* (Paris, Stock, 1975).

Boursier, Jean-Yves, *La Guerre des partisans dans le sud-est de la France, 1942–1944. La 35e Brigade FTP-MOI* (Paris, l'Harmattan, 1992).

Bowd, Gavin, 'Romanians in the French Resistance', *French History*, 28/4, pp. 541–59.

Bradley, Omar N., *A Soldier's Story* (New York, Henry Holt, 1951).

Branche, Raphaëlle, *La Torture et l'armée pendant la guerre d'Algérie, 1954–1962* (Paris, Gallimard, 2001).

Brès, Eveline and Yvan, 'Des Allemands maquisards dans les Cévennes des Camisards', in Philippe Joutard, Jacques Poujol and Patrick Cabanel (eds.), *Cévennes, Terre de Refuge, 1940–1944* (Montpellier, Les Presses du Languedoc, 1987), pp. 91–7.

Broche, François and Jean-François Muracciole (eds.), *Dictionnaire de la France libre* (Paris, R. Laffont, 2010).

Brosset, Diego, *Carnets de guerre, correspondance et notes (1939–1944)*, in Guillaume Piketty (ed.), *Français en Résistance. Carnets de guerre, correspondances, journaux personnels* (Paris, R. Laffont, 2009), pp. 103–416.

Brossolette, Pierre, 'Lettres à son épouse (1939–1943)', in Guillaume Piketty (ed.), *Français en Résistance* (Paris, R. Laffont, 2009).

Brower, Daniel, *The New Jacobins: the French Communist Party and the Popular Front* (Ithaca, NY, Cornell UP, 1968).

Brunet de Sairigné, Gabriel, 'Carnets et lettres, 1940–45', in Guillaume Piketty (ed.), *Français en Résistance. Carnets de guerre, correspondances, journaux personnels* (Paris, R. Laffont, 2009).

Buckmaster, Maurice, *They Fought Alone: the Story of British Agents in France*

(London, Odhams Press, 1958).

Burrin, Philippe, *Hitler and the Jews* (London, Edward Arnold, 1994).

____, *Living with Defeat. France under the German Occupation, 1940–1944* (London, Arnold, 1996).

Buton, Philippe, *La Joie douloureuse. La Libération de la France* (Paris, Complexe, 2004).

Cabanel, Patrick, *Histoire des Justes en France* (Paris, Armand Colin, 2012).

Calmette, Arthur, *L'OCM. Organisation Civile et Militaire. Histoire d'un movement de résistance de 1940 à 1946* (Paris, PUF, 1961).

Cantier, Jacques, *L'Algérie sous le régime de Vichy* (Paris, Odile Jacob, 2002).

Carr, E. H., *The Comintern and the Spanish Civil War* (New York, Pantheon Books, 1984).

Carré, Mathilde, *I was 'the Cat'* (London, Souvenir Press, 1960).

Carrel, André, *Mes Humanités. Itinéraire d'un homme engagé* (Paris, L'Oeil d'Or, 2009).

Cassou, Jean, *La Mémoire courte* (Paris, Mille et Une Nuits, 2001 [1953]).

____, *Une Vie pour la liberté* (Paris, R. Laffont, 1981).

Catroux, Georges, *Deux actes du Drame indochinois. Hanoi: juin 1940. Dien Bien Phu: mars–mai 1954* (Paris, Plon, 1959).

Chambrun, Gilbert de, *Journal d'un militaire d'occasion* (Avignon, Aubanel, 1982).

Chambrun, René de (ed.), *France during the German Occupation, 1940–1944*, 3 vols. (Stanford, Hoover Institution, 1958).

Chauvy, Gérard, *Aubrac. Lyon 1944* (Paris, Albin Michel, 1997).

Churchill, Winston, *The Second World War*, 6 vols. (London, Cassell, 1948–54).

Clark, Mark, *Calculated Risk* (New York, Harper & Brothers, 1950).

Clayton, Anthony, *France, Soldiers and Africa* (London, Brassey's Defence Publishers, 1988).

Clément, Jean-Louis, *Les Evêques au temps de Vichy. Loyalisme sans inféodation. Les relations entre l'Église et l'État de 1940 à 1944* (Paris, Éditions Beauchesne, 1999).

____, *Mgr Solages, archevêque de Toulouse* (Paris, Editions Beauchesne, 1994).

Clifford, Rebecca, *Commemorating the Holocaust: Dilemmas of Remembrance in France and Italy* (Oxford, OUP, 2013).

Closon, Francis-Louis, *Commissaire de la République du Général de Gaulle* (Paris, Julliard, 1980).

____, *Le Temps des passions. De Jean Moulin à la Libération, 1943–1944* (Paris, Presses de la Cité, 1974).

Cohen, Asher, *Persécutions et sauvetages. Juifs et français sous l'Occupation et sous Vichy* (Paris, Cerf, 1993).

Cointet, Jean-Paul, *La Légion française des Combattants. La tentation du fascisme* (Paris, Albin Michel, 1995).

Cointet, Michèle, *Pétain et les Français, 1940–1951* (Paris, Perrin, 2002).

Collin, Claude, *Carmagnole et Liberté. Les Étrangers dans la Résistance en Rhône-Alpes* (Grenoble, PU de Grenoble, 2000).

____, 'L'attitude des résistants face aux « libérateurs » américains: un mélange d'admiration et de méfiance', *Annales de l'Est*, 44/2 (1992), pp. 119–28.

La Colonne du Capitaine Dronne. Les hommes de la Nueve entrent dans Paris le 24 août 1944 (Paris, IME, 2005).

Comor, André-Paul (ed.), *Les Carnets du lieutenant-colonel Brunet de Sairigné* (Paris, Nouvelles Editions Latines, 1990).

____, *L'Épopée de la 13e demi-Brigade de la Légion étrangère, 1940–1945* (Paris, Nouvelles Éditions Latines, 1988).

Comte, Bernard, *Une utopie combattante. L'École des cadres d'Uriage, 1940–1942* (Paris, Fayard, 1991).

____, Jean-Marie Domenach, Christian Rendu and Denise Rendu, *Gilbert Dru. Un Chrétien résistant* (Paris, Beauchesne, 1998).

Comte, Madeleine, 'L'abbé Glasberg au secours des Juifs', in Christian Sorrel (ed.), *Alexandre Glasberg, 1902–1981. Prêtre, Résistant, Militant*, series 'Chrétiens et Sociétés. Documents et Mémoires', 19 (Lyon, LARHRA-RESEA, 2013).

Conan, Eric and Henry Rousso, *Vichy, un passé qui ne passé pas* (Paris, Fayard, 1994).

La Conférence Africaine Française, Brazzaville (30 janvier 1944–8 février 1944) (Algiers, Commissariat aux Colonies, 1944).

Conway, Martin and José Gotovitch (eds.), *Europe in Exile: European Exile Communities in Britain 1940–45* (New York and Oxford, Berghahn, 2001).

Cordier, Daniel, *Alias Caracalla. Mémoires 1940–1943* (Paris, Gallimard, 2009).

____, *Jean Moulin, l'inconnu du Panthéon*, 3 vols. (Paris, Lattès, 1989–93).

____, *Jean Moulin. La République des catacombes* (Paris, Gallimard, 1999).

Courtois, Stéphane, *Le PCF dans la guerre. De Gaulle, la Résistance, Staline* (Paris, Ramsay, 1980).

____ and Marc Lazar, *Histoire du Parti Communiste Français* (2nd edn., Paris, PUF, 2000).

____, Denis Peschanski and Adam Rayski, *Le Sang de l'étranger. Les immigrés de la MOI dans la Résistance* (Paris, Fayard, 1989).

Crémieux-Brilhac, Jean-Louis, *Georges Boris. Trente ans d'influence. Blum, de Gaulle, Mendès France* (Paris, Gallimard, 2010).

____, *Les Français de l'An 40. I. La Guerre oui ou non* (Paris, Gallimard, 1990).

____, *La France libre. De l'appel du 18 juin à la Libération* (Paris, Gallimard, 1996).

____, 'La Bataille des Glières et la Guerre psychologique', *RHDGM*, 99 (1975), pp. 45–72.

____ (ed.), *Les Voix de la Liberté. Ici Londres, 1940–1944*, 5 vols. (Paris, La Documentation Française, 1975–6).

Crémieux, Francis, *Entretien avec Emmanuel d'Astier* (Paris, Pierre Belfond, 1966).

Cukier, Simon, Dominique Decèze, David Diamant and Michel Grojnowski, *Juifs révolutionnaires* (Paris, Messidor, 1987).

Curatolo, Bruno and François Marcot, *Écrire sous l'Occupation. Du non-consentement à la Résistance. France-Belgique-Pologne* (Rennes, PU de Rennes, 2011).

d'Aragon, Charles, *La Résistance sans héroisme* (Paris, Seuil, 1977).

d'Astier de La Vigerie, Emmanuel, *Les Dieux et les hommes, 1943–1944* (Paris, Julliard, 1952).

____, *Sept fois sept jours* (Paris, Éditions de Minuit, 1947).

Dahlem, Franz, *Am Vorabend des zweiten Weltkrieges*, 2 vols. (Berlin, Dietz Verlag, 1977).

Dalloz, Pierre, *Vérités sur le drame du Vercors* (Paris, Fernand Lanore, 1979).

Debré, Michel *Refaire la France* (Paris, Plon, 1945).

_____, *Trois Républiques pour une France. Mémoires I. Combattre* (Paris, Albin Michel, 1984).

Delestre, Antoine, *Uriage, une communauté et une école dans la tourmente, 1940–1945* (Nancy, PU de Nancy, 1989).

Delpla, Claude, 'Les Origines des guerrilleros espagnols dans les Pyrénées (1940–43)', in Jean Ortiz (ed.), *Rouges. Maquis de France et d'Espagne* (Biarritz, Atlantica, 2006), pp. 163–73.

Denis, Henri, *Le Comité Parisien de la Libération* (Paris, PUF, 1963).

Desgranges, Abbé, *Les Crimes masqués du 'Résistantialisme'* (Paris, L'Elan, 1948).

Diamant, David, *250 Combattants de la Résistance racontent* (Paris, L'Harmattan, 1991).

_____, *Combattants juifs dans l'Armée républicaine espagnole* (Paris, Le Pavillon, 1971).

_____, *Les Juifs dans la Résistance française, 1940–1944. Avec armes et sans armes* (Paris, Le Pavillon, 1971).

Diamond, Hanna, *Fleeing Hitler: France 1940* (Oxford, OUP, 2007).

Dombrowski Risser, Nicole, *France under Fire: German Invasion, Civilian Flight, and Family Survival during World War II* (New York and Cambridge, CUP, 2012).

Domenach, Jean-Marie and Denise Rendu, 'Une vie', in Bernard Comte, Jean-Marie Domenach and Christian Rendu (eds.), *Gilbert Dru. Un Chrétien résistant* (Paris, Beauchesne, 1998), pp. 59–127.

Domenach-Lallich, Denise, *Demain il fera beau. Journal d'une adolescente (1939–1944)* (Lyon, BGA Permazel, 2001).

Dommanget, Maurice, *Histoire du premier Mai* (Paris, Société universitaire d'édition et de librairie, 1953).

Douzou, Laurent, 'La Résistance à Lyon (1940–1944), Colloque *Lyons dans la Seconde Guerre mondiale. Métropolis à l'Épreuve du Conflict*, Lyon, 6–7 November 2013.

_____, *La Désobéissance. Histoire d'un mouvement et d'un journal clandestins, Libération-Sud, 1940–1944* (Paris, Odile Jacob, 1995).

_____, *Lucie Aubrac* (Paris, Perrin, 2009).

_____, *La Résistance française. Une histoire périlleuse* (Paris, Seuil, 2005).

_____, 'La Résistance, une affaire d'hommes?', *Cahiers de l'IHTP*, 31 (October 1995) .

_____ (ed.), *Notes de Prison de Bertrande d'Astier de la Vigerie (15 mars–4 avril 1941), Cahiers de l'IHTP*, 25 (October 1993).

_____ (ed.), *Faire l'histoire de la Résistance* (Rennes, Presses Universitaires de Rennes, 2010).

_____ (ed.), *Souvenirs inédits d'Yvon Morandat, Cahiers de l'IHTP*, 29 (September 1994).

_____, Robert Frank, Denis Peschanski and Dominique Veillon (eds.), *La Résistance et les Français: villes, centres et logiques de décision* (Paris, IHTP, 1995).

_____ and Dominique Veillon, 'La Résistance des mouvements: ses débuts dans la région lyonnaise (1940–1942)', in Jean-Marie Guillon and Pierre Laborie (eds.), *Mémoire et Histoire: la Résistance* (Toulouse, Privat, 1995).

Dreyfus-Armand, Geneviève, *Les Espagnols dans la Résistance. Incertitudes et spécificités*, in Jean-Marie Guillou and Pierre Laborie (eds.), *Mémoire et Histoire. La Résistance* (Toulouse, Privat, 1995).

____, *L'Exil des Républicians Espagnols en france. De la Guerre civile à la mort de Franco* (Paris, Albin Michel, 1999).

____ and Émile Temime, *Les Camps sur la plage. Un exil espagnol* (Paris, Éditions Autrement, 1995).

Dronne, Raymond, *Carnets de route d'un croisé de la France libre* (Paris, France-Empire, 1984).

Drouin, François and Philippe Joutard (eds.), *Monseigneur Théas, évêque de Montauban, les Juifs, les Justes* (Toulouse, Privat, 2003).

Ducerf, Laurent, *François de Menthon. Un Catholique au service de la République, 1900–1984* (Paris, Cerf, 2006).

Eisenhower, Dwight D., *Crusade in Europe* (London, Heinemann, 1948).

Faivre, Mario, *Nous avons tué Darlan. Alger 1942* (Paris, La Table Ronde, 1975).

Farge, Yves, *Rebelles, soldats et citoyens. Carnet d'un commissaire de la République* (Paris, Grasset, 1946).

Fayolle, Sandra, 'Danielle Casanova et les enjeux de mémoire', in Mechtild Gilzmer, Christine Levisse-Touzé and Stefan Martens, *Les Femmes dans la Résistance française* (Paris, Tallandier, 2003).

Ferrières, Gabrielle, *Jean Cavaillès. Un philosophe dans la guerre, 1903–1944* (Paris, Seuil, 1982).

Ferro, Marc, *Pétain* (Paris, Hachette, 1993).

Florentin, Eddy, *Quand les Alliés bombardaient la France, 1940–1945* (Paris, Perrin, 1997).

Foot, M. R. D., *SOE in France. An Account of the Work of the Special Operations Executive in France, 1940–1944* (London, HMSO, 1966; 2nd edition, Frank Cass, 2004).

Foulon, Charles-Louis, *Le Pouvoir en province à la Libération. Les commissaires de la République* (Paris, FNSP/Armand Colin, 1975).

Frenay, Henri, *L'Énigme Jean Moulin* (Paris, R. Laffont, 1977).

____, *La Nuit finira. Mémoires de la Résistance, 1940–1945* (Paris, R. Laffont, 1973).

Fumet, Stanislas, *Histoire de Dieu dans ma vie. Souvenirs choisis* (Paris, Fayard-Mame, 1978).

Funk, Arthur Layton, *Charles de Gaulle: The Crucial Years, 1943–1944* (Norman, University of Oklahoma Press, 1959).

____, *Hidden Ally: The French Resistance, Special Operations and the Landings in Southern France, 1944* (New York, Greenwood Press, 1992).

____, *The Politics of Torch. The Allied Landings and the Algiers Putsch, 1942* (Lawrence, UP of Kansas, 1974).

Gamzon, Denise, *Mémoires* (Jerusalem, 1997).

Garbit, François, *Dernières lettres d'Afrique et du Levant (1940–1941)* (Saint-Maur des Fossés, Éditions Sépia, 1999).

Garrado, Fabien, 'Les "Mémoires" du Général Luis Fernández, chef de la Agrupación de los Guerilleros Españoles', in Jean Ortiz (ed.), *Rouges. Maquis de France et d'Espagne* (Biarritz, Atlantica, 2006), pp. 193–209.

Gaulle Antonioz, Geneviève de, *La Traversée de la Nuit* (Paris, Seuil, 1998), translated as *God Remained Outside: an Echo of Ravensbrück* (London, Souvenir Press, 1998).

Gaulle, Charles de, *Discours et messages I, juin 1940–janvier 1946*, ed. François

Goguel (Paris, Plon, 1970).

____, *Lettres, Notes et Carnets, 1905–18*, ed. Philippe de Gaulle (Paris, Plon, 1981).

____, *Mémoires de Guerre*, 3 vols. (Paris, Plon, 1954–9).

Gensburger, Sarah, *Les Justes de France. Politiques publiques de la mémoire* (Paris, FNSP, 2010).

Georges, Monique, *Le Colonel Fabien était mon père* (Paris, Mille et Une Nuits, 2009).

Germain, Marie-Odile (ed.), *Stanislas Fumet ou la présence au temps* (Paris, Cerf/BNE, 1999).

Gilbert, Joseph, *Combattant du Vercors* (Paris, Fayard, 1972).

Gilbert, Martin, *Winston S. Churchill. VI. Finest Hour, 1939–1941* (London, Heinemann, 1983).

Gildea, Robert, *Children of the Revolution: The French, 1799–1914* (London, Penguin, 2008).

____, *Marianne in Chains: In Search of the German Occupation, 1940–1945* (London, Macmillan, 2002).

____, 'Lettres de correspondants français à la BBC (1940–1943). Une Pénombre de la Résistance', *Vingtième Siècle*, 125 (January–March 2015), pp. 61–76

____, 'Myth, memory and policy in France since 1945', in Jan-Werner Müller, *Memory and Power in Postwar Europe* (Cambridge, CUP, 2002).

____, 'Resistance, Reprisals and Community in Occupied France', *TRHS*, 13 (2003).

____, James Mark and Niek Pas, 'European Radicals and the "Third World": Imagined Solidarities and Radical Networks, 1958–1973', *Cultural and Social History*, 8/4 (2011), pp. 449–72.

____, James Mark and Anette Warring (eds.), *Europe's 1968: Voices of Revolt* (Oxford, OUP, 2013).

Gillois, André, *Ce siècle avait deux ans. Mémoires* (Paris, Mémoire du Livre, 2002).

Girard, Christian, *Journal de Guerre, 1939–1945* (Paris, L'Harmattan, 2000).

Girard, Claire, *Lettres (1939–1944)*, in Guillaume Piketty (ed.), *Français en Résistance. Carnets de guerre, correspondances, journaux personnels* (Paris, R. Laffont, 2009).

____, *Lettres de Claire Girard, fusillée par les Allemands le 27 août 1944* (Paris, Roger Lescaret, 1954).

Giraud, Henri, *Un seul but, la victoire. Alger, 1942–1944* (Paris, Julliard, 1949).

Godineau, Dominique, *The Women of Paris and their French Revolution* (Berkeley, University of California Press, 1998).

Goldman, Pierre, *Souvenirs obscurs d'un Juif polonais né en France* (Paris, Seuil, 1975).

Gossman, Lionel, *André Maurois (1885–1967): Fortunes and Misfortunes of a Moderate* (New York, Palgrave Macmillan, 2014).

Gourfinkel, Nina, *Aux Prises avec mon temps II. L'Autre patrie* (Paris, Seuil, 1953).

____, *Théâtre russe contemporain* (Paris, La Renaissance du Livre, 1931).

Granet, Marie, *Ceux de la Résistance, 1940–1944* (Paris, Editions de Minuit, 1964).

____, *Cohors-Asturies: histoire d'un réseau de résistance, 1942–1944* (Bordeaux, Edition des 'Cahiers de la Résistance', 1974).

_____, *Défense de la France, histoire d'un mouvement de résistance, 1940–1944* (Paris, PUF, 1960).

Grenier, Fernand, *C'était ainsi. Souvenirs* (Paris, Editions Sociales, 1959).

Gronowski, Louis, *Le Dernier Grand Soir. Un Juif de Pologne* (Paris, Seuil, 1980).

Groult, Benoîte and Flora, *Journal à quatre mains* (Paris, Denoël, 1962).

Grynberg, Anne, *Les Camps de la honte. Les internés juifs dans des camps français* (Paris, Editions de la Découverte, 1991).

Guidez, Guylaine *Femmes dans la Guerre 4. Femmes résistantes ou le temps du courage* (Lavauzelle-Graphic, 2006).

Guillon, Jean-Marie, *La Libération du Var. Résistance et nouveaux pouvoirs* (Paris, Centre national de la recherche scientifique/IHTP, 1990).

_____, 'Les Manifestations ménagères. Protestation populaire et résistance feminine spécifique', in Mechtild Gilzmer, Christine Levisse-Touzé and Stefan Martens, *Les Femmes dans la Résistance française* (Paris, Tallandier, 2003), pp. 107–33.

_____ and Pierre Laborie (eds.), *Mémoire et histoire. La Résistance* (Toulouse, Privat, 1995).

Guldenstadt, Christiane, *Les Femmes dans la Résistance* (Herbolzheim, Centaurus Verlag, 2006).

Hamon, Léo, *Vivre ses choix* (Paris, R. Laffont, 1991).

Hellman, John, *The Knight-Monks of Vichy. Uriage, 1940–1945* (Montreal and Kingston, McGill-Queens UP, 1993).

Hervé, Pierre, *La Libération trahie* (Paris, Grasset, 1945).

Hinze, Sybille, *Antifaschisten im Camp Le Vernet* (Berlin, Militärverlag des Deutschen Demokratischen Republik, 1988).

Hobsbawm, Eric and T. O. Ranger (eds.), *The Invention of Tradition* (Cambridge, CUP, 1983).

Holban, Boris, *Testament. Après quarante-cinq ans de silence le chef des FTP-MOI de Paris parle* (Paris, Calmann-Lévy, 1989).

Hostache, René, *Le Conseil National de la Résistance* (Paris, PUF, 1958).

Hufton, Olwen, 'Women in Revolution', *Past & Present*, 53 (1971).

Hull, Cordell, *Memoirs II* (New York, Macmillan, 1948).

Humbert, Agnès, *Notre guerre. Souvenirs de Résistance: Paris 1940–41, le bagne, occupation en Allemagne* (Paris, Tallandier, 2004).

_____, *Resistance. Memoirs of Occupied France* (London, Bloomsbury, 2009 [1946]).

Huntingdon, William A., *The Assassination of Jacques Lemaigre Dubreuil: A Frenchman between France and North Africa* (London and New York, Routledge Curzon, 2005).

Irvine, William, 'Fascism and the Strange Case of the Croix de Feu', *Journal of Modern History*, 63 (1991).

Jackson, Julian, *The Fall of France: The Nazi Invasion of 1940* (Oxford, OUP, 2003).

_____, *France. The Dark Years, 1940–1944* (Oxford, OUP, 2001).

_____, *The Popular Front in France: Defending Democracy, 1934–38* (Cambridge, CUP, 1988).

Jackson, Michael, *Fallen Sparrows: the International Brigades in the Spanish Civil War* (Philadelphia, American Philosophical Society, 1994).

Jacques, André, *Madeleine Barot. Une indomptable énergie* (Paris, Cerf/Labor et Fides, 1989).

Jennings, Eric, *La France libre fut africaine* (Paris, Perrin, 2014).

Jouan, Cécile, *Comète, histoire d'une ligne d'évasion* (Furnes, Editions du Beffroi, 1948).

Jouhanneau, Michel, *L'Organisation de la Résistance dans l'Indre* (Franconville, 1975).

Joutard, Philippe and François Marcot (eds.), *Les Etrangers dans la Résistance en France* (Besançon, Université de Franche-Comté, 1992).

Joxe, Louis, *Victoires sur la Nuit, 1940–1946. Mémoires* (Paris, Flammarion, 1981).

Juin, Alphonse, *Mémoires I* (Paris, Fayard, 1959).

Kedward, H. R., *In Search of the Maquis: Rural Resistance in Southern France, 1942–1944* (Oxford, Clarendon Press, 1993).

_____, *Resistance in Vichy France: A Study of Ideas and Motivation in the Southern Zone, 1940–1942* (Oxford, OUP, 1978).

_____, 'Ici commence la France libre', in H. R. Kedward and Nancy Wood (eds.), *The Liberation of France. Image and Event* (Oxford, Berg, 1995), pp. 1–11.

_____, 'The Maquis and the Culture of the Outlaw', in H. R. Kedward and Roger Austin (eds.), *Vichy France and the Resistance: Culture and Ideology* (London and Sydney, Croom Helm, 1985), 232–51.

Kennedy, Sean, *Reconciling France against Democracy: the Croix de Feu and the Parti social francais, 1927–1945* (Montreal, McGill-Queen's University Press 2007).

Kessel, Joseph, *L'Armée des ombres* (Paris, Plon, 1963).

Kimball, Warren F. (ed.), *Churchill and Roosevelt: the Complete Correspondence* (Princeton, NJ, Princeton UP, 1984).

Kitson, Simon, 'Criminals or Liberators? French Public Opinion and the Allied Bombing of France, 1940–1945', in Claudia Baldoni, Andrew Knapp and Richard Overy (eds.), *Bombing, States and Peoples in Western Europe, 1940–1945* (London and New York, Continuum, 2011), pp. 279–90.

Klarsfeld, Serge, *Le Mémorial de la déportation des juifs de France* (Paris, the author, 1978).

_____, *Vichy-Auschwitz: le rôle de Vichy dans la solution finale de la question juive en France, 1943–1944*, 2 vols. (Paris, Fayard, 1983–5).

Knapp, Andrew, *Les Français sous les bombes alliées, 1940–1945* (Paris, Tallandier, 2014).

Knout, David, *Contribution à l'histoire de la Résistance juive en France 1940–1944* (Paris, Éditions du Centre, 1947).

Koestler, Arthur, *Scum of the Earth* (London, Jonathan Cape, 1941).

Kogon, Eugen, Hermann Langbehn and Adalbert Rückert, *Nazi Mass Murder: a Documentary History of the Use of Poison Gas* (New Haven, CT and London, Yale UP, 1993).

Kolko, Gabriel, *The Politics of War: Allied Diplomacy and the World Crisis of 1943–1945* (London, Weidenfeld & Nicolson, 1969).

Kriegel-Valrimont, Maurice, *La Libération. Les archives du COMAC (mai–août 1944)* (Paris, Éditions de Minuit, 1964).

Kriegel, Annie, *The French Communists: Profile of a People* (Chicago and London, University of Chicago Press, 1972).

_____ with Olivier Biffaud, *Mémoires rebelles* (Paris, Odile Jacob, 1999).

Krivopissko, Guy, Christine Levisse-Touzé and Vladimir Trouplin, *Dans l'Honneur et par la Victoire: les femmes Compagnons de la Libération* (Paris, Tallandier, 2008).

Kupferman, Fred, *Le Procès de Vichy. Pucheu, Pétain, Laval* (Brussels, Complexe, 1980).

Laborie, Pierre, *Le Chagrin et le venin. La France sous l'Occupation, mémoires et idées reçues* (Montrouge, Bayard, 2011).

____, *L'Opinion française sous Vichy* (Paris, Seuil, 1990).

____, 'L'Idée de Résistance. Entre définition et sens. Retour sur un questionnement', in *Les Français des années troubles* (Paris, Points-Seuil, 2003).

____, 'Qu'est-ce que la Résistance?', in François Marcot, Bruno Leroux and Christine Levisse-Touzé (eds.), *Dictionnaire Historique de la Résistance* (Paris, R. Laffont, 2006), pp. 29–38.

Lacouture, Jean, *De Gaulle. The Rebel, 1890–1944* (London, Harvill, 1993).

Lagarde, Paul de, *En suivant Leclerc* (Paris, Au Fil d'Ariane, 1964).

Lamazères, Greg, *Marcel Langer. Une vie de combats. Juif, communiste, résistant et guillotiné* (Toulouse, Privat, 2003).

Lapie, P. O., *La Légion Étrangère à Narvik* (London, John Murray, 1941).

Laroche, Gaston, *On les nommait les Étrangers. Les immigrés dans la Résistance* (Paris, Éditeurs Français Réunis, 1965).

Latour, Anny, *La Résistance juive en France, 1940–1944* (Paris, Stock, 1970).

Lattre, Jean de, *Histoire de la première armée française. Rhin et Danube* (Paris, Plon, 1949).

____, *Ne Pas Subir. Écrits 1914–1952* (Paris, Plon, 1984).

Lazare, Lucien, *L'Abbé Glasberg* (Paris, Cerf, 1990).

Lazarus, Jacques, 'Sous le drapeau bleu-blanc', in RHICOJ, *Les Juifs dans la Résistance et la Libération* (Paris, Scribe, 1985).

Le Crom, Jean-Pierre, *Au secours, Maréchal! L'instrumentalisation de l'humanitaire, 1940–1944* (Paris, PUF, 2013).

____, *Syndicats nous voilà. Vichy et le corporatisme* (Paris, Editions de l'Atelier/ Editions ouvrières, 1995).

Le Marec, Gérard, *La Bretagne dans la Résistance* (Rennes, Ouest-France, 1983).

Leahy, William D., *I Was There* (London, Gollancz, 1950).

Leclerc, Philippe, *L'Affaire des Manises* (Langres, Dominique Guéniot, 2004).

Lecoeur, Auguste, 'Les Grèves des mineurs du Nord-Pas-de-Calais' in Institut d'Histoire des Conflits Contemporains, *Séance Solennelle des Témoignages 1941* (Paris, Sénat, 1986), pp. 139–48.

Lee, Daniel, *Pétain's Jewish Children. French Jewish Children and the Vichy Regime* (Oxford, OUP, 2014).

Lefèvre, Roger, *Souvenir de maquisards de l'Ain* (St Cyr-sur-Loire, Alan Sutton, 2004).

Léo, Gerhard, *Un Allemand dans la Résistance. Le train pour Toulouse* (Paris, Editions Tirésias, 1997).

Leroux, Bruno, 'Des historiographies parallèles et concurrentes du Comité d'histoire de la Deuxième Guerre mondiale: *L'Histoire de la Résistance en France* d'Henri Noguères et *La Résistance* d'Alain Guérin', in Laurent Douzou (ed.), *Faire l'histoire de la Résistance* (Rennes, PU de Rennes, 2010), pp. 95–115.

Levisse-Touzé, Christine, *L'Afrique du Nord dans la Guerre, 1939–1945* (Paris, Albin Michel, 1998).

_____ and Stefan Martens (eds.), *Des Allemands contre le nazisme. Oppositions et résistances, 1933–1945* (Paris, Albin Michel, 1997).

Lévy, Claude, *Les Parias de la Résistance* (Paris, Calmann-Lévy, 1970).

_____ and Paul Tillard, *La Grande Rafle du Vél d'Hiv (16 juillet 1942)* (Paris, R. Laffont, 1967).

Lévy, Jean-Pierre, *Mémoires d'un franc-tireur. Itinéraire d'un résistant, 1940–1944* (Paris, Éditions Complexe/IHTP, 1998).

_____, 'France-Liberté. Franc-Tireur', in *Il y a 45 ans. L'année 1941. Témoignages pour l'histoire. Colloque organisé au Sénat le 7 avril 1986* (Paris, Sénat, 1986).

Lévy, Marc, *Les Enfants de la liberté* (Paris, R. Laffont, 2007).

Lieb, Peter, *Vercors 1944. Resistance in the French Alps* (Oxford, Osprey, 2012).

London, Artur, *L'Aveu* (Paris, Gallimard, 1972).

_____, *L'Espagne* (Brussels, Tribord, 2003).

_____, *The Confession* (New York, Morrow, 1970).

_____, *On Trial* (London, Macdonald, 1970).

London, Lise, *La Ménagère de la rue Daguerre. Souvenirs de Résistance* (Paris, Seuil, 1995).

Lormier, Dominique, *L'Épopée du Corps Francs Pommiès, des Pyrénées à Berlin* (Paris, Jacques Grancher, 1990).

Lowrie, Donald, *The Hunted Children* (New York, Norton, 1963).

Luneau, Aurélie, *Je vous écris de France. Lettres inédites à la BBC, 1940–1944* (Paris, L'Iconoclaste, 2014).

_____, *Radio Londres, 1940–1944. Les Voix de la Liberté* (Paris, Perrin, 2005).

Lusseyran, Jacques, *Et la lumière fut* (Paris, Editions du Félin, 2005).

McLellan, Josie, *Antifascism and Memory in East Germany: Remembering the International Brigades, 1945–1989* (Oxford, Clarendon Press, 2004).

Macmillan, Harold, *War Diaries: Politics and War in the Mediterranean, January 1943–May 1945* (London, Macmillan, 1984).

Malraux, André, 'Transfert des cendres de Jean Moulin au Panthéon. Discours prononcé à Paris le 19 décembre 1964', in *La Politique, la Culture. Discours, articles, entretiens* (Paris, Gallimard, 1996).

Marcot, François, *La Résistance dans le Jura* (Besançon, Cêtre, 1985).

_____ (ed.), *La Résistance et les Français: lutte armée et maquis* (Paris, Les Belles Lettres, 1996).

_____, Bruno Leroux and Christine Levisse-Touzé (eds.), *Dictionnaire Historique de la Résistance* (Paris, R. Laffont, 2006).

Marrus, Michael and Robert Paxton, *Vichy France and the Jews* (New York, Basic Books, 1981).

Martin-Chauffier, Simone, *A bientôt quand même* (Paris, Calmann-Lévy, 1976).

Massu, Jacques, *La Vraie bataille d'Alger* (Paris, Plon, 1971).

May, Ernest, *Strange Victory: Hitler's Conquest of France* (London, Tauris, 2000).

Mayer, Daniel, *Les Socialistes dans la Résistance* (Paris, PUF, 1968).

Merle d'Aubigné, Jeanne and Violette Mouchon (eds.), *Les Clandestins de Dieu. CIMADE 1939–1945. Textes rassemblés par Jeanne Merle d'Aubigné et Violette Mouchon* (Paris, Fayard, 1968).

Mesquida, Evelyn, *La Nueve. 24 août 1944. Ces républicains espagnols qui ont libéré Paris* (Paris, Cherche-Midi, 2011).

Michel, Henri, *Les Courants de pensée de la Résistance* (Paris, PUF, 1962).

_____, *Histoire de la Résistance* (Paris, PUF, Que sais'je? 1950).

_____, *Les Idées politiques et sociales de la Résistance: documents clandestins, 1940–1944* (Paris, PUF, 1954).

_____ and Marie Granet, *Combat. Histoire d'un movement de résistance* (Paris, PUF, 1957).

Middlebro', Allen, 'Choices and Actions of Members and Former Members of the French Communist Party, 1939–1941' (D.Phil thesis, University of Oxford, 2011).

Miot, Claire, 'Le retrait des tirailleurs sénégalais de la Première Armée française en 1944. Hérésie stratégique, bricolage politique ou conservatisme colonial?' *Vingtième Siècle* no. 25 (jan.–mars 2015), pp. 77–89

Missika, Dominique, *Berty Albrecht* (Paris, Perrin, 2005).

Mompezat, Roger, *Le Corps franc de la Montagne noire, journal de marche, avril-septembre 1944* (4th edn., Castres, Les Anciens du Corps franc de la Montagne noire, 1994).

Monier, Charles, Les Chemins de la Résistance à Bollène et dans Le Canton, 1939–1944 (Bollène, 2002).

Monnet, Jean, *Mémoires* (Paris, Fayard, 1976).

Monod, Claude, *La Région D. Rapport d'activité des maquis de Bourgogne-Franche Comté* (St Etienne-Vallée Française, AIOU, 1993).

Moorehead, Caroline, *Village of Secrets* (London, The Spectator, 2014).

Muracciole, Jean-François, *Les Français Libres. L'autre résistance* (Paris, Tallandier, 2009).

Murphy, Robert, *Diplomat among Warriors* (London, Collins, 1964).

Najman, Ezer, 'Capitaine Gilles du Groupe Carmagnole', in RHICOJ, *Les Juifs dans la Résistance et la Libération* (Paris, Scribe, 1985), pp. 170–2.

Namer, Gerard, *La Commémoration en France, 1944–1982* (Paris, S.P.A.G./Papyrus, 1983).

Neave, Airey, *Saturday at MI9. A History of Underground Escape Lines in North-West Europe in 1940–1945 by a leading organiser of MI9* (London, Hodder & Stoughton, 1969).

Nemirowsky, Irène, *Suite française* (Paris, Denoël, 2004); trans. Sandra Smith (London, Chatto & Windus, 2006).

Nettelbeck, Colin, *Forever French. Exile in the United States, 1939–1945* (New York and Oxford, Berg, 1991)

Niebergall, Otto, 'Der antifasciste deutsche Widerstandkampf in Frankreich – seine Leitung und Entwicklung', in Dora Schaul, *Erinnerungen deutscher Antifascisten* (Berlin, Dietz Verlag, 1973), pp. 25–34.

Noguères, Henri, Marcel Degliame-Fouché and Jean-Louis Vigier, *Histoire de la Résistance en France*, 5 vols. (Paris, R. Laffont, 1967–81).

Noiriel, Gérard, *Le Creuset français. Histoire de l'Immigration, XIXe–XXe siècles* (Paris, Seuil, 1988).

OAS parle (Paris, Julliard, 1964).

Ophüls, Marcel, *The Sorrow and the Pity: Chronicle of a French City under the German Occupation*, trans. Mireille Johnston (St Albans, Paladin, 1975).

Oury, Louis, *Rue du Roi Albert. Les Otages de Nantes, Châteaubrinat et Bordeaux* (Pantin, Le Temps des Cerises, 1997).

Ouzoulias, Albert, *Les Bataillons de la Jeunesse* (Paris, Editions Sociales, 1967).

____, *Les Fils de la Nuit* (Paris, Grasset, 1975).

Pannequin, Roger, *Ami si tu tombes* (Paris, Sagittaire, 1976 and Babel, 2000).

Passy, Colonel, *Souvenirs. I. 2e bureau, Londres; Souvenirs. II. 10, Duke Street, Londres. Le B.C.R.A.* (Monte-Carlo, R. Solar, 1947–8).

Paulin, Jean, *La Rage au cœur* (Paris, Gerard & Co., 1958).

Paxton, Robert, 'Vichy made it worse', *New York Review of Books*, 6 Mar. 2004.

Péan, Pierre, *Vie et morts de Jean Moulin* (Paris, Fayard, 1998).

Perrault, Gilles, *La Longue traque* (Paris, Lattès, 1975).

Perthuis, Valérie, *Le Sauvetage des enfants juifs du camp de Vénissieux, août 1942* (Lyon, Editions Lyonnaises d'Art et d'Histoire, 1997).

Peschanski, Denis, *La France des Camps. L'Internement, 1938–1946* (Paris, Gallimard, 2002).

____, 'La Résistance immigrée', in Jean-Marie Guillou and Pierre Laborie (eds.), *Mémoire et Histoire. La Résistance* (Toulouse, Privat, 1995).

Pétain, Philippe, *Actes et écrits* (Paris, Flammarion, 1974).

Piketty, Guillaume, *La Bataille des Ardennes. 16 décembre 1944–31 janvier 1945* (Paris, Tallandier, 2013).

____, *Pierre Brossolette, un héros de la Résistance* (Paris, O. Jacob, 1998).

____ (ed.), *Français en Résistance. Carnets de guerre, correspondances, journaux personnels* (Paris, R. Laffont, 2009).

____ and Vladimir Trouplin, *Les Compagnons de l'Aube. Archives Inédits des Compagnons de la Libération* (Paris, Textuel, 2014).

Pineau, Christian, *La Simple Vérité, 1940–1945* (Geneva, Editions de Crémille, 1972 [1960]).

Pollard, Miranda, 'A Question of Silence? Odette Rosenstock, Moussa Abadi and the Réseau Marcel', *French Politics, Culture and Society*, 30/2 (2012), pp. 113–133

Ponty, Janine, *Polonais méconnus. Histoire des travailleurs immigrés en France dans l'entre-deux-guerres* (Paris, Publications de la Sorbonne, 2005).

____, 'La Résistance polonaise: le POWN. Contribution à l'histoire de la résistance non-communiste', in Karel Bartosek, René Gallissot and Denis Peschanski (eds.), *De l'exil à la Résistance. Réfugiés et immigrés d'Europe centrale en France: 1933–1945* (Saint-Denis, PU de Vincennes/Arcantère, 1989), pp. 173–83.

Porch, Douglas, *The French Foreign Legion* (London, Macmillan, 1991).

Postel-Vinay, André, *Un fou s'évade. Souvenirs de 1941–42* (Paris, Editions du Félin, 1997).

Postel-Vinay, Anise, 'Les Exterminations par gaz à Ravensbrück, in Germaine Tillion, *Ravensbrück* (Paris, Seuil, 1973).

____ and Jacques Prévotat, 'La Déportation', in Jean-Pierre Azéma and François Bédarida (eds.), *La France des années noires* (Paris, Seuil, 1993).

Poznanski, Renée, *Jews in France during World War II* (Hanover, NH and London, UP of New England, 2001).

____, *Les Juifs en France pendant la Seconde Guerre mondiale* (Paris, Hachette, 1997).

____, and Denis Peschanski, *Drancy. Un camp en France* (Fayard/Ministère de la Défense, 2015).

Pradoux, Martine, *Daniel Mayer, un socialiste dans la* Résistance (Paris, Editions Ouvrières, 2002).

Quellien, Jean, 'Les Travailleurs forcés en Allemagne. Essai d'approche statistique', in B. Garnier and J. Quellien (eds.), *La Main d'œuvre française exploitée par le III Reich* (Caen, Centre d'Histoire Quantitative, 2003), pp. 67–84.

Questions à l'histoire orale. Table ronde du 20 juin 1986, Cahiers de l'IHTP, 4 (June 1986).

Racine, Nicole and Louis Bodin, *Le Parti communiste français pendant l'entre-deux guerres* (Paris, FNSP, 1972).

Rajsfus, Maurice, *Des Juifs dans la Collaboration. L'UGIF 1941–1944* (Paris, EDI, 1980).

_____, *La Police de Vichy. Les forces de l'ordre françaises au service de la* Gestapo, *1940–1944* (Paris, Cherche-Midi, 1995).

Rake, Denis, *Rake's Progress: the Gay – and Dramatic – Adventures of Major Denis Rake, MC, the Reluctant British War-Time Agent*, with a foreword by Douglas Fairbanks (London, Leslie Frewin, 1968).

Raphaël-Leygues, Jacques and François Flohic, *Darlan* (Paris, Plon, 1986).

Ravanel, Serge, *L'Esprit de Résistance* (Paris, Seuil, 1995).

Ravine, Jacques, *La Résistance organisée des Juifs en France* (Paris, Julliard, 1973).

Rayski, Adam, 'Diversité et unite de la Résistance juive', in RHICOJ, *Les Juifs dans la Résistance et la Libération* (Paris, Scribe, 1985).

Rémond, René, *Paul Touvier et l'Église* (Paris, Fayard, 1992).

Rémy, Colonel [Gilbert Renault], *Mémoires d'un Agent secret de la France Libre*, 3 vols. (Paris, France-Empire, 1959).

_____, *Le Réseau Comète*, 3 vols. (Paris, Perrin, 1966–71).

_____, 'La Justice et l'opprobre', *Carrefour* (11 April 1950).

Résistance et Libération. Actes du Colloque des 25 mai 1994 et 17 mai 1995 (Paris, Académie de Paris, 1995).

RHICOJ, *Les Juifs dans la Résistance et la Libération* (Paris, Scribe, 1985).

Richardson, P. Dan, *Comintern Army: the International Brigades and the Spanish Civil War* (Lexington, UP of Kentucky, 1982).

Riffaud, Madeleine, *On l'appelait Rainer* (Paris, Julliard, 1994).

_____ (ed.), *Les Carnets de Charles Debarge* (Paris, Éditions Sociales, 1951).

Rimbaud, Christiane, *L'affaire du Massilia, été 1940* (Paris, Seuil, 1984).

Romans-Petit, Henri, *Les Obstinés* (Ceignes, ETD, 1995).

Rousso, Henry, *Un Château en Allemagne. La France de Pétain en exil, Sigmaringen 1944–1945* (Paris, Ramsay, 1980).

_____, *The Vichy Syndrome. History and Memory in France since 1944* (Cambridge, Mass., CUP, 1991).

Rude, F., *La Libération de Lyon et de sa région* (Paris, Hachette, 1974).

Rudolph, Luc (ed.), *Au Coeur de la Préfecture de Police de la Résistance à la Libération III. Le Libération de Paris* (Paris, LBM, 2011).

Ruel Robins, Marianne, 'A Grey Site of Memory: Le Chambon-sur-Lignon and Protestant Exceptionalism on the Plateau Vivarais-Lignon', *Church History*, 82 (2013), pp. 317–52.

Sabatié, Norbert, 'L'Abbé Glasberg et la Résistance dans le Tarn-et-Garonne, 1943–44', in Christian Sorrel (ed.), *Alexandre Glasberg, 1902–1981. Prêtre, résistant, militant. Chrétiens et Sociétés.* Documents et Mémoires no. 19 (Lyon, 2013), pp. 59–69.

Sacotte, Mireille, *Saint-Jean Perse* (Paris, Pierre Belfond, 1991).

Sah, Léonard, 'Le Cameroun sous mandat français dans la Deuxième Guerre mondiale' (doctoral thesis, Université d'Aix-en-Provence, 1998).

Sainclivier, Jacqueline, *La Résistance en Ille-et-Vilaine, 1940–1944* (Rennes, PU de Rennes, 1993).

——, 'Le pouvoir resistant (été 1944)', in Philippe Buton and Jean-Marie Guillon, *Les Pouvoirs en France à la Libération* (Paris, Belin, 1994).

Salan, Raoul, *Mémoires* (Paris, Presses de la Cité, 1970).

Salmon, Robert, 'Défense de la France', in *Il y a 45 ans. L'année 1941. Témoignages pour l'histoire. Colloque organisé au Sénat le 7 avril 1986* (Paris, Sénat, 1986).

Samuel, Raphael and Paul Thompson (eds.), *The Myths We Live By* (London, Routledge, 1990).

Schaul, Dora, *Resistance. Erinnerungen deutscher Antifaschisten* (Berlin, Dietz Verlag, 1973).

Schor, Ralph, *Un Évêque dans le siècle, Monseigneur Paul Rémond, 1873–1963* (Nice, Serre, 1984).

Schwarz, Paula, 'The Politics of Food and Gender in Occupied Paris', *Modern and Contemporary France*, 7/1 (1999), pp. 35–45.

Sémelin, Jacques, 'Qu'est-ce résister?', *Esprit* (January 1994), pp. 50–63.

——, *Persécutions et entraides dans la France occupée. Comment 75% des Juifs en France ont échappé à la mort* (Paris, Les Arènes-Seuil, 2013).

Shennan, Andrew, *The Fall of France, 1940* (Harlow, Longman, 2000).

Sigurd Kulok, Jan, 'Trait d'union: the History of the French Relief Organisation Secours national / Entr'aide française under the Third Republic, the Vichy Regime and the early Fourth Republic, 1939–1949' (D.Phil thesis, University of Oxford, 2003).

Simonin, Anne, 'La Résistance sans fiction? *L'Armée des ombres* (1943)', in Bruno Curatolo and François Marcot (eds.), *Écrire sous l'Occupation. Du non-consentement à la Résistance, France-Belgique-Pologne* (Rennes, PU de Rennes, 2011), pp. 233–53.

Skoutelsky, Rémi, *L'Espoir guidait leurs pas. Les Volontaires français dans les Brigades Internationales, 1936–1939* (Paris, Grasset, 1998).

Sorrel, Christian (ed.), *Alexandre Glasberg, 1902–1981. Prêtre, résistant, militant. Chrétiens et Sociétés.* Documents et Mémoires no. 19 (Lyon, 2013).

Soucy, Robert, *French Fascism. The Second Wave, 1933–1939* (New Haven, CT and London, Yale UP, 1995).

Soustelle, Jacques, *Envers et contre tout II. De Londres à Alger, juillet 19–février 1943* (Genève, Editions de Crémille, 1970).

——, *L'Espérance trahie* (Paris, Editions de l'Alma, 1962).

Soutou, Jean-Marie, *Un Diplomate engagé. Mémoires 1939–1979* (Paris, Editions de Fallois, 2011).

——, 'Souvenirs des années noires', in *Les Cahiers de l'Alliance Israélite Universelle*, 201 (October–November 1979).

Spears, Edward, *Assignment to Catastrophe II. The Fall of France, June 1940* (London, Heinemann, 1954).

Spina, Raphaël, 'La France et les Français devant le Service du Travail Obligatoire (1942–1945)' (doctoral thesis, ENS Cachan, 2012).

Stora, Benjamin, *Les Trois Exils. Juifs d'Algérie* (Paris, Stock, 2006).

Stucki, Walter, *La Fin du régime de Vichy* (Neuchâtel, Editions de la Baconnière, 1947).

Suberville, Gérald, *L'Autre Résistance* (Aiou, Saint-Étienne Vallée Française, 1998).

_____, 'L'action ouvrière du Languedoc', in Jules Maurin (ed.) *Les Lendemains de la Libération dans le Midi. Actes du Colloque de Montpellier 1986* (Université Paul-Valéry-Montpellier III, 1997).

Sweets, John F., *The Politics of Resistance in France, 1940–1944: a History of the Mouvements Unis de la Résistance* (DeKalb, Northern Illinois University Press, 1976).

Tandler, Nicholas, *Un inconnu nommé Krasucki* (Paris, La Table Ronde, 1985).

Teitgen, Pierre-Henri, *Faîtes entrer le témoin suivant, 1940–1958. De la Résistance à la Ve République* (Rennes, Ouest-France, 1988).

Thalmann, Rita, *La Mise au pas. Idéologie et stratégie sécuritaire dans la France occupée* (Paris, Fayard, 1991).

Tillion, Germaine, *Les Ennemis complémentaires* (Paris, Éditions de Minuit, 1960).

_____, 'Première résistance en zone occupée. Du côté du réseau Musée de l'Homme-Haut-Vildé', *Esprit*, 261 (February 2000).

Tillon, Charles, *On chantait rouge* (Paris, R. Laffont, 1977).

_____, *Un 'Procès de Moscou' à Paris* (Paris, Seuil, 1971).

Titonel Asperti, Damira, *Écrire pour les autres. Mémoires d'une résistante. Les antifascistes italiens en Lot-et-Garonne sous l'Occupation* (PU de Bordeaux, 1999).

Tollet, André, *La Classe ouvrière dans la Résistance* (Paris, Éditions Sociales, 1969).

_____, *Ma traversée du Siècle. Mémoires d'un syndicaliste révolutionnaire* (Paris, VO Éditions, 2002).

_____, intervention. CHDGM, *La Libération de la France*. Colloque 28–31 Oct. 1974, pp. 545–9.

Torrès, Tereska, *Une Française Libre. Journal, 1939–1945* (Paris, France-Loisirs, 2000).

Toulat, Jean, *Combattants de la non-violence. De Lanza del Vasto au Général de Bollardière* (Paris, Cerf, 1983).

Trempé, Rolande, 'Le Rôle des étrangers MOI et guerrilleros', in Trempé (ed.), *La Libération dans le Midi de la France* (Toulouse, Éché, 1986), pp. 63–78.

Trocmé, Magda, Madeleine Barot, Pierre Fayol and Oscar Rosowsky, 'Le Mythe de commandant SS protecteur des juifs', *Le Monde juif*, 130 (April–June 1988), pp. 61–6.

Trouplin, Vladimir, *Dictionnaire des Compagnons de la Libération* (Bordeaux, Elytis, 2010).

Vasselot, Odile de, *Tombés du ciel. Histoire d'une ligne d'évasion* (Paris, Editions du Félin, 2005).

Veillon, Dominique, *Le Franc-Tireur. Un journal clandestin, un movement de Résistance* (Paris, Flammarion, 1977).

____, 'Les Femmes anonymes dans la Résistance', in Mechtild Gilzmer, Christine Levisse-Touzé and Stefan Martens, *Les Femmes dans la Résistance en France* (Paris, Tallandier, 2003).

Verbizier, Gérard, *Ni Travail, ni famille, ni patrie. Journal d'une Brigade FTP-MOI. Toulouse, 1942–1944* (Paris, Calmann-Lévy, 1994).

Viannay, Philippe, *Du bon usage de la France* (Paris, Ramsay, 1988).

Vildé, Boris, *Journal et Lettres de Prison, 1941–1942*, Institut d'Histoire du Temps présent, Cahier no. 7 (1988).

Villon, Pierre, *Résistant de la première heure* (Paris, Editions Sociales, 1983).

Vinen, Richard, *The Unfree French. Life under the Occupation* (London, Allen Lane, 2006).

Virieux, Daniel, 'Le Front National de lutte pour la liberté et l'indépendance de la France. Un mouvement de résistance, période clandestine (mai 1941–août 1944)' (doctoral thesis, Université de Paris-VIII, 1996).

Vistel, Alban, *La Nuit sans ombre. Histoire des Mouvements Unis de la Résistance, leur rôle dans la liberation du Sud-Est* (Paris, Fayard, 1970).

Vomécourt, Philippe de, *Who Lived to See the Day* (London, Hutchinson, 1961).

von Choltitz, *Un Soldat parmi des soldats* (Avignon, Aubanel, 1965).

____, *Soldat unter Soldaten* (Konstanz, 1951).

Wailly, Henri de, *Syrie 1941. La Guerre occultée. Vichystes contre Gaullistes* (Paris, Perrin, 2006).

Wake, Nancy, *The White Mouse* (London, Macmillan, 1985).

Walters, Anne-Marie, *Moondrop to Gascony* (London, Macmillan, 1946).

Waysand, Georges, *Estoucha* (Paris, Denoël, 1997).

Weber, Eugen, *Action française: Royalism and Reaction in Twentieth-Century France* (Stanford, Stanford UP, 1962).

Webster, Paul, *Pétain's Crime: the Full Story of French Collaboration in the Holocaust* (London, Macmillan, 1990).

Weill, Georges, 'Andrée Salomon et le sauvetage des enfants juifs (1933–1947)', in *French Politics, Culture and Society*, 30/2 (Summer 2012), 89–96.

Weill, Joseph, *Contribution à l'Histoire des Camps d'Internement dans l'Anti-France* (Paris, Editions du Centre, 1946).

Weinberg, David H., *Les Juifs de Paris de 1933 à 1939* (Paris, Calmann-Lévy, 1974).

Weinstein, Max, *Souvenirs, souvenirs* (Nice, Éditions du Losange, 1997).

Wieviorka, Annette, *Déportation et genocide: entre la mémoire et l'oubli* (Paris, Plon, 1992).

____, *Ils étaient Juifs, résistants, communistes* (Paris, Denoël, 1986).

Wieviorka, Olivier, 'A la recherche de l'engagement', *Vingtième Siècle*, 60 (October–December 1998), pp. 58–70.

____, *Une certaine idée de la Résistance: Défense de la France, 1940–1949* (Paris, Seuil, 1995).

____, *Histoire de la Résistance, 1940–1945* (Paris, Perrin, 2013).

____, *La Mémoire désunie. Le souvenir politique des années sombre, de la Libération à nos jours* (Paris, Seuil, 2010).

____, *Normandy: the Landings to the Liberation of Paris* (Cambridge, Mass., Belknap Press, 2008).

Witherington Cornioley, Pearl, *Code Name Pauline. Memoirs of a World War II*

Special Agent (Chicago, Chicago Review Press, 2013).

Zeitoun, Sabine, 'Mémoire. Des outils pour la transmission au CHRD de Lyon', *Cahiers d'histoire*, 39 (1994), pp. 317–25

____, *Ces enfants qu'il fallait sauver* (Paris, France Loisirs, 1990).

____, *L'Œuvre de Secours aux Enfants* (Paris, L'Harmattan, 1990).

Zlatin, Sabine, *Mémoires de la 'Dame d'Izieu'* (Paris, Gallimard, 1992).

Index

Abadi, Moussa 160, 203
Abbeville 23
Abetz, Otto 385
Aboulker, Henri 245
Aboulker, José 34, 245–6, 247, 248, 250–2,
   256
Aboulker, Raphaël 245–6, 247
Abwehr 103, 166, 322–3
Achiary, André 246, 247
Ackerman-Athanissiades, Blanche 35
Acre 110
Action Committee against Deportation
   (CAD) 299, 300
Action Française 44, 48, 77, 99, 111, 308
Action Ouvrière 293–5, 364, 369, 370, 389
Aden 113
Affiche rouge, the 153, 456
Africa 18
   French Equatorial 32
      rallies to de Gaulle 34–6, 37
   French West 32, 109, 256
      opposes de Gaulle 35, 36–7,
   North
      continuing war in (1940) 26–7,
         28, 32–3
      Vichy regime in 244–5
      Allied landings in (1942) 18, 71,
         128, 225, 240–1, 248–52, 260
      resistance in 245–9, 250–3
      Giraud regime in 277, 281–2
      see also Darlan deal
      see also Army of Africa
Agde 51, 182, 191
Aglan, Alya 12
Agulhon, Maurice 471
Aigues Mortes 42
Ain 369
Aix-en-Provence 456
Ajaccio 380
Alain-Fournier, Friends of 155
Albert Lake, Philippe d' 317
Albert Lake, Virginia d' 14, 317

Albrecht, Berty 98–9, 105, 134, 169, 468–9
Aleppo 109
Alès 368
Alesch, Robert 165, 435
Alexander, General Harold 279
Alexandria 33, 113, 228
Alfonso, Celestino 233
Algerian War (1954–62) 4–5, 450, 465
   and Resistance myth 455, 449–51
Algiers
   Maison Carré prison 51
   University 245, 246
   resistance in (8 Nov. 1942) 245–7,
      250–1
   arrival of de Gaulle in (1943) 277, 280
   French provisional government in 276
   Provisional Consultative Assembly in
      152, 305–7, 312
Alincourt, Jacqueline d' 304
Alliance Démocratique 276, 301
Allied Control Commission 443
Allied Military Government in Occupied
   Territories (AMGOT) 343, 345, 363, 384
Allier 406
Allies
   and D-Day 2, 313, 360
   and internal resistance 314–15, 343–5,
      373
   and landing in Provence (Aug. 1944)
      360, 379–80
   see also bombing, Great Britain,
      Supreme Allied Command, United
      States
Alligator Plan 330, 351
Alpine Chasseurs 26, 27, 265
Alsace
   annexed by Germany (1870) 180
   part of Imperial Germany 47
   restored to France (1918) 47
   evacuation from (1939) 181, 184
   annexed by Germany (1940) 22, 180–1
   refugees from 74, 76, 182

571